'This remarkable book by one of the twentieth century's leading philosophers and religious thinkers, available for the first time in English translation, is essential reading for anyone who wants to understand how the relationship between political and religious thought has shaped our world. For those who are interested in Hegel's political philosophy, Rosenzweig's book is an illuminating account of the development and political context of a way of thinking that remains relevant today. For those who are interested in Rosenzweig's own religiously inflected thought, this volume shows both the great promise and the crushing disappointment of the German political project that is the prelude to his masterwork, *The Star of Redemption*.'

— Paul Franks, Yale University, USA

'The best book on Hegel's political philosophy is Franz Rosenzweig's *Hegel und der Staat*, which first appeared in 1920. It is the most thorough in its research, the most extensive in its coverage, and the most rigorous in exposition and argument. Despite these merits, the book has not been translated into English – until now. It appears here in a reliable and accurate translation by Josiah and Jules Simon. This is a major event in Hegel scholarship, and a major contribution to the study of Hegel in the English-speaking world.'

— Frederick Beiser, Syracuse University, USA

# Hegel and the State

Franz Rosenzweig (1886–1929) is one of the most significant German Jewish philosophers of the twentieth century. Published in German in 1920 and now finally available in English for the first time, *Hegel and the State* is a major contribution to the understanding of Hegel's political and social thought and a profound analysis of the intellectual currents that shaped the German state in the late nineteenth and early twentieth centuries.

Through careful readings of Hegel's early handwritten manuscripts, Rosenzweig shows that Hegel was wrestling with the problem of how to reconcile the subjectivity and freedom of the individual within a community and ultimately the political state. According to Rosenzweig, the route out of this conundrum chosen by Hegel shaped his mature political philosophy, where he saw the relationship between the individual and the state as reciprocal. At a deeper level, the significance of *Hegel and the State* lies in the way that Rosenzweig explains the failure of Hegel's quasi-communitarian view of the state to emerge, due to the authoritarian direction of the newly unified German state under Bismarck. Anticipating the political and moral disaster that was to follow, Rosenzweig concludes by questioning the very viability of any theory of the state that relies on the pillars of bureaucratic militarism and a government-supported capitalist business culture.

With the inclusion of a Foreword by Myriam Bienenstock and a substantial Afterword by Axel Honneth, *Hegel and the State* is a ground-breaking work of early twentieth-century philosophical and political thought. It is essential reading for students of Hegel, German Idealism, Jewish philosophy, and the origins of critical theory. It will also be of interest to those in related subjects such as the history of sociology, and German and intellectual history.

**Franz Rosenzweig** (1886–1929) is one of the most original Jewish thinkers of the modern period. Following the First World War, he sought to bring about a novel synthesis of philosophy and theology he termed the "new thinking," shaping the course of early twentieth-century Jewish and Christian dialogue. His engagement with the theme of human finitude made a lasting impact on twentieth-century existentialism and he undertook two major works of translation, most notably the German translation of the Hebrew Bible in which he collaborated with Martin Buber. He founded a center for Jewish adult education in Frankfurt – the Lehrhaus – which attracted the most important young German Jewish intellectuals of its time and which is still held up today as a model for educational programs of its type. His life is marked by several extraordinary personal experiences, including a near-conversion to Christianity, an inspired return to Judaism, the composition of the beginning of his magnum opus on military postcards sent home from the Balkan front and the abandonment of a promising academic career in order to live and teach in the Frankfurt Jewish community. As well as *Hegel and the State* (1920), he is the author of what is arguably the greatest work of modern Jewish philosophy: *The Star of Redemption* (1921).

**Josiah Simon**, PhD, is an independent scholar, translator, and teacher living in Austin, TX. He has taught German, humanities, and philosophy at various institutions across the United States and conducted research in Germany at Heidelberg University and the Ruhr-University Bochum. His recent work has appeared in the *Rosenzweig Yearbook* and he is an active contributor to the *Hans Ehrenberg-Studien*.

**Jules Simon** is Professor of Philosophy at the University of Texas at El Paso. He writes, teaches, and lectures in the areas of phenomenology, ethical theory, Jewish philosophy, aesthetics, and philosophy of the city. He has published several books and numerous scholarly articles and chapters including the following: *Art and Responsibility: A Phenomenology of the Diverging Paths of Rosenzweig and Heidegger*; "Rosenzweig's Creation" in *Rosenzweig for Beginners*; "Rosenzweig's *Midrashic* Speech-Acts: From Hegel and German Nationalism to a Modern-Day *ba'al teshuvah*" in the *Cambridge Companion to Jewish Theology*; and "Rosenzweig and Benjamin, "Aesthetics and Politics: Reflections on Love and the Origins of Fascism" in *Filosofia*.

# Hegel and the State

Franz Rosenzweig
Translated by Josiah Simon and Jules Simon

Routledge
Taylor & Francis Group

LONDON AND NEW YORK

Cover image: Portrait of Franz Rosenzweig, c1902. CC BY-SA 4.0. Manuscript extract
from *Hegel und der Staat*, 1920. Leo Baeck Institute Repository, https://www.lbi.org

First published 2024
by Routledge
4 Park Square, Milton Park, Abingdon, Oxon OX14 4RN

and by Routledge
605 Third Avenue, New York, NY 10158

*Routledge is an imprint of the Taylor & Francis Group, an informa business*

First published in German in 1920 as *Hegel und der Staat.*

*British Library Cataloguing-in-Publication Data*
A catalogue record for this book is available from the British Library

*Library of Congress Cataloging-in-Publication Data*
Names: Rosenzweig, Franz, 1886–1929, author. | Simon, Josiah, translator. |
Simon, Jules, translator. | Bienenstock, Myriam, author of foreword. |
Honneth, Axel, 1949–author of afterword.
Title: Hegel and the state / Franz Rosenzweig; translated by Josiah Simon
and Jules Simon; [foreword by Myriam Bienenstock; afterword by Axel Honneth].
Other titles: Hegel und der staat. English
Description: First edition. | New York: Routledge, 2024. | Includes bibliographical refer-
ences and index.
Identifiers: LCCN 2023025257 (print) | LCCN 2023025258 (ebook) |
ISBN 9780367374969 (hbk) | ISBN 9781032602745 (pbk) |
ISBN 9780429354724 (ebk) Subjects: LCSH: Hegel, Georg Wilhelm Friedrich,
1770–1831—Political and social views. | State, The. | Philosophy, German—19th century. |
Political science—Germany—History.
Classification: LCC JC233 .R845 2024 (print) | LCC JC233 (ebook) |
DDC 320.1—dc23/eng/20230912
LC record available at https://lccn.loc.gov/2023025257
LC ebook record available at https://lccn.loc.gov/2023025258

ISBN: 978-0-367-37496-9 (hbk)
ISBN: 978-1-032-60274-5 (pbk)
ISBN: 978-0-429-35472-4 (ebk)

DOI: 10.4324/9780429354724

Typeset in Joanna
by codeMantra

# Contents

# FOREWORD

*Hegel and the State*, Franz Rosenzweig's first, brilliant masterpiece, had a significant impact upon the scholarship on Hegel's political philosophy. It is still highly regarded in our time, as is eloquently shown by the decision of the leading Hegel expert Axel Honneth, one of the best-known German philosophers today, to encourage the publication of a new paperback edition of the work by the prestigious Suhrkamp publisher (see also Honneth's Afterword to this volume). The present translation into English, competently carried out here by Jules and Josiah Simon, was long overdue, and could well become as successful in the English-speaking world as other already existing translations into foreign languages have been in other countries – in France, for example, where an eminent colleague of mine confessed to me that Rosenzweig's work, translated into French, acted upon her as a kind of revelation: Hegel had suddenly become a highly accessible philosopher, who even adopted reasonable political options.

Scholarship on Hegel has made much progress since Rosenzweig's time, without however invalidating most of his findings. This is a remarkable feat, which may be explained, in any case partly, by the fact that the young man had been formed as a historian of ideas, and taught to respect the exacting rules of "source criticism" (*Quellenforschung*), that great title of fame of German research: after he had decided to write on the genesis of Hegel's political thought, Rosenzweig went to Berlin – and became a "philologist," as he himself puts it, somewhat ironically: "I have gone among the philologists. I'm excerpting, collating, experiencing commas, pausing throughout, graphologizing, and [...] am a fool for the venerable parchment [...]" (letter dated November 11, 1910, to Hans Ehrenberg, GS I.1, p. 115): Rosenzweig made it his duty to examine not just Hegel's published works, but also all the manuscripts in Hegel's handwriting he could find in the Prussian National Library. He studied the writings of Hegel's friends and contemporaries, and the greatest possible number of books the philosopher had been able to consult (Waszek 2017); also annotating, in the copies of the books he was reading, the points that seemed important to him. Many of these marginalia are still waiting to be exploited (see however Bienenstock 2021). They show that the young man was not just a philologist, but a first-rate historian of ideas, intent upon identifying the context – theological, also political and historical – in which the texts he examined had been drafted; and then their philosophical significance.

*Hegel and the State* had been composed mainly before the First World War, but it was only published after the end of the war, in 1920; and when Rosenzweig wrote the Preface (*Vorwort*) just before that first publication, he confessed that he would not even have begun working on the theme, had he known the outcome of the conflict: the "field of ruins" the German Empire had become: "I do not know where one could find the courage today to write German history," he said, thereupon adding that if he nonetheless accepted to publish his work, this was for the sake of "science, which outlasts a life lain to ruins" (p. 12). Many, after him, did find the courage to write German history, though often after having dithered for some time. The best example of such a behavior is undoubtedly that of Friedrich Meinecke (1862–1954), Rosenzweig's thesis supervisor: the famous German historian and politician did not just go on writing books on the history of Germany; he also accepted high responsibilities within his university and even fulfilled a significant role in the political life of his country, during many years. Not so Rosenzweig: responding to his former teacher who had offered him an academic job, he refused. In a world in which "even the mountains of the spirit, which hitherto still looked like islands, are sinking into the flood," he wrote, "the only hope to survive is to take refuge in an ark, that floats on its own momentum

(*aus eigenem Antrieb*: letter dated September 17, 1923; GS I.2, p. 924 f.). To
Meinecke, who seems to have understood his attitude as a reaction of
despair after Germany's defeat, he answered that he had already adopted
such a solution before the war. He could also have added that the option
only concerned the Jewish people, not the "peoples of the world," as he
calls them in a section of *The Star of Redemption* entitled "Messianic Politics"
(GS II, pp. 328 ff.).

The *Star of Redemption*, sketched during the war and published in 1921,
contains in its third part the presentation of an eschatological conception of history whose relation to the Hegelian philosophy of history has
been, from the start, much debated: Rosenzweig seems to have intended
it to become a kind of critical counterpart to that philosophy – and also
to Hegel's system as a whole, for it is Hegel who serves, already on the
first pages of the *Star*, as his main target against philosophy, "from Ionia
to Jena" (GS II, pp. 6–12). A complete break seems to exist between the
first Rosenzweig, author of *Hegel and the State*, and the second, author of
the *Star*: this conclusion was reached by many prestigious readers of the
*Star*, among them Emmanuel Levinas, who never fails to celebrate Rosenzweig as one of his main sources of inspiration (Levinas 1990 [1959]).
The *Star of Redemption* is today much better-known than *Hegel and the State*: the
"New Thinking" it heralds (see Rosenzweig, 2000) is widely regarded
as a masterpiece of Jewish philosophy and also treated, quite often, as
a basis for understanding between Jews and Christians (Bienenstock
1998). Paradoxically enough, it even is the success of the *Star* which
accounts – for sure, only up to a certain point – for the present translation into English of *Hegel and the State*.

Still, the paradox could well reveal itself to be merely apparent: the
more recent scholarship has shown that Rosenzweig's rupture with
Hegel was much weaker than previously thought; perhaps even non-
existent on some important features of his Hegel-reception – particularly
the philosophy of history. The French Rosenzweig specialist Stéphane
Mosès, who had himself been very close to Levinas, thus famously contended that for Rosenzweig, the issue had not been "to prove that the
Hegelian view of history is false, but on the contrary, to show that it is
true, far beyond what Hegel himself could imagine [...]" (Mosès 2009
[1992], p. 38). It is indeed widely acknowledged today that the terms in
which Rosenzweig analyzed history in *The Star of Redemption* are typical of

his *Hegel and the State* and of the way in which he had retraced, in that first work of his, the genesis of the Hegelian conception of politics: Rosenzweig's characterization, in the *Star* (GS II, p. 331), of the Jewish people as already being *am Ziel* – at the goal toward which the nations are still moving and in this sense eternal, beyond history – is, at bottom, a variant interpretation of Hegel's conception of eternity as being itself in time, of history as spirit alienated in time. It would be difficult to understand his description of the state as "the attempt, which must of necessity be repeated again and again, to give nations eternity within the confines of time" (GS II, p. 332), without Hegel's discussion of the nature and role of the state in history – and the very assertion that "there is no universal history without the state" (GS II, p. 334) would not have been denied by Hegel himself. Rosenzweig had already ascribed that thesis to Hegel in his *Hegel and the State* (e.g., p. 306), the main question needing to be settled then being that of determining whether or not, or to what extent, his reconstitution of Hegel's political – and historical – conception was adequate (Bienenstock 1992).

In his 1920 Preface (below, p. 5), Rosenzweig himself explicitly acknowledged that the main impetus to his own work had been Meinecke's chapter on Hegel in his *Cosmopolitanism and the National State* (1st publication, 1907; English translation 1970, pp. 197–202) – and indeed one can only admire how carefully he developed many of the theses sketched out there, while at the same time cautiously criticizing some of them. According to Meinecke, "state and nation are so closely related to each other that the essential purpose in the existence of a nation is to be a state, and a nation that has not achieved the form of a state has no real history" (Meinecke 1970, p. 198) – but what is a "nation," according to Hegel? Endeavoring to answer that question, Rosenzweig focuses at first upon the notion of *Volksgeist*: a term on the origins and meaning of which a dispute was raging at the time (the term can be diversely rendered into English: see the translators' prudent solution below, p. xxxiii f.). Rosenzweig aptly clarifies the different options, and also renews the question: he singles out the crucial role played for Hegel by Montesquieu's definition of the *esprit général d'une nation* in his *Esprit des lois* (Book 19, Chapter 4) and brings out that which was to become, for Hegel, its main character: the *Volksgeist* always is a *result*, never a source (see below, pp. 38–41). The difference between Hegel's concept and that of the Romantic school is thereby firmly established, and the consequences are momentous, as Rosenzweig shows throughout his work.

Examining, in his 1920 Preface, three influential biographers of Hegel – Karl Rosenkranz, Rudolf Haym and Wilhelm Dilthey – Rosenzweig points out that Rudolf Haym (1821–1901), author of an influential *Hegel and his Age* (1st publication as a book, 1857), and also, one may add, of an imposing work on the *Romantic School* (1870) – had not merely perceived the danger of a "Romantic divinization of history" which permeated Hegel's age as a whole, but also tried to escape it (below, p. 9). Rosenzweig thereupon shows himself highly appreciative of the literary essays gathered by Wilhelm Dilthey (1833–1911) in his *Poetry and Experience* (*Das Erlebnis und die Dichtung*), a volume published in 1905 for the first time, and whose echoes in the whole German culture of the time were considerable: it contained path-breaking essays on Goethe and Hölderlin, also on Novalis and Lessing, and may well have conditioned Rosenzweig's own understanding of what he called "culture." But Rosenzweig also formulates a criticism – cautiously, though; for the Berlin Professor was still alive at that time, and very powerful: what Dilthey would have wanted to preserve, "despite everything presently happening and all the clear and irrefutable contradictions," was the "historical oneness" with Germany's past. Out of this strong conviction, the conscious will to secure "the continuity of our [i.e., Germany's: M.B.] spiritual development" had grown in him (below, p. 10): it is Dilthey's idea of the German national state – and of nationalism, which is criticized here.

The decade during which Rosenzweig worked on his book, between 1910 and 1920, was marked by the First World War, and by a concomitant outburst of nationalistic feelings – German, as well as French – which overwhelmed many of his contemporaries, also the philosophers (see here Lübbe 1974 [1963] on "the philosophical ideas of 1914," pp. 171 ff.); but not Rosenzweig, in *Hegel and the State*. An eloquent testimony of this can be found in a letter of Rosenzweig to his parents dated May 29, 1917:

> I deny *any* serious influence of the war on anybody. This is particularly nonsensical in my case, because I had already done much better than the war products before the outbreak of the war, which of course no

one can know. The chapter on Prussia of the Hegel (written in August/
September 1913 and March/May 1914) is much more valuable [...]

GS I.1, 411)

The letter was not originally published in full, which is unfortunate. But
the published passage, which has been much commented upon (see for
example Bienenstock 2018, p. 50 f.), already says a great deal, by referring the reader to Rosenzweig's stance in *Hegel and the State*'s important
Section 11 on Prussia: Rosenzweig had explained there that Hegel can
indeed rightly be considered as the philosopher of the Prussian state –
but only if what is meant is not Bismarck's, Treitschke's or even Meinecke's representations of it, but the Prussian state of the Reform Movement, around Stein and Hardenberg, which Hegel believed to be on the
way towards a constitutional one, a *Rechtsstaat*. "The central idea of the
coming national politics, that a people must create its state for the sake
of its history and according to the measure of its history," Rosenzweig
writes perspicuously, "was completely alien to him [Hegel]" (below, p.
306). Rosenzweig repeats, and strongly insists that Hegel's conception
of the state had definitely not been an early version of the Bismarckian *Machtstaat*, which was grounded upon *raison d'état* and exempt of all
moral obligations toward the individual. The vocabulary to which he
resorts may well have been misleading at some points – and anachro-
nistic with regard to Hegel's own vocabulary, for it was Meinecke's own,
non-Hegelian definition of "power" as *Macht* which Rosenzweig took
over. But this makes his merit as an interpreter all the more striking: at
a time when German nationalism was at one of its peaks, Rosenzweig
rightly insisted that Hegel had never gotten to the point made by later
political thinkers, who granted an unconditional right to the "nation."
It had been in the state itself – and even in a non-national one – that
Hegel had found the utter fulfillment of what the individual longed for
(below, p. 506).

Rosenzweig seems to have equated Hegel's state with what Meinecke
had defined as a "political nation" (*Staatsnation*) – and distinguished from
a "cultural nation" (*Kulturnation*: Meinecke 1970, p. 10). He was thereby
led to assert that Hegel did not relate "state" and "culture," except in
early, as yet non-elaborated Tübingen drafts, and in his later philosophy of history (below, p. 428). The conception of "culture" Rosenzweig

presupposed there seems to have been much closer to Meinecke's — and Dilthey's — idea, than to Hegel's own understanding of "culture" as *Bildung*, or "formation to culture." That conception also included the "formation to culture" through labour, as well as the development of an economic and social activity in the framework of what Hegel had called "civil society" (Bienenstock 1992, p. 178 f.) In his *Hegel and the State*, Rosenzweig even evokes Hegel's interesting solution to the "social question," arguing that with it, Hegel leaves the theories of his age far behind (below, p. 380). Crucial as this insight is, it is not the most important part of Hegel's conception, according to Rosenzweig.

What retains his interest in the last pages of his work is another question, which indeed seems to have deeply troubled Hegel himself at the end of his life: the question of the relation between religion and the state. Rosenzweig writes that Hegel changed his mind on that question in 1830, apparently after having observed the way in which the July Revolution evolved in France: merely "one decade ago," Rosenzweig writes, Hegel had been one of the "ingenious men who want to separate state and religion," but now he would argue that they are "grossly mistaken" — and resolved to require the foundation of the state upon the single Protestant faith (below, p. 477). Endeavoring to clarify Hegel's reasons, Rosenzweig writes that Hegel found everywhere the same basic error: believing that there could be a political revolution without a prior reform of the minds, a Reformation. This would explain why Hegel does not seem to have expected, even then, "after forty years of wars and immense confusion [...] a permanent end to those revolutionary confusions and wars" (below, p. 483). A lively discussion has developed in recent years on that question of the difficult relation between religion and state in Hegel (see Jaeschke 1983, p. 38; Siep 2011, pp. 28–34). The discussion is also based on Rosenzweig's pertinent remarks in *Hegel and the State* — the work has lost none of its relevance, evidently.

Myriam Bienenstock, April 2023

## REFERENCES

Myriam Bienenstock, "Rosenzweig's Hegel," in: *The Owl of Minerva. Journal of the Hegel Society of America*, 23.2, Spring 1992, pp. 177–182.

Myriam Bienenstock, "Franz Rosenzweig," in: *Routledge Encyclopedia of Philosophy*, ed. by E. Craig, London: Routledge, 1998, vol.8, pp. 357–362.

Myriam Bienenstock, *Cohen und Rosenzweig. Ihre Auseinandersetzung mit dem deutschen Idealismus.* Freiburg i.Br.: Alber, 2018.

Myriam Bienenstock, "Friendship and Religion. Some Missing Elements in Hegel's Conception of 'Lordship and Bondage'," in: *The Owl's Flight. Hegel's Legacy to Contemporary Philosophy*, ed. by Stefania Achella et al., Berlin: De Gruyter, 2021, pp. 521–533.

Wilhelm Dilthey, *Poetry and Experience*, in: *Selected Works*, vol. V. Ed. by Rudolf A. Makkreel and Frithojf Rodi, Princeton: Princeton University Press, 1985 [1905].

Walter Jaeschke, "Hegel's last year in Berlin" (translated by Norbert Waszek), in: *Hegel's Philosophy of Action*, ed. by L.S. Stepelevich and D. Lamb, Atlantic Highlands: Humanities Press, 1983, pp. 31–48.

Emmanuel Levinas, *Totalité et Infini. Essai sur l'extériorité.* Paris: Nijhoff, 1961. Translated by Alphonso Lingis: *Totality and Infinity. An Essay on Exteriority*, Dordrecht: Nijhoff, 1979.

Emmanuel Levinas, "Between Two Worlds" [1959], in: *Difficult Freedom. Essays on Judaism* tr. by Seán Hand, Baltimore: The Johns Hopkins University Press, 1990, pp. 181–201.

Hermann Lübbe, *Politische Philosophie in Deutschland. Studien zu ihrer Geschichte*, München: Deutscher Taschenbuch Verlag, 1974 [1963].

Friedrich Meinecke, *Weltbürgertum und Nationalstaat.* München: Oldenbourg, 1907, 2nd ed.; translated by Robert B. Kimber, Introduction by Felix Gilbert: *Cosmopolitanism and the National State*, Princeton: Princeton University Press, 1970.

Stéphane Mosès, "Hegel taken literally," in: *The Angel of History. Rosenzweig, Benjamin, Scholem.* Translated by Barbara Harshaw, Stanford: Stanford University Press, 2009 [*L'Ange de l'Histoire. Rosenzweig, Benjamin, Scholem.* Paris: Seuil, 1992].

Franz Rosenzweig, *Der Mensch und sein Werk. Gesammelte Schriften* (abbreviated: GS), I–IV. Den Haag: Nijhoff, 1976–1984.

Franz Rosenzweig, *Philosophical and Theological Writings.* Trans. and ed. by Paul W. Franks and Michael J. Morgan. Indianapolis: Hackett, 2000.

Ludwig Siep, "Säkularer Staat, Religion und Kirche," in: *Hegels praktische Philosophie und das Projekt der Moderne.* Baden-Baden: Nomos, 2011, pp. 28–33.

Norbert Waszek (ed.), *Rosenzweigs Bibliothek.* Freiburg: Alber, 2017.

# Translators' Introduction

Franz Rosenzweig's *Hegel and the State* (1920) is a pioneering work on the intellectual biography of Hegel.[1] Drawing from newly published editions of Hegel's works, as well as previously unpublished manuscripts, Rosenzweig (1886–1929) composed a philosophically nuanced narrative that serves as a nearly exhaustive and critical perspective on the development of Hegel's political thought and his conception of the state. Beginning with Hegel's earliest writings and placing a special focus on Hegel's theological manuscripts and the development of Hegel's systematic thought, Rosenzweig's work culminates in a detailed and historically situated account of the *Philosophy of Right* that highlights Rosenzweig's attention to historical detail, literary style, and mastery of philosophical argument.[2]

The book grew from Rosenzweig's dissertation – begun in 1909 under the guidance of German historian Friedrich Meinecke – and was written in a decidedly historicist tone.[3] Rosenzweig was also writing, however, in the wake of the publication of Wilhelm Dilthey's then highly influential *Poetry and Experience*,[4] lending his work, in tandem with its historiological and biographical form, a literary depth that Rosenzweig would continue to cultivate in his subsequent writings. In its finished form, *Hegel and the State* was published just one year before Rosenzweig's stunningly complex *The Star of Redemption* (1921), widely regarded as one of the greatest works of Jewish philosophy of the twentieth century.[5] The difference between the two works is formidable, even though Rosenzweig was editing both books simultaneously for publication. Between the time when Rosenzweig began his Hegel book in 1909 and the time of its publication in 1920, it can be said that he underwent a series of "conversions,"[6] resulting in the existential philosophy of religion configured in *The Star of Redemption*. It is thus understandable that Rosenzweig would now see himself, as he would write to his teacher Meinecke shortly after publishing *The Star of Redemption*, as an author of a "different caliber."[7] Owing in part to this statement, *Hegel and the State* has long suffered the fate of being overshadowed by *The Star of Redemption*, especially among Rosenzweig scholars, and Rosenzweig's later work has since grown into a life of its own. However, when Rosenzweig noted in 1920 in the addendum to the Hegel book that this was a work he "would no longer have written today,"[8] he was not commenting directly on his changed disposition as the author of *The Star of Redemption* – as Rosenzweig scholars have often assumed and as Rosenzweig's own confessions might lead one to believe – but rather on his overall disenchantment with post-Wilhelminian Germany itself. Prior to the collapse of the German Empire, Rosenzweig was writing on the forefront of what Wilhelm Windelband in 1910 famously called the "Hegel Renaissance" and he belonged to a group of young scholars – which included Rosenzweig's cousin and close friend Hans Ehrenberg (1883–1958), his "first teacher in philosophy"[9] – who wrote passionately "for and against Hegel."[10] When Rosenzweig decided to publish his Hegel book shortly after the end of the War, even if "a glimmer of hope" could still be gleamed from the work of his past, a new image was now before his eyes: "A field of ruins now marks the place where the Empire had once stood."[11]

*Hegel and the State* was originally published in two separate volumes: "Stations of Life" [Lebensstationen] and "Epochs of the World" [Weltepochen]. The first volume follows the "stations" of Hegel's personal and philosophical development from Stuttgart, Tübingen, Bern, and Frankfurt, leading up to the earliest versions of Hegel's system in Jena, at the end of which Hegel stands "face to face with the age."[12] The second volume shows how Hegel's thought and personality play out against the "epochs" of world history – Napoleon, Restoration, Prussia – until in the wake of the July Revolution Hegel falls to his fate at the call of the "messenger from Hades."[13] Life and death, the two poles of biography, give way to a short reflection on the legacy of Hegel's political thought in light of the new German Empire.

The form of Rosenzweig's narrative, and his explicit intention to publish the work in two distinct volumes – a gesture he would replicate in configuring *The Star of Redemption* into three separate books – suggests an insurmountable, or at the very least problematic, division between "life" and "thought," pointing towards a critique of the concept of "unity" presupposed by German Idealism. What begins as a depiction of Hegel's "stream of personal life" intertwined with his formation as a philosopher in the first volume takes on the character of a struggle for the "unification with the age"[14] in the second, through Rosenzweig's analysis of Hegel's mature philosophy of the state and of right. By framing his philosophical biography as the struggle between Hegel's personal development and the surrounding political world, and showing how this tension played out in the "actuality" of the age in the struggle between the individual and the state in the "mirror"[15] of Hegel's thought, Rosenzweig aimed to give his readers at the beginning of the twentieth century a living glimpse into their own political history, and in this way reanimate and enliven their critical engagement with German history and contemporary political communities.

In choosing the form of philosophical biography for his work and thus presenting a sweeping narrative account of Hegel's entire development, Rosenzweig imbues this narrative, to use Hayden White's technical term, with what reads like a *tragic* "emplotment,"[16] tracing the development of Hegel's thought in tandem with his philosophical character. Thus, Rosenzweig's culminating critique of Hegel's *Philosophy of Right* cannot be separated from what Otto Pöggeler calls the danger of "dramatizing Hegel's way."[17] Rosenzweig himself, however, was aware of the nuanced interpretive work that philosophical biography entails, as is attested to in his "Preface" to *Hegel and the State*, which was composed shortly after completing the work.[18] This short, literary text serves as an introductory narrative that places the authors of what Rosenzweig understood as the three classic Hegel biographies of his time into a historical constellation: Karl Rosenkranz, Rudolf Haym, and Wilhelm Dilthey.[19] These authors each made material contributions to the study of

Hegel's life, and their works made their way into the substance of Rosenzweig's critique. By introducing *Hegel and the State* with the *historical personalities* who wrote Hegel's life, Rosenzweig demonstrates his awareness
of a key philosophical claim. Namely, he implicitly argues that understanding Hegelian thought necessitates reading and interpreting Hegel's
written works, together with his intellectual friendships and adversaries, within the context of their biographical-historical development. The
overall intent of Rosenzweig's work substantiates the wise advice that
in order to best understand Hegelian thought, "one should not wish
to pull it from the stream onto a dry embankment."[20] Only in resisting
this desire – in allowing ourselves to read the work from the fused perspectives of philosophy *and* history – may we preserve the subtlety and
nuance of Rosenzweig's original work on Hegel.

In closely following Rosenzweig's gestures, as the example of the
"Preface" shows, and in learning to recognize Rosenzweig's distinctive
tone and philosophical critique, we come to know – despite the over-
whelming scope of contemporary Hegel scholarship – a different and
perhaps even new Hegel: Rosenzweig's Hegel. And while this sometimes
leaves the reader the challenging task, as Martin Kavka has formulated
it, of "untangling Hegel"[21] from Rosenzweig's own account, Rosenzweig's configuration of Hegel's philosophical biography serves as an
unmatched guide in navigating us into and through the labyrinths of
Hegelian political thought. This is especially the case if we recognize and
acknowledge that Rosenzweig, in writing *Hegel and the State*, combined the
three separate roles of historian, philosopher, and biographer. This depth
and variety of perspective, as Axel Honneth argues in his "Afterword" to
this edition, situates Rosenzweig as a central figure in Hegel studies. Following Dilthey, Rosenzweig implements a nuanced method that could
be aptly termed an "historical philosophy of life" [*geschichtliche Lebensphilosophie*],[22] setting Hegel's written works, intellectual friendships, and historical events into a productive constellation. What is unique to Rosenzweig is his acute awareness of his own position as a biographer within
an existing tradition of interpretation, as his narrative "Preface" clearly
shows. However, despite the biographical form of the work, it is easy
to agree with Honneth when he writes that "with all Rosenzweig's talent at narrative presentation, the systematically oriented philosopher still
holds the upper hand over the historian of ideas."[23] This statement strikes

at the heart of the book. Within the text, it is noticeable when Rosenzweig switches from the role of a biographical *historian* with philosophical intentions into the character of the *philosopher* himself. Rosenzweig's trust in his own capacity as a philosopher is on display, for example, when he writes, in introducing Hegel's "Metaphysics of the State," that he aims to understand what is ultimately at stake for Hegel's political thought, yet "without relying too heavily upon Hegel's own words."[24] This interpretive approach is complemented by what Stéphane Mosès called Rosenzweig's "principle of citation."[25] In how Rosenzweig balances his own words with direct quotes from Hegel's texts, he preserves a conceptual distance to Hegel that allows for some breathing room and perspective, inviting readers to follow the development of Hegel's political thought more freely, while also allowing for his own position as a philosopher to emerge. Indeed, it is precisely the philosophical expertise with which Rosenzweig carried out the substance of his task that led Frederick Beiser to laud the work as "the most authoritative on its subject."[26] However, as Axel Honneth rightly observes, "for the contemporary reader, engaging the study at hand first requires that one work through the crust of antiquated viewpoints and interpretive perspectives, before one can reach the actually productive, living kernel."[27]

Rosenzweig's generation – the first, but certainly not the last "Hegel Renaissance" of the twentieth century[28] – had already experienced what years later would be described as the challenge of future Hegel scholarship, namely that "Hegel's philosophy might no longer survive as philosophy, but only as the object of scientific, i.e. philological interest."[29] At the time of its composition, *Hegel and the State* was indeed of great philological interest, presenting the first systematic account of the genesis of Hegel's political philosophy, wed as it was to his philosophy of history. But it was, and still is, more than this: "The book on Hegel also seems to be silently determined by thoughts that later were to become important for Rosenzweig."[30] It is in view of this "silent" determination that the methodological considerations of philosophical biography, attended by a historically contextualized narrative critique, remain so important. When Rosenzweig began writing his Hegel book, he found himself in the currents of his own "stream of personal life"[31] – the "Land of Two Rivers" [*Zweistromland*], or the German Jewish "renaissance" at the beginning of the twentieth century he would help to create. Rosenzweig was a young

Jewish intellectual living in a country dominated by both Christian and secular, or deeply embedded pagan, cultural, historical, linguistic, and philosophical sedimentations. Historically, this correlates with how Norbert Samuelson describes Jewish exilic existence over the course of 2000 years, namely, that the Jewish People continuously formed and reformed their identities in dialogue with the dominant cultures in which they found themselves, as Ashkenazis, Sefardis, Americans, and today as modern Israelis.[32] The way that Rosenzweig places himself "in dialogue" with Hegel shows that Rosenzweig's book, as Wayne Cristaudo has expressed it, "is as revealing about its author as it is about its subject."[33] Readers familiar with Rosenzweig will notice how *Hegel and the State* aligns with Rosenzweig's own understanding of "narrative philosophy" [*erzählende Philosophie*],[34] his phrase for the ethical demand to take time, and thus the ethical import of the other, seriously. And those even somewhat familiar with Rosenzweig's work, even if only superficially, will notice "how various Rosenzweigs [...] jostle up against one another."[35] And what emerges from this experience is not only Rosenzweig's significance as an important interpreter of Hegel's philosophical and historical legacy, but also, in the poetical words of Shlomo Avineri, that Rosenzweig himself is "an intrinsic part of the brilliant galaxy of German philosophy."[36]

In order to understand the substance – and limitations – of Rosenzweig's critique, in order to preserve the subtlety and nuance of his interpretations in *Hegel and the State*, the narrative form of the work and the philosophical substance of the critique must be taken as a whole. The aim of the *Philosophy of Right*, as Hegel claims in the Preface, was nothing less than "the *reconciliation* with actuality."[37] Among the many faces of Hegel displayed for us by Rosenzweig is one that reveals Hegel's self-understanding – as one called "to comprehend" [*begreifen*] – that was coupled with his workman-like commitment to help his listeners and readers "preserve their subjective freedom in the realm of the substantial."[38] Pöggeler asserts that "Hegel's sole aim is to seek rationality in what is actual, and he has no desire to stray beyond what is actual or is becoming actual."[39] From that perspective, the lasting contribution of Hegel's political thought, simply put, would be to help orient thinking individuals in the basic relations of humankind – to other humans, communities, and our shared political world. That is already an ethically infused task. In this sense, Rosenzweig was also inspired by Hegel to "seek rationality in what is actual," laboring for many years on a penetrating and original study on Hegel's life and political thought. However, as explicitly worked out in his original reading of Hegel's "double-dictum" in the section on "Prussia," Rosenzweig also worked through the ways in which Hegel came to realize that the ultimate importance of the relation between rationality and actuality was in actualizing the rational.[40] This demand, which became the quintessential contribution of Hegel's idealist thought to and from the history of philosophy, supports the task of ethically educating individuals to trust in their cultural education as a ground for the personal commitment to freely choose to work in their own individual ways – and thus to thrive – in and with the state.

It is our hope that our translation will render visible the "living kernel" of *Hegel and the State* to our readers and that the work as a whole can show how Rosenzweig's own productive encounter with Hegel continues to be a fertile source for navigating Hegelian thought, as well as the fruitful "entanglement" of Hegel and Rosenzweig. With respect to Rosenzweig scholarship, to understand the impact of Hegel for Rosenzweig requires one to work from the direction of Rosenzweig's own engagement with Hegel's thought, even explicitly bracketing this encounter and resisting the desire to read another "Rosenzweig" back into it. And with respect to Hegel scholarship, unearthing the "living kernel" of Rosenzweig's critique requires, in the spirit of Hegel himself, to recognize in what manner "the interest of the whole realizes itself through the particular ends."[41] For both thinkers, what Rosenzweig writes about the legacy of Hegel's thought in the wake of the publication of the *Philosophy of Right* still applies at the beginning of the twenty-first century: "Life had to first break apart the unity of thought in order to construct these broken pieces anew."[42]

Looking back upon the early twentieth century – one hundred years after *Hegel and the State* appeared and two hundred years after the publication of the *Philosophy of Right* – Rosenzweig's Hegel book has exceeded the limited hopes of its author, who had seen in his own work a dispassionate service to "science, which outlasts a life lain to ruins."[43] Yet Rosenzweig could not have been aware of the many competing forms Hegel's legacy would take or even that the thinking demanded by his philosophy would not be "abandoned by reason." Rather, in a world fraught with contradictions and competing ideologies, Hegel's philosophy is once again called to task, although the historical conditions have drastically changed: "In endeavoring to conceptualize the upheaval that marked the end of the eighteenth and the beginning of the nineteenth centuries, Hegel hands down to us a task that, following two world wars and in the light of the ongoing political, economic, and environmental catastrophes that threaten us, has become almost inconceivably more difficult."[44] Indeed, to put the normative guidelines more clearly, the ongoing task of disentangling the threads of Hegelian thought remains relevant because of how the dialectical passages and provisional reconciliations that deeply characterize Hegel's philosophy provide powerful models for constructively thinking through the problems of emerging worlds. Not only has Rosenzweig provided us with a work that still serves to help navigate the "rationality" of Hegel's thought for understanding these "actual" emerging worlds and institutions, but this work deserves to be read on its own terms – first in bracketing *The Star of Redemption* and only then in tandem with this book – to help us better face the entanglement of Rosenzweig's own philosophical legacy with Hegel and German Idealism, as well as articulate the nexus of religion and nationalism in twentieth century Europe. And only in this regard – as a testament to both Hegel *and* Rosenzweig – may we rightly situate *Hegel and the State* among the "classics of philosophy."[45]

* * *

This translation was begun in working with the facsimile reprint of the original 1920 edition of *Hegel and the State*, first published in this form in 1962 and again in 1982. As Axel Honneth notes in his "Afterword," the German Gothic script contributed to making the text both less accessible and, in the reprints published well into the twentieth century, certainly gave it a less modern feel. When in 2010 Suhrkamp Verlag published a new German edition of the book, edited by Frank Lachmann, we shifted our focus and began working with this new edition of the text. Not only does the Suhrkamp edition present Rosenzweig's text in modern typescript, but Lachmann's editorial work, primarily through an extensive reworking of the endnotes, helped to better align Rosenzweig's *Hegel and the State* with modern Hegel scholarship. We retained all of the endnotes from the Suhrkamp edition, including the exact numbering, in order to faithfully align our translation with Lachmann's scholarly edition. The endnote numbering, for those interested in referencing the German text, may also serve as a means of orientation between the Suhrkamp edition and our English translation.

In shifting from working with one edition of the text to another, when any discrepancies between the 1920 and the 2010 editions arose, we chose to defer to Rosenzweig's 1920 edition. Perhaps the most important and substantial discrepancy between the Suhrkamp edition and our translation is the curious omission of Rosenzweig's two epigraphs, which he took from Friedrich Hölderlin's poem *"An die Deutschen"* [To the Germans], and which we have included in our edition. The epigraphs are not merely ornamental. They function as the "motto" of Rosenzweig's book and form a substantive part of Rosenzweig's narrative. As Rosenzweig even alludes to them within the main body of the text itself, we thus deemed their inclusion essential.

Although there are various standard English translations of Hegel's works, the literature is far from uniform. In our own work, we have drawn from a circle of various Hegel translators. The most important of these translators for our work are: H.B. Nisbet (*Elements of the Philosophy of Right; Political Writings*); Alan White (*The Philosophy of Right*); T.M. Knox (*Early Theological Writings; Natural Law; Political Writings; Hegel's Philosophy of Right*); J. Michael Stewart and Peter C. Hodgson (*Lectures on Natural Right and Political Science*); and Brady Bowman and Allen Speight (*Heidelberg Writings*). While our translation choices only occasionally coincided directly with the work of these fellow translators, more than anything, their work was helpful in keeping track of technical terms and cross-checking several obscure or challenging passages.

All in all, in translating *Hegel and the State*, we chose to treat Rosenzweig's work as a primary source itself. Rosenzweig wrote his text on Hegel before the version of "Hegel" that evolved into the twentieth and twenty-first century existed – a Hegel now almost unreadable without referring to Marx, for example – and before the language used to speak about Hegel and even Hegel's philosophical terms themselves had become calcified, for better or worse, within our modern minds. There is a certain fluidity of meaning to Rosenzweig's text which a strictly technical coherence to the various standard translations of Hegel's technical terms would suppress. As Rosenzweig's translators, we have thus attempted to lend Rosenzweig's language, and indeed preserve in this language, the excitement and tone of discovery and not paint over this language in too modern a manner, thereby turning Rosenzweig into just another Hegel interpreter among many. In other words, we worked to retain the unique tone of Rosenzweig's interpretation.

In order to aid the reader, we have chosen to include several key German terms in brackets to help better trace these terms throughout. This occurs, for example, when the English translation was ambiguous, or when an important German term was introduced for the first time in the text. Less often, we set a German term in brackets to help the reader recall our translation, or even give the curious reader a point of contact to the original German.

The English translation of *Hegel and the State* has presented problems both unique to this work and ones common to all translations of Hegel – and to German philosophy and literature more broadly. Rosenzweig's ability to conceptualize and structure historical events philosophically lends this work a linguistic complexity that, while perhaps not lost on the trained German reader, is difficult to replicate in English. In translating the text, we were confronted with the unavoidable issue of how both Hegel and Rosenzweig respectively embraced German culture and its linguistic medium and with determining how to deal with certain ambiguous or equivocal terms. It is not only the common translation problems of terms like *Bildung* or *Geist* that proved difficult, but the fact that Rosenzweig's study is so comprehensive – spanning each stage of Hegel's development – and that Rosenzweig himself becomes deeply merged in the linguistic medium of the age. Moreover, underlying this cultural depth and complexity is the immanent challenge of Hegel's philosophy and philosophical system itself. On the level of language, since Rosenzweig was tracing the development of Hegel's system – understood most broadly as spirit coming to recognize itself as an evolving process of historical self-actualization – this carries with it the consequence that terms which might have had one meaning at a certain stage of this process gradually change their meaning at a later, or higher, stage. While these problems are not new to Hegel and Rosenzweig, and certainly not new to translating itself, this text did provide us with specific terms that remained challenging or even inadequate throughout. Thus, what follows below is meant to give several concrete examples of our thinking as translators, while also showing how our decisions were bound up with our own philosophical interpretations of the text.

Above all, what readers of Hegel will soon notice is our choice to translate *Sittlichkeit* – which could be taken as the central term of the book – with "ethicality." In doing so, we have diverged from the now standard translation of "ethical life" and followed Alan White in his translation of the *Philosophy of Right*. In our understanding, this choice preserves the more deliberate phrase "*sittliches Leben*" ("ethical life"), does not conflate notions of "life" and "ethics," and better draws out the dialectical relation between "morality" and "ethicality" as two technical terms in Hegel's vocabulary. Furthermore, the term "ethicality" may even allow some readers to approach the concept of *Sittlichkeit* with new eyes and heighten the appreciation of Rosenzweig's pioneering spirit. And finally, we hold "ethicality" to be a more accurate and useful translation of *Sittlichkeit*, as it holds the conceptual space of this term without linking it unequivocally to the concept of "life." Following this reasoning, we also chose to render *sittlich* as "ethical."

As consistently as possible, we chose to translate the verb *erkennen* as "to recognize" and *anerkennen* as "to acknowledge," aware of the limitations of both English terms. For the term *Bildung* we have oscillated, depending on context, between "culture," "education," "cultivation," and "formation," and marked the term in brackets when we deemed it important. The noun *Geist* we translated consistently as "spirit," while the adjective *geistig* is mostly "spiritual," and in a few instances "intellectual," "academic" or even "lucid."

A central term in Rosenzweig's text, and a tricky problem for us, was the translation of *Gewalt* and its use in several compound nouns. Accordingly, again depending on context, when *Gewalt* appeared on its own, we translated it as "authority" or "force." The noun *Staatsgewalt* we translated as "state authority" and the plural *Staatsgewalten* as "powers of the state" or "state-powers." Another central term is *Gesinnung*, which we translated as "disposition," and the central concept of *Staatsgesinnung* we translated as "disposition towards the state" and at times "state-disposition."

Hegel's concept of *Volksgeist* provided us with a good challenge, as this term evolves in meaning over the course of Hegel's development and in translating the term, we have tried to capture Rosenzweig's account of this evolution. For example, in earlier sections, we have translated *Volkgeist* as "folk spirit," where it denotes a more pagan, ethnic understanding of *Volk*, and in later sections, where Rosenzweig sees Hegel grappling with the national-ethos emerging from the French Revolution, as "spirit of the people." We marked this distinction in brackets at certain junctures to avoid the German term being lost in ambiguity. Related to this, we translated *Volk* as "people" and *Völker* as "peoples," and resisted the terms "nation" and "nations." Significantly, Rosenzweig is diligent in showing that for Hegel *Volk* does not equate with "nation," and that Hegel's state doctrine is therefore not a model for the modern national state.

This same logic of linguistic evolution in Hegel's understanding applies to the evolving nature of a *Verfassung* ("constitution"), a term which carried considerable ambiguity in nineteenth century Europe. The notion of a *Verfassung* is situated somewhere between a living engagement with the evolving history of a people and a living document that corresponds to the self-governing "lived world" of the people who form and live by the constitution. As this term evolves for Hegel, in addition to the more common *Verfassung*, he uses the modern French word and conception of "constitution" [*Konstitution*] and thus we have used brackets to mark the different notions of *Konstitution* and *Verfassung* in the text.

Another central problem for our translation was the evolving nature of what Hegel terms *Stand*, and *Stände* in the plural, along with a series of associated compound nouns and adjectival phrases. While the term "estate" captures the term *Stand* in a technical sense, not only is the notion of an "estate" foreign to contemporary minds, it obscures the modern notion of "class" that was emerging in the changing socio-economic world of nineteenth century Germany along with the evolution of Hegel's philosophical thought. Thus, we opted to also selectively employ the term "class" to account for Rosenzweig's analyses of Hegel's own understanding of the evolving semantics of that phrase, especially as it applies to evolving socio-political conditions reflected in Hegel's later writings, noting that Hegel also occasionally uses the German term *Klasse* ("class") interchangeably with *Stand*.

While the occasional use of brackets is meant to aid the reader, we also avoided overusing this practice as not to take away from the readability and flow of the text. Overall, given what we deem to be a highly challenging, complex, and yet significantly rewarding text, we worked to the best of our ability to remain consistent in translating Rosenzweig's work while providing the reader with a clear and accessible text. To the reader, we hope that our translation will open new interpretive pathways into the existing historical context and ongoing relevance of Hegel's thought as well as Rosenzweig's philosophical legacy. For both those with only limited knowledge of German and for those with a command of the language, it is our further hope that our English translation will provide a new and complementary view on Rosenzweig's text that will bring – in the spirit of Rosenzweig's own thoughts on translation – something new to the original itself.

Josiah Simon (Austin, TX) and Jules Simon (El Paso, TX), May 2023

## NOTES

1   Rosenzweig, Franz. *Hegel und der Staat*. Berlin: Suhrkamp Verlag, 2010. First published: München and Berlin: Verlag von R. Oldenbourg, 1920. Facsimile reprint: Aalen: Scientia Verlag, 1962 (1984).

2   See: Roberto Navarrete Alonso, "'Der Jude, der in deutschem Geist macht.' Das Hegelbuch Franz Rosenzweigs und seine Wirkung." *Naharaim* 2016; 10 (2): 273–302. Navarrete Alonso's meticulously researched essay on *Hegel and the State* serves as a first class source on situating Rosenzweig's Hegel book within both Rosenzweig's intellectual biography and within Hegel scholarship. The present introduction is written in the same spirit of working with the "Rosenzweig vor dem historischen Rosenzweig [...] der weit bekannt ist" (277).

3   In this regard *Hegel and the State* belongs to the tradition of German historiography that was thrown into crisis at the beginning of the twentieth century. See: Paul Mendes-Flohr, "Franz Rosenzweig and the Crisis of Historicism," in: *The Philosophy of Franz Rosenzweig*. Hannover: University Press of New England, 1988.

4   Wilhelm Dilthey. *Das Erlebnis und die Dichtung*. Stuttgart: B.G. Teubner Verlagsgesellschaft, 1957 (1906).

5   For a nuanced account of Rosenzweig's view towards his own Hegel book, see Navarrete Alonso, "'Der Jude, der in deutschem Geist macht'", 291–292.

6   See here: Benjamin Pollock, *Franz Rosenzweig's Conversions*. Bloomington: Indiana UP, 2014. Especially pgs. 51–58 on "Hegel and Hypochondria."

7   See Nahum N. Glatzer, *Franz Rosenzweig*. New York: Schocken Books, 1970, 96.

8   Page 12, this volume.

9   Wolfdietrich Schmied-Kowarzik, "Brief Illuminations on the Dialogue between Franz Rosenzweig and Hans Ehrenberg," in: *Rosenzweig Jahrbuch* 8/9 (2014), 87–111.

10   Wilhelm Windelband, *Präludien. Aufsätze und Reden zur Philosophie und ihrer Geschichte*. Tübingen: Verlag von J.C.B. Mohr, 1921. See here also: Otto Pöggeler, "Hegel Editing and Hegel Research," in: *The Legacy of Hegel. Proceedings of the Marquette Hegel Symposium 1970*, 23.

11   Page 12, this volume.

12   Page 249, this volume.

13   Page 497, this volume.

14   Page 340, this volume. [*Vereinigung mit der Zeit*]

15   Page 136, this volume.

16   See Haydn White, *Metahistory: The Historical Imagination in Nineteenth-Century Europe*, 1973, 7.

17   Otto Pöggeler, "Between Enlightenment and Romanticism: Rosenzweig and Hegel," in: *The Philosophy of Franz Rosenzweig*, Ed. Paul Mendes-Flohr (1988), 121.

18   Shlomo Avineri writes that the "the whole *Vorwort*, is itself a chapter of German *Geistesgeschichte* [...] a reflection of the spiritual as well as political development of Germany in the 19th century." (Avineri, "Rosenzweig's Hegel Interpretation," in: *Der Philosoph Franz Rosenzweig, Bd. II*. München: Verlag Karl Alber, 1988, 832.

19   Karl Rosenkranz, *G.W.F. Hegels Leben* (1844); Rudolf Haym, *Hegel und seine Zeit* (1857); Wilhelm Dilthey, *Die Jugendgeschichte Hegels* (1905).

20   Page 19, this volume.

21   Martin Kavka, "A Note on Religion and the State in Rosenzweig's *Hegel und der Staat*," in: *Rosenzweig Jahrbuch*, 8/9 (2014), 150.

22   See Otto Bollnow, *Die Lebensphilosophie*. Berlin: Springer-Verlag, 1958.

23   Honneth, "Afterword," Page 523, this volume.

24   Page 418, this volume [*ohne allzu unmittelbaren Anschluß an das Hegelsche Wort*].

25   Stéphane Mosès, "Hegel beim Wort genommen," in: *Zeitgewinn. Messianisches Denken nach Franz Rosenzweig*. Frankfurt am Main: Verlag Josef Knecht, 1987, 75.

26   Frederick Beiser, "Introduction: The Puzzling Hegel Renaissance," in: *Hegel and Nineteenth-Century Philosophy*. 2009.

27   Honneth, "Afterword," Page 510, this volume.

28   Beiser, "Introduction." See also: Slavoj Žižek, Frank Ruda, and Agon Hamza, *Reading Hegel*. Cambridge: Polity Press, 2022.

29   Otto Pöggeler, "Hegel Editing and Hegel Research," 23.

30   Pöggeler, "Rosenzweig and Hegel," 120.

31   Page 19, this volume.

32   Cf. Norbert Samuelson, *An Introduction to Modern Jewish Philosophy*. Albany: State University of New York Press, 1989, 212 ff.

33   Wayne Cristaudo, *Religion, Redemption, and Revolution*. Toronto: University of Toronto Press, 2012, 296.

34   See here Rosenzweig, "Das Neue Denken," in *Zweistromland: Kleinere Schriften zur Religion und Philosophie*. Berlin: Philo Verlag und Buchhaltung, 1926.

35  Kavka, "A Note on Religion and the State in Rosenzweig's *Hegel und der Staat*," 133.

36  Schlomo Avineri, "Rosenzweig's Hegel Interpretation," 836.

37  G.W.F. Hegel, *Elements of the Philosophy of Right*. Cambridge: Cambridge University Press, 1991, 22.

38  Hegel, *Philosophy of Right*, 22.

39  Otto Pöggeler, "Editorial Introduction," in: *Lectures on Natural Right and Political Science: The First Philosophy of Right*, Trans. J. Michael Stewart and Peter C. Hodgson. Oxford: Oxford University Press, 2012, 42.

40  Page 424, this volume. See also: Fackenheim, "On the Actuality of the Rational and the Rationality of the Actual." In *The Hegel Myths and Legends* (1996).

41  Hegel, *Philosophy of Right*, 302. For an alternative perspective on this point, see Eric Weil, *Hegel and the State*, 1998 (1950), viii. Weil comments that Rosenzweig's Hegel book is "a work that is notable for the perspicuity it displays in its treatment of individual problems but in my opinion is mistaken in its overall conception of the issue." It thus seems clear that Weil is critiquing (rather than honoring) Rosenzweig in naming his own book *Hegel and the State* (!).

42  Page 435, this volume. [*Das Leben mußte erst die Einheit des Gedankens sprengen, um die versprengten Stücke neu einzubauen*]

43  Page 12, this volume.

44  Pöggeler (2012), 42.

45  See Klaus Vieweg, *Das Denken der Freiheit* (2012). In a subtle and idiosyncratic gesture, Vieweg lists Rosenzweig's *Hegel und der Staat* not among his "Sekondärliteratur," which might be expected, but together in rather exclusive company – along with Aristotle, Rousseau, Kant, and Nietzsche, among others – under the heading "Further classics of philosophy" [Weitere Klassiker der Philosophie]."

# Translators' Acknowledgements

This translation was conceived of while painting a fence in the desert of New Mexico – as a conversation between a father and son. Shortly thereafter, in 2005, Jules was invited by Heidrun Hesse to co-teach a graduate seminar on *Hegel und der Staat* at the University of Tübingen and Josiah, having secured a modest travel grant from his graduate department at the University of New Mexico, was quickly in tow. This marked the beginning of a collaboration and long-term commitment inspired by Franz Rosenzweig's own experiences of working in a *Zweistromland*, of dialogically bringing together two streams of thinking throughout the course of his short but highly productive life. In presenting our translation of Rosenzweig's *Hegel und der Staat* from German into English, we recognize that this speech-thinking project could only have occurred because of the confluence of two cultures – the language, history, philosophy, and literature of modern Germany and of the United States – and because of the confluence of two generations, a father and son who came together to inspire each other to take on the ethical task of translation.

After this marked beginning in Tübingen, which for Jules was a return to the city where he had first studied Hegel's *Phänomenologie des Geistes* with Heidrun Hesse on a Fulbright Grant from 1989–1991, and which for Josiah proved to be the inheritance of Jules' passion for Rosenzweig, each followed their own paths for a time. While Jules pursued other projects connected to Rosenzweig's work, such as his book *Art and Responsibility: A Phenomenology of the Diverging Paths of Rosenzweig and Heidegger* (Bloomsbury, 2011), Rosenzweig's *Hegel und der Staat* gradually shifted towards the center of Josiah's academic and professional life. After a one-year residence at the University of Heidelberg, where as an undergraduate he took his first translation course with Andrew Jenkins, and after studying Hegel's *Phenomenology of Spirit* and Nietzsche's early works under the guidance of Iain Thomson, Josiah would go on to write a Master's Thesis on Rosenzweig's Hegel book, and eventually his dissertation, *Franz Rosenzweig's Hegel and the State: Biography, History and Tragedy* (University of Oregon, 2014).

Withal, some of the most important institutional support for work on this translation came from the leadership and various members of the International Rosenzweig Society. First and foremost is Wolfdietrich Schmied-Kowarzik, the first president of that Society, who supported our work on and from *Hegel and the State*. Wolfdietrich invited Jules to present a talk to a faculty colloquium that he hosted at Kassel University on an interpretation of "Hegel's Concept of the Family" and, separately, invited and financially supported Josiah to a year-long residence at Kassel University to engage in a Rosenzweig-related research project which served as the impetus to pursue his PhD in German Studies. Wolfdietrich also published a co-authored chapter by Josiah and Jules, "Hegel und der Staat," in *Franz Rosenzweig: Religionsphilosoph aus Kassel* (Euregioverlag, 2011). Josiah and Jules are thankful to the International Rosenzweig Society in general for its ongoing support in providing a venue for a number of presentations they made over the years interpreting various aspects of *Hegel and the State*. Some members in particular were especially supportive of their translation efforts, such as Wolfgang Herzfeld and Myriam Bienenstock. Through Wolfgang, Jules and Josiah co-authored the "Foreword" for *Franz Rosenzweigs Jugendschriften (1907–1914) Philosophie: Teil II – Hegel: Schriften zur politischen Philosophie* (Verlag Dr. Kovac, 2015). And Myriam deserves a special thanks for her ongoing support from the very beginning of the project and for her gracious acquiescence in writing the "Foreword" for this translation. Other philosophers from the Rosenzweig Society who encouraged our work on this project include Christoph Kasten, who was also an early reader of Josiah's dissertation, Inke Sauter, Wayne Cristaudo, Michael Gormann-Thelen, and Petar Bojanic.

Thanks are also in order for our editors at Routledge, Tony Bruce and Adam Johnson, whose support for the translation and patient understanding while we brought the manuscript to completion was invaluable. Our correspondence with Axel Honneth on the translation of his "Afterword" was helpful and underscored the importance of the work in the field of Hegel scholarship. Along those lines, we are especially thankful for the extraordinary support of our translation offered by Charles Rodger. He not only provided encouragement at a critical juncture as we were working in the trenches of translating, so to speak, but provided extensive editorial and style suggestions for more than half of the text as we brought it into its final shape. His voice is woven into the fabric of this translation.

In closing, we have a few final, personal recognitions that we would like to mention.

For Jules, that begins with his former mentor and long-time friend, Norbert Samuelson (1936–2022), who first introduced Jules to Rosenzweig's thought and place in the universe of Jewish philosophy. Although he dissuaded Jules from his initial interest in pursuing Rosenzweig's work on Hegel, Jules persevered, and Norbert became one of his most constructive critics. The struggle to meet Norbert's formidable challenge led, inevitably, to enhancing the excellence of this translation. Further support came from a group of Jules' graduate students who emerged out of a seminar Jules had offered on Hegel's *The Phenomenology of Spirit*. Those students became a reading group which met with Jules weekly to discuss, at first, Hegel's *Philosophy of Right*, and then served as the First Readers of the translation of *Hegel and the State*, reading it in its English translation from start to finish. They anointed themselves *Border Hegelians* and consisted of Omar Moreno, who has never missed a meeting of the reading group, and the other members: Juan Carlos Duran, Edgar Llamas, Frank Hernandez, and Matthew Rethorn. Finally, recalling the many, many days and nights toiling alone at his writing desk wrestling with the task of translation, Jules is deeply thankful for the unreserved support and encouragement of his partner and wife, Kim Diaz.

For Josiah, he would first like to thank his German teachers, all of whom inspired him to pursue the language and culture beyond what he could have imagined: Keith Cothrun, for never allowing him to speak English in his high school German class; Katrin Schroeter, for encouraging him to pursue graduate studies in the first place; Jeffrey L. High, for stirring and reawakening his passion for research and scholarship; Jeffrey Librett, for allowing him the freedom to craft his own dissertation project; and Martin Klebes, for his unwavering support and belief. Josiah would also like to thank his international colleagues in Bochum: a lucky confluence of both the Hans Ehrenberg Society and the Hegel Research Colloquium. It was here that he connected to the deep traditions of Hegel scholarship and German Idealism and gathered the courage to finish the translation. He would thus like to expressly thank Andreas Losch and Traugott Jähnichen for their support in his studies of Hans Ehrenberg and Birgit Sandkaulen and Johannes-Georg Schülein for their invitation to join the Hegel Research Colloquium. Josiah would also like to thank Richard Haw, who offered him his first translation commission for a project on John Roebling (himself one of Hegel's students in Berlin). For the early stages of the project, Josiah is indebted to Kirstin Vasgaard for her support. And this translation would have proven impossible without the personal support from Kate, Josiah's mother, and Josiah's siblings Rebekah and Jared. As each project draws to a close, it is the people we hold closest that we ask the most of and who prove the most supportive. For this, Josiah thanks Heather Tone, for her loving support, her inspiration as a writer herself, and her deep patience and understanding. And he thanks Eliot, for bringing him tea. Finally, Josiah would like to thank his daughter Iris for her unending creativity and curiosity. He hopes one day she might read this book.

In the end, befitting of our commitment to this work, our deepest thanks are to each other.

# HÖLDERLIN, "TO THE GERMANS," ("AN DIE DEUTSCHEN") 1800

**1909:**

But, as lightning from clouds, does the act perhaps follow
Lucid and mature from thoughts?
   Does the golden fruit, as from the orchard's
     Dark leaf, follow from the written word?

*Aber kommt, wie der Strahl aus dem Gewölke kommt,*
*Aus Gedanken vielleicht geistig und reif die Tat?*
   *Folgt der Schrift, wie des Haines*
     *Dunkelm Blatte, die goldne Frucht?*

**1919:**

Our lifetime is indeed narrowly limited,
We see and count the number of our years,
   Yet the years of the peoples,
     Has these a mortal eye seen?

*Wohl ist enge begrenzt unsere Lebenszeit,*
*Unserer Jahre Zahl sehen und zählen wir,*
   *Doch die Jahre der Völker,*
     *Sah ein sterbliches Auge sie?*

Friedrich Meinecke

In grateful
Admiration

# PREFACE

The first to write the life of Hegel was the Königsberg professor Karl Rosenkranz. His book appeared in 1844. The author had even known Hegel himself. Among the students who remained personally faithful to Hegel, he is one of the more unreserved. Without taking into account that, according to his views, he would be counted among the Hegelian Left, he nonetheless does have something in common with them; not simply a certain independence over against the systematicity of the master, but even more, a peculiar dispersion and mobility of the senses, a restless grasping and seeking for materials within the treasures of time and the past. And finally, the strong inclination towards absurdities rich in spirit places the author of the *Aesthetics of the Ugly* almost more in line with Strauss, Bauer, and Feuerbach than with Marheineke, Gabler, and Henning. His book on Hegel shows comparatively few of these characteristics; they are held in restraint by the pious respect of the student for the dead master and that seriousness of attitude that comes, so to speak, from writing on official behalf of the school: Hegel's life story was made public as a supplementary volume to his works. The quantity of handwritten material, which the book reprinted or summarized, also had the effect of constricting the space for the author's own excursions. Nevertheless, because of how it distinctively illuminates the typical character of that time, the book remains indispensable and can never be rendered completely superfluous. The reader will find many delightful insights in this book, but what might be mentioned here is how Rosenkranz recognized in the fact that his hero, having gone to Tübingen in the autumn, to Bamberg in the autumn, to Nurnberg in the autumn, to Heidelberg in the autumn, to Berlin in the autumn and having died in the autumn, "one of those curious tendencies of human destiny," a tendency "for which one would gladly like to discover a ground in individuality itself and accordingly, demand that Hegel have a full and harvesting autumnal nature." The move into and away from Bern, completion of the first major work, and marriage all remain curiously unmentioned, perhaps because the theory already seemed sufficiently provided for. Altogether, though, the book did not suffer as much from these peculiarities as one might assume. Mental fireworks fly throughout the account, without confusing this account itself. In applying his own standards to the material, Rosenkranz showed restraint. It would almost be possible to separate the author's independent remarks cleanly from the book and one would then be left with a collection of materials that would be typical of a biography for that time. Rosenkranz's reserved approach makes it difficult to infer from the book alone how he himself actually stands to any one of the many sides of his subject. It could be the case that his external, and especially internal, distance was not yet great enough to allow him to formulate an intellectual history of a more comprehensive and universal scope. He only knew how to situate his hero in terms of a history of philosophy, but here his hero had already done the decisive work – the pupil merely followed the master's lead. Admittedly, he is occasionally driven to a clearer position by a pupil-like question or an idle remark, but these always remain mere details. All of this is also valid for his treatment of the political. Rosenkranz gives us the material and adds an observation here and there, but all in all the state rarely appears. One is even tempted to say that its rare appearance is remarkable if one considers that the book appeared in those early years of Friedrich Wilhelm II where we are accustomed to see the powerful breakthrough of political interest in Germany. Yet it is not quite so remarkable, for deep into the movement of 1848, the political interest of this decade still carried strong humanist tendencies. And far removed from the fact that it had already stained the view of extra-political areas of life, it is yet itself entwined in the entire web of culture. The great battles of the 1830s and 1840s took place on religious and not political grounds. Throughout both decades, in the public battle for Hegel's legacy, the conflict broke out and was fought around the philosopher of religion and his unfinished works – a storehouse of weapons. Consider the words that Friedrich Förster spoke at Hegel's gravesite: "Was it not he who led those who doubted the Fatherland back to trusting it, in that he convinced them that the great political movements of foreign countries would not compromise the reputation of Germany for having called forth the by far more successful movement in the church and in science?" These words were consequently validated in that decade. And the year 1848 then became significant for the judgment on Hegel precisely because it made the thinker of the state into a coveted icon.

Rudolf Haym was the first to draw out the consequences from the new situation. The lectures on *Hegel and his Age* that he held in 1855–1856, and published as a book in 1857, determined the opinion on Hegel up until the beginning of the twentieth century. Only rarely does the biography of a philosopher end up being the work of such political passion; perhaps an even rarer case might be that from such an attitude a great biographical work of art would eventually emerge, a complete picture, in which hardly a driving force of the life presented is completely suppressed, a work simultaneously filled with such a depth of intuition and passionate one-sidedness of judgment. Love and resentment rested on the scale of this book such that, even more than his earlier biographical work, it became a testament to the author's own personal becoming and the passage of time.

Haym's formative years occurred before the year of the German revolution, which he experienced as a twenty-six-year-old. When he entered the university, the reputation of the Hegelian system stood nearly unshaken. Conflicts took place more over the conclusions not drawn out by the creator himself than over the stability of the system's founding presuppositions. Haym, who was at first superficially impressed by the direction taken by the Young Hegelians, then by Feuerbach, and even more deeply by Strauss, eventually turned toward the system of the master himself, and began burrowing deep into the passages and arteries of its richly mysterious formations. His spirit, originally more inclined toward thinking than observing, was drawn in by the dialectical versatility and keen sharpness of the Young Hegelian critique. At the same time, his insistent longing for fulfillment and materiality then appeared to have found, in the magically powerful method of the master, its divining rod, by means of which a contemplative spirit could draw out and appropriate the treasures of historical life. The more that original contemplative direction receded, a direction which had been, from childhood on, impressed upon him by his father – a school director with devout faith in reason – the more a new drive in his personal development pressed forward, the drive "to carry [his tent] from one epoch of humanity to another and again, and again to the next – not like the eternal Jew, rather like the eternal human, like the becoming, striding history of humanity itself," the more he had to turn away from the system in disappointment, a system which in the end appeared to exhaust the depth of life only to sacrifice the extracted goods upon the altar of the concept. When the year 1848 then came, bringing the young members of the hereditary-imperial party in the church of St. Paul their first political activity and deep political disappointment, this hazy historical outlook, in which the youth relived in themselves the romantic beginnings of the century, then began to assume more secure goals, goals of a new, narrower yet more virile epoch. The darkness of the reaction, which broke over the valleys of the present in the fifties, enabled the heights of the past of the Prussian state, for which his national hopes were now threatening to shatter, to shine forth more brightly. The promising marriage of Prussian politics and the German spirit, which took place at the beginning of the century, became the subject of Haym's first great work, *Wilhelm von Humboldt*. If here he could avoid testifying to his threatened belief, it was his lectures on Hegel which brought the root of evil to the surface, and that hope for Prussia's German calling now began to waste away. For whose spirit was it other than that of the Prussian philosopher of the state from the twenties, who, with rigid adherence to what was only at one time actual, still dared to carry out the reason of history! Where else could the inability of this government to act procure a better appearance of justification than from the tranquil world-observer, the "world-finisher," who distorted the aesthetic view of life of Weimar classicism into a political ideal? And so it came about that the book, which matured out of the lectures, had, according to Haym's own later admission, a double face – it was as much a philosophical as a political polemic. And furthermore, it was an act of self-liberation for the author. For, again in his own words, to finally come clean with respect to Hegel had been his most pressing concern for a long time. The act of virile resentment, its wellspring in the old love, flowed deeper than the reader could immediately discern. The same danger appeared to him in the life of Hegel from which he himself, indeed from which the entire age, had only recently wrested itself free, namely, the danger of a Romantic divinization of history, indeed everything considered as the grandeur of culture in the classical moment of 1800. It was, in essence, from this that the new generation freed itself as it placed its life under the rule of the grand objectives of the state and the people. It was this danger which one felt the need to oppose with the entirety of one's existence. Moreover, if one wanted to solve the task of the present and prepare the way for a future idealism, then a conscious will towards actuality had to be established within the state, science and art, which would oppose the high-flown ideals of that youthful age. These things were expressed in the remarkable opening and concluding pages of Haym's book. In these pages, the essence and task of the present were, at that time, illuminated in almost uncanny clarity. Through the "progress of history," Hegel's philosophy is "more than refuted: it became judged"; the spirit must now "fulfill" itself in "what is real [im Realen]"; one's duty is to battle "for the sake of that one thing which is necessary, for the sake of a more rationally measured and ethical structuring of our life in the state"; from the "general shipwreck of the spirit and of the belief in spirit in general," it follows, precisely when one grasps the collapse historically, indeed recognizes it actively, that "the inextinguishable embers of the idealist view should thereby be all the more rigorously kindled."

It was from within the world of thought framed by Haym that Wilhelm Dilthey, our third biographer, found the point of departure for his own work and personal development, and thereby, in his old age, placed research into Hegel's life on a new foundation. Despite Dilthey being twelve years younger than Haym, that opposition of epochs before and after 1848, with reference to which Haym tuned the fundamental tone of his book, also became Dilthey's driving experience, albeit in a totally different sense. Haym's intellectual beginnings, his awakening to his own life of the mind, were still deeply rooted in that old epoch and he drew part of his scholarly passion specifically from the conscious will to overcome that epoch, as much internally as externally. Dilthey's youth

already stood under the full mastery of the new epoch. He was receptive, all too receptive, to what really spawned from the new spirit –
"positivism" and "empiricism" – which, at that time, began to spread
throughout Germany as a slave revolt of the besieged West against the
European victory of the German classical spirit. Yet, despite such dependency on the historical events of his age, Dilthey held within himself
a deeply personal impulse to fix his vision on the image of the peak of
1800, even though it was disappearing more and more with time. He
also held onto a belief in the historical oneness with that past which
was to be preserved despite everything presently happening and all the
clear and irrefutable contradictions. From this belief, there grew within
him the conscious will to secure "the continuity of our spiritual development," resulting in his first great work, a history of the young Schleiermacher.

This historical context perhaps shows that even though he swam
along with the currents of his age as an adult, Dilthey only first began to
broaden the horizons of his work in his later years. Only then had the age
become oversaturated with and scornful of the sense of actuality of the
last half century, seeking once again to take up that broken continuity. A
new generation then found their leader in Dilthey, who had from early
on struggled to keep this path to the past open. He himself should have
wondered how he could have published his Novalis and Lessing essays
out of the 1860s, nearly unchanged, together with his newest work in
the year 1900. And for the younger among us, the surprisingly immediate and contemporary appeal of those old essays is still fresh in our
memories. And so it came about that for a generation who sought the
way back to the old idealism through a newly fashioned longing, Dilthey
was called upon to renew the historical memory of Hegel.

Already in 1887, when the collection of Hegel's letters appeared, Dilthey had stated that the time for fighting with Hegel was over, and that the
time of his historical recognition had come. Although this still sounded
similar to Haym's position, it was already something quite different. For
Haym, the historical recognition itself was to end the fight, whereas Dilthey pulled out of that fight altogether. But, as far as one can tell, only
in the years after 1900, after Kuno Fischer's two volumes on Hegel had
appeared, did Dilthey begin to fulfill the task which was set in 1887. This
resulted in the History of the Young Hegel, which appeared in 1905.

It is characteristic of Dilthey's historical and personal context that his book traced the development of the metaphysician, on the one hand, and the philosopher of history, on the other. For Rosenkranz, in accordance with the direction of that decade, it was the philosopher of religion, for Haym, the politician. That distinctive inner departure of German culture from the state, which occurred as a reaction to the close relationship of the two during the founding years of the empire, found its expression in Dilthey. For him, the political in Hegel was more a piece of Hegel's development than a founding force. And characteristically, he expressed it, where he does express it, less in terms of a new sense for the power-state, the beginnings of which Meinecke would soon articulate, than in the early soundings of a wish for a cultured nation, a wish which had just recently awoken in the past decades.

Yet overall, it was now a totally new Hegel that Dilthey's book presented. It is not as if those beginnings, which show Hegel sharing paths with Hölderlin and the early Romantics, remained unnoticed by the older biographers. Rosenkranz had already lingered with them not without being impressed, and in Haym's work they are placed as a decisive factor in Hegel's development from world-improver to pious Quietist. It is rather the crude methods of presentation of the two – for Rosenkranz, essentially a naïve wondering about the conceptuality of such historical detours, for Haym a rashly judged insertion within the much too linear path of Hegel's biographical development – that Dilthey, a contemporary of Nietzsche, then brought to bear, purely as such, over against the vulnerable sense of spiritual actuality taught by positivism. And so, it was he who first recognized how that connection between Hegel and Hölderlin was more than a biographical curiosity and more than the cause or mark of an anomaly of nature. It was he who first, with gentle hand, raised the veil and showed how, from the great rigid pictures of the historical Hegel, which remained just as soulless and untransparent in Rosenkranz's panegyric as in Haym's pamphlet, a stream of hidden sorrows and hidden passions poured forth from those days of Hegel's youth.

\* \* \*

The book before you, whose earliest parts reach back to 1909, was in essence finished as the War broke out. At that time, I did not think I would need to add a prefatory note. Today, this cannot be avoided. For the reader has a right to discover, already at the threshold, that in the year 1919 this book could only be brought to an end. I would have never begun it today. I do not know where one could find the courage today to write German history. At the time when this book came to be, there was hope that the internal as well as external, breath-robbing narrowness of the Bismarckian state would expand itself out into a free empire, breathing the air of the world. This book was meant, as much as a book can, to play its own small part in preparing for this. The inflexible and limited Hegelian thought on the state, which came more and more to be the leading thought of the past century, and from which, on January 18, 1871, the world-historical act sprang "as lightning from clouds" – this thought, in its development throughout the life of its thinker and at the same time under the watchful eye of the reader, was supposed to undermine itself so as to open the outlook upon an internally as well as externally more spacious German future. It worked out differently. A field of ruins now marks the place where the Empire had once stood.

This book, which I would no longer have written today, I could equally not revise. There remained only the choice to publish it as it once was, that is, in its origin and intention, as a testament to the spirit of the pre-War years, not the "spirit" of 1919. Only through the addition of a second motto and a few clearly recognizable addenda did I believe it necessary to mark the tragic moment of its appearance. That I am still even publishing the book is due to the fact that the Heidelberg Academy of the Sciences, through a generous guarantee to assist in the cost of printing, awoke the trust in me that a certain service would be rendered, if no longer to German life, then surely to science, which outlasts a life lain to ruins. The Academy, in particular Counselors Rickert and Oncken, should receive express thanks from the author.

For the internal development of the book my thanks are due in the first place to my highly honorable teacher, Counselor Meinecke; I received the first impetus to write it from the eleventh chapter of the first book of his *Cosmopolitanism and the National State*. Among friends, I was helped by the philosopher Hans Ehrenberg, the jurist Eugen Rosenstock, and the national economist Emil E. von Beckerath. I am indebted to Pastor Lasson for valuable suggestions. Handwritten materials were made available to me by:

- The Prussian State Library of Berlin
- The Prussian State Archive of Berlin
- The City Library of Leipzig
- The University Library of Heidelberg
- The Bayern State Archive of Munich
- The Kreis Archive of Bamberg
- The University Library of Tübingen.

I express my thanks to all of them.

Dr. Franz Rosenzweig
Kassel, in the month of May 1920

# Volume I

## Stations of Life (1770–1806)

# 1

## PRELIMINARY REMARKS

What is rational ...
and what is actual ...

Twice in the course of its history, a thought common to all of Europe with respect to its origin and goal inundated the German state. The first time it was the dream of a universal empire, based on a religious natural right, under whose effect German royalty cast an enclosing arch over the landed nobility, such that this subordinated entity could grow to unheard-of autonomy. The great schism in the church of the sixteenth century, in that it drove back the Empire even further, eternalized this condition. Consequently, the second of these movements common to Europe, that based on secular natural right, only found in Germany the stump of the great tree that had once cast its shadow over Europe. It became Germany's fate that the new movement annihilated even those remains of their predecessors' creations, whereas its constructive energies flowed into the new state, which arose from the landed nobility – at first from within, then against, the Empire. While this movement powerfully expanded the state

DOI: 10.4324/9780429354724-2

internally, it initially only drew the firm external borders of peoplehood
[Volkstum]. Only when the state filled out these borders did it begin
anew to direct its act and will towards the world.

This homecoming of the Enlightenment within the borders of peoplehood was in its essence already predetermined. There were, indeed,
two currents that ran alongside each other in this river. Simultaneous
with the liberation of one's conscience, which led to ecstatic pride in a
newly born, fearless, and unbounded rationality, there also occurred that
awakening of a sense for the world. This sense for the world soon spread
from an artistic grasp of nature to the recognition of the state, in both
its essence and history. Machiavelli as well as Luther stand on the scale of
the eighteenth century. Therefore, those who only follow the direction
of the inspired rationality of this time will misunderstand the richness of
its political thought. Next to Rousseau stands Montesquieu, next to the
*contrat social*, with an equal share in immediate and lasting influence, the
*esprit des lois*. Next to the ideal of the state of the one, passionately fulfilled
and coldly calculated, was the political museum of the other, a treasury
of immeasurable materials of experience brought together with a true
joy in collecting the multifarious, the colorful, even the bizarre. Indeed,
it was brought together much more in the manner of an ingenious col-
lector, lucidly integrated and indexed, rather than being united in one
structure by the creative power of the thinker. Those who wish to speak
of the dominating tendencies of the political thought of that time must
at least have this double countenance before their eyes: a Janus-head,
whose two faces never view the same object. The one, which looks out
towards the state for how it should be according to reason, prefers to
see, or oversee, all actuality of political life in the state with the eyes
of a revolutionary. The other, in that its glance through this actuality
strays from here to there in curiosity, would rather not feel the historical
rationality within this manifold life; rather, it only finds a confusion of
strange things which long for that richly spiritual, enlightening inscription. To unite this double countenance, to change the breaking apart of
the two viewpoints into a joining together, became the project of the
nineteenth century. And if one makes use of the right of history to seek
out the spiritual kernel in acts and thoughts that were, and had to be,
foreign to the consciousness of the actor and thinker, then one may see
the guiding saying for that century in the famous dictum from Hegel's

*Philosophy of Right*, the actuality of the rational and the rationality of the actual. One could even say this was the motto for those contemporane-ous movements that Hegel fought against in that very work, and indeed, even the motto for movements that later proclaimed themselves to have superseded his philosophy. If one thus extracts this particular Hegelian illumination, then the Hegelian paradox would encompass the view of the state held by men such as Haller and Stahl, Savigny and Ranke, Dahl-mann and Treitschke. It would set this otherwise fractious group in com-mon over against the eighteenth century, and they would share in both the insoluble entanglement of a value-setting will and the historically conscious observation – the "rational" and the "actual" – however dif-ferently the knots were tied each time.

It is no coincidence that among the three peoples in whom the spirit of the eighteenth century made itself so powerfully apparent, it was pre-cisely in Germany where the new century's idea of the state won an espe-cially forceful, and in many ways – at least in theory – a most forceful life. In France, the distance between the political thought of these two centuries seems minimal compared with the distance that France's sci-ence and art had to overcome in order to join the Romantic movement of the new century. Politically, if Tocqueville's thesis is correct, it seems here that the nineteenth century essentially took up the inheritance of the eighteenth. In Germany the opposite is true. The general intellectual development since the middle of the eighteenth century actually runs without a visible break right into the nineteenth. But for the state, and especially for the ideas of the state, which means here for the relation-ship of the human being to the state, the distance between the centuries seems at first glance immeasurable. The chasm was so wide that it could only be crossed with a leap. And so, some came up short, others jumped further than necessary, and almost everyone took a strong charge. For the most part, the unfolding of this new view did not play itself out in thought as a dry, conceptual process, but was rather deeply embedded in the stream of personal life. In order to understand this unfolding, one should not wish to pull it from the stream onto a dry embankment. Precisely therein lies the irresistible charm of intellectual scholarship in those decades of German development.

So what was it, then, that so strongly divided political thought in Ger-many in the second half of the eighteenth century from that of France and

England at that same time? German political writing is also characterized
by that drifting apart of concept and experience, which was portrayed
in the great figures of Rousseau and Montesquieu above. The two directions remain estranged from each other, even where they are found side
by side in the same personality. Think of how the young Kant seems in
some of his writings to be so completely devoted to the abundance of
the actual – in reading Herder one cannot miss the image of the teacher
that the greatest of his personal students carried in his memory. And yet,
think of how foreign that other Kant, the lawgiver of reason, grew next to
this one, the Kant from whom the old Herder unwillingly departed and
from whom Fichte and the younger generation kindled their fires. And
Herder himself, think of how helpless this spirit is when he takes flight
from the ground of philosophy of history into the land of political ideas.
No section of his work cost him such "dreadful" trouble as the one on
"governments" – and in what incomprehensible constructions he moves
about here! And finally, how when writing on politics the protest against
the eighteenth century is itself so – eighteenth century! Yet, as has been
said, the double countenance of academically exploring the state is not
particular to the German Enlightenment. Although resolving this schism
certainly took great intellectual effort, it was carried out in the closed-
off workings of science, one is even tempted to say, on its own accord.
But another, deeper schism still remained in Germany. To overcome this
deeper schism required the winds of the times, the waves of events –
even more so, personal experience. This latter schism was the hostility
or indifference of the individual towards the state, the abyss between the
personal life of ethics and the public life of the state. Such a divide did not
occur in France, nor in England. In those cases, the Enlightenment was
from the beginning much more also a movement of the state – in England, the intellectual foundation of a powerful political party, in France,
minimally, a church-state opposition. In both England and France, the
Enlightenment never completely estranged its supporters from the state,
indeed, it could never teach them to be proud of the estrangement. But
in Germany the heritage of the Christian European task of the Empire
had lasting effects and merged with the new way of thinking. This led far
more than in the west to a purely spiritual and intellectual movement.
The earth from which this movement grew, and whose energies it in
turn nourished, was also not really on the state and societal level. There

emerged, rather, a community of the educated, which spread from Riga to Zurich beyond the borders of individual states with no concern for the borders of the Empire. It was a very unified collective which helped move along with certainty any and all inspirations without essentially changing them. This was a community the likes of which had not shown itself since the age of the Reformation — the collective of our classical writers. One could think of the Hofmeister at the end of the eighteenth century, the widespread visits and letter-writing that we notice both in the beginnings of the classical age of literature, as well as deep into the Romantic years. There are significant traits of this new conviviality and commerce of spirits in the area of German culture.

Undoubtedly, a specifically German culture arose here. In certain courts, the creative centers of an entirely, or at least primarily, French Enlightenment were only islands, and all in all they remained meaningless for the spiritual life of the nation. And despite the fact that the national accommodation of culture became infinitely important for the rise of an entirely German state in the next century, this new collective remained very much a stranger to the state in the century of its emergence. With regard to the political conditions in Germany, perhaps it could have not been possible otherwise. This culture was alienated from the state, not simply its enemy. Indeed, the tepid appreciation of the state with regard to the business of its "policing," bound up with an ignorance towards the intimate reciprocity of state life and culture, is in the highest sense an essential tendency of this Enlightenment. A stranger to the state, but not its enemy. This new generation was not yet ripe for a deep antagonism towards the state, because it had not yet lived trustingly enough with the state and as it still had the nineteenth century before it. Kant could serve as the classical example for this disposition. In the 1784 essay "What is Enlightenment?" Kant praises Friedrich's Prussia as the genuine state of the Enlightenment, in that Friedrich says to his subjects: argue, but obey. This "but," this complete disjunction between "arguing" and "obeying," is expressed in Kant's essay with a most unselfconscious brevity.

Of course, even before world relations changed and German culture awoke in shock out of this still life, a warning had already been issued. The guilty conscience of its statelessness had already condensed into a solid figure and sat, like an armor-clad spirit, among the guests at its table: into the mores of German Enlightenment entered the Polis, the image of antiquity. Most likely this occurred only gradually. At first it seems that the new humanism is only interested in inheriting a new cultural object, without necessarily assuming that it was the greatest thing of its kind. A pronounced passion for all material was hidden within this new current. In the area of education, this passion aligns well – up until the end of the century – with the philanthropist belief in actuality and usefulness, even if, according to their later educational doctrine, they saw in this belief outright evil. But the closer we get to the end of the century, the more exemplary antiquity becomes for the present, the more the Greeks – who at first appeared fused with the Romans – resolved themselves as the true image of antiquity. And the image of antiquity's "love of the fatherland" shone forth in ever-brighter colors. What is at stake here is not so much those lingering tones of an artful renaissance of poetry, for which the Berlin of the Seven Years War became the "Sparta," as those are in essence really only lingering tones. What is new, rather, is the expression of a disposition which served to transfigure antiquity, a disposition which, in that it was turned towards the present, had to recognize that Berlin is through and through not "Sparta." What is new is the measurement of the state of the present against the standard of the Polis. At first the comparison does not necessarily favor the ancients since far too many people were dominated by an enlightened opinion of the splendor of the present. However, the balance gradually shifts. Herder provides a concrete picture of this change. In a talk that the 23-year-old gave in Riga, he addresses the following topic: do we still have the public and fatherland of the ancients today? He answers the question in favor of the present: the famed freedom of the ancients is only "a boldness of desire to guide the wheel of the state itself." Over against this "untamed insolence" there is measured freedom which, today, every patriot wishes for themselves: the freedom to create one's own happiness and comfort, to be the friend to those closest, and to be the father and guide of one's children. This was the case in 1765. Thirty years later the same man asked himself the same question, but the answer turned out to be entirely different. Certainly – this much remained from the earlier view – we should perhaps not wish to have the Greek state back, for "we would hardly obtain that which we really desire from the exchange." But the reader will not be easily convinced that there is no internal connection between the hymn which the great writer had just written, intoning the ancient Polis as "a moral fatherland," and the demands he immediately thereafter placed upon the state of the future, demands which stood apart in their prophetically bold view in taking the national state and the national culture in this decade together. That the seer entirely misjudged the essence of this future national state need not bother us here. Indeed, insofar as he denies the future national state the "spirit of conquest" of the old power-state, he actually anticipated, even if only vaguely, a contrast between the new national state and the *ancien régime*. History has thoroughly proven this contrast, which brought about the subversion, or at least a strong transformation of the concept of a "European equilibrium," to be true. But completely aside from this: look how extensively – compared with 1765 – Herder's demands for an individual reach, an individual who is "no longer [allowed] to stand idly by and count the waves, as if he were on the shore, no longer [allowed] to imagine himself in the haven of a select riparian society, which here is not at his disposal"; look how spirit and state come together here in the concept of the "culture of the fatherland": "light, Enlightenment, civic sense; the noble pride to not let oneself be regulated by others but rather to regulate oneself, as other nations have done for time immemorial; to be German on one's own *well-protected* ground and soil."

The eighteenth century, Rousseau's spirit of rational certainty and Montesquieu's spirit of joyful experience, the political homelessness of Germany's new national culture of the spirit, the appearance of antiquity viewed through the eyes of German classicism – these forms arose for us on the horizon, their shadows lie over the landscape that we now take into view. From Germany of the eighteenth century, we turn our eyes to the land of Württemberg, from the forces of German culture to a schoolboy from Stuttgart, G. W. F. Hegel.

# 2

# STUTTGART

Hegel was born in 1770, in the same year as Friedrich Wilhelm III and Hölderlin. This year marks the middle of a decade that includes the birth of Schleiermacher, W.v. Humboldt, K.L.v. Haller, F. Schlegel, Novalis and Schelling. When Louis XVI lost his head, the youngest of these men was 18 and the oldest 25 years old – thus all in that span of life where a person is often still searching for their relationship to the world. None of them remained untouched by the culture of the Enlightenment, all of them grew beyond these beginnings of their inner being, and each of them laid for their part a piece of the foundation on which the history of the new century was built. However, there remained in all of them enough of this spirit of the old century – even if it was only scars that the fighters took with them as keepsakes from the fight – that none of them ruled over the entire development of the century they helped introduce. Beginning in the 1840s the age seems to have overcome them – certainly following the paths they opened, but now with new goals. That is the difference between this generation and the next one – the generation of Dahlmann and Uhland, Savigny, Grimm and Böckh – which, as it

DOI: 10.4324/9780429354724-3

took the stage, already found the battle with the "Enlightenment" over and which, from the beginning, could already let the victorious winds of the new century fill the sails of its life. Its effectiveness was not fatefully bound to the year 1848 as it had been for so many of those introduced earlier in our account. And as Hegel's contemporaries were split from those that came after them due to their relationship to the culture of the eighteenth century, so too were they split from their immediate predecessors – the generation to which Stein and Gneisenau, Schiller, and Fichte belonged. These men were already finished as the great event in France first began to unfold. Each fit it into their circles, they certainly still learned from it, but – unlike the following generation – it didn't add anything to their inner development. And so, none of these men actually outgrew the eighteenth century entirely. They represent its highest peak and its completion. And if some of the lasting strengths of the culture of the eighteenth century were safely brought over to the nineteenth century, despite the victorious battles of the next generation, then it is thanks to these great educators.

With such an overview it may become clear what it meant or could have meant to be born in Germany in 1770. In the history of Württemberg the year 1770 marked a year of change. In this year the long-standing feud between Duke Karl Eugen and his estates, the "provincial assembly" as they would say in Württemberg, was settled through an inheritance agreement. The following years then brought the Duke the internal reversal, through which the former picture his people had of the tyrant receded behind the figure of the robust, affable, and well-meaning old man. For the people of Württemberg these late years under Duke Karl, the years in which Hegel grew up, are remembered as the happiest time that Old Württemberg ever experienced. And the historian can also claim that in this epoch, for the first time, the duchy was bestowed with the blessings of enlightened absolutism, an absolutism from whose greatest advocate the young Duke had once taken, as a "mirror for princes," the sum of his teachings with him on his way – blessings of princely sovereign power, whereas up until now it had almost exclusively known its curse. But the blessings were of course only granted him in limited radius. Not taking his personality into account, the Duke was missing the most important precondition: radical legal and actual authority. The Prince was not the one and only master in his state. The inheritance agreement

of 1770 from which the good will towards the Duke grew gradually
stronger was at the same time, indeed in the first place, a fundamental
self-assertion of the secondary rule of the estates. During a century in
which the growth of princely power was otherwise so favorable overall,
there was hardly another German land in which this secondary rule held
similar importance. Full of civic and Lutheran spirit, as was exhibited in
the century of the Reformation, oligarchically rigid, as it would become
more and more with the increasing importance of the narrow Committee, it had the ability to stand its own ground against the princely power
of the eighteenth century. It was supported above all through the help of
foreign powers: Prussian and England-Hannover, who believed that the
Protestant character of the advanced southern German land's provincial
assembly was guaranteed; Austria, with the legal means of their empire,
gladly helped secure princely power for the sake of their own unaban-
doned claim to inheritance; and finally, certainly also supported by the
defiant manner of the Swabian race, who, in the old constitution, true to
the saying "*parta tueri*," defended, unseen, the jewel of the good old right.
In truth, it was not so much princely excesses that stood in the way of
this holy relic than a current development of the state. The parallel placement of the constitutions of Württemberg and England – coming from
the Fox himself and accepted with pride by Württemberg, also visibly
dominating the view of the state held by the famous Swabian historian
Spittler – had a very unwanted truth: England as well as Württemberg's
estates were both, under the banner of "Freedom," a closely knit oligarchy. In England, as well as in Württemberg, the discord in the state
was rendered harmless where it was beneficial or seemed beneficial to
the advancement of business by the coarser and finer means of personal
influence. The Duke and the Committee of the Estates had, for the most
part – the provincial Estates Assembly was not called up for 26 years
after the inheritance agreement despite two changes in government –
the wool pulled over their eyes.

Through his parents, Hegel stood in a close relationship to the two
powers of Württemberg's life of the state[1] – yet it would hardly prove
momentous for the development of his political view. His father was a
fiscal officer to the Duke – secretary of the retirement division – and his
mother came from a family of the Landed Estate's civil service. It was
his father who directed him to an intellectual post – his mother died

early. In terms of how his way of life and the mode of this philosopher's thought would come to be seen, Hegel's biographers have often spoken of the influence of Swabian folk art and the old Protestant faith that ruled over his parent's house. School was then added to these edifying forces of birth and the parent's house. When Hegel attended the "*Gymnasium Illustre*"[2] of Stuttgart, it was still officially untouched by the new philanthropic and humanitarian pedagogical thoughts of the time. It was seven years after Hegel's departure that the school first took up changing its prevailing "position according to funds." But at the same time, the institution was not closed off to the currents and events of the age. Worth mentioning here are a few graduation speeches shortly after the time of Hegel's departure, which dealt with highly political subjects, subjects such as the "*nova rerum* in the French Revolution." In order to discern how Hegel himself directly and indirectly absorbed the school's cultural and educational material, we are instructed by sources that reach broadly across various periods, sources from which the narrative of the formation of Hegel's view of the state could very well begin.

We have at hand a journal that Hegel began as a fourteen-year-old and continued until he left the Gymnasium, a few more or less independent school essays and finally a pile of excerpts and notes that the boy gathered from a wide range of materials. This was a boy in whom the generally naive practicality of his age had already come into a peculiar sort of union with the dormant seriousness of a born scholar.[3] One cannot expect to find in these records things that would enrapture someone with no idea of what was to become of this child. It is only through the forward-looking glance, which later readers can hardly avoid, that some of these things take on an unfounded relationship and importance. The earliest preserved note is already of a political nature: a little dramatic scene entitled "A conversation between three people" – Antonius, Lepidus, and Oktavian.[4] The manner in which the three historical personalities are conveyed shows the influence of Shakespeare as well as the Enlightenment's pragmatic conception of history.[5] Everything is taken as human, personal, from a later point of view one could even say without background. The political act appears only as the product of personal drives and nothing more. Correspondingly, we also discover from the journal that this little serious man often reflected on and researched in books, *quaenam sit vehementissima animi perturbation, quae plurimas intulerit in hominess, urbes, civitates, regna calamitates* [what is the most violent disturbance of the mind, which has inflicted the greatest number of calamities upon men, cities, city-states, and kingdoms]. He takes it upon himself to research, *quae effecerint honoris libido, auri amor, superbia, invidia, desperation, odium, ira et ultionis libido* [what created the lust for honor, the love of gold, pride, envy, despair, hatred, anger, and a lust for revenge], and then began immediately with the *honoris libido* [lust for honor]. Alexander, who waged war upon Darius, *a quo numquam laesus fuit!* [...] Timur, *praestantissimi Romanorum duces* [by whom he was never injured! Timur, the most outstanding of the Roman leaders] the old Germans, and – the student duels must serve as closing proof.[6] Over and against the droll, censor-like disregard of what was actually political, there now turns up, likewise very early, a noteworthy tendency towards the history of culture and civilization. It sounds like an offshoot of Voltaire's sense for history when we hear that the boy liked Schröckh's account of world history above all others because it avoided "the loathsome many names," wisely left away "the many kings and wars where there are often a few hundred men romping around etc." and, "that which is most splendid," it combined education with history and always carefully adduced "the status of scholars and science."[7] The future philosopher of history thus also believed that he himself had a sense, "although rather dark and one-sided," for what pragmatic history was: namely "when one does not just tell the facts, but also the character of a famous man, an entire nation, its customs, traditions and religion, and articulates the various changes and differences of these aspects from other peoples. When one follows the fall and rise of great empires and shows what effects this or that event or what a change of political state had for the constitution of the nation, for its character and so on."[8] One can hear in such words the tenor of the times, the influence of Montesquieu and Voltaire or the tenor of the future, the later Hegel, the philosopher of history, for whom "thought was to become the most powerful epitomist."[9] The former is justified because, as the narrative will show at the point we now find ourselves, the future lies much further away than the past. With the help of our interpretation, Hegel's earliest efforts, although merely random insights, are not so much general remarks in the sense of the century's great west-European thinkers and writers of history and their German successors, but more so speak to this same sense of history with regard to specific

questions. Above all, two passages of the journal come into view as such
attempts to present the relationship between the life of the state and the
life of the spirit. Both are historical reflections on a favorite subject of
the time – language. The fourteen-year-old is searching for the historical
causes for that "*opulentia*" of the Greek language that make it so difficult.
He finds two reasons: on the one hand, the disdain of the Greeks towards
the barbarians whose language they did not learn, resulting in the Greek
language developing undisturbed in ever richer ways, and then on the
other hand, the internal conditions of the Greek states where rhetori-
cal abilities would become the means to influence the decisions of the
people. Hegel, again entirely in the spirit of the historical mode of the
century, aims to bring the development of language and the character of
politics into relation with each other.[10]

These types of questions now come again and again to the fore. In the
later school years, they address, so it seems – we are dealing here more
with excerpts than with Hegel's own writings – the concept of enlightenment and its relation to culture and the state. From the year 1786 we
find notes on "Enlightenment through Science and Art" and also especially on "Enlightenment of the Common Man" (which was certainly
"always directed towards *the religion of its age*").[11] Regard for the belief of
the "rabble" was the reason for Socrates' sacrifice of the rooster.[12] From
1787 a larger group of excerpts are extant that can serve as testimony of
Hegel's tendency with regard to the aforementioned question. To begin
with, Hegel draws from an essay by Mendelssohn: enlightenment of the
human being is in general without difference in the estates [Stände],
while that of the citizens is altered according to estate and profession.
That state is then unfortunate where enlightenment, which is indispensable for humankind, cannot spread itself out across all estates without
endangering the state constitution. Yet a truly cultured nation knows in
itself no other danger than an excess of national happiness. When it has
reached this peak, it falls into danger precisely through this achievement.[13] The last sentence may remind one of Hegel's mature doctrine
on the death of the spirit of a people [Volksgeist] that has fulfilled their
world-historical task. The sentence on the danger of enlightenment in
general may remind one of the position that the philosopher of history gave Socrates in the development of the Greek state. But again here,
these reminders can only serve to clarify the great distance at which

the future still lies. Shortly after the Mendelssohn excerpt, Hegel writes
out remarks by Nicolai on culture, enlightenment and the "veneer" of
a nation. A nation can receive the "veneer" from without; culture, on
the other hand, must be brought forth by internal strengths.[14] A further
excerpt from Nicolai says: well-intentioned improvements to the culture
of a nation and enlightenment in scholarship and religion arise most
securely from the middle class of a people when it is not imperative
that they concern themselves with the most necessary needs of the body.
Only then can and will they be prepared to be reflective and active. To
bring these people to such a condition is the highest art of a regent and
certainly promotes the well-being of a nation more than all direct ordinances and commands.[15] These examples shall suffice. For it is less the
details of the excerpts that hold our attention than the common subject-
matter, which lets us conclude with certainty the presence of a tendency
that raises the question of the relationship between spirit and state – to
now use the later expression.

Additional excerpts from the year 1787 also show a tendency towards
the other side of politics, the side of natural right. The future theology
student makes consecutive excerpts from the Berlin academic Sulzer's
book, *A Short Notion of all Sciences*, which begin at §186 of the book with
philosophy; arrives with §219 at the theory of human duties, natural
right and the right of peoples; from §231 on, tackles the concepts of a
science of the state and police; from §240 onwards, develops the tasks
of jurisprudence up until the concept of ecclesiastical law; but then very
questionably breaks off in the book with §259 where the section on
theology begins.[16] The eager student had appropriated a series of the
most up to date ideas on the science of the state from Sulzer's book. He
discovered in that book that the law of nations was an applied natural
right, which viewed "independent civil societies as individual people."
The science of the state was "the theory of the happiness of entire states
or civil societies." He heard there of a natural right of society that comes
to be "from the nature of a civil society in general" and is "also common
to all states." In constitutional law, which entails "the obligation of the
citizen to the regent and the regent to the citizen," he learned of differences between "the natural or universal constitutional law" that flows
"from universal concepts and from the universal composition of a state
in general" and the "particular constitutional law of free states," which

is founded "on the particular laws and contracts between subjects and regents." Hegel wrote out all of these sentences.

Going along with the spirit of the times in general, a lively idea of antiquity now began to take shape for the schoolboy in his reflections on the historical and legal make-up and tasks of the state, whose beginnings we just observed. However, this idea was still only quietly stirring and had hardly imbued his image of the state. Already at the Gymnasium, to judge by the books he bought then, Hegel had pursued Greek above and beyond the limited demands of the school.[17] Two talks on questions from the history of classical civilization are available to us. The one deals with the religion of the Greeks and the Romans.[18] The veneration for the ancients, whose superstition and all too human representation of divinity the young man of the Enlightenment could not and must not disavow, makes a timid and somewhat clumsy entrance, even if the ideas of the majority of the people of our so famously enlightened times were made up of nothing less – Hegel makes this evident here, as he did earlier in the journal. Here the Greeks and the Romans went the path of all nations. Before Hegel then blocks any historical understanding of this "path of all nations" with the unavoidable idea of the deceit of the priest, he lingers on an investigation which is psychologically not entirely superficial. In doing so, he also shows an understanding for purely emotional phenomena, for primitive inclinations that later "more intelligent and cunning people who were chosen to serve the divine" take advantage of. In this part of the investigation there then appears a noteworthy thought with regard to our context, where Hegel attempts to explain the origin of polytheism in state-historical terms (for only the thought of divinity in general comes entirely natural to humans). He finds the cause therein, that "the Greeks and the Romans [were] a mix of so many different peoples." For the first time one hears a favorite historical thought of the later Hegel: the Roman pantheon as the symbol of a Roman Empire that fuses together many peoples. But once again one must note here that it is only an echo. This was not the spiritual permeation of a past actuality, but the understanding-based explanation through a historical process of a phenomenon that seems unnatural to the enlightened mind. Again, the step away from Montesquieu is smaller than that towards Ranke.[19]

In the talk given one year later, shortly before the end of school, entitled "On some Characteristic Distinctions of the Ancient Poets" (namely, from the moderns), the new humanitarian movement appears more prevalent than in the essay just discussed.[20] The young speaker praises the kind of destiny of the ancients that unified the general interest of humankind with local interest. Over against this, "the famous deeds of our older, as well as our more modern, Germans are neither intertwined with our political constitution nor is their remembrance preserved through oral propagation." The self-contained formation of the ancients becomes the model. Yet a model – and this is new for the aptitude of the time – not of imitation, but rather of comparable development of the people: "Had the Germans refined themselves again and again without a foreign culture, then their spirit would have without a doubt taken another path and it would have its own German plays instead of us borrowing the form from the Greeks."[21] And so the Greeks become here for Hegel what they were to become for this generation: a reminder of their own Germanness. And we also notice another thing in these words: the idea that the historical past must be "intertwined" with the modern political constitution.[22] We notice nothing of the "negative" recognition[23] that ruled the relationship of the eighteenth century towards history. The sentence unconsciously anticipates the historical aptitude of the next century.

With such budding ideas in his heart, Hegel now set off to the *Stift* in Tübingen. And looking down upon the new arrival from the entrance, still from earlier times and uniting paganism to good humanitarian Christianity, was the inscription: "*Aedes Deo et Musis sacrae.*"[24]

## NOTES

1   Klaiber (1877), 65f.
2   Paulsen (1897), Vol. II, 153 f.; Klaiber (op. cit.), 70–83.
3   GW I, 1–50; GW III, 1–205.
4   GW I, 37 ff.; Rosenkranz 451–454.
5   Hegel owned a copy of Wieland's Shakespeare translation already in 1778 (Rosenkranz 7).
6   GW I, 16 f.; Rosenkranz 438 f.
7   GW I, 3: Rosenkranz 438.
8   GW 1, 5; Rosenkranz 433.
9   Introduction to the *Philosophy of World History* (GW 18, 133 (Introduction 1822–1828: "the thought the understanding the most powerful epitomist"); HW 12, 16).

10    GW 1, 13f.; Rosenkranz 437 f. – On the connection between republican free-
      dom and Pseudo-Longinus oratory in the last chapter; whether Hegel had
      already read it at that time [i.e., at the beginning of 1787], I do not know (GW
      I, 30 f.; Rosenkranz 446). [In Rosenkranz's transcription of this diary entry, a
      sentence is missing (GW I, 30f.) in which Hegel refers to the "hours allotted
      to the winter half-year 1786–87" (ibid., 31), noted in the margin of the sheet,
      from which it emerges that he was busy almost daily with pertinent reading
      and instruction.]

11    GW I, 29 f.: Rosenkranz 445; cf. Thaulow (1854), Vol. III, 30.

12    GW 1, 5f.; Rosenkranz 433 f.; Thaulow (op. cit.), 33 ff.

13    GW 3, 169–174; Rosenkranz 433 f.; Thaulow (op. cit.), 120 ff.

14    GW 3, 177f.; Rosenkranz 433f.; Thaulow (op. cit.), 125 f. [on the "veneer"
      concept, cf. the Mendelssohn excerpt already transcribed on May 31, 1787
      (GW 3, 170)].

15    GW 3, 179; Rosenkranz 433f.; Thaulow (op. cit.), 126

16    GW 3, 115–225; Thaulow (op. cit.), 89–95.

17    GW 1, 6f.; Rosenkranz 11, 434; Klaiber (op. cit.), 72, 81.

18    On the following, cf. GW 1, 42–45; Rosenkranz 454–458.; Thaulow (op. cit.),
      153–158.

19    The thought can be found in Montesquieu's text, "Dissertation sur la poli-
      tique des Romains dans la réligion" (Montesquieu (1949 ff.), Vol. I, 81–92).

20    On the following, cf. GW 1, 46–48; Rosenkranz 458–461; Thaulow (op. cit.),
      158–161 [Thaulow erroneously dates the lecture at 1787].

21    GW 1, 48; Rosenkranz 461.

22    GW 1, 46; Rosenkranz 459.

23    Cf. Rexius, G.: "Studien zur Staatslehre der Historischen Schule" in *Histo-
      rische Zeitschrift* 107 (1911), 500 ff. (cf. Section 3, note 32).

24    On the inscription, cf. Klaiber (op. cit.), 159. [JS & JS: "A house sacred to God
      and the Muses."]

# 3

## TÜBINGEN

The schoolboy had dryly and precociously absorbed certain views on the essence and life of the state from the culture of the times. Yet shortly before his departure from school he began to develop a disposition that brought him into hostile opposition against the "cold book-knowledge" of this very culture. Hegel's time in Tübingen, which we are now entering, is in essence a further development of this disposition. But the young man had yet to realize the actual depths of that culture against which he now took up arms. Kant, who brought the Enlightenment to its apex and then buried it, surely did not go unnoticed – this is evidenced by the excerpts of the schoolboy[1] – but the young man of the Enlightenment was still unaware of the seriousness and reach of Kant's thoughts. Even as in Tübingen he occupied himself more closely with the new philosophy[2], yet according to the judgment of his comrades only superficially, what he discovered aligned happily with the other thoughts he possessed – and especially with those of the Enlightenment. However, he was not yet unsettled by that new philosophy. This is shown by the Tübingen writings, which we will soon take into account. For now, his spirit lived

DOI: 10.4324/9780429354724-4

according to its own inner necessity. He could not be misled by what
was not, or not yet, in alignment with him. Hegel stood open towards
other influential powers than those of Critical Philosophy. These powers
are anticipated in the cultural-revolutionary tone of that talk the schoolboy held in 1788, shortly before graduating. For Hegel, the early days
in Tübingen really do seem to have been the epoch of an inspired soul,[3]
albeit a still well-tempered one. While a club of young Kantians met
together in the Stift, he read Rousseau. And Rousseau allowed him and
his comrades to see in a radiant light the things that would then occur in
the following eventful years over in France. A political club formed in the
Stift and French newspapers were carried around. The entries of friends in
Hegel's yearbook show the spirit that then ruled over them. *Vive la liberté!*
*Vive Jean Jacques! In Tyrannos!*[4] Hegel himself took a lively part in the disputes
of the club. He also came into heavy altercations with his father,[5] the
official to the duke, who was through and through hostile towards revolution. Of course, the often-retold story of the freedom tree that he and
Schelling supposedly planted near Tübingen and danced around seems
somewhat unbelievable.[6] But this much is certain: Hegel always preserved
the memory of the first swigs from the still potent intoxicating drink of
these great years. Even later in Berlin he purportedly explained to his
circle of students how every year on the day of the storming of the Bastille he raises a glass of wine to the ideas of 1789.[7] And even if this is not
true, in the Berlin lectures on the philosophy of history, which we have
available in his printed works, we at any rate find the words: "This was a
magnificent sunrise. All thinking beings celebrated this epoch together.
A sublime emotion ruled in this time, and an enthusiasm of spirit shud-
dered through the world as if it had now first come to an actual reconciliation of the spirit with the world."[8] Even with the progression of the
events of the Revolution, Hegel did not allow this first image to cloud
over. Its reflection becomes visible in his yearbook, when at the end of
1793 the troubled entry of a friend quotes Rousseau's words by adding the emblem [Symbolum] "*liberté raisonée*": *S'il y avait un gouvernement des
anges, ils se gouverneraient démocratiquement* ["well-reasoned freedom": If there
were a people of gods, they would govern themselves democratically]."[9]
Although we have a remark from Hegel on the "whole shamefulness of
the Robespierrians"[10] from the year 1794, we will still see that he hardly
became untrue to the ideas of 1789 as he perceived them.

The ideas of 1789 as he perceived them in Tübingen: with this we articulate our next question. The extant handwritings allow for an answer, and we are led along the right path by the important reports, although there are not many, on Hegel's relations and reading material during his years at the Stift. In 1790 Hegel became closer to one of his comrades at the Stift, the young Hölderlin, who had then also wanted to "learn a little about human rights from the great Jean Jacques."[11] The two students were so different in nature. Hegel was serious, congenial, and even if he hastily took the lead sometimes, still cumbersome. Hölderlin was strange and Apollonian among his companions,[12] "with modesty, indeed with open anxiety"[13] in the face of greatness, perhaps most beautifully summed up in Hyperion's words: at rest and moved.[14] These two found themselves, above and beyond "Jean Jacques," united in the common religion of Greek rapture. The new-humanist wave had just broken through to Tübingen. The professor of Greek limited himself to the explanation of the New Testament, but the poet Conz held lectures on Euripides. Hölderlin attended these lectures, and together the two friends, to whom Schelling – barely grown out of boyhood – came as a third, read their Plato. Reading Kant was most likely balanced by Jacobi's novels and his Spinoza book.[15] And Hegel also encountered Herder at this time. The aspirations of these young men were far removed from the spirit of theology that permeated the Stift. But how the ideas of the Revolution certainly must have played out in these minds, as they coincided with the forces churned up in the German "Storm and Stress" movement and with the newly born classical ideal. "Reason and freedom remain our watchword and the rallying point of the invisible church," Hegel later wrote Schelling from Bern in remembrance of this time.[16] Let us see how "reason and freedom" come together with the "invisible church" in Hegel's manuscripts, in which he wrote down his ideas for himself during the end of his time in Tübingen and at the beginning of his time in Bern.

At hand is a collection of manuscripts that were compiled by the editor of the early writings under the title "Folk Religion and Christianity" ["Volksreligion und Christentum"].[17] Hegel found the historical impulse for this writing, which is certainly the earliest of his intellectual oeuvre, in the same religious-philosophical discourse that the old Kant and the young Fichte were simultaneously undertaking at the beginning of the

1790s.[18] But mind you, the first flames of Hegel's spirit were not ignited by the new Critical Idealism as a whole, nor by the new world view, and not even by the new theory of morals, but rather by the attack on an area that was only marginal for the founder of Critical Philosophy himself: the question of the relationship between positive and natural religion. And so, we begin to understand that the task for the young Hegel falls almost completely outside the entire field of Critical Philosophy and comes to a head more sharply than with Kant and Fichte in the investigation into the essence of the church. Thus, we further understand how in this context, next to Kant and the fledgling work of his greatest student, there could emerge a thoroughly pre-Kantian book as a third and equally important starting point: Mendelssohn's *Jerusalem* with its portrayal of the relationship between state and church.

These are the literary influences.[19] We will discuss them on later occasions, but we can look away from them for now. For as telling as they are and as worthy to be pursued individually – the spirit of the whole flows from other sources.

To begin with we will hold to the oldest collection of fragments still likely to have originated in Tübingen. The investigation begins with the relationship of human beings to religion. For the young man – and here, already in the beginning we find the roots of a contrast to Kant, who will only allow the strict separation of reason and sensuality in a "System of Morality" – human nature is "more or less only impregnated with the ideas of reason as salt imbues a dish."[20] And so for the sensuous human being, religion will also be sensuous. And "public religion" – "the concepts of God and immortality, insofar as they make up the conviction of a people, insofar as they influence the actions and thoughts of that people" – this public religion does not just immediately affect the morality of the individual, but rather ennobles the spirit of a nation, "so that the so often dormant feeling of their dignity is awoken in their soul, so that the people does not throw itself away and does not let itself be thrown away."[21] Of course, the effectiveness of a "folk religion" can only be realized by a religion where the genius of a people has not yet lost its youthful strength under the weight of its chains.[22] But – the reader of Kant asks further – will not a folk religion precisely as public religion and understood as pure religion of reason, which worships God in spirit and in truth and which serves only in the name of virtue, necessarily degenerate into "fetishism"? Certainly, he answers himself, and all that remains is that folk religion gives as little cause for this as possible and that it prepares the people to take up the religion of reason[23] So how must folk religion be constituted? Its doctrines must be authorized by universal human reason. They must be "simple" because then they will "have more of a share in the formation of folk spirit [Volksgeist]" than if they were "amassed." They must be "human," and indeed be so in the sense that Hegel once excerpted from the essays of the Enlightenment writers in Berlin, that they "are commensurate with the cultural spirit and the stage of morality at which a people stands."[24] The impact of the doctrines on the spirit of the folk should only happen on a "large scale," they should not mix in with the practice of civil justice and through their nominal "positive" content should also not lend support to the priest's lust for power.[25] This much about the doctrine. But furthermore, a folk religion must also occupy the heart and fantasy; its customs should actually have sprouted just as much from the spirit of the folk as they are connected with religion. The most appropriate of all ceremonies would surely be – because of the minimal risk to degenerate into fetishism [Fetischdienst] – "holy music and the song of an entire people."[26] Finally, a third and most essential part of a folk religion: "It must be so constituted that all the needs of life and the public affairs of the state are connected to it."[27] No partition between life and doctrine![28] "Folk spirit, religion, degree of political freedom" cannot be considered separately. "They are woven together into one strand like three colleagues who can do nothing without the others."[29] "Folk religion – which generates a large-minded disposition – and nourishes it – goes hand in hand with freedom."[30] Folk religion and political relations together form the spirit of the folk. How sad the spirit of the Christian peoples, how majestic the image of that genius, which radiates – "oh, from the distant days of the past" – before the soul, that folk spirit, for whom its *Politeia* was a lenient mother, not a scolding, firm woman—one who did not force its tender limbs into confining swaddling clothes. That genius, to whom the coarse threads of necessity, which bound it to nature, were hardly something oppressive, but rather, in that it processed them through "self-activity," finds an extension of its enjoyment and an expansion of its life in the spontaneous proliferation of the threads.[31]

Let us take pause with this image of Greek humanity. It suggests itself as an irrefutable assumption that someone who had sketched out such an outline carried Schiller's "Hymns to the Gods of Greece" in his heart. And as Hölderlin's friend, whose poetry in Tübingen sprouted entirely from the strophic form that was disclosed in that very poem, this is a certainty. We may take pause, for already the first piece gives an answer to our question on Hegel's conception of the ideas from 1789. For him, the religious-philosophical subject matter of Kant and Fichte shifted into the cultural-philosophical. The idea of freedom circulated in his thoughts, but it becomes shrouded and overgrown by the new view of the "folk spirit."[32] For Hegel, the folk spirit was then not really the secret root of all national existence, as the Historical School would later define the concept, but rather a component of this completed existence or, according to most passages, its greatest blossom. It is not so much a cultivating force but rather cultivated folk life itself. It becomes "cultivated," "produced," "raised" and then works freely back again — we cannot push the contrast too far — on the individual, and then through the individual back upon those powers that produced, raised, and cultivated it. Indeed, in one passage it even goes above and beyond the individual, namely, there where it is demanded from the customs of religion that they germinate from the folk spirit. But as the prominent, and for Hegel's intellectual development, determinate side of the conception, we must hold on to the following: folk spirit appears to him as product, as the visible, living entirety of a national ethos. With this the context of Hegel's concept of "folk spirit" within a history of ideas also becomes clear as day. For the folk spirit as result coincides with Montesquieu's definition of the *esprit général*: "*plusieurs choses gouvernent les hommes: le climat, la réligion, les lois, les maximes du gouvernement, les exemples des choses passées, les mœurs, les manières; d'ou il se forme un esprit général qui en résulte.*"[33] In contrast with Montesquieu, the components and how they fit together were changed for Hegel, but the concept retained the character of a result. The issue is how the question was posed and formulated by the great historical works of the eighteenth century as the disentanglement of a richly formed historical figure into clearly arranged and countable "causes." This manner of posing the question coalesced to some extent in Montesquieu's definition of *esprit général* into a leading idea of the philosophy of history. Eventually, it was adopted by Herder and finally grew over into the nineteenth century in the form of the Hegelian concept of folk spirit. From there it then later flowed together in its effects with the folk spirit of the Historical School. This concept, however, issued from much different sources of

the eighteenth century, namely, from the resistance against that splinter-
ing of the living into its component parts that was itself exemplified by
that prior direction of historical-philosophical questioning. We connect
this resistance with such names as Hamann, Herder, and Goethe. After
Voltaire, one became accustomed to see in the "*génie*" of a people, of an
age, a root of their historical life. Herder taught one to recognize in the
original God-created "genius" of a people, in the "genetic character,"
an "inexplicable," "inextinguishable" element of historical occurrences.
Those of the "Storm and Stress" movement plunged their new knowledge about art and life into the foreign word "*Genie*," such that quite different, partially English[34] and even neo-Platonic influences ran together.
Kant gave the concept of the new doctrine of art a broadly visible place
in his *Critique of Judgment*. Precisely from this book and from the concept
of genius, Fichte, and then later Schelling, were strongly stimulated in
a general philosophical manner. And finally, what Schelling presented
about the unconscious emergence of art in the artist, this and perhaps
also his recently published exposition on how the goal of world history
is unconscious to the individual, these all fell as seeds into the soul of
the twenty-year-old future founder of the Historical School of Law. And
so, the history of the Romantic idea of the folk spirit also issues from
the eighteenth century, an idea that knit the living dress of national life
– woven in the dark depths, not in the bright of day – in this regard,
fundamentally and continually separated from the folk spirit of Hegelian
character. Now admittedly this Hegelian folk spirit, despite that in contrast to the Romantic concept it comes from the prevailing tendency of
the eighteenth century and unmistakably bears the marks of this descent,
is already no longer under the influence of its Enlightenment origin
at that time in Tübingen. Already now, to anticipate a technical term
first used by Hegel later on, it is "living totality," indeed, a product, but
already more than a mere product: despite its put-togetherness it is a
once-again-unified entity. The poetical image-like quality that is used to
talk about it allows this entity to appear entirely above and beyond the
mere "*ce qui en résulte*" of Montesquieu. In contrast to the "*plusieurs choses*"
whence it comes, it does not have the lower, but rather the higher grade
of liveliness. The Hegelian concept which, according to its form, stems
entirely from the Enlightenment, belongs in this striving for concrete
unification within the circle of the German revolution of feeling against

the Enlightenment. But of course, the same impulse towards unity again expels it from this circle. For in that Hegel is now looking above and beyond Montesquieu for a unified source in the unified result, he names as the inner root of the whole of national life that is viewed together in the "folk spirit" – "universal reason."

Reason! The circles of the Enlightenment, Kant, and the Revolution appear hard to separate there. National culture and folk spirit are always determined according to the attained degree of universal reason. With this, religion wins its place. As folk religion, religion is, besides political relations, the most important mediator between the roots of reason and the blossom of life.[35] It is itself, with regard to its content, determined by reason. Its historical, accidental essence is conceived of as something less than reason, as something left behind from the ideal of Kant's pure, moral religion of reason. Admittedly, the effects that are expected from this pure religion of reason are really themselves – and this is what is entirely new – something different and more than pure reason and pure Kantian ethicality. What is expected is an entire national life, where for the individual the iron bond of needs is entwined with roses, so "that he feels as comfortable in these chains as if they were his work, as if they were a piece of himself."[36]

Those who know Hegel's doctrine of the state, as he more or less presented it in the introduction to his Berlin lectures on the philosophy of history, will have heard multiple preludes in the foregoing. The relationship between folk spirit and reason, even the placement of religion between the two, almost forces one to recall Hegel's later statements on these questions. Nevertheless, one could say that the similarities are certainly present, but that they are emphasized much too strongly through our ordered presentation. At one point the rational core of cultural life was still conceived very abstractly as "Enlightenment," as knowledge, whereas later it appears to him in the form of the state, as "ethicality." Moreover, it is in no way a coincidence that at the center of these pages, which to some extent preserve for us Hegel's first social-philosophical system, we find Hegel's view of the folk spirit and the relationship of the individual to this spirit, while the state is almost only ever discussed in relation to the folk spirit and hardly or never to the individual human being. And what an image of the relation between the state and folk spirit Hegel gives us! The state really only has the task to watch over "the mood, the inspirations of its darling"[37] as a good mother. The good mother Politeia should leave the upbringing of her darling as much as possible to nature, "which nurtures every plant best the less it is grafted, the less it is affected."[38] So this is the "freedom" that "goes hand in hand" with folk religion. And the remarkable future-sounding thought, that the folk spirit finds the "extension of its life"[39] in the multiplication of the threads which connect it to nature, refers, and here one should take note, not to the political but rather to the cultural "threads."

Within this ideal of society, with which the student of the Tübingen Stift answered the ideas of 1789, it is precisely the idea of the state that remains undeveloped. Here Hegel is just as blind as this entire generation. It will always remain remarkable, how from the countless bright eyes that looked over from Germany to France at this time, none saw the world-historical process that was taking place there behind the fog of phrases and steam of blood – the emergence of the new nation-state. Over there, one only saw that which one already possessed and guarded in one's own bosom, one saw the victory – and soon the failure – of one's own well-trusted ideals. One saw freedom, but not the state – freedom in the sense of the blessed personality, as Wilhelm von Humboldt understood it in his famous essay from 1792.[40] And it remains characteristic of Hegel, in contrast to Humboldt's ideas, that here this idea of freedom matured into an image of a new humanity and stopped revolving around the individual person and their formation: that here the new humanity immediately became the highest image of a new community, the folk spirit. This step came almost too rushed and too forced. As naturally and smoothly as this transition from humanity to folk happened here, one could almost expect that the ethical-personal part would easily be completely left behind while that idea of the folk spirit would continue to develop in the Romantic sense towards a natural, all-encompassing totality into which individual life would be absorbed without will or coercion. To a certain degree that is what indeed happened, but only to a certain degree. The thinking and willful "I" remained a power in Hegel's developing thought structures. That all-encompassing totality consciously received an ethical, not a natural being. But at the moment, nothing points to such a future. The beautiful and free folk community [Volksgemeinschaft], as Hegel then had in mind, was still missing. Precisely the firm skeleton of the legislative and coercive state, the sober

light of political thought had not yet shone into these dream images of a
new national cultural life. For the Tübingen theologian, the austere strict-
ness of Kantian ethicality in its exclusive seriousness and its virile and
proud opposition – this we must add – had not yet become a concrete
experience in contrast to the feeling-enraptured dreams of community.

Before we go on, we still have to cast a glance on some thoughts from
texts that are connected to those we just discussed. Chronologically, they
in fact already belong in the first year of residence in Bern. According
to their content, however, they still stand in closer connection to the
first fragment insofar as they also essentially deal with the comparison
between Greek culture and Christianity. The tone, of course, changes. The
mood of the glance to the past, the mourning that recalls Hölderlin, the
guiding charm of images influenced by Wieland now begin to give way
to a much sharper critique, a dry and level-headed language. The new
wave that would reach its high point in Hegel's years in Bern is already
surging forth. The state enters into the center of the field of vision much
differently than in the Tübingen piece. It receives its due share of responsibility for the discord between what is ideal and life. Hegel's letters from
the end of the year 1794 and beginning of 1795 show the writer in the
midst of falling out with Protestant orthodoxy. The hellenizing enthu-
siast has become a modern revolutionary. The fight against orthodoxy,
likewise, becomes also, at least indirectly, the fight against the state of the
present age, for "orthodoxy is not to be shaken as long as its profession,
tied to worldly advantages, is interwoven in the whole of the state."[41] Yet
things will change: "The system of religion, which has always taken on
the color of the age and state constitution, will now attain its own true
dignity."[42] "Reason and freedom" – hereby we can understand the passage from the letter introduced earlier – must assert themselves in the
state for the sake of the "invisible church." This gives the sharp sweeping
political thoughts that Hegel takes up and expresses their special personal coloring in that they are in unceasing relation to the theological
battle, the battle for the "invisible church." This becomes even more clear
in these early fragments than in the related notes from 1795 and 1796.
The historical view of the emergence of the state is also similar to the
one carried out in Herder's *Ideas for the Philosophy of History of Humanity*. Despotism develops from the misuse of the originally patriarchal conditions
of trust between people and prince which the people then try to legally

limit.[43] A state then emerges in which "no one is provided more good than is allowed or commanded." The emergence of religion follows the same path. Also, here the innocent childish spirit is lost to the class of priestly leaders, who now use their power to oppress and depreciate the people who still live in antique simplicity.[44] The state's immediate purpose is not inner "morality," but rather merely outer "legality"[45] and precisely because of this it will also try to pull religion into its circle of power. And, especially as a monarchical state, through its concern for the propagation and maintenance of religion, would impede religion's own further inner development. Without the state, religion would perhaps experience such development in the context of the changing public spirit, that is, of universal Enlightenment.[46]

If, on the one hand, the state is criticized here in relation to religion, so also, on the other hand, religion, at least the Christian religion – although not the religion of antiquity – is criticized in its relation to the state. Here, for the first time, the thought appears for Hegel that in the following years ever more exclusively occupies his theological-political reflections and, fused ever more strongly with personal experience, ferments the clarification of his view of the state: the thought of the incompatibility of Christianity with the state. It first emerges in the comparison between Socrates and Christ, which makes up the content of the second fragment[47] and comes to a head with this contrast. Socrates allows his students to continue to function in civil life – "he who was a fisherman, stayed a fisherman, no one had to leave their house and home" – whereas Christ is someone who "would have become the laughing stock of the Greeks." This fragment, which is the sharpest expression that his hellenizing aversion to Christianity had found as yet – for the person of Jesus himself is otherwise held in high regard in the most passionate outbursts of these sketches – follows chronologically immediately after the oldest Tübingen fragment.[48] Emotional judgment is replaced with more factual observation in the next fragments that concern us. "A state, which today would usher in the commandments of Christ – it could only do this externally, for this spirit cannot be commanded – would soon disband on its own accord." The principles of Jesus only worked for the formation of individuals. Already the early Christian community within the heathen world negates the authentic spirit of the law of the community of goods, the spirit of universal human love, by being closed off from the world. The Reformers, in their Christian policing institutions, also overlooked the difference between the necessary institutions for a ruling folk religion and the private laws of a partitioned society, a club.[49]

It is a major piece of Enlightenment polemic that Hegel takes up here, originally brought up by Bayle, known to Hegel at least through Montesquieu's refutation[50] and through Rousseau[51] and Gibbon.[52] Hegel fuses it with Mendelssohn's construction of church and state as a voluntary and a coercive society.[53] What is peculiar to Hegel, is that this critique of the church does not stand alone, but rather next to the earlier discussed critique of the state. Indeed, to complete the opposition, the critic always rejects the one for the sake of the other: he fights against the church for the sake of the state and against the state for the sake of the church. It is not our task to settle the opposition – the young thinker is not conscious of it himself. At present, the inviolable inner and outer freedom of the human is really the driving, almost all-powerful thought. In comparison, the reasons for this become secondary. That conceptual opposition is thus the correct expression of the feeling that overcomes Hegel in Bern. Only now, and only thus prepared, is he ready for the full effects of Kant's philosophy. We learn from a letter to Schelling dated January 1795 that Hegel has recently taken up Kant's philosophy again in order "to learn to apply its most important results to some of our customary ideas or to elaborate such ideas according to those results." We have followed the beginnings of the inner upheaval he pronounces here. We will begin to see how the image of a folk community that he instinctively realized in Tübingen now recedes and how this first beautiful world, where it is not destroyed, is yet overtaken by other growths.

## NOTES

1   GW 3, 184–190, 191–200; Thaulow (op. cit.), 129–146.

2   Rosenkranz 28, 32 f.; Klaiber (loc. cit.), 190 f.

3   Rosenkranz 28 ff; confirmed and supplemented by Klaiber (op. cit.), 204, 206. Cf. Hegel to Niethammer on April 19, 1817: "after one and a half years at the university [...]. During this time, my father also could not have been satisfied with me." (BR, II).

4   Rosenkranz 34.

5   Rosenkranz 33.

6   Rosenkranz 29; Plitt (1869), Vol. I, 31. The following is an entry from Hegel's student album shared there (Vol. III, 251; cf. also Br IV, 66) from 1793: "Long

lives he who does what is right / And sets his sights firmly on the German cap of liberty."

7   Varnhagen von Ense (1868 f.), July 16, 1826.

8   HW 12, 529.

9   Rosenkranz 34 [The quote reads in the original: "S'il y avait un peuple de dieux, il se gouvernerait Démocratiquement." (Rousseau [1959 ff.], Vol. III, 406)].

10  Hegel to Schelling, December 24, 1794 (Br I).

11  Hölderlin to Neuffer, November 28, 1791 (Hölderlin [1992 f.], Vol. II, 475 – verbatim: "Otherwise I have done little; let the great *Jean Jacque* teach me a little about human rights [...].").

12  Klaiber (loc. cit.), 208, II.

13  Goethe to Schiller, August 23, 1797 (Goethe [1985 ff.]), Vol. IV, 31).

14  Hölderlin (1992 f.), vol. I, 653 – "Like the starry skies, I am at rest and moved." ["Wie in Sternenhimmel, bin ich still und bewegt."].

15  Rosenkranz 40.

16  Hegel to Schelling, late January 1795 (Br I).

17  GW I, 83–164; Nohl 1–71.

18  For dating see Nohl 404 [According to Nohl it was written in 1793, during Hegel's last year in Tübingen. Along with analyzing the handwriting, Nohl leans on Hegel's familiarity with Fichte's "Versuch einer Critik aller Offenbarung" of 1792 and Kant's "Religion innerhalb der Gesetze der bloßen Vernunft," which appeared in 1793; the GW edition follows this dating at least for Text 16 ("Religion ist eine der wichtigsten..."), which corresponds to the first part of the fragment Nohl recorded as "Volksreligion und Christentum" (cf. the editorial report in GW I, 469).].

19  For instance also the 24th Book of Montesquieu's *"De l'esprit des lois"* (Montesquieu [op. cit.], Vol. II, 714 ff.), which is cited by Nohl (Nohl 40). [According to RB Rosenzweig owned a copy from the publisher "Firmin Didot fréres" from 1859. Such an edition does not seem to have existed; it is likely the case of a typing mistake in RB. It is possible that Rosenzweig referenced the edition from 1849, which was indeed published there.].

20  GW I, 84f.; Nohl 4.

21  GW I, 86; Nohl 5.

22  GW I, 87; Nohl 6.

23  GW I, 99 f.; Nohl 17.

24  GW I, 104; Nohl 21.

25  GW I, 106; Nohl 23.

26  GW I, 109; Nohl 26.

27  GW I, 103; Nohl 20.

28  GW I, 109; Nohl 24 (cf. also Mendelssohn [1783], 95).

29  GW I, 111; Nohl 27 [In the first manuscript, the quotation still reads "folk spirit, history, religion, degree of political freedom" – Rosenzweig also alludes to this (cf. GW I, 112 note 2; 475)].

30  GW I, 110; Nohl ibid.

31  GW I, 110ff.; Nohl 27ff.

32  A clarifying dispute over the concept of *Volksgeist* [folk spirit or spirit of the people] for Hegel and for the Historical School played out between Brie (Brie, S.: Der Volkgeist bei Hegel und in der historischen Rechtsschule. In: Archiv für Rechts- und Wirtschaftsphilosophie 2 [1908/1909]) and Loening (Loening, E.: Die philosophischen Ausgangspunkte der rechtshistorischen Schule. In: Internationale Wochenschrift für Wissenschaft, Kunst und Technik, 3/4 [1910]). Loening's conclusions essentially concur with those arrived at by Landsberg (Landsberg [1910], vol. III/2, 213 ff.); Landsberg placed Loening's assumption of Savigny's relation to Schelling's System of 1800 on sure footing in that he brought to light Savigny's travel letters from 1799 and 1800, which had been buried in the 1889/90 Program of the Lyceum Fridericianum in Kassel; the annotations of this publication, for which we have Herr Professor Stoll to thank (Stoll 1890) already contained what was essential in deciding the dispute between Brie and Loening. More recently Kantorowicz (Kantorowicz, H.: Volksgeist und historische Rechtsschule. In: Historische Zeitschrift 108 [1912], 295 ff.) alluded with desirable clarity to Hegel's remarks from 1793 already discussed early by Dilthey and Eber (Eber 1909).

If, however, with regard to the transference of Schelling's thoughts to Savigny, Loening and Landsberg point towards Schelling's lectures from 1802 (Schelling 1803) on the method of academic study, then it is to be added that these lectures provide something new in their conception of the state in comparison with the System of 1800; and what is new, as G. Mehlis (Mehlis 1906) already expresses, is presumably already the outcome of Hegel's influence upon Schelling; so that, if following Loening and Landsberg we also wanted to ascribe to the book from 1803 a part played in the advancement of Savigny's ideas, then Brie's thesis would in a certain sense need to be established retroactively against Loening and Landsberg; then Hegel would have indirectly had an effect through the Schelling of 1803 upon the first formation of Savigny's concept of a *Volk*. The question can only be answered if one knows when and in what form Savigny had confused the thought of cosmopolitanism, which still held sway over him in 1799 (cf. Stoll [op. cit.]), with the thought of peoplehood; Schelling's System of 1800 still essentially held the same position as Kant's "Idea for a Universal History with Cosmopolitan Purpose"; it was first the lectures of 1802 that went beyond this position.

It is not entirely impossible that Savigny would have taken notice of Schelling's new remarks. It is actually an erroneous assumption that we have no evidence of Savigny's philosophical interest from a later time. In the year 1802 he writes to Fries, whom mutual friends had praised, with a series of questions on general metaphysics and legal philosophy and is then evidently disappointed with Fries' reply. As it is, in the first of these letters (cf. Henke, P.J.: Jakob Friedrich Fries. In: Monatsblätter für innere Zeitgeschichte. Bd. XXXI [Jan. – Juni 1868], 293 ff. [letter from February 3, 1802]), he formulates his wishes regarding legal philosophy as follows: "The division of right from morality appears to me to be endowed with more meaning than it requires; much more necessary is a thorough presentation of the relation to politics." In saying so, must he not have been captivated by Schelling's 10th lecture?

It is also to be noted here that the occurrence of the expression "state-individuals" [Staatsindividuen] that Loening as well as Landsberg had established in using it against Brie is not to be used in the same sense with Schelling in 1800. In context the expression has a meaning that goes directly against the romantic concept of "state-individuality" [Staatsindividualität]: given that individuals states are perishable, at that time for Schelling the ideal state was thus not an individual, but rather a universal state [Universalstaat]; Hegel (cf. p. 151) is prioritized over Schelling in the doctrine on the "ethical individuality" of the *Volk* especially emphasized by Brie.

The presentation in the text could only minimally take into account the amendments and adjustments that Kantorowicz (op. cit.) sought to supply to Landsberg. What deserves thanks, among other things, seems to me to be his rejection of the relation between Savigny and Herder established by V. Ehrenberg and the relation between Savigny and Wilhelm v. Humboldt established by Kunze. On the other hand, I hold his most important positive contribution (op. cit., 323), namely the relation between Savigny and Montesquieu, to be misguided. According to Kantorowicz (op. cit., 296), the dependance of right upon the *Volksgeist* is clearly taught as a demand (Montesquieu [op. cit.], Book 19, ch. 21f.) as well as a regular fact (ibid. Chpt. 23ff.) and accompanied with many examples in the 19th Book of the "Espirit des lois," as is likewise the possibility of the reverse relationship (ibid., ch. 27). The correct reading of the 19th Book, however, was already given earlier by E. v. Möller. According to him, with Montesquieu "the origin of laws is not transferred into the *Volksgeist*, but rather in contrast laws are presented as among the constituent elements that bring about the *Volksgeist* and even at times solely determine it (v. Möller, E.: "Die Entstehung des Dogmas von dem Ursprung des Rechts aus dem Volksgeist" in: *Mitteilungen des Instituts für österreichische Geschichtsforschung* 30 [1909], 30). For Montesquieu, it is never the case of "right," but rather of the law set by the legislator (Landsberg, E.: "Artikel Savigny, Friedrich Carl v." in: *Allgemeine Deutsche Biographie*). Furthermore, for Montesquieu the clinging of the legislator to some natural or historical conditions is only a concession or convenience (cf. Rexius [op. cit.], 496 ff.; the quotes that Wahl presents from Montesquieu against Rexius [Wahl, A.: "Montesquieu als Vorläufer von Aktion und Reaktion" in: *Historische Zeitschrift* 109 (1912), 135 f.] can serve as evidence of the accuracy of Rexius' thesis). Yet in addition, the chapters 21 and 23 ff. that Kantorowicz (op. cit.) draws upon for the "independence of right from the *Volksgeist*" in no way establish a relation between right and *Volksgeist* but rather that between laws and customs. Montesquieu strictly distinguishes *moeurs* and *manières* from *espirit général, esprit de la nation, caractère de la nation*. For Montesquieu, the relation between customs and laws is a relation between two "*choses*," both of which form the *Volksgeist* (cf. Montesquieu [op. cit.], Book 19, ch. 4). An independence of laws from the *Volksgeist* is only expressed by Montesquieu in one sentence of chapter 5 (the one quoted by Kantorowicz), which is to be understood entirely how G. Rexius does, namely as a rule of wisdom for the legislator. The idea that laws or the legislator proceeds from the *Volksgeist* is also foreign here; when Kantorowicz, and following him Wahl (op. cit.), invokes the justification of this sentence as an instance against Rexius, it almost appears as if he connects the "*nous*" to the legislator as opposed to the enforcer of the law; only in this case would the objection be valid (cf. also the passage v. Möller [op. cit.], 30). By contrast, the independence of the *Volk* character from the laws is shown in great detail in the main chapter and in the closing chapter of the entire book.

Unfortunately, Hildegard Trescher (Trescher 1918; cf. also this: "Montesquieus Einfluß auf die philosophischen Grundlagen der Staatslehre Hegels" in: Schmollers Jahrbuch 42 [1918], 471–501, 907–944) is also mistaken in answering this question, at least in the assertions she provides. Within her implementation she then wonders herself how that pre-claimed "impact" (namely claimed only by her, not by Montesquieu) of the *espirit général* upon all expressions of life "is nowhere to be seen." Montesquieu is robbing the whole of the *Volk* of its soul. Certainly! Only he cannot rob from them what it had never possessed. It should not be disputed that although intellectually there is no relation between Montesquieu's and Savigny's concept of the *Volksgeist*, that nevertheless some impulse, even influence may have been *possible*. For the history of ideas, fruitful relations often come about through misunderstandings. But in order for that to be the case here, and before declaring it, it would first need to be proven. Until then, one must stay with the confirmed connection to Schelling.

And with regard to this connection, Kantorowicz is mistaken in relating what Schelling says about "higher nature" in 1801 with what Savigny says about the same in 1814, a relation which moreover he himself thinks is not entirely secure (Kantorowicz [op. cit.], 314: "it is not entirely clear in what sense." For Schelling, "higher nature" stands in contrast to the nature of the *Philosophy of Nature* and is history which converges with the general situation of law, as later through the state he finds a "second nature" represented through the state within the higher ethical order. For Savigny, by contrast, the "higher nature of a *Volk*]" (the "higher *Volk*") is the *Volk* as a unity above and beyond all ages of its history in contrast to a *Volk* of the momentary present. For Savigny, however, the doctrine of freedom and necessity is not exactly the same as with the Schelling 1800; but it was also not mere "catchwords" that remained with Savigny from Schelling, nor did Schelling's thoughts from 1800 "lose their deep meaning" or become "devoid of all problems." Rather, what happened was a transformation of Schelling's ideas, especially those which Schelling himself had already undertaken in 1802. In 1800, Schelling did not teach the unconscious development of right, but rather the ideal condition of international law; and at that time it was not the states which carried this development, but instead that this development was to bring about the destruction of the same. It was first in 1802 that Schelling brought together right and the state, and now no longer treated state-individuality [Staatsindividualität] as a transitory appearance on the path towards the final cosmopolitan condition of history.

33    Montesquieu (op. cit.), Book 19, ch. 4. [JS & JS: "the general spirit: Many things govern men: climate, religion, laws, maxims of government, examples of things past, customs, manners; from which a general spirit is formed which results from it."]

34    Shaftesbury (cf. Schlapp [1901], 125; on this in general: Weiser [1916]).

35    GWI, 103; Nohl 20f.

36    GW I, 114; N 28 [the quotation is noted in the margin, according to the GW edition; the main text reads: "that it seemed to be entirely his work."]

37    Ibid.

38    GW I, 111 [this passage of the text was not transmitted by Nohl].

39    Ibid. [in both the first and the second version; on the latter, see ibid. 112, footnote 2].

40    There is nothing to say for or against that Hegel was familiar with the sections published at that time. I cannot find any "influence." [What is at stake is v. Humboldt's text on the theory of the state, "Idee zu einem Versuch, die Grenzen der Wirksamkeit des Staates zu bestimmen," which was published in excerpts during Hegel's lifetime.]

41    Hegel to Schelling, late January 1795 (Br I).

42    GW I, 164; Nohl 71.

43    Herder (1844 ff.), vol. V, Book 9, ch. IV–V, 310–326.

44    GW I, 123, 125; Nohl 36, 38.

45    GW I, 138; Nohl 48.

46    GW I, 153 f.; Nohl 61 f.

47    GW I, 115–120; Nohl 30–35 [Rosenzweig's numbering of the fragments goes back to Nohl; in GW, Text 17 ("Ausser der Mündlichen Unterricht ..." is intended].

48    [Cf. the dating in Nohl (Nohl 404) and the Editorial Report in GW I (475 f.)].

49    GW I, 128 f. further 134, 121 f.; Nohl 41 f., further 44, 360.

50    Quoted after Nohl 40; in addition Montesquieu (op. cit.), Book 24, ch. 6.

51    Rousseau (1959 ff.), Vol. III, Book 4, ch. 8.

52    Gibbon (1776 ff.), Vol. II, ch. 15, para. IV ("Their [early Christians'] aversion to the business of war and government.").

53    Mendelssohn (op. cit.), 28 (cf. GW I, 134; Nohl 44).

# 4

# BERN

It was not Kant himself, not the historical Kant in Königsberg, who now entered Hegel's intellectual development in a rigorous and exclusively powerful manner, but rather a Kant who himself had already been received into the stream of history. For Hegel, the first Kant was only a force next to other forces – he had endured gods next to him. Now it was different. Fichte, the ethicist, and under whose influence he knew Hölderlin to then be in Jena and Schelling in Tübingen, now became for him the translator of Kant. Fichte will lift philosophy, so Schelling prophesied in January 1795 to his friend in Bern, to a height at which even most of the current Kantians will become dizzy. And he will definitively destroy the orthodoxy that already believed to have made its peace with the new philosophy.[1] Hegel's answer is less assuring: the orthodoxy is not to be shaken as long as its profession, tied to worldly advantages, is interwoven into the whole of the state.[2] But Schelling, certain of victory, is not to be discouraged: Kant was the dawn, Fichte the sun who must and will disperse the murky fog. In a few heavily laden sentences Schelling gives the outline of his own philosophy, which is also without doubt

DOI: 10.4324/9780429354724-5

that of his friend – he has become a "Spinozist." God is nothing other than the absolute "I"; there is no personal God; the human is guaranteed immortality by the eternal impossibility of going over into the absolute which is, however, his highest aspiration. From the dissemination of these thoughts, the young Schelling expects the downfall "of the hitherto entire conception of the world and sciences," the downfall of the "moral despotism" of the philosophical half-men, that is, the pseudo-Kantian theologians who pressed freedom of thought down even lower than any political despotism.[3] Nothing is more telling than the reverberation that Schelling's fanfare finds within Hegel: he also awaits a "revolution" from the completion of the Kantian system, yet the system itself, as well as Schelling's critical thoughts on it, will remain esoteric.[4] But through the implications "some gentlemen will be left astonished." And now, having arrived at the "implications," the full stream of Hegel's own thoughts is suddenly set into motion. I quote the paragraph in full: "One will get dizzy at this highest height by which the human is being so greatly exalted. Yet why was one so delayed in placing a higher value on the dignity of the human, in recognizing the human capacity for freedom, which sets humans in the same order as the spirits? I believe there is no better sign of the times than this, that humanity is being presented as so worthy of respect in itself. It is proof that the aura of prestige surrounding the heads of the oppressors and the gods of this earth is disappearing. The philosophers are proving this dignity, the peoples will learn to feel it and not only demand their rights which have been trampled in the dust, but rather themselves take them back again and make them their own. Religion and politics have joined in the same underhanded game. The former has taught what despotism willed, contempt of the human race, the incapacity for it to attain anything good, to become something on its own. With the spread of ideas of how everything *ought* to be, the indolence of people, who, set in their ways, always take everything as it is, will disappear. The enlivening strength of ideas, even if they are in themselves still limited, such as the idea of the fatherland, its constitution, and so forth, etc. – will lift up the minds of the people, and they will learn to sacrifice themselves for such ideas. For presently the spirit of constitutions has made a pact with self-interest and has founded its realm upon it."[5] Hegel, with his feet on the ground, carries on the theme of his friend, who himself is housed high in the ether of thought. He has nothing to say about the sun and worlds and quickly moves on from the "esoteric" comparison of God and the absolute "I." The dignity of the human – this is the point where the ideas of his friend really affect him and where he summarizes them himself, raising them to a storm-swept challenge to the "gods of earth."[6] The initial signs of tranquil humility in the face of "fate," which appeared here and there in the Tübingen writings,[7] have disappeared. The "how it ought to be" lifts itself against the "indolence, to take everything as it is," against the hope that everything will work itself out in time – "off the seat of your pants, gentlemen!"[8] Thus speaks the same person, who, seven years later, would see the goal of the science of the state in the "understanding of that which is," and who then would pour out the full vessel of his disdain over "its pretend philosophers and teachers of human rights."[9] But at that time in Bern, in close view of the workings of a small aristocratic republic, where admittedly – just as in Hegel's homeland – the spirit of the constitution had made a pact with self-interest,[10] Hegel was living entirely in a feeling of opposition to his surroundings. Alienated within the family of his employer, clouded by impulses of human hatred, Hegel sought salvation – now really experiencing the mood of Rousseau internally for the first time – in the arms of good mother nature.[11] Thus attuned to those inner notes, he was inclined to take up the doctrine of the unconditional self-legislation of the individual, the dignity of the human, in its entire disregard for all other values and goods of the internal as well as external world; to apply this to his present world view, to his still "customary ideas"; and to reshape these ideas according to the demands of this doctrine. We have the results of this desire at hand in the work of the summer of 1795 and the winter from 1795 to 1796. The first, a "Life of Jesus,"[12] we can leave aside in our context. But the other, known under the title "The Positivity of the Christian Religion," contributes to the questions surrounding the older manuscripts and demands careful observation.[13]

The questions of Tübingen have won a new form. If, at that time, the spirit of antiquity and the spirit of the present, folk religion and Christianity, stood rigidly across from each other as two closed worlds in claim and counterclaim, a historical element now breaks in upon the formulation of the question. This spirit of the newer peoples, this Christian church, is itself something that has developed over time. In its beginnings,

Christianity was the elevation of the religion of reason against the dead positivity of Judaism. It is a task of the history of dogma to depict this process of devolution, that is, how the religion of Jesus, instead of becoming "folk religion," could become positive religion – could become the Christian church of the present. Hegel chose a more narrow task out of the great thematic of the history of dogma and the church: to search in part in the religion of Jesus itself, in part in the spirit of the times, for some universal reasons "through which it became possible that early on one could mistake the Christian religion for a religion of virtues, and at first make it into a sect, and then later into a positive faith."[14] This formulation is more momentous for Hegel's development than its Enlightenment tone lets on. It was decisive in general that he changed from forming concepts through comparison and contrast, as in the earlier fragments, to a historical form of questioning, even if his conception of history itself was still inextricably linked to his contemporaries' conception of history. This is admittedly no longer the case when Hegel goes beyond the viewpoints of contemporary ecclesiastical history in not allowing an originally pure Christianity of Jesus to become reshaped and tarnished from without. Rather, over and above this, he looked to find the points of "misjudgment" in the religion of Jesus and in the Christianity of the early congregation itself. Even Herder, in his famous seventeenth century book *Ideas*, had not preceded him in this. Thus, we have here the seed of Hegel's concept of historical development before us and, in general, one of the paths that leads out of the eighteenth century's conception of history. Admittedly, at that time, the way that Hegel posed his questions was still aligned with how he had done so earlier. In particular, in Bern his questions hardly took his views on the state into consideration, whereas a few years later in Frankfurt these views would become exceptionally important while treating the same subject in a wholly new manner. For Hegel in Bern, Jesus' personal relation to the state was not as fundamental to the coming history as was his performance of miracles and his own statements. One could even say that at that time the individual's unconditional right for freedom over and against the state was much too self-evident for Hegel to have been liable to foresee any, or even the, driving force of the development to come. The political problem is signaled only quietly in the treatment of the disciples: "they didn't have an interest for the state like a republican has for his fatherland; all of their interest was confined to the person Jesus."[15] But this condition only becomes consequential as one among others in that it leads to the deification of the "teacher of virtues" and thereby to a "positive" part of the doctrine. Only after the congregation had taken up the positive in their faith and their order, and furthermore when they had also learned to observe the pure laws of virtue as positive, did they enter into the decisive relation with the state. We are already familiar with this line of thought: as the congregation grows and finally encompasses all citizens of the state, "ordinances and arrangements that did not bother anyone's rights when the society was still small become duties of the state and duties of the citizens which otherwise could never have occurred."[16] But with this, the investigation leaves its historical course. Here, at the point where the sect becomes the church, the jurisprudential critique on the concept of the church and its relationship to the state sets in. Here, the conceptual proof of the proposition that was used earlier to historically describe the expansion of Christianity holds true: what is applicable in a small society is unjust in a state.[17]

This part of the essay, which is important for us, entitled "How a Moral or Religious Society Grows into a State,"[18] shows Hegel fully under the dominion of contract-thinking. And yet, this thinking is not, as one might expect out of someone from Württemberg, about the thoroughly living principle of Württemberg constitutional law, namely, the idea of a contract between the prince and the people, but rather, in the spirit of Rousseau, the thought of a contract of every individual with everyone else. Yet in addressing the particular question of the position of the church to the state, as well as both of these to the people, Hegel again distances himself greatly from Rousseau. It is rather the influence of Mendelssohn's *Jerusalem* that is noticeable here.[19] But what is new with regard to Mendelssohn is the core tone of Fichtean pathos and, likewise, the main line of Hegel's argumentation is now particular to him. For while Mendelssohn essentially undertakes the separation of state and church on the basis of the concept of contract and the impossibility to draw up a contract on internal matters, here that separation for Hegel is derived from the concept of society, namely out of the differentiation between a voluntary society and a coercive society. The state is a coercive society, for in it the duties of one are the rights of another, and for that reason their fulfillment must be enforceable, which it would not be as

the fulfillment of a mere ethical duty.[20] We thus have before us, starting with the individual, the conceptual construction of coercive state
force. The force over the individual, which is derived from the natural
subjective rights of the individual, is then, of course, simply the highest
force; it allows no equal power next to it, no state within the state. Legal
claims that are based on freely undertaken duties and forces that allude
to such legal claims, such as the church, are not equal to the force of
the state: The rights that I "concede to" in such a society into which I
freely enter "cannot be the rights the state has over me; for then I would
recognize a force in the state that is different from the state but with the
same rights."[21] In that it is thus built up as an unconditional power, its
conscious purpose remains, as the disciple of Montesquieu also admits,
that through the invisible influence of the state constitution "a virtuous
spirit of the people [can be] cultivated," albeit only as mere "legality,"
an external lawfulness of affairs. Only as the means to this end does the
state also become "ethicality," the good disposition of being inclined
towards the direct fostering of its citizens. Now, it can bring about this
fostering, as it will be carried out in relation to Mendelssohn, not in its
own person, not as a state. Rather, this fostering needs religion. But even
if religion can guarantee the state the real ethical disposition of its citizens, it cannot itself be the subject of civilian laws. For "if the religious
ordinances of the state became laws, it would again progress no further
than with all other civilian laws: to legality."[22] This is the relationship of
church and state as it should be, but it came about differently in history.
The church, the Protestant as well as the Catholic, became a state itself.
Its contract only differs from the civilian contract in that it aims at the
protection of a certain universal belief, not every personal belief.[23] So far
there would be nothing to criticize. The church, however, does damage
to the natural rights of humans and the state through the fact that the
entry into, as well as the exit from the church contract was not left to
the arbitrary will. Thus, neither state nor church law remained "pure";
state and church are in conflict. The state, whose laws affect the security
of the person and the property of every civilian, entirely aside from their
religious opinions, has the duty to protect these rights. But the church,
which encompasses the entire state, excludes from the state that person
who leaves the church as well. And in most Protestant as well as Catholic
lands, the civilian element of the church–state has withdrawn from its

right and office, not only when both come into collision, but also, as with birth and marriage, when it needs the sanction of both. Just as how the state abandons the right of its citizens in favor of the guilds, whereas it should be its duty to protect everyone who, without offending the civil laws, wants to support themselves however they wish, so the state, in the selection of its educated officials, gave up its right in favor of the universities, who thus exclude everyone who is not "properly" from the state.[24]

This state ideal is so entirely unromantic, and also, thus removed from Montesquieu, so hostile towards all powers that could intervene between the freedom of the individual under contract and the omnipotence of the state born from contract. But the omnipotence of the state is now certainly not only responsible for itself but it finds its task and limit in the natural rights of the individual person. For this state, the concession of civilian rights to those of other faiths is nothing more than the "suspension of a great injustice and thus a duty."[25] The thought of human rights breaks into the enclosure of the *contrat social*. To the natural rights of humans, besides the right of "bestial preservation," belongs the right to develop one's abilities, to become a human being. Insofar as the state gives its duty, which comes from this human right, over to the church, even if it is well-meant, it becomes a traitor with regard to this right.[26] For whereas the state – and here this conceptual construction's defiant "I" reaches its highest point – whereas the state thus grounds independence from the law on the free decision to live under the law – for example, the freedom to emigrate (which, by the way, was really a law in Württemberg) as a philosophical justification of the state![27] – the church, on the other hand, through that authority over school, robs the individual of the inner freedom to choose to become a member. Yet it is solely on the basis of such free decision that the church can and wants to justify its claims on the individual.[28] Whether or not Rousseau's contract theory is right or wrong as a historical theory – a question, which is shoved aside as carelessly by Hegel as by Rousseau himself[29] – in either case, the essence of civil society entails that "the state makes it its duty to claim and protect my rights as its own."[30] Yes, Hegel bemoans the fact that the basic laws of the German Empire assure the churches, as such, free religious practice rather than entrust the states with the protection of freedom of religion. Because only hereby "would one have had the delight [...] to see a fundamental article of the societal contract developed, celebrated and purely recognized in the contracts of the nations, a human right, which cannot be given up by entering into a society of any kind."[31] The state also has the duty, and this is almost a given after all that has come before, to protect a newly formed church against the dominant one from which it had separated.[32] Of course, to protect the people in general from church legislation that is hostile to reason, to prevent them from renouncing the right "to give oneself one's law, to alone be held accountable for the wielding of the same": that "is not the affair of the state – this would mean to want to coerce people to be human and would be an exercise of force."[33] The cold, almost deliberately matter-of-fact manner of the conceptual investigation gives way in the last pages, as can already be recognized in the passage cited above, to a tone of passionate accusation. In this concluding section, Hegel spells out "which form morality must take in a church."[34] "The state, or rather the ruling powers in the state – for the state is thereby destroyed – gains an advantage in this case through the intention of the church to have an effect upon people's dispositions – namely as a sovereignty, as a despotism that has won complete free play after suppressing all freedom of will through spirituality – the church has taught people to scorn civil and political freedom as excrement over and against the heavenly goods and pleasures of life."[35] – The state is "destroyed" when the "inalienable human right" to "give oneself laws from one's own bosom!"[36] disappears. Hegel's belief in human self-rule [Selbstherrlichkeit] has now climbed to such heights. He now loudly raises his accusation against the state, which "mistakes the extent of its rights and either allows a ruling church to emerge in a state or even associates itself with this church and thus oversteps its powers."[37]

The state ideal of the Revolution stands before us: the state that flows from the free individual and issues into the free individual, almighty against everything that tries to insert itself between it and other humans and against all that aims to plug up its source or dam up its outlet. We recognize the spirit of Rousseau in the hostility against the forces that try to plug the source, the ideas from 1793. We sense the spirit of the declaration of human rights in the hostility against the powers that threaten to dam the outlet, the alienation of the state from its true purpose. No doubt that this second aspect, the Germanic soul of the Revolution, seized the young German more strongly, and therefore the tone here is more personal. For he knows how to translate the French *droit de l'homme* into a phrase nourished from deeper wells: into Kant's, Fichte's, and Schiller's "dignity of human beings." But admittedly, the human being is as great and the content of his demands as rich as this apparently almighty state is poor and soulless. It is as if the state were only the rigid cliff over which, like a waterfall, that proud human striving flows, in order to flow along further with strengthened momentum but unchanged in essence. This striving does not circulate as enlivening blood through the body of the state, creating an independently breathing being. Missing in the relationship of human beings to the state is the ethical, through which that all-pervading power of the state over humans would itself first become ethically ennobled. It must have been precisely during this summer, shortly after the text just discussed, that Hegel copied "The Oldest System-Program of German Idealism" from his friend Schelling.[38] In this text it is said that there is no idea of the state, because the state is something mechanical — just as there could be no idea of a machine. "Thus, we must go above and beyond the state! — for every state must treat free humans as mechanical wheelwork; and it should not do so; and thus it should *cease*."[39] It is the same passionate accusation against the state that erupted for Hegel. But for Hegel the confrontation could not end here. For him, the hate for the state could not become the denial of the state. How Hegel settled things is shown by the text that immediately follows the notes just discussed, and which we may presume was composed at the end of Hegel's time in Bern.[40]

Arguably, in his early period, Hegel had not written anything so comparably complete. Such beautiful mastery of the writer over his material, with language neither shallow nor overconfident, is seen neither in the older manuscripts — often so cold and dry, internally fragmented, and rambling off uncontrollably — nor in the forthcoming drafts of the Frankfurt years — flowing with profound difficulty.

The subject is the old one. Yes, materially the thoughts are more closely connected to the Tübingen and early Bern texts than the large-scale manuscript of Bern that we just came to know. They come across as a more richly historical attempt at the Tübingen investigations on the folk religion of the ancients. It is now the reader of Gibbon that takes up this material again, except of course that Gibbon would have provided more than just historical material. The thoughts with which Hegel orders things, the questions that he asks, are not raised in the same way by Gibbon.[41]

Hegel attempts here to bring his older inclinations, engendered by his feelings during the Tübingen time, into harmony with Kant's and Fichte's more rigorous belief in the "I" as well as with the sharp political turn of the Bern years. Let us recall that during the time in Tübingen there was hardly any talk regarding the state. The state's job was then limited to make itself as little noticed as possible. Now the state becomes the center of attention for this set of ideas as well. The older question of the relationship of the folk to religion expands to the task of understanding the interrelationships of these essential entities: folk, religion, and state. The historical problem whereby this relationship comes to view is the old question, excitingly renewed by Gibbon, of the cause of the Christianization of the ancient world. But where the great English successor of Voltaire sets up his famous five points of natural causes, here Hegel looks for one reason, for the "quiet, secret revolution in the spirit of the age that is not visible to everyone, least of all to contemporaries, and is just as difficult to represent with words as it is to summarize." "How could a religion be displaced that for centuries had set itself firmly in the state, that was most intimately connected with the state constitution, that [...] was intertwined with a thousand threads into the fabric of human life?"[42] Hegel easily dismisses the answers that try to dispose of the historical riddle from the world with expressions such as "enlightenment of the understanding, new insight and such": those pagans also had understanding; religion, even a fantasy-religion, "is not ripped out of the hearts and entire life of the people by cold conclusions."[43] He knows another answer. The religion of the ancients was only a religion for free peoples and with the loss of freedom, the meaning, the driving force of this religion, must also have gone missing. Of what was the freedom of the people of antiquity composed? "The idea of his Fatherland, of his state, was the unseeable, that higher thing for which he worked that drove him on; this was the ultimate purpose of his world [...] His individuality vanished before this idea."[44] But the states forfeited their freedom; the people lost the consciousness "which Montesquieu makes the principle of the republics under the name of virtue and that is the skill to be able to sacrifice the individual for an idea, which is realized by republicans in their Fatherland [...] The image of the state as a product of its activity vanished from the souls of the citizens."⁴⁵ Usefulness in the state — no longer the active production of the state — becomes the great purpose that the state sets for its subjects, whose own activity is accordingly merely good for "the individual," for "acquisition and subsistence, even vanity."⁴⁶ "All political freedom fell away, the right of civilians only secured a right for the security of property that now filled up his entire world."⁴⁷ Death now became something terrible for him, "for nothing outlived this — the republic survived the republican and he had the idea that it was his soul, something eternal."⁴⁸ The human being also no longer found refuge in his gods, for they were "single, incomplete beings that could not satisfy any idea."⁴⁹ The citizen of the Polis could be content with these weak, human-like gods, for he carried the eternal in his own bosom; what the comic could scoff at in his gods was not what he held as most holy. The sacred shrine of the human will, "the freedom to obey self-given laws, [to follow] self-chosen authorities [...] to carry out self-coordinated plans," is now destroyed.⁵⁰ "In this condition, without belief in something lasting, in something absolute, in this habit to obey a foreign will, a foreign legislation, without Fatherland, in a state where there could be no lasting joy, whose pressure the citizens alone felt,"⁵¹ the new religion presented itself to the people and showed them that absolute, namely that which was "independently practical,"⁵² which they once possessed in the free state, and without which reason cannot live, and which from now on they possess in divinity. The new god, who did not replace the gods of antiquity but rather the state of antiquity, or more precisely: the free state-controlling will of the citizen — in opposition to that which was formerly "absolute, independently practical" within co-determination in the republican state — is now out of reach of our will; the human relates "passively" to the "revolution to be brought about through a divine being."⁵³ Even the people in whom the representation of such a helper from above, a messiah, first came about, only took refuge in such comforts when first subjugated by foreign nations; "as a messiah was offered to them who did not fulfill their political hopes, the people still thought it was worth the effort that their state remained a state; those peoples that are indifferent to this, such a people will soon stop to be a people."⁵⁴ If we dare, in response to this conduct, to prescribe a people "not to make its matters its own matter, but rather our opinions," then we only show how the feeling of "what a people can do for their independence"[55] is so foreign to us. Thus, this is the end of the old world: the violation of freedom forced the people "to flee from their eternal, their absolute, into divinity,"[56] in place of a Fatherland, of a free state, came the idea of the church, which had no place for freedom and which was most intimately bound to heaven, while the former found itself completed on earth.

That is more or less the core of what we observed from the notes. What leads up to this are well-known items from Tübingen, the reception of the old cultural-national thoughts, which only now, elevated from their then background of religious belief in reason, are placed in the pure light of beauty-inspired observation. "Those who lived one year within the walls of Athens, unversed in its history, its culture and legislation, could get to know them pretty well from the festivals."[57] But we are without religious fantasy, which would have grown on our ground and been connected with our history and "simply without all political fantasy."[58]

Let us stick with the core piece, in which we find what is really new in comparison with the beginnings in Tübingen. Great things are said of the state here. The ethical relation of the individual to the state, which was missing from the previously discussed Bern writings, is discussed here with utmost vigor. The idea of the state is the good for which the individual works, the ultimate purpose of his world in front of which his individuality vanishes, that which survives him, his soul, something eternal. There is no doubt that the spirit of reason-measured construction that dominates in those other drafts is silent here. There is hardly a sharper emphasis on the interpretation of the ethical relation of the human to the state thinkable than here, where Hegel praises the Jews in the age of Jesus for their rejection of the unpolitical messiah. At the same time, one would be mistaken if one merely saw a contradiction between the image of the state of this section and the admittedly somewhat older lines of thought on the state and the church; indeed, I would not even like to speak of development without further details. We cannot forget that in this earlier text it is the interpreter of history and not the researcher of concepts who speaks. In the background of these Hegelian reflections there stands a very particular view on the world-historical process, and indeed a view that is far from the one that will later dominate his famous lectures on the philosophy of history; this first comes up in a manuscript from the time of Jena. If Hegel later understood the Christian epoch of world history as the completion and in a certain sense the conclusion of the development of humanity – as the world in which the ruins of oriental as well as classical antiquity were built into a higher and richer structure – then in the manuscript at hand he still saw world history entirely from the viewpoint of the classical ideal. The pure humanity of Hellas and the undivided strength with which the individual there took part in the state as a complete personality, was followed, in the Roman Empire, by an epoch that neither recognized the people in their wholeness nor let them take part in the state; only the partial-human counted, only as "acquisition and subsistence"[59] was his activity allowed to enter the monarchy. Only life and property were secured for him by the constitution, and private right became the ruling power of life.[60] Into this condition Christianity brought that which was lacking, the certainty of the absolute – without, by the way, infringing upon it. On the contrary, it solidified and preserved this condition until the present day. For the present – and here the emotional starting point of this view of history is easily recognizable for those who are familiar with the Tübingen Hegel – with its monarchies, its inclination towards acquisition and property as the highest goods of life, its separation of the people into estates and careers, the banishment of the individual from participation in public life, or rather limitation of the individual in this participation to the post of a cog in the machine, this present still stands essentially within the age of the Roman Imperium. And so, at that time, what dwelled in Hegel as hope and belief was pushed into the future. The lofty task of the time ahead is to reclaim the lost unity of the Greek people. If one can talk of a completion, a conclusion of the history of humanity, a third world-year, then such an epoch begins only now, in the immediate present. It is this age that first holds the right "to vindicate, at least in theory, as property of the people, the treasures that have been squandered on heaven" – freedom of the will resting upon itself.[61]

Now, how much this articulation of history, which still shows up for Hegel even after the emergence of his definitive historical-philosophical division and alongside this, how much of this grew forth from Hegel's particular being, how much of it was the intellectual expression of an enraptured longing for Hellas and a view towards a future, simultaneously opened up by the Revolution, in which those dreams of longing could be actualized: one can hardly go wrong in assuming an attachment, maybe even a decisive influence on this classical philosophy of history through the great work that took up a world-historical interpretation for the first time upon the foundation of the new philosophical movement. Hegel read Schiller's *Letters on the Aesthetic Education of Man* when they appeared in the first issues of the journal *Horen*, which Hegel, as the only private person in a terribly unartistic Bern, had obtained.[62] Of course, one must be careful – here as always – to not immediately draw connections and dependencies from individual instances and relations. That said, Schiller's division of the entire course of history up until the present into the Greek epoch and the following period, which serves as the premise for his thoughts on aesthetic education, is much too bold and, despite the connection with Rousseau, really without predecessor – indeed, even for Schiller himself it was an entirely fresh product stemming from his acquaintance with W.v. Humboldt – to not connect the recurrence of this fundamental view in Hegel with Schiller's text.[63] This is especially so considering that antiquity and the present were juxtaposed in elegiac opposition in Hegel's older writings, but not tied into the historical arrangement like now. Additionally, Hegel agrees with Schiller in contrasting both ages according to the view of the inner all-sidedness or one-sidedness of its people, even to the point of depicting the clockwork of the moderns in opposition to the "polypoid nature" of the Greek states. They both further agree in the hopeful longing for a rebirth of that beautiful fullness of the Greek people. And finally, they agree in the belief that the day of completion for humankind is dawning in the present moment.[64]

In the section just discussed Hegel thus sketches the relief of the state of antiquity. In contrast, the portrait of the relationship between the state and the people in the preceding parts of the manuscript is seen from the perspective of the present. The pulse of the entire view of history from that time is thus, that here the magnificence of Greek antiquity has become simply impossible in the Christian world. For here the place of the absolute, which in the consciousness of antiquity the state could seize and, as long as it was a republic, actually did seize, was otherwise occupied. Christianity historically comes into contact with an entirely different kind of state, namely that of the Roman Imperium, and it created preconditions in the consciousness of the individual that demand an entirely different state. The state can no longer be something divine, as it was back then when the gods were not yet divine to the people. Rather, in the modern world it falls to the state to protect the sacred relics, belief, and human rights which lie outside of its precinct all together. Ultimately, however, it is satisfied with its own unholy sphere of power. This is the modern ideal of the state which Hegel does not find cause to develop in the purely historical section of his text, even more so since he fully established and presented it in the preceding parts. And of course, as the concluding parts of the text reveal, Hegel looks back with longing on that unbroken unity of the entire civilian and religious life in the free state of antiquity, but – we would like to say – with a longing that is aware that the lost paradise cannot be restored.[65] The rejection of Christianity, of course, did not merely apply to the church but, rather, to the forms of personal religion that spread and developed in and next to the church, that is, it applies to the Christian people in general who have "absolutely no unity."[66] However, the accrual of personal freedom of conscience, the sense which "great men of newer times have given the name Protestant,"[67] the Bern individualist wants least to abandon this advance. So, for the present he can only erect the strict goal of the image of the state known to us which, willed by the will of all, finds its task in the protection of the natural rights of the individual. A different, opposing understanding of Christianity would have led and will lead to another image of the new state. At this time Hegel is just as far from the one as from the other.

In conclusion, let us continue to try to show the extent to which the outlook towards the future, rather than just being the afterglow of the sun that has set, itself colors the image of longing for the state of antiquity. For the main outlines of the paintings are more related than they may at first glance seem. What separates them for Hegel most essentially is this: for the people of antiquity the active production of their states signifies the crown of life – "the ultimate purpose of their world"[68] – but for the post-Greek people, the work in the actual state of the present is only the unconsciousness – to speak with Schelling – of the little cog in the machine,[69] whereas the active production of the state, as it should be, could only mean for them the dry fulfillment of the societal contract. The height of ethical being lies for these people in a circle that the power of the state is only allowed to protect, not enter. This divides the two ideals, the past and the present one. But these ideals concur in that there, as here, the state is in the first place a "product."[70] It is made and, indeed made by individual people, whether on the one hand the making has the value of the highest ethical activity into which individuality is merged or, on the other hand, is only the distant achievement of a duty. The state of antiquity is also only an ideal as a free state. Only through the fact that the citizen produces it himself, that he co-operates to present it in reality and to preserve it, does the state become his eternal, "his soul."[71] By all means, freedom of the state means freedom, the republican freedom of its citizens, freedom to obey self-given laws, to work together on the entirety of the state and not on just some particular point. The thought of the free individual human thus also dominates the conception of the Polis. The state is powerful but is not power: it is not the independent being, strolling about, that could also use its right against the rights of the individual, that lives its own life and is unconcerned if this individual perhaps unconsciously affects it as a little cog in a subordinated position of the machine or even at all. We are still far away from that Hegel who was set to create the effective formula for the political thinking of the nineteenth century.

## NOTES

1   Schelling to Hegel, January 6, 1795 (Br I).
2   Hegel to Schelling, January 1795 (ibid.).
3   Ibid.
4   Cf. the conclusion from Schelling's letter of July 21, 1795 (ibid.).
5   Hegel to Schelling, April 16, 1795 (ibid.).
6   This formulation comes from a Mendelssohnian statement on Hobbes (Mendelssohn [op. cit.], 12).
7   Nohl 10 (belief in fate, natural necessity), 20 (trust in God's providence), 22 (faith in a broad and good providence, complete devotion to God), 23 (respect for the stream of natural necessity), 29 ("but it taught him iron necessity, it taught him to follow this inalterable fate without complaint").
8   Hegel to Schelling, August 30, 1795 (Br I).
9   GW 5, 172; HW I, 479.
10  Hegel to Schelling, April 16, 1795 (Br I).
11  Hegel to Nanette Endel, July 2, 1797 (Br I).
12  GW I, 205 ff.; Nohl 73–136.

13  GW I, 281–378 (listed here under the title "Studien 1795–1796"); Nohl 152–232
    [in Nohl the new version of the beginning of the first fragment, dated Septem-
    ber 24, 1800, is printed on pp. 139–151 and later this is included in vol. 2 of the
    GW edition (cf. GW I Editorial Report, 495)].
14  GW I, 286; Nohl 156.
15  GW I, 294; Nohl 163.
16  GW I, 298; Nohl 166.
17  Ibid. [Nohl changed the manuscript version of this marginal heading from
    what is now printed in GW I ("Was anwendbar in einer kleiner [sic] Gesell-
    schaft ist, [ist] ungerecht in einem Staate.") to "Was anwendbar in einer
    Gesellschaft ist, ist ungerecht in einem Staat."].
18  GW I, 306; Nohl 173.
19  It is also explained here (Mendelssohn [op. cit.], para. I, 28) that the state
    possesses the right of coercion, but not the church. – I do not wager to say
    to what degree Hegel is directly influenced by the collegial tendency of eccle-
    siastical law, which underlies Mendelssohn's text, and which was accepted in
    general at that time (see Landsberg [op. cit.], vol. III/I, 308). Its first serious
    representative, Pfaff, had taught in Tübingen. With regard to the relation of
    the state to morality and legality expressed by Nohl (Nohl, 175/GW I, 308) see
    for instance Mendelssohn (op. cit.), 26: "[Thus], at most the state is satis-
    fied with dead practices," admittedly it "only halfway [attains] the final aim of
    society in this manner," for "external motives do not make those they affect
    *happy*" (which is the "final aim of society [Ibid. 25 f.]). On the relation between
    ecclesiastical and political constitutions see: Ibid., 56 ff. and GW I, 350 f./
    Nohl, 212. On the impossibility of forcing ethical duty cf. GW I, 306/Nohl, 173
    and Mendelssohn (op. cit.), 31 f. – Incidentally, during the course of the expo-
    sition, Hegel adopts Mendelssohn's central idea on the internal impossibility
    of a church contract, see GW I, 326 ff., respectively Nohl 191 ff. (esp. 192, 195
    bottom, 199 bottom, 204).
20  GW I, 306; Nohl 173.
21  GW I, 306 ff.; Nohl 173 ff.
22  GW I, 308; Nohl 175.
23  GW I, 310 f.; Nohl 177.
24  GW I, 319; Nohl 185.
25  GW I, 320; Nohl 185.
26  GW I, 323; Nohl 188.
27  According to Uhland in his poem on "the good old right" (Uhland o.J.):
    "Right, which leaves everyone open / to migrate around the world, / holds us
    firm to maternal soil / through love itself alone."
28  GW I, 322 ff.; Nohl 188 ff.
29  Nohl 191; Rousseau (1959 ff.), vol. III, Book I, ch. I ("*je l'ignore*" [I do not
    know]).
30  GW I, 327; Nohl ibid.
31  GW I, 335; Nohl 198 f.

32   GW I, 339 f.; Nohl 202.

33   GW I, 351; Nohl 212.

34   GW I, 342; Nohl 205 (marginal heading).

35   GW I, 345; Nohl 207.

36   GW I, 351; Nohl 213.

37   GW I, 349; Nohl 211.

38   "Das älteste Systemprogramm des deutschen Idealismus" [JS & JS: "The
     Oldest System Program of German Idealism"] pub. by F. Rosenzweig,
     Heidelberg 1917 (HW I, 234 ff.) [On the controversy over the actual authorship
     of the text, see e.g. Jaescke (2003), 76–80].

39   Ibid. 234 f.

40   GW I, 359–378; Nohl 21. 4–231 [for dating, cf. the Editorial Report to GW I,
     500].

41   Nohl 362 ff.; Hegel is quoting from the Basel edition of 1787. The sketches of
     his own thoughts are inserted together with the notes from Gibbon.

42   GW I, 366; Nohl 220.

43   GW I, 367; Nohl 221.

44   GW I, 368; Nohl 222.

45   GW I, 369; Nohl 223. The description of the political-societal condition in the
     Roman Imperium corresponds to Gibbon's second chapter and Montes-
     quieu's "Considérations" [Montesquieu 1949 ff.], vol. II, ch. 14, 146: "Le
     peuple romain qui n'avait plus de part au gouvernement, composé presque
     d'affranchis [...]"), as well as in ch. 13 (ibid. 136 ff.) The religious side of the
     matter is missing there, however.

46   GW I, 369; Nohl 223.

47   GW I, 369 f.; Nohl 223.

48   GW I, 370; Nohl 223.

49   Ibid. – verbatim: "[...] which could not satisfy an idea."

50   GW I, 369; Nohl 223.

51   GW I, 370; Nohl 224.

52   GW I, 371; Nohl 224. – This is how [the manuscript] should be read, since
     Hegel's common practice is to use the lowercase when writing adjectives as
     nouns and he himself crossed out the comma separating the words "inde-
     pendently" and "practical" [so also GW I: "the independently practical" – in
     Nohl the wording is: "the independent, the practical"].

53   Ibid.

54   GW I, 371; Nohl 225 – Just as Cato turned to Plato's Phaedo only "when what
     had hitherto been for him the highest order of things, his world, his republic,
     was destroyed" (GW I, 361; Nohl 222; cf. also GW I, 197; and Nohl 362 as
     antecedent of this version).

55   GW I, 378; Nohl 225.

56   GW I, 375; Nohl 227.

57   GW I, 370; Nohl 215; cf. note 217: "Is then Judea the Fatherland of the
     Teutons?"; cf. also the beginning of Appendix "2" GW I, 359 (GW I, 80).

58  GW I, 360; Nohl 215.
59  Nohl 223.
60  The sentence to which I am referring here (Nohl 71) belongs within this context. [What is meant with this "sentence" is probably the following: "In private
life, the love of life, the ease and adornment of the same, would have to be
our highest concern (which when brought into a system of intelligence would
comprise our morality), now – in the case that moral ideas can gain ground
for someone, such goods sink in value, and constitutions that only guarantee
life and property will never be taken as the best – the entire anxious apparatus, the artificial system of motivating forces and grounds for solace, wherein
so many thousand weak ones found their relief, becomes more dispensable."]
also cf. Nohl 222, 229, 230, resp. GW I, 368 f., 376 f.
61  GW I, 372; Nohl 225.
62  See the list of subscribers to the first volume; for further references to Hegel's
acquaintance with the "Horen," cf. Hegel to Schelling April 16, 1795 (Br I) and
GW I, 341 (Nohl 204).
63  Cf. Walzel's notes in the Vol. 2 of the "Säkular" edition (Schiller [1904 f.], vol.
XI, LXI ff.) [according to RB, Rosenzweig apparently owned a four-volume
Schiller edition from the Bibliographical Institute, Leipzig/Vienna 1890].
64  Cf. especially the 6th letter of Schiller's "*Briefe über die ästhetische Erziehung
des Menschen*" (Schiller [2004], Vol. V, 581 ff.).
65  Cf. Schiller (ibid. 586). Gladly I will [...] admit that [...] the genre could not have
progressed in any other way."
66  Nohl 210; cf. ibid. 366.
67  GW I, 368; Nohl 199, cf. also ibid. 194 [The quotation reads in Nohl: "[...]
great men in recent times have given the meaning to the concept of the name
Protestant to denote a person or a church that has not bound itself to certain
inalterable norms of faith, but which protested against all authority in matters
of faith, against all obligations that contradict that sacred right [...]"].
68  GW I, 368; N 222.
69  Cf. the "System Program" [JS & JS: see note 38 above].
70  GW I, 369; Nohl 223, cf. also GW I Appendix "5", 366 f.
71  GW I, 370; Nohl 223.

# 5

# TWO POLITICAL WRITINGS

Two political writings from the year 1798 show how also now, as the armies of the New-Franconians poured over the neighboring lands in victorious advance and the Revolution had evidently secured the heirship of Louis XIV, Hegel remained spellbound by the idea of the state of the early Revolution, intoxicated by freedom and faithful to justice.

In Bern, Hegel was a private tutor in the Steiger family. His students were the grandchildren of the honorable Nikolaus Friedrich Steiger, the last mayor of Bern before the arrival of the French. Just as Hegel had no personal connection to this family, he only looked upon the state of affairs in Bern, to the extent he was afforded a view, with coldness and animosity. A letter to Schelling from the year 1795 reports to the friend how "humanly" things are going with the expansion of the *Conseil souverain*, how "all intrigues between the male and female cousins of princely houses are nothing compared to the matches that are made here [...] the father appoints either his son or his daughter's husband, depending on who brings the highest dowry."[1] The republican who we encountered in the former section had now become familiar with "an aristocratic constitution,"[2] a republican constitution, however, where the

DOI: 10.4324/9780429354724-6

high republican demand for justice was scorned and disrespected. With regard to this state, which did nothing to fulfill his ideal, Hegel may have searched for an opportunity to urgently exclaim to the world the warning *"discite justiciam"* and this opportunity was given by a work of translation that appeared in a Frankfurt publishing house for Easter in 1798: "Entrusted Letters on the Former Relationship under Constitutional Law of Vaud to the City of Bern. From the French of a Deceased Swiss Man."[3]

This Swiss man, who, by the way, was not yet dead at that time, was named Jean Jacques Cart. He was a Vaudian lawyer who, after a failed attempt to protect the rights of his homeland against the government in Bern, pertaining to a certain case with regard to some new money for roads, retreated from this latter place to Paris and, in that there he sided with the Gironde, was driven further to America on account of Robespierre's victory. Just then, as Hegel's translation appeared, the content of the piece was assured universal interest in accord with the recent and newest upheaval in Switzerland, which had come from Vaud. Posselt's European annals refer at the beginning of March to the author and his piece, which had appeared five years earlier. – Cart's book is a brilliant piece of attorney's literature. The author, although convinced that according to natural right the actions of Bern against his homeland were and are outrageously unjust, still does not balk from supporting his further conceptual derivations on historical right and unlimited privileges. Indeed, the natural right of the individual and the peoples (those united by culture, history, descent, and/or language) actually only help him to bend his bow back further. The arrows themselves were then taken almost entirely from the quiver of historical right. With this, his accusation is so finely tuned to the note of honorable indignation that, even today, it evokes nearly this same indignation in the outsider as well.

Beginning in 1564, Vaud stood in a subservient relationship to Bern through its contract with Lausanne.[4] The judgment of historians is varied as to how this rule was carried out in eighteenth century Bern or, more precisely, how this rule was implemented by a third of the half-hundred families capable of office in Bern. Actually, however, only a selection from the 68 ruling families ultimately held office. Nonetheless, in general, that the "honorable gentlemen" of Bern must have made use of their position to some degree is shown by the strict manner in which the ruling class already suppressed every independent uprising in their own citizenship, by the complaints that were brought up here as well as in Switzerland's other subjugated lands against the tyranny of the corruptible governors and their greedy wives, and last but not least by the rebellion against the spiritual pressure coming from the insurrection of the noble Vaudois folk hero, Jean-Abraham-Daniel Davel. Still today, the most beautiful vineyards of the Canton of Vaud are owned by the old families of Bern. In a lawsuit between his father and the men of Bern that lasted years, Benjamin Constant, perhaps the best-known future resident of Vaud, first attracted the eyes of the public and perhaps also the attention of Hegel.[5] – In the decades between Davel's unlucky insurrection and the outbreak of the French Revolution, Bern's pressure on Vaud became, if not heavier, then surely more perceptible. And at that time, towards the beginning of the French Revolution, La Harpe, the famous son of the land, brought the old alienated rights from Petersburg to the memory of his homeland. What occurred, of course not without the influence of immediate propaganda coming from France, was that on the second anniversary of the storming of the Bastille the tense mood in Vaud was vented in great public demonstrations. A "conspiracy" was hardly at the base of the rather harmless ecstasy, but Bern felt itself obligated to sharply intervene. The military and harsh judgements of a special court of law restored quiet again. However, a silent rage lingered, and Cart's text hit on this mood of the land. The hope expressed in this letter was fulfilled five years after its appearance: the old regiment in Bern was toppled and the subservient relationship of Vaud to Bern dissolved.

The foreword shows in what sense Hegel had wanted to present the text to German readers. After a description of the publication's author, fate and content, the German publisher comes to speak of its literary form: the letter-form has the effect that the presentation "also contains the sensations that sprung from those events and conditions," but in this case this does not reduce its believability. On the contrary, "for a lot of people an expression of sensation [is] necessary," especially for those who "don't believe that one could lose one's patience over certain things and, even if they know about what is going on very well, are still highly astonished at the results."[6] This blow of the "unconcerned carelessness" towards the "results"[7] leads over into the strong closing lines, which we may relay in full:

> From the comparison of the contents of these letters to the newest affairs in Vaud, from the contrasts of the appearance of the forced quiet

in the year 1792, the pride of the government towards their victory –
many useful applications would result: yet the affairs of the age speak
loud enough for themselves; it can only remain to become familiar with
them in their entire fullness; they scream loudly across the earth:

*Discite justiciam moniti,*

but the deaf will find it hard to grasp their fate.[8]

One would mishear the overarching tone of those calm, powerful sentences if one connected too closely the observation that all that was happening here was becoming familiar with the affairs in their entire fullness, with
the resigning self-limitation of an "understanding of that which is,"[9] to
which the politician later succeeded. The tone here was still entirely of the
will and the act: of course the affairs should speak, but they should do more
than speak; they should "scream," openly instruct, and warn: *discite justiciam
moniti!* The revolutionary, future-shaping will of 1795 – "lift yourselves up
by the bootstraps, my dear gentlemen"[10] – is still unbroken. But we can
just as little allow one to conclude from the "positive-historical character
of his argumentation, from his constant reaching back to that which was
handed down from earlier times" that at that time Hegel "in no way paid
homage to an abstract radicalism" and that "the revolutionary intoxication
of ideas of the Tübingen period only made use of serious historical studies to quickly fly away." Hegel's intellectual development did not unfold so
superficially.[11] Even the serious historical studies of his Bern years, if they
had any effect at all, did not have such an instant and immediate effect. The
positive-historical character of the argument comes much more from Cart
and is not altered by Hegel; but for Cart this character of the argument only
provided the means to a fight. Moreover, human rights are always standing
as reserves in support, for the weakness of the enemy proves itself precisely
therein that the positive-historical proofs already suffice to destroy the simple people. Thus, Hegel himself is also far removed from accepting historical right in place of the right with which we are born. As evidence for this,
we have the testimonies from the late Bern period and we will also find it
confirmed that his views on these points have not yet changed since Bern in
the text on the Württemberg constitution, completed in a few months after
the appearance of the Cart translation.

Hegel is not only the translator, but in a narrow sense also the editor of Cart's text. He abbreviated it rather extensively and added annotations. The abbreviations did not change the essence of the text; the closing sentences of individual letters, in which the writer mostly turns personally to the reader and glances forwards and backwards towards the course of his discussions, are left out on a regular basis. The omissions within the individual letters fall equally on the positive-historical sections as upon the outbreaks of indignation that pepper the text. Regard for the censor may have been decisive for some of these omissions. Two letters are left out entirely, the eighth and the ninth. They contain two great digressions from the theme: the one concerns the French immigrants, in whom Cart sees the originators of the intervention of Bern's government in Vaud country, to which Cart also had to yield. The other digression is concerned with the damnability of war and the monarchy as well as the nobility, and is richly spiced with insinuating historical remarks according to the taste of the Enlightenment. If the omission of both letters, precisely because they do not bring anything to the actual theme, is not explanation enough, one could still at least suppose with some right for the second that a deeper historical insight had spoiled Hegel's pleasure in translating Cart's provincial wisdom. One could suppose – but, of course, at that time Hegel's recognition of monarchy was not that far along. If he soon thereafter describes the position of the prince within the Württemberg constitution as that of a person "who *ex providentia majorum* unites all forces in him and gives no guarantee for the recognition of human rights,"[12] then the distance between Hegel and Cart is rather insignificant.

This much on the treatment of the body of the text. For the annotations, Hegel could have used all sorts of materials, perhaps already collected in Bern. One learns the origin of most of them from Hegel's own list of sources and from some excerpts preserved in the posthumous works.[13] Besides Müller's history of Switzerland[14] and the Swiss journey of the tireless book-producing Professor Meiner of Göttingen[15] – incidentally, a glowing admirer of the patrician authority of Bern[16] – the material for the annotations was provided by a few local literatures, namely the old Lausanner judge Seigneux's *System of Criminal Law*, alluded to by Cart himself, and a text which appeared in 1793 by an unnamed supporter of the government of Bern, referred to by Cart in an angry footnote: "du *gouvernement de Berne.*" Finally, Hegel used the old, collected volume *L'etat et les délices de la Suisse* in its 1730 edition. That which Hegel himself saw or heard during his years in Bern was also of particular benefit to the annotation. Thus, there is also a very detailed comment on the expansion of the Great Counsel, about which Hegel also speaks in the letter to Schelling mentioned earlier[17] – it is also mentioned here that to get a picture of everything that is interconnected, one has to "have seen it oneself." And so we find further, also relying on local inquiries, comments on the secret treasure of the state, on tenure-track appointments,[18] and on a legal case from 1794.[19] Hegel also reports on scandalous details from the investigation and punitive quartering after the celebration of the day of the storming of the Bastille.[20] The tendency of the annotations naturally follows what is expressed in the "prefatory thoughts." It becomes openly visible in drawing upon the American War for Independence, only remotely alluded to in the text: The taxes that the English parliament put on the tea to be imported into America were very low, but the feeling of the Americans was that, even though the cost of the taxes was little and in itself unimportant, at the same time, to capitulate would mean that the most important right would have been taken away. This is what actually led to the American Revolution.[21] – The detailed comprehensiveness of the annotations reveals the quiet discipline that Hegel used then, as throughout his life, in mastering the material of experience, a skilled discipline that led a modern researcher, overreacting against the commonly held view, to speak of Hegel as the "great empiricist."[22]

The annotations do not bring particularly much to our main theme. What is nearly most remarkable is a stray light that occasionally falls on Hegel's participation in the parliamentary events in England, particularly because none of the notes on English affairs, which Rosenkranz provides as testimony to these Frankfurt years, are preserved. Cart's praise of English freedom is furnished by the editor with the comment that the last years may have changed a lot here. In opposition to Pitt's recent measures of force, Hegel weighs in on the side of Fox, who he soon thereafter cites in the text on the Württemberg constitution. He explains, entirely in line with the Monthly Journal,[23] which at that time supplied the German world of letters with reports on the proceedings and conditions of European states, that it was generally noticed "that a minister is able to defy the opinion of the people through a self-made majority in the parliament, that the nation is so incompletely represented that it is not able to make its voice count in the parliament."[24] It is the oldest reference by Hegel to the English parliament that has been preserved for us, – curious is the fact that the theme that may be discerned here in his first published text will also make up the subject of his last published text, albeit in a more expansive context and with precisely the opposite point of focus: when in 1831 he wrote the essay on the British reform-bill for the Prussian state newspaper, he gave his highly dubious expert opinion on the undertaking to make that partial representation of the nation a little more complete. Was the sixty-year-old then still thinking of his first public statement on the subject? One would like to think so; along with the off-putting examples of pure aristocratic government, he also names there, beside Venice and Genoa, Bern.

The text on the relations of Vaud was already made obsolete by the current events when it appeared: the title spoke of the "former relationship of Vaud to the city of Bern." A different, albeit not a better, fate was in store for Hegel's second foray into politics.

During the move from Bern to Frankfurt towards the end of 1796, Hegel stayed for a few months in his homeland, Württemberg, and found a land in political upheaval. For the first time since the Inheritance Agreement [Erbvergleich] of 1770, an Estates Assembly was again called into session. Since the beginning of the French Revolution, Württemberg was affected by subversive republican agitations. Let us recall the sentiments that were none too secretly cultivated among those of the Tübingen Stift. The connection of the Upper Rhine with Montbéliard made the transmission of the "New-Franconian" ideas even easier. And then it happened that Württemberg, in the year after the peace treaty in Basel, which it did not join, was flooded over with Moreau's troops and as the fortunes of war changed in favor of the Austrians, its legions hung around no less forcefully than the displaced French. In the resumed armistice negotiations with France, the dual powers of the duke and the Estates Committee then led to an ominously pivoting politics. The Committee drew nearer to France, while the hereditary Prince, who decisively influenced ducal politics, sought salvation in holding on to Austria, as was already the case at the time of the peace treaty in Basel. The College of Privy Councilors, which in comparison was at liberty with respect to the duke, did things in common with the Committee. Finally, in the autumn of 1796, the duke decided to call up an Estates Assembly. It seemed that the war compensations demanded by France could only be covered by new taxes. However, for this to happen, in accordance with what the estates fought hardest to gain from the Inheritance Agreement, the consent of the Estates Assembly was necessary, even while at war. In calling an Estates Assembly, one would like to think that the ducal government had also hoped to break the deeply rooted power of the Committee, from which there was no escaping in these hard times, and perhaps hold a freer hand over and against a partially scaled-down Committee. At any rate, the appointment into the Privy Council of the Göttingen historian Spittler, once a member of the Tübingen Stift, could point in such a direction; assuming it was not simply meant to prevent the estates from taking him into their service.[25] Among the countless pamphlets that began to appear immediately after the calling of the Estates Assembly, Spittler's is the most remarkable, on account of both the personality of the author as well as his appointment to follow. Spittler wanted to uphold, untouched, the "foundations of the distribution of power" between the ruling sovereign and the Estates Assembly as they were wisely drawn up by the fathers; thus, he also did not touch upon the root of evil, which is the "distribution of power." Rather, he strongly supported strengthening the power of the assembled provinces over and against the Committee. Hence, he desired intermittent elections and thereby stronger supervision of the administration of the Committee's funds through the Estates Assembly. Spittler therefore supported the utilization of the estates' rights to rejuvenate the Committee. Additionally, he wished for the preservation of the current – unwritten – civil servant law that guaranteed higher ducal officials a certain independency over and against the duke, the restraint of foreign nobility in military and state service, and subjecting this nobility to taxation.[26] The pamphlets that appeared between the calling and the meeting of the Estates Assembly naturally went further, to some extent.[27] Already here, voices ventured forth that wanted to see the step taken from the mere allegedly elected representation of the estates to the actually elected representation of the people. The preferential right of the magistrate, which for this little circle connected the active and passive right to vote, seemed to them outdated or at least improperly appropriated. At least those magistrates who were eligible to vote on representatives, so others demanded, should be elected by the people, not as they had previously been only through an internal appointment.[28] In pamphlets at that same time, perhaps through a person who stood close to the government, the wedge between the old Committee and the imminent Estates Assembly was also driven even deeper, after Spittler, and if the government had hoped to get rid of the unpopular Committee through such means, then this is what was now achieved.[29] The new Estates Assembly called the present Committee to account and chose a new one. But in the end, the hereditary prince was proven to have been correct from the onset in his critical stance against the idea of calling up an Estates Assembly: the conflict intensified since the estates were not shy, supported as they were by the mood of the land, to advance their own politics in foreign affairs without informing the government. An agreement was also never reached on the distribution of war debt, for the estates had wanted to tax ducal property. And they tried to thwart the duke's efforts towards electoral dignity, admittedly with the aim of preventing their opponent from becoming too power-ful. While in this manner the internal conflict of the Old Württemberg state showed itself in all its intensity, in the final days of the year 1797 the man came to power who would end this conflict with an iron fist: Duke Friedrich. He first tried, in deference to France and to put pressure on Austria, to cooperate with the Estates Assembly. Yet it soon came out that the agreement would not last long and, above all, suspicion arose in the duke's circle, and not without reason, that the land was rummaging for a Swabian republic.[30] The establishment of Helvetia cast its shadows on the neighboring land and raised hopes on the one hand, concerns on the other. The Estates Assembly seemed to be involved in subversive plans. Towards the beginning of June, the duke began the fight with the estates and in September, the agreement, which until then had still been externally maintained, became an open quarrel.

During the first half of the year, in the time when a preservation or reestablishment of the endangered agreement could still be hoped for, is when Hegel must have composed a text with which he also wanted to add on to the many "wishes, pointers and suggestions" of the mean-while already ebbing flood of pamphlets. There are unfortunately only a few preserved pages, namely, the handwritten opening, and a piece from the body of the text reprinted by Haym. Incidentally, we must rely entirely upon Haym's quotations and statements, which we must also, albeit cautiously, follow here.

Let us remember the motto of the Cart translation: *Discite justiciam moniti*. The preserved opening of the Württemberg text could be described as a complete modification of that motto.[31] Hegel starts from the prevailing mood of the people of Württemberg, as it was in the second year since the beginning of the Estates Assembly, and adds to this his impatient *Quousque tandem*: "It is time once and for all that the people of Württemberg step out of their vacillation between hope and fear, their oscillation between expectation and error in these expectations."[32] He demands that at least the better ones "focus their undirected will on the parts of the constitution that are grounded on injustice and apply their efforts on the necessary change of such parts."[33] It seems time – and now comes an ominous description of the general widespread mood – for "[t]he quiet satisfaction with the current reality, the hopelessness, and the patient surrender to an immense, all-powerful fate has changed into hope, expectation, and courage for something else. The picture of better, more just times has vibrantly come into the souls of the people and a longing, a sighing for a more pure and free condition has moved all the minds of the people and divided them from the current actuality."[34] Hegel himself, as he so described that "sighing for a more pure and free condition," had the pleasure of knowing the person who gave this sentiment its purest artistic expression, the Hyperion-poet Hölderlin. Hegel continues: "The feeling is universal and deep that the structure of the state, as it still stands today, cannot be preserved."[35] Justice is "the sole measure"[36] by which to judge which parts of the old constitution have become untenable because justice is the only power that can bring about a secure condition. Whoever wants to artificially uphold the old conditions that "no longer agree with the morals, the needs, and the opinion of the people," only clears the way for violent upheaval. Therefore, one should raise oneself from "fear and obligation to courage and will" and everyone should begin with themselves, each individual as well as every class, giving up their unjust property, "to raise [oneself] above one's small interests to justice." Those who hold "inequitable" rights, "strive to set yourself in equilibrium with the others."[37]

Justice, again and again justice! The word never ceases to strike our ears. After this introduction, there can be no doubt regarding the basic disposition from which the text grew. But what was its particular content? Let us first observe the second, larger piece that is preserved for us in Haym's reprint. It deals with the Estates Committee and the authority of its officials, in particular the often appointed "lawyers." We know that this post and its occupants also experienced other sharp attacks. Hegel sees in the "hubris of the higher officials"[38] nothing short of the basic mistake of the entity of the estates, as it hitherto existed. In contrast to the pamphlets, which did not go beyond their attacks on lawyers and legal advisors,[39] Hegel describes the actual danger of this relation more directly: in that lawyers and legal advisors do away with the Committee, and "thereby with this, the land," they offered the court the easy opportunity to reach its aims, if it merely knew how to win over these few executive estate officials, especially the lawyers.[40] No clergyman has ever had "a greater power over the conscience of his penitents as these political confessors have over the official conscience of those related to the Committee."[41] Of late, their position between prince and Estates Assembly is still secured: they know how to make themselves almost independent from the Committee.

This paragraph, without even drawing initially upon the information provided by Haym, throws some light on the particular political stance of the text. Admittedly, Hegel sees the imperfection of the old committee very glaringly, as we would certainly expect based on his known comment on the "incomplete representation of the English nation in parliament."[42] But apparently, he still sees the most dangerous enemy in the court, in the princes by whom the interest of the Estates Assembly is betrayed. Hegel, as little as Spittler, had freed himself from the idea of a necessary, mutually opposed position of prince and people, "ruling power" and "provincial assembly,"[43] just as the thought of justice as a guiding political principle could easily take on a sense of a fragmenting state. The entire constitution, as Hegel holds in the passage already known to us and shared by Haym, revolves "around a person who unites all forces in himself *ex providentia majorum* and gives no guarantee for his recognition of human rights."[44] The vote for the Estates Assembly – this is the only clear demand passed on to us by Haym – must occur independently of the court; until now, this was only the case in Württemberg on limited occasions. Hegel neither awaits reform from governmental councils, nor from civil servants: they have lost "all sense

for innate human rights," for in wrangling between office and conscience they always look only for "historical reasons for the positive."[45]
Thus, he places all of his hope, in accord with the republican spirit, with
which we know him to still be imbued, on the estates. We already saw
from the attack on the committee officials that Hegel does not therefore
overestimate the quality of their current constitution. Apparently, for the
time being, his call for justice is aimed at the estates. There, in similar
fashion to Cart's letter, the word displays a two-fold meaning: the claim
of innate human rights based on natural right is, for Hegel, bound to the
reliance on the good old right, that of privileges; the text was to have
contained detailed arguments on the content and legal consequences of
the old contracts between the duke and the estates, but it is certain that
here for Hegel, as for Cart, natural right supervened over the historical.
How else is the stab at a civil service, which is always looking about for
merely historical grounds for the positive, to be understood? What else
should the demand on every individual and every estate mean, towards
which the opening of the text leads: to check one's own possession of
rights against the criteria of justice and to renounce unjust possession
itself before one demands it of others? But of course, even as much as
natural right held priority over historical right, so it met its limit with
the cold actuality of the present. The student of the ideas of 1789 knows
very well that he would actually need to demand an election of the
Estates Assembly by the people, but he does not believe that this people,
descended from centuries of a hereditary monarchy, has the capacity for
it and appeals for the justification of such concerns to the most unsuspi-
cious of sources: Fox. In his powerful talk for parliament reform in the
previous summer he himself had once casually admitted that one could
not, concerning the dangers of contemporary compliance, compare two
peoples, England and France, of which the one has, throughout many
centuries, crept along in the barbarism of slavery, whereas the other, for
just as long, has enjoyed the light of freedom.[46] And so Hegel demands:
"as long as everything else stays in old conditions, as long as the people
does not know its rights, as long as a common spirit is not present, as
long as the power of the officials is not limited, popular elections would
only serve the purpose of bringing about a total collapse of our constitution."[47] The power towards which Hegel's attack is primarily aimed, the
court, would hold onto victory precisely if the revolutionary demand for

popular elections prevailed. And he admits accordingly: "The main point would be to lay the right to vote into the hands of a body of enlightened and virtuous men who were independent of the court. But I cannot understand from which manner of elections one could come to such an assembly, even if it was so that one could carefully determine the active and passive ability to vote."[48] This helplessness, from which the essay, according to Haym, who had the handwritten copy before him, tapered off, really seems to first fully develop for Hegel in the course of the work. For originally he titled his text: "That the magistrate of Württemberg must be elected by the citizens," indeed, instead "by the citizens" he first wanted to write: "by the people." As subtitle to this heading still came the words: "To the people of Württemberg"[49] This is also telling – the majority of the older pamphlets carried on their title page a dedication to the Estates Assembly, which even though adjourned, still existed. But more important than such a small sign of the mood is the material content of this heading. Accordingly, Hegel, as it seems, would of course initially not have wanted to infringe upon the election of the delegates of the Estates Assembly by the city and provincial magistrates. But through the replacement of the government dominated "internal election" of these officials through some actual voting procedure, initially thus only a local reform, an up-to-date reshaping of the old provincial representation would have come about indirectly. Such suggestions, as mentioned, already come up here and there in the pamphlets of the winter between the calling up and the opening of the Estates Assembly. Hegel also seems to have originally demanded for Württemberg, in agreement with Spittler and many other voices of the time, the other major characteristic of a modern representation of the people, namely term limits.[50] Haym has nothing more to say of either demand; one could perhaps assume that the copy that laid before Haym was either not complete or was based on a later version of the text. With regard to the first demand, the election of the magistrate by the people, it would still have been possible that initially Hegel himself wanted to lead off his essay this way but allowed it to take a step back during the course of the work. Somehow this would also explain that in the preserved opening to the manuscript the previously mentioned original heading, including the revolutionary dedication, was crossed out and in its place a clear demand – election of the magistrate by the people – was placed by a foreign hand, in another

ink, along with the words: "On the recent Domestic Affairs of Württemberg, especially on the inadequacy of the Municipal Constitution." The
new title, which now promises only a critique and no longer a concrete
practical demand like the first one, corresponds better to that copy of the
text that Haym seemed to have before him and in which Hegel likewise
does not conceal that every true representation "presupposes the indirect
or immediate choice of those who are to be represented," but no longer
dares to offer a definite proposal.

Some things remain unclear for us. Above all, the reason why Hegel
did not publish the text. Rosenkranz shares a letter to Hegel from a friend
in Stuttgart, unfortunately left unnamed, from the 7th of August, 1798
to whom Hegel had sent the text. According to this friend, the publication, under current conditions, would be "more a calamity for us than a
benefit." Who is this "us" in which the letter-writer includes apparently
both himself and the recipient Hegel? Rosenkranz speaks of three friends
from Stuttgart; why does he not name them? Did Rosenkranz perhaps
fear exposing those still alive in 1844? One could almost think as much
when one finds in the letter to Hegel that he shares the "conditions" so
described that make the publication of the text unfeasible: "Of course,
my dear friend, our reputation has suffered deeply. The agents of the
great nation have surrendered the holiest human rights to the contempt
and scorn of our enemies. I know of no revenge that could do justice to
their crime. Under these conditions the disclosure of your essay would
be more a calamity for us than a benefit." In what relationship to the
"agents" of the French Revolution does the letter-writer believe himself,
and perhaps Hegel, to stand? And who are these "agents" supposedly so
influencing the course of Württemberg's internal battles? Are they those
sent by France, or the secret friends of France, who are making a stir in
the land for a Swabian republic? Then the letter-writer would be playing on the mistrust of the duke, recently awakened by these activities,
over and against the Estates Assembly, and on the futility of his enacted
reforms, which, according to Hegel, would have to had come from the
Estates Assembly. To be sure, the sentence on the holiest human rights
"[surrendered] to the contempt and scorn of our enemies" seems to
point less towards secret activities than towards public acts; in that case,
with the term "agents" one would have to think of France's representatives at the Congress of Rastatt. This would not necessarily imply a direct

practical influence by France upon the Württemberg movement, even if at that time the internal fight between the duke and the provincial assembly had transferred its central stage to Rastatt, where the French appeared as their arbitrator. However, such a close connection is made impossible by the intellectually excited tone of the letter's sentences. I would like to understand those sentences as follows: the cold political realism that the new France avowed at the Congress and the publication of the exchange of pamphlets we just followed, which could open the eyes of the most gullible minds, appeared to Hegel's Stuttgart friends as a soiling of their own ideals, which would rob these of the strength to set themselves through. According to the apt view of the letter-writer, this practical renunciation of the lofty ideas of 1789, whose practical realization Hegel's text was supposed to serve, is the "crime" to which no revenge could do justice. And where France is now giving up on the matter of the "holiest human rights," Hegel might as well, so advised the friend, remain silent; now there can only be talk of calamity.[51]

Thus, Hegel experienced the backlash of external life against the ideas that had determined his political thinking up until then. He did not immediately succumb to this backlash; we will see in the next chapter how slowly and personally his view of the state continues its development in the coming winter of 1798 and 1799. We cannot even detect an immediate impact that the text on Württemberg made upon his experience; things continued in their own internal connection. The most that we can assume is that this experience opened the way for the coming changes in thought, hardly more.

But it was these coming changes that transformed the politician Hegel so much that, when nineteen years later he again took up a question on Württemberg, he then sides with that very force against which, in 1798, he had expressed his strongest mistrust: the side of the "ruling power" [Herrschaft].

## NOTES

1   Hegel to Schelling, April 16, 1795 (Br I).
2   Ibid.
3   The exact title is, "Entrusted Letters ... City of Bern. A Complete Expose of the Former Oligarchy of the Estate of Bern. Translated from the French of a Deceased Swiss Man and Annotated. Frankfurt am Main. In der Jägerschen

Buchhandlung 1798" [Hereafter cited as CH]. The discovery of this writing is owed to H. Falkenheim, who reports on it (Falkenheim H.: "Eine unbekannte politische Druckschrift Hegels" in: *Preußische Jahrbücher* 138 [1909], 193–210) [Hegel's comments are now in HW I, 225–268].

4   On the following, see Dierauer (1887) vol. IV.

5   Rosenkranz 62.

6   HW I, 256 f.; CH III – verbatim: "to a high degree."

7   Ibid.

8   HW I, 257 f.; CH, III f. [JS & JS: "Having been warned, learn justice"]

9   GW 5, HW I, 463.

10  Hegel to Schelling, August 30, 1795.

11  I am polemicizing here against Falkenheim's point of view (Falkenheim [op. cit.], 204 ff.). Falkenheim also seems wrong when it comes to Cart when he designates the theoretical authority to whom the latter defers as "not Rousseau, but rather Montesquieu." Admittedly, Rousseau is never mentioned. However, it suffices to read the 9th letter (not translated by Hegel), or even just the closing lines of this letter, to see how strongly Rousseau's spirit prevails over Cart's text. Here the relation is again thus, that the doctrine of the sovereignty of the people [Volkssouveränität] dominates Cart's polemic and that the doctrine of the division of powers [Gewaltenteilung] is only used as the means of the polemic. – I believe I agree with Max Lenz, who in his short overview of Hegel's life sets the major turning point of Hegel's political development first after the two political writings of 1798 (Lenz [1910/1918], vol. II, 1st half, 189).

12  Haym 67. [JS & JS: "from the providence of the elders."]

13  Among the preliminary studies for the translation of Cart's text the following are extant: 1. ms XIII, 57a–b: Excerpt from "*L'état et les délices de la Suisse par plusieurs auteurs. Amsterdam 1730. Tome I, chapt. XIII. Sur le gouvernement des cantons*" (GW 3, 225 ff. [Excerpt 41]). As with the rest of the volume, the section is compiled from a dismissive judgement of the political relations of Switzerland and an apology directed against this. The excerpt begins at "*bei uns*" (p. 216) until "*défie*" (p. 217), continues on p. 217 with "*presque*" until "*proposent*" on p. 218; then on p. 223 from "*A l'égard*" until "*lieux.*" Hegel comments in the margins on the word "usage": un abus, pas un droit"; he writes with regard to this paragraph of the excerpt in general and also again with regard to the paragraph after the next: "belonging to XIII"; thus, these parts of the excerpt were to be used in the annotation to the 11th letter, which is the 13th letter in Cart's original text, thus on pp. 194–198 of the translation. The excerpt then provides p. 228 from "celui" (with the omission of the words "ou" until "soit") until "inconnu" – a passage that Hegel may very well have thought of when writing the closing sentence of his first annotation to the 5th letter (p. 81f.). From there follows p. 232 "Les revenus" until "sordide," whereby likewise as mentioned the note "belonging to XIII" can be found on the margin; then comes p. 239 "Le pouvoir" until p. 240 "gouvernement"; finally, derived from p. 241 the words "on ne peut pas dire que toutes les

familles qui non part du gouvernement ne"; with this the excerpt stops at the end of the page, the second sheet of paper is empty.

2. ms XIII, 59–60. Excerpt from "Système abrégé de jurisprudence crimi-nelle accommodéaux loix et à la constitution du pays par Fr. Seigneux. Lausanne 1756." (GW 3, 228–233 [Excerpt 42]) (Only the edition from 1796 was available to me, to whose page numbers I have added those provided by Hegel). The excerpt features a sentence from the Foreword X (VIII) "des juges" until (IX) "de la justice"; there then follows "p. 5 ff." (5) "la Suisse," with omissions, until (12) "je pouvrais," as well as "belonging to IV. p. 90" written by Hegel, the passage of the original corresponding to p. 54 of the translation. Hegel's annotation to this on p. 58 is translated from the first half of this section of the excerpt. The inscription "belonging to p. 184" refers to the second half of this section of the excerpt, which is p. 131 of the translation. The beginning of the annotation Nr. 2 on p. 138 is taken from this part of the excerpt. – The following section of the excerpt is composed of the sentences (18) "Les seigneurs" until "réservé," and added to this "p. 20" (16) "le Sou-verain" until (17) "delégation." The inscription "belonging to VI, 140" is found in this section, which is p. 91 of the translation. It is used in the opening of annotation No. 1 on p. 116. What follows is the paragraph (18f.) "Je dois" until "Coutumier," which according to the comment belongs to "p. 180," that is p. 127 of the translation. A comment by Hegel does not refer back to this part of the excerpt. The end of the excerpt is composed of "p. 28" (23), "Fief et Jus-tice" until "sans Jurisdiction" and (24) the comment on "adjudication," both without inscription and unused.

3. ms XIII, 62 a–b. Excerpt from "Du gouvernement de Berne. En Suisse 1793. chap. 4. des contributions publiques" (GW 3, 223f. [Excerpt 40]). It con-tains p. 17 "Les impôts" until p. 18 "prospérité publique"; p. 18 "il n'en per-çoit" until 20 "Hollande." The omitted passage on p. 18 deals with the price of salt. In 1798 it was out-of-date, as it had since (1794) been increased. Hegel may have been thinking of this chapter, among other things, when he write the following indignant remark: "In that, when the topic was on the bad form of government of the canton Bern, one received the answer that the subjects pay almost no tax [Abgabe], and that they were therefore extolled to be happy or enviable, only proves in general how much lower it was still valued to enjoy no political rights than to receive a few Taler a year less in one's pocket" (HW I, 258). CH, 82 (Annotation 3 to p. 79) refers to the excerpt.

14   Cf. CH, 59.
15   Meiners (1791 f.) – Meiners' Swiss trip is probably the source for the story of the child murderer told in CH, 118.
16   Meiners (op. cit.), Vol. II, 162.
17   Ibid., 194–198.
18   Ibid., 83 f., 96. f.
19   Ibid., 118 f.
20   Ibid., 121.
21   Ibid., 82.

22  Plenge (1911), 36 [Plenge literally referred to Hegel as an "empiricist of over-whelming greatness"]; cf. on the other hand Lasson's contradiction in the introduction to the *Philosophy of Right* (Ww. VI, IX).

23  Posselt (1795 ff.), Heft 6 (1796), First Part, 42 f.

24  CH, 81; cf. additionally, on England, Rosenkranz 85.

25  For Spittler, see Pahl (1840), 401 ff.; Strauss (1876 ff.), vol. II, 168 ff.

26  The pamphlet is printed in Spittler (1827 ff.), vol. IVX, 168 ff. Spittler's state-ment opposing the committee had already appeared in 1794 (in Göttingische Anzeigen von gelehrten Sachen. 70. Part [1794], 699 f.; cf. Spittler [loc. cit.], 490).

27  A very convenient overview of the contents is provided by the document "Inbegriff von Wünschen, Winken und Vorschlagen in Bezug auf den Bev-orstehenden Landtag Württembergs. 3. Abschnitt: von Schäden und Kosten, welche der Französische Reichskrieg dem Herzogthum Württemberg verursa-cht hat, und insbesondere der für den Waffenstillstand entrichteten Kriegss-teur oder Kontribution." (Speiedel 1797).

28  At the very least, Spittler's pamphlet demanded of the committee an expan-sion of passive suffrage.

29  "Etwas über die bisherigen landschaftlichen Ausschüsse," and "Freimütige Betrachtungen über die Organisation der landschaftlichen Ausschüsse," both writings, anonymously by W.A.F. Danz (1797). Although Danz had incurred the disfavor of Karl Eugen as a Professor in 1792, he became a Court Assessor in 1796 and a Government Councilor in 1797.

30  Dizinger (1833), 29; Pahl (op. cit.), 125; *Historische Zeitschrift* (op. cit.) 46, 407; Hegel (1881) vol. II, 310; List, A., in: *Württembergische Vierteljahreshefte* (1916), 522 ff.

31  On the following, see HW I, 268–273 (also Rosenkranz 90–94; Haym 65–68, 483–485; Ww. VII, 150–154).

32  HW I, 268; Rosenkranz 91; [JS & JS: "For how much longer"]

33  HW I, 268; Rosenkranz 92.

34  HW I, 268 f.; Rosenkranz 92.

35  HW I, 269; Rosenkranz 92.

36  HW I, 268; Rosenkranz 92 f.

37  HW I, 271; Rosenkranz 93.f.

38  HW I, 271; Haym 484.

39  For example, the two mentioned earlier (Section 5, note 25–26).

40  HW I, 272; Haym 484.

41  Ibid.

42  CH, 81.

43  Haym 67.

44  Ibid.

45  Ibid.

46  Posselt (op. cit.), Twelfth Part (1797), 278. This is the only passage I can find to take into consideration. 195 HW I, 273; Haym 66.

47  HW I, 273; Haym 66.

48    Ibid.

49    [On the title, see Jaeschke (2003), 82 f.].

50    This is what it seems according to the first sentence which Rosenkranz
(Rosenkranz 91) quotes from a letter to Hegel (fragment "unknown to Hegel"
dated August 7, 1798 [Br II]). *Unclear* to me remains the sentence from the
same letter: "the dismissal of the landed estates, which you have rattled off
quite generally, is likewise nothing other than arbitrary." Also unclear is Rosenkranz's remark, admittedly rejected by Haym, that Hegel oscillates between
the principles of "Rousseau's politics [...] and between the Platonic one of an
ideal and real estate [realen Standes]" (R 91). Rosenkranz will presumably
have thought of the selection of a "corps of enlightened and righteous men,
independent of the court," from the remaining people, to whom the right to
vote would belong. (HW I, 273; Haym 66).

51    On France's "Realpolitik," see Posselt (loc. cit.), Issue 6 (1798), 270, 300, 308
f.; the third text had already been printed in the "Moniteur" at the beginning
of the year.

# 6

## FRANKFURT

The thoughts of the preceding section were already with Hegel during his time in Frankfurt. Nothing in the political writings from 1798 seemed to point beyond the political ideas of the theological drafts just observed. Nevertheless, around this time we stand directly before the turning point. In those years in Frankfurt, the general foundation of Hegel's associations of ideas experienced its second, and this time decisive, blow. Of course, at that time his definitive system was not yet actually formed, but his thought was moving into the constellation that would rule over his later system: the idea of the unity of all life gained force. The straight-laced ethical will of freedom of the Bern Kantian gave way to a peculiar belief in fate. It was the old historical-religious riddles, which had previously initiated the turn towards Kantianism, that now formed the basis of the turn away from Kantianism. The questions of the content of Jesus' teaching, its place in its time and its advance into the world, already frequently addressed, were raised anew by Hegel, and now everything became new under his quill: Jesus stopped being the teacher and preacher of Kantian morality for him. Rather, Kant and the

DOI: 10.4324/9780429354724-7

orthodox teaching of sin, punishment and redemption now collectively made up the colors for the image of the Pharisees and Jesus became the teacher or, more precisely, the personal bearer of the new ethical system that Hegel put in place of both Kantian ethics and the orthodox ethic of "separation and incomplete unification." Instead of sin it was now called guilt. In place of the sin-punishing God or the rigid uncompromising moral law now came fate. Guilt and fate – an ethic that summarizes personal life under the same concepts through which art history tries to illuminate the essence of tragedy. And then, even above guilt and fate, issuing from them, dissolved and restored in them and through them, *the unity of life*. Every separation of the human from this unity is guilt; indeed, guilt is, all in all, nothing other than such a separation, an injury to this never-to-be-divided life. But the injury does not affect some foreign thing, some God who reigns in infinite distance from the earth. It is also not a categorical moral law, which stands, unreachably sublime, over and against the reality of a life ruled by instinct and inclination. The injury affects the injurer himself: for all life is one. And so, guilt brings forth fate from itself; the guilty one feels through his own life that he has placed himself out of life. This fate cannot, as with the God of orthodoxy, be deceived through representative penance, but neither does it remain eternally irreconcilable, like the injured outer or inner law, like Jewish or Kantian law. Rather, as fate immediately grew forth from the guilt-ridden separation of the human from "life," so too does reconciliation occur immediately through the reunification of the human with life, through the restoration of the relationship torn apart through guilt: love. Life can again heal its own wounds. And thus, guilt and fate are connected with one another in the thought of life, and life is itself nothing other than the movement from guilt to fate. The individual cannot avoid this movement. He cannot be guilt-free, precisely because he is an individual. But if he still wants to, if he wants to save himself from the stream of life onto the shore, then it is this very sought-after innocence, this desire to withdraw from life, that is his guilt. And he who hopes to remain fateless will suffer the greatest fate of all.

This is, in a rough outline, Hegel's ethical metaphysics as it was developed up to the beginning of 1799 in Frankfurt. The distance from everything we have seen until now appears, and indeed is, enormous. How Hegel's spiritual relationship to the state developed in this connection can perhaps already be anticipated from what has already been said. But we will understand it completely if, in what follows, we dig up the personal roots of his metaphysics. Just as before, this metaphysics still carries the seal of experience on its brow. We must also dig up the personal roots if we seek to uncover the delicate side-paths on which these roots branch out to other independent growths in the soil of the age.

It is clear from what has already been said how Kantian philosophy now also provided its impulses. Clear as well is that this philosophy was now no longer only received, as it had been in Bern when Hegel allowed his still customary ideas to be reworked by Kant, but rather, was now strongly critiqued. But even that is going too far. In actuality, Kant's philosophy now suddenly became a mere object of conflict. It cannot be proven that Hegel's new standpoint came from this critical engagement with Kant; it is more likely that Schelling's continuing strides in the scientific world, which Hegel carefully followed from his solitude, provided him important impulses. However, it is hard to distinguish just how much of this was impulse, that is, how much on Hegel's side was his own accommodation, if not his rushing-ahead. We cannot forget that in the end – if one focuses only on the major things and looks away from the minor ones – Schelling and Hegel lived in the same spiritual world in those years, and that the truly great currents of the Weimar-Jena life were carried, barely weakened, to the reader of the *Horen* in Bern, the comrade of a Hölderlin who had just returned from Jena, and perhaps even carried more purely than they were in local proximity, where the daily and personal reverberations sometimes sounded too loudly.

But the significance of the relations with Hölderlin are to be valued the most. It seems difficult to observe, separated from the others, one of the great men through which the German spirit spoke in that overrich decade of Schiller and Goethe's friendship. The tasks that they set themselves touched so closely, and the paths they traversed crossed so many times. Even their goals and solutions often stood so close together. Nevertheless, the first commandment of the researcher always remains this: one should, initially, understand everyone from out of themselves and their most intimate circle. The change in meaning that the same word often undergoes when passing from one circle to the next already necessitates this. In what follows, the expert will come across many Fichtean and Schellingian, as well as Schillerian technical terms. However, it is not the words, but the sense that matters, not the tools, but the will and the work, the need and the act. And in this sense, if anyone comes into question for understanding Hegel in the next few years, then it is Hölderlin, even if his actual influence cannot be proven with certainty.[1] All in all, where the ideas of the two touch, it can be said that Hölderlin was ahead of his friend. As we will see, Hegel did not therefore follow on the same path. Rather, even where he arrived at the same conclusion, the path was always his own. – The fact of their friendship does not go far enough to explain how their ideas touched. This friendship was indeed, at least from Hegel's side, the most warm and personal of his youth. One can trace throughout the letter of Bern to Schelling, besides the respect for the young genius, whose first system program he carefully transcribed at that time,[2] a conscious distance of the older to the younger. By contrast, in the few preserved letters between Hegel and Hölderlin, there is purely the feeling of the relationship of equal to equal; the brother opens his heart without reserve to the other brother.[3] The verses directed towards Hölderlin in August 1796 express what Hegel felt for him and with what an unchanged communion of ideas he believed this feeling to be congenial:

> Your image, loved one, appeared before me,
> And desire for the days that have escaped. But soon it will give way
> To reunion's sweet hopes.
> Already the long-awaited, fiery
> Scene of embrace is painted; then the scene of questions,
> of secret, mutual detecting,
> What here in attitude, expression, and temperament
> Has changed in the friend since that time; – the joy of certainty,
> to find the old bond stronger, even more mature,
> The bond that no oath had sealed:
> To live only the free truth,
> At peace to never, never enter into the standing rule
> Which regulates opinion and feeling.[4]

> *Dein Bild, Geliebter, tritt vor mich,*
> *Und der entfloh'nen Tage Lust. Doch bald weicht sie*
> *Des Wiedersehens süßern Hoffnungen.*

*Schon malt sich mir der langersehnten, feurigen*
*Umarmung Szene; dann der Fragen, des geheimen,*
*Des wechselseitigen Ausspähens Szene,*
*Was hier an Haltung, Ausdruck, Sinnesart am Freund*
*Sich seit der Zeit geändert; – der Gewissheit Wonne,*
*Des alten Bundes Treue fester, reifer noch zu finden,*
*Des Bundes, den kein Eid besiegelte:*
*Der freien Wahrheit nur zu leben,*
*Frieden mit der Satzung,*
*Die Meinung und Empfindung regelt, nie, nie einzugehn.*

But already then, as Hegel wrote these lines to him, Hölderlin had grown internally beyond that confident defiance against the "standing rule" [Satzung] in which Hegel sought the spiritual content of their union in friendship. That which still stood firm for Hegel, that which now had become perhaps even more acute and one-sided for him in contrast to when the friends first took leave from one another, precisely this had become questionable for Hölderlin. While still in Jena, it is probable that Hölderlin wrote a few pages of a draft for his novel Hyperion, containing a highly personal critique of the Kantian–Fichtean life-law of defiance against the standing rule.[5] The young Hyperion – we can repeat Hölderlin's words almost unchanged[6] – had become more serious and more free, yet strict beyond measure and, in the full sense, tyrannical against nature. He had lost practically all sense for the quiet melodies of life, home, and childhood. It was unfathomable to him how Homer could have once so fully consumed him. And so, Hyperion meets a "good man" and listens to his teaching: surely, we should preserve the ideal of everything that appears to us as pure and holy, surely, we should subdue the resistant nature of the spirit that rules in us. But even in battle with nature we can depend on her willingness. Does our spirit not encounter in everything that there is a friendly, related spirit? And is there not hiding, when it turns the weapons against us, a good master behind the shield? Certainly, we feel the limits of our essence, and the hemmed-in energy impatiently struggles against the chains. Yet there is also something in us that gladly bears the chains; for if the spirit was not limited by some opposition – if it did not suffer – then we would not feel ourselves and others. But to not feel oneself – is death. We cannot deny the drive to free ourselves. Yet we also cannot proudly exempt ourselves from the drive to be limited. This conflict of drives is united by love. And therefore: the spirit of the human is great and pure and unconquerable in its demands; it never bends to the force of nature. But heed also the aid that comes from the land of the senses. When what you carry in you as truth comes to meet you as beauty, accept it thankfully, for you need the help of nature. – But remain free in spirit! Never lose yourself! Do not forget yourself in the feelings of your poverty!

These teachings and warnings, which opened the version of the novel from that time, touch upon the theme that is realized through the life of the hero. It is likely that the heart-felt experience of the poet in Frankfurt coupled with the complete internal detachment from Fichte delayed the content and plan of the work of poetry. But even so, at the time of the publication of the first part, the poet must have had a balance of will and receptivity in mind as the goal of his hero's development. Indeed, in the contrast between Hyperion and Alabanda, Hyperion's friend of forceful will, the book gained new content as their internal quarrel finds external presentation. The two ways of life that the "good man" instructively lays down in that first draft now become part of the story, they become living, human opposition.

Those riddles of personal life, around which Hölderlin's novel of 1797 circles, also appear repeatedly in Hegel's writings from 1797 to 1800, and not just those initial riddles, but also Hölderlin's further development of the same over the coming years. And yet, despite all agreement, they are developed by each in accordance with their own unmistakable lived content and meaning: the explanation is to be found in what is common in the lives of both. Both experienced a time in the beginnings of their spiritual being where "Homer" completely won over their young hearts. For both, the Kantian-Fichtean philosophy moved into their lives as a strict, mostly internal, foreign-felt mistress and tried to topple over their "customary" ideas. Both, among others, came to the aid of Schiller in his *Aesthetic Letters* in order to help free him from the autonomy of Kant and Fichte; Schiller's *Aesthetic Letters*, and Schiller's previous text *On Grace and Dignity* had a fundamental effect on Hölderlin. Hegel seems to have grasped Schiller's writing less in its ultimate philosophical sense, and he would not so much have found the overcoming of Kant in the book as the possibility of reconciling his old dream of beautiful Greek humanity with the harsh pride of the "I" of the newer times through the view Schiller opened into the future of a third Empire. This raised new questions for both Hegel and Hölderlin. For the poet it was immediately the personal: how to preserve oneself in the shock of conflicting life-views? how to fulfill Kant's rigid law without disturbing Schiller's beautiful freedom of play? how to give oneself over to this beautiful play without forgetting that strict law of ethical freedom? To love limits and sorrows without denying the limitlessness of the free act. For the philosopher things moved more slowly, by way of a remarkable intertwinement of interpretive work in history and the development of a new image of humankind.

In Bern, Hegel's sense of self was one of defiantly pushing forward. Although the first signs of his humility towards fate can already be found in his oldest papers still belonging to the Tübingen period,[7] the Kantian-Fichtean wave washed away these stirrings, together with the traces, also perceptible in Tübingen, of an ethics of feeling and inclination. As mentioned, Schiller's *Aesthetic Letters* probably moved him, above all through their focus on a philosophy of history. But embedded in this philosophy of history, they also brought Hegel a new concept of the ideal: "totality," the unity of life, and indeed, the unity of personal life. At that time, Schelling had already formulated the following moral imperative in his text *Of the I as Principle of Philosophy*: become simply one, raise the plurality in you to unity, that is, become a self-enclosed totality. Nothing other than the essential characteristic of the "simple organization of the first republics," the internal unity and wholeness of humanity, was placed over and against the fragmenting division of labor in contemporary society.[8] The task of the future was to renew that beautiful unity. This more blissful task than the Kantian sense for the ethical appraisal of humanity now inserts itself during Hegel's last year in Bern in connection with his then-proud consciousness of the ethical dignity of humanity as a new strength that, nevertheless, first appeared like a stranger among friends. Already before the end of April 1796 the Christian human is simply identified as having "more or less no unity"[9] and the "republican" boasted that "his entire circle of influence [possesses] unity."[10] At the same time, isolated thoughts of mysticism from the Middle Ages are called to Hegel's attention by several quotes in Mosheim's ecclesiastical history. In his excerpt from there, Hegel particularly emphasizes the sentence that God begot the son *"sine omni divisione"*[11] – because, perhaps there, for the first time, a worldwide-embracing meaning of "unity" dawns, which at first had only been directed towards the soul of the human. Still, as already mentioned, these thoughts are scattered among the mass of Hegel's musings at that time. And it even appears questionable whether he did not just copy the sentences for the sake of their mystical consciousness of freedom over and against Scripture and "statute" and for the Christ-identity of the "divine" human expressed in them than for the metaphysical feeling of the All promoted by them. Especially a few Latin sentences, with which the statement – for Hegel as well as for Mosheim – closes, would lead us to think so. However, his personality is much too abrasively closed off to the world in that span of his life for the new idea of the "unity" of the human to already be able to develop into the life-unity of the human and world. Eventually, when he seems to directly touch on the feeling that "to give oneself up is pleasure," as he does in the poem "Eleusis"[12] from August 1796 – "I give myself over to the immeasurable, I am in it, am everything, am only it" – the unfamiliar mood slips from him almost in the same moment: "recursive thought alienates and shudders before the infinite." Or when, on a hike in the Jura plateaus in July 1796, he reflects on the residents of this region, that they "live in the feeling of dependency on the power of nature and this gives them a calm devotion during the destructive outbreaks of that same power," in the exact preceding sentence he had mocked the physicalist-theology of the age, which looks to satisfy the pride of humans through the idea that everything is done for them by a foreign being, rather than finding satisfaction "in the consciousness [...] that it is actually he himself who has bestowed all of these purposes on nature."[13] And it is exactly on the same piece of paper on which he cited the mystic passage that he writes out several sentences, with apparent approval, from Forster's *Views of the Lower Rhine* where the Greeks are praised as "humans who can stand for themselves" in contrast to our need for help.[14] We may recall, in this regard, that republican passion for the life of antiquity with its active generation of the state through the individual, which was described in those writings that were already discussed from the final period in Bern. And so, he chides in a somewhat later note on the Mosaic state, that here the individual was "completely shut out from active interest in the state."[15] As we already know, in his hurry the writer may have omitted the word "active" as self-evident in this republican judgment, but he then expressly adds it and thereby shows the manuscript's reader what was important to him. Accordingly, as he continues in his description of the Jews, setting republican existence as equal to activity: "the political equality [of the Jewish people] as citizens was the opposite of republican equality, it was only the equality of insignificance."[16]

The piece, from which the previously mentioned sentences come, draws the line of history further up until the appearance of Jesus. The final words are laid down here – and what matters is to adjust the ear to what is personal- and confessional-like: "In such a period where he who is thirsty for inner life (he could not live in friendship with the objects surrounding him, he had to be their slave, and in conflict to living with that which is better inside of him, he is only treated by those objects adversely and treats them likewise –) is looking for something better, and is then offered cold, privileged dead things and told this is life; in such a period, the Essenes, John the Baptist, and Jesus created life in themselves – and rose up in the fight against the eternally dead."[17] The distinct tone of the feeling of the I is not difficult to discern through the historical interpretation of the soul. The human is driven back from an adverse world, adversely poised against it. All "life" is on the side of humanity, the world is only the "eternal dead," and "battle" is the only possible answer for this world. He continued to express the old aggressive sentiment, ill-disposed towards all restfulness, which we know from his letters to Schelling from Bern: "lift yourselves up by the bootstraps, my dear gentlemen." But this sentiment is expressed here with great clarity and for the last time. What also appears for the last time in this manuscript on Jesus, who is seen purely as a fighter against his time, is undivided hostility, the undivided will to act. From now on a displacement of the lights in this image of Jesus begins and a new image of our hero from his own relationship to the world now exerts itself as a feeling, which then – definitely not immediately, but rather gradually and on a winding path – also reaches the thoughts on the relationship between the human and the state and fundamentally changes it.

We mentioned earlier that Hegel felt very unhappy at his post in Bern. Apparently, afterwards he had not even kept the smallest connection to the family in whose house he had lived for three full years. This can be inferred from his way of life in the Steiger house – even more so in that the dissolving of his relationships to the family certainly took place in an orderly fashion. He even blamed the family itself for the unsatisfactory outcome of his pupils' lessons.[18] According to his sister, when he returned home again after his long absence, the previously always cheerful and harmlessly good-humored Hegel, who, according to Hölderlin's testimony never lacked joy,[19] was introverted and seemed almost dismal. But then, he arrived in Frankfurt and received a friendly reception in the house to which Hölderlin's efforts had brought him and found in Hölderlin himself and his friend Sinclair sympathetic companions.[20] We may ask what effect this had on the hostile feelings towards the world into which the revolutionary courage for the future of the early period in Bern had condensed for him over the years. It wouldn't be impossible to figure out the answer from his changed interpretation of humankind in his religious-historical manuscripts.[21] But as chance would have it, we are even more favorably placed, as a very remarkable testimony is preserved from Hegel himself from the first year in Frankfurt. This testimony is found in a letter to a young girl towards whom the almost twenty-seven-year-old had developed a gentle inclination during the winter in his homeland. "From Frankfurt," he writes, playing on country life as he had come to know it during his time in Bern on the Steiger property, "from Frankfurt I am now always driven by the memory of those days lived in the country and how there, in the arms of nature, I always found peace with myself and with humanity, and thus I often flee here to this faithful mother, so that I can again separate myself from the people with whom I live in peace and protect myself from their influence and counteract a union with them under her aegis."[22]

What is ultimately inexplicable in personal life eludes analytical treatment. Such matters want simply to be recorded. Accordingly, the quoted passage from the letter is for us a source of the first degree. Hegel looks back on his relationship to people during his time in Bern as if on something past. It lies behind him. But the rupture between him and the surrounding world has remained; indeed, it has now become very deep, now become incurable. For it is no longer the fault of the world. It meets him with open arms and at the same time wrests from his hands the weapons with which he had formally threatened the "eternal dead." But he disdains the unification, the union that the world offers to him. Indeed, he counteracts it and flees from what is friendly under the aegis of solitude – "he wants his suffering," so we may describe it with the words with which he later tries to articulate this conception of soul.[23] This condition is, namely, perceived as suffering, but as a suffering for which there is and can be no remedy or fight, precisely because the human wants suffering. He tries to keep himself pure of the world, to preserve his foreignness over and against it. The words with which Hegel tries to define Jesus' relationship to the world: "he could not live in friendship with the objects," are words that are changed, upon reworking the manuscript, into: "he cannot unite himself with the objects about him."[24] Certainly, one can live with the world "in friendship" as one who is "thirsty for inner life." The writer was convinced of this among the people with whom he lived in peace. But to "unite" oneself with this friendly world, Jesus can do this no longer according to Hegel's new consciousness of self and life. It is clear that Hegel has now grown on his own into a similar knowledge of life as that which arose for Hölderlin-Hyperion in Jena out of the contrast between Schiller and Kant: "remain free in spirit, do not leave the helm when a joyful wind blows in your sail."[25] It sounded as though it had sprung more from the moment and, I would almost like to say, was more accidental and personal in Hegel's letter. He was already beginning to look into the dangerous depths that lurk beneath this consciousness. What Hölderlin earlier planned in the draft of Hyperion which he had then begun to outline after the publication of the first part of the novel – really since that summer of 1797 – as a particular dramatic poem, was the further development of this condition up until his strange breakdown. At that time, as the coming chain of events will show, Hegel had not yet anticipated anything of the sort. This new feeling spread its influence only very gradually, and only very gradually did it transform itself. But compared with the Hegel of Bern whom we have come to know, we already now see an escalation and a transformation. His feeling of self becomes internalized, and the earlier impetus was lost to him. In return, there was no longer a binding union to his surroundings and the world to which there would be an answer or repercussion. It gained a totally universal, perhaps the most universally thinkable, meaning, abstracted and removed from the world, and had become the tragic knowledge of that which is above and beyond all contingencies of one's surroundings – the necessary isolation of the inner human being. Hegel himself states shortly before that letter that "the other extreme of being dependent on an object" is this: "to fear the objects and that the flight from them, the fear of unification," indeed, that this is actually "the highest subjectivity."[26] Now, according to his own admission, Hegel had ascended to this "highest subjectivity." In his development, this feeling of life is only a moment but, if I am not mistaken, the decisive one from which he emerged in overcoming it as a mature human being.

Let us continue to follow this development. We already saw previously how this self-consciousness works itself over into the understanding of a historical condition of the soul in discussing the modification of the words "could not live in friendship" into "cannot unite himself." It is a shift in the same sense when a new version of the overview of Jewish history considers that the consciousness of the Essenes is no longer characterized simply as "a rising up in the fight against the eternal dead." Rather, Hegel says of the Essenes that they "saw the objects as either hostile or at least entirely irrelevant."[27] For us a fog lies over the further formation of Hegel's new self-consciousness in the year from the summer of 1797 until the summer of 1798. Only here and there – few remnants of that time may be ascertained with any certainty – does the view briefly open upon that formation. Surely, in all probability, both political texts discussed in the previous section originated in this year but they are still to be understood purely as the outcome of the standpoint won in Bern. Indeed, the content of the one text is drawn directly from Hegel's stay. In connection with the present section, they can only show us that the transformation of the human introduced above is still far from taking hold of the political thinker, and that it is even further still from reaching the philosopher. Only in the late summer of 1798, after putting the finishing touches on the text on the Württemberg constitution, did that change advance far enough that it no longer bears the Kantian-Fichtean moral doctrine next to it – that forceful, world-forming certainty of reason – but now challenges it to a process of critique. Thus, although we have little to say about the intervening period, there is nevertheless still something. On the page that stands closest in time to what was preserved in that letter from July 2, "fate" appears for the first time,[28] which for Hegel had previously appeared only in the oldest manuscript

from Tübingen, mostly as "necessity," but also as "providence" or "fate."
At that time in Tübingen, these were names for the power to which the
human of antiquity as well the true Christian joyfully gave themselves
over. It is one of the impulse-like anticipations of much later thoughts,
found in abundance in this Tübingen piece. This idea also disappeared
along with its comrades in Bern. "Fate," as it first comes about in Frankfurt, is something different: it is the unknown power, in which nothing
is human, and yet from which the individual suffers, and who, if he
is conscious of his purity and has enough strength to be able to bear
this complete separation between himself and the cause of his suffering,
powerfully confronts it "without subjugating himself to it or reaching
some unification, which, with a more powerful being, could only be
slavery."[29] In this idea of fate there is nothing yet of "fate's pious goddess," which can already be found in Hölderlin's Hyperion fragment from
Jena.[30] Rather, this idea reminds one here of what was shortly before
expressed by Schelling. For Schelling, fate in the tragedy of antiquity is,
in contrast to the gods who are close to humans, the actual meta-natural
[Übernaturliche].[31] And so, for Hegel, fate is entirely meta-natural here,
an "unknown power, in which nothing is human," and behind whose
designs, in that he turns the weapons against us, a good master is not
concealed – in contrast to Hölderlin's fragment. It is really that same
idea of fate found in the letter from July 2, 1797, which the writer had
to formulate thus in order to counteract the union with fate, in order to
be unable to reach a unification with it. But precisely this consciousness
of the "I" will be shaken down to its foundation and here fate will stop
being simply that which is foreign, beyond human and meta-natural.
From what follows chronologically after this passage on fate, we receive
an idea on the tendencies that the shock and transformation of this consciousness will instill in the eternally lonely human in counteracting his
union with humankind.

The dark weight of the new style prefigured in that passage of the
letter now shows itself fully developed in a fragment on love. This fragment reminds one of Plato in its sensual, meta-sensual ambiguity of
expression, and yet in contrast to Plato, the secretive meta-sensual meaning is not found in the picture of longing for love, but rather in that of
the unification of love. "As living, the lovers are one."[32] All of a sudden,
that previous "inauthentic" love lies far behind, that love whose "essence

lies therein, that the human in his most internal nature is oppositional and independent, that everything is outer-worldly to him, which is then as eternal as himself."[33] Indeed, "*fabula narratur*," we know of whom the tale is told. "Actual" love is different. It seeks to unite all differences; it "storms over individuality"; it is "fear of one's own." If previously we could sense in the letter from July 2, 1797, that the "highest subjectivity," the "fear of one's own,"[34] would be only a moment in Hegel's development, here we see this stage surmounted. The concept of fate will likewise soon gain new coloration. At that moment, however, a resting point entered into the movement of thoughts. The concepts of living, of love, and above all the new evaluation of "individuality" and "one's own," all of this was now far enough developed to impel Hegel towards articulating a strict, general pattern of the existing view of the ethical, and that meant moving towards a confrontation with Kant. An external incident certainly contributed to this: Kant's *Doctrine of Right* (*Rechtslehre*) had just been published in a second edition, which included some important additions. Hence Hegel, who had just finished the work on the constitution of Württemberg, began an examination of the Kantian ethical doctrine based on his new concepts. We can surmise the manner of this confrontation to some extent from Rosenkranz's intimations, who still had the now lost manuscript before him, and from a likely repetition of the same in the pieces soon to follow. The only preserved piece of the entire work fortunately contains Hegel's critique of the Kantian doctrine of the state. And so, in this we may see if the new views have already become strong enough to not merely unsettle general ethical individualism, but also political individualism and, above all, to already move the view of the state essentially away from that point at which we last saw it arrive in Bern. If we recall, there was nothing of this sort to notice in the text on the constitution of Württemberg, which was written shortly before, nor in the Cart translation, which appeared a few months earlier. To anticipate it directly: this is the case only with one point in the fragment under discussion.

What is under critique is Kant's conception of the relationship between state and church, and Hegel repeats this conception in a correct, yet questionably compact summary: "Both should leave each other in peace and have nothing to do with one another."[35] This view was, in essence, Hegel's view in Bern, and is thus certainly well-known to us.

Now, however, he himself is fighting against this view, claiming that such a pure separation could not be possible. And indeed, such a pure separation is not possible, entirely regardless of whether the state "has the *principle of property*"[36] or whether "its *principle [is] a complete whole*."[37] This is nothing more than the familiar distinction from Bern between modern monarchy and the republic of antiquity. Yet in the latter case, where the state has a complete whole as its principle, state and church cannot possibly be different – for the same whole that rules over state is represented in the church as a living whole by the imagination – indeed, in this case the ideal image of the Polis of antiquity is nothing new for us after Bern. Nonetheless, we must surely be surprised after Bern that a separation for the modern state is also not possible, that indeed here the human "acts in the spirit of the church, not only against individual laws of the state, but rather against the entire spirit of the state itself; *against the whole*."[38] The reason for this irreconcilability is that here the state presupposes the people "very *incompletely* as those who *have*" while the church presupposes the people "as a *whole*" to whom "the feeling of this wholeness is to be given and preserved."[39] Thus, the new anti-Kantian view of the human as an indivisible unity asserts itself here. This anti-Kantian view sharply rejects, along with every hard separation in the human, the disintegration of the people "into a particular state and especially into church people" and, therefore, generally speaking, denies the ability of the state, which rests on such "disintegrated" people "to hold off the overflowing church from its banks."[40] Admittedly, this already appears to be distant from the bold and conceptually certain draft from Bern, which refrained from a questioning tone as far as possible. But it is nevertheless not a new solution to the problem of the state. For despite the new stance towards the question of the church and state, the view of the relationship of the state to the people in the sole fragment that has been preserved is still the old view. At that time in Bern, the separation of state and church was possible and necessary for the sake of the Kantian separation prevailing within modern Christian humans. Now in Frankfurt, this separation is impossible due to the in-ethicality [Unsittlichkeit] of such an inner-human duality. But then as now, the human, whether divided or whole, is the starting point for the development of thought. The question is not what the state is for the human, nor what kind of relationship the individual has to the whole, rather, as before, the state adjusts itself to the essence of the human such that the question of the state is answered from the viewpoint of the essence of the human. For Hegel, that "the individual human [and] human relations are in the power of the state" is still merely a fact he knows, and that as yet means nothing for his view of the state. That becomes very clear when he warns that the state which wants to hold off the overflowing church from its banks will become, thereby, "inhuman and monstrous."[41] It does not become conscious to the writer here that the state does not have the duty to simply just be "human" and "safe." The human is still the measure of the state. It is clear that the personal effects of Hegel's thought are at this point sufficient for a critique of the Kantian ethical doctrine, but not yet sufficient for the construction of a new view of the state. He was still missing a concept through which the thought of the inner unity of the human could come into contact with that other aspect of metaphysical unification, the overcoming of the "fear of one's own," through love. The dissolution of "one's own" into the whole of the world still happened itself more or less within the windowless four walls of the "I": the image of love under which the thinker tried to accomplish the process already demonstrates as much. The devotion itself to the world and its value still occurred within the blind intoxication of the feeling of self – a leap into the ocean. The moment is yet to come where the world confronted the human in a sharply illuminated form, where it forced him to look it in its eye and not shy away from its "inhuman-monstrous" greatness. What is still lacking is the concept that would complete the framework of ideas and thus serve as the supporting arch for the planned religious-historical work: a concept for the actual world in its relationship to the new consciousness. But this concept soon begins to form.

We still recall where we last encountered the thought of fate, namely prior to the effusion on love. At that time, fate appeared to the human as something foreign and harsh, something immense, the unknown cause of his suffering, and something he consciously and powerfully set against his purity without trying to find some unification with it. We saw how the self-consciousness to which fate necessarily appeared in such a form became rooted in its internal solitude and how it began to sense the blessedness of "unification." At that time, we foresaw a renewal of the image of fate. Now, in the fall of 1798, fate reenters, and at that in a two-fold connection.

After more than a year, Hegel takes up anew some drafts, already known to us, on Abraham and the spirit of Jewish history, so as to work them into a finished form.[42] And now he does this under the dominion of the concept of fate. In the drafts, as far as we can see, the historical connection between Abraham and the Jewish people was conceived of as equality of character, as having the same idea of the divine. But now this connection is revealed infinitely deeper to Hegel as the unity of fate. The spirit of Abraham is the unity, the soul, which rules over the fates of all his descendants. Of course this fate itself, in the particular manner it takes on in the Jewish consciousness, is drawn here by Hegel entirely according to the image that he himself connected to the concept of fate until now: fate is the particular form, be it "armor and conflict," or the manner by which the human "carries the shackles of stronger ones."[43] However, the capacity of the concept expands itself as it no longer merely describes the relationship of the individual human to the "cause of his suffering." Fate becomes the bond of unity of an entire history of a people over the ages. And so, we learn how the original spirit of the nation, namely the spirit of Abraham's worship of God, which exhausts itself in enslaved dependency to a foreign being and hostile violation by the environment, again and again becomes the fate of the people. Those who were at first wanderers become settled: they succumb to the fate "against which their nomadic ancestors had fought for so long and through which resistance to which their daemon and the daemon of their people only became more and more embittered."[44] They grasped their fate anew during the epoch of Solomon, in whose "decline" Hegel – in contrast – sees a rise, when they sensed more beautiful spirits and served foreign gods: they cannot become worshipers, only slaves to these gods. Where they again submit to their fate, the old covenant of *odium generis humani*,[45] there "their God awakens again."[46] As the national daemon tires, the scourge of its fate turns against itself through its own hands. It is "the fate of Macbeth, who stepped out of nature itself, clung to foreign beings and thus in their service crushed and murdered everything holy in the nature of what it means to be human. Finally abandoned [...] by his gods and smashed to pieces by his very own belief."[47] – The fate of a people is understood here as such: originally outward-bound from the spirit of their ancestors, like circles from a stone thrown into water, this original spirit of the people later masters itself. But then when it wants to go its own way, it is daemonically forced along the old path. In trying to evade this path, it encounters an embittered daemon, in submitting to this path anew, a reawakened God. Finally, the people pull this spirit down with them into the abyss through the very fanaticism of their submission to it.

Before us lays the first great example of an interpretation of history particular to Hegel, the first specimen of his skill in crafting precious jewels of past events into golden chains, and nothing more. However important this essay is for the development of the concept of fate, however strong the conception of history is guided here by the fresh strength of this concept, this concept has little influence on the ideas of the state, especially on the relationship that stands in the moment at the core of the investigation, the relation of the individual to the state. But what the essay says about this still does not diverge one bit from the old ways already known to us. Freedom of the citizen is still the "great purpose" of the state's legislation;[48] political laws are still one and the same with laws of freedom.[49] Moreover, the republic is still the ideal of the state because the introduction of a monarchy in a free state reduces all citizens into private persons.[50] And again, in a leaflet written almost simultaneously with this draft and very much like in the fragment on the critique of Kant written not long before that, we hear the final judgment on the bad state, it is "something foreign, external to humanity,"[51] – what was called "inhuman" in the critique of Kant.[52] But precisely in the winter in which we now find ourselves, the concept of fate is deepened one last time, leading us further along.

In the essay on the Jewish people, the concept of fate grew into a historical life. In another manuscript[53] he now goes into the connection with personal-ethical life that, as we will see, is more consequential for the subsequent development. This happens in connection with the newly undertaken inquiries into the history of Christianity, to which the inquiries on Judaism were to serve as the introduction and which the editor collected under the title "The Spirit of Christianity and its Fate."[54] Again and again, Hegel feels pressed to grasp the content of Jesus' teachings. As in Bern, where he had previously made Jesus into the proclaimer of Kantian principles, which he is now aware of, especially Jesus the synoptic,[55] – now, where the Kantian ethic is a standpoint that he himself has overcome, he places his own overcoming of Kant and his own, new, ethical consciousness into the Johannine Jesus. Forgiveness of sin – as it is called in these sentences that spill entirely untamed from his pen – is not the transformed emergence of punishment, but rather fate reconciled through love.[56] Guilt and punishment must be connected to one another "of complete necessity." Therefore, the act is the punishment itself – as much as I have injured life that appears foreign to the act, so much have I injured my own. Life is, as life, not different than life, and so the injured life faces me as fate. This fate can be reconciled because a separation which I myself have made, I can also eradicate.[57] For the sinner is precisely more than a sinner – to draw on a somewhat later formulation, he is a human being. Crime and fate are within him, and if he once more turns back to himself through love, beneath him.[58] And so Hegel sets up, here in the first draft – because the last sentence, which we took from the concluding version, also corresponds to a passage of a draft[59] – the concept of personal fate which is one with the act of the human being and which alienates the human being and reconciles him again. In this manner, in the sphere of personal life the image of fate had now transformed itself. Out of the fate that had opposed the human as unknown and foreign there now has evolved an entity which is closely related to that which is most intimate to this human. Here, as in the previously considered image of the fate of a people, fate and the bearer of fate are moved closer together. Here as there, separation from fate is guilt, reunification is atonement. The manuscripts do not provide clues as to which of the two meanings of the concept is older, the historical or the ethical. And as a matter of fact, given the close intertwining of conceptual and historical thinking which is particular to the young Hegel, I would not even dare to presume to side with one or the other.[60] Here as previously, only a first attempt is made at the deepening that the concept of fate would experience during the course of this winter, so that the two directions that the new idea had made use of until now, the historical and the ethical, will themselves attempt a common task, namely, a task that follows from fate as content of the teachings of Jesus to the question of the fate of Jesus himself. We now follow this new turn.

In the main draft for "The Spirit of Christianity and its Fate," which we just looked into, as well as in the somewhat later and indeed even oldest parts of the composition, no attempt was made to apply the concept of fate to Jesus himself. Surely the personality of Jesus had also changed with the teachings. His essence was no longer, or at least only in the earliest parts of the first draft,[61] embodied self-determination or self-activity. No longer was his essence purely absorbed in the fight against time and surroundings. Rather, Hegel was inclined to linger on such turns of Jewish history and the Protestant account, which allowed an interpretation along the lines of that familiar attitude wherein the human finds a sorrowful fortune in removing himself from the influence of humankind and counteracting a union with it. And so, the Either-Or of antagonism and indifference against the "objects" now also disappears from the description of the Essenes, wherefore we had already seen the initial conception of the sects mitigated as fighters against their time. From now on, entirely unequivocally, they "do not enter the fight" with what is Jewish, "but rather disregard it."[62] And now Jesus demands we should be ourselves and disdain every dependency and every union with objects. We should also remain unconcerned with the distress that results for those who disdain every union with objects.[63] One of the joys of his disciples must remain to be pursued by the world, in order that they show their resistance against it.[64] He tears them away from all human relationships, all holy relations of life.[65] – Such is the new challenge for personality.

Yet, towards the beginning of the draft, Hegel still conveyed the total view of the life of Jesus that was entirely in line with his earlier manuscripts: "someone finally had to appear who attacked nothing short of Judaism itself, but because he did not find in the Jewish people that which would have helped him to fight it, that which he could hold onto and with which he could have brought it down, he had to perish, directly establishing only a sect."[66] After internalizing the thought on personality, which emerges in the course of this draft, and above all in the renewal of the concept of fate laid down here and in the essay on the spirit of Judaism, the restructuring of the view of the life of Jesus now comes into play. We now pick it up, beginning in the oldest part of the composition that the manuscript allows us to draw out. The ethical concept of fate and its reconciliation, already known to us from the draft, is here initially developed broadly as the content of the teachings of Jesus. However, a new turn already appears to us here: "fate comes from either one's own act or that of another."[67] Until now, with fate we had only come to know the overcoming of the concept of punishment, and thus, only understood it in connection with the concepts of sin and guilt – that is, as a human act. Now we hear that fate can also arise for humans in sorrow. "He who suffers an unjust attack can defend himself and proclaim himself and his right or he can also not defend himself. With this reaction, be it to tolerate or fight, begins his guilt, his fate."[68] Be it to tolerate or to fight! The new concept of fate has also extended its dominion over that soul who – according to the words from the letter of July 2, 1797 – counteracts its union with the world. Even such suffering as the "highest subjectivity" is not able to escape the force of the world. They who do not themselves rise up in the fight against the eternal-dead, but merely tolerate in silence its unjust attack, they have thereby become guilty, precisely in this will-to-suffer, and thus are subjugated to fate. Giving up one's rights and fighting for rights – both are an equally "unnatural" condition. And so now, within the course of the composition, the idea of a fate of Jesus suddenly emerges. Its oldest version can be found in some jotted-down lines:

> The fate of Jesus – renunciation of the relations of life – (a) civilian and civil, (b) political, (c) living with other people – family, relatives, and nourishment.

> The relationship of Jesus to the world – part fleeing, part reaction, and fighting against the same. As long as and as far as Jesus did not change the world, so much did he have to flee it."[69]

It is evident how the newest development of the concept of fate, according to which silent suffering is also guilt and summons up fate, already plays a part here, at first, of course, without shaking the older conception that saw a fighter in Jesus's relationship to the world. This transitional character of the sketch is characteristic of the composition. Also therein, the "renunciation of the relations of life" is certainly shifted more broadly than before into the fore, but the end result shows both conceptions, older and newer, still next to one another: "In that Jesus disdained to live with the Jewish people, but at the same time always fought against their actualities with his ideal; thus it could not be avoided that he had to be defeated by them."[70] The old image of the fighter is still unobstructed; and that is again completely characteristic of the fact that, in this connection, Jesus is still "agitating for a great plan."[71] For the last time, the Enlightenment-inspired observation of life is noticeable according to its plan and intention.

For the last time. For in that same winter, as Hegel enhances the manuscript with a first level of major additions and entirely rewrites extended sections, there comes about, one would almost like to say, that which had to come about. If a deepening of the thought of fate was initiated in the first manuscript, seeing guilt also in suffering and soon with this the highest guiltlessness as precisely the highest guilt, we would see the elevation over all fate directly connected to the highest, most unfortunate of all fates: thus, the consummating concept of fate now begins wholly and exclusively to rule over the contemplation of the life of Jesus.

"Empedocles, disposed towards a hate of culture through his temperament and philosophy, towards contempt of everything specifically business-like, towards every kind of interest differentially directed to objects; an enemy until death of all one-sided existence and therefore unsatisfied in actual, beautiful relationships; restless, suffering, simply because they are special relationships [...]" – this is the beginning of Hölderlin's first plan of his tragedy and, as a result of this first draft, the roots of its tragic passage from guilt to fate.[72] And these are the words with which Hegel introduces the new treatment of the fate of Jesus in the final version of the section of his work: "This confinement of love to oneself, its fleeing from all forms, even if its spirit was already breezing through them, or originated from them, this distance from all fate is precisely its greatest fate; and here is the point where Jesus is connected to fate and of course in the most sublime way, but suffered from it."[73] In the older version of the fate of Jesus, the "disdain of the forms of life" was still justified in that they had all been, even the most beautiful of forms, "tarnished," "soiled," "desecrated."[74] Precisely this justification, and any particular justification in general, has now disappeared; the "fleeing" applies to all forms in general, because they are forms. Irrespective of whether they are in themselves "impure," they are in any case impure "for love."[75]

Everything that was earlier effectiveness and act in the life of Jesus for Hegel is now driven back as far as possible. After the first appeal among the Jewish people found no believers, he left the fate of his nation untouched and intact. In so far as he does not see the world as changed – the original draft reads "had changed [the world]," essentially more of a belief in action[76] – to that extent "he flees [the world]."[77] He stands with the state "in the only relationship, residing within its jurisdiction, and he submits himself to the consequences of this power over him – consciously suffering."[78] Given that "he consciously suffered from the state, with this relationship to the state a great part of living associations are thereby already [...] cut off."[79] That which "[goes missing] with the variety of joyful and beautiful bonds is replaced by the acquisition of isolated individuality and the narrow-minded consciousness of idiosyncrasies. Admittedly, all relationships established through a state, which stand infinitely deeper than the living relation of the divine union and can only be disdained by the same, are ruled out from the idea of the Kingdom of God. But if it was available and Jesus or the community could not take it up, the fate of Jesus and his community that remained faithful [would thereby result in] a loss of freedom, a limitation of life, a passivity in being dominated by a foreign power [...]."[80] "The fate of Jesus was to suffer from the fate of his nation; either to make it his own and to bear its necessity [...] to unite its spirit with his own, – but to sacrifice his beauty, his connection with the divine – or to push the fate of his people away from himself and, thus, to keep his life in himself as undeveloped and unenjoyed [...]."[81] "The existence of Jesus was thus separation from the world and escape from it into heaven; [...] in part an activity of the divine and in this way a fight with fate, in part in spreading the Kingdom of God [...], in part immediate reaction against individual parts of fate as they directly affected him in the moment; except against that part of fate that immediately appeared as the state and also came to consciousness in Jesus, against which he reacted passively."[82]

We can break off there, for we do not wish to give an exhaustive presentation of this Hegelian text here. And so for now we will no longer follow how the fate of Jesus expands, how it becomes the fate of the community and finally the founding historical essence of the Christian church, whose fate it is "that church and state [...] can never blend together into one."[83] For now we can let this stand on its own, for in the section presented above we now have before us the turning point of Hegel's view of the state. The state is a part of fate! And fate in the highly charged sense to which the word had developed around that time for Hegel: the entirety of life as it confronts the individual, something unavoidable from which he cannot escape – for a "union" [Bund] with the world alone does not create the "possibility of a fate." He who counteracts the union with the world, he who is elevated above all fate is also met by fate, and the most sublime, the fate of this highest guilt that is made up of the highest innocence: he who wants to save his life will lose it. And thus, this fate is something unavoidable. It is not only that from which the individual cannot escape, it is that from which he is not allowed to escape. It looms before us.[84]

And this fate, a part of it, is the state!

That is the moment when every view on the state that would place the individual before the whole has become an absurdity. It is unthinkable that what "fate" is in this monstrous sense could still be a contract. The state has grown above and beyond all dependency on individual humans. And just like that, the thinker will now find something more and something different in the state than a guarantor of human rights and will no longer subdue himself by holding on to the rules of justice as the highest measure.

Immediately after Hegel had worked his way to this view along the winding paths upon which we followed him – the beginning of 1799 – he turned his eyes anew to the actuality of the state which surrounded him. How might it have unfolded for him now? A valuable piece from Hegel's posthumous writings allows us to answer this question.

The Congress of Rastatt was still in session and the Empire was supposed to pay the cost for its fall from supremacy. In those years, the war was within reach of the private tutor of Frankfurt. In 1797, Hoche had even advanced up until Frankfurt. It was not yet a year since Hegel, on a stay in Mainz, had seen everything around the quiet stream ravaged and destroyed – "[there was] no village on its banks that did not lay half in ruins, whose tower and church could still have a roof, could still have more than barren walls."[85] So now he turned his view, already engaged in the proceedings in Rastatt, to the subject of those proceedings, namely, the German Empire and its constitution. A single page is preserved from the beginning of the text and what follows. On the first page, if we approach from the perspective of the text on the constitution of Württemberg, written barely three-fourths of a year earlier, we already find ourselves standing under a much different sky. The confident will that spoke from that previous text, desiring to improve the world, has given way to deep resignation. An indescribable air of melancholy wafts over these pages; the look of a heavy face that does not want to pry itself loose from the seer. "The following pages carry the voice of a certain mood, a mood which reluctantly parts from its hope to see the German state lifted out of its insignificance, takes leave and yet, prior to the total separation from this hope, wanted one last time to vividly recall its ever-weakening wishes and to once more enjoy in an image the weak faith in the fulfillment of this hope."[86] In this voice, Hegel contemplates the most miserable of all constitutions, aside from those of the despots, whose flaws were apparent to everyone through the continuous peace negotiations that ended the war. One of Hegel's most cherished thoughts, which he also includes in the text on the Württemberg constitution and in the major theological work, again finds confirmation here: a revolution comes about when the spirit has disappeared from a constitution. This time, with the pressure of the belief in fate weighing upon him, he reflects on the essence of such a condition, unlike before, when he focused on the searching and striving that grows out of it. "The structure [Gebäude] of the German constitution of the state is the work of the wisdom of centuries, it is not carried by the life of the present time. The entire fate of more than a thousand years is contained in it and the justice, bravery, the honor and the blood, the necessity of long-decayed generations still lives in it [...] it stands in the world isolated from the spirit of the times."[87] He who writes like that has learned to moan under the burden of history. The steeply walled-in "I," towards whose dark depths Hegel had directed his senses in the previous months – see how in these years they attracted the glances of the young Romantic school again and again, and how at that time and in Hegel's most intimate proximity these dark depths transformed into tragedy for the poet of Empedocles – this "I" now gives the writer the coloring to depict the fundamental historical essence of the German constitution: "The legend of German freedom has once more made its way to us from that time in Germany when the individual, unbent by any universal, stood for himself and his honor, and when his fate touched upon himself alone. He struck his strength upon the world [with] his sensing mind and character or constructed them to his liking – in that the individual belonged to the whole through character, but in his activity and act, in his counter-effect against his world, suffered nothing from the whole, but rather without fear and without doubt in himself, limits himself only through his sensing mind."[88] But for this individual who "suffers" nothing from the whole, from the universal – let us remember well the burden of this word "to suffer": it is the word that describes the relation

of the beautiful soul, the utmost innocence, to the surrounding world
– for this individual the "universal" now becomes master, or should at
least become it. Precisely because this did not happen in the German
Empire, that there the individual acquired their rights for themselves
and did not get them handed out "by the universal, by the state as a
whole," that, according to the original legal basis, German constitutional
law is private law, – all of this is the cause of the hopeless condition.[89]
And this power of the universal over the individual, the state over the
people, is now the affirmed thought on the state in general, the thought
that now stands behind all complaints, descriptions, and reproach. In
the fight between the part and the whole, which in the summer seemed
to still be decisively favoring the part, the whole has now, after the shift
in thoughts over the last few months, definitively won. Sovereignty has
become the "necessary character" of the state.[90] Not too long ago, Hegel
had demanded the improvement of the Württemberg constitution in the
name of justice. The words "*discite justitiam moniti*" stood at the head of his
publication on the violation of the old rights of Vaud through the aristocracy of Bern. Now he had an image of the state before him that could
fully appear, in that "every right to a share in the authority of the state
[Staatsgewalt] is precisely determined,"[91] a constitution whose principle,
whose soul, is justice. And the view of the sad outcomes of such a constitution, where the entire structure of the state rests on the preservation
of the inviolable rights of the separation of the estates from the whole,
has the effect that the sentence "justice is the principle, the soul of the
constitution," which only a few months ago would have been a quite
remarkable statement, is now expressed in the voice of most bitter scorn.
The standard of justice slips away with the state that is recognized as the
"fate" of the individual.[92]

We do not know to what degree this first version of the work blos-
somed, as well as whether or not it was a satisfactory description of his
then current conditions, or if, when Hegel took it up again later, this
same work led into thoughts on reform. That Hegel initially had such a
conclusion in mind – to once again enjoy the image of its weak faith in
the fulfillment of this hope – is nevertheless probable. It is also probable
that he soon renounced this intention, as he crossed out the paragraph
that expressed it shortly thereafter and likely even before the new outbreak of the war caused him to lay the pages aside. The only preserved

page of the next installment presumably asks: "should not Germany's path still be found at the crossroads between Italy's fate and the union into *one* state?" and references "two factors" that give hope to the latter – without, by the way, it yet being obvious to us what these factors would be "that could be considered as the inclination against its disbanding principle."[93] But the way that Hegel introduces the question allows us to again recognize how far removed the mood of the entire piece was from any courage towards reform: if the drive to isolate oneself is "the only moving principle in the German Empire, then Germany finds itself unstoppably sinking into the abyss of its disbanding, and a warning for this would of course show zeal, but at the same time the foolishness of unnecessary labor."[94] That is no longer the man who would like to lead from the "fear, that must" to the "courage, that wants to." And although the dominant idea of the state as fate certainly allowed, in accordance with the connection between fate and character, moving principles and tendencies to count against it as unchangeable powers in the lap of the state, it was not yet inclined to already trust the state with its own, unlimited life, the capacity to change and develop above and beyond all inborn "principles." It still knew nothing of the comprehensive power of history. Initially, it shaped the side of the new image of the state that turned more towards the people: only the right of the state over the individual was divined in it and soon brought to light in these pages on *The German Constitution.* Even with the word sovereignty Hegel appears to emphasize almost nothing other than the power of the whole over its parts, not yet independence, the power of the whole over itself and directed outwardly. Overall, in the following period Hegel still wrestled with that painfully enduring bearing towards the world and life. By no means did he personally leave "suffering" from the whole and the world behind him, for he had learned to see it as guilt. And another manuscript, which is even more important to us in that it represents the only certain remnants for over a year's time, shows how deeply Hegel's view of the state was still entangled in personal turmoil from which it grew into new life, and how little it could solidify into an objectively clear form.[95]

Once again, it is only the beginning of a text on *The German Constitution.* However, that only becomes clear from the last lines, shortly before it breaks off. The immediate political starting point, which for the first version of the text could be found in the peace negotiations of Rastatt and its expected outcome for the Empire, no longer exists, as the war was newly reignited. And there is also no talk of war in the manuscript. Rather, the actual subject of the manuscript takes shape in an unexpected turn towards the end from extremely dark and viscous movements of thought on the place of the individual in the present age: *The German Constitution*.

Hegel again outlines the contours of the condition already familiar to us wherein spirit no longer feels at home in the old forms. This time, the attention of the thinker is focused on the position of the individual within such a condition. At this stage, Hegel finds a striving of reciprocal convergence in the dull impulse of both the stirred-up masses and individuals towards change and in the longing for life of those spirits wandering in the light of the idea. The former strive from their imprisonment within actuality towards clear consciousness, the latter towards the actualization of what was seen in the spirit. In this striving, they meet each other half-way. It is the contrast that Hölderlin embodied in his novel within the pair of friends: Alabanda is here the strongly impulsive noble revolutionary; Hyperion is pulled by him into his circle – by him, he who draws the soft-spirited friend through a touching love, a longing towards his unblemished purity. The specific contrast of these two figures may have come to Hegel's mind here and in what follows: "He," so Hyperion himself describes the relationship in the novel, "he who is hounded from home to and fro among strangers by fate and the barbarism of humans, from his youth on embittered and made wild, and yet also the internal heart full of love, full of longing to penetrate from the inner rough sheathes to a friendly element. Myself, already so deeply cut off from everything, so foreign and lonely with my entire soul among humans, so ridiculously accompanied by the sounds of the chains of the world in my heart's most dear melody; me, the antipathy of all blind and lame, and yet too blind and lame to myself, yet myself so superfluous to all that was from afar related to the intelligent and the rational, the barbarians and the jokers – and so full of hope, so full of the singular expectation of a more beautiful life."[96]

In Hegel's manuscript, the Hyperion-characters, those "who have worked nature into an idea within themselves,"[97] are discussed further, and in a confessional way worth noting: they "cannot live alone, and the human is always alone if he has represented his nature to himself, made this representation into his companion, and enjoyed himself in it;

he must also find what is represented as something living."[98] They cannot live "alone"! The step has been made that even leads over the guilty consciousness to the "highest subjectivity." For Hegel was still detained by that guilty consciousness in the winter from 1798 to 1799. And certainly, with this the inner solitude, the "highest subjectivity," to which he confessed in the letter from July 2, 1797, was definitively negated. But this negation did not lead any further at this time; it remained in painful subservience to a fate which was always justified over and against human suffering – for "innocence has never suffered, every suffering is guilt."[99] The negation taught Hegel to grasp the state as a part of an always necessary and just fate and lent it a dominating force over humankind. In this way, it retained a painful pull; it was not a joyful submission to the fate of the world, no *amor fati*, even though the fate was known and felt as the only one justified.[100] And yet, it was actually from the inner direction of these ideas that the step towards joyfulness, towards complete reconciliation of humans with the world was made. Already then, fate was reconciled in the reconciliation of humans with themselves through "love"; yet it remained a compromise within the walls of the I, which was still without external consequences, so to speak. But now a reconciliation readied itself that truly went beyond the I. Here, the human being had finally stopped wanting to counteract his union with the world. He no longer wants to "be alone," he wants to find his own nature, that which is represented in him, "worked into an idea" outside of himself and as something living. The drive and will towards that so long disdained union with the world has arisen in our hero and will now become the determining force of his life.

But admittedly, it was initially only the drive and the will. And so here we now see a still uncertain will, still doubting itself, and above all unsure as to the point at which it should tackle the matter. The dichotomous situation of humans, "who the age has driven into an internal world," is now depicted. If a human being wants to preserve himself in his internal world, his position can be only either "an ever-enduring death, or when nature drives him to life, only an endeavor to lift up the negative of the existing world in order to find and enjoy himself in it, in order to be able to live." Hegel now designates as "ever-enduring death" the counteraction of the union with the world, which once appeared to him as the highest personal life – and he now posits the great "or" against this "either."

Yet precisely this "or," the striving to pass from the idea over into life, is made infinitely more difficult for this human being through his clear awareness of the fate under which he stands: "his suffering is bound up with the consciousness of limits, on account of which he disdains life as it is offered to and allowed for him." And so, the drive to "preserve" himself in his internal world, be it as it may, always remains alive in him; his clarity always drives him from what is new back into himself. "He wants his suffering," Hegel says of him – the same words with which we once tried to grasp the mood of the confession in the letter from July 1797.[101] Yet how much easier do those others have it who are led on their turbulent paths to an unknown, which they "unconsciously seek," by a force that "holds [them] prisoner."[102] Let us recall in the description that Hegel gives these others the words that Alabanda's comrades speak as they try to persuade Hyperion to join their secret society: "We are here to clean up the earth, here to rip up the weed with the roots attached, so that it withers in the burning sun. Not that we want to harvest, the reward comes too late for us; the harvest is no longer ripe for us. We acted daringly rather than merely reflecting. We played with fate, and it did the same with us. We have stopped speaking of luck and misfortune. We do not beg for the heart of the human. For we do not need his heart, do not need his will. If no one wants to live where we have built, we are not guilty for that. I often told myself, you sacrifice decay and I still did my daily tasks."[103] And now Hegel writes about these people, to whom the internal inhibitions of those others he depicted remains unknown: their suffering is "without reflection on their fate," and thus "without will" – namely without the will to "suffer," which for the people of Hyperion's lineage bars the way to act. They honor the "negative," the negating, revolutionary strength of their own essence, suffering dully and unconsciously in the bonds of fate. The limits, which have something unassailable for those living in the idea, those who want their suffering, they do not take these limits for outright unconquerable as such, but only externally, "only in the form of their legal and powerful existence,"[104] and thus they can believe in the possibility of clearing them away. This stands in deep contrast to the spiritual people who recognize in fate, that is in the "limits," something "absolutely" necessary and never to be "subjugated," above and beyond all right and all power of the contingent present. In contrast, they take as absolute their own "determinations" and therefore their own person and its "contradictions." And so, this human is prepared to sacrifice himself and others for such absolutely imagined personal goals, regardless of whether they hurt his "drives," or his lower, accidental will, or emotional needs. This is quite like Hölderlin's Alabanda, and in this regard similar to Schiller's Posa as well, and how he initially brings Hyperion's friendship into the service of his own revolutionary plans and then, in turn, sacrifices himself for the friend. The stance of such humans against prevailing life is unconfused; they act and know how to recognize and accept the consequences of their actions, even if it "hurts their drives." But how is moving above and beyond that which exists to be possible for the person ruled by spirit, he whose nature drives him to live! Of course, the surroundings are as good to him as they are to the blind, heroic revolutionary, who "would rather live daringly than reflect," so that his nature stands hostile – "negative" – over and against him. But at the same time, he is internally moved through his clear intellect to recognize these surroundings that limit him: for him, the world is "positive with respect to the will" – indeed he "wants" his suffering. He is filled by the knowledge that for him the sublimation of hostile external things cannot be brought about through force, neither his own nor another's. What would his will even be in the face of force![105] It would be the revolt of the human against fate, the distancing from which is precisely the sum of all guilt and a hopeless beginning at that. It would be hopeless if force attacks fate from the outside for fate "remains what it is" while force only removes the limits of life in order to set new ones and with these new limits new suffering. It would also be hopeless if the revolt of the suffering one himself is against his own fate because "the enthusiasm of one bound up is a horrible moment for him, a moment in which he loses himself." Thus, Hölderlin had formerly taken the un-Fichtean wisdom from Fichte that we are only certain of ourselves in the consciousness of our limits.[106] We became familiar with the usage of this thought in that earlier version of Hyperion that we introduced at the beginning of this section. Hegel similarly reasons here: the enthusiasm of one who is bound is a horrible moment, for he possesses the consciousness of his personality only in the limits of his fate, and so he would shatter his highest life along with it if he revolted against these limits. Only when he again remembers the simply forgotten certainties of his personality will he again find the self which he had lost in the revolt against these limits.

So, what hope still remains for him in the drive of his spiritual nature towards life, he who "wants" his suffering, now that the paths of force against that which exists are closed for him? Hegel gives a new answer: fate must turn in toward itself, "the existing life has lost its power and all its dignity," has been left by all fortifying strengths, all that is awe-inspiring. Fate is no longer reconciled by the I, no longer achieves this reconciliation through love, but rather in itself and through itself: fate becomes – history. For Hegel, in this moment history acquires an ethical, indeed an almost religious meaning, which it retains for him throughout the rest of his life. It is the great basin in which the human is washed clean of all guilt, it is the stream into which it is both a duty and blessing for the individual to flow. The walls of fate, within which the spiritual human saw himself hopelessly trapped, fall of their own accord. This is Hegel's new, and for him definitive, solution!

Hegel is instructed by "all appearances of the age," which he allows to pass over him in one great image, that the present time in which he now finds himself is a historical epoch "wherein one no longer finds satisfaction in the old life" and that the epoch has been breathed upon by "a better life." We are no longer surprised after what has preceded that "nature in its actual life [is] the only attack against or refutation of the inferior life" and that this refutation cannot be "the subject of an inten-tional activity – as such, a "natural" "refutation" is, after all, precisely the work of history, which pours forth over the intentions of the individual human. The individual may then do nothing but take from existing life that whereby it was invulnerable to its spiritual concerns, that "truth," "dignity," and "honor," which, in coming into contradiction with exist-ing life, makes "the demand of the drives as timid as going against one's conscience." The internal right, which the old life had "vindicated" for itself, must be taken away from it and lent to the life being called for. So, with the German Empire – and here the introduction begins to approach the subject-matter – the task of those longing for "life" is to show that and to what extent the claimed dignity already no longer resides in the individual parts of the constitution: that, perhaps, the Kaiser's power is no longer the true "universal" of the state, but in contrast is "isolated in itself and had made itself into something particular" and thus is "now present only as a thought, no longer as an actuality." The introduction breaks off in the middle of the page and in the middle of the sentence with this discussion of the intended process.

We tried to indicate how there is also belief within this process and how this belief was the result of Hegel's personal development. The hopeless resignation to the limits of a terrible fate that dominates the introductory fragment to the text on *The German Constitution* from the beginning of 1799 and stemmed from the new view of the state just emerging at that time, has given way. That mood is itself followed here in its final psychic and temporal connections and thus, recognized and grasped, thrust aside. A new door opens, a movement occurs within "fate," the rigid metal begins to stream forth. And to knowingly follow this stream is the ful-fillment of the longing of those people thirsting for life from the realm of the idea, the goal of their actions. What emerged here from entirely personal perils and doubts, the new philosophical valuation of history, was perhaps simultaneously carried out scientifically by Schelling with his *System of Transcendental Idealism*, following Kantian ideas.[107] For Schelling as well, history is here the liberator from the labyrinths of the doctrine of ethical volition. "[T]he most holy cannot be entrusted to chance." With this, Schelling, still entirely caught up in Fichte's ethical pride, justifies history's philosophical positioning. It cannot be determined if Hegel was already familiar with this text by his old friend as he wrote those pages. The entirely individual wording, the work with concepts and images whose meaning only opens up to the expert on Hegel's older manu-scripts, would in any case disallow the thought of influence. It is even doubtful itself whether the more general meaning of those sentences for the view of history even entered into the consciousness of the writer at all – so entirely are they still filled with his own experience.

The new bearing of the "I," this last and total melting down of the "highest subjectivity" of 1797, now quickly arrives at its fundamen-tal conclusion. In September of 1800, Hegel finished a larger work which, since Dilthey and on the basis of two preserved pieces, one has come to maintain as the first draft of his philosophical system. It cannot be deduced from the remnants if the state was given special treatment when grappling with its issues. It is almost likely that the entire work revolves around the concept of religion.[108] The preserved, concluding words of this work now add the final touch to the picture of the new self-consciousness, which we were able to sketch out on the basis of the pages observed above. They describe, in verbatim to a work by Fichte,[109] the standpoint of the "I," which sways "above all nature,"[110] only to elevate it in a last turn in a surprising sudden manner with Hegel's new world view: "And thus the blessedness, in which the I has everything, everything in opposition beneath it, is the most dignified and most noble when the union with the age would be ignoble and base."[111] If it were so! But it is not so. The sentence once again presents in compressed form the beginning and end of the mental and spiritual development to which we bore witness in this section, and crafts a name for the result: "unification with the age."[112] It was at that time that those verses appeared from Hölderlin, who – in Hegel's words – the age had driven into an internal world, in which Hölderlin fruitlessly searched for a way to the "God of the age," from whom his drives turn away trembling: "I look to save myself from you in the cave, and would like, stupid me, to find a place, you-who-are-omnipresent, where you couldn't be."[113] At that time, Hölderlin had also already begun to look for his path, albeit in a different, but correspondingly exact manner. His great goal in the years to come, after he had attained from the Greeks the freedom they had once lost, was to become patriotic. The most difficult and highest thing is to "freely use" what is closest, what is most one's own.[114] "Forbidden fruit like the laurel is yet most often the fatherland. But this is only ever tasted at the end."[115] In this way he was reconciled, albeit not with "the age," but with the "fatherland," whose "holy earth" becomes for him the guarantee of a future that is already slumbering in the bosom of the present. Indeed, it lives in the new songs that he is now intoning. This turning point that rounds out the poet's last productive years corresponds exactly to the one that happened to Hegel in 1800. The present moment provides him with the security that his friend, whose ways had separated from his own, gained from his native soil. He now writes to Schelling that his current intent is "to find [a] return to an engagement with the life of the people."[116] The actualization of this intent leads him to Jena. And here, not too long thereafter, he wrote down the outcome of his years in Frankfurt, the will to live, which he captured there, and which he wrote down in an epigram "Resolution":

Bold may the gods' son of battle for completion trust himself. Break the peace with thee, break with the works of the world. Strive, try more than today and yesterday, and you will not be better than the age, but this at its best.[117]

"Break then the peace with thee!" This is in a powerfully concise way the opposite goal to that past one of 1797: "to separate oneself from the people and to counteract a union with them." The compass of the soul has turned its focus in the opposite direction, the "highest subjectivity" of before has given way to the striving towards highest materiality. The star towards which the needle now points is "the age." The new magic phrase is "to be this at its best," to unite oneself with it. And we will soon see how this firm stance of the personality achieved in this manner also brings the image of the state above and beyond the idea of a state based on fate into its ultimate form.

And yet another observation finds its place here, where Hegel's life crosses over from the years of development into those of a man. How Hegel had sketched his personal hardship into the picture of the entire age, how he uncovered there a striving of mutual reconciliation between those hungry for life, coming from the realm of the light of reason, and those longing for spiritual consciousness from a dull imprisonment in the actual, to finally find in the "unification with the age" the most personal answer for the most personal hardship: all this may remind us of the attempt at a description of the relationship between human and state in the German eighteenth century that introduced our narrative. There we tried to depict the Janus face of that century's conception of the state, the divergence of the reason-oriented and material-bound endeavors of its thinkers on the state. We indicated that the defining act of the German nineteenth century's great state thinkers was merging the separate ways of viewing. If we recall this, then it certainly may seem here as if Hegel's questioning and solutions, lifted above and beyond the frame of individual life, achieved a universal historical significance.

## NOTES

1 Cf. Zinkernagel (1907).
2 Cf. Section 4, note 38.
3 Cf. the important letter to Hegel from July 10, 1794 (Br I).
4 Hegel to Hölderlin, August 1796 (Br I); Rosenkranz 79.
5 Against Zinkernagel's conception as a frame narrative, cf. Joachimi-Dege (1908), 23 ff.; as far as the relationship to Fichte is concerned, Hölderlin remains thoroughly dependent on him with respect to his conceptual material, even by contradicting him in content; he seeks, as it were, to beat him

with his own weapons; the entire doctrine of the limit, the two drives, etc., is Fichtean (cf. Hölderlin's letter of April 13, 1795 in Hölderlin [1992 f.], Vol. II, 577–579); but the peculiar emphasis on the ethical value of passivity is quite foreign to Fichte. To put it compactly: using concepts from the *Wissenschafts-lehre*, Hölderlin seeks here to assert the ethics of *Briefe über ästhetische Erziehung* against the ethics of "Bestimmung des Gelehrten."

6   Joachimi-Dege (op. cit.), 175 ff.; only the sentence on "Homer" according to an older version (ibid. 204, cf. Hölderlin [op. cit.], vol. I, 523–526.

7   Nohl 10 (GW I, 91 f.; HW I, 18f. ["Bei viel sinnlichen Völkern ..."]); N 20 (GW I, 102 f.: HW I, 32 f. [ab "b Wenn die Tugend ... ]), N 22 f. (GW I, 104 ff.: HW I, 35 ff. [ab diese Lehren, so sehr sie ... "]) N 29 (GW I, 112: HW I, ab "Wir kennen diesen Genius ..."]).

8   Cf. Schiller (2004) vol. V, 583 (6th letter on "Aesthetic Education").

9   GW I, 348; Nohl 210 – The date, "April 29, 96," as inspection of the manuscript teaches, in fact goes with what follows.

10   HW I, 207; Nohl 366, Appendix "5."

11   Nohl 367. [JS & JS: without any division].

12   GW I, 399 ff.; Rosenkranz 78 ff; cf. Br. I, 38 ff. – the view given in the text, which deviates from the common one, has since been most beautifully confirmed by the manuscript that has again come to light in the meantime: in it – it is a concept – the whole passage from "Der Sinn verliert sich" to "vermählt es mit Gestalt," which for Dilthey is still decisive in determining the chronology of Hegel's inner development – is crossed out! Is it too bold, incidentally, to refer with respect to this dialectic of pantheism and individualism to the eighth of Schelling's "philosophical letters," published shortly before? Compare especially the fourth to last paragraph "Anschauung überhaupt ..." (Schiller [2004], vol. III, 94 f.) [(on the manuscript of the poem, see Editorial Report GW I, ibid. 503]).

13   GW I, 391; Rosenkranz 482.

14   GW 3, 218; Nohl 367.

15   Nohl 370, Appendix "7" – there "from the active."

16   Ibid.

17   Nohl 371.

18   Hegel to Hölderlin, November 1796 (Br I).

19   Hölderlin to Hegel, July 10, 1797 (ibid.).

20   Rosenkranz 80 f.

21   Indeed, interpretation of humanity [Menschendeutung] and sense of self [Selbstgefühl] for Hegel stood in very intimate connection. This is wonderfully illustrated by the following anecdote (in Köpke [1855], Vol. II, 70 and Varnhagen von Ense, K.A., handwritten. Royal Library of Berlin [now in the holdings of the University Library Kraków; cf. Stern (1911)]. Tieck was reading *Othello*. At the end Hegel commented on the character of Iago. He saw therein proof for the unsatisfied temperament of the poet himself. Tieck responded: "Professor, are you of the devil?" What Hegel takes here to be self-evident with Shakespeare certainly applies to his own art of characterization, and the amusing horror of the artist [Tieck] must have somewhat bewildered him.

22 Hegel to Nanette Endel, July 2, 1797.

23 GW 5, 16; HW I, 457.

24 Nohl 371.

25 Joachimi-Dege (op. cit.), cf. at 113 f. The quotation is a combination of two sentences (ibid. 178, 180; Hölderlin [1992], Vol. I, 526, 528).

26 Nohl 376; the comma placed by Nohl before "the highest subjectivity" is missing in the manuscript.

27 Nohl 373.

28 HW I, 243; Nohl 377, appendix "9" – Prior to 1795, Hegel had once wanted to deal with the concept of providence himself (cf. Hölderlin to Hegel, January 26, 1795 [Br I]).

29 HW I, 243 f.; Nohl ibid.

30 Joachimi-Dege (op. cit.), 180; Hölderlin (op. cit.), Vol. I, 528; actual wording: "Do not dishonor the good goddess of fate!"

31 Cf. the 8th letter on "Dogmatismus und Kritizismus," published in 1796 (SHK 1/3, 85 ff.).

32 Nohl 379; this and the following quotations are from the first version of the text (ibid. appendix "10. Love," 378 ff., c. November 1797), unless otherwise indicated.

33 HW I, 245; Nohl 378.

34 Nohl 380 (second version of the text).

35 HW I, 433 f.; Rosenkranz 87 – verbatim "both, state and church, [...]."

36 HW I, 444; Rosenkranz 87.

37 HW I, 444; Rosenkranz 88 – verbatim: "*But if the principle of the state is a complete whole ...*"

38 HW I, 444; Rosenkranz 87 – verbatim: "Acting in the spirit of the Church, the human being as a whole acts not only against individual state laws, but against the entire spirit of the same, against *its whole.*"

39 Ibid – verbatim: "whereas in the Church the human being is a *whole.*"

40 HW I, 444; Rosenkranz 88.

41 Ibid.

42 Nohl 243 ff.

43 HW I, 274; Nohl 243.

44 HW I, 286; Nohl 252 – The passage belongs to the (somewhat later) additions; in its basic version, however, it corresponds to HW I, 281/Nohl 248 ("Dem Schicksal ...").

45 *Odium generis humani* [JS & JS: hatred for the human race] is "the soul of Jewish nationality" (HW I, 293; Nohl 257); an early occurrence of the word "nationality" (cf. Meinecke (1908), 141 note 3).

46 HW I, 294; Nohl 258.

47 HW I, 297; Nohl 260.

48 HW I, 290; Nohl 255 (the passage belongs to the somewhat later additions).

49 Ibid.; so self-evident is the equation to him that he had first simply wanted to write "political laws."

50 HW I, 294; Nohl 258.

51 This passage is missing in Nohl (Appendix "8," 373 f.).

52   HW I, 444; Rosenkranz 88.
53   HW I, 297 ff.; Nohl Appendix "12," 385 ff.
54   GW I, 241 ff.; Nohl 241 ff.
55   HW I, 354 f.; Nohl 289.
56   Nohl 393, crossed out in the manuscript; cf. HW I, 346 note 256 HW I, 305; Nohl 392.
57   HW I, 305; Nohl 392.
58   HW I, 353; Nohl 288 – In the manuscript, instead of "sinner," the word "crimi-nal" is used.
59   Namely, the sentences starting with "Die Strafe ist ..." (HW I, 396; N 392 f.).
60   [On the dating, see Jaeschke (2003), 86]
61   HW I, 298 ("Es mußte endlich ..."); Nohl 386.
62   Ibid. Verbatim: "do not allow themselves into combat with it."
63   HW I, 309; Nohl 395.
64   HW I, 312; Nohl 398.
65   HW I, 309; Nohl 396.
66   HW I, 386; Nohl 298.
67   HW I, 346 note; Nohl 283 (crossed out in the manuscript).
68   HW I, 387; Nohl 284.
69   Nohl 305 (marginal note in the manuscript; not included in the HW edition).
70   HW I, 405; Nohl 331.
71   Ibid.
72   Hölderlin (op. cit.), Vol. I, 763.
73   HW I, 397; Nohl 324.
74   HW I, 404; Nohl 326.
75   HW I, 404; Nohl 331.
76   Nohl 305 Annotation.
77   HW I, 399; Nohl 327 – the wording of the following quotes corresponds to HW I.
78   Ibid.
79   HW I, 399 f.; Nohl 327.
80   HW I, 399 f.; Nohl 327 f.
81   HW I, 401; Nohl 328.
82   HW I, 402 f.; Nohl 329.
83   HW I, 418; Nohl 342.
84   HW I, 350; Nohl 286.
85   Hegel to Nanette Endel, 25. Mai 1798 (Br I).
86   GW 5, 6; HW I, 452 Annotation [The following quotations from "Fragmenten einer Kritik der Verfassung Deutschlands" are taken from Lasson's edition of Hegel's works (Ww. 7). Here, however, the citations are given according to GW 5, since from there all stages of editing of the text are provided and not only the first stage provided by Lasson – see Editorial Report on GW 5, 552 ff].
87   GW 5; HW I, 452 f.
88   GW 7 f.; HW I, 453.
89   GW 9; HW I, 454 f.

90   GW 13; HW I, 456.
91   GW 12; HW I, 455.
92   GW 14; HW I, 456.
93   GW 15; HW I, 604.
94   Ibid.
95   Namely, until the fall of 1800 (cf. on the dating GW 5, 668 f.). Lost to us from this period is a commentary on Steuart's theory of the state (Rosenkranz 86), written from February 19 to May 17, 1799; cf. on this p. 180.
96   Hölderlin (1992 f.), Vol. I, 631 f.
97   GW 5, 16; HW I, 457.
98   Ibid.
99   HW 347; Nohl 284.
100  As late as 1801, he interwove the following thesis into his habilitation: "*Principium scientiae moralis est reverential fato habenda*" [The principle of moral science is to hold fate in reverence] (GW 5, 227; Rosenkranz 159).
101  GW 5, 16; HW I, 457. – "Fate" and "limit" are here one and the same; the "consciousness of limits" stands in contrast to the "without reflection on his fate."
102  Ibid.
103  Joachimi-Dege (op. cit.), 55 f.; Hölderlin (op. cit.) Vol. I, 638 f. (different wording).
104  GW 5, 16; Rosenkranz 89 – The important "only" is emphasized by Rosenkranz.
105  "Life in struggle with life, – which contradicts itself." – Cf. HW 348; Nohl 284 – verbatim: "again contradicts."
106  Cf. Section 6, note 3; related to this in the piece at hand is the striking ambiguity of "determinacy" – at once character, at once world; at once "I," at once limit – upon which the explanation given in the text partly rests.
107  SHK I/9 1–2.
108  "Systemfragment von 1800" – HW 419–427; Nohl 345–351.
109  "Die Bestimmung des Menschen" (in FW I/6, 145–311) [Rosenzweig mistakenly referred here to the lecture "Bestimmung des Gelehrten" first published twelve years later as that "Fichtean writing"].
110  HW 426, 427; Nohl 351.
111  HW 427; Nohl 351.
112  Ibid.
113  Hölderlin (op. cit.), Vol. I, 228; Joachimi-Dege (op. cit.), 126.
114  Hölderlin to Böhlendorf, December 4, 1801 (Br I).
115  Hölderlin (op. cit.), Vol. I, 398.
116  Hegel to Schelling, November 2, 1800 (Br I).
117  GW I, 511; Michelet (1884) Vol. I (Wahrheit aus meinem Leben"), 87. The *Vossiche Zeitung* of November 16, 1841, from which Michelet quoted the epigram, "Bricht dann ... "; Michelet reading seems preferable to me. [GW also shares "Bricht dann ..." with; cf. editorial report on GW I, 716 f.].

# 7

# JENA (UNTIL 1803)

At a much later time, Hegel would sketch out a kind of philosophy of the stages of life for the psychological part of his lectures, and said of the passage from youth to adulthood that there "the completed development of subjective individuality has to fight against its absorption into universality and objectivity, still adhering and lingering in empty subjectivity – against hypochondria." And he added to this as a comment: "This hypochondria occurs most often around the twenty-seventh year of life, or between this year and the thirty-sixth; – it can often be insignificant, but an individual cannot easily avoid it, and if this moment occurs later on, it shows up with serious symptoms. But in that it is [...] essentially of a spiritual nature [...] this mood can spread and penetrate underneath the entire shallowness of a life that has not withdrawn into itself into subjective inwardness."[1]

Very personal experiences are mirrored in these apparently very factual sentences. The noticeable emphasis on the twenty-seventh year of life, given that we know of the confessional letter from July 2, 1797, provides us with a sure clue about this personal moment of impact. And following

DOI: 10.4324/9780429354724-8

upon this a further self-testimony, which comes up in a letter from the year 1810 and describes rising out of this "hypochondria," may lead us into the Jena years. This time, according to the occasion, Hegel emphasizes not so much the universally human aspect of this development as the special case of the educated person, when he writes: "I know from personal experience this mood of the mind or much more that of reason, when one day it enters with interest and its intuitions into a chaos of appearance and [...] while internally certain of the goal, has not yet come to clarity and specification. I suffered to the point of exhaustion for a few years from this hypochondria. Generally, every human being has such a turning point in [their] life, the nocturnal point of the contraction of his essence, through whose narrowness he is forced and then becomes solidified and assured in the surety of his self, in the surety of his ordinary daily life – and if he is already in such a condition as to be unable to be completed through the same, then in the surety of an internally noble existence."[2] It was this last surety that Hegel had now won for himself. His personal development proper is complete. Lifted up and out from the intense heat of experience, his thought is now hammered into shape on the anvil of philosophical thinking. From now on there are no longer any cliffs of inner experience through which the stream of ideas must break. The obstacles that will still distract and divide him in the coming years are the difficulties of the matter itself [die Sache selbst].

An early, almost instinctual grasp of the connections between cultural life and national community did not immediately lead, as one might assume, to an intuition of state-life built upon these connections. A strong awareness for the "dignity of the human being" became the foundation of Hegel's first independent political thoughts and interrupted that earlier direction. A double ideal of the state sprang from this awareness, different for the ancient and the modern human being. For the former – the state which produces its free activity: the height of existence; for the latter – the agreement of all to protect natural rights, especially the freedom of conscience of every individual. In the end there was no shorter way from the "more modern" ideal to the living state of the present than from the ancient ideal. The vein of trust in freedom which ran through these images of the state now died off in Frankfurt. In the "state as fate" the ground was laid for a new view, which did not take its start from the individual human but rather from the state itself. And so, the focus of the idea of the state definitively shifted; the will towards "uni-fication with the age," which was based on the rational governance of history, was driven towards the reflective grasp of the actual state of the present. But by no means was the fundamental world-historical view of the difference between the ancient republicans on the one hand and the people in the Roman Empire or the modern monarchy on the other, nur-tured by Gibbon and Schiller and from which the double ideal of the state proceeded, already done away with. Of what was once carried out in the oldest drafts from Tübingen, the thought to attune the entire being of the people – religious, private, public life – into a beautiful harmony, we now hear towards the end of the time in Frankfurt that this is only "possible with peoples whose life is as little torn apart and divided as possible, that is, with happy ones; unhappier ones [...] in the division of preserving a part of the same [...] must concern themselves [...] their highest pride must be to securely preserve the division and the One."³ With such words in September 1800 and on the same pages on which the answer to the "unification with the age" was given for the first time, the claim is made for the modern independence of the "I." The steadfast division of the individual from the whole, beyond all needs of a highly-tense inward-ness, and the grand view of this whole as "fate," which for the individual is an ethical necessity to honor, these are the two impulses for the further formation that the idea of the state now undergoes, as well as the thematic material for the contrapuntal treatment. The conscious will to be "not bet-ter than the age, but this at its best" then sets the work under a formal law to expunge from the thought of the state the last remains of the original experience that is still visibly clinging to the idea of the state as fate and to form them into a calm objectivity for the intuition. From the experience of the state as fate comes the recognition of the state as power. This shift now begins in the drafts of a critique of The German Constitution, again taken up in the winter from 1800 to 1801.⁴

We have already encountered them many times. Their beginnings go back to the time shortly before the end of the Congress of Rastatt, which among other things brought Hegel the knowledge that the thousand-year Holy Roman Empire of the German Nation was now really coming to its long-prophesied end. At that time, the renewed outbreak of war took the quill out of Hegel's hand. Only once, as far as we can see, he again turned to the subject before the fall of 1800 in those remarkable pages on the age and the placement in it of the intellectual human. There it was perceived from a very general point of view, and in a narrower sense, without any connection to the political events of the time. Now, at the end of 1800 or the beginning of 1801, after the weapons of war had sounded for the last time, he turned to the work again, and this time did not take his eyes off it for a year and a half. The question arises for us, after we have accompanied Hegel right up to the threshold of this undertaking, whether or not, in working on a subject so clearly arising from the age, certain influences from the time and surroundings may have made their way in, more than are noticeable in our account, which up until now has advanced in strict connection with immediate sources, therefore only barely lifted its view in the last few years above the writing desk of the private tutor of Frankfurt. It must be seen here, if anywhere, if this limitation to internal events has corresponded to our subject, or, as much too faithful slaves to the *quod non est in actis, non est in mundo* [what is not in the records is not in the world], we have failed it. Accordingly, an attempt should therefore be made to set up the framework in which Hegel's interest in the German constitution could have shifted, without taking into account what is known to us about his particular internal development. We find him first engaged with work on the manuscript in Frankfurt, in the immediate vicinity of the French border and beyond the theater of war. Here, in the old city of coronation, he was still surrounded by the living signs and memories of the glories of tradition. Only a few years ago the last imperial coronation had taken place. Here, one still clung to the Empire and the old constitution – the frenzy of Mainz in 1792 did not infect its neighboring city. Still further back we may recall Hegel's Swabian heritage. For in Swabia in the eighteenth century the Empire was certainly still a living entity. The duchy was interspersed with countless knightly and city areas immediate to the Empire. During the Seven Years War, of course contradicting the mood of the Protestant land, the duke stood on the side of the Kaiser. The unique fight of the provincial assembly against the duke helped enliven the thoughts of the Empire in contrast to the newer thoughts on the state, perhaps here more than anywhere else in one of the bigger German lands. For the German eighteenth century, the Empire was, and not unjustly so, the protective power against the sultan-like appetites of the minor princes. Beyond this, the Swabians in particular had their own kind of historical connections to the old Empire. And even the name of the "empire" itself had remained especially tied to the vernacular of these Swabian, Frankish, and Rhenish lands. And the memories of Swabia's role in the most magnificent time of the old Empire had been newly reawakened. Already in the 1780s, Thill, Conz, and Reinhard praised the age of Stauffer, all predecessors of the later Swabian school of poets. Schubart's easily inflamed singer's blood greeted the confederation of princes with overflowing joy and hope, in which a strangely future-oriented romance for the Empire mixed with an enthusiasm for Prussia. Even the scholarship on the state took a patriotic turn for the Empire here, especially with both Mosers. The younger one, in his writings, tried to advance political-educational work. But the father, perhaps the most influential state teacher of Germany at that time, collected the documents of imperial law with endless industry, meanwhile rejecting every attempt to grasp this law conceptually as without "actual benefits," and in this way became rather isolated from the scholarship of his age.[5]

In that the efforts of the German constitutional lawyers indeed went together with Moser in that one direction, one grasped and presented more the law that was available in documents than the law that was actually current under the state law of the Empire. But for the Göttingen school,[6] which even among outsiders was recognized as the leading school in scholarship, next to this there still lay the old doctoral question of the essence of the Empire in terms of constitutional law.[7] We do not need to go into the history of this conflict of schools here. It suffices to know that at the end of the century in Germany it was the view of Pütter, who viewed the Empire as a state made up of states, that was almost exclusively accepted. Still, simultaneous with Hegel, in 1802 the old Pütter explained the German Empire as a "*regnum divisum in plures respublicas plane diversas, quae tamen adhuc unitae sunt in modum reipublicae compositae*" [the kingdom was divided into many distinct republics, which, however, were still united in the form of a composite republic]. That this view of the Empire was taken up without exception is all the more noticeable in that the general doctrine of the state was otherwise in no way compatible with the concept of *civitas composita* [composite state]. Rather, it remained standing on the ground of the strict idea of sovereignty under international law, stemming from Pufendorf's formerly developed concept for the Empire of *systema civitatum* [system of states] of even if one – Schlözer

– considers that such an authority-less union of states without the right of majority, into which, according to Pufendorf, the German Empire would transform itself "at an unstoppable pace and as if by itself," and thus would not hold up in the world of actuality. It was now also Pütter who, through the three slender volumes of his *Historical Development of the State Constitution of the German Empire*[8] tried to revive an interest for the national antiquities of the state in the educated circles. It was precisely from this work that Hegel drew a good portion of his knowledge, but also merely knowledge.[9] Hegel could not adopt the comfortable confidence in the vitality and indispensableness of the ancestors, which was expressed by Pütter in his fading book in an homage to "Joseph, George and Friedrich Wilhelm." And when Pütter earnestly leaves the future of the Empire to the discretion of divine foresight, which "until now has visibly guarded over our nation,"[10] Hegel could only ridicule this call for a "special divine Providence." In general, one has to keep the entire status of contemporary scholarship on the state laid out here before one's eyes. One has to view the reference books, which in these dying years of the Empire still discuss its claims to Burgundy and Arelat[11] or the placement of the Kaiser above all princes of Christianity, in that they gave the Imperial war constitution a modest little place at the end of the book.[12] One has to keep all of this in mind in order to perceive the cutting sharpness of the statement "Germany is no longer a state" with which Hegel intended to open his work, and in order to appreciate what it meant when, at the very beginning he dealt with the armed forces, even before the usual section on territory.

But admittedly, it would be a mistake if we intended to bring Hegel's manuscript in too close a relation to the learned knowledge of the state of the time. Always anew, it does away with "the" teachers of constitutional law. The manuscript presents itself as a pamphlet and wants to be seen and judged as a pamphlet.[13] Indeed, if one had said about the Württemberg manuscript from 1798 that it was the sole word in those proceedings that pointed candidly to the seat of evil, in the end one cannot make the same claim for the text on *The German Constitution*. For the daily banter of the times between the Congress of Rastatt and the Principal Conclusion of the Extraordinary Imperial Delegation cannot be said to lack candidness. But Hegel's manuscript stands out from the scholarly literature through its unjuridical and powerfully uninhibited tone. At the same time, it is in a good sense more scholarly, richer with historical connections and general relationships, than any of the writings of the day that I had before me. And, as far as I can see, in its suggestions for reform, it stands completely alone. For me, immediate influences from the writings of the day appear to run over into it even less than from the scholarly works. What remains after this double exclusion is the impact of the age, the living present, which pulls genius into its stream before it is paralyzed by textbook formulas and certainly before it seeps away into the broad expanses of the writings of the day. But with this we would be thrown in our conclusion back upon the personal history of our hero, for we had left him precisely with this decision for unification with the "age"– to be "not better than the age, but this at its best." How this unification now occurs within the region of the idea of the state and at the same time how the last lingering tones of that highly personal conception of the state as fate, in which the meta-personal conception of the state came to a breakthrough, how these became concentrated in the brazen building of the state as power – that is now to be told.

To begin, the presentation will not commence with the part of the manuscript entitled "Concept of the State," but rather with the original version of this section, which most likely comes from the winter between the move from Frankfurt to Jena.[14]

Germany, this is certain for Hegel, has lost the right to still call itself a state. "A group of people can only be called a state when they have unified themselves in general in communal defense of their property [...] the establishment for this defense is state power; this must be enough in part to work against internal and external enemies, in part to preserve itself."[15] In our draft, in which Hegel is on the whole content with the simple arrangement that the state is power, and for now only power, he is still wrestling much more strongly than in the final version with the difficulty of the connection of the individual to this state purpose and to this state. Certainly: "Every individual wishes [...] to live in the safety of his property by means of the state."[16] But from such a wish it is very far to the insight, that it really comes down to him, the individual, down to his decisive input: "The power of the state is something that for him is present outside of himself, he allows this thing found outside of himself to care for him, as he cares for himself."[17] And thus, the state must "preserve itself against the isolating drive of each and everyone."[18]

This is a strong sentence, probably with an intentionally pointed critique of the "isolating drive of all" directed towards Rousseau's *volonté de tous*. And so, Hegel initially arranges the state as a power in opposition to the individual; the concept of the state as power allows its own origin, already known to us, to shine through once more. Then, after a quick side-glance to the meaning of the internal administration of justice and the meaninglessness of its counterpart in the external life of the state, namely in the contracts of the state, it directly proceeds further on to the bare version of the concept of the power-state, from which Hegel wishes to proceed: the power of the state to preserve itself against other states, "the power of war and what is related to this."[19] Everything in political life receded in comparison to this. "No other branch of connection to a whole, not the legal constitution, not religion, etc., makes up the essence of the state as does communal defense, the ability to uphold its independence against foreign states."[20] In a broad presentation it is proven from within the political actuality of Europe that in the end it doesn't matter for a state if legal unity prevails, if there exists regional or provincial differences in contributions to the debts of the state, if within the state there are still other justified levy recipients beside it. The feudal constitution showed how the state could still be very powerful without state levies and under the right conditions the state could support itself alone in its land-domain ownership, the latter of which was a recognized right in Hegel's homeland. And finally, the powerful Austrian and Russian monarchies or even England with its regions in Wales show that in our age, in contrast to the city-states of antiquity, it is unimportant if "with regard to customs, the way of life, languages, and so on, [...] a loose or absolutely no connection" occurs.[21]

On this point the draft leaves us in a bind, and thus we may also give pause to our considerations for a moment. It is not difficult to name what we have seen. Before us stands the state of the eighteenth century with its fresh willful power, with its indifference towards the task of a state unity carried through to the end, its underestimation of national drives and its lack of understanding for the spiritual powers which unfold in national life. "Power, power and once again power" is written above the entrance to this structure [Gebäude] of the state. All internal diversity of political life and all spiritual wealth of national life disappear, for the blinded glance of the thinker, in the light of this sun. There seems to be no notion in him of that which he almost simultaneously shapes into a philosophical doctrine: that this wealth, coldly shoved to the side, is the heart from which warm blood could flow into the veins of the Leviathan.[22] The task of "a unification with the age" appears to be strictly, indeed too strictly carried out. Too strictly – for the age already carried in its lap new political ideas which were to break up the old forms and put them together anew. And it would be a mistake if one thought that, in his striving to master "the age," Hegel had only held onto that which was already overripe in it. He also knows to rediscover in the lap of the age the fermenting ideas of freedom that had once almost exclusively dominated his view of the state. These also receive a place in the new image of the state. Admittedly, he is not very successful in internally connecting them with the dominant concept of the state as power. Ununited as within the age itself, the old and the demand for the new lay side by side. The philosopher acts as a faithful mirror for this unsettled condition and, therefore, a valuable witness for the backward-glancing scholar.

It is not surprising that nothing more shines through from the former limitation of the state to the protection of human rights. Nonetheless, rights such as these are still discussed in great detail. And indeed, Hegel adjoins these considerations to his view on the triviality of all that which remains untouched by the state's essence as power by making reference to the opposite of his idea of the state in the "theories of the state that are posed in our days by pretend philosophers and teachers of human rights, [which] have been partially realized in monstrous political experiments." There, "with the exception of the most important things – language, education, customs, and religion – everything else that we have excluded from the necessary concept of political authority is subjected to the immediate activity of the highest political authority."[23] Against whom is this short-fall directed? With respect to the monstrous political experiments, clearly the administrative despotism of the new French state is meant. With the phrase "pretend philosophers and teachers of human rights," the young philosopher is aiming at a more proximate target. A comparison with a similar shortfall in the text written before July 1801, *The Difference Between Fichte's and Schelling's System of Philosophy*,[24] shows that he is thinking of none other than Fichte, who had recently departed from Jena. Fichte sketched out a rational state in his "Foundations of Natural Right," in which, according to a passage mentioned by Hegel, "the police more or less know where every citizen is at every hour of the day and what he is up to."[25] There, in a long footnote, Hegel mocks Fichte's individual suggestions for currency exchange and coinage. Through this shortfall, the pamphlet's concept of the state now experiences an internal shift whereby the elevated position of power, the indifference of all that does not evidently benefit it, receives a new sense. Things that seemed unimportant until now become meaningful; a state-free sphere circumscribes itself within the power state.

State authority must "leave to the freedom of its citizens what is not necessary for its purpose, [namely, ] to organize and maintain authority for its internal and external security." Indeed "nothing [should] be holier [for it] [...] than to grant and protect the free actions of the citizens in such things, with no regard to benefit, for this freedom is holy in itself."[26] One almost imagines that one is hearing the young Humboldt. The individual turns against the state's imperiousness and at present seems only to have declared the state as indifferent towards the inner life of the nation in order to now declare, inversely, that this inner life is indifferent and free with regard to the state. At the same time, compared to Humboldt's concept of freedom from 1792,[27] there is in this concept something more and something less. Something less: he does without the spiritual glimmer which overlays Humboldt's concept. Rather, Hegel's animosity against the "basic prejudice that the state is a machine with one single spring"[28] has a moral-satirical tone. He accuses this state of "unfree jealousy" and "ignoble carping" and whose model, in addition to the French republic, he above all designates as Prussia. One wanted that "in the entire state every bit of earth that nourishes it would be led to the mouth in one line, would be investigated, calculated, reported and commanded by the state and law and government."[29] And something more, compared to Humboldt: in that Hegel delineates a state-free sphere within the state, he does not allow the state to count merely as a necessary evil within its own domain, but observes it with great and calm acknowledgment. So, it is no surprise if now the free individual is not perceived in complete separation from the state – which would mark the condition of "barbarism" – but rather, if not for their own sake, then indeed for the sake of the state, that they take part in the state.

Admittedly, "with the size of the present state," a direct participation of all individuals is a thoroughly impossible ideal. Conversely, to be able to calmly tolerate the self-governance "of the subordinate systems and bodies" – "estate, city, village, and commoners" – is an advantage of the old hereditary monarchy.[30] And if the state must also respect and protect this freedom, "without all regard to utility," then as far as it does no harm, the state thereby also finds its own advantage. Many administrative costs are removed from it by the special councils, which, incidentally, in contrast to the state, can honorarily occupy many positions. In that way, then, only those involved spend money, and unnecessary expenses do not easily accrue. And finally, in participating in the general affairs through one's own will, there will arise a contented spirit and "the free, self-respecting sense of self."[31] The people must not feel that they are being treated merely "with reason and according to necessity," which is also more surely achieved through self-governance than through the patronizing wisdom of a government, but rather they should be treated above all with "confidence and freedom," for trust will inspire trust.[32] "The difference is infinite: whether political authority institutes itself such that everything it may count on is in its own hands, and that also because of this it can count on nothing else, or if in addition to that which is in its hands, it may also count on the free devotion, the sense of self and the self-striving of the people – an all-powerful, insurmountable spirit, which that hierarchy chased away, and which has its life only there where the highest political authority leaves as much as possible to the citizens' own conduct of affairs."[33] We feel ourselves suddenly displaced from the milieu of the young Humboldt's *The Limits of State Action* into the world of Prussian reform. And if we look more closely, we can recognize the manner in which this occurs. Hegel certainly sees that the state, supported "by the more free and unpedantic spirit" of the people can become "infinitely strong."[34] However, that the individual, through participation in the state, does not merely become "happy,"[35] but rather – to use the words of the mature Humboldt – "becomes more ethical in himself and achieves a higher validity for his occupation and individual life,"[36] Hegel seems to still barely notice this more ethical than political side of the relation, even if we desire to hear in the words "free and self-respecting feeling of the self" a soft intonation of these notes.

In that we know the personal origin story of this conception of the state, the question arises with regard to how it fits into a general history of ideas. We looked for the source of the group of thoughts just presented, that worship of power in itself, in the state idea of Absolutism. One may also remember that Hegel knew Machiavelli and that he cites Frederick the Great's sentences on the non-binding character of international treaties.[37] And here one may also think of Hobbes[38] and Spinoza.[39] On the level of freedom within his view of the state, some things point us back to the years in Bern, but the difference from then is that the freedom of the individual is now only a constraint on the state and no longer its purpose. Also in Bern, according to a statement by Rosenkranz, there would likely fall the beginnings of an enduring interest in the writings of Benjamin Constant.[40] As for the manuscripts from Bern, the influence of Constant upon them is, chronologically, not a possibility. Later on, Constant's stance against the reestablishment of the monarchy could have perhaps strengthened Hegel's republican sentiment, which still suffused both political writings from 1798. The guiding idea of Constant's first political period – lawfulness and not arbitrariness – whose representation ultimately drove him from France and with which he began his historical calling of mediating between Rousseau and the French liberalism of the next century, finds its counterpart with Hegel when, in the later version of the pamphlet, it is said that laws come between the personality of the monarch and the individual, insofar as, through the individual act of the monarch as law not only the individual, but rather all are affected, the individual is not oppressed. With Rousseau, the unconditional arbitrary freedom of the "general will" is justified in that it is "the will of all." In similar fashion, and yet differently, Hegel positions the will that proceeds from "all" as the law that connects to "all." According to Hegel, the justification of the state over and against the individual reads: "The contradiction that the state is the highest authority and that individuals are not oppressed by it is resolved by the power of the laws."[41] And finally, what Hegel brought forth in favor of local self-governance conceptually moves partially in line with Montesquieu.[42] Several remarks show that Hegel, very generally, had in mind conditions of prerevolutionary Europe, rather than exclusively those in England: low levels of jurisdiction, rights of city administration, churches, and caring for the poor – everything that Absolutism more or less allowed to persist.[43] This much need be said on the approximate context on which the thought of freedom in the state here rests for Hegel.

More challenging will be determining how German-idealistic ideas merged with Jacobian-absolute ideas as these came into historical importance in the age of Prussian reform. Of course, the entity of Württemberg's estates is not to be considered here. Rather, one could point towards Hegel's interest in the English Parliament. At that time in Germany, Hegel was not alone in this interest which, as we know, was subject to critique. It suffices, in this regard, to name Rehberg and Brandes. Hegel's fellow countryman, Spittler, also praised the English constitution. Spittler's ideal of a constitutional state as a product of historical development was actualized in the English constitution, which gradually "changed from a feudal system into a successfully developed constitution of a free people." Hegel also adopted from his reading of Montesquieu the derivation of the representative system from the "Germanic forests" through the mediation of the feudal system, yet first disposing of Voltaire's mockery of it.[44] Yet if one asks if for an observer viewing England the coupling of freedom and power could so easily have arisen in the passing of years, then it would certainly have to be denied, precisely for a time of such difficult internal pressure. In the end it is likewise to be accepted for Hegel – and of course also no less difficult to prove in detail – as with the men of the Prussian reform, that the connection of national power politics with ideas and phrases of freedom, which at that time experienced its high point in France, also somehow affected him despite all his objections to the new French state. For us, in that we have followed the internal development of his ideas, these somewhat arbitrarily placed questions regarding external and general "influences" come less into view.

Here, we again get a deeper explanation from viewing the sources themselves. It was apparent how easily both main groups of thought, those of state power and those of freedom, went together. It was above all apparent how both times the thinker really put his foot on the threshold of the political nineteenth century, albeit without crossing over this threshold. The national soul was still withheld from the power-state, while the individual human is still granted entrance into the state but solely for the sake of the power of the state. The ethical importance of the union of the state and the individual intoned, at most, only quietly. Here as there, Hegel was still too strongly – and too consciously – biased toward his own age. Both biases were indeed internally connected: both times it was the soul, that of the people as well as of the individual, which had not yet struggled to open the path to the state. The path for the soul in Hegel's doctrine of the state is opened only slowly, and to put it bluntly, never completely. In the following years, he labored in the difficult task of thought and observation for the sake of opening up this path. Figures of a philosophy of state, often of almost the most shocking greatness and strangeness of form, marked the stopping points on his path. Precisely now, almost incidentally and only shortly after first composing the concept of the state in the critique of The German Constitution, does there appear the first of these testimonials of his efforts towards conceiving an internally unified image of the state, one inclined towards the spirit of the age. In the publication The Difference Between Fichte's and Schelling's System of Philosophy,[45] with which Hegel, even before his habilitation, introduced himself into a philosophy-infused Jena in 1801, one can recognize Hegel's own ideal of the state in his comments with respect to Fichte's contested ideal of 1796.

According to Hegel's accusation, Fichte, in how he built up the community of people on the self-limitation of the individual, "negated [...] every truly free, of-itself infinite, and unlimited, that is, beautiful, inter-relationship of life." For "the community of the person with others must [...] not be seen as a limitation of the true freedom of the individual, but rather as an expansion of the same."[46] This is reminiscent of the earliest of Hegel's papers, wherein the student of the Tübingen Stift saw in the Greek folk spirit's proliferation of bonds that shackled it to nature not a limitation, but an expansion, of its essence. Yet then it was not the state, but rather only the bonds of cultural life that were being considered. But now Hegel fixes his glance on the community of the state, and the following sentence actually provides the motto of the philosophy of state for the following years: "The highest community is the highest freedom."[47] This is the embryonic thought that Hegel will henceforth draw upon in seeking to make the state, which was once fate and became power, into something ethical. What does freedom mean for him here? "Through a truly-free community of living relations, the individual has relinquished his indeterminacy (that is: his freedom)." Hegel now calls freedom, that same freedom that earlier Fichte and Hegel himself had granted the state coercive force to protect, he now calls this freedom indeterminacy! "There is," Hegel continues, "freedom in [a] living relation alone in so far as it contains the possibility to give itself up and to enter into other relations"[48] – a sentence that is illuminated if one remembers that second introduction to the text on *The German Constitution* from Frankfurt, which proceeds from the two forms of dissatisfaction with the present. In that text, for humans who embraced that idea, that is, those who recognized the desire to attack fate externally as foolish, redemption was promised in the notion that fate turns in upon itself. In this way, history became the tool, indeed more than a tool: it became the essence of freedom. This is the only way to understand it if the freedom of living relations is conceived of as the possibility of the entire relation being sublimated, being changed. It is a very delicate concept of freedom and, with regard to its scientific meaning, closely related to that concept of philosophy of history developed by Schelling in 1800 of the "neither free nor unfree, but rather *absolutely* free and for this reason also necessary" action, which Savigny later built into the foundation of the Historical School of Law.[49] But here, on his own initiative, Hegel takes the step that Schelling had not taken at that time, and which, soon emulated by Schelling, perhaps decisively determined Savigny's concept of a folk. Where Schelling had only seen a relationship between humans and history, Hegel inserts the state directly in the middle. For Schelling, this only came up in 1800, at the distantly dawning end of history in the Kantian configuration of the "universal legal constitution." That Schellingian action of individuals in history that was "neither free nor unfree, but rather *absolutely* free" is already actualized for Hegel in its relation to the state, in the non-arbitrary ordering of the individual in the "living relationship," in the entirely free, self-transformative, ethical essence of the state. The state is "the true infinity of a beautiful community" in which "laws are made expendable through customs, the extravagances of unsatisfied life through holy enjoyment and the transgressions of oppressive strength through possible activity for great objects.[50] And if we still doubt how we are to name this image of the state, then we gain certainty from the sentence where Hegel describes the "self-formation into a people" as the "most complete organization" that reason could give itself and demands of this people that it be "the organic body of a communal and rich life."[51] This is Hegel's first attempt to inwardly fuse the pieces of the image of the state which are falling apart in the text on *The German Constitution* into the concept of a national state organism.

And he again brusquely emphasizes here the meta-legal dignity of this state and fights against the "*fiat justia pereat mundus*" positioned so highly by Kant, which claims: right must come to pass, even if therefore trust, desire and love [...] are destroyed.[52]

From the sentence last referred to, we can easily find our way back to the critique of *The German Constitution*, which is much more sober in its concept of the state. Here the almost continuous theme is the fight against the violation of the idea of the state by private right. As with the introduction to the major manuscript of 1801/02, which is most likely from the beginning of 1801 and thus stands chronologically in close proximity to the text just discussed, the critique begins powerfully. Its basis is a transcription of the oldest introduction from Frankfurt. It inquires into the "peculiar principle" of German constitutional law[53] and finds it very natural – as already in that draft from the beginning of 1799 – that the newer teachers of constitutional law gave up trying to comprehend the German constitution and that they merely describe imperial law.[54] It can henceforth be seriously comprehended only historically: from the German character, from its "drives toward freedom," its "tenacity in particularity."[55] The strongly colored painting of this character, which Hegel had still sketched in that earliest draft entirely out of the passionate after-feeling of suffering consciously and with will in the solitude of self, goes almost unaltered into the new version. Only now, corresponding to the liberation from that inner darkness that had since come to pass, the tragic element in the relation of humans to the world fades away and the "suffering" of the whole weakens to "become limited."[56] From the original character and its self-willed action there forms "circles of authority over others [...] with little limitation of that which one calls political authority."[57] And finally, the present condition is formed, where constitutional law is nothing but an "herbarium of the most diverse private rights" or at least "constitutional laws acquired in the manner of private right"[58] and where the German Empire is in the right "like the empire of nature in its productions, unfathomable in greatness and inexhaustible in smallness,"[59] and its constitution "the sum of rights, which the individual parts have taken from the whole," or the "justice which carefully assures that no authority remains for the state."[60] Just as the "unlucky manner with which war is waged" was indeed entirely in accordance with constitutional law.[61] *Fiat justitia pereat Germania* – as Hegel mocks the hated saying again and again – would have to be the inscription on this structure of right [Rechtsgebäude], this "system of right against the state."[62] Hegel wanted to add the older section on state and power, which we already discussed, to the end of these deliberations on state and right, so as to show the different components of state power in thoroughly separate treatments and that something as such does not exist in Germany, to show that Germany is "no longer a state." It would lead too far astray to follow these remarks individually. The basic idea remains the rift between formal right and actual power. Every means to make this rift urgent is welcomed by the pamphleteer: at times historical declarations on the connection between present conditions and the original character of the folk; at times conceptual developments on the incompatibility of the general idea of the state with rigidly upheld particular rights; and at times harsh mockery. And so he goes down the row: the imperial army, the finances of the Empire, the results of the Imperial Empire since 1648, the legal constitution, the religious conditions in their development since the schism in the church, fiefdom, and the body of estates.

The closer Hegel approaches the suggestions for reform that are intended to make up the conclusion of the text, the more precisely will we follow him once more. After he had recognized in fiefdom, this predecessor of a representative constitution, the new political "principle" which Germany had brought into the world, he now asks how in the German Empire, where the feudal constitution had not advanced to a modern state, the result had been its decay and disintegration, and comes thus to speak of territorial sovereignty. Its pillar of support is not right, but rather power, and most of the time not its own, but rather that of foreign countries. "Richelieu had the rare fortune of being seen as the greatest benefactor of that state for whose greatness he laid the true foundation, as well as for that state at whose cost this came."[63] That talk is now of him, the great creator of states and his work. However – characteristic of a Hegelian consideration of the past – this was without the evident thought that such a man was missing for Germany. Rather, Hegel takes things up just as they happened and not otherwise: in Germany, as in France, Richelieu brought "the principle, on which they were internally grounded, wholly to fruition," there monarchy, here the formation of a host of independent states.[64] After the counter-example of France, Hegel presents the likeness of Italy, and after the man Richelieu, Machiavelli's book *The Prince*: fate led Italy to the earlier development that completely escaped Germany. For us, the Ghibellines and the Guelphs correspond to the Austrian and Prussian parties in the eighteenth century. The turmoil of the independent states, from which the imperial power had withdrawn, provoked the obsession for conquering from the ruling powers. And so, they experienced the fate of "guilt that pygmies direct upon themselves when they are trampled underfoot next to giants."[65] For a while, through constant partial submission, the larger states could hold off full subjugation, but could not avoid it in the end. From the deep emotions of this condition "an Italian man conceived with cold composure the necessary idea of the salvation of Italy through the union of the same into *one* state,"[66] a man who knew that "burning limbs [...] cannot be healed with lavender water": Machiavelli.[67] Hegel cites the words with which he invokes his prince "to assume [...] the sublime role of a savior of Italy"[68] and then continues: "One can perceive that a man who speaks with the truth of sincerity had neither baseness in his heart nor jest in his head."[69] No, his work "remains a great testimony to the fact that he rejected his age and his own belief that the fate of a people, whose political downfall is closing in fast, could be saved through genius."[70] The sideswipes directed towards the moralizing opinions of the book, especially towards Friedrich's "school-exercise," as well as towards the view on the ironic intention of the work, are understandable.[71] The entire paragraph is remarkable as being the second appearance of Herder's interpretation of the "Prince," brought into prominence in the nineteenth century by Ranke. With Herder, the drive to measure past times by their own standards was also the guiding thought here. Hegel is led along through the rigorous insight that according to its essence, the state "has no higher duty than to maintain itself."[72] He appeases the remainder of his conscience for freedom with the idea that "freedom should only be possible in the lawful union of a people to a state,"[73] and thus, that it is now time to create this state. The historical circumstances have to then justify the recommended means, for the book is not "one for all conditions, that is, not to be handled as a fitting compendium of moral-political principles. One has to approach reading *The Prince* [...] directly from the history of Italy, and it will not be justified, but rather appear as the most high and truest conception of an authentically political mind of the greatest and most noble sensibility."[74]

Germany shares Italy's fate, but its destiny differs from that of Italy in that, although it came to pass later, it will be decided more quickly; for the present does not tolerate any small states. Thus, the masses did not "remain dismembered, but rather [...] new seeds were formed around which the parts were collected [...] into new masses."[75] And with this, Hegel moves from the critical consideration of 'that which is' towards the possibilities which lay hidden in the lap of 'that which is,' which comes to its highest point in the pamphlet. Towards what will it be aimed? Four political systems appeared in Germany during the last war, by way of which, in general, "more truth came into the relationships between states":[76] the Austrian, the imperial, the neutral (Bayern, Baden, Saxon), and the Prussian. Austria, for which the "weight of infinite rights"[77] is connected to the imperial crown, is at a disadvantage against Prussia, which does not have to take any precautions. But in its inherited wealth, in this "majestic principle"[78] of its politics through which it is capable of "magnanimity,"[79] it also holds an advantage over the new-comer, Prussia. The German estates find themselves between two powers that no longer exist, but earlier had sometimes led the smaller states to Prussia's side. The Protestant concern[80] had become irrelevant since Joseph II, as had the fear of the Jesuits. And the idea of a "universal monarchy" – against which Johannes von Müller considered the Prussian union of princes necessary[81] – had always been an empty word. In their mania for growth, "Austria and Prussia stand at least as equals, even if the former still has some advantages."[82] And so Hegel chooses Austria, which had again turned towards "the great interest of the people."[83] Hegel's disregard for Prussia at the time was in no way universal; on the contrary, in the preceding years Prussia's coming domination was only infrequently mentioned. The reason for his partisanship is, then, noteworthy enough: even if, since the Revolution, public opinion had become suspicious towards "shouts of freedom" and towards "anarchy," it also became "deeply embedded, that the people must participate in the most important affairs of a state."[84] Without a "representative body," which "most German states possess," that "concedes part of the government's levies, but especially the extraordinary ones to the monarch," "freedom [is] no longer thinkable."[85] This basic principle "has become part of common human sense."[86] And because the Austrian states now have landed estates, which just recently granted the monarch special contributions

to the war, this German freedom – "this" here standing in opposition to
the old "liberty"– will search in its interest for protection from a state
that is itself based upon this system. The despotically assembled Prussia,
whose landed estates have lost their meaning, this "leathery spiritless
state" with its "complete lack of scientific and artistic genius," this Prussia, "whose strength one cannot account for according to the ephemeral
energy by way of which a single genius knew how to raise it up for a
time,"[87] cannot protect "with a highly attuned interest, what is truly
enduring in this age."[88] "No Prussian war can any longer [...] count as a
German war of liberation."[89]

But how could the uniqueness of a collection of individual states,
which has already been "universally nested in the spirit of the people,"[90]
now be overcome? One has to inspire the landed estates with interest for
Germany again but allow them to help make decisions and participate.
"A manner of participation in the general affairs would have to be created for the estates."[91] Here Hegel turns to practical suggestions. Above
all, one thing and one thing alone is necessary: a "state power led by a
sovereign with participation of the parts," so that "the German people
would again come into relation with the emperor and the Empire."[92] In
carrying out this thought, Hegel combines sweeping innovations with
the careful preservation of whatever is somehow able to be preserved. All
military should be put under control of the emperor, the princes acting
as born generals. The costs would be allocated annually by the general
landed estates, which, however, would not have to be composed of the
existing landed estates, because certain lands do not have estates and the
very small ones could not come up with the cost of a representative.
Rather, on the basis of the new division of the military, to be formed
independently of the existing territorial boundaries, they could be chosen according to the number of residents. Therefore, a high-profile proposal, which, through the disregard of the borders of the member-states,
even goes above and beyond Bismarck's parliament towards the erection
of a unified state. These general landed estates – here the connection
to the historically given becomes visible – would then be connected
with the city bank of the parliament. The disparity that the smallest cities of the Empire would then have a vote could be avoided by spreading
out their right to vote onto the surrounding land. The canton of knights
would send their representatives to the college of princes. The latter and

the electoral college would be transformed into a kind of upper house following the English example, in which the rulers themselves would have to appear, possibly also represented by princes or the most distinguished vassals and would vocally advise and vote – a thought that was significant for Friedrich Wilhelm IV and in 1870 for the crown prince: "the talents and the radiance of the representatives [...] would grant such a royal meeting a sublime position."[93]

But a turning point follows from these suggestions for reform, and this lends this text its entire significance. Hegel expresses already with complete certainty the deep insight into the workings of history, long before Fichte demanded Germanness of the oppressor, that "even if thereby all factions would have gained thereby that Germany would have become one state and even if the need was felt deeply and with certainty,"[94] nevertheless, deliberation will not bring about the event, but rather only force [Gewalt]. "Concept and insight carry along something so mistrusting against themselves, that they have to be justified through force: then the human being will submit to them."[95] The force of a conqueror would have to collect "the common heap of the German people" into one mass, together with its landed estates, which are only filled with a special spirit, and force them "to regard themselves as obedient to Germany."[96] This "Theseus" would have to "have magnanimity" and "grant a share of that, which applies to everyone," that is, to the very people he created. He would need to have enough character "to want to carry the hate with which Richelieu and other great individuals, those who destroyed the characteristics and peculiarities of the people, burdened themselves."[97] Thus, the series which runs from Richelieu to Machiavelli's *The Prince* culminates here in the demand through which Hegel certainly would have reached the intention that his first biographer suspected of him of, namely, to become a German Machiavelli.[98] For his voice would have also, like that of the Italian, at least indirectly "died away without effect,"[99] and only a succeeding generation, one who saw the fulfillment with their own eyes, would have first honored him as the prophet of the nationally unified state.

The unconditional conviction of political thinkers had admittedly also emitted the cry of distress for a magnanimous tyrant. Already Plato had awaited the actualization of his beautiful state solely from the son of a tyrant. And so, according to Machiavelli, the new birth of a republic, from whose forms spirit has escaped, could likewise only come from a dictatorial authority. The longing for enlightened despots was certainly in the blood of the eighteenth century. However, due to its historical position, Hegel's idea was different from such apparently similar thoughts. This becomes clear when one remembers that Hegel employs the same ideas a few years later against the establishment of a state based on contract.[100] One should recall the dominance that the idea of the contract held over the predecessors of the historical worldview in the eighteenth century. One should also recall that both Kant and Fichte still made the idea of the contract the basis of their works on the philosophy of state. In the swelling choir of dissent that now arose from the most diverse camps against this form of thinking, undisputed for centuries, Hegel had his own particular voice. Hegel's new solution is for a great man who the many obey against their will rather than sealing state contracts among themselves, as this great man has their unconscious will on his side, the will that one day is also to be their own. The attitude of Hegel's position in the coming decade is somewhat explained by the fact that in 1857, Haym can see nothing in this appeal to the superiority of authority, this appeal to the practical genius of the individual over the particular will of the many, other than Hegel's own mistrust with regard to the value of his own suggestions, which Haym also does not value in their scope and importance.[101] It is not mistrust in the value of his thoughts that allows Hegel to promote their forceful actualization, but mistrust in the strength of the insight to actualize itself on its own. How mistaken is it, then, to observe this closing turn only as a kind of appendage, as a "disclosure of doubt." Even if one could question the seriousness of the Italian Machiavelli's closing chapter, this same doubt does not apply to the German Machiavelli. He remains so strictly bound to his view of state power throughout that it will later form the core of his proposed reforms. And the concluding appeal to power, to authority, proceeds with internal consistency precisely from this essence of the state as power.

And to whom is this appeal directed? We tried above to locate it within the movement of the science of the state, yet by no means could we thereby write off the immediate temporal conditionality and tendency. With this we arrive at a question that was not even asked by the older discussions of the text.[102] Dilthey was the first to risk a guess here and looked to recognize the Consul Bonaparte in the conqueror and magnanimous Theseus.[103] What was for Dilthey merely a guess has since been repeated, albeit likely unjustly.[104] The two times Napoleon is mentioned by name in our text[105] already indicate that, besides the strength of the conqueror, Hegel did not ascribe to the Corsican the character of "magnanimity."[106] Yet this was the other part of the equation, which Hegel had found wanting in the "entirely calculating" politics of France, that he then explicitly attributed to Austria's German politics. And above all, how was Hegel – whose goal in this text was entirely certain with regard to how he hoped to unify the future Germany under Austrian rule – how was he to pass the actualization of this task into the hands of that power that Austria had been at war with until recently and whose intentions could in no way be pointed towards a strongly unified Germany, especially compared with the age of Richelieu that Hegel, in this connection, had just discussed so thoroughly? No, if a specific name is to be named, one must look in Austria's camp for the conquering founder of Austria's German dominance. And there is certainly only one person Hegel could have thought of: the victor of Amberg and Würzburg, of Stockach and Zürich, who since Hohenlinden guided Austria in state chancellery and courtly council on as it came up in the future of the all-powerful minister. In the previous years the patriots attached their hopes to the archduke Karl and since then, especially in the German southwest, he long remained the only popular national hero.[107] With regard to the Corsican, if one even still grants him that much magnanimity, a turn towards describing him as a conqueror would have been impossible. And if, in 1802, Hegel had identified the word "conqueror" with a foreigner, then in 1805, given the newly surfaced "indifference of the subjects towards their princes, and then the indifference of the princes to be princes, that is, to hold themselves as princes," he never would have declared that the previously demanded "tyranny" for Germany was "superficial."[108] Indeed, subsequently, the new hereditary Empire of Austria began to visibly withdraw itself from German affairs, while at the same time a wild *ruere in servitium* [rush into service] set in for the future states of the Confederation of the Rhine. Now, more than ever, things were ripe for a French attack. The Germans – he evidently adds sometime later, likely around 1806 or 1807 – have disappeared as a people, because they could not endure tyranny: this is another allusion that clearly shows that, in 1802, he could have only been thinking of a native conqueror. Thus, in

1802, if a specific assumption had to be made, then ultimately the only possibility for the role of "Theseus" would have been the Archduke Karl.

Yet something more general could be alluded to with this passage. Although not explicit, with this conclusion Hegel in fact puts the last touch on the introduction's image of the state. There the state was recognized as power, yet in a certain sense, it was actually still up in the air. There was a certain paleness in those chains of thought, difficult to grasp and yet distinctly perceptible to the reader. One did not see the ground upon which these entities that breathe power, and only power, moved. The closing passage puts an end to this uncertain feeling. With a firm hand, Hegel now moves the state into the gears of history. Of course, it is not yet the philosopher of the state who raises these matters, as they have not yet become cemented into the foundational materials of the concept of the state. In the interim, it was the pamphleteer who spoke the great, conclusive words: "concept and insight must be justified through authority [Gewalt], then the human will subject himself to them." Concept and insight, here those of the writer himself, later for the philosopher, concept and insight in general – and these justified through authority. Here is the watchword of this new doctrine of the state, which taught the coming generation to see within world history the connecting bridge between the realms of spirit and power, between concept and authority.

Of course, the new view of the state required a sacrifice. The passion for historical observation crippled the hands of the seer himself, as the deep infusion from the momentum of the course of history held the thinker spellbound, in the position of the observer. This was distinct from the accusation leveled against him by the leading voice of a later generation. The historical worldview that was the property of this generation, which accused Hegel that he dealt with the misery of the state of the present by resigning himself to quiet observation, made it so that the passion of its first observer could hardly be captured.[109] There really is no need for such auxiliary devices which aim to interpret internal drive through the pressure and counter-pressure of external forces. The final version of the introduction – upon which Haym based his accusation – makes clear Hegel's own relationship to his proposals for reform: yet the internal reconciliation with things that Haym raises is in no way predominant. This is shown through a comparison with the oldest opening of the text, which is partially integrated into the introduction. The deeply painful mood laying over the draft from 1799 – the voice of a mind that "wanted to once more enjoy in an image the weak faith in the fulfillment of his hopes, prior to the total separation from this hope" – this mood has since retreated. The sentences above were already blotted out by Hegel in the draft.[110] Admittedly, during that winter in Frankfurt, Hegel perceived that which he saw, that which weighed upon him personally, as a burden. At that time, he may have wanted to save himself from this pressure by escaping into the dreamland of his hopes. But now things have changed. If he could then bracket his "ever-weakening wishes"[111] solely on the grounds that the principle of separation was perhaps not the only foundational direction of the German state, he has now long overcome such a belief in an unchangeable character that determines the history of a people for all time. He knows that, if such a historical "principle" is "brought to complete fruition," that history can then create something new out of its own womb. The pressure of the world no longer surges across his chest. He has now learned selfless observation. It is this Hegel that will be shown to us by the new introduction.

Germany is no longer a state. It experienced this in the last war. To reflect upon the "spirit" of this experience is "worthy of those […] who do not give themselves over to what happens, but rather recognize the events and their necessity, and distinguish themselves through such a recognition from those who only see arbitrariness and chance for the sake of their vanity so as to convince themselves that they would have carried out everything that happened more cleverly and more success-fully."[112] The value of such a recognition would not be that one learns from it "how one could act better in a future case; for those that act in such a way in these great events that they could manage the same are very few, the others have to serve the events with understanding and insight in their necessity."[113] For whoever makes mistakes through "internal weakness and imprudence,"[114] strengthens, at most through experience, the habit of perpetrating them. But whoever is able, and also "has the external means," to draw benefit from the insight into mis-takes others make, already possesses the insight "which the thoughts of a civilian can do without."[115] Hegel then directs his text towards private citizens, herein very different from the Florentine model, not towards the leaders, not towards "Theseus" himself. He wants to lead private citizens to "understand that which is," by way of which they "serve the events with understanding and insight in their necessity."[116] One cannot forget which violent "events," according to Hegel's expectation, lie ahead of the "general masses of the German people along with their landed estates." More than anywhere, there rules in Germany the vice to place their own concepts and purposes "between the events and the free interpretation of the same."[117] Moreover, the Empire, this thought-state – as it is described with partiality in the manuscript – specifically entices such a pairing of dead concepts and living events. For here the laws have lost their old lives and what is new had not yet been captured in laws or, moreover, old and new life have each gone their own ways, have settled on themselves, "and the whole is in decay, the state is no longer."[118]

A harsh, feelingless denial of will towards the unshakable way of things – this is now Hegel's relationship to his own desires for reform. He is convinced of the correctness of his suggestions. Even more, he believes he is doing nothing but preparing minds for what is certainly coming. That "which is" [was ist], and which Hegel would like to guide us to understand, contains not merely the shadowy old Empire, but rather the "new life" as well, and the draft from 1799, which lies here at the direct basis, still knew nothing of this. And the "new kernels" of both major states, one of which will absorb the fall of the Empire in ruins, also belongs, along with the people's longing for participation in the state, to that "which is." Hegel hopes his text will help prepare for this development. The "understanding of that which is," moreover, already implies, coming from Hegel, something of that revolutionary tone which it was later to take on as the "expression of that which is" under the pen of his greatest student, the founder of German social democracy.[119] For Hegel, the underlying tone is already not tranquil perseverance in the old conditions, but rather an unlimited trust in the course of history and its strength to allow for something entirely new. Admittedly, the individual, and thus Hegel himself, steps silently to the side of the authoritative force of this process. He himself does not feel called to participate, but in doing so also does not relinquish the forces of the past to the present, but rather to the powers that are capable of bringing about the future: to history itself and the great historical personality.

It is not as if Hegel had been entirely safe from the threat of a "unification with the age" directed merely towards completion. As he now turned to the representation of his ideal of the state, while not having the particular designs and possibilities of an actual state before him, he is confronted with a future that, at least in principle, had recently been so clearly revealed to him only to now veil itself again. In light of the newest science, that is, on the basis of the foundational concept of the organism breathing in living beauty, Hegel transfigures [verklärt] a state entity which was to carry away or certainly at least shake up the storms of the coming years everywhere they still existed: the absolute state based on the foundation of a society of estates, which the Protestant Northern Germany, above all Prussia, had shown him. This state, and not as one might think, the Polis, neither the historical nor the Platonic, is the actuality which shines through the dark and heavy thought-images of the "System of Ethicality."

"System of Ethicality" is the name of a manuscript that Hegel must have written down in preparation for the lecture on natural right in the winter semester from 1802 to 1803, probably during the lecture-free summer.[120] It constitutes the first preserved formulation of the part of the system that Hegel later called "Objective Spirit" and which, perhaps more than anything else within the system, opened up new philosophical territory and material for the Idealist movement. We must still attend to the question of whether the manuscript deals only with this specific part of the system. It begins with three levels, ordered more or less into three parts each, in accordance with that familiar form that Kant once introduced as a logical division, which Schiller used to divide history, which was animated by Fichte into the logical procedure of development, and which was suffused with the material of actuality by Schelling at the cost of its internally moved vitality. In that in general this manuscript corresponds methodologically to Schelling, the course of the thinker is not accompanied for Hegel by a movement of things, rather he wanders through them like the well-positioned images of a museum, here comparing, here observing a new one – yet without the rigid images, enlivened by his glance, climbing down off their pedestals, and beginning to dance. In order to reach the object of our interest, we must swiftly follow the philosopher's path until reaching the state, whereby, admittedly, Hegel's own process can hardly be taken into account.

The presentation of ethicality, culminating in the "people," rests on two initial levels. The first consists of those human relations that carry their concealed ground within the completed "ethical totality,"[121] that is, within the people, just as with Schelling nature has its concealed ground within God, whereby the detached individual seems to operate freely within these relations, just as nature appears to exist without God. For the sake of comparison, Hegel also describes this level as the "natural."[122] Natural ethicality begins with the first awakening of the willing I, with "feeling"[123] – need and satisfaction in pleasure – which is followed by the most simple work and its product, including the means which the working human acquires: tool and speech.[124] To those who are thereby lifted above the moment through language, there arises work that no longer merely serves the moment of need and its tool, the machine.[125] As language arises for him from the lowest level of the economy, so now the spiritual tools of a higher economy arise: the legal recognition of ownership in property;[126] becoming mobile in trade[127] and, even more universally, contract.[128] A step further up, and one comes to the monetary economy of exchange.[129] There emerges here, observed only according to form – what one would call "sociological" today – the relation of master and servant, wherein it still remains internally unfounded who is master and who is slave, which is different than with the state.[130] The ethicization, the internal necessity which in general is already possible within this world of "natural ethicality," gains that relation, together with everything that preceded it, in the family.[131] To be sure, this is also bound by strong chains to the dark ground of the natural. For it, the true ethicality of the community of the people is likewise only a secret background. Compared to the depth of this ethical life, the family is only a superficial appearance. Nevertheless, within the substructure of ethicality, the family is closer to ethicality than anything that came before. Family is something that persists within the eternal change of generations, just as ethical life persists within the whole of the people.

Until now, individuality, particularity was the ruling determination. The universal, the whole, was only a secret root, nowhere visible itself. Negation of individuality now emerges as the basic determination of the second level. Here, the "universal" also does not come to light in visible form, as it does in the end with the state. The state resembles the world of "natural ethicality" in that in the latter a diversity of human relations is also developed, albeit without unity. The world of the second level, titled "The Negative or Transgression,"[132] points to the state insofar as it negates self-satisfied particularity, albeit not in order to confer upon particularity a higher ethical life. Hegel then develops the connection of life, transgression, conscience, and reconciliation, which he had already done in Frankfurt, yet within this account, in contrast to before, vengeful justice now also receives a place.[133] From purposeless rage,[134] transgression proceeds from the consciously-purposeful transgression of property,[135] to murder,[136] which really applies to the whole, and then peaks with the duel,[137] and ultimately in the highest duel, that of ethical totalities: war.[138]

Here, at the height of transgression, we stand at the entrance to absolute ethicality. If we apply the highest point for each level, hereby in the sense of Hegel, then we can say: the philosopher builds up the essence of the state from family and war. The family is the hearth presiding over the feelings which issue from and lead back to the individual; war is the negation of the particular being of the individual: above both rises the "idea of absolute ethicality," whose "intuition is an absolute people."[139] An absolute people – not an absolute nation. For Hegel, "people" [Volk] means something like nation-state [Staatsnation] at that time, in contrast to "nation," by which he means cultural-nation [Kulturnation].[140] This use of language creates a bridge between the concept of the state in the text on The German Constitution and the concept of the state in the system. Here as there, the state does not rest upon the "nation" – which, moreover, people and state can outlive – does not rest upon the "folk spirit" [Volksgeist] of the Historical School, but upon the "people" [Volk]. The strength of the political idea has made the "folk spirit" of the time in Tübingen, which stands mistrustfully over and against the intervening power of the state, into its servant. And, just as in the text on The German Constitution, this state is built up upon weaponry. Already the two-part prelude, which ascended ahead of its appearance in the system, closed with the sounds of war: "The equality before which the side of right [...] disappears, is war" with its "absolute disquiet" in which the "deserter," Mars, "constantly goes from one side to the other" until the opponents again move away from each other in peace.[141] And because war is constituted as defense, the presence or absence of war-like virtues generally determines the outline of this state structure.

The people, the political community, is, of course – different than in the text on The German Constitution – more than a mere "quantity" that "is formed by a common defense and political authority."[142] There, Hegel thought to show that the Empire, even in its most modest demands, could no longer count as a state, even if it could still be called so, and he tried to define it as such. Here — as already hinted at already in the publication from the summer of 1801 — he sketches out the image of the perfect state. And here he rejects directly from the beginning, like Aristotle and Cicero, the concept of mere "quantity."[143] This people is "not a relationless quantity nor a mere majority," rather "the connection of a quantity of individuals." As mere "quantity," the people would stand "foreign" over and against the individual rather than "having reality for its consciousness, being one with it, and having power and authority over it." As mere "majority," the people would be a multitude which loses itself in the undetermined rather than a circle closed in upon itself.[144] And within this people there is no equality of individuals, no "equality of civility." Instead, the equality that is at work here is the unity — "identity" — of all in the divided whole, wherein they do not lose, but rather find, themselves. The equality presents itself precisely "in the consciousness of particularity."[145] This ethicality then, this "living independent spirit," which appears as a Briareus with a myriad of eyes, arms and the other limbs, each of which is an absolute individual"[146] — this ethicality is actualized in the perfect state. Thus, Hegel now weds the state and the individual soul with one another. What is merely a faint echo in the critique of the German constitution, namely that through the state the citizen can attain a "free, self-respecting feeling of self,"[147] has moved to the center, and done so with such force that all ethicality external to the state becomes inferior. This doctrine of virtues appears in this system first in the doctrine of the state: the content of morals "is completely within natural right."[148] The "virtues" of the individual are something impermanent in the face of the ethicality revealed by the state.[149]

What applies to "ethicality" is actualized in the "people." Each of the three ways in which ethicality can position itself in relation to individual virtues must therefore "organize for itself, be an individual [Individuum] and take on a configuration": the people divides itself into estates.[150] Just as nature generates a realm of configurations, so too does ethicality. That this comparison rules over Hegel becomes visible in what he proposes here. Admittedly, in nature one recognizes the necessity of such individuation because one admits there the incompleteness of each individual appearance. Within the ethical, however, each individual is supposed to be a whole, and not merely a part that first becomes a whole when joining the others. The objection cuts deeply. Precisely for the sake of inner universality and wholeness, which is set as the goal of humans, in those days the most noble minds in Germany attacked such incompleteness in the old state's composition of estates. It was also the philosophical task of our thinker to fuse that same inner fullness of personality with the power-nature of the state, each of which in the text on *The German Constitution* he had only placed next to each other. How will he justify the division of estates there? They are, so he explains, not separated from each other in the sense that each is somehow incomplete until they first appear as a whole to the synthesizing observer. Rather, each estate is a "totality" and it carries "the others [...] in it,"[151] and does so not only in connection to a part of the whole, but rather to the whole itself in all its splendor. Only the manner and meaning, not the content of this connection, is different for each estate. Unlike Plato, for whom particular virtues fit each estate, here there is rather the differentiated order of the same entirety of virtues – and moreover an overall differentiated ethical level than differentiated, individual virtues formed as working parts. As far as one can tell, this is only a secondary consequence, not as with Plato the root cause of the separation of estates. Thus, the individual, "too poor" "to comprehend [ethicality] in its entire reality," finds his ethical completion in that he belongs to an estate." Only because of this is he "a true individual and a person."[152]

Hegel's conception of the division of the state into estates is strikingly innovative, that is, as new in the relation of the estate to the individual as in the connection of the estate to the state. To think here of Plato or Aristotle actually allows only for the formulation of the question, but nowhere the answer. And we are just as far away from the view of a state with a substructure of community-estates, according to which Frederick the Great ruled his Prussia and which essentially rested, more Platonistically than Hegelian, on the thought of a division of labor. Here, the fullness of life of the new philosophical spirit created much deeper possibilities of understanding. But of course, as far removed as the form and meaning of this doctrine of the state and estates is from the age of Frederick, the content corresponds almost entirely to the great king's still existing state.

Hegel's state is comprised of three estates [Stände]: nobility, citizen, and peasant. Within nobility, the "absolute estate,"[153] the ethicality of the state is truly embodied in actuality. It is not the sum of all virtues, but rather the sublimity over all particular virtues. The rule of this estate is not "love of the fatherland and people and laws," but rather "the absolute life in the fatherland and for the people."[154] The sublimity over all "particularity" finds its expression as "bravery" and its work in the destruction of a particular living thing, the enemy: this noble is a noble of war.[155] Yet this is not just any fight. For example, the "absolute ethical" activity" is not the hate-filled "war of families against families,"[156] but rather, since the ethical itself is "people," so the enemy can be "only an enemy of the people and must itself be a people."[157] In such wars hate is impersonal and the rage of war is only a passing rush. "Death goes into the universal just as it comes out of the universal [...] the pistol is the invention of [...] impersonal death, and it is national honor which drives it, not the injury of an individual."[158] This estate must be lifted above all individual work, which is bound to things; it is only suited for the work of war, which destroys individuals, and the training of others for war. Both of the other, lower estates must afford it what it needs. It is "useful" for those others, and above all "in the highest manner," for through its existence it grants them the intuition of the highest ethical life, and with this the participation in this life, which is only accessible to their consciousness. For its own participation − the truth, that this state which comes before their view in nobility is also their "absolute internal essence" − remains hidden to them.[159] If this is the "highest manner" by which the nobility "uses" citizens and peasants, then it also uses them indirectly, as Hegel puts it with dry contempt, "in their own manner." It does so in that it protects property and possession for them and, at least for the second estate, the citizen, spares it from bravery.[160]

We now descend to this estate spared from bravery. "The work of needs, possession and acquisition and property" − nothing but things that cannot become the internal content of life for the individual,[161] who rather must be entangled in ethically meaningless relations of master and servant.[162] But while the state takes up the economy within itself and subordinates it to the right of citizens, the economy receives an ethical "reality," and its bearers, the owners, having thus become an estate and, "acknowledged as universal," are no longer enslaved with their entire personality to the play of economic powers.[163] For this estate, the form under which the virtues of the individual appear is righteousness, just as bravery was for the first. It produces right and also gives equity a voice. It lays the highest value on the preservation of the "empirical existence" of the individual and takes care of the livelihood of the family and of fellow citizens, befitting one's social status.[164] However, everything that it undertakes has a limit: since for it mere life counts as the highest good [Gut], it can thereby be unselfish, indeed sacrificing, albeit "[with] neither the entirety of its possessions nor life."[165] Nevertheless it reaches a kind of ideal height where it sacrifices from its own, whether it is in contribution to the needs of the first estate or for the individual poor and suffering.[166] Admittedly, the "general" sacrifice for the state lacks "vitality," and in "living more" for the poor it lacks "universality."[167] So much for this estate of "relative ethicality," which "cannot be brave."[168]

Finally, there is the "raw ethicality" of the peasant.[169] Like the citizen, the peasant is also assigned to work and acquisition, but in place of the impersonal dependence which economic life brings to the citizen there appears for the peasant a patriarchal relation of dependence. Its activity does not fall under the gears of general economic life like that of the citizen but is, rather, "a great and more encompassing totality," as it is incorporated into what is living itself and leaves nature something to do.[170] The ethicality of the peasant is simple and undivided: "trust" is the form by which its virtues appear.[171] The individual "is not to be moved through understanding – for by this it fears, however fairly, that it will be betrayed – but rather through the entirety of trust and necessity, through external drives that also connect with the whole."[172] Civil law does not approach the peasant, because, in the end, strife is mediated "according to passion and discussion."[173] And on the basis of trust he is "also capable of bravery and may in this work and in the danger of death join the first estate," for to this he dedicates his trust, according to the related undivided manner – the "totality" – which suits the nobleman as well as himself.[174] –

This is how society is arranged in Hegel's state. A nobility which pays no taxes, practices no civil trade, holds the position of officers; a peasantry which, in connection with a patriarchal relation of dependence, follows the commands of noble officers in war, are trained by them in peace, foreign to the life of civil law, directs its work in trusting obedience or is otherwise forced through castigations which "connect to the whole"; a citizenry – acquiring, tax paying, free of military service, strictly separated from the two other estates, a pure spectator over and against political life, with its own civilized ethos foreign to the state. We now have a clearly recognizable portrait of conditions which as a whole could already be familiar to Hegel from his dealings in Frankfurt with Prussian Common Law.

At first glance, it must be confusing that the philosopher eternalizes here a state entity upon whose soulless workings the writer of the pamphlet had also passed such devastating judgment. But we may already recall that the philosopher had left the intellectual circles of the eighteenth century entirely behind him in the way in which he carried out this division of society. Of course, the original image of that which he now placed upon a pedestal was already present in the Prussian state, but unfelt, ungrasped, and therefore without life, and so in truth skies away from his portrait. Similarly, in the text on The German Constitution he had recently acknowledged, with frank disdain for all petty means of justification, the bare power-state of the eighteenth century, which even eighteenth-century thought had perhaps never brought itself to do – even if the great king, who dwelled in equal amounts in both the state and the spirit of the century, admitted, not without regretful gesture, that Machiavelli was right. And similarly, here Hegel found tones of the glorification for the old state, which in the time of his full powers he never would have perceived that way. The new spirit misappropriated the object, but it was nevertheless the new spirit. Actuality still had to change in order that this spirit could find an agreeable object.

The ideas of the state of the pamphlet and of the system visibly connect in the thought that the state is essentially power. The pamphlet represents it conceptually and builds its suggestions for reform upon it, while the system leads it broadly into the particulars of the division of society. Just as in the pamphlet, this side of the state as power is placed over and against all content and goals of civilian life as indifferent, so in the system a high wall is erected between the estates, in that the power of the state is ordered according to war and the estates according to civilian and peasant acquisition. For the third estates, capable of bravery, if also only a vague follower's bravery, this is a wall which can again be broken through. For the citizenry, however, with their specific

purposes and insights, this wall remains firmly upright. Hegel also occasionally acknowledges a special placement of nobility in the text on *The
German Constitution*, also under the condition that there it really fulfills the
duties of the state and cannot simply be content with the pleasures of
its privileges, as were the French nobility, who thereby precipitated the
Revolution.

Freedom and power were connected to each other easily enough in
the image of the state found in the pamphlet. When Hegel now undertook to fuse these elements, it basically happened along the path he
had already traversed in the publication from the summer of 1801. But
above and beyond that universally valid concept of freedom, which sub-
sisted in the mere participation in the free development of the people,
he now, in accordance with the division of the ethical substance into
estates, allowed freedom to have its own coloring within each estate.
In the first, it became the truthful ethical release from all anxiety about
worldly things. In the third, what counted was solely that frail concept
of freedom, which counted for all estates, without the addition of a
freedom specific to this particular estate. Finally, within citizenry, the
unconditional validity of the "empirical existence" of the individual was
added to the common freedom of the life of the people. And here we
again most likely find, admittedly desecrated, the state-free sphere from
the pamphlet, now in the realm of ethicality and no longer as a universal
demand, but specialized into estate and estate customs. And in general,
this is the relation between the two texts. For just as here – in accordance
with the need of our philosopher to configure, to "individualize" – there
has evolved out of a demand that the pamphlet universally imposed on
the citizen of the state the ideal of an estate, so the democratic demands
in general, which the writer of the pamphlet brought against the claims
of the philosopher with an open sense and apt obstinacy, are taken from
the age and completely absorbed into the system. There is no longer any
talk here of the participation of the people in legislation and the approval
of taxes, which was acknowledged there as a demand of the spirit of
the age and sunk into the foundations of the future state. But even if the
democratic demands have been absorbed into the system, they have not
disappeared. They have only changed in the same designated way that
the entire state was changed in the pamphlet. The indirect participation
of all has become the organic "totality" of the whole, which is foreign

to none and in which everyone finds themselves, whether one "lives"
therein – as in the first estate – or whether it is in "viewing" – as in
the two lower estates. Next to the state of the pamphlet, which on all
accounts is still to be viewed as state, there then came the beautiful state
of the system. The pamphlet, in the certain simplicity of its thoughts on
power and in the self-evident connection to existing powers without
concern for theories, in the living individual state as well as in the living
wish of public opinion for political co-activity, this pamphlet was related
to the works of Bismarck, allowing them to appear as nothing other than
fulfilled prophecy. The state ideal of the system has become, according
to its contents, a transfiguration of dying-off conditions. However, in
the light which touched upon that which was descending, there lay the
enlivening powers of a rising political spirit which, reaching out into the
future, would prepare and accompany the work of Bismarck. Between
the demands of the pamphlet and the work of Bismarck there is, at first
glance, a surprising and yet almost coincidental agreement. There thus
runs a subterranean line of development from the system's image of the
state through St. Paul's Church to January 18, 1871.

Until now, we have become acquainted with the state of the system
only in its societal structure. Apparently, Hegel had originally wanted
to separate this part out as a "state constitution" from a second part on
"government,"[175] an opposition which, still unusual then, became popular in the nineteenth century through a shift of meaning as "constitution
and administration." Hegel would have acquired it personally or through
reading from Majer, the constitutional lawyer of Tübingen, who, for his
part, adopted it from Pütter's magnum opus on imperial law. Also here,
Hegel's engagement with the German constitution might perhaps have
influenced the system. This first planned division was to now oppose
the structure of the estates, the "system of ethicality in its repose"[176] to
the "government," which places the reposing system in motion, subordinates the estates to each other and the whole and simultaneously
allows them to come forth in their particularity and thus actually first
makes up the life of the state.[177] But now the change in meaning of the
word constitution [Verfassung] made this division ambiguous. Hegel
recognized that that which was newly called "Konstitution" and which
began to play such an enormous role in political thinking, was not to be
grouped in the sense of Pütter and Majer's division with "constitution,"

but rather with "government," and that it was not related to the resting existence of the people in the state, but rather was the law according to which the state acted against that being at rest.[178] So he allowed the title "The Constitution of the State" [Staatsverfassung] to span over both parts and called that first one, for which he originally wanted to preserve the name constitution, now, in a visible predicament with the technical term coming from the scholarship on the state "Ethicality as System, at rest."[179] The government, if it otherwise represents through its composition the whole of the state together with the tasks into which it divides itself, represents not merely power but, according to the spirit, "is the true constitution [Konstitution]."[180] So according to Hegel's view, the best constitution would be a good system of administration. He rejects the – new French – concept of a constitution as "something crude," where the state as such immediately effects the individual. That which was already rejected in the pamphlet would be "formlessness, and a negation of freedom." That was rejected because freedom "is formed (in der Form), and therein that the individual part, a subordinated system of the entire organism, is self-acting."[181] Thus, the government must divide itself and do so "according to necessity."[182] Thus it collapses into a fixed center point of movement and into the bearers of this movement itself: "absolute" and "universal" government.

The "absolute government" is not somehow one with the first estate. On the contrary, it must be recognized exactly how far it should stretch out its "negation" of the lower estates. "But law is such a recognition."[183] The absolute government thus cannot itself become an estate, rather the "empirical" freedom of all estates, including of the first, must be negated, negated precisely through the limiting law. "This absolute preservation of all estates must be the highest government."[184] And so this highest government is made up of those "who, as it were, have given up real being in an estate and basically live in the ideal, the elders and the priests, who are actually both one."[185]

The elders and the priests – the former from nature, which they will soon enter into, the latter through God, to whom they alone are ordained and so lifted above life and its particularities – are "alone capable of persevering the whole"![186] There, all modern relations seem to get out of hand and the influence of antiquity seems undeniable. Is Haym then correct when he claims that this Hegelian ideal state is drawn "not merely according to the pattern, but almost according to the template of the Platonic"?[187] An antiquating tone is certainly not to be mistaken here. But is this move also supposed to be Platonic? Apparently, Haym is thinking about the famous passages on the necessity that philosophers become kings or kings become philosophers. Because here alone perhaps, if anywhere at all,[188] Plato demands state authority over the estates, including authority over the ruling ones. This would certainly be a meaningful similarity, but then the difference would be even more important. Plato places demands on the "man who is wise and kingly,"[189] because only the philosopher has true knowledge, which, itself raised above the existing laws, is capable of giving the lawless drives of the human being the right direction. But with Hegel there stands on the corresponding place of his state not the wise man, not pure "ethicality," but rather, as he himself says: here at the highest point, where the subject is the preservation of the whole, "ethicality [appears] to have to flee to nature, to the unconscious."[190] Not the philosopher, but rather the priestly old man, he who is above the particularities of ethical existence, above the estate, lifted out and up not by ethicality but by nature or God, he is the reposing middle point of the movement of life in the state. With Plato, a higher ethical will is supposed to rule over the base naturalness of life, to set the law for it. With Hegel, there rises out of the given and "presupposed"[191] higher ethicality of life a pure natural knowledge, which is capable by nature of recognizing that ethicality of the given life – "but law is such a recognition"– and thus is capable of guarding over its preservation. The Platonic philosophers can lower themselves to give a bad world the good law, whereas Hegel's old men preserve and develop the existing best constitution.

But hereby this thought, seemingly eccentric and foreign to the times, fits into the context of the age. It is the Hegelian attempt to solve a task upon which the doctrine of the state of the entire last decade in Germany as in France labored: to protect and develop the constitution through the constitution – to add a "pouvoir constituant" to the constitutionally related forces.[192] The constitutions of the Revolution, in that they wanted to bring ideals of natural right into the actuality of the state, had let a light fall upon the difficulties of the relationship between written constitution and unwritten life. One searched for formulas and arrangements in order to hold both powers in lockstep. That led to the right to amend the constitution, first suggested in 1789 and 1791, but first recognized in 1793, which, according to Condorcet's formulation, established that no future generation could overthrow its laws. It led by convention to Condorcet's idea to constitutionally renew the constitution every twenty years – to change the unruly course of history more or less into a strictly well-timed piece of music. It then subsequently leads in 1795, in connection with Rousseau's "Tribunat," which was to hold the powers of the state in balance, to the idea of an independent administrative body in Siéyès' plan of a "constitutional tribunal," which would simultaneously serve both powers, the powers of preservation and development, holding the constitution of a people as well as that of any other form of life within itself. Siéyès then finally realized this, his favorite concept, in the "senate of preservation" of the consular constitution. Only recently, while observing the Wetzlar Imperial Chamber Court, Hegel was reminded of this point of the consular constitution, as well as of the plan of the Constitutional Court of 1795. It is likely that he now thought of these French ideas and efforts.[193] He expressly recalled the forceful information that Fichte had pondered for the protection of the constitution of his rational state, the "Ephorate,"[194] "old mature men" whose only and "purely negative" power lay therein, that at any moment they could declare the "suspension of the state," through which the government would be placed before the court of the sovereign people.[195] Hegel calls this idea "entirely empty [...] in its negative bearing."[196] This authority is granted the "administration of the government in all branches," since it is supposed to function as commanding and superior "and at the same time be nothing with regard to power."[197] Hegel's absolute government is not a power such that it is all and nothing, but one which assumes the difference of the estates that Hegel originally described as "constitution." It is "law-giving and regulatory where a relation develops that wishes to organize itself separately or where a previously meaningless aspect develops itself little by little in its previous unrestrictedness and begins to become powerful. Above all, it makes decisions in all cases where different rights of systems come into collision and the present time renders them impossible in their positive existence."[198] So it forms, dare we say, an authority which, on the one hand, upholds the estate-based order of the state and, on the other hand, secures the whole of the life of the state in opposition to the independent life of the estates. It preserves the constitution in that it renews the same. Here its contrast to Fichte's Ephorate—and with this the difference between the Fichtean and Hegelian idea of the state — now becomes very clear. The Fichtean Ephorate is the power which appeals to the eternal law of reason, effective within the sovereign people, from those currently in power. Hegel's absolute government aids, precisely in the opposite way, the historical movement, the "present," in its right against the forms of the estate-based order of the state which rest in the womb of ethical reason. There is no further justification for that which Fichte's "people's community" [Volksgemeine] decide. But this highest power of the Fichtean state only then appears when something extreme, an injustice, occurs. Hegel's absolute government, equally raised above all responsibility, is active in every moment; uninterrupted, the life of the state flows forth from it. Both authorities are lifted above all responsibilities and the Hegelian also above all justification and above all responsibility. It can be that because, indeed, it does not establish the constitution anew like Fichte's people, whose declarations always have the strength of constitutional law but, rather, only continuously preserves that which was "presupposed." The people's vote, legal determination, and military force would only take away its "holiness."[199] "It is the immediate priesthood of the most high, in whose sanctum it takes counsel and receives its revelations," it is "divine, sanctioned in itself and not made."[200] Hegel's state concentrates itself into this absolute peak. Unlike Fichte's revolutionary state of 1796, it does not get its right and its justification from the absolute ethical law that stood as an eternal standard next to it, or as eternal good before it, but is itself absolute. From the ethical order of the reposing life of the estates in the state there rises the natural peak, through which the whole first attains "reality" [Realität].[201] The state, as internal ethical order, becomes, as a whole in the world, a natural being with the unquestionable and unanswerable forcefulness of the same. It is, despite all metaphysical play of light, still the state of the pamphlet, still the state as power.

Just as the power-state of the pamphlet was indifferent towards forms of government, even if monarchy was visibly featured on occasion, this is now also the case with the state of absolute ethicality. Democracy, as well as monarchy and aristocracy, can be "forms of a free government." Whether they are so in fact hinges on the opposition between government and governed being "only superficial" and "the essence of the same" – which is not the case in the unfree forms of ochlocracy, oligarchy, and despotism.[202] Under the three free constitutions, for which the natural "reality" of the ethical presented in the system of wise old priests is embodied respectively in one, several, and in all individuals, the one which seems externally closest to the absolute, the aristocracy, now receives, strangely enough, the worst mark. It may be an echo of the experiences in Bern when it is said of it: "it differentiates itself from the absolute constitution through heredity, even more through possession; and because it has the form of the absolute and not its essence, it is the worst."[203] In the same way, democracy is to be objected to because government, in that it is made up of "all," cannot be made up purely from possession, and further that here no "absolute estate" can be singled out.[204] Only monarchy, which can do without private possession, is not expressly criticized in this context. Indeed, the absolute constitution, although it would be a kind of aristocracy, appears to Hegel to be equally well-actualized in the forms of aristocracy and monarchy.

It also becomes clear from these comments on the indifference of the absolute constitution towards the individual forms of government that Hegel draws up his best idea of the state without regard to the path from thoughts to actuality. On this point, Fichte's doctrine of the state from 1796 also deviates in its entire mood. Fichte's ideas are conveyed to the reader with such intruding, restless logic, which turns the details to and fro, that one is forced to continually think through and affirm the possibilities of application. With Hegel there is no trace of such a desire to convince. According to his own words, the strength of ethicality lies in the "strength of intuition and the present."[205] And yet – or perhaps because of this – there is more life in his image of the state than in Fichte's bold demands. Precisely the comments on the absolute government show it again. It is, as we saw, perhaps most closely represented in actuality by a monarchy. It is really true of kingship that it, issuing from the first estate, still stands over the estates, because in lawgiving activity it preserves and renews the relation of the estates to each other and subordinates them all to the whole of the state. Through birth, it is the "natural" peak of the state, "sanctified in itself and not made," the soul of the movement of the whole. This applies, we must add, precisely to a kingship such as Friedrich's. And on the other hand, it should be said that this ideal monarchy of the eighteenth century could not itself have been seen in the eighteenth century. Rather, again here, the new philosophical knowledge regarding the "identity" of government and people pours its gilded semblance over the much more sober hardness of historical actuality. With the great thinker of the state of the German nineteenth century, it becomes clear here how the scholarly justification of our new kingship grew forth without interruption from the intuitions of the state of Friedrich and how, indeed still here, the disposition of the classic-romantic philosophy became the necessary mediator between the old and the new century.

Under the name "universal government" Hegel deals with government as cause and bearer, not as before as mere center point, of the "universal movement." Whereas the "absolute," hereby arguably comparable to hereditary kingship, is the power which secures the continuity of the life of "the people" over the ages, the activity of the "universal" is entirely absorbed in the "specificity of the people for this age,"[206] that is, in the work of the point of life just arrived at. To say it in advance: if behind the "absolute government" there stood the kingship, then the "universal" would become the ideal likeness of officialdom, which the sovereign kingship had formed for its purposes.

If one wanted to divide the universal government according to the three powers of government and at the same time, with Kant, into the three premises of a syllogism,[207] then one would see the universal in legislation, the "ideal" [ideell] subordination of the particular under that universal in jurisprudence, and finally the "real" [reell] subordination of the particular under the universal in executive power. Hegel himself reminds us that although Kant also understands legislation as the "major premise," he understands both other powers in opposite order: the executive as the "minor premise" and jurisprudence as the "conclusion."[208] Thus, it is easy to perceive the meaning of the division for political science behind the rattle of the conceptual mill. For Kant, the maxim of justice is the goal of the state; for him, executive authority is only the link between legislator and judge, more or less only a bailiff. But Hegel, corresponding to his disdain for justice as a political ideal, which is already known to us, places judicial decision in the more modest position. In this state, which is power [Macht], the other powers [Gewalten] converge in executive power. On its own, each of the three is a mere abstraction; the actual action of government unifies all three functions in itself at all times. And if one tries, as Montesquieu taught, to artificially hold them together through the division into representatives, then the representatives will of themselves be the executives of the government and it will depend on them to what degree the activity of the others means something. The distinction of an externally and internally oriented activity of the state seems to penetrate the thinker deeper than Locke's and Montesquieu's division of powers; deeper, because it conceives of the state every time as "totality" – on the one hand as particular, a state among states, on the other, in relation to the individual person, as universal. Nevertheless, at that time, Hegel rejects this later-adopted division, and with significant reasoning: the actual life of the state is a continual change of both activities; a "specificity" which still only seemed to concern the external government suddenly becomes "immediately that of the people."[209] A true division must result in "organic systems," "to which these forms of outer and inner are subordinated,"[210] so that every "system" of state activity encompasses both external and internal political life within itself. Hegel sets up three such "systems": one of need; one of justice and war; and one of upbringing, education, conquest and colonization. To recognize here the reflection of a historical order of officials is made difficult by the basic idea of this division, namely, to continually integrate the external and internal life of the state under each government activity, which, in general, is so important for the science and history of the state of the next century. This basic idea leads to the surprising, indeed later rarely executed coupling of war with the administration of justice, of conquest and colonization with upbringing and education. In what follows, we will go through the systems one by one.

Hegel, in his lost commentary on Steuart's work on national economics, had once applied the thoughts of "life" against the objectifying direction of mercantile doctrines.[211] One can certainly understand that the newest doctrine, which was just beginning its triumphant march through Germany, attracted even him. He was captivated by Adam Smith,[212] in that the Scotsman did not proceed like the physiocrats from the production of goods in general,[213] but rather from the work of the individual person. The death of the concept of "wealth" that dominated the old doctrine of national economics was and remained the wealth of the state. It seemed to be displaced in the book The Wealth of Nations by the living image of a self-generating, world-embracing economic whole, which itself emerged from various individual needs, poised in its own equilibrium. Hegel now proceeded from this image as well when he, typical of the individualistic features of his new philosophical conception of the state, already composed this section under the heading of "Need."[214] But, typical for his economic policies,[215] which again deviated from Smith's economic theory as it was generally formulated, the individual person is for him not merely the starting point, instead Hegel advances the question of the individual person within this whole of needs, certainly harmonious in itself, and there finds the individual helplessly facing a "foreign power over which he has no influence."[216] Thus, the government was presented the task of taking control of this "unconscious, blind fate."[217] It can do it, for it can recognize which are the respective needs of the whole and which are the enduring needs of the individual. On the basis of this knowledge it will intervene, regulating and bridging space and time, into the vacillating equilibrium of economic life. If it wanted to let it come to the natural establishment of equilibrium, then in the meantime the unprotected individuals, indeed entire estates, would have to atone for the inappropriate trust of government in theory. It is a case which we have already encountered many times in this text: the thinker again appropriates the new thoughts as his own and then justifies an older politics on the basis of these new thoughts. He demands the regulatory intervention of the state into economic life and demands it as much for the sake of the state as for the helpless individual. Steuart generally demanded of the "statesman" that he secure "physical necessities"[218] for the worker, and mercantile practice had also followed this goal. Hegel could not have attained these thoughts in such fundamental universality from Smith. Nevertheless, the turn to what is past is less sharp than usual. After the instance of a moderate mercantilism, precisely as Steuart represented it with his separation of "economy" and "governance," of "statesman" as steward and as head of the house,[219] Hegel limits himself to the regulatory intervention of the state. He does not want to make the state into the uninhibited master and ultimate author of national economic life, as true mercantilism tried to do in doctrine and deed.

If the state fulfills in this work of regulation a more "incidental" duty,[220] imposing itself from case to case, then a deeper task arises for it from the eternally necessary difference between poor and rich, especially at the point where this opposition reaches its greatest dimensions: in "trade."[221] The trade class, divided in itself "into many special classes of trade, and these into classes of different wealth and consumption,"[222] produces, as we have already recalled from earlier indications and as Steuart likewise already pointed out,[223] relations of a bare, unimaginative command: on the one side the monstrously rich individual, and on the other side the masses, degenerated into the most crude, "inorganic" machine-work, into the "bestiality of despising everything elevated."[224] And then "that which is without wisdom," wealth, has become the essence of all things, and "the absolute bond of the people, the ethical, is gone and the people dissolved."[225] What is the government to do in this case? It must, "if it sacrifices a part of this estate to mechanical and factory work [...] preserve the whole as such in the liveliness possible for it. But this happens [...] through the constitution of the class in itself."[226] Hegel's remedy against the dangers to the state and society of factory life may be found in professional codes that encompass the employers and employees and in which impersonal dependence is displaced through a living relation of person to person, in an "internally active connection, which is not physical dependency."[227] To now form from the trade class such "a living universal" and thereby to certainly make the individual "partly [...] dependent, although ethical in confidence, respect and the like,"[228] is not the task of government, but rather the constitution of the class in itself," which must proceed from its own nature. If this "living relation" exists, then "the rich person is immediately obliged to reduce the power-relation and even the suspicion of the same through a more universal ability to participate – a marginal note recalls the Athenian establishment of liturgy[229] – and through the personalizing of relations, where the will no longer throws itself upon bare earning as such, but rather "exists as living activity," "the drive towards boundless wealth itself is eradicated."[230]

It is tempting today to overestimate the significance of these thoughts, with their mix of deeply penetrating insight and hopeful utopia, for the whole of Hegel's idea of the state. It may therefore be necessary to say immediately that later on, without exactly disappearing in detail, these thoughts considerably receded for Hegel. In the coming years, one can already recognize a progressing displacement of the mercantile aspects in his economic philosophy. That the politician so passionately felt the necessity of social balance at that time was perhaps due to his engagement with English workers' relations in Frankfurt from 1795 to 1797 and, incidentally, the parliamentary debate over the tax on the poor. Then, he may have also learned of those local support associations, the *friendly societies*,[231] themselves proceeding from the bosom of the work force, which widely established themselves as predecessors to the later worker's associations. If Hegel did have these new English developments in mind, it nevertheless now seems certain that with his factory associations, which were to tie a bond between the contractors and workers, he thought especially about the old guilds, once discarded by himself, in which the absolutist state really found something rising up without its influence from the "organic essence" of the estates, something which it only had to preserve and watch over. Again, old images are thrust before the eye of one who had recognized here such a peculiarly modern need of political life.

The state takes immediate part in economic life to the extent that it itself has needs. Thus, fiscal authority comprises the conclusion of the section. For Hegel, the three needs of government – corresponding exactly in number, manner, and order to Smith's famous three tasks of the state: *defense, justice, public works and public institutions*[232] – are preservation of the class of war, remuneration of the class of civil servants, and the needs of the entire people.[233] Hegel adds to the purposes of the state – like Adam Smith, as well as following him in the main division – the doctrine of state funds. The government cannot work as a "universal," it can only take into possession through taxes "the ripe fruits directly, without work."[234] If it acquires something itself, then it can only do so because it rents out property, "in order that thereby it does not receive direct earnings and work, but rather these in the form of emolument, corollary and the universal."[235] In that Hegel essentially adopts a line of argumentation with which the fledgling national economy was fighting every form of state monopoly and possession of provinces – as a universal the state cannot and should not profit through the private economy – he justified precisely with this reasoning the possession of provinces in the form of leasing, as the age had showed it to him. The already so often noted procedure becomes even more clear with the doctrine of taxation. Fundamentally, disregarding the freedom from taxes of the first class, the fiscal requirement of liberalism was that taxation "must have the form of formal universality or justice."[236] But in life "the system of stipulations [falls] immediately into contradiction"[237] in that it should, but cannot, be just. Indeed, "absolutely just" would be that "each should contribute in relation to the size of their property; but this property is nothing landed or firmly situated, but rather a living unboundedness, something unpredictable within the industry of acquisition."[238] To meet this "living unpredictability" through a taxation of income would be "formally possible," but not in actuality, as Hegel now lays out following Smith. For income is not "something objective, known and recognizable"[239] like landed goods. Thus, in the end he comes to the requirement to assess the landed goods, that is, what is "objective," according to the average profit. However – an objection against the "only stipulation" of the physiocratic tax – as this taxation would not incorporate skill as such, there is in addition to this a second taxation procedure to be applied, one which incorporates skill, namely, through that "which it spends" because that "passes through the form of universality [...] it becomes a commodity."[240] In order not to upset the equilibrium of the economy, this consumption tax must extend "to the most possible particularity"[241] of the commodities, which would also give the government a ready means to regulate the details of economic life.[242]

Thus, after advancing the principle of "absolute justice," at the end there comes the juxtaposition of land and consumption tax, divided into two different population groups. However, here Hegel followed Adam Smith in all the details of his line of argument. Smith, likewise proceeding from the principle of taxation of income and recognizing the practical impossibility, recommends land and consumption tax in the end.[243] Here, the new doctrine and the old actuality with contribution and excise tax showed Hegel for once the same image. It is noteworthy that, despite this, it is precisely here that he comments on the "contradiction" between the starting point and the result. In comparison with the actually political thoughts, frequently stuck in the *ancien régime*, in these economic thoughts there is an altogether stronger, more modern element. Adam Smith demanded entrance into Hegel's state and gained admission.

Hegel then deals comparatively briefly with the "System of Justice." What was incidental possession in the system of needs becomes here justly acknowledged property. Justice now "must itself be something

living and look to the person."[244] Law, as "right in the form of consciousness,"[245] is thus necessary but something indifferent in comparison with
living justice. The government could leave the acquisition classes alone,
for whom civilian right is at stake, in their futile endeavors to take the
mere incidental possession in right "up into infinity" through such an
unbroken "completeness of civilian laws [...] that [...] the judge [...]
would become a pure authority without vitality and intuition."[246] But
the government would do better to overcome this false striving "through
what is organic in the constitution,"[247] in that it establishes the administration of justice according to the principle of freedom, that is, the
"identity"[248] of government and governed. To that end, the one searching for justice must see its own kind before it in the court of justice:
desirable are "the same class, equality of birth [...] living within the
same citizenry."[249] And even further, "abstraction of law" must not rule,
but rather "an accommodation towards contentment which includes
the satisfaction and agreement of those involved according to fairness,
that is, seeing the whole of the same as individuals."[250] Curiously, the
acknowledgement of the necessity of written law which Hegel would
later uphold against Savigny connects here with thoughts on free right.
In the composition of the courts of justice, an old actuality again merges
with a new ideal: the personal legal venue becomes based on the great
modern thought that the governing and the governed should be one.[251]

The goal of right is punishment, which in civilian procedures affects
only the restoration of the disrupted "determination"[252] and in criminal
procedures affects the personality itself. But in its third form, in accordance with the principle of unification of inner and outer life of the
state under every "system," it appears as war. The "people" are judged in
war, both as personality and property owners. Thus, they are comparable
to the criminal as well as to the civil defendant.[253] For the first estate,
which indeed "lives in the people," war is actually the appropriate form
in which right approaches it. This is a claim that Hegel later applies only
still to the state itself, namely, that "there is no praetor over states."[254]

Finally, in the third "system" the government acts through the individual upon the people as a whole: upbringing, education, colonization. "Conquest," which according to the introductory outline should
also appear here, is left out in the admittedly fleeting sketch of this version. Particular forms of upbringing, "talents, inventions, and science,"[255]

have little consequence. True education is that which the people, the "self-educating and consulting and conscious people,"[256] bestows upon themselves. Next to the "police," which may exercise discipline upon individuals, there thus stands as the truly "great" discipline "universal customs, order, education about war and, based upon this, the verification of the truthfulness of the individual."[257] Finally, in colonization the state fulfills consciously and according to external plan what happens internally through the begetting of children: the people "becomes objective to itself" and brings forth "another people."[258] In these intimations, in which the ideal image shines more brightly than before away from the narrow actuality of German life, the text trails off. What follows are those jotted down sentences on the form of government with which we already dealt, and tacked on to these a few more, which will still occupy us, on the relation of the forms of government to religion.

In that we now turn to the major essay "On the Scientific Ways of Treating Natural Right,"[259] which Hegel published in the winter from 1802 to 1803, we can relate frequently back to the discussed system. For the essay presupposes the main part of the system, even if, in its scientific intimations, it also contains the first signs of the future overcoming of that form of the system. The first part of the essay critiques the "empirical" manner of treating national right.[260] Hegel conceives this more or less as all older attempts at natural right, in contrast to those of Kant and Fichte, which he critiques in the second section, and of course also in contrast to his own attempt, which he will present in the last part of the essay. In the "empirical manner," an isolated fact is brought forward out of the fullness of actuality, whether it is a condition or whether it a human drive or wish, and the structure is built based upon this secure point.[261] As the prime example, Hegel chose to tackle Hobbes' doctrine on the state of nature. The sense of Hegel's critique becomes visible when he explains that in truth it is not a matter of finding passage from the chaos of a natural condition to the majesty of the condition of right: for in true ethicality "the state of nature and majesty [...] [are] simply identical."[262] And if one already senses here in this characteristic revaluation of the state of nature into the idea of ethical nature the philosopher's quiet delight in the "empirical" streak within the concept of the state of nature, it becomes entirely clear when, immediately following, he finds the greatest sin of this older natural right in its "consequence" – only through inconsequence could "the violence done to intuition"[263] become good again. And connected with this praise of "inconsequence" there logically follows a powerful defense of the "old, through and through inconsequential," pure empiricism.[264] For the first time, we encounter there the equation of the actual and the rational in its original freshness: "A great and pure intuition may [...] in the pure architectonics of its presentation, in which the connection of necessity and the rule of form do not become visible, do not express the truly ethical; like a structure that presents the spirit of its author mutely, without the image of the same being positioned in it."[265]

Kant and Fichte, the representatives of the second manner of treating natural right,[266] then have it much worse. Indeed, Hegel also recognizes in them a "great side," namely the thought that "the essence of right and duty – and the essence of the thinking and willing subject are in general one."[267] But Kant and Fichte did not remain faithful to this great thought of setting a single essence as the goal and bearer of ethicality. They destroy it through the fatal separation of legality and morality, which found its scientific expression in the separation of ethics into the doctrine of right and of virtues with Kant and into natural right and the doctrine of customs with Fichte. Over and against the possibility of this oneness of consciousness and duty, that is, morality, there stands the possibility that they are not one, or legality; and along with this a system of coercion arises alongside the system of freedom. And as Fichte himself sees the precondition of the system of coercion in that "loyalty and belief"[268] have vanished, with this "the inwardness, the reestablishment of the lost loyalty and belief, the oneness of universal and individual freedom and ethicality, are made impossible."[269] The basic idea of the Hegelian attack is, accordingly, that it is nonsensical to want to preserve freedom through coercion. For from here on the main thrust against the "Ephorate" already known to us is then carried out. The Ephorate does not have the power to oppose a state coup – Hegel calls to mind the Brumaire incident[270] – nor do they accord the security that they are the voice of the true universal will and, even more so, this security is not offered by the people they have called together, this "rabble, which [...] was plainly not brought up in order to act in the spirit of a whole but rather solely for the sake of the opposite."[271] Ethical freedom is not composed of a decision to act this way or that. Rather, it is beyond the possibility of such decisions. The free "individual" can no longer be "*coerced*" [gez-wungen] because they are "*subjugated*" [bezwungen].[272] This true freedom now constitutes the subject-matter of the section. The polemic gives way to the presentation.

While leafing through this third section we happen upon well-known things. Here we encounter remarks on right and judges, closely related to those of the system, and above all we again encounter the estates. They are the same as in the system. Only here there is really a slight convergence with Plato and Aristotle's estates, in that the third estate is sometimes added to the second and the first estate of the free is dif-ferentiated as unfree from the two lower estates.[273] In contrast, however, there is no thought of slavery because for Hegel slaves do not constitute an estate.[274] In an estate as such the individual is free; only the entire estate, "whose work aims at individuality and as such does not hold the danger of death within it"[275] may be regarded as unfree. This is where, incidentally, the third estate, which during war "may increase the first accordingly *en masse*,"[276] separates itself again from the second. In general, then, the tripartite nature of the estates, corresponding to present actual-ity, still holds sway. The connection to the present, unlike in the system, is now expressly established here: "among the most recent people, the wage-earning class has gradually stopped performing duties of war, and bravery has formed more purely into a special estate [...] which is ele-vated through those of the wage-earning class and for whom possession and property are minimally something incidental."[277] The more modern form of absolute ethicality is then very clearly separated from the Greek form, in that the line of history from the one to the other is drawn out. The sharp separation of the free, who "live in the state," and those of servant-nature, which the Platonic as well as Aristotelian state touch on, was lost at the point at which Hegel, beginning already 1796, had set the great break in world history, namely with the passage from the free state to the Roman Empire. "In the loss of absolute ethicality and with the degradation of the noble estate, both previously particular estates have become the same and, with the cessation of freedom, slavery neces-sarily ceased."[278] There then did not immediately come about "those set above," namely the new division of estates known to us, even less the true ethical form of this division wherein an estate is only dependent upon another estate and not an individual upon another individual. Rather, in place of the Polis, in which the unfree in such personal slave-relations were dependent upon those who constituted the estate of the free, there now came at first a general mixture of estates. Gibbon again lends the philosopher the colors for the image of this condition, where in fact "the people is comprised only from the second estate"[279] and where accordingly private right becomes the ruling power of life.[280] And in that this rule of private right, which had once come to be in this way and which was ridiculed by Plato as a condition of sickness of a people, has become lasting, so there is only one way out: "that this system be consciously taken up, recognized in its right, closed off from the noble estate, and be granted its own estate as its realm."[281] This is the historical-philosophical conception of absolute ethicality, as demanded by the current age in contrast to the epoch of the Polis. If in the system the division of estates seemed to still be crafted out of the conditions of the eighteenth century without much reflection, then here it is different. The division of estates now contains a substructure of world history. The importance of these matters becomes even more noticeable with this deepening of history, in that from now on they prove themselves for Hegel as the unchanging middle point from which the philosophy of spirit reconfigures itself. The internal displacements which the main part of the system undergoes in the following years have their common origin in the following question, an attempt at which was first made in 1802 with the structure of the estates: the question on the relation between political and economic people, state and property.

State and economic individualism may appear to share a philosophical manner of observation, but history will not confirm such an unconditional fellowship. So, for the German nineteenth century until 1878, the union of economic-societal freedom and concise stately synopsis is nothing short of "tendency" in the sense of Ranke. It would accordingly be unfruitful to want to explain such an alliance of forces through conceptual generalities. Instead, it may suffice to approach the phenomenon there where it becomes scientifically most graspable: in the intellectual history of the individually great person.

When Hegel speaks of the political "basic right" of property in his notes from Bern – older testimonies are missing here – one almost believes one sees a scornful smile glide over his face. He knows well enough that in more recent times, the state grants humans "the rights of property and the protection of the same,"[282] however, full of internal wrath, he refuses to consider constitutions that "only guarantee life and property"[283] as the best. That is precisely the unhappy inheritance from the age of the Roman Imperium from which we still suffer today: general private life without participation in the state, without "moral ideas,"[284] with a religion which, "without its own truly independent dignity," "awaits everything from somewhere else."[285] The view that state and property stand in an unnecessary, almost unethical relation to each other, is still dominant late into Hegel's Frankfurt period. This view comes from the same place of ridicule as a comment from the Cart-translation, which Hegel shares in response to the idea that the constitution of Bern is good because the citizens there did not have to pay any taxes.[286] In the fall of 1798 Hegel still praises the wisdom of Solon's code of laws, which, because the acquisition of property could disturb the equality of the citizens, upheld the equality of the shares of inheritance.[287] This conception of property stands in clear connection with the main political thought of this early period: that each constitution of the state must touch upon the holy principle of all justice, namely, upon equality.[288] Justice is thus understood without regard for property, the state is governed according to justice, and property, standing in the way of the higher goal of just equality, is something subordinate.

As this political concept of justice disappears during the course of the winter of 1798/99, so too does the political concept of property change. Of course, at first it looks as if the gap between state and property would still expand. Precisely in that section on the fate of Jesus, which encompasses the great change in the idea of the state, the thought of the ideal political community sways, so it seems, far above and beyond all connections with property. This is the case when Hegel speaks of those who "were never active in such a unification, never enjoyed this union and this freedom, particularly when the civic relation is suitable only to property."[289] Even in the oldest introduction to the text on *The German Constitution*, in the beginning of 1799, Hegel still saw in civic property "a universal only in regard to the side of right, and merely as an object that is isolated and unrelated."[290] And from this precondition of the "unre-latedness" of private property, the core of the German constitution as private right counted for him as the cause of German misery. Later, however, he had to eradicate this conceptual foundation, this "unrelatedness" of private property. For precisely now the idea of fate, by which Hegel learned to recognize the powers of the world, began to draw its circles wider and wider. And thus, this idea also reaches the concept of property in the last layer of the major theological manuscript and reshapes it. Let us listen to the sentences in which we encounter for the first time how the concept of property is inundated with the new feeling for the world: "There is indeed nothing to say [...] about the [...] demand to throw off the worries of life and to disdain riches; it is a litany that will only disperse in sermons or in rhymes, for such a demand has no truth for us. The fate of property has become too powerful for us for reflections about it to be bearable, its separation from us to be thinkable."[291] Thus, property is now given the same form as the state was before the state; both are fate to us, from both we cannot and are not allowed to think ourselves divided. The opportunity that the two hitherto foreign concepts find each other is now granted. Not that Hegel no longer felt the weight of the problem. Quite the opposite. In the second introduction to the text on *The German Constitution* he describes the "old life" of the German eighteenth century, wherein the new spirit no longer finds "satisfaction." It was "a limitation to an ordered reign over its property, a contemplation and enjoyment of its completely subjected small world, and then also a self-annihilation which reconciled this confinement and elevation in thoughts on the heavens."[292] The grounding of this sentiment of the citizens, which is satisfied in private life and calms all further longings in reverent piety, has now begun to waver under the movement of the world: the limitation of humankind to an ordered reign over its property, which it thus made to some extent into its "absolute,"[293] now gives way to a bad conscience about this limitation of life to possession. The human desires more than this. And nevertheless – so we hear repeatedly in September 1800 – the "necessity of property" is its irrevocable "fate."[294] How it raises itself above this fate in religion, at least in spirit, is explained here. The third introduction to the text on *The German Constitution* provides a first explanation of how fate in life unites with the state, which is also fate. "A mass of people," so it begins, "can only then be called a state if it has first united to a communal defense of its property."[295] The property which the thinker had earlier cared to see purely as a strength that is foreign, indeed dangerous to the state, makes its appearance in the conceptual determination of the state itself.

Admittedly, the connection that Hegel allows between state and property, after many attempts, is a very raw one, as in this pamphlet the conception of the state we are dealing with is by no means the ideal state but rather a state that can still only "be called" a state.[296] And one can already expect that Hegel will not adopt it in similar fashion into the image of the state of his system. However, his system will also not entirely disown this state, which is to protect the property of the people, as the most profound result of Hegel's development culminating just now is that valleys and peaks, appearances and ideas are not held internally separate from one another. Rather, Hegel will ground the protection of property more deeply in the essence of the state, no longer in the "wish of each individual to live, mediated by the state, in the security of his property."[297] And he already allows this individualistic justification to fall silent in the pamphlet in 1802.[298] Indeed, the outline of the new image of the people in the text from the summer of 1801 still shows no attempt to balance the "self-configuration of reason into a people"[299] with the fate of property. But the System of 1802 takes up the task, and with this begins a development that will first reach its completion in the separation of "state" and "civil society."

Economic life is initially dealt with in the first part of the system without any connection to the state in a kind of history of economic phases. After the economizing human is introduced into the system in this manner and then transgression startles him from his peaceful rest in the next part, the state appears in the third part, armed, initially a war-state, and seemingly without economic connections. These connections then become visible in the content of the estates, which are the state's societal "precondition." And these connections appear in broad-ranging manner in the first section on the functions of government. Whereas we already saw in the first section, and likewise in the "System of Justice," that there was a noticeable indifference of the state towards that which lay hidden under the wings of the economy and right, and a tacit approval, which was then also carefully qualified, now, while writing the essay on natural right, the philosopher has become conscious of the scientific task of reconciling this indifference of his state towards economic individuals through the great thought on the "identity" of the state and the human being.

The division of estates is the fixed point.[300] With this as a starting point, the foundation of the system is now changed: instead of resting upon "natural ethicality" and "transgression," the estate-based state in our essay rests upon a "system of needs" and a "system of justice." The one relates to the other not in simple opposition as natural ethicality and transgression do in the system of the manuscript. Rather, the "needs" are lifted to a higher level in "justice," and brought as close as possible, and integrated into, the absolute ethicality of the state. When the estates are then explained as the reflection of this entire philosophical and spiritual foundation at its highest level – the peasant as the representative of the purely natural economy, before right and beneath the state; the citizen as representative of the economy in the state, private life secured by right and left in peace by the state; the noble as the embodiment of the absolute ethicality of "life in the state" itself – we must not be confused by such a derivation. Indeed, we know that the division of estates is in truth older than the new system as a whole. The System of 1802 still contained that noticeable echo of the ideas from Frankfurt that circled around the mystery of the I, and that inserted "transgression" as philosophy of personality in general between the "natural" ethicality of the economy and family and the "absolute" ethicality of the state. That has now disappeared. The question of how the economic individual relates to the state now dominates the entire design. Between life beneath the state and the state itself there emerges, in the place where previously the relinquished force of transgression was allowed to rage, a middle-realm of connections which are neither thinkable without the state nor without the human prior to the state. Before us is the formative outline of the philosophical and spiritual System up to 1805, and of the state-philosophical system up until the end.

What Hegel actualized for the first time in the act of writing the system will open up to us if we now perceive how he himself articulated this philosophical act by way of which the doctrine of estates, with its separation of political and economic ethicality, would be removed from its previous isolation and become metaphysically anchored. The division of estates is "nothing other than the enactment of tragedy within the ethical which the absolute plays eternally with itself, in that it eternally [...] surrenders itself to suffering and death and lifts itself from its ashes into majesty."[301] And, "captured more closely for the ethical," Hegel finds the image of this tragic drama [Trauerspiels] in the "ending of the trial of the Eumenides."[302] Through his command, Apollo, the god of pure, originally undivided light, entangled humans in action and guilt and thereby gave the Eumenides, as the powers of rigid right, authority over them. The "people" of Athens acknowledge "human wisdom as the Areopagus of Athens," the equality of the bright god, from whom the human was sent forth, and the dark many-sided powers of life, in whose snares they stepped. "But divine wisdom as the Athene of Athens," the divinity of the state, gives the god of light back to them and reconciles the feuding parties in that she confers divine honor and residence in the city upon the powers of right, "so that their wild nature may delight in the contemplation of Athene sitting on her throne high on the citadel opposite their own altar, which is erected down in the lower city, and in this way be calmed."[303] Thus, ethicality sacrifices a part of itself, in that it "separates [its inorganic nature] from itself as fate and places it in opposition to itself, in order that it not be entangled thereby."[304] Property has become the fate of the state, which it has consciously placed over and against itself, thereby "preserving its own life and holding itself pure from it."[305] Thus the movement that began in Frankfurt ebbs away. At one time the state as well as property were the "fate" of humankind, to which they had to give themselves up, willingly or unwillingly: they could not and were not allowed to remain "fateless." Now the state has long since moved from within the circle of this consciousness of fate and leads a proud, satisfying life in its own sphere; but property has remained fate. Yet property is now no longer the fate of the human being, but rather of the state, and this fate does not seize the state inescapably, but it is a fate from which it can preserve itself "purely" in that the state grants it its own sphere of existence and thus opposes it "as objective."[306] Fate has become again what it was before the winter of 1798/99: namely, something "objective," standing in foreign opposition. It has lost its omnipotence over the highest life, which is now life in the state. This life has now risen above it and holds itself pure from it – we could say "fateless," had this word from the Frankfurt period, as we will soon see, not since taken on a new meaning.

Thus, the essay definitively forms one side of the Hegelian thought on freedom. The idea of a state-free sphere in the modern state, which was inspired by the political notes from Bern, and which surfaced anew in the concept of the state in the text on *The German Constitution*, here, however, no longer idealistically tinged as in Bern but tinged with civil-liberal ideas – namely, an indifference of the power-state towards the private life of its citizens – now becomes a metaphysically supported idea. A partition is erected between political and economic ethics. The state sees in the world of private right its lasting opposition, an opposition it will admittedly include in its circle of dominion but recognize and "divinely honor" it within this circle. Rousseau's great mistake – so it was written at one point around this time by Heeren, the historian from Göttingen – is that he "regarded the members of civil society as people [Menschen] but not at all as property owners."[307] The common aspiration of the Prussian reformers, which was passed along all the way to the party that founded the Empire, was to build up the state upon free property owners, to make the economically freed individual serviceable to the state with their overly economic and spiritual powers. Here, Hegel embodies this idea of the state in a state which was to uphold the "independence," the "freedom" of the individual in the second estate as a lower but necessary form of ethicality next to the absolute appearance of ethicality in the warring estate.[308] If the state "wanted to "completely penetrate the being of the individual as a perfect police force [...] and thus destroy civilian freedom," that would be "the harshest despotism."[309] Such an intervention of state right into private life would be just as objectionable as the intervention of the private concept of justice into state life, which is advanced in the doctrine of state treaties and in the overestimation of the binding strength of international contracts, or present as the interference of morality in private, state or international law.[310] The separation of a state-free sphere, which happens here under the form of a division of estates, was expressed in the text on The German Constitution more smoothly and more soberly, however, the same thing was meant both times.

Already around the time of the text on The German Constitution the individual in the state had still recognized other starting points for his will towards freedom than the two forms of existence of the second and first estate, the state-free sphere and the "life in the state," bound to each other on the same pole. We know how, already in July 1801, Hegel understood "freedom" as the unconscious devotion of the individual to the course of the free, self-fulfilling development of the whole. We followed this idea of freedom, within which history and the individual soul united into a singular marriage, from its first intonations. It also receives sufficient attention in the essay at hand, in which many previously scattered rays of the Hegelian image of the state are now collected.

Just as Hegel's "absolute ethicality" disregarded what philosophers called morality at that time, in so far as he saw in this only the ethicality "of the *bourgeois* or the private person,"[311] thus of the second estate, so it is also not the mere "ethicality of the individual."[312] Rather, the essence of absolute ethicality is "to be *customs* [Sitten]"[313] and it can only be the soul of the individual if it is the "spirit of a people" [Geist eines Volkes].[314] What Hegel now understands by the spirit of a people becomes clear with what he says about upbringing, law-giving, and cult. The essence of upbringing is that the child, "imbued from the breast of universal ethicality, [...] comes to know it more and more and thus passes over into the universal spirit."[315] What the Pythagorean answered to the question of what would be the best education for his son is valid: if you make him into a citizen of a well-organized people.[316] – If upbringing provides "its peculiar [...] body for individuals" for the ethical, then it presents itself as a "*system of law-giving*" "in the form of universality and of knowledge."[317] "So that this system completely expresses the reality or the living customs at hand: in order that it does not occur, as is often the case, that that which is right in a people and in actuality cannot be recognized from its laws, whose ineptitude in bringing the true customs into the form of laws and the fear to think these customs, to see and acknowledge them as their own, is the sign of barbarism."[318] We know in which people the author of the pamphlet saw this schism between actuality and the embodied laws. And the view on law-giving already clearly shows the point at which the opposition between Hegel's spirit of the people and that of the Historical School would later erupt. It cannot then be emphasized how much with the spiritualization of customs into laws the unity of both itself must in the end receive a very intuitive form and "be seen and prayed to as the god of the people, and this idea [...] [must] have its activity and joyous movement in a cult."[319]

Customs, laws, religion – absolute ethicality appears in these three overlapping forms for Hegel as the spirit of a people. We learn from a passage in the system manuscript how, conceived as national cultural unity, the spirit of the people [Volksgeist] relates to the state. There Hegel described the highest government as the "negative," that is: as the animating strength of the body of the people and added to this in passing: "the absolute positive soul of the living is in the whole of the people itself."[320] "Positive," contrasted like this with the "negative," means the

moved contrasted with the mover, the animated contrasted with the ani-
mator. And, accordingly, in the essay on natural right, Hegel likes to use
the designation "ethical totalities"[321] for peoples. For him, the spirit of
the people, as already in Tübingen, is not the root but rather the blossom.
It was not the secret of national life but its visible revelation to all: customs, laws, cult. Not without reason does Hegel mention here Montesquieu's "immortal work."[322] Montesquieu thus conceived the *esprit général*
as a total occurrence and so one is reminded of him and not romantic
ethnology regarding the emphasis of law-giving. One is reminded of
him when the "totality of the extended image"[323] is referred to in justifying a historical detail. There where the "folk spirit" [Volksgeist] of the
Romantics spins forth the visible life of the nation and the state from the
dark womb of being, another power is at work for Hegel: the "absolute
government." This power, the living soul of the entire people, immediately receives the "revelations" of the "most high."[324] The largely common approach of the polemic leaves no doubt as to the roots of the political opposition that would be contended over beginning in the 1820s in
Berlin at both the heights of science and in the lap of the government:
Hegel and Savigny, the enlightened-absolute wisdom of officialdom and
the "estate-liberal" tone of Friedrich Wilhelm IV or the young Bismarck.

At that time, in the winter of 1802 to 1803, Hegel could of course have
known nothing of this opposition. The fight was as yet purely against the
political individualism of the mature eighteenth century, against Kant
and Fichte.[325] The investigation pivots on the placement of the individual
in the "people" and at the same time that of the "people" in history. We
know how in a certain sense both of these questions were intertwined
into one. Insofar as they are, here the soul of the people and individual
souls are wandering a common path towards the state.

The task of the state that our essay assigns to history is not dissimilar
to the one that is solved by "absolute government" in the system manuscript. History makes the individual circles of political life palpable, how
they are dependent upon each other and how they are interdependent
upon one another. Thus, it repeatedly restores the equality of the whole,
and this equality is likewise repeatedly destroyed. It itself, the "world
spirit," is what remains and that which "has enjoyed itself [...] in every
people, under every totality of customs and laws."[326] It is not too great of
a risk to assume that this "world spirit" is really that "most high" which

reveals itself through the mouth of the "absolute government." The last pages of the essay present an account of how history now carries out its task towards the people. Of course, these pages likewise mean something else for Hegel: in them he evidently parts with the plans of his pamphlet. For example, now at the beginning of 1803, he weaves in the image of the German constitution, something he once wanted to work out in a text of its own. And here it becomes perceptible how closely the emergence of the new historical worldview and view of the state in Germany were connected with the drama of the sinking Empire.

Every present age of a people is destined to perish: "According to necessity [...] each single member of the chain must pass over and another must enter."[327] It thus happens that certain life-circles come forward and others recede more strongly. This division, "wherein some things grow towards new life, while others, which had established themselves at a stage of certainty, remain behind and witness as life flees from them,"[328] leads to consequences that the second introduction from Frankfurt to the text on The German Constitution already described with almost the same words: "The form of the law which was given to a specific custom [...] gives it the appearance of something existing in itself." The conscious strength of such a law "holds great weight over the unconscious character of newly emerging life."[329] If "in the present moment of the whole there is no longer an absolute connection and necessity,"[330] and the new law is only to be explained historically, on the grounds of past life, then it is no longer justifiable for the present. On the contrary, so concludes the pupil of the Enlightenment in an unconscious attack against the future Historical School of Law, "on the contrary, this historical knowledge of the law, which is grounded alone in lost customs and an expired life, proves exactly that it is now lacking understanding and meaning in the living present"[331] – that the power which it still holds is "shameless."[332] And likewise those laws are invalid which, like those of the Empire, admittedly seem to have truth – for they are the laws of dissolution precisely "within a dissolved people"[333] – which in fact estrange the parts from the whole. In such a people, through the innermost "untruth of the whole [...] also [...] within the science of philosophy [...] within ethicality, and likewise within religion, there could no longer be much truth."[334] Thus, Kantian philosophy, with its belief "that reason recognizes and knows nothing, exists solely in empty freedom [...] in nothingness and its appearance," is the exact likeness of the dying Empire with its "negative law-giving," whose content and essence is "that there be no law, no unity, no whole."[335] But the age is already ripe, and with a "jolt"[336] the new configuration will emerge. Admittedly, philosophy knows that every configuration is transitory. Its task remains to conceive, above and beyond all actuality, of the image, as Hegel himself well knows, of the never-reached agreement between absolute spirit and its configuration. "However, to attain this absolute configuration it cannot flee to the formlessness of cosmopolitanism, nor to the emptiness of the rights of humanity" – Fichte – "nor towards the same emptiness of a league of nations and world republic"– Kant, and up to 1800, Schelling – "but rather, to attain the high idea of absolute ethicality it must also recognize the most beautiful configuration."[337]

The most beautiful configuration! The aestheticizing tendency of these words has often been raised. Yet under this shell a political kernel lays hiding; the closed-wholeness of the work of art is, as the concepts brought in opposition show, the form with which the philosopher grasps the closed-wholeness of the national state and raises it up not as a precursor or constraint, but as the ideal itself.[338] And cultural-nationality and its state stride, hand in hand, on the same street, proceeding towards this unreached goal; the history of the one is the history of the other. This is shown precisely by the adventurous coupling of a Kantian critique of reason with a German constitution. The highest inner "truth" of education would correspond to the most beautiful configuration of the state.

Beginning with history and its movement, Hegel feels out the cohesion between nationality and state. This same historical movement had already dawned upon him earlier as the reconciler between personal freedom and the existing order. And finally, in a particular case, personal character also now establishes the path towards the state. With the great political-historical personality – "like that of Epaminondas, Hannibal, Caesar and some others"– even "virtues" themselves are acknowledged, that is, individually heightened characteristics, which Hegel otherwise does not allow to count as ethical in the highest sense.[339] There are then no longer any virtues remaining in the now rejected meaning; they have "individualized" themselves again and, "even though within absolute ethicality," they have likewise become "their own living configurations."[340] Entirely analogous, the sentences on Richelieu in the text on

*The German Constitution* had already seen the political genius therein, that "the individual identifies himself with a principle."[341] The person who in this manner "intermeshed his individuality with fate" thereby grants this individuality "a new freedom."[342] This is the fourth form which the ethical freedom of the individual takes on in this state. There was the freedom of the economic "bourgeois," foreign to the state, and the bearer of Kant and Fichte's "morality"; the freedom of the warring class from all of those earthly shackles of possession and righteousness, which make up the content of freedom for the "bourgeois"; the freedom of the individual to drink from the breast of universal ethicality. There now joins these three forms, as the fourth, the freedom of the great statesman. If one ignores the activity of the "bourgeois," foreign to the state even if acknowledged and protected by the state within its class, then the personal character of the great statesman is the only form acknowledged as ethical within Hegel's state. And this fourth form is also only acknowledged because and insofar as it is "intermeshed with fate." Moreover, this form also does not contain its legal ground within itself, but solely in the overarching whole, in the state and its history.

It is not easy to empathize with a disposition which tends to only acknowledge individual human character as valuable in its subordination to the necessary path of the whole. However, it helps to remember how, at that time, this in some regard personality-negating belief was the common property of the best minds. Gneisenau called it the "world-historical view of the present age"; Bismarck's *"fert unda, non regitur"* [a wave happens, it's not controlled] was the innermost conviction and ethical impetus within the circles of Prussian reformers. One is tempted to recall these people, who truly thrust themselves against the great historical wave in hero-like solitude, as witnesses against the view that only understood humankind as representative of the age and of history – they themselves would have denied such testimonial roles. What seemed to be refuted as doctrine through their lives was for them itself something deeply rooted, a feeling of life ruling over them. And, we must add, this feeling dominates the coming century of Ranke as the doctrine of historical personality. To perceive human nature as valuable in itself, without connection to an overarching historical whole, this was denied to an age which saw even in "heroes" only "representative" human beings. The century was familiar with those personalities who were of little value with respect to their individual uniqueness, yet nevertheless honored as free with respect to their morality, those members of that "great, for us most noteworthy multitude," in accordance with Kant's beautiful expression. And it was familiar with the valuable individual character of the historically great man, but valuable precisely only through that connection to the whole, to that multitude. Both of these views of personality found their place in Hegel's doctrine of the state, the one as the second estate, the other as the great statesman. But another view of personality also emerges, one imbued with that feeling of personal uniqueness that recedes in the coming century, perceived as valuable in itself, without a meaningful connection to the whole. And it is infinitely telling how that happens. If the philosopher allegorized the relation between the state and the freedom of civil commerce and the autonomy of the subjects as the tragedy in the ethical, then "comedy" acts as the relation of the state to humans who are recumbent in their personal uniqueness, lifted internally above and beyond the state in the highest sense.

The comedy of the ethical differentiates itself from tragedy therein that it is "fateless,"[343] that its players are only "shadow-images"[344] and not taken seriously by the poet or audience. The comedy of antiquity and modern comedy – Aristophanes, for instance, and Moliere – fantastical comedy and character comedy are differentiated along the lines of the individual within the state of antiquity and of modern life. Modern life, albeit, understood in the encompassing sense: from the Roman Imperium until the present, from the emergence of life determined by private right until the fall of the state, which sacrificed constitutional law itself to these powers of private right – from Julius Caesar until Kaiser Franz. In the foreground, the comedy of antiquity shows a light-hearted play of dream-like liberated individuals, powerless, however, against the unshaken "divinity, foreign [...] but standing in absolute certainty"[345] in the background. In Greek life this corresponds to the quiet self-certainty with which the Polis, well aware of its "admirably strong nature" – to speak with Plato – "sets with absolute carelessness for some its members the task of achieving a certain prize [...] and, certain of its absolute reign over every singularity and intemperance, regards the loss as nothing."[346] "Such an ethical organization will thus drive, without danger and fear or envy, individual members to the extremes of talent in every art and science and skill and thereby make them into something special: certain of itself that such divine monstrosities do not harm the beauty of its configuration but are, rather, comical traits which amuse a moment of its configuration. We may, to invoke a certain people, look to Homer, Pindar, Aeschylus, Sophocles, Plato, Aristophanes etc. for examples of such cheerful enhancements of individual traits."[347] Very rarely has such an absurd explanation of genius been proposed as this, which understands it as comical in the strictest sense. Within this worldview, which is focused on the political whole, what is reserved, at best, for great individuals who are not political is the position of "divine monstrosity." And it is questionable whether one may acknowledge such greatness in the state in this truly modest role. For precisely in Greece the "play of shadows" soon turned into something of fatal seriousness. Already the "sweeping multitude and high energy of the emergent individualization" and further, a "more serious nascent individuation" like Socrates and even the remorse of the people of Athens for his death, are signs that someday the Polis would eventually have to recognize in the "play of shadows," "a fate which was becoming all-powerful."[348]

It is otherwise with man in the modern comedy. Here he does not practice his light-hearted play, only the audience member takes him comically. Rather, in all seriousness, he holds his small, accidental nature to be absolute, and thus falls all by himself into the hands of that order in which the accidental commands unconditional validity, into the world of private right. And in it he now finds himself "constantly disappointed and dismissed."[349] Thus, comedy is an image of life in this age, where the individual believes himself to be firm and secure in his particularity until he is taught otherwise "through the next reversal or even upheaval of the earth spirit."[350] And in this role, similar to the comedic hero, he then has the choice, when "his well-earned and most secure possession of principles and rights are ravaged," either to convince himself "that it was his own efforts of reason and will swaying above fate that [...] brought about such changes, or to explain them away as something unexpected and out of place, and then call up all the gods against such necessity and submit himself to this."[351] What a despicably grandiose view on the invalidity of individuality! This is how, in the text on The German Constitution, Hegel described the powers that move humankind – politics, religion, necessity, virtue, authority, reason, cunning – each of which carries itself as an absolutely free and independent power, "unaware that they are all tools in the hands of higher powers, of primal fate and all-conquering time, which laugh at such freedom and independence."[352] It is the same "laughter" that resounds through that description of comedy. Hegel took the sovereign tone of this laughter with him into those storms that, only a few years later, would descend upon Northern Germany.

In order to be able to write such pages on the comedy of the ethical, Hegel must have been far removed, further still than we saw at the end of the last section, from that feeling of life of those first years in Frankfurt. What is now comedy for him, the closing-in-of-oneself in the "I," the "fear of one's own,"[353] this he perceived four years ago as the most personal tragic element and represented it as the tragedy of Jesus' life. "Fatelessness," the word once shared in common with Hölderlin, was filled to the brim with the content of that tragedy – the poet also found in this word the entire weakness of the age and therefore gave it the task "to be able to affect something, to have destiny"[354] – fatelessness: for Hegel, this word now becomes the heading of the comedy of the ethical. I don't know how the revaluation of thoughts, as well as feelings, between 1797 and 1802 could be illustrated with greater clarity.

Thus, in this manner, with the configurations of the state-free sphere, the political estate, upbringing through the spirit of the people, the great statesman and the comedy of the ethical, the essay rounds out the thoughts on the relation between the human being and the state: in acknowledgement and dismissal, it was the sound of the new century.

## NOTES

1   GW 15, 231 f.; HW II, 537 f.: "in the 27th year": the original "in" is then changed into an "around"!
2   Hegel to Windischmann, May 27, 1810 (Br I); the sentence "every human being ..." should begin with: "I am" – making the personal connection even stronger. Cf. also Gabler's account (handwritten copy at the Royal Library of Berlin), who Hegel had spoken to in 1805 about his "futile attempts at deeper recognition" and his "hypochondria": "the latter," Gabler tells, "he took on mentally, phenomenologically, and remarked that probably everyone who had some potential had to go through such a hypochondria once in his life, in which his previous world and his inorganic nature would crumble."
3   HW I, 426; Nohl 350 f.
4   GW 5, 1–219; in parts also HW I, 451–611.
5   Moser (1766), Vol. I, ch. 27, § 1, 4, 15.

6   Cf. Moser (1770), 37.

7   V. Gierke (1902); Brie (1874) – among older literature, Hegel mentions Conring and Hippolithus a Lapide as his predecessors in the distinction between Roman right and state law; but they made this distinction "more to dissolve the state than to connect the same." (GW 5, 37).

8   Pütter (1786 f.).

9   A densely written sheet of excerpts from this work in Hegel's hand has been preserved (GW 5, 207 ff.). Among more recent literature, Hegel cites (ibid., 123 f.) J.v. Müller's "Darstellung des Fürstenbundes) (v. Müller 1787) and (ibid., 43) D.F. Haas' "Vorschläge, wie das Justizwesen am Kammergerichte ... zu verbessern sei ... Wetzlar 1786–1788 (Hass 1786 ff.); the latter work seems to have been the basis for Hegel's criticism of the Imperial judicial system (cf. in addition to the cited § 347, for example, § 346).

10   Cf. the section "Historische Entwickelung" at the end (Pütter loc. cit.).

11   Häberlin (1794 ff.), § 14, esp. p. 54; Leist (1805), § 14, Annotation 9. On the placement of the Kaiser, cf. Häberlin (op. cit.), § 21 conclusion; Leist (op. cit.), § 16a II.; v. Gönner (1804) § 99.

12   Leist (op. cit.), 249 ff.; v. Schmalz (1805), § 439 ff.

13   Guglia (in: Euphorion [1894], vol. I, 415) and Bitterauf (Beilage zur Allgemeinen Zeitung [1904], 498) judge the form of the text on The German Constitution in a similar manner as in the text; on the extent of political insight similar to Treitschke (1912 f.), vol. 1, 194, who incidentally depends upon Haym's understanding, and different from Bitterauf (loc. cit.).

14   GW 5, 66–70 (cf. Editorial Report, 582); HW I, 582 ff. I follow the oldest version of the [heavily revised] manuscript [cf. the annotation apparatus to the quotations from GW 5].

15   GW 5, 66 f.

16   GW 5, 67.

17   Ibid.

18   Ibid.

19   GW 5, 68.

20   GW 5, 70.

21   GW 5, 72; HW I, 585 – In the wording of the manuscript: "An equally loose ..." 338 Cf. pp. 149–152.

22   Cf. pp. 149–152.

23   GW 5, 172; HW I, 479.

24   GW 4, 1–92; HW 2, 7–139.

25   GW 4, 56; HW 2, 85.

26   GW 5, 175; HW I, 482.

27   Cf. Section 3, note 40.

28   GW 5, 174; HW I, 481.

29   GW 5, 174 f.; HW I, ibid.

30   GW 5, 173; HW 2, 479 f.

31   GW 5, 175; HW 2, 482 – verbatim: "the free and self-respecting sense of self." 348 GW 5, 176; HW 2, 483.

32  GW 5, 176; HW 2, 483.

33  GW 5, 177; HW 2, 484.

34  GW 5, 178; HW 2, 485.

35  Ibid.

36  V. Humboldt, W.: "Denkschrift über Preussens ständische Verfassung vom 4. Februar 1819. "In Humboldt (1903 ff.), vol. XII.

37  GW 5, 5–135; HW , 558.

38  Rosenkranz 159 (on Thesis IX).

39  Ibid. 48.

40  Rosenkranz 62; the French essay printed by Rosenkranz (Rosenkranz 62, 532) on the changes in warfare during the transition from monarchy to republic is more likely to be an excerpt than a work of its own. I have not succeeded in proving it as Constant's work, just as Rosenkranz has not. It is quite wrong when Mayer-Moreau ([1910], 74–76) claims the influence of Constant (1814) on the view of the special nature of the modern state compared to the ancient one; he lacks any proof that this idea appears earlier in Constant than in Hegel; although he at least emphasizes the occurrence of the idea in Hegel for 1801/1802 – the other pieces of evidence escaped his attention [Mayer-Moreau], 41 ff).

41  GW 5, 202; HW I, 597.

42  Montesquieu (op. cit.), book 8, ch. 6; the belief that it is inexpensive is also common at that time (cf. Lehmann, M: Freiherr vom Stein. Vol. II. Leipzig, 1903, 69).

43  GW 5, 173; HW I, 481, on the care of the poor; but cf. p. 156 f.

44  GW 5, 111 f.; HW I, 533 f.; Montesquieu (op. cit.), book 2, ch. 6.

45  GW 4, 1–93; HW 2, 9–141.

46  GW 4, 54; HW 2, 82.

47  Ibid.; on the interpretation cf. GW 4, 72; HW 2, 108: "Freedom is characteristic of the absolute, if it is set as something internal [...] thus considered in opposition to its being [...], consequently with the possibility to leave it and to pass over into another appearance." This Hegelian text offers many occasions to refer to the second introduction to The German Constitution written in Frankfurt.

48  GW 4, 55; HW 2, 83.

49  SHK 1/9–1, 301 – Literally it says: "The Absolute acts through each individual intelligence, that is, its action is *itself* absolute, insofar as it is neither free nor unfree, but both at the same time, *absolutely* free, and for that very reason also necessary. Cf. also Section 3, note 32.

50  GW 4, 55 f.; HW 2, 84.

51  GW 4, 58; HW 2, 87 – "Organization" is here expressly opposed to the "machine."

52  Ibid. [JS & JS: let justice be done even if the world shall perish].

53  GW 5, 58; HW I, 456.

54  GW 5, 161; HW I, 461. – Cf. Moser (1766), Vol. I, p. 550. Hegel may have been particularly impressed by Majer, who wrote in the *Teutsche Staatskon-*

*stitution* (Majer [1800], p. 57 f.): "However, in the meantime, the sources of German history have gained ever greater publicity. One gradually grew tired of the argument about the very problematic German state constitution, and the statesmen calmed themselves down at last with the fact that the practice could leave this point all the more completely put aside, as it was to be regarded as a mere academic question. On the other hand, the German study of history became more and more important." What Hegel says about the popular designation of the Kaiser as "head of the empire" among the scholars of state law may also be attributed to Majer (GW 5, 63; HW I, 469).

55  Majer lectured in Tübingen several times on Tacitus' "Germania"; the views on the ancient Germanic sense of freedom were common property of the age.
56  GW 5, 8 Annotation.
57  GW 5, 60; HW I, 467.
58  GW 5, 61 (cf. Annotation); HW I, 468. – (cf. Note); HW I, 468 – on this idea, cf. Majer (op. cit.), 51: "The romanizing publicists often applied principles from Roman private law to state relations in a rather unfitting manner."
59  GW 5, 62; HW I, 468.
60  GW 5, 63; HW I, 469.
61  Ibid.
62  GW 5, 63 f.; HW I, 470; [JS & JS: Let justice be done to Germany]
63  GW 5, 126; HW I, 548.
64  GW 5, 127; HW I, ibid. – cf. J. v. Muller's account of the federation of princes (v. Müller [op. cit.], book 2, ch. 13).
65  GW 5, 130; HW I, 552.
66  GW 5, 131; HW I, 553.
67  GW 5, 132; HW I, 555.
68  GW 5, 131; HW I, 553.
69  GW 5, 131; HW I, 554.
70  GW 5, 135; HW I, 557.
71  GW 5, ibid.; HW I, 557 f.
72  GW 5, 133; HW I, 556.
73  GW 5, 132; HW I, 555.
74  Ibid. – verbatim: "One must approach reading *The Prince* directly from the history of the centuries preceding Machievelli and the history of Italy from that same time, with the impression that these have given."
75  GW 5, 137; HW I, 559 – verbatim: "gathered."
76  GW 5, 131; HW I, 563.
77  GW 5, 144; HW I, 567 – verbatim: "infinitely many" or "infinite many."
78  GW 5, 143; HW I, 566.
79  GW 5, 144; HW I, ibid.
80  Which at least "surfaced in popular opinion and did not fail to have its effect" during the Seven Years' War – this is what the Swabian meant (GW 5, 145; HW I, 567 f.).
81  Cf. Section 7, note 9.
82  GW 5, 149; HW I, 572 – verbatim: "stands."

83   GW 5, 152 f.; HW I, 575.
84   GW 5, 149; HW I, 72.
85   Ibid.
86   GW 5, 150; HW I, ibid.
87   GW 5, 177 f.; HW I, 484 f. [Rosenzweig quotes here *mutatis mutandis*. In the HW edition the sentence reads as follows: "How when in such a modern state, in which everything is regulated from above, nothing that has a universal side is left to the administration and implementation coming from sections of the people that are interested in it – as the French republic has done – a leathery, spiritless life is the result, this, if this tone of pedantry in ruling can remain, will only be experienced in the future; but what kind of life and what aridity prevails in another equally regulated state, in the Prussian state, is apparent to anyone who enters the first village of the same, or sees its utter lack of scientific and artistic genius, or does not consider its strength according to the ephemeral energy to which height a single genius had known to raise it for a time."]
88   GW 5, 150; HW I, 573.
89   Ibid.
90   GW 5, 153; HW I, 576.
91   GW 5, 154; HW I, 577.
92   Ibid.
93   GW 5, 157 (cf. annotation); HW I, 580.
94   GW 5, 157 (cf. annotation); HW I, 580.
95   GW 5, 158; HW I, 581 – verbatim: "the concept and insight," therefore later "leads," "must" and "submits to it."
96   GW 5, 157; HW I, 580.
97   Ibid.
98   Rosenkranz 236, 245.
99   GW 5, 136; HW I, 558.
100   Cf. Rosenkranz, 195.
101   Haym 209.
102   Not even in Treitschke (loc. cit., 194).
103   Dilthey (1905), 150 f.
104   Mayer-Moreau (op. cit.), 45.
105   GW 5, 141; HW I, 564; Ww. VII, 121.
106   GW 5, 143 f.; HW I, 566 – Austria "a power, whose politics and magnanimity are capable and incline towards protecting its" – the small estates – "existence" (ibid.). Of course, at that time Bonaparte also attributed the common voice to that same "magnanimity"; cf. Holzhausen, P.: "Literatur- und Stimmungsbilder aus den ersten Koalitionskriegen" in: *Beilage zur Allgemeinen Zeitung* (1898) and the same (1900); cf. as well Heigel (op. cit.), 399f.; v. Dalberg (1802), 40: "And the exceptional man, whose merit as producer is even greater as victor, who makes possible what appears impossible, who established order upon the ruins and atrocities in France, who gave his contemporaries freedom, this extraordinary man has enough greatness of soul to

rise above the class of benefactors of individual nations in order to become a benefactor of humanity, to widely support constitutions, calm, peace and concord."

107 Groß-Hoffinger (1847), 257; Österreichische Rundschau XXXI, 427; In 1799, Dalberg, eager to scheme and versatile, had wanted for him the position of a "dictator" of the anterior imperial circles (Krämer [1821], 28 ff.; v. Beaulieu-Marconnay [1879], Vol. I, 234); in 1800, and again just then in 1802, there were already plans at the Imperial Diet to honor him through a national memorial (Heigel [op. cit.], 429). From Dalberg's pamphlet, just cited, immediately before the adoration of Napoleon: "the upright German may hope that [...] Germany's hero and savior Karl will also be its preserver" (v. Dalberg [1802], 39). Hegel himself might well have hesitated a moment, if he should designate the brother of the rightful head of the Empire as "conqueror"; he crossed out the harsh word in the manuscript and then, led by an austere political sense of reality – which also taught him to see in this future Austria, in contrast to the German states, a power alongside others – put the word back (GW 5, 157 [cf. annotation]; HW I, 580). [JS & JS: Lachmann edited this endtnote from a passage that Rosenzweig had originally included in the main body of the text].

108 GW 8, 259; SE III, 237.

109 Haym 77 ff.

110 GW 5, 6 (cf. annotation); HW I, 452 Annotation.

111 Ibid.

112 GW 5, 162; HW I, 462 f.

113 GW 5, 162 f.; HW I, 463.

114 GW 5, 163; HW I, ibid.

115 Ibid.

116 Ibid.

117 Ibid.

118 Thus the original version (GW 5, 165; HW I, 465).

119 Lasalle (1863), 35, who, however, quotes Fichte for this purpose.

120 [JS & JS: "System of Ethical Life"] GW 5, 277–361; SdS, 3–85. [On the dating, see GW 5, 660 ff.] – The manuscript presents itself as the continuation of a longer manuscript, published by Ehrenberg and Link, [JS & JS: Hegels Erstes System (1915); Eingeleitet von H. Ehrenberg], which contains a Logic, a Metaphysics, and most of a Philosophy of Nature. Yet internally it is not a continuation. Haym was already successful in showing (Haym 170ff.) that there is a noticeable difference between the academic method of the larger and the smaller manuscript; the smaller one, which we are dealing with here, works entirely with the philosophical concepts which Schelling had quite recently used as the foundation of his lectures (beginning in 1801) and his writings (in the "Darstellung meines Systems der Philosophie" at the end of 1801). However, a gap in time, as Haym assumes, is not therefore a given; throwing himself consciously into the thoughts of others is not uncommon with Hegel; indeed, in "The Life of Jesus" from Bern, Hegel had made the

world of Kant's language and thoughts his own, to the point of complete self-renunciation. And in this case with Schelling, we are even dealing with thoughts that Schelling had developed in intimate connection with Hegel, indeed, the expert on Plato whom later, according to his own testimony, he would say inspired him. One could even hold it to be highly probable (cf. the article – by J.E. Erdmann and by Jodl – in the ADB) that Schelling was driven towards this truly independent step in his philosophizing, which until then still depended upon Fichte ("even since I had seen the light of philosophy" he writes about this moment in 1805) precisely by Hegel's text from July of 1801, in which Hegel had grasped the contrast between Fichte and Schelling much more deeply than Schelling had yet been able to express himself; at that point Hegel had boldly interpreted his friend's philosophy, much like Schelling had once done with Fichte's system in 1795, in the direction that Schelling himself was soon to take. In that Hegel, in contrast to Schelling, had then developed Logic, Metaphysics, and Philosophy of Nature independently according to form and content, whereas his Ethics was thoroughly dependent upon Schelling in terms of its form and especially its language, although admittedly not its content, that may have had its own reason. The logician, the metaphysician, as well as the philosopher of nature entered a living philosophical movement; he almost had to, in order to be understood, make use of the linguistic tools which had been forged by Kant, and even more so by Fichte, and which Schelling had adopted from both. Thus, Fichte's well-known technical terms whirr around us here with Hegel and are only occasionally mixed with Hegel's own influence. It is otherwise with the philosophy of the ethical [Philosophie des Sittlichen]. Here Hegel must have felt like a complete beginner; what Schelling had produced before the reunion with Hegel in this area, with the exception of the fundamental questions, was without autonomy and breadth; and Fichte the ethicist appeared at such infinite distance from the ground of his own knowledge that he had to reject even an apparently external connection. And moreover, Hegel was far removed from understanding language as something purely external. Just as he was the first one to introduce the linguistic-philosophical tendencies of the bygone century into the new philosophical movement, at that time he had also struggled consciously and seriously himself to "teach [philosophy] to speak German"; he testifies to this himself in a letter to Voß, the translator of Homer into German. In that, in the area most his own, which he was now preparing to decipher, a connection to the language at hand did not come into question, in that it was impossible for him here to connect to the philosophy at hand, he was forced to rely upon new means of language. And therefore, it seemed obvious to him to reach for Schelling's newest language, which was free from all memories of a foreign ethical doctrine, to which Fichte's language inevitably clung. But all of this has only the value of conjecture.

121   GW 5, 340; SdS, 63.
122   GW 5, 280; SdS, 4.
123   GW 5, 281; SdS, 5.

124   GW 5, 290 ff.; SdS, 14 ff.

125   GW 5, 297; SdS, 21.

126   GW 5, 298; SdS, 32.

127   GW 5, 301; SdS, 24.

128   GW 5, 302; SdS, 25. – The idea of economic stages points as much to the Steuart, which Hegel himself worked through (cf. Roscher [1874], 592), as to Plato, whom Eber holds entirely responsible (loc. cit., 81).

129   GW 5, 304; SdS, 27.

130   GW 5, 305; SdS, 28 f.

131   GW 5, 307; SdS, 30.

132   GW 5, 309; SdS, 33.

133   GW 5, 312; SdS, 36.

134   GW 5, 314; SdS, 37.

135   GW 5, 315; SdS, 38.

136   GW 5, 319; SdS, 42.

137   GW 5, 319 annotation; SdS, 43 annotation.

138   GW 5, 322; SdS, 46.

139   GW 5, 279; SdS, 3.

140   A nation can exist as a nation and simultaneously perish as a people: "Germans disappeared as a people – were only a nation" (from the undateable marginal note to a manuscript from the end of 1805 [marginal notation from the "Jena Systementwürfen"; cf. GW 8, 259 Annotation; SE III, 236 Annotation. For dating cf. the editorial report to GW 8 or the introduction in SE III, XX ff. In context, the quote is as follows (according to SE III): "Realization of the northern stubbornness of the Germans, because they could not bear any tyrants they disappeared as a *people*; – they were only a *nation* [...]]); "if Germany [...] completely perishes [...] as a state [...] and the German nation as a people" (GW 5, 64; HW I, 470). And, like Tacitus' Teutons, they can make up a people without being a state (GW 5, 59; HW I, 466), i.e., they can be politically organized but not into a single state. Furthermore, it is telling that Hegel translates Polis with "people" [Volk] in Aristotle (cf. end note VII/314). The connecting link is likely Cicero's "*populus*"; as a schoolboy Hegel had already read the fragments of his book on the state. Thus from 1800 to 1801, "nationality" (cf. end note VI/45) ("in other countries [...] nationality, the state, was victorious over the wreckage" – namely the schism in faith), is combined directly and without a conjunction with "state" (GW 5, 46; HW I, 609) – it is not to be judged in what sense.

141   GW 5, 322 f.; SdS, 46.

142   GW 5, 166; SdS, 473.

143   Aristoteles πληθος ου το τυχον; Cicero: *non omnis hominum coetus qopqo modo congretatus* [JS & JS: not every group of men is gathered together in the same way].

144   GW 5, 325; SdS, 49.

145   GW 5, 326; SdS, 49.

146   GW 5, 328; SdS, 51.

147  GW 5,175; HW I, 482.
148  GW 5, 328; SdS, 52.
149  GW 5, 329; SdS, 53.
150  GW 5, 333 f.; SdS, 56 f.
151  GW 5, 333; SdS, 56.
152  GW 5, 334; SdS, 57 f.
153  GW 5, 334; SdS, 58.
154  GW 5, 328; SdS, 52.
155  GW 5, 330 f.; SdS, 53 f.
156  GW 5, 331; SdS, 54.
157  GW 5, 329; SdS, 53.
158  GW 5, 330; SdS, 54.
159  GW 5, 335 f.; SdS, 59.
160  GW 5, 336; SdS, ibid.
161  This is the sense of the sentence "Since the unity, which is in these relations, is something ideal as such, something thought, for the sake of the difference being fixed, it alone receives a reality in the people."
162  GW 5, 336; SdS, 59 f.
163  GW 5, 336; SdS, 60.
164  GW 5, 331; SdS, 55.
165  GW 5, 332; SdS, 55.
166  Ibid.
167  GW 5, 338; SdS, 62.
168  GW 5, 332; SdS, 55.
169  GW 5, 338; SdS, 62.
170  Ibid.
171  GW 5, 332; SdS, 55.
172  GW 5, 332; SdS, 56.
173  GW 5, 333; SdS, 56. – The third estate is "within the first" in civil law (GW 5, 338; SdS, 82).
174  GW 5, 339; SdS, 62.
175  The original disposition plan can still be recognized (GW 5, 327; SdS, 50); "first the repose of the same or the state constitution, thereupon its movement, or the government" [in the wording "as then"].
176  GW 5, 339; SdS, 62.
177  GW 5, 327; SdS, 50.
178  GW 5, 339 f.; SdS, 62 f. – On what has been said about Pütter and Majer (cf. Section 7, note 54), see Landsberg (loc. cit.), Vol. III/2, 340 and 454 (on this, for example, Majer [1800], 16: "through the person of the regent, the state receives life and activity").
179  GW 5, 327; SdS, 50 f.
180  GW 5, 340; SdS, 63.
181  GW 5, 340; SdS, 63 f.
182  GW 5, 340; SdS, 63.
183  GW 5, 341; SdS, 65.

184   Ibid.

185   Ibid.

186   GW 5, 342; SdS, 65 – verbatim: "By the loss of the reality [des Reellen] of indi-
      viduality, of the particular, is it alone capable, outside of its estate, which is the
      form and particularity of its individuality, to be above all in indifference and to
      retain the whole in and through all its parts."

187   Haym 166 – actually: "above the template."

188   On this question see Zeller (1903) Part 2, Dept. I, 901 (note 5) – Hegel him-
      self, by the way, did not presume a separation in Plato (HW 19, 85 f.) and
      already in 1802/03 in HW 2, 490 ("The constitution [Konstitution] of that sec-
      ond estate ...") (corresponds to Ww. VII, 380). That Hegel himself regarded
      the difference between the Platonic "philosophers" and his "old men" as a
      characteristic difference between ancient and modern statehood is shown by
      HW 19, 11 ff, which possibly go back in part to a Jena notebook.

189   GW 452 f.; HW 2, 485 – cf. the passage in the Dialogue *Politikos* (in Plato
      [2005], vol. VI, 522–525-294 a–c).

190   GW 5, 342; SdS,65.

191   "Absolute government is not formal merely because it presupposes the differ-
      ence of estates." – GW 5, 345; SdS, 68 f.

192   Cf. Zweig (1909) [JS & JS: constituent power].

193   GW 5, 88 Annotation.

194   Cf. FW 1/3, 440.

195   Cf. GW 4, 445; HW 2, 275.

196   GW 5, 344; SdS, 68. – verbatim: "entirely formal and empty."

197   GW 5, 344 f.; SdS, 68.

198   GW 5, 44; SdS, ibid. – GW "[in which] various rights ..."

199   GW 5, 346; SdS, 70.

200   GW 5, 345 f.; SdS, 70.

201   GW 5, 342; SdS, 65.

202   GW 5, 360; SdS, 84 f.

203   GW 5, 361; SdS, 85.

204   Ibid.

205   GW 4, 440; HW, 67.

206   GW 5, 346; SdS, 70.

207   Kant, *Rechtslehre*, § 45 (Kant [1902 f.], Vol. VI, 313).

208   GW 5, 348; SdS, 72.

209   GW 5, 349; SdS, 73.

210   GW 5, 349; SdS, 74.

211   "With noble pathos [...] Hegel fought against the deadness of the same (the
      mercantile system) by striving to save *the temperament* [das Gemüt] of the
      human being in the midst of competition and in the mechanism of labor
      as well as commerce" (Rosenkranz 86). This is to be combine with what we
      know about the role that the concept of "life" played in Hegel's thought at
      that time.

212   Roscher (1874), 598 ff.

213 Had Hegel been affected by their thoughts? In terms of contemporary history, it would be expected (cf. Roscher ibid.). In Bern Hegel had read Rayn as a work of history (Rosenkranz 60). The manuscript at hand explicitly rejects the "single edition" and otherwise shows no specific physiocratic traits, except perhaps one reminiscence noted in Section 3, note 233.

214 Roscher (op. cit.), 928 – For the section of writing discussed here, the first editor Mollat lists the heading as "a. The System of Need"; in the wording of the manuscript, the section is simply titled "A." However, the words "The System of Need" form the first words of the running text (GW 5, 350; SdS, 74).

215 That Hegel proceeded from Smith directly and not only from Sartorius' hand-book (cf. Roscher [op. cit.], 615) seems to me to emerge from the doctrine of state-needs, which Sartorius brings into a series deviating from Smith.

216 GW 5, 350; SdS, 74.

217 GW 5, 351; SdS, 75.

218 Cf. Feilbogen, S.: "James Steuart und Adam Smith" in *Zeitschrift für die gesamte Staatswissenschaft* 45 (1889), 236. Mention should also be made here of Whitbread's Minimum Wage Bill in the House of Commons in 1795 and the Poor Law introduced by Pitt in 1796; Rosenkranz reports that these negotiations greatly stirred Hegel's interest (Rosenkranz 85).

219 Steuart in the Introduction to Book I (Steuart 1913 f.).

220 GW 5, 352; SdS, 77.

221 GW 5, 353; SdS, 7.

222 GW 5, 353; SdS, 78.

223 Steuart (op. cit.), Book II, ch. 26.

224 GW 5, 354; SdS, 78.

225 Ibid.

226 Ibid.

227 Ibid.

228 GW 5, 354; SdS, 79 – verbatim: "ethically, in confidence."

229 This side glance, as the only explicit mention of ancient Greek conditions, is a main support of the thesis that the System of Ethicality is "a [...] description of the private, public, social, artistic and religious life of the Greeks" (Haym 160). In contrast to such evidence, referencing that the word "rifle" [Schießgewehrs] is mentioned (GW 5, 331; SdS, 54) might be an equivalent counterargument.

230 GW 5, 354 f. ("marginal addition": footnote to 355); SdS, 79.

231 Brentano (1871 f.), Vol. I, 100, 105f. – Eden (1797) gave a detailed account of the same.

232 Smith (1810), V, I, 1–3.

233 "[...] e.g., its residences etc., i.e. its temples, its streets etc." (GW 5, 355; SdS, 79 – the wording: "its temples, streets") – "temples" sounds antiquated. However, in Karl Friedrichs von Baden "Abrégé des principes de l'économie politique" (In: Daire [1864]) *patrimoine public* is explained as follows: "*C'est ce dont tout le monde a l'usage et qui n'est proprement et exclusivement à personne; les chemins, les rues, les temples, les quais, les ponts, les rivières*" (ibid., 377);

the explanation is also cited in "Leçons economiques" by the older Mirabeau (cf. Leser [1874], 91). Smith, under the third task of the state, also takes up commerce [Verkehr], instruction of the youth, and (as "instruction of adults") the church all together. He acknowledges that the church is supported by the state, even if he does not hold it to be exactly necessary.

234    GW 5, 355; SdS, 79.
235    GW 5, 355; SdS, 79 f.
236    GW 5, 355; SdS, 80.
237    GW 5, 356; SdS, 80.
238    Ibid.
239    Ibid.
240    Ibid.
241    GW 5, 356; SdS, 81.
242    In that "skill" would thereby not be incorporated, then the products of the soil would be overburdened; for the quantity brought to the market would not be adjusted according to the exchange value, as is the case with pure products of skill; cf. Smith on this reasoning (op. cit.), V, 2, 2, I, I: "[The (English) land tax cannot] prevent the possibly largest proliferation of the products of the land. Just as the land tax does not influence the reduction of the number of products, so it also cannot influence raising their prices. It does not in any way obstruct the purchasing diligence of the people." Hegel also justifies a taxation based on different kinds of estates in the text on *The German Constitution*: the reasoning for this may be found, entirely "separate from all that is called privilege" (GW 5, 169; HW I, 476), in that work cannot be calculated as something "subjective"; and in that one cannot grasp the "the natural side" of that which is being taxed, taxation is limited to what is objectively at hand, the "product" (ibid.) of work, by way of which – so we must elaborate – in view of the deep difference between what citizens, peasants, intellectuals, and nobles produce, implementing a uniform taxation would be pointless. The argumentation is similar to that found in the "System of Ethicality," in that it admits equal taxation in principle, and yet acknowledges it as impossible in practice, thereby seeking to justify the existing condition of the differences between estates.

243    Reasons to hold against capital interest tax: "In the first place, the quantity of the tracts of land one possesses cannot be held in secret, rather this can be determined with certainty. Yet what monetary capital one possesses is almost always a secret and can almost never be reliably determined." (Smith [op. cit.], V, 2, 2, 2 [I]); "Capitation tax, if one bases it on the assets or the revenues of the taxpayers, becomes almost inevitably arbitrary" (ibid., V, 2, 2, 4 [I]; "The impossibility [of levying] residents [...] with a capitation tax exactly relative to their income seems to have created the opportunity for the invention of consumption tax" (ibid., V, 2, 2, 4 [2 beginning]). Cf. the simplified summary from Sartorius (1796), §125: "In that all previous taxes, excluding those from basic pension, are more or less unequal [...], none other remain [...] except for

[...] consumption taxes." Admittedly, Hegel wishes to apply excise duty on the "largest possible particularity" of commodities, Smith only on luxury goods.

244  GW 5, 357; SdS, 82.
245  Ibid.
246  GW 5, 352; SdS, 82.
247  Ibid.
248  Ibid.
249  GW 5, 352; SdS, 82 f.
250  GW 5, 352; SdS, 83.
251  In the same context, Hegel later declared that the demand for jury courts was justified; but it seems doubtful to me that he had done so already at that time; at the very least the peasantry "is within the first estate in civil law."
252  GW 5, 359; SdS, 83.
253  GW 5, 359; SdS, 84.
254  Cf. "Elements of the Philosophy of Right," § 333 note (HW 7, 500): "There is no praetor, at most arbitrators and mediators between states, and even these only by chance, i.e., according to particular wills."
255  GW 5, 360; SdS, 84.
256  Ibid.
257  Ibid.
258  Ibid.
259  GW 4, 417–485; HW 2, 434–530.
260  GW 4, 421; HW 2, 440 ff.
261  Cf. also Schelling's criticism of the "previous treatment of so-called natural right" in the tenth "Vorlesungen über die Methode des akademischen Studiums" (Schelling [1856 ff.], vol. I/5, 315 f. [1990], 108 f.).
262  GW 4, 427; HW 2, 448 – verbatim: "the majesty."
263  GW 4, 428; HW 2, 449.
264  GW 4, 428; HW 2, 449 f.
265  GW 4, 428; HW 2, 450.
266  Cf. also Schelling (op. cit.), 316/(1990), 110.
267  GW 4, 441; HW 2, 470.
268  GW 4, 442; HW 2, 471 (cf. FW 1/3, 139 ff.) – (cf. FW 1/3, 139 ff.) – verbatim: "that loyalty and belief will be lost."
269  GW 4, 443; HW 2, ibid.
270  [Napoleon's coup of 18 Brumaire (November 9) 1799].
271  GW 4, 445; HW 2, 475. – verbatim: "what could one do with such rabble that ..."
272  GW 4, 448; HW 2, 479 [emphasis by Rosenzweig].
273  Vgl. Schelling (op. cit.), 314/(1990), 107 f.
274  GW 4, 334; SDS 58.
275  GW 4, 455; HW 2, 89 f.
276  GW 4, 455; HW 2, 490.
277  Ibid.

278   GW 4, 456; HW 2, 491.
279   GW 4, 457; HW 2, 492.
280   Gibbon (1776 ff.), Vol. I, ch. 2.
281   GW 4, 458; HW 2, 493 f.
282   GW I, 200 annotation: Nohl 365.
283   GW I, 164 annotation: Nohl 365.
284   Ibid.
285   Ibid – verbatim: "The System of Religion, which was always colored by the age and the state constitution, whose highest virtue [was] humility, consciousness of its incapacity, which expects everything from elsewhere, evil itself in part, will now receive its own true, independent dignity.
286   HW I, 258.
287   HW I, 289, N 284.
288   HW I, 331, N 271.
289   HW I, 400, N 327.
290   GW 5, II annotation.
291   HW I, 333, N 273.
292   GW 5, 17, HW I, 458.
293   Ibid.
294   HW I, 424; N 349 – verbatim: "and therefore he [the human being] gives up property, whose necessity is his fate, as a sacrifice."
295   HW I, 582; Ww. VII, 17 – verbatim: "A crowd of people can only call itself a state if it is united in the common defense of the whole of its property."
296   Cf. again, for example, the Tübingen professor Majer (idem 1782), 137 "[...] since, after all, it is precisely for the sake of this (property) and its security that the union of the state was established."
297   GW 5, 67.
298   Cf. Ww. VII, 17 where he repeats the definition almost verbatim, only that – incidentally, already in an older revision of the original draft – the "to have been joined," which still felt too much like the overcome idea of a contract, has become "to be joined."
299   According to GW 4, 454 ff., HW 2, 487 ff.
300   Cf. on the following: GW 4, 454 ff., HW 2, 487 ff.
301   GW 4, 458 f.; HW 2, 495 – verbatim: "to suffering and to death."
302   GW 4, 459; HW 2, 495.
303   GW 4, 459; HW 2, 495f.
304   GW 4, 459; HW 2, 496.
305   GW 4, 485; HW 2, 530.
306   Ibid.
307   Heeren (1803–1808) Vol. II, 240.
308   Cf. GW 4, 461 f., 468; HW 2, 499 f., 504 f.
309   GW 4, 459; HW 2, 496.
310   GW 4, 485; HW 2, 530.
311   Ibid.
312   GW 4, 467; HW 2, 504.

313  Ibid.
314  GW 4, 467; HW 2, 505 cf. the quotation from Aristotle's *Politics* (Aristotle 1991 ff.), 1253a (GW 4, 467 f.; HW 2, 505.
315  GW 4, 469; HW 2, 507.
316  GW 4, 469; HW 2, 508 – the quote stems from Diogenes Laertius (1998), book 8, § 16.
317  GW 4, 459; HW 2, 495.
318  Ibid.
319  Ibid.
320  GW 4, 467; SDS, 67.
321  GW 4, 477; HW 2, 519.
322  GW 4, 481; HW 2, 524.
323  GW 4, 480; HW 2, 523.
324  GW 4, 345 f.; SDS, 70.
325  GW 4, 477; HW 2, 519.
326  GW 4, 479; HW 2, 502.
327  GW 4, 481; HW 2, 525.
328  GW 4, 481; HW 2, 525.
329  GW 4, 481 f.; HW 2, 525 f.
330  GW 4, 482; HW 2, 526.
331  GW 4, 482; HW 2, 526.
332  GW 4, 483; HW 2, 527.
333  Ibid.
334  GW 4, 483; HW 2, 528.
335  Ibid.
336  GW 4, 484; HW 2, 529.
337  GW 4, 484; HW 2, 529 f.
338  Cf. also Schelling (1990), Lecture 10: "The State as a Work of Art."
339  GW 4, 469; HW 2, 507.
340  Ibid.; verbatim: "living" [lebenden].
341  GW 5, 127; HW 1, 549.
342  Rosenkranz 190.
343  GW 4, 459 f.; HW 2, 496 – verbatim: "without fate."
344  GW 4, 459; HW 2, 496.
345  GW 4, 460; HW 2, 496.
346  GW 4, 460; HW 2, 497.
347  Ibid.
348  GW 4, 460; HW 2, 497 f.
349  GW 4, 461; HW 2, 498.
350  Ibid.
351  GW 4, 461; HW 2, 498 f.
352  GW 1, 95; HW 1, 517.
353  HW I, 247 – verbatim: "Fear of mortality, of one's own."
354  Hölderlin (1992 f.), Vol. II, 374 ("Anmerkungen zur Antigone").

# 8

# JENA (AFTER 1804)

The preceding section accompanied the development of Hegel's idea of the state until its individual details became clearly visible for the first time. Up until this point, Hegel's image of the state appeared in three successive phases. The first, the "concept of the state" in the pamphlet, was not systematically developed and was never intended to be a philosophical ideal. We discovered from the publication of 1801, at least suggestively, in what connection the state stood for Hegel at that time. We encountered a systematic philosophy of state in broad detail for the first time in the manuscript of 1802. In contrast to this manuscript, the text on natural right, published in the beginning of 1803, enabled us to already recognize a new phase of the system. It is here where we begin again and, based on truly rich, if also incomplete sources, follow the subsequent development of Hegel's philosophy of state, as it was presented on the lectern in Jena from extensively detailed notebooks.

In what preceded, we recognized as the core of Hegel's view of the state the doctrine of the three estates which, as Hegel developed them, clearly showed themselves to be a heightened likeness of northern German, in particular Prussian, relations of the eighteenth century.

DOI: 10.4324/9780429354724-9

In this division of estates, the contrast between an ethics of personality and an ethics of society, between a state-free sphere and "life in the
state," which in a certain sense already became visible at the end of the
time in Bern in the juxtaposition of the modern and classical image of
the state, was systematically configured and thereby overcome by the
philosopher. This was possible because in Frankfurt the middle point
of both ideals of the state, the individual and the state as a whole, came
into contact in a very personal manner through the thought of the state
as fate. Thus, hereafter it is no longer the case of a contrast or juxtaposition. The state and the human being were systematically held distinct,
systematically united. The division of estates, in 1802 only a part of the
doctrine of the state – "Constitution" – next to which the doctrine of
"government" stood as the other part, appears in 1803 to make up the
entire content of the doctrine of the state. On this basis, the systematic
foundation was also reconfigured: "transgression" does not appear there
as the second preliminary stage to the state, as it did in 1802 as the
last and only systematic echo of the ideas from Frankfurt; rather, in its
place is the world of right. And while in 1802 "natural ethicality" still
included the entire sphere of economics and right, apart only from its
relation to the state, as the first preliminary stage, apparently in 1803
a separation emerges between phenomena occurring before right and
before society, and phenomena occurring within right and society. From
now on, the former inhabit the first part of "Natural Right," the latter the
second. The problem of the state-free sphere and the disposition of the
citizen, which in the system of 1802 only determined the structure of
the estates, now dominates the entire systematic plan in 1803 and finds
in the state itself, through the structure of the estates, only its concluding
solution. This first fundamental change in the system between 1802 and
1803 shows the central importance that the problem holds for Hegel's
political thinking. The previous sections attempted to show how it came
to have such importance.

The essay on natural right only provides a few clues on the closer
explanation of both first stages. He calls the first the "real *practical*" and
lists its content as perception or physical need and pleasure, work, and
possession. He designates the second as "*right*," insofar as it is possible
within the "real practical," that is, within the realm of the first stage:[1] the
manifestation of the absolute ethicality of the state, to a certain extent

the pre-ethical realm of the "real practical." One can assume that at that time Hegel had pictured in detail this middle realm between life below the state and the state as a simple repetition of that life, but now in its relation to the state. The assumption becomes almost certain as we now turn to the next preserved version of the essay on natural right.

This next version is preserved as a quarto manuscript which was apparently prepared for the purpose of lecturing.[2] The parts that will come into consideration for us were not formulated before 1804, and so it is possible that we have before us a work from the lecture-free summer semester of that year. And similarly, we may assume that the first Jena system, of which the "System of Ethicality" makes up one part, is probably the outcome of such a lecture-free half year, the summer of 1802.

The manuscript contains, aside from the missing opening, a complete philosophy of nature followed by the philosophy of spirit beginning in the middle of the page. This is designated as the third part, so that, as already in 1802, one can imagine as an overall design that a Logic preceded the preserved manuscript as the first part,[3] a supposition that is confirmed by Hegel's lecture notes. In the division of the philosophy of spirit we now in fact find the differentiation, which was already in place in the essay on natural right in 1803 and unknown in the System of 1802, between a sphere beneath the state, and a higher one in which the life of the first sphere now appears again within the state, although not yet as the state itself. This first sphere is designated here as the "formal existence"[4] of consciousness and establishes itself in the three stages of language, the tool, and possession. Language is no longer, as in 1802, and apparently even in 1803, conceived in close association with the most practical relationships of the human being.[5] Instead, language appears in connection with a psychology of intelligence: perception, imagination, sign, etc.[6] The psychology of practical consciousness – "animal desires," "work," etc. – is addressed with the tool.[7] Into the doctrine of possession Hegel brings marriage, the relation of parents and children, the family estate and the utilization of life for the acknowledgement of possession.[8] This last part is elaborated on disproportionately, which is explained in that this part partially accommodates the missing doctrine of "transgression" from 1802. It is precisely the contradiction that here the whole of life is appointed to something individual, possession, that allows for a second sphere, that of private right, to emerge. This is taken here, however, already as nothing less than the existence of consciousness in the people. Since the concept of the "people" already appears at the second stage, rather than, as in 1802, only appearing at the third stage, the universal doctrine of absolute ethicality is therefore already introduced and dealt with at this point. It is not entirely clear how Hegel imagined what came next, as our manuscript is no longer complete. It seems as if at that time he would have wanted to more closely incorporate the second and third part of the system of the philosophy of spirit or, in the terms of 1803, right and absolute ethicality, in contrast to the first part, perhaps almost as its own main part. It is nevertheless certain from the text that he places a break between the sphere of right of 1803 and the sphere of the state. He conceives of the sphere of right as the development of the spirit from its mere "formal" existence described in the first part and, here, the sphere of the state for Hegel is the absolute self-indulgence [Selbstgenuß] of the spirit. "Spirit being judged according to its inorganic nature"[9] occurs such that he allows it to subsist, but designates it with the character of "universality." This operation is sequentially undertaken on all three stages of its "formal existence" – language, tool, and family. They all first attain "real existence" in the people. It is only primarily in the people that language is truly language. Similarly, it is only primarily in the people that the immediate instinctive work for one's own needs becomes "universal." It becomes learned work; the tool becomes the machine. Between the needs of the individual and the satisfaction of the same comes the work of the entire people. The division of labor, the dulling of the individual worker, monetary economy, and the dependence of all upon all, so that the human being, in that he subjects himself to nature as a species, only increases his interdependence to it as an individual.[10] "Raised to this universality, need and work form for themselves an enormous system of communality and mutual dependence in a great people, a life of the dead moving within itself, which moves in its consciousness blindly and elementarily to and fro and like a wild animal requires constant strict tempering and taming."[11] And like language and work, possession also becomes "a universal in its particularity"[12] in the whole of a people – it becomes rightful property. The individual no longer instantiates their entire natural personality for the recognition of possession, as in the condition prior to right but, rather, possession is solely tied to the legal person. Here the last preserved page of the manuscript breaks off.

For us, its importance lies primarily therein, that here Hegel makes the first attempt to describe in detail the middle-realm, which he will later designate as "civil society," between the state and the human being before the state. He does not yet look to give it its own structure, but rather – and here it shows that it is a first attempt – he simply repeats the structure of the sphere prior to the state and designates it "with the character of universality."Thereby, for example, he comes to the idiosyncratic and later unrepeated double-placement of language as language in general and as language of a people. In terms of content, the manuscript does not offer much that is new. The view of national economy is the same as in 1802, stemming from Smith: on this basis the demand to the state is then founded to govern and tame the "wild animal" of economic life.[13] Things that were addressed in part, like the concept of property and machine-work in 1802 in the first part of the system, the dulling of the working masses and the abandonment of the individual to the harmony of the economy in the closing part of the system, are now found together in 1804 in the new middle realm.

The next shape of the system on the philosophy of spirit, calculated from the first Jena system as the fourth, is preserved as a revision of the manuscript just discussed. It deals essentially only with the first part. The triple-division of language, tool, and possession is replaced by a double division of theoretical and practical consciousness[14] already initiated in the previous shape.[15] The "spirit of a people" now emerges as the fusion of this theoretical and practical consciousness. Due again to the fragmentary record, it is not certain whether Hegel wanted to develop this double division only within the first or as the first and second part of the whole. The wording of the additions speaks to the second possibility. It would then follow, in accordance with Hegel's intention at that time, that the doctrine of what would later be called "society" would have introduced the concluding part of the system. The next shape of the system, which we now turn to, speaks very emphatically for the other possibility – the double division within the first part.

It is the last configuration that the system in Jena reached. One can place it with relative certainty in the year 1805.[16] Here, at least for the parts of the system important to us, we finally find continuous material. As we came to know through the disjointed folios pages, Hegel had lectured on the doctrine of the state during his final years in Jena.

All previously observed phases of the system were either carried out in fragments or passed down in fragments. Even the System of 1802, the comparatively most complete, was lost towards the end to aphoristic insinuations. On the basis of the manuscript to be discussed below, we can first look to answer certain questions preserved until now regarding the older phases of the system.

In the part of the manuscript at hand, the double division of the first section of the philosophy of spirit into a theoretical and practical part, "Intelligence" and "Will," which was first carried out in the revision of the previously observed manuscript, is also its basis. In the manner already discussed, the section "Will" encompasses simple work, the tool, nature-based relations of family life and finally, as the freely acknowledged individuality that asserts itself in conflict, the person in the legal sense. With this we cross the border of the first part and find ourselves at the entrance to the second part: "actual spirit." "Spirit is neither actual as intelligence nor as will, but rather as will which is intelligence [...] Possession transforms [...] into right, [...] work [...] becomes [...] the work and satisfaction of all; – and the difference between individuals becomes a knowledge of good and evil; – personal right and wrong."[17] Here machine-work, contract, crime and punishment all initially only unfold in their relation to the person. Behind this there surfaces the realm of "authoritative laws"[18] and now the concepts just addressed are run through a second time, now in relation to this realm, albeit in new arrangement. One already sees from this complication of the entire division which the "actual spirit" experiences here, in contrast to the arrangement of the first stage simply repeated as "real existence of consciousness" in the previous phase of the system, how much the independent importance of this middle-realm has grown. Under "authoritative laws" we first find the family, now no longer an appearance of nature but rather a right-based religious union of people and in addition inheritable family property. With the departure of the children from their parent's family a new sphere, whose limits coincide more or less with the outline of "civil society" from 1820, now appears under "authoritative laws," inserted between family and state. Insofar as the "person" is assigned its own world within "actual spirit," which was not the case in 1804, the later independence of right within the doctrine of "objective spirit" is initiated. In this manner there already appears in 1805, with the separation of the spheres of family and the supra-familial, an essential trait of the final version. But while in 1805 this sphere beyond the family had its own place for Hegel, it did not yet have its own name. Just as in 1803, and even in 1804, he conceived of this sphere only as the reflection of the state in the natural-ethical realm, or as the development of the state from this, so that now he only has the name of "state" for the existence between the family and the state: whereas in the family individuals were what was actually living, the "existence" [Dasein] of the family, here "law [...] emerges as existence: the state."[19] This realm, where the whole carries out an "unconscious guardianship" in "strict necessity"[20] over the human, is divided in detail into the three worlds of national economy, civilian, and criminal administration of justice. Hegel's views on national economy are known to us from before. As in 1802 and 1804, he describes the de-ethicizing consequences of the division of labor and machine-work. There is now no longer any talk of the guilds which, in 1802, were supposed to provide relief. Only the state-based politics of economy is introduced here: "the authority of the state enters and must assure that every sphere is preserved, takes the middle ground, looks for outlets, channels of reason in other lands, and so on – impeding some insofar as it overreaches too much to the disadvantage of others."[21] But now – and here the effects of the new economic doctrine already visible in 1802 break through – "*freedom of trade*, intervention must be as inconspicuous as possible. Because it is the field of caprice – even the appearance of force must be avoided – and do not desire to save what cannot be saved, but instead engage the suffering classes differently."[22] The government is capable of guarding individuals within certain limits only through its "universal oversight."[23] In contrast to 1802, a turn from what was contemporary also enters into the doctrine of state-income. Indeed, already in 1802 Hegel agreed with Adam Smith on the theory of taxes. Now, he even polemicizes expressly against the physiocrats. But whereas in 1802, here like almost everywhere with a dependence on the actuality of the state, he had practically acknowledged the emoluments from the domains, Hegel now states, radically and only differing from Smith in the justification: "The wealth of the state must be based as little as possible upon the domains and instead be based upon bonds. These are privately owned and fortuitous, and thus excluded from dissipation, because no one seems to lose anything, but rather wins or hopes to win.

Everyone feels good about bonds and wants to see that they are used well."[24] We hear nothing that is new, or at least nothing that is important to us, about the civil administration of justice. The state is "the power of right,"[25] it coerces and has to make sure that "whoever has the desire"[26] can be surrendered to the entire length and breadth of litigation which "is almost more essential than the law itself."[27] The state finally shows its true face in the administration of criminal justice, as far as it can even show it at this stage. It is the "power over life and death"[28] and, indeed, in pardoning it expels actuality itself from the world – "the act is [...] as if it never happened."[29] There the state is "master over evil" and, Hegel adds, thereby certainly taking up the thread from Frankfurt: "like pure life."[30] Of this the same was said as now of the state, namely, that as fate of the individual it had healed the very wound that it had made.

"This power over all *existence*, property and life," so Hegel now summarizes, "and even over thoughts as well, over *right* and good and evil, is the body politic, the living people."[31] As "wealth"[32] the state coolly leaves the earning individuals unbothered as much as possible. This is Hegel's emotional emphasis on the acknowledged freedom of trade. As a civil right worth respecting it maintains in the citizen the source of its opinion of itself as a person worth attending to. Finally, it intervenes in the outer-stately life of the individual as a punitive and pardoning power over life and death. Those are "its *authorities*," not yet itself, not yet its existence. These it first attains in the "Konstitution."[33]

While the overall design of the system of the philosophy of spirit from 1802 until 1803 could be followed in its gradual transformation, this is impossible for the internal structure of the main division. This is evidenced only somewhat for 1803 by the essay on natural right. For the subsequent period we are almost entirely abandoned by the sources. We could nevertheless conclude that large sections of the doctrine on absolute ethicality from 1802, namely at least the doctrine on the "universal government," were shifted in 1803 and certainly in 1804 from the ending to the middle stage of the system and to the later doctrine of society. Now, in 1805, the third and last part of the philosophy of spirit entitled "Constitution" provides the confirmation of such conclusions, and even more.[34]

In contrast to 1804, the last system of Jena is entirely free from the shackles of the Schellingian method. That can be seen even in the use of language which, admittedly already in 1804, showed an important Hegelian trait in how strongly the concept of consciousness was utilized, but also clearly betrayed the connection with the System of 1802 in the external joining-together of the "potencies." At that time in 1802, the construction of the individual "potencies" followed, corresponding respectively in relation to "concept" and "intuition." According to the basic characteristic directed towards "intuition and the present" of that draft, the stages of ethicality were constructed from purely knowledge-based components. It appears in 1804, as far as the fragmentary material allows for such a claim, that this work with the fixed pieces "concept" and "intuition" gives way to a livelier understanding of the individual stages as forms of consciousness. Hegel later attempted to universally carry out this manner of understanding the world in the work that concluded the Jena epoch, *The Phenomenology of Spirit*. What was already begun with the revision of the System of 1804, namely the consistent division of consciousness into intelligence and will, now dominates the entire structure of the System of 1805. Just as Hegel had worked with concept and intuition in 1802, he now works with intelligence and will. They are now the basic forces according to whose relation the systematic placement of the individual appearances of spirit are ordered. The knowledge-based characteristic of the System of 1802 is laid aside here in favor of a philosophical counterbalance of knowledge and will. This incidentally does not exclude that the historian, despite Hegel's academic counter-balancing, may sense how here, and indeed everywhere with Hegel, the personal and prevailing undertone of passionate recognition forcefully holds sway. Intelligence and will, separated from each other, and in fact the will here as the higher stage, now make up the content of the first part of the philosophy of spirit; the will, "which is intelligence," [35] fills the middle part as "actual spirit": the will, which is no longer the "abstract" will of the individual. Instead, the will operates within the framework of the community. Finally, the "constitution" shows the will how it not only prevails within the framework of the spiritual community, but rather how, as the will of the individual, it stands in the most internal connection with the will of the spiritual community, indeed really becomes one with it. When Hegel now prefaces his philosophy of state with an introductory section on the concept of the universal will, then this closely correlates, as we will see, with the basic characteristic of this phase of his philosophy of spirit. At the same time, it marks the moment when Hegel erected the scientific foundation of the structure of his state which, from now on, he will not abandon.

The relation of the individual will to the collective will is described as threefold: individuals divest themselves of their will with respect to the whole; they make themselves into an essential component of the collective will; and finally, they acknowledge the freedom of the collective will in the same manner as they acknowledge their own.[36] Or, compared with the individual, the whole is "master, public authority and regent."[37] This is now carried through.

To begin with, let us consider the "master." What does it mean that the whole dictates the will of the individual, that, as Hegel says with Aristotle, it "comes earlier than the parts"?[38] The doctrine of state contracts attempts to explain this, and thereby establish "the principle of the true, free state."[39] Hegel dismisses this. The theory of state contracts presupposed what it wanted to explain,[40] namely, the obligation of individuals, the universally valid content of the individual will. Every individual has the right "to run away and come to an agreement with others about something else,"[41] and yet the theory requires that they do not exercise this right. Thus, universal will cannot be understood as the product of the individual will prior to the state but, instead, solely as a preexisting "authority, which coerces it."[42] And with this there originates, already known to us from the critique of *The German Constitution*, the doctrine of the spiritual coercion of the state, emerging in the contract theory from that still unexplained contradiction between the natural will of the individual and the collective will: "Thus all states were founded upon the sublime authority of great men, not physical strength, for many are physically stronger than one."[43] In this sense, the "Natural Right" essay already rejected deriving the passage from the state of nature to the state of right from a subjugation of weaker to stronger. The spiritual element in Hegel's doctrine of the state went into effect with this point: "physical strength" does not explain the success of the great man of power. Instead, he has "something in his features, for which others want to call him master; they obey him against their will; contrary to their will, his will is their will; their immediate will is his will, but their conscious will is different; the great man has these people on his side, and they must be on his side, even if they do not want to be. This is the leading nature of the great man: to know the absolute will and to express it. Everyone gathers around his banner; he is their God."[44] As examples, Hegel names Theseus,[45] as well as Pisistratus, who made "the laws of Solon the citizens' own"[46] – thus actually justifying concept and insight through authority! – and additionally, the "terrible force" of Robespierre: "*Tyranny, purely appalling reign, but* [...] *necessary and just insofar as it constitutes and preserves* the state."[47] Power is "evil in itself," thus taught a great historian later on in strongly felt contrast to the sentiment of his age.[48] Hegel, who himself would become one of the originators of this sentiment, thought otherwise. His state knows "no concepts of good and evil, harmful or wicked, malice and deception; it is elevated above all of these, for in it evil is reconciled with itself."[49] Praise of Machiavelli and a strike against the "northern obstinacy of Germans"[50] easily follows such an estimation of power as good in itself: they have "detested such doctrines the most and Machiavellianism expresses the most evil, as they are suffering from precisely the same sickness and have died from it."[51]

Tyranny makes itself superfluous; it is merely "cultivation towards obedience."[52] Therefore, the tyrant, who should indeed abdicate, but does not, can and must be overthrown. With this, however, the state ceases to be merely "master" and now shows the human being a new face: "public authority and regent," reign of law.[53] The soul of the relation between the state and the individual is no longer the self-externalization of the individual will towards unconscious obedience, but rather trust to find one's own will in the will of the whole. In contrast to that other "positive" relation, now this can take on two different forms, and indeed has taken them on in history. Government and governed can be externally the same people: "the same person provides for himself and his family, works, enters into contracts, etc. and precisely thereby he also works for the universal and this is his purpose; on the one hand he is called *bourgeois* and on the other *citoyen*."[54] Admittedly, in democracy the unity of the individual will and collective will is still not completely actualized. With democracy, the will of the individual is devalued by the possibility to be outvoted, the necessary independence of the executive and the unpredictability of the success of the vote. Nevertheless: "this is the beautiful, fortunate freedom of the Greeks, who were, and continue to be, so very envied; the people at once dissolved into citizens, and the people is, at once, the same individual, the government; it simply stands in reciprocation with itself."[55] But this living "ingenious"[56] unity of the human being and the state, this Empire of the old ethicality has vanished and had to vanish: "A higher abstraction is necessary, a greater contrast, a *deeper* spirit"[57] – it is not enough, as in the Polis and its most internal portrayal, the Platonic state, that the individual relinquishes his particularity. Rather, he must know his particularity, "this," his personal self, as the "essence" of the state.[58] This occurs within the second form which the "positive" relation of "trust"[59] between the individual and the whole may assume: within modern monarchy.[60]

It is the first very basic acknowledgement of monarchy that we find in Hegel. Of course, the pamphlet of 1802 had already found in modern monarchy, in that which is connected to the representation of the people, the true guarantee of personal freedom. Hegel had even attempted there, for the first time, to construct world history according to oriental despotism, the Greek municipal republic, and the Germanic estate-based monarchy – a construction that, two decades later, would form the basis for his lectures on the philosophy of history. But next to this philosophy of history, which appears only occasionally, there still stands that older one, nurtured on Rousseau and Schiller and on the experience of the magnificent sunrise from 1789, and held in common with Hölderlin and Schelling. For this philosophy of history the present was not regarded as fulfillment, but rather as an epoch of transition from the deepest decline, namely from the Roman Imperium and absolute monarchy, to a more beautiful future. And with this philosophy of history, upon which, as the "Natural Right" essay clearly showed, the ideal of the state from 1802 and 1803 rested, the older, republicanizing construction of the head of state was salvaged and incorporated at least into the first system of Jena. In this system, the absolute government was described as an aristocratic, unhereditary body of priestly sages, even though Hegel himself admitted that this aristocracy of the ideal corresponded in actuality precisely to the worst constitution, a hereditary oligarchy, which he was indeed familiar with from Bern and, moreover, that practically the monarchy of the ideal would come next. At that time this was merely a supplementary observation. Only now do we find monarchy taken up into the ideal of the state without digression and reservation. Various older tendencies of Hegel's thought are intertwined in its justification.

With the sketch of the priestly-sage of 1802, a specific thought was already active: the ethical organism should receive in them an outer-ethical, more or less natural, pinnacle. Thereby its life in actuality should be secured such that with this, the human would become woven into the trans-, and sub-human – the divine and natural – course of things. We had previously pointed out how a theory of hereditary monarchy was being prepared in 1802. Now, what had previously been primed for, breaks through. Within the commonwealth, the prince represents the "immediate, the *natural*": "*nature has fled hither.*" Otherwise, the family is regarded with respect to the state as "something to leave," as a pre-, and sub-stately community. With respect to the state – one is reminded of certain aphorisms by Novalis[61] – that of the prince alone is an abiding, "*positive*" greatness which does not disappear in it. Every other individual is regarded only as that "*which it has made of itself*," as cultivated [gebilde-tes].[62] The prince alone is already born into that which he is regarded as, he is "*immediate will, absolute resolve.*"[63] And now comes the supplement to these thoughts on the political meaning of heredity: just as the personality of the prince has little to do with the polity, so too with the individuality of the citizen: "the commonwealth is closed in itself," prince and citizen "may be constituted as they desire."[64]

This applies to citizens as well. That is the other side of this theory of monarchy, whereby it makes way for the later theory of state sovereignty. The monarchical thoughts receive new strengths which, in 1802, showed themselves only to be active in the doctrine of the estates, not in absolute government. At that time, the thought of freedom from the state received a highly individual configuration in the division of estates. We saw in 1803 how the juxtaposition of political ethicality and private life already dissolved in the doctrine of the estates and generally became the foundational idea of the system of natural right. Admittedly, we will now further see how, in 1805, the content of the doctrine of the estates does not change in its essentials, although the strong ethical accent it contained in 1802, and even in 1803, has somewhat diminished. Besides growing throughout the entire system, the ethical idea which was embodied in the doctrine of the estates now receives its own dwelling place, namely, in the doctrine of the monarch.

The historical course from the Polis to the modern state demolished the "ingenious" unity of the Greek people. However, it had a "*higher principle*

[…] with which Plato was unfamiliar."[65] A "higher divide" was created which entails that "everyone […] knows their self as such as the essence, arrives at this obstinacy […] to be separated from the universal and yet to be absolute."[66] The "universal" is now no longer, as in democracy, composed of individuals but, rather, "free from everyone's knowledge."[67] Thus, it is free on both sides: free with regard to the self-assured modern individuals who have lost their external freedom "but have retained their internal freedom, namely that of thought,"[68] and free with regard to the constitution of the regent, who is only the "empty knot"[69] in which the threads of the living state are entwined. Both hereditary monarchy and freedom of thought correspond to each other, being merely the most external poles, the "extremes" of the life of the state. The "spiritual union" that connects them is not to be found in the immediate participation of the people in the government, for instance – Hegel wishes only for local and corporate self-government – but rather in "public opinion." It is "the true legislative body, national assembly […], declaration of the general will."[70] But as the institution of this "public opinion" Hegel designates here – civil service: "Governmental civil servants belong to this spirit; today, governing and living are different in states whose constitutions are still the same, and these gradually change over time. The government does not have to stand on the side of the past and stubbornly protect it – but also need not be the last to be convinced and to change."[71] The aristocratic and estate-based image of the state of 1802 turns into a monarchical-bureaucratic state, which was certainly a transformation in line with the transformative times. Specifically, the last referenced passage on public opinion and civil service is probably, to judge according to the manuscript, a later addition, possibly already from the time around 1806. But let us not forget one thing here. The aristocracy of the System of 1802, like the bureaucracy of our manuscript, are themselves only husks, beneath which dwells, essentially unchanged, the same idea of the state with its uniform problems as we came to know them throughout the entire time in Jena. The grand view of the autocratic state, the classification of the internally free individual personality in this state, who indeed no longer wants to accept external obedience, but instead wants precisely to make use of the internal, human "will" – these things remain as the foundation. This time, however, the elements are no longer interlocked, as they were in the System of 1802, into an envisaged political cosmos.

Everything has become more relaxed, externally more multifaceted, and less monumental. It is telling that the unsystematic preliminary remarks, which alone occupied us previously, are now almost more politically substantial in comparison with the systematic discussion, which they are only meant to prelude.

These remarks convey much already known to us. Let us remember that the heading of the entire concluding section of the philosophy of spirit was called "Konstitution." In 1802, Hegel had thereby only designated the division of estates and differentiated the government from it. This time the division of estates only makes up the first sub-part. The estates are separated, as already in 1803, into two groups, into the "lower" estates. Now, however, it is the "estate of universality," the estate of civil servants, rather than, as in 1803, the landowning officer-nobles, that stand opposed to the "lower" estates. Peasant and citizen are again arranged to an almost humoristic vividness, and here it was harder to misconstrue than in the System of 1802 that modern actuality is the archetype of the description.[72] But above the peasant and the citizen, there now comes a separate estate: the merchant estate, whose activity appears more or less as the liberation of work from that of the earth- and place-bound peasants and petit bourgeois. Here, the thinker's paradigm was also provided by the social actuality of the age: lower and higher civil status was an important distinction within the law of the German territorial state. Thus, in the merchant class, acquisition reaches the kind of "universality" possible for it, and thus shows its true face. And this arises from it when "complete ruthlessness" is named here as the disposition of the estate – together with the trust of the peasant and the righteousness of the citizen. Only strict law applies. "Trade must be honored, let perish what may [...] factories and cottage industries are grounded precisely upon the misery of a class [Klasse]."[73] With its non-native manner the merchant systematically oversees the "estate of universality," the estate of civil servants. The division is already the same as in the section on "Universal Government" from 1802: financial administration, administration of justice and the police, as well as the system of needs, justice, and education. "The strength of the government entails that every system, as if it were alone, freely and independently [...] cultivates itself and the wisdom of the government, to likewise modify everything according to its estate [...] as the veins and nerves submit to the various viscera and direct and develop themselves according to these."[74] However, it is not insignificant that Hegel now provides the above things while characterizing the estate of civil servants. As with the thoroughly psychologizing treatment of the estates in general, it is also seen here that this time, and unlike in 1802, Hegel does not actually conceive of a monumental-objective picture of the state organism, but instead gives us more of a moral-psychological systematic of the dispositions appearing within the state.[75] Following the existing German conditions, Hegel addresses in detail how the estates are to be treated differently with regard to taxes and the civil and criminal administration of justice. The name of police, which has sunken from the elevated meaning of the Greek word to now mean care for public safety, is mainly accorded the oversight of trade, economic commerce, terms of employment, and guilds. The disposition of the civil servant is that he "*fulfills his duty,*" that he sees "*the absolute* in his particular actions."[76] In his particular actions: because although his actions are realized in the truly universal object, the state, they themselves are not truly universal, "his work is [...] very divided, [it is] machine work."[77] Thus, he stands on the border between impersonal ethicality and true "*moral* disposition": "spirit has lifted itself over character"[78] – namely over the particular character of the estate.

With this we enter into the middle section of the part called "Constitution": in the manuscript Hegel left it without a heading, which is not coincidental. As the manuscript shows, he often went back and forth regarding its content. At first, so it seems, he intended to describe the division of estates and the efficacy of the government towards the estates in the first part, and the disposition of each estate in the second part, its "self-consciousness," its spiritual "elevation" over its existence; thus, in the first part "ethicality," in the sense of antiquity as a basic element also of the modern state, in the second part modern "morality," in the elevated meaning that Kant and Fichte had given the word. Yet, in contrast to those great thinkers, morality is also a basic and grounding element of human communal life, and is also a part of the "Konstitution."[79] In execution, however, matters turned out somewhat differently. In the first part, estate and the disposition of each estate were dealt with together. For the second part, those circles of life remained whose estate-dispositions had to be free from all the limitations, surely befitting the citizen, peasant and civil servant as well: "*scholar, soldier, government.*"[80] But the differences in disposition remain as planned in the first draft. Looking back from the second part, the entire path of the first part we have observed constitutes the beginning of the self-liberation of spirit from the "life of a people." Here it is indeed noticeable that Hegel obviously still places an individualistic morality, derived from Kant and Fichte, above the "ethicality" of the divided estates and the bureaucratic machinery. It almost seems to be a reversal of the accentuated values when, in contrast with 1802, Hegel sees a necessary task in the elevation of spirit over the dispositions of the estates to "morality": spirit "is the life of people in general, it is to free itself from this."[81] Yet, initially, the contrast cannot be seen so clearly. For, just as in 1802, at least in the execution, "morality" remains bound to the estates. In the end, then, morality remains firmly anchored within communal life. Nevertheless, this pressing down of the ethical value of societal organization, held together with an unusually strong emphasis on personal freedom of thought as the basic essence of the modern state, is highly curious. It is also of great consequence for the further development of the system, for which, in the end, the division of estates, insofar as this division is not active in the representation of the people, is banished entirely out of the state into society, corresponding to the prevailing development of the idea of citizenship of that age. We will have to keep a close eye on this point in order to understand the political content of Hegel's next major work, and above all Hegel's relation to Napoleon, and then, looking back, to first completely understand what was just discussed.

With regard to the particular political content of the middle division of the text, the "educated person" is ranked along with the civil servant, for the latter is "in part educated person as well."[82] Insofar as he is an educated person, insofar as he recognizes the universal in the particular duty that he fulfills in his position, he already has that freedom in his actions which strictly speaking first characterizes an educated person. But higher than the free activity of the educated person, which is still only an intellectual devotion to the universal, there stands the ethical essence of the soldier estate, where the "actual self" gives itself over to the "individually existing whole," the "people."[83] What Hegel adds here on the natural condition of the states against one another, that is, on the "eternal deception"[84] of treaties, is mostly known to us. Even the rejection of the idea of an eternal peace does not surprise us. In contrast to the

System of 1802, an important difference is that now the soldier estate is no longer situated along with the landowning nobility. In general, it stands out that we only hear of the noble once, and at that in passing, namely, that his tax privileges are dangerous to himself. The air of the Napoleonic age becomes noticeable here as at other points. In place of the first estate, which was occupied in 1802 and 1803 by the landowning nobility, civil service now enters into our system. And – a further noteworthy move – the difference upon which the contrast between citizen and peasant came to a point in 1802, the inability of the first to be brave, is not mentioned this time. Of the peasant it is said that in war they constitute the mass, but nothing at all is claimed of the citizen in connection with the military. The civil servant, who in 1805 took the place of the nobility, was previously modeled in the "universal government" from 1802. Yet, whereas then he was actually only in the closest connection to the "absolute government" as its voice [Organ], he has now become an estate and has his own disposition within that estate. However, insofar as he is "in part educated person as well," he is, in the same manner as the officer and the highest government, again more than an estate. If, in 1802, we found civil servants within the description of "universal government," gathered as they were around the royalty of the old state as its "domestic servants," then now, in 1805, the civil servant is something new, even with respect to how closely they are situated to "public opinion," whose voice he represents. Indeed, in the manner they do business they still correspond to the civil servants from 1802, yet they have outgrown them through a sense for their own estate, through the elevated meaning which is attributed to learned education, and through the relation with "public opinion," this "true" lawgiving body and universal will. It is the ideal of a civil service which Hegel may have believed to be actualized in the Napoleonic state council at that time,[85] and certainly later in Prussia.

The immediate motivation for the reformulation and renaming of the estates with respect to 1802 seems to have come to him from a quite specific, determinable point. Through Napoleon's grace, the Italian Republic established electoral colleges, from which – as in France – the pseudo-parliaments of this constitution proceeded.[86] But in Italy, in contrast to the French model, the structure of corporations [Körperschaften] was not democratic, but instead based on estates: there was one college each for the "*possidenti*," "*merchanti*," and "*dotti*." Connecting Hegel's thoughts to this actualized constitution is also made probable by the segregation of the merchants into an independent estate, as well as the omission of the connection between land ownership and noble officials, and especially by the strangely intentional emphasis that the "civil servant" is likewise "an educated person" – *dotti*! It is not the case that Hegel emulated this precisely, but probable that he remodeled his division of estates from 1802 with this in mind. Just then, in May 1805, on the occasion of Napoleon's royal coronation in Italy, which was carried out with all arrays of pageantry along with the simultaneous renewal and change in the constitutional laws, this piece of Napoleonic governmental wisdom was introduced to a wide-eyed Europe through receptions, speeches and replies. Hegel himself subsequently only brought that division of estates into connection with the constitution from 1805, although it was not first created at that time.[87]

In war, where everything is sacrificed to the whole, "government is complete."[88] Precisely here, where individuals are let loose against each other, where they have their "absolute freedom,"[89] the government shows its strength as the free spirit "certain of itself."[90] But it is not yet the last stage of spirit; the state does not complete itself in it but, rather, it completes itself in the third section of the third part of the philosophy of spirit titled "Constitution" – namely through "art, religion, philosophy."[91] The last five pages of our manuscript are dedicated to these matters; thus, valuable material finally comes to hand for answering that long postponed question on how the philosopher thought about the relation of the state to the ultimate things at that time.

In mentioning Hegel's critique of Kant's *Metaphysics of Morals* from August 1798, we discussed a paragraph dealing with the state and the church. In contrast to Kant's demand for the separation of church and state, once shared by Hegel himself in Bern, in 1798 he declared such a separation as an internal impossibility: the church, in that it captures humanity in its wholeness, would constantly flow over and beyond the artificial borders that are supposed to cut it off from effecting a state, which, like the modern state, can only lay claim to part of humanity. The critical fragment does not allow one to recognize how Hegel himself thought about the relation at that time. The full weight of the question only became clear to him when he saw in the state, including in the modern state, a world that captured humanity in its wholeness just as well as the church could: only when the state became for him the "fate" of the human being. In the summer, he still asserted the oneness of church and state for the city-state of antiquity, which presupposed an internally unified human as its producer. There, the church represents precisely the same thing for an intuiting imagination as the ruler does for the state. In that the state now became "fate" for Hegel in the winter – something all-powerful which is indeed at the same time a vital necessity for humanity – with this issue the historical riddle grew to a dominating magnitude for him, namely, the riddle of how the Christian church is to relate to this state, which henceforth was to be acknowledged in its externality as ethical as well. The coinciding of both powers in the Polis – Athene, as Hegel would later readily say, both the state and its deity – no longer applies here. For this new conception of the state, an internal ordering of one over the other, namely of the church over the state or, more exactly, of personal religion over the state – as Hegel had accepted it in Bern and, still in the summer of 1798, in requiring the state to protect the religious freedom of conscience within and beyond the church – was now no longer permissible. Hegel now had to conceive of the historical relation between the state and the Christian church as an unresolved dissonance: this is how he sketches it in the final pages of the major theological-historical manuscript from Frankfurt. We would now like to resume the observation of this text from the point where we had previously left off.

The "guilt" of Jesus had attached itself to his separation from the connections of life, to his suffering behavior in response to the powers of the world. His "fate" thus grew for him precisely within these powers from which he fled. His fate becomes the fate of his work. A stone thrown into water makes rings, which, spreading out, finally cover the entire surface of the sea – this is more or less the appearance of these Hegelian contentions which, proceeding solely from a conception of Jesus' consciousness guided by Hegel's own experience, expanded in ever greater circles to the early congregation, to early Christianity and to the early church. The fate of Jesus, internally transformed only through the multitude of those carrying it, became the fate of the congregation.[92] Even the congregation, which "seemed to escape all fate in preserving love unmixed and outside all union with the world,"[93] is seized here by its fate: its ideal of a closed-off love within its own circle, which it could no longer afford owing to the living feeling of an outward expansion of the circle, rigidifies through the worship of its founders into dogma. But now this fate is one "whose middle point was the expansion of a love that flees all connections into a community, which developed in part through the expansion of the community itself, coinciding in part with the fate of the world through this very expansion, and in that it had unconsciously absorbed so many sides of this world, as well as fighting against the same, had in this way become ever more impure."[94] Thus, the church, for the last lines make reference to this, is the encounter of the internal and external fate of Christianity. The former is what is actually new in Hegel's formulation. The transition of feeling into existence, the deific removal of that which was originally immediately present in human love, this inner fate becomes the "essential character" of the Christian church. Its history moves within this contrast between God and the world. It contrasts its essential character "to find rest in an impersonal living beauty; and it is its fate that church and state, religious practice and life, piety and virtue, spiritual and worldly acts, can never fuse together into one."[95]

Thus, Hegel understood the fight between state and church as an internal historical necessity and thereby, for him, also as "fate." The former longing for the separation of the two powers, acknowledged as impossible already in the summer of 1798, now became not a demand for the conjoining of the two but the acknowledged necessity of their antagonism. The starting point was reached for the systematic treatment of this relation in the coming years.

The remains of the "system" finished in Frankfurt in September 1800 show Hegel to be at this point. At the same time, another force becomes active which proves decisive for the relation in the following years, namely, the historical-philosophical image of the present. According to whether Hegel saw in the historical epoch since the founding of Christianity the second or third age of the world, according to whether for him Christianity was merely one, even if a very important, stage of the world-historical process, or rather the ground from which this world-historical path would no longer stray for all eternity – according to all of this, the contrast between church and state had to appear in an array of varying light. To say it now without delay: the final decision on the historical-philosophical question first came about for Hegel after his Jena period.

At that time, in 1800, the older view alone dominated, the view turned towards the future which saw in the Christian epoch of world history a decline from the beautiful vitality of the Greek Polis. This corresponds to the moment in the "System Fragment" when Hegel describes with innermost participation the beauty of a cult in which the entirety of natural life becomes transfigured to an "elevation of finite life to the infinite, so that so little of what is finite [...] remains as possible."[96] Admittedly, he also acknowledges here, as we have already heard, that this "most complete completeness"[97] has no place in the present age: it is only possible with peoples whose life "is as little torn and disrupted as possible, that is, with fortunate ones; less fortunate ones cannot reach such a stage, instead [...] their highest pride must be to maintain [...] the separation."[98] Thus, it pertains to the present to place itself on the ground of "separation." And Hegel does so visibly in a noteworthy historical exposition that he had written in the winter of 1800 to 1801, thus immediately after composing the above conclusion to the system, as he, for the third time, as far as we can see, again worked on the text on The German Constitution.

At hand is a pair of quarto-pages with the heading "Religion," which would later serve as the template for a part of the discussion on church relations in the Empire. Hegel explains how the religious divide of the eighteenth century indeed bears the most blame for the rupture of the German Empire. However, insofar as religion ruptured the state, it helped to advance another separation "which thereby strengthened some principles that are necessary conditions for the emergence of a state."[99] For in "weaving" Protestant religious rights into the state, the basic principle was found, "which itself was in fact handled very adversely, that a state was possible despite different religions."[100] Thus, at that time, the independence of the state from the church "was admittedly not fixed but certainly prepared for."[101] Thus, at that time, he designated independence from the church as the necessary condition for the existence of a state, restricting it only minimally, and in the last version in 1802 he calls this independence the "principle of modern states." If previously religion was virtually the only bond in Germany, then from now on, after this has now become ruptured, the modern principle of the state had arisen "in order to unify itself externally above external things, such as waging war etc."[102] It is fitting that with this simple recognition of the modern principle, Hegel, in this text and for the first time ever, now interprets the Christian age as something with finality, as an historical completion.[103] Yet with this first appearance of the new construction of history the old one is not yet done away with. The first preserved system draft from Jena is the stage upon which something almost like a fight between the tendencies underlying both images of history then plays itself out.

It should be remembered how many threads run back and forth between the state ideal of this system, on the one side, and the concept of the state from the pamphlet, as well as the actual German territorial state of the epoch. In this sense the Hegelian text was also an attempt to unify the ideal with the "age." If this could be overlooked, then this is due in part here to the place that the systematist gave to the idea of the state. When one read that in the absolute ethicality of the state "the view of philosophy [...] according to which all things are in God [...] [is] completely realized for the empirical consciousness,"[104] when one found it described as the "absolute truth," the "absolute education," the "highest beauty and freedom," "without suffering and blissful," indeed as the "divine, absolute, real [...], existing, under no shroud,"[105] then it was certainly easy to believe that in this system Hegel assigned the state the place of the absolute. One would then, of course, give little thought to the four weighty words according to which it is only "for the empirical consciousness"[106] that the state actualizes the philosophical view for which all things are in God, even if these four words could have led one down the correct path. But in overlooking this, one would allow Hegel to see the absolute in the state here – the statements just cited do indeed actually remind one of the Aristotelian metaphysics of the resting God – and once this is accepted it was justified to describe this image of the state from 1802 as a renewal of the state theory and praxis of antiquity, which is even in good accord with Hegel's own view on the difference between the ancient and modern state. Yet this then, of course, obscures the path towards understanding the details themselves. It was initially misleading that one treated that system, as it lays before us, as a closed whole. We already saw how the section on government towards the end was still in rough outline. Likewise, the section on religion was certainly planned, but only executed in part towards the end of the manuscript. That it was planned out, and indeed from the very beginning, is proven by a few anticipatory sentences in the first part of the system.[107] The notion that Hegel had then wanted to completely leave out religion from a philosophical system is nonsensical with regard to the development observed until now, as well as untenable in view of the approximately simultaneous drafts of the pamphlet, as also in view of the essays for the philosophical journal. He who in a political pamphlet describes religion, from which he simultaneously wishes to distinguish the state as independent, as the "most internal of humankind," as the "most personal," would hardly deny its place in a philosophical system that makes a claim to universality. But admittedly, everything depends upon which place.

Initially, this much seems certain: the place is to be found within the system, in that it displays no gaps in its development, after – which means in the sense of the Hegelian method, above – the stages of absolute ethicality that we came to know, and thus above constitution and government. Nevertheless, as a result, the assumption is suggested that, as the system from 1805 also shows, religion was to be inserted as the third and closing subsection of the third part of the entire system. As we will subsequently see, this would also better correspond to the presumed content of a section on religion from 1802 than is the case in 1805. For it certainly seems that the intention was there in 1802 to deal with religion primarily in its relation to the state ideal.

Hegel connects the question of state and religion directly to the discussion of the various forms of the state. With democracy, he only has the democracy of antiquity in mind. When he attributes "absolute religion"[108] to it, then he understands by this that here divinity is worshiped in human form. For Hegel, there first emerges with this idea a lasting adherence, most strictly in 1806, to a religious-historical construction, according to which the actual source of Christianity is not to be seen as Judaism but rather Hellenism, and indeed not, for instance, Greek philosophy, but rather – most surprisingly! – Greek sculpture. Accordingly, in 1802, it is not Homer's religion, not Greek religion itself, within which the gods are still presented as natural forces, that Hegel describes as "ethical," but rather the "imagination" [Phantasie][109] of this religion, its plastic arts. This "separation" between the ethical and the natural, first realized with the statues of the Greek gods, then comes to completion within Christian dogma, the becoming-human of God, which first began with the mundane crimes and weaknesses of Homer's gods so as to become "absolute" with the death of Christ.[110] It is within aristocracy and monarchy that Hegel now sees the modern constitutions. He makes short work of the former, which he describes here as the worst of all constitutions, doubtlessly remembering Bern. In contrast, he makes an important observation about monarchy. As we know, monarchy is the actual form of the state of that "second" world age of the early Hegelian philosophy of history. The character of this epoch, which arose with the Roman Imperium and faded out in the process of dissipation of the German Empire, is thus determined, as is likewise already long known to us, in that here the monarch does not truly have the same essence as the whole, and hence there is still place next to him for religion. Now, the more that the internal unity of the "people" constitutes itself, the more the condition becomes truth which, precisely in this system, Hegel struggles so forcefully to look into within the society and state of his German environment, and all the more must, and indeed will, the independent placement of religion next to the state fade, all the more will "the people take up the divine in themselves."[111] The reconciliation of the world that thus comes about, which had been divided in Christianity into the true community of the state, will admittedly first lead to an "unimaginativeness of irreligion and the understanding."[112] It becomes clear how Hegel sees this future as already present when, in his philosophical journal, he himself turns his attack precisely against that "unimaginativeness." But this enlightenment is only an accompanying and passing appearance. Hegel does not say at this point what will come next. It is not being too bold if we suppose that he is awaiting a unification of Christianity and paganism: the dogmatic truth of the "absolute religion" in the form of a cult born forth from national life. Too much pushes towards this, including the threads that weave over and across to the early Schelling, as well as to the later Hölderlin, and above all, a few pages preserved in print by Rosenkranz and from which, according to him, Hegel lectured at the beginning of his Jena period.[113] While Rosenkranz's statement cannot be verified,[114] there are also internal reasons that would mandate placing the fragment in the early Jena period, perhaps even still at the end of his time in Frankfurt.

Hegel divides the world-historical path of religion very clearly here into three stages, the first of which, the pagan "religion of nature," culminates in the ideal forms of a "beautiful mythology."[115] Since the Romans had "crushed the living individuality of the peoples, driven away their spirits, [and] destroyed their ethicality,"[116] there within this "infinite pain"[117] of the spirit, which had lost its home in living nature, the world was ripe for a new, second religion. Christianity, born from infinite pain, had as its original content precisely the reason for this pain, namely the de-deification of nature, the contempt for the world and, as its necessary supplement, the certainty of belief that nevertheless in this infinite separation a person carried within themselves the assurance of being one with the absolute. These two forces, the feeling of separation and the belief in reconciliation, now play out within the history of Christianity, which reaches its internal middle point in the Catholicism of the Middle Ages, the beautiful religion. Here, as far as it can even occur in Christianity, whose basic essence is simply separation, the divine has returned to its home in nature. "The new consecration is given to all. The ruling-force of the monarch is consecrated by religion: his scepter contains a piece of the holy cross. All of the land has an eye toward the special messengers of God and is marked with their traces. [...] All things of the highest and lowest acts are given a new consecration, which they had previously lost. The old curse, which spread over everything, is resolved, [as] all of nature has come into grace and its pain is reconciled."[118] But of course, this consecration only comes externally, nature is blessed but not through its own spirit. And so, the essence of Christianity, as the religion of separation and pain, is only first entirely unveiled in its last historical configuration, in Protestantism. It again sublated the poetry of consecration and within it nature is now only "blessed by the Fatherland," whereas the "religious Fatherland and the appearance of God are again banished into the distance from one's own Fatherland."[119] It is then no wonder when, finally, in that it thus lost the Catholic "vitality, assurance and peace of reconciliation, that it passed over, through the "infinite longing" of Pietism, into the common Enlightenment from that "sabbath of the world" of the Middle Ages, into the "common, unholy work-day."[120] Even if at that time Hegel saw in Protestantism, in contrast to Catholicism, a decline, it is nonetheless the higher form within the entire history of religion, precisely because for him Christianity is dissolving and the third religion, the religion of the future, is announcing itself. There is no bridge that leads between these ideas of the young lecturer in Jena and the soon commencing flight of the Romantics into the womb of the old religion: "Because such beauty is down below, it can thus no longer return nor be mourned, rather only the necessity of its passing can be recognized and anticipated as that which is higher, which must take its place and for which it is to prepare the path."[121] Protestantism, precisely in that it "extracted" the foreign and external "consecration" of Catholic Christianity from the world, has prepared this path – now "spirit can dare to bless itself as spirit in its own configuration [Gestalt] and establish the original" (and actually present within classical paganism) "reconciliation with it in a *new religion*, in which the infinite pain and the entire gravity of its opposition is taken up, and purely dissolved."[122] And this moment has arrived when the basic feeling of Christianity will be entirely taken up into a new religion but will also become entirely dissolved, when the system's ideal of the state will have become actuality: "when there is a *free people* and when reason will have its reality reborn as an ethical spirit, which can have the audacity to take up its pure form [Gestalt] upon its own ground and from its own majesty."[123] This third age of the world is already dawning, and philosophy stands at its gate.

That is the historical-philosophical view of the present under which we have to place Hegel's first philosophical system of the state. It is also attested to for us by Hegel's first years in Jena. I am thinking of the great concluding essay of the treatise on "Faith and Knowledge" in the philosophical journal,[124] of Schelling's journal essay "On the Relation of Philosophy of Nature to Philosophy, in General,"[125] which corresponds exactly to Hegel's construction, and of the striking use of the word "Protestant" at a point in Hegel's essay on "Natural Right."[126] In general, the positive valuation of Catholicism from the Middle Ages, which goes almost as far as to philosophically construct the adoration of Mary, is a characteristic trait unique to Hegel in these years. Yet it is infinitely important for understanding his view of the state at that time to keep this one thing in mind: how entirely future-oriented his view was then.[127] The Hegel of these years was consumed, one would like to say, with such an apocalyptic sense of the present, which barely possessed even the likes of Nietzsche to such a degree. Hegel believed to be experiencing in his present age the conclusion of an eighteen-hundred-year-old world epoch and that he himself, with his philosophy, was helping to weave the living cloth of the new world age. The unity of the state and "the divine," which was supposed to become an actuality in the coming year of the world, was already once present in the Greek Polis, but then

it was another divinity and also another state that were connected in
unity. It was up to the state and the church to carry over the configured
products of the second world-year into the third. Not the beautiful configurations of the old gods but rather the religion of suffering, "of Good
Friday," and not the state of antiquity assembled from slaves and free citizens "living in the state," but rather the state of newer times organized
into estate divisions: these were the religion and the state which were
to grow internally together in the coming age of the world and thereby
become "absolute."

But for the contemporary observer, it is precisely here that an internal
schism is revealed, a schism which would further carry Hegel's thoughts
on the ultimate questions of the philosophy of state, in particular those
of state and church. Not without reason did we previously call the system from 1802 the stage for the battle between two images of history.
The sense directed towards the future still took the elements that it
wanted to plant in the future from the life of the present. It was precisely
the system from 1802 that allowed us, under the husk of a philosophically eternalizing style, to repeatedly discover the state and society of the
German eighteenth century. Already in the pamphlet, Hegel had actually
gone quite a bit further than the German constitution. Here, he frankly
acknowledged the constitutional monarchy and the freedom of the state
from the church. And that recognition of the constitutional monarchy
did not merely pertain to a state of the future but, rather, in distinct
alignment with Montesquieu, Hegel shifts the roots of this form of the
state into German antiquity and conceives of it as the state form of the
Germanic-Romanic Europe in the past and present. For Hegel, this was
an understanding that had to take on the shape that the history of this
Germanic Europe, together with the present and beyond this into the
future, is grasped as a "third" world-historical epoch.[128] Even if here in
its first appearance this new plan of history was perhaps nothing more
than a quickly erected construction for the purposes of the pamphlet,
it, together with the constitutional royalty for which it was to serve as
the historical-philosophical basement, nonetheless gradually established
itself against the older view in Hegel's world of thought. Admittedly,
this older one rules initially undisturbed. This is shown by the System
of 1802 with its "absolute government," as well as by the lectures and
journal essays. But we already showed how this older division of history

contained in itself the impetus, against its actual intention, to immediately eternalize the present. The newer division, which performed this intentionally, was almost certain to triumph. Nevertheless, it would take a long time until it was the victor across the board.

In the System of 1805 – the sources forsake us with respect to what directly preceded this – two important positions are dealt with in light of the new view of the present. We already addressed the henceforth unrestrained acknowledgement of monarchy. Here we only still need to address the final systematic acknowledgement of the juxtaposition of state and church[129] and, in connection with this, an oncoming change in the placement of the state in the system.

The conclusion to the manuscript of 1805, from the heading "Art, Religion, Science" onward,[130] fundamentally differentiates itself from all older Hegelian remarks on these subjects, at least those on art and religion, in that the connection to the state, to the "people," no longer visibly forms the only noted target of the observation. Of course, this connection still plays an important part; indeed, significant remains of the original systematic formulation, as we had to imagine it in 1802, are preserved, above all, in the placement of the section in the overall part called "Konstitution." However, in the execution, in contrast to the systematic structure, the independence of regions later encapsulated within "absolute spirit" is as good as decided. What is of concern for us here is above all the independence of religion. We already noticed a strong individualist strain in the overall design of the doctrine of the state. "Morality," which is raised above the estate, came to be above the "ethicality" of the estates. This line now reaches its high point in the new conception of religion. Religious life is no longer understood as beginning from a cult of the "folk," no longer as the self-view of its political existence in common service of the folk gods, but as beginning from the faithful individual soul. What the government as such only possesses within the state, namely the unconditional moral self-determination and sublimity over each limited ethicality of the estates, this the individual person as such possesses in religion. Here, "everyone rises to this intuition [...] – their nature, their estate sinks like an image in a dream, like a distant island appearing as a cloud of air on the edge of the horizon – they are equal to the ruler – they are regarded by God as much as everyone else."[131] And what this new foundation of the concept of religion already allows us to anticipate here is that the absolutization of Christianity, albeit it without being specifically stated, proves entirely advantageous to Protestantism. Only a few fragmentary lines on the margins of the notebook show that Hegel even still included the Catholicism of the Middle Ages in the lecture at all. Regardless, if he himself had then already taken the change into the general view of the universal religious-historical picture, which we will encounter a year later in *The Phenomenology*, however that may be, at that time the philosopher of religion had made his sincere and henceforth unbroken peace with the present. But only the philosopher of religion. Indeed, the state thinker confessed himself unapologetically to the state of the present, but this only happened, as we will still see more closely, to the detriment of the high placement that the state had held for him in the first years in Jena, and again later on. A detriment which was signified by the overgrowth of the free disposition over the bound ethicality of the estates and which, for its part, was also eased by the outgrowth of religion from the circle of the political. The historical-philosophical consequence of the new valuation of monarchy, although it flashes up already once in the pamphlet of 1802, was at this time not yet systematically drawn out, as *The Phenomenology* again shows. For the time being, all of these stimulating and inhibiting forces of the biographical course now influenced the treatment of the relation of state and church.

"The church has its opposite in the state,"[132] so begins the composition now. What was once, as he first expressed it in 1799 and 1800, the final outcome for the thinker, the self-denial of "unhappier peoples" in a historical fate, is now calmly placed as the starting point of the whole: "the human being lives in two worlds."[133] Yet the position of the two worlds towards each other, as Hegel once saw them in Bern, is now distinct. At that time, he had only fought against the external conflict and did not want to acknowledge its internal necessity. Now he does just this. He understands that both church and state are, in the end, of the same essence: "the church is *the state*, raised into thought."[134] In this he now allows their opposition to take root. This internalization of the problem was not possible as long as he denied to the Protestant, as was the case in the first years in Jena, the ultimate "identity" between the church and the state, indeed denied it the entire Christian epoch altogether, and only wanted to accept this "identity" for a just glimmering future. That the unity of essence, which for Hegel was earlier only considered for the state and the church of antiquity and for the free people of the future, may now also be conferred upon them in the Christian world, this was connected for Hegel to that force of disposition that now emerged for both. Until now, the two forces stood opposed to each other in their entirely unmediated greatness and only now do they find in their relation to the individual a point of mutual and innermost contact. The human has "his actuality" in the state, "his essence" in the church. In the former he is to offer himself up, in the latter his "absolute preservation" is guaranteed. But the eternal, which he wishes to acquire through his conscious rejection of the state in the church, still has "its existence," its earthly actuality in the state, in the "*spirit of the people.*"[135] And so both are in the right: the state is in the right insofar as it asserts its essence of actuality against the "fanaticism" of a church that wants to introduce the Kingdom of Heaven on earth, as well as against the conscience of the individual, which it does not need to respect.[136] Indeed, the state's grandeur goes so far that it may coerce religion into its service, may "use" it, insofar as it – as that without actuality – "is in need of existence, of immediate actuality."[137] But in contrast to this state, in which the ideas of Frederick's and Napoleon's church politics appear to be found together, the human of the church is also in the right who, in internal obstinacy, "surrenders his existence and is prepared to die for his thoughts."[138]

Even if the state and the church can stand opposed to each other, this will not be the case if they are both "complete." And the reconciliation, whose image Hegel is now sketching no longer as the face of the future but rather as a possibility of the present, is likewise the first appearance of a thought which from then on exerted a determinative power over Hegel's views. The church may not for its part, therefore, wish to introduce the Kingdom of Heaven on earth, because this actuality of heaven on earth should be the state. Rather, its great work rests in the obligation to make the state into the Kingdom of Heaven for the individual: to bring forth the reconciliation of state and the Kingdom of Heaven "in thought."[139] In thought – thus to reconcile in consciousness both worlds in which the human being lives, that is the task of the church. In this manner it becomes the "internal *absolute security*" of the state. The human being now no longer fulfills his duty to the state in the limited ethical disposition of his estate but rather through a kind of "self-thinking" [Selbstdenken] – "through religion."[140] Religion can only complete this work if it, itself complete,

works in a complete state. Hegel's state has become Christian. Not in
the sense that it is somehow religiously directed or distracted, but in the
more internal sense that it attains its ultimate guarantee, its anchoring
in the consciousness of the individual, from the hand of religion. And
with this, something has certainly occurred in the system that, even if
Hegel so strongly emphasizes the autocracy of this state which is the
"spirit of actuality,"[141] still contains in itself a philosophical depreciation
of the state. "[S]ubjective internality" [subjektive Innerlichkeit], to use a
Hegelian technical term, which had already strongly asserted itself in the
doctrine of the state in comparison to before, in joining with religion,
which is nevertheless still treated under the section "Constitution," is
effectively something beyond the state. According to Hegel's own summary, the entire doctrine on the "Constitution" contains nothing but the
self-liberation of the spirit from the "life of a people," and thus from the
state – moving from the bound ethicality of the "natural" to the freedom
of the "moral" estates and arriving at its goal in art, religion, and science.
The soul thus finds a position, not hostile to, but internally removed
beyond, the state. Hegel now moves from this persuasion towards developing the image of world history and deciphering the nebulous countenance of the present. As the Corsican rode into Jena, this new work was
completed. But Hegel, as he saw him passing by, knew that the fate of
this man, his rise and fall, was recorded in his manuscript.

The Phenomenology of Spirit – for this was the manuscript – does not
belong as a whole within the succession of phases by way of which
Hegel's system developed; it is a work of its own species. This is attested
to by remarks of the author, and especially by the circumstance that in
the summer semester of 1806 he simultaneously lectured on phenomenology and logic on the one hand and on the philosophy of nature
and spirit on the other, the latter two, by the way, from the preserved
notebook. Hegel thought of The Phenomenology as a kind of introduction
to the system. Before allowing the essences of heaven and earth to pass
before his eyes as their philosophical world-ruler in a long, well-ordered
procession, he puts himself, so to speak, into the soul of these essences
themselves. However, he does this not as they proceed along already in
rows and groups, but rather as they continue to hurry from all the ends
of the world to the gathering place: he makes himself at home in the
inner life, in the "consciousness" of all these essences, and searches for

the image of the world as it paints itself in their souls in order to purely express the world as it "is for consciousness." He is driven again and again through his own restlessness from every consciousness in which he had begun to settle down, outward and further into a new circle of inner existence, until his urgent progression from appearance to appearance, from configuration to configuration, from consciousness to consciousness, finds its peace with the ultimate and highest configuration at which the path arrives. But this does not belong to the procession; it takes its place on the throne that is prepared for it and allows the procession, which now comes into motion, to pass before its seat: it is philosophy, "absolute knowledge" itself. This much on the path as a whole.

The law of this path, the order and grouping in which the configurations enter into the gathering place, is not so easy to recognize in the details. For half a century one tirelessly repeated the judgment that *The Phenomenology* was "a psychology brought into confusion and disorder through history and a history brought into ruin through psychology."[142] In truth, the following is the case: *The Phenomenology* initially wanders through those "configurations of consciousness" that critical philosophy first taught us how to understand as such, preconscious "transcendental-psychological" capacities, through which lived actuality changes into something universally valid and necessary and is constituted into "nature" in the Kantian sense. From there it passes over to practical feelings, as yet unknown in the common literal sense, and becomes more or less a psychology of primitive life. And, belonging here quite well, the end of this section forms a group of primitive-emotional worldviews, which appear in the garments of historical configurations – the Stoicism and Skepticism of antiquity, the Catholicism of the Middle Ages – and which are not strictly bound to their bearers, precisely because of their pre-intellectual, emotional and feeling-oriented essence, but instead can appear in a certain sense always and everywhere. For example, just as at the end of the first section, "nature" was "constituted" in a Kantian sense, so at the end of this second section Schopenhauer's "metaphysical need" is thus more or less constituted. But with this *The Phenomenology* steps out of the circles of dark, instinctive experience into the freer air of intellectually conscious being. Three groups of configurations appear here, and already a fourth configuration becomes visible in the distance, the elevated configuration of the queen, philosophy herself. The configurations of the first group are the representatives of the directions in which the awakened modern human being exerts their youthful self-confidence: the investigation of nature, the self-discovery and development of the soul in boundless enjoyment and unconditional action – the Faust of Goethe's fragment also strides into this swarm – finally, Kant's great proclamation of unconditional ethical freedom. In that here the demand peaks for the "I" to give law to the world, the next group already approaches. One could say: just as a century of "historical" worldviews followed the century of "individualistic" worldviews in the development of the modern spirit, so the group now arriving encompasses the historical forms within which, according to Hegel's view at the time, the naturalization of reason in actuality was, and continues to be, fulfilled. Thus, in this section, and nowhere before, *The Phenomenology* becomes for a certain span a philosophy of history, and it is this section above all that we are to address.

"Spirit" – this is what Hegel calls here in a narrower sense the consciousness that world history experiences and into which *The Phenomenology* will now feel its way. Unlike earlier, its configurations are not only configurations of consciousness, but rather "*actualities*" – "configurations of a world."[143] In that we are given the names of these spirits – "the ethical world, the world ripped into a here and beyond, and the moral world-view"[144] – we immediately recognize that, again here, Hegel's philosophy of history will be under the spell of his earliest awareness of time, which was intertwined with Schiller's *Aesthetic Letters*. This is so, for it does not begin with the world of the orient, but rather with the "ethical world" of the Greek Polis. The ideal picture that Hegel outlines of it is, with respect to its political content, fully known to us. What is above all new here, and also systematically fruitful for what follows, is the treatment of the individual. Just as, on the one hand, Hegel had long ago seen in the absorption of the individual into the life of the state a characteristic trait of the Polis at the time of its peak so, on the other hand, the "moral" individual in the state and opposed to the state only recently took on a stronger position for the philosophical systematist of the state. Thus, in fact, the problem of the individual in the new description of the Polis now shifted more earnestly for him than before into the focal point of the observation. However, due to a historical-philosophical theory that simply did not wish to acknowledge this problem for the Polis, it receives a highly peculiar formulation. It was not the individual human as such that opposed the Polis but, instead, the human as a member of the family, the ethical world of the woman and the man. If Hegel later brings family and state into close systematic proximity, then the roots of this systematic lay in the profound comments in *The Phenomenology* on the ethicality of family and state as reconciled or discordant elements of the life of the Polis. The quarrel between divine and human law in Sophocles' *Antigone* is woven so artfully into these lines of thought that even within general consciousness today the true threads of the Sophoclean tragedy are difficult to separate from the thought fabric of the German philosopher. We need not follow these things further. Simply put, the beautiful world of ethicality had to go under because it was beautiful, because, one would like to say, it led a plant-like natural existence. Its fate is thus the fate of everything natural. "Just as before only the Penates perished in the spirit of the people, so now through their individuality the living spirits of the people perish in a *universally* common essence whose [...] *universality* is spiritless and dead, and whose vitality is singular for the *single* individual."[145] We already know that Hegel is thinking about the Roman Imperium with its civil law. He does not bring it up here as before, as the beginning of the second world epoch, but rather as the conclusion of the first, and yet explicitly separated from the "ethical configuration of spirit" as "another" configuration.[146] The affiliation of the Caesars with the Polis instead of with the *ancien régime* had become necessary because in the meantime monarchy was now recognized as the ideal form of the state of the present and the future and thus the non-ideal Tacitus-Gibbon-like picture of Caesarism had to be banished behind a high epochal divide.[147] In that monarchy as such could no longer be described within the Roman Imperium, Hegel more sharply emphasizes its singular historical traits: universal equal rights and universal deprivation of rights over against the one, the "master of the world,"[148] who is sketched more or less after the model of a Heliogabalus.[149] Thus, the individual who is not yet prefigured in the Polis has indeed come into appearance, but either only as an empty "formal" legal personality or as a likewise empty "monstrous aberration"[150] of the master of the world. Thus, a rupture has entered into the world; personality has appeared, yet it does not find the space for living or activity suitable to it. It is and feels itself to be internally empty. The living whole personality of the Polis had to go under so that the individual person could come into being. But now, that perished ethical homeland is missing on this side for the one that has come into being. The second world day of the spirit has dawned: "the self-alienated spirit: culture."[151]

The world events since the fall of the Roman Empire are seen as a single long prehistory to the great turmoil in France, standing at the end of this epoch, for which the German philosopher, serenely certain of the future in the most absurd manner, erects a giant historical-philosophical grave, and which now prepares to impose its iron law upon the last unconquered German state! How does Hegel integrate these historical appearances, and above all the development of the modern state, into this purposeful course? The world of the self-alienated spirit is torn into two worlds, into a de-deified realm of actuality and into an actuality-less otherworldly world of belief. Hegel had long since accused the Christian human of having "no unity"; an accusation, which later would only be made of the human of the Middle Ages, and of them to an essentially limited extent. Here it again rules over the entire description of the spirit of the Middle Ages and of the contemporary age. Indeed, one could not say that overall in this general view a sharper line is drawn between the Middle Ages and the contemporary age. We are carried in both circles, that of actuality as well as that of belief, in an almost unnoticeable movement across this watershed of the ages. Hegel designates "culture" [Bildung][152] as the fundamental essence of the new "world of actuality" as well as of the existence of the individual in it. For his part, Hegel also gives this newly formed word, into which the early Romantics had already poured the heaviest of content, a widely encompassing historical meaning. He calls culture the production of the universal spiritual world which occurs in conscious devotion. Culture for the individual thus means that he first becomes what he is for his world through the sacrifice of his "natural self."[153] Culture in both senses is that which was missing in the old world. It is missing from the "ethical world," for it did not know the individual as such at all. Its heartbeat was not nurtured by the single spirit [Einzelgeist], but by the "native spirit"[154] of the commonwealth and of the family. Culture was likewise missing from legal status, for in this condition the individual indeed counted, but not according to his culture, and rather as an empty person in the legal sense. In the world of culture the "commonwealth" and the "family" in the realms of ethicality do not correspond to such "native spirits," powers existing above and beyond the individual, but rather to authorities that the individual consciously creates and consciously makes useful for himself: "*state-power and wealth*."[155] This new opposition within culture is nothing other than that between state and property, public and working life, well known to us from all of Hegel's system drafts: later between state and society. This opposition is used and contained here historically almost more sharply than ever; the old world of ethicality, and even the world of legal status, did not know it like this at all. The great historical opposition which played itself out in the latter is an entirely different one and the chaotic monotony of the Roman Imperium entirely lacked the enlivening power of a great opposition as such. Only the spirit of contemporary history, insofar as it took place in the world of actuality, yet for this entirely and utterly, is to be understood from those two powers, their battle, their equilibrium, their change of roles. We do not need to follow the details of how typical attitudes of consciousness now develop in relation to these two powers of life, nor how also here, as is to be expected from our knowledge of the history of the system, the estates are integrated initially as "organized masses," before state power has become "actual state power," a "*government*" "always rising towards revolt,"[156] and then, in the end, yielding to the state. France's absolute monarchy now becomes the subject of description. The thoughts that great historians would later bring to the prehistory of the Revolution are anticipated here in highly idiosyncratic remarks: the literary idealization in which the unrestricted power of the crown in the age of Louis XIV and classical tragedy are brought internally to completion, the "*heroism of flattery*,"[157] the language of the price of state power is the immediate precursor to the "language of inner strife,"[158] in which, just like in its spokesperson, the true nature of the disintegrated spirit of the eighteenth century first comes to light. Taine's view of the *esprit classique* already appears here essentially formed. Similarly, it is surprising that when the royalization of the French noble is itself immediately understood as an internal transformation of the essence of state power it becomes "wealth"[159] and, transformed as such, royalty again slips into the hands of the nobles. This conception of the prehistory of Revolution is indeed older than Tocqueville's book in general, almost as old as the Revolution itself.

Thus, the state, the external world, is now matured towards revolution. In the other world, the internal, the development moves towards the same goal. In contrast to the de-deified world, belief is damned to a flight from the world, and in this manner comes into contact, and finally into battle, with the other residents of the transcendent region, with *"pure insight."*[160] The pure insight of the older German rational belief – one should especially be reminded of this here with the overly dark and heavy remarks – shows itself as the first source of the Enlightenment of the eighteenth century. The entire following section is then dedicated to this, its fight against the two worlds of belief and actuality, which it successfully leads, because it unifies under its banner the two final spiritual results of those conflicting worlds, the forces of serious rationality and the frivolously spirited "arguing and babbling."[161] But it completes its actual work in that it erects its own idol, that of universal utility,[162] over the demolished old existence. In this, its highest thought, more or less the ideal of perfected non-ideality, was finally able to bring together the circles of the godless actual world of culture and the actuality-less world of pure thought and belief, seemingly separated forever in the old life. "Both worlds," so the section closes, "are reconciled and heaven is planted down upon earth."[163] And with this bright trumpet cry the presentation arrives at the year of the "magnificent sunrise,"[164] 1789. Here the concluding part on the "self-alienated spirit" begins, entitled: "Absolute Freedom and Terror."[165]

With the thought of "utility" the absolute making-worldly of the beyond was still an ideal. Now this becomes configuration and an acting historical subject, Rousseau's "general will" – "not the empty thought of the will, which is placed into tacit or represented consent, rather real universal will, the will of all individuals as such"[166] – which is no longer bound to anything but itself. It "lifts itself onto the throne of the world," the sole heir of the entire now-fallen "system, which organized and preserved itself through the division of the masses."[167] It can only do "whole work" because in its absolute freedom "all estates, which are the spiritual essences into which the whole divides itself, are eradicated."[168] After such a thorough sublation of the entire past, this general will, if it stays true to its essence, can create nothing positive, because that always had to be something determinate and individual. And here, for the first time, Hegel interjects significantly into this depiction of the Revolution. For this will, if it would only abandon its Rousseauian emptiness and allow itself a configuration in an ethical structure, would then be the very will that Hegel himself had sunk into the foundation of the state. If this absolute freedom could "give [itself] *consciousness*," could become "work," then it would divide itself "into existing spiritual masses and into the limbs of various powers"; into the "*thought-things*" of the three powers and into the "*real essences*" of the different estates.[169] But it is just this individualization that the general will cannot do; it "does not [...] allow itself to be cheated out of actuality through the *idea* of being obedient under *self-given* laws [...] nor through its representation in lawgiving – cheated out of the actuality to set its own law."[170] Since universal freedom cannot bring about any positive work, "it is [then] left only with the negative act"[171] and this is directed towards its only remaining object after the eradication of all existing organization, namely towards the individual will contained within its general will. Thus, it becomes "terror"[172] and its sole work death – "with no more significance than cutting off a head of cabbage or swallowing a mouthful of water"[173] – this is the entire wisdom of a government, which is always the currently winning party, and for which being suspected must take the place of being guilty. But in that the general will fully enjoys life in this manner and becomes the "Fury of disappearance,"[174] the "terror of death,"[175] it reveals its true nature that was unrecognized by Rousseau, namely that it is not merely the subsumption of individual wills but, rather, at the same time their annihilation. And with this the absolute freedom of the Revolution has reached its third stage, where it again consciously recognizes the thought of the "nothingness" of the individual, but with this also the basic principle of "the organization of the spiritual masses,"[176] the estates, which now reestablish themselves. The individuals, "who have felt the fear of their absolute master, death, again acquiesce to the differences, subordinate themselves to the masses and again return to a divided and limited work."[177] The new monarchy – there is no doubt that the description written in 1806 refers to this – is established.

But what meaning does this entire turmoil have, from which spirit appears "to have been hurled back to its starting point, namely to the ethical and real world of culture"?[178] Is it really "only refreshed and rejuvenated through the fear of the master, which has again entered into consciousness?"[179] A "cycle of necessity"[180] henceforth to be run through always anew? It is Hegel himself who poses these questions. Here, for the first time, we stand at the decisive point of this entire philosophy of history: here it first takes hold of the present. Hegel negates the questions asked. Certainly, spirit would have to always repeat the development of the Revolution, which came to rest in royalty, if the entire fruit of the Revolution was to be found in the rejuvenation of the old world in "culture," in the *ancien régimé*, if its entire work was supposed to more deeply convince humankind of the order that goes beyond and even excludes it. But that is not the case. With the "absolute freedom"[181] of the Revolution something completely new has appeared in the world and, because new, determined to carry the future: consciousness purely bound to and referencing itself. That is the "most sublime and ultimate"[182] configuration that the human spirit can reach, self-denial no longer as in the world of culture for the sake of some worldly or otherworldly goods but, rather, to finally use Kantian words for the Kantian matter at hand: the denial of the empirical character for the sake of the intelligible character, the free self-legislation of the "I." As the ethical world of antiquity perished in the atom-like isolated "person" of Roman law, and this person then built up their new world, the double-world of "culture," so this world of culture perished in the French Revolution in the *volonté générale*, acknowledging neither outer- nor inner-worldly powers next to it, and this now becomes the cornerstone and foundation of the third Empire. But not as *volonté générale*; it destroyed itself when it became actuality in France and there, out of the cauldron of the Revolution, the old state and the old life emerged again refreshed and rejuvenated. Rather, absolute freedom now leaves this land where it destroyed itself in the attempt to become actuality and goes "into another land" where, in its "lack of actuality"– enclosed in self-consciousness – "it counts as what is true."[183] "The new configuration, that of *moral spirit*, has emerged."[184] The third year of world commences; its ground is Germany, its formerly world-historical content the new self- and life-feeling of the Kantian-Fichtean philosophy, or early Romanticism; its coming completion – and here, according to its nature, *The Phenomenology* leaves the historical configurations of the section "Spirit" and enters a sphere laid out beyond the philosophy of history – its completion is the absolute religion of Christianity, which is one with absolute philosophy.

With this overview of history, Hegel seldom, if ever, distanced himself to such a degree from his earlier and later expropriation of the ethical to the state. The observed attempts in the system to lift "morality" above "ethicality" are fully actualized here, at least in a historical-philosophical sense. This is not to be understood as if now Hegel had suddenly imagined the third world-historical epoch without a state as purely individualistic, solely filled with religious and philosophical forces. To attribute that to him would mean to strongly underestimate his sense of actuality. In this post-revolutionary epoch, the state will not cease to occupy its place in human existence and, exactly as in the System of 1805, it is a state that went through the Revolution, embodying its universal will in the person of the monarch, inwardly preserving or reestablishing the pre-revolutionary societal division of estates. This last point is especially noteworthy; yet it unequivocally follows from The Phenomenology that Hegel believed himself to see in Napoleon's monarchy a restoration of the old stratification of society coming into being. His own political systematic, familiar to us, with its already modernized division of estates around 1802, may have led him to recognize precisely in this the meaning of the new royalty with its new nobles, its renewed bureaucracy, and its distortion of the revolutionary thought of universal military service, which went beyond the idea of estates. But the greatest impression seems to have been made by Napoleon's Italian constitution with its three estate-based electoral colleges. This constitution is certainly the first attempt to come from the Revolution towards a reclamation of the old estate-principle for the new state, or in the words of its author: for the creation of colleges "*où nous avons réuni les différents éléments qui constituent les nations*"[185]; and if one considers how, at least in the first half of the century, this thought never came to rest, then one cannot entirely disagree with the spokesperson for the "*possidenti*" who explained in Milan before Napoleon that this institution, which replaces the old and "frivolous" differences between estates with more grounded and just ones, and thus increases the strength of the entire people, would be epoch-making.[186] Hegel, at any rate, accepted it.

If from The Phenomenology it again becomes entirely clear that in 1806, as already in 1802, Hegel believed that the state of the future, the third epoch of the world, would – at least according to its body – be the same as the state of the second, pre-revolutionary epoch, and only the spirit that animates this body would be different, then the meaning of this state for the overall life of the third epoch has indeed become a very narrow one. Hegel certainly no longer postpones the moment of its completion as he once did until the point in time "when there will be a free people," but sees this moment as dawning now, immediately now, in this epoch of German spiritual life. From France, where it prepared the state and the social life of the coming epoch from the material of the past, the spirit of history has gone over into Germany in order to begin there the work of the new, highest age: first as "moral spirit" to set the human on their own and then, thus prepared, to bring about the ultimate: to become absolute religion, absolute knowledge. Furthermore, this last thing does not first come about in the distant future. Absolute religion is no longer something that has to first become: no new creation going beyond the Greek religion of beauty and the Christian religion of suffering, no result of a "free people" of the future first unifying both. The last system already showed us that the philosopher has made peace with Christianity, and with Protestantism in particular. The Phenomenology demonstrates for us further the highly important fact in this connection, namely, the philosopher of history carries out the construction plan that had still been discarded for the whole of history within the history of religion: Christianity as the historically concluding fusion of the "natural religion" of the old Orient and the "religion of art" of the Greeks. Thus, now that the historical human being, the bearer of "spirit," is stepping into their mature age, absolute religion is already prepared for them – they only have to reach out their hand.

And absolute knowledge? Hegel concluded his summer lecture in 1806 with the following words: "This, my dear gentlemen, is speculative philosophy, as far as I have come in the formation of it. Consider it as a beginning of philosophizing that you are to carry on. We stand at an important epoch, a time of fermentation where spirit has been jolted and arisen above its previous configuration and won another. The entire mass of previous ideas, concepts, the ligaments of the world, are dissolved and collapsing like a dream upon itself. A new emergence of spirit is in the making. Philosophy must above all greet its appearance and acknowledge it, whereas others, powerlessly resisting it, cling to the past and the majority unconsciously detect the weight of its appearance. But it is the task of philosophy, recognizing it as the eternal, to show it honor."[187]

The self-consciousness of the thinker has now swelled to such heights. He stands face to face with the age. Even more so: he talks to it, and it speaks to him. He really has become prepared, and capable of entering into it: "to be" it. He has crossed the Dantean middle of our life's journey. The stations of life transform for him into the epochs of the world. The stream of thought has broken the barriers of its banks and now saturates the thirsting fields of the age.

## NOTES

1 GW 4, 454 f.; HW 2, 489.
2 [This refers to the first "Jenaer Systementwurf" (GW 6, SE I). For the history of the edition and its dating, see the editorial report on GW 6 (340–357), the introduction to SE I, and Jaeschke (2003). 15 ff., esp. 160 ff.]
3 Perhaps the same as in 1802. Only an exact expert of that logic could decide whether the modification of the natural philosophy would be compatible with a retention of the old logic.
4 GW 6, 282, annotation; SE I, 197 annotation.
5 Namely, where "need" and "pleasure" are still conceptualized together with "perception."
6 GW 6, 282 ff.; SE I, 197 ff.
7 GW 6, 299; SE I, 210.
8 GW 6, 301 ff.; SE I, 212 ff.; the words "and the family" connected by commas are an addition; before, the comma was obviously a period.
9 GW 6, 317; SE I, 225 – verbatim: "... *its being judged against the appearance of the other as it is itself, or its inorganic nature.*"
10 GW 6, 321 ff.; SE I,228 ff.
11 GW 6, 324; SE I, 230.
12 GW 6, 325; SE I, 231 – verbatim: "Possession similarly becomes [...] in its individuality something universal."
13 GW 6, 324; SE I, 230 – verbatim: "[...] like a wild animal requires constant strict control and taming."
14 Cf. before the conclusion of "I. Potenz" (GW 6, 296; SE I, 208).
15 And this is done by additions on consciousness (GW 6, 273–279; SE I, 189–194) before the first "potency," by concluding this first "potency" (GW 6, 295 f.; SE I, 207), and by a transition from the first to the following two (GW 6, 297 f.; SE I, 208 f.).
16 [Jenaer Systementwürfe III. Naturphilosophie und Philosophie des Geistes (GW 8, SE III). Cf. also here on the dating and history of editions in the editorial report in GW 8 (ibid., 312–322), Kimmerle's remarks on the "Chronologies der Manuskript Hegels in den Bänden 4–9" (ibid., 348–362 as well as the Introduction to SE III.]
17 GW 8, 222 f; SE III, 204 f.
18 GW 8, 236 ff.; SE III, 217 ff.
19 GW 8, 242; SE III, 222.

20  Ibid.
21  GW 8, 244; SE III, 224 – verbatim: "[...] that each sphere will receive [...] outlets, seek new channels in other lands for sales [...]."
22  GW 8, 244 f.; SE III, 224.
23  GW 8, 245; SE III, 224.
24  Ibid.
25  GW 8, 246; SE III, 225.
26  GW 8, 249; SE III, 227.
27  GW 8, 248; SE III, 227 f.
28  GW 8, 253; SE III, 230.
29  GW 8, 249; SE III, 228.
30  Ibid. – verbatim: "[the law is] as much master over evil as pure life."
31  GW 8, 249 f.; SE III, 228.
32  GW 8, 250; SE III, 229.
33  GW 8, 253; SE III, 231 –verbatim: "these are their [the power-state's] *authorities* [...]"
34  GW 8, 253 ff.; SE III, 231 ff.
35  GW 8, 222; SE III, 204.
36  GW 8, 253; SE III, 231.
37  GW 8, 256; SE III, 234.
38  GW 8, 257; SE III, 234 (annotation on Aristotle).
39  GW 8, 257; SE III, 235.
40  In the margin (GW 8, 257; SE III, 234) "Es ist *vorausgestz* was werden soll"; similarly to what is already in the essay on "Natural Right" [GW 4, 426; HW 2, 447].
41  GW 8, 257; SE III, 235.
42  GW 8, 258; SE III, 235.
43  Ibid.
44  GW 8, 258; SE III, 235 – verbatim: "[...] their *immediate* pure will is his will [...]."
It is tremendously instructive to place these thoughts next to their "model"
with Aristotle (1991 ff.), 1288a; the distance gives measure to the deepening
that the human mind has experienced during these two millennia.
45  Ibid.
46  GW 8, 258; SE III, 235 annotation – verbatim: "According to Solon Pisistratus,
each of the citizens made the laws their own."
47  GW 8, 258; SE III, 236.
48  [This claim is often attributed to Friedrich Christoph Schlosser (1776–1861);
cf. Burkhardt (1905).]
49  GW 8, 259; SE III, 237.
50  GW 8, 259; SE III, 236 (marginal note).
51  Ibid.
52  GW 8, 259; SE III, 237.
53  GW 8, 260 ff.; SE III, 237 ff.
54  GW 8, 261; SE III, 238.
55  GW 8, 262; SE III, 239.
56  GW 8, 263; SE III, 240

57  GW 8, 262; SE III, 239 – verbatim: "But it is [...] a greater contrast and educa-
    tion, a deeper spirit."
58  Ibid.
59  GW 8, 260; SE III, 238.
60  GW 8, 262 ff.; SE III, 240 ff.
61  And, for example, the historical and constitutional remarks on the concept of
    the royal "house" in Rosenstock-Huessy (1914).
62  GW 8, 264; SE III, 241.
63  Ibid, in the margin – verbatim: "this alone, born for this purpose, immediate
    will – or great individuality – energy of willing absolute resolution, in itself, of
    a will – we command."
64  GW 8, 264; SE III, 241 – verbatim: "the prince may be constituted as he
    desires, the citizens as they desire."
65  GW 8, 263; SE III, 240 – verbatim: "This is the *higher principle* of the *newer
    times*, with which the *old ones* were, *with which Plato* was unfamiliar."
66  GW 8, 262; SE III, 239.
67  GW 8, 262; SE III, 240.
68  GW 8, 264; SE III, 241.
69  GW 8, 263; SE III, 240.
70  GW 8, 262; SE III, 240.
71  GW 8, 263; SE III, 240.
72  Also the allusion to the (in Prussian Common Law permitted) corporeal pun-
    ishment of the farmer is there, even more clearly than in 1802: "a crude moti-
    vation, so that he notices a force is present here, must be attached to this
    form." (GW 8, 267 f.; SE III, 244)
73  GW 8, 270; SE III, 246.
74  GW 8, 271; SE III, 247 – verbatim: "[...] each likewise to modify according to
    the estate."
75  Cf. already the heading: "The lower Estates and Dispositions" GW 8, 267; SE
    III, 243).
76  GW 8, 273; SE III, 249.
77  Ibid – verbatim: "very divided, abstract, – machine work."
78  Ibid.
79  [Cf. what Rosenzweig termed the "margin draft" section, originally in the mar-
    gin (GW 8, 265; SE III, 242) as well as the annotation apparatus to the pages
    mentioned.]
80  GW 8, 273 annotation – verbatim: "*scholar, soldier,* and *government*."
81  Ibid. annotation.
82  GW 8, 273; SE III, 249.
83  GW 8, 274; SE III, 250 – verbatim: "the existing whole."
84  Ibid.
85  Hegel was interested in this: "*incompatibilité d'humeurs*," as a ground for
    divorce, which was proposed in the state council, but did not pass (GW 8,
    240; SE III, 220).

86  Cf. also the "Tagespolitische Notizen" of 1802; cf. the texts of November 1802 listed in Kimmerle H.: Zur Chronologie von Hegels Jenaer Schriften (in: Hegel-Studien [1967], 141) under "B. 42" and "43."

87  GW 16, 363 ff.; HW II, 107.

88  GW 8, 276; SE III, 251 – verbatim: "the government, the epitome of the whole, is completed."

89  Ibid.

90  GW 8, 277; SE III, 252.

91  GW 8, 277; SE III, 253 – verbatim: "C. Art, Religion, and Science."

92  HW I, 401 f.; N 329.

93  HW I, 412; N 336.

94  HW I, 412; N 337.

95  HW I, 418; N 342.

96  HW I, 425; N 350.

97  HW I, 425 f.; N 350.

98  HW I, 426; N 350.

99  HW I, 599; Ww. 7, 79 annotation.

100 HW I, 599; Ww. 7, 79 f. annotation – in the wording: "[...] what was treated adversary therein, is [...]."

101 HW I, 599; Ww. 7, 79 annotation – verbatim: "[...] partially not even fixed [...]."

102 GW 5, 99; HW I, 521 – verbatim: "externally unify."

103 GW 5, 111; Ww. 7, 93

104 GW 5, 325; SDS, 48.

105 GW 5, 329; SDS, 52.

106 GW 5, 325; SDS, 48.

107 GW 5, 308, 312; SDS, 31, 35.

108 GW 5, 361; SDS, 85 – Here, Schelling's 10th lecture on academic study offers worthy parallels, with its striking reference – is he thinking of his friend's manuscript? – to a possible "existing document" on the "true synthesis of the state" (Schelling [1990], 109).

109 GW 5, 361; SDS, 85.

110 Ibid.

111 Ibid – verbatim: "[...] the [people] take the divine into themselves [...]."

112 Ibid.

113 Rosenkranz 133–141.

114 Haym, who still had the manuscript (cf. 9th lecture, Annotation 7 [Haym 206] and 16th Lecture, Annotation 13 [ibid., 416], follows it. There (and in the associated text) still further messages from the lost manuscript.

115 Rosenkranz 135.

116 Rosenkranz 136 – "[...] crushed, so that their spirits were driven away [...]."

117 Ibid – verbatim: "The ethical pain had to be infinite."

118 Rosenkranz 135; verbatim: "all individual acts and all things of the highest and lowest acts [...]."

119 Ibid.

120    Rosenkranz 140.
121    Ibid – verbatim: "nor mourned, rather."
122    Rosenkranz 141.
123    Ibid.
124    GW 4, 315–414; HW 2, 287–433.
125    SHK, Bd. I/XII, 2, 530.
126    GW 4, 484; HW 2, 530.
127    Here, above all, Haym's picture, whose simplistic contours cannot be denied, is fatefully misdrawn, and Dilthey has anticipated the decisive correction here.
128    GW 5, 111; HW I, 533.
129    In the margin (GW 9, 283; SE III, 258); "Synthetic connection of the state and the church."
130    GW 8, 277 ff.; SE III, 258 ff.
131    GW 8, 281; SE III, 256.
132    GW 8, 284; SE III, 259.
133    Ibid.
134    Ibid.
135    Ibid.
136    Ibid.
137    GW 8, 285; SE III, 260 – verbatim: "utilize."
138    Ibid.
139    GW 8, 284; SE III, 259.
140    GW 8, 285; SE III, 259.
141    GW 8, 284; SE III, 259.
142    Thus the judgment of Haym (Haym 243).
143    GW 9, 240; HW 3, 326.
144    GW 9, 240; HW 3, 327.
145    GW 9, 260; HW 3, 354.
146    Ibid.
147    Moreover, because now that the third epoch is monarchical, monarchy may also occur in the first.
148    GW 9, 263; HW 3, 358.
149    Schelling (1856 ff.), II/1, 545 (corresponds to Schelling [1985], Vol. 5, 555).
150    GW 9, 263; HW 3, 58.
151    GW 9, 264; HW 3, 359.
152    GW 9, 266 f.; HW 3, 362 f.
153    GW 9, 267; HW 3, 364.
154    GW 9, 269; HW 3, 367.
155    GW 9, 270; HW 3, 367 – verbatim: "Thus, the first entity is *state-power*, the other is *wealth*."
156    GW 9, 275; HW 3, 375.
157    GW 9, 278; HW 3, 378.
158    GW 9, 282; HW 3, 384.
159    Ibid.
160    GW 9, 289; HW 3, 393.

161 GW 9, 293; HW 3, 399.
162 GW 9, 304 ff.; HW 3, 415 ff.
163 GW 9, 316; HW 3, 431.
164 HW 12, 529.
165 GW 9, 316; HW 3, 431.
166 GW 9, 317; HW 3, 432.
167 GW 9, 317; HW 3, 433.
168 GW 9, 318; HW 3, 433.
169 GW 9, 318 f.; HW 3, 434 f.
170 GW 9, 319; HW 3, 4351.
171 GW 9, 319; HW 3, 436.
172 GW 9, 321; HW 3, 437.
173 GW 9, 320; HW 3, 436.
174 GW 9, 319; HW 3, 436.
175 GW 9, 321; HW 3, 437.
176 GW 9, 321; HW 3, 438.
177 Ibid.
178 Ibid.
179 Ibid.
180 Ibid.
181 GW 9, 321; HW 3, 439.
182 GW 9, 322; HW 3, 439.
183 GW 9, 323; HW 3, 441.
184 Ibid.
185 Galais (1819), 190. [JS & JS: "where we have brought together the different elements that constitute the nations"]
186 Aldini, A., May 19, 1805 (in *Gazette nationale* 13, 1022, Sp. I).
187 Rosenkranz 214 f.

# Volume II

Epochs of the World
(1806–1831)

# 9

# NAPOLEON

On March 9, 1802, Goethe wrote to Schiller on the French Revolution, which had again come to his attention on the occasion of reading a memoir on the age of Louis XVI: "Altogether, it is the monstrous view of brooks and streams which, through the necessity of nature, came rushing down against each other from many heights and out of many valleys, finally causing a great river to overflow and a flood, in which both those who anticipated it, as well as those who had not, went under. One sees in this monstrous factuality nothing but nature and nothing of that which we philosophers so gladly like to call freedom."[1] Such words are worth remembering if one wants to know what this age, what its "philosophers" had missed in the swell of outrageous events and what the void was which Napoleon – not the acting human, but rather the image that etched itself into those minds, which was not the giant himself but rather the shadow of the giant – filled for a generation thirsting to intuit the idea. Goethe, after he had confessed to have found only "nature" and not "freedom" in the pandemonium of the Revolution, thus continues: "We eagerly await whether Bonaparte's personality will still further

DOI: 10.4324/9780429354724-11

please us with this magnificent and ruling appearance."[2] In response to this testimony, it would be presumptuous to situate oneself at any other standpoint than that of the observer. Goethe had learned again and again to see in the Corsican more, and something other than the magnificent and ruling appearance of human freedom in a world of forced coercion and was doubtlessly confident that his work was of world-historical duration. It was with great difficulty then, as he was convinced by the process of things that world history was moving on from that man, that he turned back to the old view: Napoleon no longer appeared to the old man as the bearer of historical life but, rather, detached from his specific work, as a sign of that which humankind is capable. He thus names him alongside those others who the daemons have put here to tempt us: Shakespeare, Rafael, Mozart.

It is, as we will see, a similar development that Napoleon's image undergoes for Hegel. Admittedly, how he may have followed the rise of the young general is not known to us. It would be barely permissible to supplement our memory with those verses that his Frankfurt companion, already a shadowed spirit, wrote on the heroes of Lodi and Arcole, whom poets should leave untouched "like the spirit of nature."[3] Disregarding a fleeting mention in the text on The German Constitution – for we did not believe ourselves allowed to identify him with the closing promise of "the conqueror"– we hear only now for the first time, in 1806, that Hegel calls Napoleon the "Universally Named." But it already happened there in full feeling that this name meant more than a man, it meant history. What Hegel thought of and viewed as the state until then was unified in front of this image. The unavoidably great figure forced him, as well as the entire range of his contemporaries, to show their true colors. Indeed, no one was permitted to remain neutral; the individual had to reveal the deepest forces of their disposition towards the state.

"The emperor, this world-soul," so Hegel wrote two days before the Battle of Jena, "I saw him riding through the city on his way to reconnoiter; it is certainly a wonderful sensation to see such an individual, concentrated here into a single point, sitting on a horse, who reaches out into the world and reigns over it."[4] The emperor, the world-soul! What did this mean to him? For it is more than an admiring exaggeration, also more than an empty platitude. And being satisfied to designate it as patriotic indignation, as Haym was, is certainly not an exhaustive assessment of this paradox. Rather, there is a much more definite view of the past and present bound together in that phrase, one of the German and Roman worlds, and one even of the relationship between state, religion, and philosophy. This view is worth understanding. And only after being understood may those who must and desire to feel indignant towards this view still do so.

At that time, in his *Addresses to the German Nation*, which was to teach a downtrodden people to again believe in their future, Fichte had emphasized the thought that the German people had received their greatest encouragements – renaissance and revolution – from Roman Europe, out of which this "humanistic people" was then set to form the effectively dominating experiences of the genus through the German Reformation and German Idealism. It seems highly unlikely to then encounter Fichte, the orator to the German Nation, and Hegel – who would travel in the coming decade with full sails in the wake of Napoleon and now so gladly greeted the collapse of Prussia – to encounter these two on one and the same path in the history of philosophy. And yet, it is so. In the previous section, we heard how Hegel had understood the world-historical meaning of the present moment. For him, the French Revolution marked the end of a world-historical epoch beginning with the collapse of the Roman Empire. With the concept of the general will, a will that only wanted itself, its own actualization, the French Revolution introduced the new, simple thought into the world that would necessarily blow apart a world constructed upon oppositions: state-power and wealth, belief and insight, this world and the beyond. But the world freed of oppositions, which was formed by the new thought, cannot be the world of the state. As the general will wished to configure itself in the state through the form of "terror," it destroyed itself. The old state emerged again, now rejuvenated through the Revolution. And yet, from then on, spirit no longer effectively lived its life in the state and above all no longer in the world of educated culture, of which this state was a part. Rather, spirit "passed over into another land" – Hegel himself had expressly declared that he indeed had another land in mind – into another land where, precisely in its revolutionary denial of all independent actuality outside of itself, which had to fail in the world of the state, it "counts as the truth." Rousseau's general will became Fichte's "I," and from this the movement directly arose which led to absolute philosophy and to the religion of the future. The beating heart of history that had last sounded within the modern state, brought to its completion by Louis the XIV, will henceforth sound within German philosophy. "Spirit" has migrated from this world into the beyond, from the state to philosophy, from France to Germany. For Hegel, Napoleon can thus only be the prince of this world. But his world-historical significance consists of the fact that he is precisely this. He has restored the state, essentially the old state, even if in his monarchy – other than in the kingship of Louis the XIV – state-power did not establish itself in opposition to wealth, but rather, as with the priestly old men in the System of 1802, embodied itself above the estates in the position of the elevated "universal will." That is Napoleon's greatness and likewise the reason he would fall. It was in this sense that in 1814 Hegel himself referred to these sentences from The Phenomenology, as though they were the prophecy of what had since then occurred. That Napoleon preserved the state was his greatness, but just at that moment the state ceased to be the middle point of human history. According to Hegel's interpretation of 1814,[5] Napoleon's downfall became in a deeper sense more necessary than the downfall of others who had saved the state through the establishment of tyrannical authority. Of those – perhaps the likes of a Robespierre – it could be said that they were overthrown not because they were tyrannical or appalling, but because they were "superfluous." However, Napoleon would not merely make himself superfluous as an individual. Instead, his work itself, in the deepest sense, would become superfluous. But for now – we find ourselves in the year 1806 – for now this "extraordinary man," who Hegel saw riding forth, is still the middle point of world history, the world-soul, the "individual, sitting on a horse, who reaches out into the world and reigns over it." He still holds the reins in his hand, and he is still "the great teacher of state law in Paris."[6]

What could the great teacher of state law directly teach the philosopher? The last summary of thoughts on the state in the System of 1805 had already, with the expulsion of the antiquated features from 1802, yielded a general view that very nearly corresponded to the very being and appearance of the Napoleonic state. In particular, we might see the treatment of the relationship between public opinion and civil service in the System of 1805 as mirroring the Napoleonic variety of enlightened despotism. Whereby even then we had to leave open the possibility that the manuscript in question might be a later addition and therefore might not be from the time in Jena. We believed to have directly shown the influence of Napoleon's Italian constitutions through the division of estates in the System of 1805, as well as through the determined manner with which *The Phenomenology* attributed the estates their role in the contemporary state. And in view of the inner life of the state, at least in the move from an aristocratic to a bureaucratic ideal, Hegel's philosophy had turned towards Napoleonic actuality. But in the following years, Hegel either did not notice or did not desire to notice the will towards world-empire, that very aspect that appeared to Hegel's contemporaries, as well as to those who followed, as the actual hallmark of the Napoleonic system. The faithlessness in the possibility of this form of state was too firmly grounded in the essence of Hegel's entire view of the state for it to be shaken by the impending actualization of events. In order to correspond to its fundamental nature of war-like self-preservation, the state had to be one single state. The result of Hegel's newest view of the state and history was that, if beyond this he could, indeed had to, prescribe tasks to the state, the essence of power would be made subservient to the goals of education and culture. And it was already decided in the context of his newest thoughts that this task could only be solved in a German state, for the intellectual life of the coming world was the life of the German spirit.

In a German state – by no means in the one German state. If Hegel could have hoped for a nationally united Germany several years earlier, it now seemed that such hopes were entirely cut off for him. Already in 1805, he had bid farewell to such hopes under the twofold influence of the establishment of the Austrian hereditary empire (which, in general, could be taken as the departure of the Habsburgs from their connection to German politics) and the attitude of the German princes and peoples in that time of preparation for the Confederation of the Rhine.[7] But the equation of state and nation was never made in the essence of Hegel's philosophical image of the state. Therefore, no longer staying in Jena, Hegel could uncritically turn himself toward one of Napoleon's southern German satraps, which, just at that time, had widely opened its doors to non-local scholars: Bavaria.

The newly minted Kingdom endeavored to fuse its Catholic territory with the largely Protestant influx over the last few years. The channels were finally to be opened to the long pent-up stream of Northern Germany's heretical culture. Montgelas, the "first German minister of revolution," as he was named by the somewhat spiritually akin Hardenberg, who was also his cousin in Prussian office, effectively ruled over Bavaria and was hardly obstructed by a King who was happy to just have his rest. More important was the consideration given to the almighty French emperor who, through his envoys, delivered to Montgelas occasional directives or indications. Personally, the enlightened minister gladly surrounded himself with the new Protestant scholars and defended them against the machinations of the long-established clerics, who were beginning to feel shoved aside. Schelling, Jacobi, and Thiersch were the beacons of the Munich Academy of Sciences. The Swabian Niethammer, friends with Hegel since Jena, was to rejuvenate the secondary school system of the Protestant parts of the country based on the new humanism. Paulus, also Swabian and similarly connected with Hegel since Jena, worked under Niethammer on the provincial school council. Hegel would have gladly become a professor at the newly founded university in Würzburg, or even in Erlangen, for that matter. But this was blocked by the financial difficulties in which the state found itself due to uncertain external relations, and simultaneously through new establishments in the interior. Thus, it was to the liking of Niethammer, who had become Hegel's advisor and supportive friend in all conditions of external life and bureaucratic affairs, that the younger countryman at least positioned himself on the horizon of the Bavarian government. As a very well-paid interlude, necessary to secure life's necessities after he was left fortuneless by exhausting his father's inheritance, Hegel assumed the position of editor at the Bamberg Newspaper.[8]

The small paper – four quarters, four pages – had, in the twenty-two years since it was founded by an emigrated French priest, already changed its chief editor six times. Under Hegel's direction, it appeared every weekday, printed in the morning and delivered in the afternoon. It was not the actual local gazette of Bamberg, the "Bamberg Correspondent" fulfilled that role. The "Bamberg Newspaper" provided Bamberg, and above all Bavaria's Main Administrative District, with news on the home-state and especially on European events. In this function it was quite significant for relations at that time – the Bavarian government found it to be an inheritance of the time when Bamberg was still the city residence for the

Empire's princes. It was considered by the citizens as belonging "to that which was long ago allocated to the local city" and was "granted advantages" by the new ruler himself. One even read the paper outside the borders of Bavaria, at least outside of the Main Administrative District, such that the citizens felt themselves in tune with the economic happenings "which brought foreign money into the land and especially into the Main Administrative District itself."[9] Nevertheless, the portrayals that appeared in the obituaries after Hegel's death and claimed to uncover the "deep spirit" of the editor[10] in his "clear and sharp essays, probing into the age," were already false, because the paper – in line with the press in general at that time – really contained no "essays." And if the newspaper itself, under Hegel's direction, had already "elevated itself to one of the most important papers in Germany,"[11] then this went unnoticed by Hegel himself: the complaints about the "newspaper galleys," about the spirit-less poverty of his business, go on and on in his letters for more than a year and half after he left. In truth, his task was limited to merely compiling news stories. His sources were foreign newspapers, as well as his newspaper's own correspondents, whom Hegel, through his old connections, eagerly sought to increase. Knebel in Jena, among others, was solicited and helped guide things, albeit admittedly not enough for Hegel. At most, the editor appended a short embellishment to the report to help orient his readers. At that time, even a paper dedicated purely to news stories did not lack in world history. When he took over the editorship, the last events of the Prussian–French war were still playing out, including the sieges of Danzig and Kolberg. Then came the Treaties of Tilsit, and Hegel, writing to Jena about the hardships of a newspaper writer in times of peace, movingly complained that he had to be content with merely reporting on the occasion a French Marshall would travel through the city. Admittedly, there was no shortage of troops and prisoner transports traveling through Bamberg, and they were duly recorded with the greatest exactitude.[12] The columns were also filled with reports on festivities for the birthdays of kings and queens, or a previous report when a Bavarian prince had moved into town and took up residency with his young wife in the house of the former bishop.[13] Less often, it was reports on some kind of scientific phenomenon which could be seen in Bamberg, such as a comet[14] or a hermaphrodite.[15] And finally, in the late summer of 1808 came the Spanish battles, albeit reported with caution, as well as the festivities in Erfurt.[16] In those cases, the editor had something to do again. Admittedly, it is astounding enough to see how so few events excited Hegel politically, namely, how few of the steps that Bavaria took in the direction of becoming a modern state made it into the newspaper, even in the form of a simple report. That there was talk "in several states of the Confederation of the Rhine about the introduction of a *Napoleonic Code* and constitutional forms" was in fact all that a reader of the *Bamberg Newspaper* learned about it.[17] Neither the King's Ordinance from May 1, 1808, which announced the rendition of a constitution, nor the publication of this constitution, which admittedly never came into effect, were even mentioned at all in the government paper's edition from May 25, and just as little on the reforms that were then occurring in the government.[18] And nevertheless, despite express caution, there were still clashes with the censor.[19]

Right at the beginning of his work in Bamberg, in the neighboring Erlangen, Hegel had seen a cautionary example of how it could turn out for a careless newspaper writer during these times of war. There, the French governor suppressed the *Erlangen Newspaper* and threw the chief editor – Stutzmann, a fellow companion in philosophy with Hegel – along with the censor, into prison for eight days "for improvement," because they "allowed false news and remarks to spread into their public writings, which were capable of disturbing the public peace."[20] Hegel, therefore, knew exactly what he was in for. The censorship for newspapers in Bavaria was based on an edict issued through Monteglas in 1799 which, for something of that age, showed quite a significant broadmindedness in handling the press. It allowed, in general, the reprinting of foreign sources and was content with the qualification that with "conspicuous and unauthenticated reports" the precise origin should always be given.[21] This was the aspect where things could occasionally be reined in. Through the increase in Protestants in Swabia and Franken, Bavaria had gained an important daily readership, albeit first in 1799. In fact, the *Augsburger Allgemeine* newspaper and the *Korrespondent von und für Deutschland*, which was published in Nuremberg, were being read in all of Germany. The second of these also worked very closely with its own correspondents. At first, the current law, according to which the business of censorship was incumbent upon the censor appointed as the highest provincial official by the regional commissioner, appeared to suffice. But dissensions soon arose among foreign countries. Napoleon, as an upstart, suffered from a nervous over-estimation of public opinion, foreign to older governments – Monteglas called him "drunk-on-praise and always oversensitive to lampooning" – and from the middle outwards this new spirit of suspicion against the evil newspaper writers spread even among the dependent governments. The Erlanger affair was merely a prelude. Next, in the spring of 1807, a complaint of the Swiss government, albeit unofficial, came from the Bavarian envoys in Bern on account of a very short article in the *Augsburger Allgemeine*. This led in Munich to the occasion of tightening censorship rules and all content, "in order to avoid all vexations often caused by reporting false and rash news in public papers," was henceforth only to be included if it was an official report from an official source.[22] Because it was uncertain what the concept of "official" really meant – in the strictest sense, the only official newspaper until now was the French *Moniteur* and its counterpart in the Kingdom of Westphalia – this was used as a lever to find occasion to arbitrarily intervene in any given newspaper issue. More than this was admittedly not wanted. For even if the high provincial officers looked with disdain, due to the work it caused them, upon the papers under their censorship,[23] the economic significance of some of these was already so significant that one could hardly wish for their demise. As of the fall of 1808, so it seems, Hegel's paper had still not entered into the purview of the Munich foreign ministry office, to which the censorship complaints of foreign governments were sent; "petty annoyances," caused by the president of the provincial regional office – whether out of personal aversion or "out of pure fervor for service and submissiveness" – remained without further consequence.[24] But then suddenly, in the fall of 1808, and very much against his will, the editor aroused the attention of the government. It was the point in time when the storm of the Austrian uprising became concentrated. In the summer, reports about it were passed on from the Bavarian emissaries in Vienna to Montgelas, who then passed them on to Napoleon.[25] Then, from Paris, came the "invitation" to the Confederation of the Rhine "to be prepared to defend against any attack." Bavaria amassed all of its troops into three observation camps in a calculated distance from the Austrian border. Naturally, it was undesirable that official attention be directed towards these preparations, although the displacement of troops in these days already betrayed enough to the attentive

observer. Hegel also had his own thoughts on the matter when he found
out about the simultaneous withdrawal of Bamberg's military and the
break-up of the French camp near Berlin, together with the departure
of the marshal to Dresden. In any case, the veil was to be lifted as little
as possible. Unfortunately, on August 19, Hegel's newspaper published
an article on the Bavarian camp, wherein some exact details about the
partition of the troops from the (of course secretive) royal decree were
repeated word for word.[26] Hegel had unsuspectingly taken them from
a torn off piece of a transcription of the decree, brought to him by an
employee of his press, who claimed to have found it. This was noticed
in Munich. An intense investigation into the origin of the article was
demanded by the ministry for foreign affairs; evidently, they were looking to uncover treason in the military administration. The newspaper
was threatened with suspension if it did not reveal the "military person" from whom it had gotten the decree. Hegel, who knew from the
cases of the Bayreuth and Erlangen newspapers that the ministry would
make good on any given threat, could nonetheless admit only what was
known to him. On any account, he sought to secure for himself Niethammer's advocacy, but whether it was necessary cannot be determined.
In any case, Hegel's hope that more important political matters, which
were becoming increasingly tense by the day, would prevent the authorities from further handling the matter, was not met. The "difficult story"
led in the second half of December to an inquiry from Munich and
repeated replies from Bamberg. Then nothing further is heard regarding
the matter. But the attention of the ministry had now been awakened,
and Hegel would feel, once again and now with this story, "the indignity of his situation." On November 1, 1808, a royal edict was issued
from Munich to all of the general county commissioners that instated
anew the decree from March 16, whereby all that was to be published
were official reports from official sources, which would also have to be
listed and that – and this was new – the troubled leaders of the provincial authorities themselves were to be tasked with the censorship of the
newspaper![27] And the occasion for this decree was provided, apparently,
by none other than the unlucky author of The Phenomenology.

On October 26, Hegel's paper published an article "out of Erfurt"
which described, in a strict reporting tone, but effective precisely
thereby, the manner in which Napoleon dealt with his princely vassals:

"Around ten o'clock the invitees came together in the great audience room of the emperor. However, it took nearly three hours before the very busy monarch appeared before them. He came around one o'clock, sat himself down at a table, ate, drank, again withdrew himself, and the gathering came to its end." Additionally, the article also reprinted some rumors on the Congress of Erfurt: "that a northern alliance had formed under the protection of his majesty, the Roman emperor; that all post offices in Germany would be given back to the prince of Thurn and Taxis; and that Erfurt would remain a free city and would be tax-free for ten, or as others said, for twenty years." Whether the report on the Munich government's breakfast was intentionally spiteful cannot be deduced from the records; these allow it to appear as if the storm broke out only on account of the "rumors." Among these rumors, one was indeed of special interest to the Bavarian state, namely that having to do with the postal service. A little over a half year earlier, it had suddenly and without compensation removed the postal right that had been given to the house of Thurn and Taxis in 1806 as a "fiefdom of the throne" and itself taken control of the profitable business. This was reason enough to sense in the Bamberger paper's dry remark a stealthy attack on one of the Kingdom of Bavaria's most holy goods. In Bamberg, Hegel himself had already immediately found out, most likely through the regional commissioner, with whom he was on good terms, that without intending to do so he had again caused distress by reprinting the notice. Thus, immediately in the next issue of the newspaper there appeared, attached in a seemingly harmless manner to a report on similar rumors from a Parisian paper, a withdrawal of the one published yesterday from a public German paper, classifying it "as a totally empty rumor unsupported by any authority." Despite this prompt denial, and even given the innocuous origin of the report from officially censured papers of the Confederation of the Rhine, or even from "those controlled by the government of his imperial French majesty," Hegel still felt called, in a "most reverent" letter of justification from November 9, to add the insurance that he, "through the punctual compliance with the orders handed to the editors of the newspaper, would take the trouble to carefully avoid any cause whereby the highest disapproval could fall upon me."[28] After he had stood out so disagreeably once, it was no longer so easy to fulfill this promise. Even before he had sent off the letter of justification, on November 8 the newspaper had to again publish an amendment from a "higher place," this time out of Leipzig, because it had designated the existing prohibition against the importation of English goods as ineffective in a commentary on cotton trade. The magistrate from Leipzig let it be known very clearly that the existing law that restricted English business would be administer in the strictest manner. Fortunately, at the end of the month, the start of Hegel's position in Nuremberg extracted the philosopher from a situation which had become increasingly difficult. The newspaper quickly met its fate. The last incident, which led to an intervention from Munich, appeared to have concluded with Hegel's response and the connected investigation that continued until Christmas. But on January 27, 1809, the French diplomatic representative in Munich recalled how often he was brought to complain about the terrible spirit of some Bavarian newspapers, especially those of Nuremberg and Bamberg. And it was again the "*Gazette de Bamberg*" that this time aroused the highest scorn of Napoleon himself, albeit with two issues that had been published perhaps a week after Hegel's departure: news from the Pyrenean Peninsula that appeared suitable "à relever les espérances d'un parti à la vérité expirant mais à jamais incorrigible";[29] and – terrible, most terrible! – an article wherein Friedrich Wilhelm III's magnanimity was praised, who remained loyal to Alexander after Eylau in response to Napoleon's promises. The emissary "suggested" suppressing the newspaper – which had aroused the lively "indignation"[30] of the emperor – and critically added that the minister was not strong enough to be able to put enough weight behind his own opinions and actions in the new provinces. The emissary knew why he was being so forthright: on January 16, Napoleon had made him personally responsible for all future perfidious and dangerous articles published by Bavarian newspapers. That was close to the last straw for the Bamberger Newspaper. The final blow, in case it needed any, came from a complaint by Prince Hatzfeld,[31] which was passed on to Monteglas by the Bavarian emissary in Berlin.[32] The complaint was about an article published during Hegel's departure, and therefore most likely still came from one of his correspondents.[33] The hidden malice Hatzfeld claimed to see could have only been understood, however, by those who were well acquainted with Berlin's conditions and its people at that time. In any case, on February 7, the dissolution of the newspaper was decreed and reported to the French emissary on that very same day.[34] But even if

Hegel was completely free of guilt regarding the Hatzfeld incident, for Monteglas the people of both editorial staffs were fused into a single person. He recognized the "just indignation" of the emperor against "the" editor, who had already been issued multiple calls for greater "*circonspection*." As far as the records permit us to ascertain, the above statement really only applied to the old and not to the new editor. Thus, Hegel blamed himself, and with good reason, that the suspension issued upon his successor was due to his own time as editor. And thus, in calming his conscience – and quieting his concerns – his friend Niethammer was actually wrong.

When those events happened in Bamberg, Hegel was already in his third month as rector and teacher at the Royal Gymnasium in Nuremberg. He would live there for eight years, longer than anywhere else besides his birth city. This was the first time that he had come into a real position and in Bamberg Hegel also found himself – from the Tucher family – a wife. And it was Hegel himself who viewed these two events together.[35] When Hegel wanted to delay publicly announcing his engagement until he had obtained the professorship in Erlangen, which was in prospect at that time, Niethammer had to allay Hegel's doubts as to whether an aristocratic child from an imperial city could offer him her hand, pointing out to Hegel that this was a time when kings themselves were no longer required to have any ancestors in order to attain the free right for the king's daughters and a time in which personal merit and self-acquired rank without ancestors was more noble than all ancestors. When Niethammer asked Hegel the following question, it captured the moment in Nuremberg's history well at which Hegel entered into the city: if Hegel did not, as teacher and rector of the Gymnasium in Nuremberg, consider himself reputable and worthy enough "to publicly and solemnly be accepted as a member of a family which had occupied a very reputable place in the previous glory of the imperial city of Nuremberg."[36] Indeed, Hegel came to the venerable city as a member of the new, but not at all revered Bavarian administration. An administration which, in essence, was considered there to be a rotten and run-down entity. Hegel, who at that time, in a city recently rediscovered by the young Romantics, could only bring himself to give the city the beautiful title of "the old pâté," seemed to see it almost the same as the city commissioner who arrived along with him. The latter, in a long report to

Munich,[37] could not emphasize enough the alleys which were empty of people, poorly laid out, badly plastered, and even more poorly lit[38]; the nearly deserted aristocratic houses with their at-most two heated rooms, where "vast forecourts, darkened chambers, darkened plastered stones and great show kitchens" that filled the rest of the space[39]; the "pompous resort-addiction" of the foundation managers[40]; guild constitutions in need of deep reaching reform[41]; the fifty-nine nightwatchmen, who are no longer found in any other capital city of the empire.[42] Hegel's own assignment for "deep reaching reform" now lay in that part of the new Bavarian Nuremberg which, according to the well-understood intention of the government, and again in the words of that report, was "not to be regarded as a local institution, but rather as belonging to the broader circle, indeed to the Kingdom": the secondary school system. This was also run-down. Even in the second winter of Hegel's rectorship, the "singing of the Gymnasium students on public streets" could not be suppressed because "the essential income that would thereby be lost to the institution itself could in no way be covered."[43] Hegel then sought to lead the general goodwill of the government in a continuous small war against local insufficiencies, always and above all with his ally Niethammer by his side. From this, the entire reorganization of the secondary school system in Bavaria proceeded. Hegel was also concerned here with introducing the new humanistic-Protestant idea of education into the darkness of "Barbaria," as Hegel called Bavaria. Initially, the task of the new rector was above all of an organizational nature: he had to establish a decent existence, worthy of the great tradition going back to Melanchthon, for the Gymnasium, which eked out a miserable life in the city, and which was to be united from the remnants of three schools into one. Once again, at the beginning of Hegel's third year of activity, the institution was even threatened with complete dissolution; the city commissioner himself advocated to the King for the preservation of the Gymnasium. We are instructed by some characteristic accounts from students on Hegel's strict and objective manner of administration, which probed each detail of school business, by way of which and over the years, according to the testament of the board,[44] he won over "the disposition of the local, educated public."[45] His innate administrative talent could more or less work itself out during those years. Yet, after the interlude in Bamberg, in addition to the practical thinker, the lecturing theorist also had his say – even if on a lowered lectern. While he really never stopped searching for a professorship at a university, from year to year at the Gymnasium he had the opportunity, as "Professor of Preparatory Sciences," to present his system anew to boys and half-grown youths, a system which Hegel had last lectured on more than two years earlier, on the basis of the notebook from 1805, in the summer of 1806. Not only had his audience changed, but in the meantime the world also appeared to have changed. This was especially true of one major event, "the likes of which comes about only once a millennium," which occurred between that summer of 1806 in Jena and this winter of 1808 to 1809 in Nuremberg: the Battle of Jena.

The sections on the philosophy of state found in the oldest preserved version of the system from Nuremberg are only available to us in the form Hegel used to lecture to his students in the lower grades. However, it is certain that precisely on the point that is noteworthy for us the simultaneous presentation to the upper grades did not deviate. To a certain degree, even if not entirely, the presentation to the lower grades may be regarded as a source for Hegel's system of the philosophy of state in the Nuremberg years and, with regard to the main points, up until at least the Winter Semester of 1812/13.[46] The content is divided into teachings on right, duties and religion. As in Kant's *Metaphysics of Morals*, the philosophy of state is also located within the teachings on right. However, unlike Kant and also in opposition to Hegel's own view held in previous years, and to which he would later return, the doctrine of duty, that is "morality," was placed above the state. On the path from the ethicality of the state to the consummation of Absolute Spirit, we now find with the systematician Hegel – and only now – the morally free individual. Already in the last Jena system we believed to have perceived probing attempts in this direction and, under the impression of the figure of Napoleon, *The Phenomenology* had found formulas for a philosophy of history which strongly inclined towards the displacement of value considerations in favor of the state and in favor of free morality. Now the systematic consequences, which were still being circumvented in 1805, were drawn out. Napoleon's sun stood at the zenith above Hegel's system.

Of course, it is not the case that the state is understood here by Hegel purely and exclusively as a legal institution. Here, Hegel also deals with the relationship of the human being to the state as an ethical one. Duties towards the state form a part of the doctrine on duty, albeit admittedly not the highest part. But Hegel conceives of the state here only as the actuality of the "concept of right." The human being has duties towards this state, but the state itself is not the highest and most perfect human duty.[47] An initial approach in this direction was already brought about by the previous Jena system, even though at this point – admittedly under the common title "Constitution" – Hegel thought to order the estates and estate-oriented dispositions above those "moral," absolutely free dispositions, the "self-liberation of the spirit from the life of a people," which were elevated over the estates. But now this separation and superordination has become much clearer. The old division of duties into perfect and imperfect, if thereby legal duties and morals duties were to be differentiated, could now, so he explains, "likewise be switched." Where here Hegel addresses the state under the category of law, a higher valuation of "*disposition*" in contrast to legal duties, which exact "only an external necessity,"[48] comes as a great surprise. And it is perhaps even more striking when Hegel designates only "pure personality" and "abstract freedom" as the subject of right (and thus here also as the subject of the state), whereas the actualization of that "pure concept," that "abstract person," indeed the "specific determination of existence and existence itself"[49] is reserved for morality. One need only remember what connotation the words "abstract" and "concrete" possess in Hegel's vocabulary in order to recognize how outrageous it is that Hegel refers the state to the "abstract" human being, indeed, ascribes the state only prohibitive strength, as with the rule of law in general. In comparison to this surprising aspect, dealing with the details becomes of secondary importance.

In contrast to what was still the case in 1805, this time – and so from now on in general – the treatment of the "origin of right in state society"[50] begins with the family. For the Polis, The Phenomenology had first recognized in the ethicality of the family the sustaining ground, as well as the permanent opposing pole of the ethicality of the state. Now, the systematic outcome of that profound discussion on the conflict in Sophocles' Antigone stands before us. The family is "the natural society,"[51] the state the "society of human beings subjected to relations of right, wherein they are valid for each other not on account of a particular relationship with nature according to natural inclinations and feelings, but rather as persons."⁵² But this contrast is now bridged, and for the first time, through a concept, albeit conditionally introduced into the system, which just at the time of Napoleon's rule is indeed striking: the nation enters between the family and the state. "When a family has extended itself into a nation and the state coincides as one with the nation, then this is something very lucky."⁵³ The "commentary" that immediately follows shows that it is admittedly nothing more than good luck, and certainly not a necessary condition of the state: "A people is connected through language, customs and manners and education, but this connection does not yet form a state."⁵⁴ And characteristically enough, in the same passage where Hegel dismisses the national foundation of the state as incidental – it really is only "good luck," and for Hegel "luck" means very little, as expressed during these exact years in a wonderful letter to his bride⁵⁵ – in the same sentence he also keeps the ethical and civilizing tasks of the state in their place. Admittedly, the "morality, religion, prosperity, and wealth of all its citizens is very important to the state. The state must also show care to promote these conditions, but they do not constitute its immediate purpose, but rather right [das Recht]."⁵⁶ For Hegel, the natural as well as the ethical sides of the state are likewise – the first in general, the second at least at that time – deferred behind its "immediate purpose": right. We have seen how this devaluation of the concept of the state – for that is what it is, based on everything that we know about Hegel's view of right – is related to the merely external meaning of Napoleonic power. In the present age of the world the state is no longer the highest, it has vacated its place in the spiritual structure of things for morality, which in the near future, according to Hegel's conception, will then yield its place to religion.

The essentially legal conception of the state is explicated in the following paragraphs through short remarks on the state of nature, out of which humanity must pass into a condition "in which the rational will is the ruling one,"⁵⁷ and further on, law as the "abstract expression of the universal will";⁵⁸ finally, "government," that is, the state as power, is not in opposition to the state as law, but rather the actualization of the same universal will, whose "abstract essence" was law.⁵⁹ Hegel, then, still deals in detail with the powers of state and constitutional forms. For the former, this time he does not depend upon the customary three, in that he adds a fourth to Montesquieu's three powers, which, in characteristic underestimation of independent administrative practice and arguably also dependent upon the parliamentary usurpation of the administration then blossoming in England through "private bills," he had forgotten: the administrative and financial.[60] Already in 1805, Hegel had designated civil service as its own power [Macht] within the overall life of the state; the "fourth power [Gewalt]" – incidentally, he orders it as the second – is a new attempt in this direction. The constitution of the state is then primarily derived from the grade and type of distribution of power [Gewaltverteilung] and only secondarily according to the common Aristotelian grouping of the share of citizens in governance, and incidentally, as already familiar, preference is given to the moderate hereditary monarchy. The limitation of the monarch is carried out through laws, which protect the rights of the citizens, additionally through the release of a part of the exercise of governance to "colleges or also imperial estates,"[61] whereby, in comparison to 1805, the mention of imperial estates at this juncture represents a novelty, hardly unrelated to the aforementioned constitutional plans and attempts of Bavaria and the Confederation of the Rhine in general of these years. In 1805, the only thing opposing the prince was civil service, now introduced as "colleges," in which public opinion admittedly found its voice. Within the system we now have the first appearance of the representation of the people [Volksvertretung], whose necessity the journalist Hegel had long since recognized. Accordingly, the share of citizens in the state is now fundamentally comprehended within internal state law. In general, in the account we have on hand here, the central division of the doctrine of the state into "internal and external state law," which will remain so in the future, is hinted at for the first time.[62] With regard to the position of the state among other states and to the significance of war, we learn that which is already known to us.[63]

That side of the state life which earlier enjoyed with Hegel its superordination over right and morality, indeed its proclamation as God's governor upon earth, namely the ethical side, now appears, as already noted, only as a part of the doctrine on duty. It is only here that we actually first learn what the state means for the individual and the individual for the state. Admittedly, the cold truth is expressed right at the beginning that the state aims "to be able to do without the disposition of its citizens,"[64] but on the other side, at least in this context, the main content of the old ethics of the state is provided. It turns out that the state "cannot do away with the disposition of its citizens," it "grasps society not only under relations of right, but rather conveys unity as a truly higher moral community in customs, culture, and universal ways of thinking and acting."[65] But this is now addressed only in connection with the doctrine on duty, not within the doctrine on the essence of the state. And above all, within the doctrine on duty it does not denote the completed end, but only the transition, from "family duties" to "duties for others."[66] One could stress as much as one wants that the character of this philosophical propaedeutic is typical of a puerile understanding – but by no means can this cause us to find such a fundamental deviation in the systematic structure.

After we have thus become roughly acquainted with the systematic formulations, we can now examine with a keen ear the direct sources of Hegel's political disposition. A main source flows to us from his school addresses. As rector, he was obligated to regularly hold a public speech at the student awards ceremony at the end of the school year, "to present the history of the secondary school in the past year and to touch upon that which would be useful to hear for the public's relation to the school."[67] Hegel carried out this task, which he had to fulfill five times from 1809 to 1816, in a manner that made it impossible for his listeners to ignore that a philosopher was speaking to them. And from Hegel's philosophy of education, some quite significant rays illuminate Hegel's views on the essence of things in general.

The first of these talks, held on October 29, 1809, extolled education in the humanities on account of its spiritual content, "which has value and interest in and for itself." This content forms "the soul nurtured thereby into a core of independent worth [...] which constitutes the foundation of usefulness for everything else."[68] The implication that follows subordinates the state to higher purposes to such a degree that it still comes as a surprise, even after all that has been said before. Whereas earlier Hegel readily allowed the state to evoke ethical powers among its citizens simply through its existence and ethical order, he now demands that it should explicitly, indeed for the sake of its own preservation, nurture the spiritual-ethical culture of the individual beyond the proper political sphere: "this independent support, this substantial inwardness, which is the mother of the composure, prudence, presence, and wakefulness of the spirit."[69] It is only from this more general perspective that the words he used to allude not only to the Austrian defeat of this year, but especially to Prussia, should be understood: "have we not even seen in these recent times states themselves neglect and scorn what their inhabitants sought to preserve and build up out of the inner backdrop of their soul, direct their inhabitants towards mere utility and towards the spiritual only as a means, and cluelessly stand in the face of danger, collapsing in on themselves in the very midst of their multitude of utility?"[70] The state is to deal with the "spiritual" as an end in itself, as something lying beyond itself, it is to "build up" the "inner backdrop" in the soul of the individual: the state itself apparently no longer dwells within this inner backdrop – it has become the mere foreground of inner life.

It follows from this that religion now becomes the most central point of focus for Hegel, to the extent that, in accord with his current views, for him religion is the key to the future of Germany, as well as the world. "Fatherland, rulers, constitution and the like do not appear to be the levers by way of which to raise up the German people," thus writes Hegel in January 1807 to the most sympathetic of his Jena pupils, "the question is what will follow when religion is stirred up."[71] And now quite crucial for him – as we already know from the final Jena system – is that Protestantism is the bearer of this future, but a Protestantism, admittedly, which has moved heavily towards philosophy, indeed one which more or less coincides with freedom of thought. Due to the way in which he conceptualized Protestantism, he felt an elementary hatred against Austria's upheaval of 1809, supported journalistically by Friedrich Schlegel, and rejoiced that "this liberation and Catholicization of us all endorsed by Friedrich Schlegel has gone to the dogs and he will have to consider himself lucky if he stays free from the gallows."[72] How does skepticism against Prussia on the one side and trust in Napoleon on the other connect with such Protestant conviction, which almost turns here into the Jesuit-fear once mocked by the reformer of the Empire precisely in favor of Austria? A letter to Schelling from January 1807 sheds some light on this. According to that letter, "nothing proper is to be expected anymore [...] from the spirit of Northern Germany; formal culture seems to have fallen to its lot, and this service seems to have been allotted to it exclusively – though enjoyment of its fruit is reserved for a higher genius."[73] What that means, and especially what that means in a letter to the then still befriended Schelling, is clear to see for those who are familiar with Hegel's thoughts and way of speaking in Jena. Formal culture, which seems to have been allotted to Northern Germany, is the ethical individualism brought to its peak by Kant, Fichte, and Jacobi, which *The Phenomenology* placed at the beginning of the transition of spirit from Germany to France. In that text, whose publication Hegel was overseeing at that time, just as this individualism was only the forerunner of absolute religion and of absolute knowledge, so now, in the quoted passage from the letter, a higher genius than that of Northern Germany, namely that of Southern Germany – Hegel writing Schelling![74] – will enjoy its fruits, namely absolute religion and absolute knowledge. That only the German spirit comes into question for this world-historical emergence, for this we have full proof, by way of which Hegel's assertion from the year 1814 that he predicted the fall of Napoleon in *The Phenomenology* is also cleansed of the suspicion of being simply *vaticinatio ex eventu*.[75] The same person who celebrated the victory of culture and spirit over crudeness and sophistry in the Battle of Jena, and could see "no other prognosis" for the Prussians, this same person expected – in 1807 – that the Germans, pressured by France, would be forced "to give up their inertia towards actuality, emerge into it and perhaps, in that interiority preserves itself in exteriority, even surpass their teacher."[76] Provisionally, at least, they will be fully consumed by what they learn. The great teacher of state law, sitting in Paris, will be there to fulfill the historical mission through them. Beyond all personal admiration that Hegel held for "this extraordinary man," political conviction is at work here. It is remarkable – and yet not unjustified – how concern for a "Catholicization" did not appear to come to him at all here. He holds himself to Napoleon's protection of the Protestant university organization – again we see how in this connection for Hegel Protestantism and education are one and the same. The only authority in Protestantism "is the intellectual and moral education of all, and this is assured through the institutions, which Napoleon hated, but [...] saw solely from the aforementioned side and therefore learned to spare them, spared institutions in Holland and Göttingen, etc."[77] If Napoleon thus appeared harmless to him at that time in this most important relation, and if his general devaluation of the idea of the state had allowed him to believe in the possible independence of intellectual cultivation from the prevailing "state establishments," Hegel now found unconditional trust in

Napoleon regarding the questions on the development of a constitution, which now occupied a more secondary place in his thinking. The striking characterization of the emperor of the army as the "great teacher of state law" was meant by him in all earnestness.

Even if, as indeed we know, the Corsican appeared to him as the one who tamed the Revolution, and thus as a power of restitution, Hegel was in no way calmed to see Napoleon's domestic political work completed in the restitution of the old state, especially in the differences between estates. Although it may have almost seemed so in The Phenomenology, in truth, as his letters from the following period reveal, Hegel did see in Napoleon the savior of the Revolution's fundamental ideas from their own ramifications – if one may, the savior of the Ideas of 1789 from those of 1793. Rather shortsightedly, he thought he could recognize the essential content of Napoleon's political will in the shadow-images of a parliament that Napoleon allowed to subsist in France and advanced in the satellite states. This delusion shows us just how strongly Hegel's image of the state was now colored by constitutional thinking. This can be explained to some extent by the fact that Hegel, true now as then to the impressions from his youth in Württemberg, found that the participation of the people in the state was equally met by an advisory college of civil servants, as in an elected body of representatives. With the privy council, Napoleon's monarchy had itself created a political body that best of all corresponded to Hegel's requirements, definitely more than is the case with its tribunals and senates. At that time, when Hegel was waiting for the "key decision"[78] from Paris for Bavaria and the Confederation of the Rhine in general, which, according to his hope, "would not only have an effect on the foreign division of land, but would also, for the salvation of the people, also influence internal organization,"[79] he noted with pleasure Napoleon's purported words to the minister of Württemberg on the intended annulment of the landed estates by his king: "I made your master into a sovereign, not a tyrant."[80] His "entire political temperament"[81] depends upon whether or not the Napoleonic code would be introduced, and furthermore, also whether "additional parts of France's or Westphalia's constitution would be instituted."[82] "Only if it is the will of heaven, that is, the will of the French emperor!"[83] – for admittedly, as the recent events in Württemberg have shown: "the German princes have not yet grasped the concept of a free monarchy, nor sought its realization – Napoleon will have to organize all of this."[84] With the previous German imitations of the French, one half was always left out, and indeed that half "which contained that which is most noble, namely the freedom of the people, their participation in voting and resolutions, or at the very least an explanation of the reasoning for governmental measures for the discretion of the people."[85] In short, "*publicity*," that "conversation of the government with the people about their own and its own interests [...] this is one of the greatest elements of the strength of the French and English people."[86] And accordingly, he urgently questions his friend from the Munich government whether or not the forthcoming reorganization of Bavaria will really only result in twelve prefects and not "also a state council? not also representation of the people?"[87] And this is again indicative of how here collegial-bureaucratic ideas coalesce with parliamentary ideas, both as the cornerstone of a "free monarchy." How thoroughly modern he thereby conceived of the relation of the people and of civil service to the highest level of government, how totally free from any dualistic impulse, which would have been only too understandable for someone born in Swabia, this is shown – if we didn't already know it – by the formula by way of which he conceived the "key moment of freedom," namely, that restriction of the highest authority of the state: "The self-confidence of the state in itself, which leaves its parts to do as they like."[88] The government does not trust the people nor the people it, rather, the state trusts itself: a self-contained circle.

But given all of that, according to these testimonies from the letters, the state also no longer fulfills the innermost part of life. The Battle of Jena was certainly an event that "would not occur again in a hundred or a thousand years,"[89] but even this apocalyptic designation of the age already shows that Hegel sees more in the battle than a political event. It is known to us which people and which ideas had their day in history with this battle. It is not without meaning that he called it an event "*too big*" for a political newspaper writer.[90] It is not the longing for peace of a philistine when Hegel then regrets that the miserable war could again disturb what is "best, namely the arts and the sciences."[91] And when he really assigned the state the task of developing the "inner backdrop" of the soul of its citizens, when he wished for Bavaria to have a literary review in part of the government newspaper, as was the case with the Moniteur[92]: within all of this there appears the superordination of the spiritual over the state, that demotion of the state to the role of a simple caretaker of spiritual life, which is not of this world, briefly, that shifting of the weight by way of which we came to know the actual hallmark of Hegel's Napoleonic period. One feels oneself to be transported into Hegel's radical revolutionary beginnings as a student and private tutor when one reads how he convinces himself more and more each day that theoretical work brings about more in the world than practical work: "once the realm of ideas is revolutionized, then actuality cannot resist."[93] At first, it might seem strange that Hegel could go so far as to one-sidedly overvalue thought in favor of actuality while under the impression of Napoleon's omnipotence. Apparently opposing motives, namely the happy surrender to great men of action and actuality along with the conviction of the autonomy, indeed the priority, of spiritual life over all actuality, are intertwined here. We saw how this intertwining of a more or less Fichtean theory with the most un-Fichtean attitude thinkable could, and did, result in a single historical-philosophical knot.

But history itself sliced apart this artificial knot with a sharp sword. The year 1813 arrived. It found Hegel – something other could hardly be expected – rigidly incredulous at first, then increasingly more stunned. He had become much too obsessed with his own thoughts to be so easily led out of this magic circle. The word "liberation" now regularly appears in his letters with ironic cadence. He had not perceived dependency on a Napoleonic France as a lack of freedom – we know why. When he now writes about the approach of the "Cossacks, Bashkirs, and also other admirable liberators,"[94] this combination, to which he introduces the Prussian patriots, already shows how little he himself, like Goethe, could imagine liberation through these liberators.[95] As his own state then joins up with the allies, as its youth from his closest circle thronged to the flags, he knew of nothing else to do than to point out to one of these young friends a "soldier" passing through and to draw his attention to "which society he would be entering if he joined it voluntarily."[96] And, sullenly, he comments on the news that the "liberators" are marching through: "if I ever by chance should see someone who is liberated, I will also take to my feet."[97] And yet, the first yield of the new freedom that he experienced in Bavaria was for him an occasion for mockery. On the instance of the "Field Marshall Wrede," he remarks: "The French emperor did not tolerate that minor powers should have a

Field Marshall. But now, after such a total turnabout of things, after such brilliant victories, such heavy burdens and abundant blood, we have one."[98] And he could not overcome his mistrust in the successes of the Allies for a long time. From a comment he made about the final battle of the 1814 campaign, it even sounds like he still considered an eventual defeat of the Allies possible, indeed even probable. When everything was nonetheless decided and Napoleon was undeniably defeated, he then finally sought an explanation for what had happened and sought after a stance for himself. The following important passage from a letter – from April 29, 1814 – is quoted in full below. It also signifies the end of the episode outlined in this section: "Great things have happened all around us. It is a tremendous drama to see an enormous genius destroy himself. That is the τραγικωτατον [tragikotaton] that there is. The whole mass of mediocrity, with its lead-like weight, presses down without rest or reconciliation, and continues on in a leaden manner until that which was once elevated descends to the same level, or lower. The turning point of it all, the reason that this mass has authority and remains at the top, as the chorus, is that the great individuality himself had to give it the right to do so, thereby bringing himself into ruin."[99]

So dramatically, one might say – individual and mass, hero and chorus – does the great event present itself to the philosopher. Not one force that wears itself down in battle with equal forces, as the historian would see it and as Hegel himself had later seen it, not the revolution in battle with the nationalities. Instead, it is simply the one and the many. At first, it nearly appears as if Hegel forcibly avoids drawing consequences from what had happened, as if he evades everything by way of the aesthetic, the "tremendous drama." In truth, this subordination of Napoleon under the tragic law of history expressed something that until now Hegel had not expressed, and something more than he meant to express here. Namely, he "praises himself" for predicting all of this in that passage from The Phenomenology, which we choose to set as the basis for this entire section, and we were not in line to believe him, in so far as it is believable and insofar as such predictions are at all believable: but he really did predict in that passage the course of events in the broadest strokes. What Hegel did not foresee and what he could not have foreseen was the mood with which he himself would perceive the events. That the tyrant who had done his work would become superfluous and experience his downfall because of his superfluousness; that the great individuality must give himself the right to his own destruction, thus the factual necessity of the current victory of Germany over France; all of this was expressed in *The Phenomenology* as the necessary triumph of spirit over power. And this is what happened in 1813. But as it was happening, Hegel was blind to this fulfillment of his own maxim, he saw only "Cossacks, Bashkirs, and also other admirable liberators." And the fact that the destruction of Napoleon was not a destruction from the inside out, not through the spirit, but rather, as it appeared to him, that it would be through the mass of mediocrity with their lead-like gravity, this he had never divined in 1806. And this now made him sullen and, as he tried to sort things out, gave him the feeling of having lived through a tragic drama.

But in this moment of fulfillment – and we have to skip ahead here a bit – the foundation upon which he had expressed his prophecy slipped out from under his feet. The fact that remained for him, namely that the fall of Napoleon was a victory of mediocrity over genius, indeed that this mediocrity could only have been victorious over genius in that the latter – again, utterly in the style of tragedy – had done the former the favor of destroying itself. This view, which again placed the emphasis of what had happened upon the individual, could no longer tolerate in the long run the thoughts of the pivotal world-historical character of the last quarter century. Hegel could no longer call the Battle of Jena, which was followed seven years later by the Battle of Leipzig, an event which "would not occur again in a hundred or a thousand years." For him, the present could now move from the apocalyptic illumination of the birth of a third Empire into the earthly light of day. Even if the events Hegel had experienced were still meaningful for the present, the great turning point of world history could no longer lie here. What he had believed to have seen in the transition of world history out of the realm of the state and into the realm of the spirit, this fluttered away in face of the impact of events. A structure for the historical process, which had posited the last major turning-point in the emergence of the Germanic peoples and their ideas on the state, was already lying in wait for him from a much earlier time. He now had to return to this view, whose religious-historical parallels he had already drawn in *The Phenomenology* in 1806. The belief that in the present moment he was experiencing an infinite beginning, the beginning, as it were, of a timeless epoch, a thousand-year empire, this belief, which had fueled his political thinking and thought in general in the previous years, this historical, trans-historical belief now had to go. What remained was the belief in the power of history. The recognition that the "chorus remains at the top" had desacralized the present moment for him. And if history, understood as the chorus, was right, then its living content was henceforth no longer a present which would become future, but instead a present as heiress of all the past! The powers of the Restoration, and yet also the powers of the century's historical worldview, now entered their realm.

## NOTES

1   Goethe to Schiller, March 9, 1802 (in Goethe [1985 ff., vol. XXXII).

2   Ibid.

3   Hölderlin, "Buonaparte" (Hölderlin [1992 f.], Vol. I, 185).

4   Hegel to Niethammer, October 13, 1806 (Br. I). The letter begins with the words "Jena, Monday, October 13, 1806, the day Jena was occupied by the French and the Emperor Napoleon arrived within its walls."

5   Hegel to Niethammer, April 29, 1814 (Br. II).

6   Hegel to Niethammer, August 29, 1807 (Br. I) – verbatim: "The great teacher of state law sits in Paris."

7   Cf. Vol. I, p. 159.

8   Cf. on the following the Yearbook of 1912 of the Historical Society of Bamberg (in: *Bericht und Jahrbuch des historischen Vereins,* [1911 f.], 64 ff.) as well as Beyer (1974).

9   Bavarian State Archives, Munich, M Inn 25 098/I, sheet 62 ("Bamberg February 23, 1809") (petition of the citizens for the lifting of the ban) [the file contains a petition together with a list of signatures].

10  *Neuer Nekrolog der Deutschen* (1824 ff.) IX (1831), 963; see also Eduard Gans's "Nekrolog" for Hegel in the Allgemeinen Preußischen Staats-Zeitung, Dec. 1, 1831 [see Nicolin (1970), 490–496].

11  Frankische Merkur 1831, Supplement No. 49.

12  Bamberger Zeitung 1807, Nr. 121, 123, 126 bis 128, 130, 133, 134, 136, 138, 142, 146, 149, 151, 157, 161, 165, 174 (Spanish corps, in Germany for the first time since the Thirty Years' War), 192 334, 349, 351, 353, 359. – 1808, nos. 180, 237 f., 273, 275, 279–282, 284, 288. 308.

13  Ibid. 1807, No. 132, 161, 171, 174, 180, 189 f.; – 1808, No. 50, 196, 289.

14  Ibid. 1807, No. 117, 283.

15  Ibid. 1808, No. 169.

16  See below.

17  Ibid. Issue from February 8, 1808.

18   Administrative forms not mentioned: Division of districts (June 21 and September 23, 1808), abolition of serfdom and formation of municipalities (August 31, 1808). Mention is made, however, of the organization of the medical profession (Bamberger Zeitung 1808, no. 279). For this compilation, the estate of Marschalk v. Ostheim kept at the Bamberg District Archives was valuable to me (see Fischer 1911 f.).

19   Bitterauf, Th.: Censorship of political newspapers in Bavaria 1799–1825. In Bitterauf (1913), 304–351.

20   Fränkischer Kreiscorrespondent 1807, p. 306.

21   Heigel (1886), 436 (cf. Hilsenbeck [1913]).

22   Bavarian State Archives, Munich, M.A. ("General Acta of the State Ministry of the Royal House and the Exterior. Negotiations on the Censorship of Newspapers. 1799 – May 1819"), sheet 22 (March 16, 1808).

23   Thürheim to the Ministry, Nuremberg Nov. 23, 1808 (ibid., sheet 46) "[...] only with this limitation [...] do the editors face the demise of their papers, which I for my part sincerely wish, but which would be very sensitive to the proprietaries of the correspondent and to the Arario of the Ober-Postamts-Zeitung.

24   Hegel to Niethammer, July 8, 1807 (Br.I).

25   Montgelas' Memoirs (in: Historisch-politische Blätter 83 [1879], 188).

26   We are only informed about the following affair by letters to Niethammer from September 15 (Br. I) and October 1 (ibid.). I have found nothing in the files (State Archives and District Archives Munich and District Archives Bamberg).

27   Bavarian State Archives, Munich, M.A. 25 001, sheet 33. – The causal connection with the Bamberg Newspaper from October 26 seems to be refuted in that the related rebuke from Munich addressed to the commissary general of the Main Administrative District, Baron v. Stengel (ibid., sheet 34 [transcription]) has the date of November 2. But the text of this edict describes the ordinance from November 1 as "enacted today"; furthermore, the draft of the Munich ordinance from November 1 has the note "Sent 11/4" (ibid., sheet 33), even if according to Stengel he first received the ordinance as well as the edict on November 7 (Stengel to the Ministry, November 11, 1808 [ibid., sheet 40]); and above all, the copy of the ordinance sent to Stengel from November 1 (Royal District Archive Bamberg, Acta der K. Gen. Comm. Am Retzatkreis, Die Zensur der Zeitungen betreffend, 1808, 154/I), shows that the "1" of the date is written over an original "3," which aligns with the postmark "R. 4. München, 4. Nov. 1808" and the note "Praes. 6/11. 1808" (which differs from what Stengel declares!). The ordinance thus seems to be postdated, possibly with the intention to disguise its causation through a single incident. But of course, it is also possible that the ordinance is really from the 1st and that it was delayed in being issued.

28   Hegel to Commissary General of Bamberg, November 9, 1808 (Br. I).

29   Cf. Section 9, note 9, sheet 51 [JS & JS: to raise the expectations of a party with expiring but forever incorrigible truth].

30   Ibid.

31   Ibid., sheet 47.

32  Rechberg to Montgelas; the incriminating sentence was in No. 338 of the newspaper.
33  The correspondent was Capitaine Baron von Sellentin (Bavarian State Archives, M Inn 25 098/I, sheet 58).
34  Ibid., sheet 55 (report to Stengel) and 56 (report to Otto).
35  Hegel to Niethammer, April 18, 1811 (Br. I).
36  Niethammer to Hegel, May 5, 1811 (ibid.).
37  Bavarian State Archives, Munich, M Inn 15 245/I ("The situation of policing in the cities of Nuremberg, Fürth, and Schwabach, Nuremberg February 20, 1810"), 32 sheets.
38  Ibid., sheet 16.
39  Ibid., sheet 15.
40  Ibid., sheet 5 f.
41  Ibid., sheet 13.
42  Ibid., sheet 3.
43  Ibid., sheet 14 – Hegel's own view, for example, in the letter to Niethammer May 7, 1809 (Br. I).
44  Bavarian State Archives, Munich; M Inn 15 255/II ("Police report for the last quarter of the year 1810. Nuremberg, January 15, 1811") without sheet or page number.
45  The passage quoted comes from Hegel's personal file and there from the endorsement of his application for dismissal, in which the "p. Hegel's departure from here" is regretted (Bavarian State Archives, Munich; M Inn 23 299).
46  The reclamation of the *Propaedeutic* published by Rosenkranz in Volume XVIII of the *Werke* [now: GW 10 resp. HW 4] is made possible for the purposes of the book at hand by the official letter Hegel sent to Niethammer on October 23, 1812, published in Volume XVII of the *Werke* [GW 10, 824; HW 4, 403]. There it states in relation to the "doctrines of religion, right, and duties," which were written out for the lower grades: "I [...] know nothing other than to begin with right, the most simple and most abstract result of freedom, thereupon moving to morality and from there to religion, as the highest stage" (HW 4, 404) and [later] he explains the doctrine of the spirit in the encyclopedia intended for the upper grades "upon closer inspection as superfluous," because it is already "*present*" "1. in doctrine of psychology, 2. In the doctrine of right, duties, and religion" (GW 10, 826; HW 4, 408). He attempts thereby to bring aesthetics into the curriculum for his pupils in place of the mandatory encyclopedia. But we observe here from the second passage quoted as well as from the self-evident manner, vis-à-vis Niethammer and unencumbered by pedagogical concerns, with which he orders right beneath morality and gives no special place to ethicality, in the (earlier and) later sense, that in 1812 Hegel apportioned the outline of the philosophy of the spirit no differently than he had carried it out in the extant *Propaedeutic* for the lower grades. The Encyclopedia published in Volume XVIII of the *Werke* by Rosenkranz, which indeed proves itself to be a precursor of the *Encyclopedia* published in 1817, is thus not to be dated before 1813, whereas the "doctrine of right, duties,

and religion," as is already evident by the relation in the text to the rudiments of the *Encyclopedia* from 1805 and *The Phenomenology of Spirit*, provides us with the systematic that prevails until at least the end of 1812 [cf. the editorial report to GW 10, 851 ff.].

47    GW 10, 414; HW 4, 265.
48    GW 10, 403; HW 4, 251 f.
49    GW 10, 404; HW 4, 252 f.
50    GW 10, 389; HW 4, 232 – verbatim: "It is necessary to consider: (1) right in itself; and (2) its existence in state society."
51    GW 10, 399; HW 4, 245.
52    GW 10, 400; HW 4, 246.
53    Ibid.
54    Ibid – verbatim: "[...] education together. This connection [...]."
55    Hegel to Marie von Tucher, summer 1811 (Br. I).
56    GW 10, 400; HW 4, 246.
57    GW 10, 400; HW 4, 247 – verbatim: "within which"
58    Ibid – verbatim: "expression of the will existing in and for itself."
59    GW 10, 401; HW 4, 248.
60    Ibid.
61    GW 10, 402; HW 4, 249.
62    GW 10, 403; HW 4, 250 f.
63    Ibid.
64    GW 10, 414; HW 4, 265 – verbatim: "the disposition of the citizens."
65    GW 10, 414; HW 4, 266 – verbatim: "the unity in customs."
66    GW 10, 415; HW 4, 267.
67    GW 10, 455; HW 4, 312 – speech given on September 29, 1809.
68    GW 10, 460; HW 4, 319.
69    Ibid.
70    Ibid.
71    Hegel to Zellman, January 23, 1807 (Br. I).
72    Hegel to Niethammer, May 7, 1809 (ibid.).
73    Hegel to Schelling, January 3, 1807 (ibid.) – verbatim: "and this service was to be directed to it alone."
74    This may explain the little sentence sketched out only in 1806 or even later in the margin of GW 8, 259 about the "Germans" who had now "disappeared as a *people*" and their "Northern obstinacy": "The principle of absolute singularity brought into the world – the *existence* of the *concept* of the Christian religion," corrected to: "The *existence* of the thought in the South.
75    [JS & JS: after the event] Another counter-instance to this suspicion is the following passage from Schubert's self-biography (Schubert [1854 ff.], vol. II, 316), who communed with Hegel in Nuremberg (the time around 1809 is mentioned): "although his judgments on the relations of German territories and other European powers to France at that time displayed such clear and sure knowledge of the actual standing and situation of things that we had to agree with him, if not immediately, nevertheless in due time."

76   Cf. Section 9, note 64.
77   Hegel to Niethammer, October 10, 1816 (Br. II).
78   Hegel to Niethammer, August 29, 1807 (Br. I).
79   Hegel to Niethammer, October 13, 1807 (ibid.).
80   Cf. Section 9, note 78.
81   Hegel to Niethammer, February 11, 1808 (Br. I).
82   Ibid.
83   Ibid. – verbatim: "but only if."
84   Cf. Section 9, note 78.
85   Hegel to Niethammer, November 1807 (Br. I).
86   Hegel to Niethammer. January 22, 1808 (ibid.).
87   Ibid.
88   Hegel to Niethammer, November 1807 (ibid.).
89   Hegel to Knebel, August 30, 1807 (ibid.) – verbatim: "comes about once in a hundred or a thousand years."
90   Ibid.
91   Hegel to Niethammer, August 20, 1808 (ibid.).
92   Hegel to Niethammer, January 22, 1808 (ibid.).
93   Hegel to Niethammer, October 28, 1808 (ibid.)
94   Hegel to Niethammer, May. 21, 1813 (Br. II).
95   Cf. Treitschke (1912 f.), vol. II, 36: "mischievous volunteers": "Cossacks, Croats, Kashubes, and Sambians, brown and other Hussars."
96   Hegel to Niethammer, December 23, 1813 (Br. II) – verbatim it reads "liberator" instead of "soldier."
97   Ibid.
98   Hegel to Niethammer, Easter (April 10) 1814 (ibid.)
99   Ibid.

# 10

## RESTORATION

In the Germany that now surrounded Hegel, and with which he was forced to come to terms, one could hope for everything or fear everything, depending on one's mood. The Congress of Vienna was in session. It was the same Vienna of "Friedrich Schlegel" from which Hegel had feared a general recatholicization just a few years earlier. The fear of Jesuits, indeed, the fear of an Inquisition, now also played a role in his thinking, and even made its way into his dreams.[1] In the – erroneous – news that the hereditary Grand Duke of Mecklenburg had become Catholic, Hegel also saw "a sign of the times." What he had heard, also erroneously, about a miniature *coup d'état* of the Duke of Brunswick against his Estates seemed to him "a good preview."[2] He waited for the results from the Congress with extreme skepticism. In only one passage does Hegel seem to express hope for the Congress as an "eternally memorable experience that the people would now have of what their princes are capable of when they come together and deliberate with personal spirit and mind on the salvation of their peoples and the world, and indeed counsel according to the noblest expressed principle of general justice and the

DOI: 10.4324/9780429354724-12

good of all," which, he says, exacts a "brilliant result."[3] But this passage cannot be taken otherwise than ironically, especially since in the context immediately preceding it the progress of congressional affairs is given the predicate "makeshift."[4]

If something held Hegel the politician inwardly upright during this time, it was that belief in history to which he brought himself upon the fall of Napoleon, the conviction of the right of the chorus. It is expressed in full in that remarkable letter in which one has rightly sought a key to Hegel's political attitude in the following period. The letter is in answer to Niethammer's complaints that the clerical reactions in Bavaria were looking to destroy his organizational work for schools. Niethammer, who saw the German princes erecting dams against the peoples' struggle for political freedom with the same negative success as was the case three hundred years ago in the struggle for religious freedom, asks full of fear: "who all will drown in the lake that is now collecting?"[5] Hegel, who did not differ from Niethammer in his assessment of the current state of affairs, was prompted by this to "more general reflections," which show him to be a hard-headed optimist in the face of his friend's concerns. He adhered to the fact that "the world spirit of the age gives the command word to advance; however, such a command is being parried while this essence strides irresistibly like an armored, tightly locked phalanx but with such imperceptible movement, like the striding sun, forward through thick and thin. Innumerable light troops against and for the same essence flank around it, most of them knowing nothing at all about what [it] is, and receive only jolts through the head as if from an invisible hand."[6] The reaction can "perhaps only reach the shoelaces of this colossus and smear a bit of shoe polish or mud on them, but it cannot untie them once he puts them on and much less take off these shoes of gods, which have [...] elastic soles or are themselves even seven-league boots."[7] His conviction of the gradual, yet inexorable, course of history is now so firm, but at the same time also so degraded in value that, only a few years earlier, he had still attributed to the "imagination" in contrast to actuality, that he now simply declares that it is inwardly, as well as outwardly, safest to "keep a firm eye" on that giant, namely the "advancing" age that is at the command of the world spirit: "one can even stand there and help, for the edification of the entire busy and eager assemblage, to spread the shoe pitch which is supposed to stop the giant, and for the sake of one's own peace of mind lend a hand to the enterprise that is being taken so seriously."[8] With this almost uncanny irony, Hegel had found a personally stormproof angle from which he could watch things play out in peace. It was only shortly before his death that an unforeseen event would seriously startle him again.

His readiness to go along with the course of history, which he had learned to acknowledge as the ruling force above and beyond the will of the individual, now finally made it possible for him to accept, yet admittedly in a rather unpolitical manner, the spirit of the Wars of Liberation, which he had long rejected. In his inaugural address in Heidelberg, he was able to call nationality "the foundation of all living life,"[9] which the German nation had preserved for itself. This retraction does not compare to the great confession Goethe had made when proudly and humbly apologizing before the national community. Goethe, who well knew that, apart from the historical event, a great national asset had been calmly preserved in him and in his strength to be able to "feel purely," and who now nevertheless saw and confessed that those who had groaned under the chains and had finally torn them apart were "greater" than he was owing to the pain that they felt. But Hegel deemed the youth who sat at his feet to be lucky, in that they could now devote themselves "unconcernedly"[10] to truth and science, and basically rejoiced in the victory only because now, after the nation had "hewn itself out of the worst,"[11] it was to be hoped "that next to the state, which had swallowed up all interest, the church would also rise up; that next to the kingdom of the world, towards which all thoughts and efforts had hitherto been directed, the Kingdom of God would again be considered. In other words, that next to the political interests and other interests bound to common actuality, now science, the free rational world of the spirit, would blossom again."[12] This was still very much in the mood of the previous decade, during which time Hegel had subordinated the state to the spirit. And this mood was distinctly audible when, following the sentences just quoted, Hegel assigns to the German nation the preservation of the sacred fire of philosophy as its world-historical task. Now – after Leipzig and the Belle Alliance! – he thinks he should be permitted to compare his people, for the sake of glory and hope, to the Jewish people, for whom the world spirit had likewise reserved "the highest consciousness," so that this world spirit would emerge from them "as a new spirit."[13] Hegel still wanted his nation to be so unlike a state, so entirely only a people of the spirit, that he now saw the state as something small next to the *"Kingdom of God."*[14] Thus, it was likely his preoccupation with the latest events in his old homeland that then allowed him to gradually, and unnoticeably, again gain a lively interest in the state.

It has been a long time since we have seen Hegel inwardly involved in the political events of Württemberg. Great changes had occurred there since he had desired to intervene in the dispute between the Duke and the Estates in the summer of 1798, to the harm of both, but filled with a deeper mistrust of the Duke. After all kinds of confusion, the Duke had finally dissolved the Estates without further ado, resolutely sided with Napoleon and, through the grace gained from the fall of the Empire, won a considerable enlargement for Württemberg and kingship of the "sovereign" state of the Confederation of the Rhine. A hitherto unheard-of military effort was expected of the land in the following years. Under Napoleon's banner, the Swabians again proved their old martial prowess, for the first time in a long time. King Friedrich's internal despotism, no longer limited by the Estates' counter-management, created for itself the necessary civil service and sought to merge the new territories with the old in every way possible, especially by abolishing the privilege of the Protestant Church. Of course, the fat gentleman also gave in to his personal desires with an intemperance the likes of which even Württemberg of the eighteenth century had never seen. A quite considerable part of the taxes, which had increased tenfold in comparison to earlier times, seeped through this channel. It is understandable that the land, which was already familiar with the allure of a public and ruthless treatment of political grievances from the agitated 1790s, was under great pressure. But Friedrich knew how to silence his subjects: the famous decree of 1809, issued at the beginning of the war with Austria, which made any talk of political matters punishable, is only the peak of a long series of administrative measures. When the new Battle of Hermann had rung, the King of Ubier, unlike his counterpart in Kleist's drama, quickly annexed himself to the victors, thereby gaining confirmation of his European sovereignty, which seemed to him the most precious achievement of the French alliance. The negotiations at the Congress of Vienna must have frightened him, since a strong imperial power seemed to be at times dangerously close. It was all the more important to prevent this,

as dreams of restoring Württemberg's previous legal status were beginning to take root in the land. Thus, at the beginning of 1815, the King
published a decree in which he promised to give Württemberg a constitution "of its own accord, without outside influence." He was met most
unexpectedly with success. The Estates, however, instead of giving their
jubilant approval, which the old tyrant was contently counting upon,
met in March and declared with deep mistrust, only waiting to be confirmed, that they could not adopt a constitution unilaterally mandated
by the King. Rather, a new constitution could only be adopted upon the
firm ground of the old statute of limitations, and only by way of the con-
ventional means of establishing contracts in the old Württemberg. The
King was furious. However, under the impression of the indispensable
necessity to come to an agreement with his people before the dreaded
Federal Act forced him to do so, he sought to give in on the matter and
accepted the complaints of the Estates about his government, making
concessions on some controversial points. The Estates, however, in an
inextricable intertwining of loyalty to their paternal heritage and stub-
born obtuseness, relied upon the contract and the old law. They lightly
brushed aside the major transformations in the actual conditions of history, which made it impossible to go back to the constitutional status of
1770. The opposition came to a head when, in July, the King adjourned
the Estates and they called upon the foreign governments that had previously taken on the European pledge to defend the old constitution in a
Protestant and anti-Austrian manner. In the meantime, a flood of writings and essays on the matter had arisen in Swabia itself, as well as in
other German lands. The Estates were uncritically supported by liberal
public opinion, which represented a certain power in Germany in those
first uncertain and forward-looking years after the Wars of Liberation,
and even by the Romantic-Conservatives, who, as advocates of the old
law, could not refuse their participation. Just then, in July, under carelessly preserved anonymity, a document was published that in principle
acknowledged the validity of the old law, but in fact sided completely
with the king in practice. The author was the curator of the University of
Tübingen, Karl August von Wangenheim. This drew the King's attention
back to the former, but now neutralized, minion of Tübingen. Wangenheim was a committed pupil of the Schellingian Eschenmayer, and Wangenheim's mad formulas of a philosophy of nature, into which he folded

a bureaucratic, courtly, and feigned constitutional absolutism, seemed suitable to the King to lend a certain intellectual glimmer to royal policy. Thus called upon, Wangenheim succeeded in getting the King to yield in principle to the Estates and, at the reconvening of the Estates in October, to acknowledge the validity of the old constitution and the necessity of a contract-based agreement. The entanglement seemed to have dissolved itself. But the distrust against the King was too strong. The Estates could not be put off by the basic acknowledgment of their position. Instead, the dispute continued throughout 1816, whereby the Estates, committees, and the press debated over the relics of the old Estates' subsidiary government, namely over an independent treasury and a permanent committee, as well as over Wangenheim's pet idea of a House of Lords. And then, in November, the King died. As was the case in 1797, a change of throne seemed to bring the struggle between rulers and Estates to a new stage. And yet, just as before, this hope proved deceptive. The new King appointed Wangenheim, who was already on his last legs, to the Ministry, and in March he presented the Estates with a draft constitution that went a long way toward accommodating them in matters of the treasury and the committee. However, in his personal dealings with them, the King could not find a tone they would respond to. Furthermore, enough factual differences remained in detail, with the question of a House of Lords remaining completely irreconcilable. And finally, the necessity of a contract, which was now basically acknowledged by the government, presented itself to the Estates in a much more legitimate and formal way than in the soldierly sense of the King. Thus, in the summer of 1817, a rupture occurred here as well, under similar guise as had occurred two years earlier. The Estates appealed abroad. The government tried to have its constitution adopted directly by the electoral bodies, bypassing the Estates. Both failed. Then the King and the Ministry began to govern with deliberate intent according to the constitution rejected by the people, as far as it was possible. The beginnings of a pro-government minority party, which had first emerged in the decisive final vote of the Estates, continued to develop quietly under the impression of this shrewd policy. Meanwhile, the literary battle had continued with undiminished vehemence. The November and December issue of the *Heidelberger Jahrbücher*, in which Wangenheim's paper from 1815 had recently been torn thoroughly apart by the theologian Paulus from the standpoint of the Estates, published "Proceedings of the Estates Assembly of the Kingdom of Württemberg, 1815–1816,"[15] a pointed essay antagonistic towards the Estates. It remained no secret that the author was none other than Hegel himself.

Hegel had followed the changes in his homeland with some interest. Since he had taken that fundamentally unambiguous position in the summer of 1798 – antagonistic towards the Duke out of principle and only towards the Estates on account of their mismanagement (which, however, was a mediating rather than a decisive position) – he had deeply changed his political views. However, if we did not already know this, then we would not have been taught otherwise by the first remark he again devotes to the relations in Württemberg. In August 1807, Hegel said that the German princes had not yet grasped the concept of a free monarchy, that Napoleon would first have to organize everything, and he proved this by saying that Napoleon, after the annulment of the landed estates, had grimly said to the Württemberg minister: "I made your master into a sovereign, not a tyrant."[16] Even if this anecdote turns Napoleon's actual relationship to that event in Stuttgart on its head, in any case, one can see that at that time Hegel sharply disapproved of King Friedrich's arbitrary regime. Therefore, it is certainly to be understood that Hegel is referring primarily to Württemberg when, soon after the above anecdote, he sees in the fact that Germany, in their political imitation of the French, have omitted precisely "the most noble half," namely, the participation of the people in the state. And thus, this caused the other half, the strictly unified state, to also become "utterly amiss, arbitrary, coarse, crude, especially dumb, hateful of publicity, draining, and wasteful."[17] He seems to have re-entered into a personal relationship with Württemberg only around the turn of the year between 1811 and 1812. At that time, already under the curator Wangenheim, Tübingen had started negotiations with the Nuremberg rector about the philosophical chair there, but they fell through. When Hegel came to Heidelberg in 1817 and joined the editorial staff of the *Heidelberger Jahrbücher*, he clashed with his older friend and compatriot Paulus over the criticism of Wangenheim, which Hegel found "*quoad personam* malicious [...] and *quoad rem* highly philistine and commonsensical."[18] The philosopher, who until then had agreed with the rational theologian on some points, especially on his hostility to clericalism, had in the meantime deviated so much from the position in the Württemberg affair that he himself had taken in 1807 that the actions of his colleague, who had become the "god" of the landed estates, was now highly aggravating. Some wanted to attribute personal ambition as the cause for Hegel's current intervention, but there is no evidence for this. However, it can be assumed that his anger towards Paulus caused Hegel himself to take a stand in the same journal. It happened, in accord with where it was published, in the form of a review. The opportunity to do so was provided by the recently published minutes of the negotiations from the years 1815 and 1816 which, with an addendum published in September, covered the entire course of the affair up until the dismissal of the Estates Assembly in July. Hegel did not address the addendum. He was accused by friends[19] and opponents[20] alike that he would not have been able to make certain accusations against the Estates had he included their conduct in the last session. Hegel himself evenly explained this constraint of the issue by the fact that the epoch, thus judged by its successes, forms "a historical whole," which was brought to conclusion on the one hand by the death of the King, and on the other when the Estates' completed their own draft of a constitution.[21]

It was not without purpose that the transpersonal, historical context of King Friedrich's resolution on the constitution was emphasized above. For it was characteristic of the Hegelian view,[22] in contrast to all other voices that were raised for and against Friedrich's plan, that it was based on the historical thinking effectively underlaying the King's action, and thus, from the outset, gained a standpoint beyond the participating parties – beyond the parties, and especially beyond the government standpoint itself. The following must form the firm ground for understanding Hegel's intervention: he placed the will for European independence, the actual, and barely admitted, reason behind all that work on the royal constitution, openly and without inducing national shame, at the center of his observations. But in doing so, in being, as we shall see, more governmental than the government itself, in occasioning the possibility of understanding the government's viewpoint in a politically deeper and more brilliant manner than the government itself could or would dare to justify, Hegel had dangerously strayed in the details down the wrong path. It happened to him more than once that he allowed the historical necessity of the matter and the personal cunning of its royal representatives to merge all too completely together. Thus, the essay was as rich in brilliant political highlights as it was poor in embarrassing sophistic distortions. And therefore, one can only agree conditionally with the judgment of a recent historian, who calls the essay one of the best pamphlets to ever come from a German pen.[23]

According to its external form, Hegel's essay is a review. It essentially follows the course of events by way of what the negotiations "published in print"[24] can illuminate. Hegel expressly declares that he does not want to trace hidden psychological connections but, instead, considers it the task of history, and here also his own task, "to present the nature and course of the substantial matter and to reveal the character of the acting persons according to what they *do*."[25] This portrayal of the course of events is, however, interrupted often enough by doctrinal and polemical digressions and, moreover, the largest part of the essay, by far, is nevertheless devoted to the first days of the negotiations. One can thereby see that what captivates Hegel most is the process of contending powers and the fundamental contrast between the old estate-based view and the modern view of the state, which emerges here. Even such important events as the royal concession of November 1815 are treated with surprising brevity, and the battles of 1816 are addressed only in summary. But even such inequality did not contradict the critical practice. One would have to provide substantive reasons if one wanted to claim that the essay provided something more than a position on the political factions of that time, effective because of its own emphases, that instead it consciously intervened in a very specific situation, and that what was hiding under the shroud of a review was not a treatise on politics, but a political pamphlet aimed at the present moment. Allow us to postpone an answer to this concern for the time being and first present the purely political content of the essay.

The fall of the Empire, the world-historical event that consciously, even unconsciously, informed Hegel's overall historical view for so long, provides the starting point for his understanding of the events in Württemberg. After the Empire "had finally reached its deserved and shameful end, which was also in accordance with its outward manner," Württemberg passed from its previous feudal relations "into sovereignty and into the position of a state – one of the actual *German empires* that took the place of the absurdity that had only carried the empty name of an empire."[26]

It was upon the ground of this new actuality that Hegel gained his footing. At the same time, however, he now based his argumentation on a view of the old Empire that consisted of the constant choral refrain of political science in the eighteenth century, which was indeed sympathetic to the Empire. The learned gentlemen in and around Göttingen were infected by the Enlightenment and the idea of the constitutional state [Rechtsstaat] to such a degree that they could note with pleasure that in Germany a subservient citizen could seek justice against his prince before a higher court, and thus that a major requirement of the Age of Enlightenment was actualized there in Wetzlar. Hegel attached his justification of the royal politics to this exact thought, which he implemented in a similar sense. The Empire is no longer, and what was missing was the supreme judge between prince and subservient citizen, between the government and the Estates. A mutual coexistence and opposition, as it existed in the old Württemberg with its separate administration of ducal and county funds and with its constitution based on contracts, had become absolutely impossible since 1806. Contracts require a higher power who, in cases of doubt, decides on their validity and application. Precisely this higher judicial power of the Empire had now also legally ceased to exist. The New Württemberg was forced by the "storm wind," which blew away the protective roof of the Empire that had shielded it, to be a state, a sovereign state that cannot be based on contracts between two independent powers within it, but must be internally, as well as externally, one. Therefore, when the king eliminated the old Estates in 1806 and established that "strong ministerial government,"[27] it was only the first step on the path to becoming a sovereign state. This is how Hegel describes the period without Estates beginning in 1806. It was now nothing but the second step on this same path when the King allowed the "will" of the state to come alive, adding it to the "power"[28] of the state by providing the state, which he still had to create, a constitution. It was not a constitutional promise, like the princes had now made to their peoples, that drove him towards this second step, a step that carries in itself a higher necessity than the merely "positive"[29] necessity of a promise, namely the necessity to create the monarchic state and to also do so "inwardly."[30] For the Estates – and just why, we will soon learn – are indispensable to the concept of a monarchic state. But of course, when the King now convened the Estates and wanted to integrate them as an important "life element" into the "organism" of the new state, the Estates opposed him because they did not want to acknowledge the very life force of this new state, namely, the unity flowing from sovereignty. They indeed declared themselves to be landed estates, "but of another world, of a past age," and demanded "that the present should be transformed into the past, actuality into non-actuality."[31] Therefore, this is how they acted in response to the pending individual questions regarding the internal unity of the state. They indeed acknowledged the unity of the territory but did not want to recognize the strong growth of Württemberg in its own right. Instead, they would rather apply the old constitution of the land to this territory, whereas the government sees in this very growth an occasion to renew the constitution for the entire land in a uniform manner. Moreover, they simply do not want to resign themselves to the idea of administrative unity. "The ideas on the opposition between national interest and state interest, between a national treasury and a state treasury, taken from past relations and now changed in the even more confused present," stand as impediments in the way.[32] Above all, however, they lack the concept that the people and government must stand together in opposition to foreign lands, for better or for worst. When Napoleon returned from Elba, they employed that "pernicious, unpatriotic, indeed in the higher sense, often criminal artifice" of the old Estates, "wanting to use the compulsion of political circumstance [...] in order to wrest advantages for themselves from the government, and at the same time to produce an internal embarrassment through external events."[33] Moreover, this disposition shows itself as completely disgraceful in how they also took the foolish step of appealing to the old pledging powers, a step by way of which a people surrenders to the "ultimate humiliation of itself."[34]

One must acknowledge that this thought effectively captures the core difference between the old estate-based state [Ständestaat] and the new people's state [Volksstaat]. The demand for the unity of the people and the government, both internally in their mutual relationship and externally vis-à-vis foreign powers, was just as unfamiliar to the Estate-based state as it was essential to the new state, which emerged from absolutism. The fact is that the "strong ministerial government" was the first step toward a constitution and the representation of the people in the modern sense, and that this in turn meant the completion of what the latter had only been able to initiate, namely, the implementation of the idea of unity in the state, which was recognized here as clearly as anywhere else in Germany at that time. In addition, when Hegel now conceptualizes the necessity of a parliamentary institution as something internally factual, we may recall Hegel's own youthful political thoughts while at the Stift, notes now more than a quarter-century old, which had then reminded us of a particular man. This necessity, just as with Humboldt and his great constitutional memorandum from February of 1819, departs from the "external," merely "positive" necessity of fulfilling an incidental constitutional promise. Hegel summarizes this inner necessity as an indispensable part of monarchic state life, insofar as he takes it purely as a conceptual necessity, and expresses it briefly and most sharply in the following formula: the will of the state also belongs with the power of the state.[35] The notion that the will is alive in the representation of the people, but as the will of the state, is really the gathering place of everything that this fellow heir of the Revolution had to contribute from his endowment into the new century's debate over its legacy.

What Hegel holds against the Estates is first and foremost not that they discuss, but that they do not discuss enough, that they are "mute."[36] Namely, that it is not an essential purpose of contemporary estates to draft written legal petitions in the manner of lawyers but, to use an older Hegelian word, to bring "publicity" into the life of the state. Certainly, it would have been most comfortable for a contemporary Machiavellian prince to rule together with estates in the old sense. It would have been the "most perfidious advice"[37] that one could have given to such a prince: to rule like Augustus and Tiberius under the form of the old constitution. A "rational monarchic state" would then, of course, not have been possible and the late King deserves thanks for having "shown himself above the temptation of this deception."[38] But the Estates so little understand their own nature that they themselves seek to eliminate the public and open illumination of state relations and, instead of developing a lively opposition party from among their own, they would rather suppress the beginnings of such a party. And yet, the striving for power of a proper parliamentary counterparty of the English kind is precisely its justification, in contrast to the rigid unity of the old German Estates against their government, which even now in Württemberg is considered praiseworthy by the Estates. Without political parties, the Estates themselves are only a political party.

Now how does one obtain such desirable Estates, as they are described here? Hegel does not exactly reject the "*democratic principle*"[39] of equal suffrage, however, in sharp criticism of the royal draft of 1815, he declared himself to be an opponent of the tax limit and the age limit, both of which conceive of the individual only as an "atom" instead of according to his "*validity in the civil order.*"[40] These "French abstractions" had to be abandoned in favor of the existing cooperatives, guilds, and municipalities which had to be "restored to a political order and honor by an electoral procedure based on membership and purified of privileges and wrongs. They had to be inserted into the state as an organic formation."[41] The justified prevalence of property would be better secured by omission of per diems than by the census. Furthermore, it is regrettable, and does not correspond to the newer concept of the state, if the eligibility of civil servants to stand for election is taken away. One is more likely to find the "sense of the state"[42] in civil servants, those who today are no longer princely servants in the old sense, than in the privately appointed advocates and notaries, from whose excess numbers the Estates now suffer. In general, however, the abstract principles according to which the people appear to be dissolved into a "heap"[43] – number, wealth, and age – should not be rendered ineffective, but should be pushed back by making them electoral conditions for the lower bodies, from which, in connection with the old Württemberg electoral law of the magistrates, the new landed estates would also have to emerge. In this way, those "dry," "external,"[44] "insignificant" conditions would not be so "harshly contrasted with the elevated interest of the member Estates."[45] This alone could prevent atomistic, fragmented voters from feeling indifferent towards their own electoral rights, which would otherwise soon be the case. With these observations one can glimpse the inner workings of this line of reasoning. Hegel, just as little as anyone else at that time, did not suspect that corporate formations, which mediate between the voters and popular representation, could again arise directly from the "atomistic" electoral law. Therefore, that a popular party system had not yet developed alongside the parliamentary system, effectively explains why the most diversely ranging minds met in the desire to establish direct elections on existing corporate foundations. One did not suspect the possibility that living corporations could exist on a purely political foundation, and thus one looked for ways to insert the existing social structure, as well as the circles of local self-government, into the correctly perceived gaps between the two "harshly" opposed powers of popular representation and of voters. And Hegel did the same.

If earlier, despite his insistence on a "restricted"[46] right to vote, we could not ascribe to Hegel a simply dismissive relationship to the "democratic principle," then this was due to his view of popular representation in the state in general, in contrast to the powers of kingship and aristocracy. Here he swims with the great current which, starting from absolutism, had spread by way of the Revolution over Europe as a challenge and doctrine. He starts here from the thought that in great political movements prince and people had usually united against the aristocracy, against this "middle class," which, "instead of forming the bond between both, as it is determined to do, stiffened itself with privileges and monopolies, and hindered, even nullified the actualization of the principles of rational law and general welfare."[47] Hegel now found a similar aristocracy in Württemberg, corresponding to the nobility and clergy in old France, consisting of those who were once immediate to the Empire and of the "bourgeois aristocracy of the notary."[48] Hegel poured out the full scale of his scorn over the latter, in particular. Through their administration, they brought the entire people into "notary allegiance"[49] and degraded the Estates Assembly to class representation through their massive predominance. Even nobility laws in their old scope, quite apart from the fact that they could only be founded on positive state law, would "contradict every state organism."[50] But the royal constitution, namely the first one of 1815, had very much restricted these privileges, above all through the unicameral system and through the smaller number-votes for non-elected members compared to votes for the representatives.

What are the rights of this popular representation? What are the rights of the citizen in general? How does the "will" in the state express itself against the "power" in the state?

The royal constitution was very generous with regard to the basic rights of the individual. In this way, the constitution did not merely accommodate the desires of the contemporary age, but also the spirit of the old Estates, as it had developed in Württemberg under the influence of natural right. Here, with Hegel, the constitution finds an enthusiastic supporter. The paragraphs in question "speak for themselves." They constitute "the rational basis of a constitutional order."[51] And even if they are also contained in part in the old constitution, they are to a certain extent only incidental, not formed "out of the principle"[52] – and it is the principle that matters. One should hang this *"elementary catechism"*[53] outlining the foundations of the state on plaques in the churches and teach it to the youth. In carrying out this ground plan for an organic legislation, the Estates would have had an appropriate object for their function. But instead, they became fixated upon those rights which were bound to be rendered obsolete by the fall of the old Empire, they strove for a power of the crown, which only remains harmless in the English Parliament because of the general "sense of national dignity" there.[54] This applies to the right to approve taxes, where a European sovereign state requires "completely new guarantees against the private sense and the presumptuousness of the Estates,"[55] which were not necessary in the placid life of the former imperial fiefdom of Württemberg: the Estates are now displaced "into an entirely new element, namely the political."[56] The right to approve new taxes and to agree to increase existing ones is thus a major and candid concession on behalf of the government, regardless of whether the Estates, which can be debated, even had these rights under the old constitution. These rights now denote "an infinitely higher, more independent capacity than before: an influence on war and peace, on foreign politics in general, as well as on the inner life of the state."[57] Furthermore, Hegel declares that the compliance granted in the first royal constitution concerning laws of liberty, property, and the constitution, as well as the right to non-binding legislative proposals and grievances, are nothing less than "general truths of a constitutional-like condition."[58]

All in all, the "will of the people" is certainly a great statement, but precisely for this reason it should not be desecrated. Just as it is one of the greatest things that can be said of a human being that they *"know what they want,"* so a representative of the people must be "among the wisest, not because they know [what they want], but because they should know what their *true* and *actual* will is, that is, what is *good for them.*"[59] Therefore, even if the demand "seems absolutely just that a people must examine for themselves the constitution that is given to them,"[60] it is to be fundamentally deplored that the representatives of the people "demand from the King that he should unquestioningly and unconditionally accept the constitution which they and the people deem to want."[61] Popular sovereignty [Volkssouveränität], to introduce the word Hegel does not use here, is "revolutionary" only because it means "stepping out of the organism of the state,"[62] which includes the people and the government. In the end, it is the idea of organic state unity that here determines this condemnation of "democratic informality,"[63] even more than disdain for the people's natural lack of insight.

If the Ministry has constantly sought to circumvent breaking with the unmanageable and undiscerning Estates, Hegel assigns it a purpose that sheds a final light on his constitutional idea: the people, like their leaders, need *"political education."*[64] This takes place through political work: it is "education through oneself" – a path "to which people also certainly have the right."[65] Thus, the constitution itself has to affect what is actually the prerequisite of its healthy effectiveness: the development of a sense for the state, which is a "sense of governing and obeying."[66] The Estates must be torn out of their private sense, their natural propensity towards passive neutrality concerning the great questions facing the life of the state. And with this, the most fundamental aspect of Hegel's position on a question which split opinions becomes clear, namely his position on the question of the validity of the good old law. The old right must give way, not because or at least ultimately not because the circumstances in Württemberg have changed, not because abuses have taken root (it is through its "abuses" that the English constitution has been preserved), but because historical law as such cannot be valid in a people that has not yet had any history at all – for this people has never had a state.[67] Thus, this last, and most profound thought of this Hegelian text connects to the thought with which it began: Württemberg became a state only through the fall of the Empire. Only now does its history as the history of a state begin. Now everything must become new, and what is old does not, as it may appear, have the right of history on its side, but instead history is against it. The history of a people begins only when it becomes a state. Hegel systematically configures this thought in the outline of his philosophy of state, which he was writing simultaneously for his *Encyclopedia of the Philosophical Sciences*. In this work, the state is the philosophical precondition of history. And it is now the same in his critique. From now on, the new constitution will develop further within this history and through this history. And while appended general clauses determine that all older laws, as far as they are not affected by the constitution, remain in force, a constitution is nevertheless "indeed something fixed, but not something that is simply dormant." And this, as Hegel concludes with one of his great Baroque turns of phrase: "this is the true *general clause* that the world spirit itself appends onto every existing constitution."[68]

Thus far, we have intentionally tried to work out Hegel's theory of constitutional kingship, which is the basis of his critique, in order to detach his point of view, as much as possible, from the relations of the day. What now remains is the second, no less important task, of again placing it into this contemporary context. For the first task, we depended upon the philosopher of state, for the second, we depend upon the politician. Only such separate treatment will allow us to decide the extent to which the one outweighs the other. And yet, only in taking the two together are we able to situate this episode within the life of Hegel, the man, and to understand its place along Hegel's path from Napoleon to the Prussian state.

In writing the essay, Hegel comes into contact with four powers from the life of his native state: kingship, the Ministry, the Estates Assembly, and public opinion. In the period between 1815 and 1817, all four of these powers certainly did not remain rigidly unchanged. Hegel himself rarely refers directly to the present, instead he cloaks his views in the discussion of negotiations that largely took place one and a half years earlier, in the spring of 1815. Thus, based on the historical narrative, it will be somewhat difficult to deduce the present conditions in the autumn of 1817, even if the text as a whole seems unambiguous with regard to the conditions in the spring of 1815.

What is most characteristic is the relationship to kingship. At that time, all complications proceeded from this. When Friedrich proposed it, the constitutional idea was a work most his own. We know the purpose that he connected with it: a stark closure of his Württemberg against possible German nationalist efforts, which in the beginning of 1815 could still be feared from Vienna, or at least from the Prussians in Vienna. For such a purpose, a constitution seemed to him good enough. Hegel's joyful agreement now came to greet him. For the philosopher, the state was so strongly rooted in the system that Hegel could hardly conceive of its subordination to the idea of the nation: a people without a state has no history. The central idea of the coming national politics, that a people must create its state for the sake of its history and according to the measure of its history, was completely alien to him. For him, the German Empire, which was not a real state, had been replaced by "German empires," which appeared to him not as political hybrids, transitional states at best, but rather as states in the full sense of the word, and for him even beyond this. Thus, the king's territorial-egoistic fear of a future comprehensive German state and the philosopher's statist contempt for what was old, and thus for any newly forming German empire, met at the same point. And what the imperial fox did not dare to confess as the reason for his liberal impulse, the philosopher was able to express with the naiveté of an idealist as the last and decisive reason for the necessity of a constitution: Württemberg was a real "German empire," closed off externally and internally. It is highly significant that in his report Hegel silently ignores the Estates' exasperated complaints from June 1815, when Württemberg had not co-signed the Federal Act on the grounds that "the great principle stating that all Germans are children of one fatherland"[69] was not included – what does Hegel care about the German Confederation. And it is almost moving to see with what zeal the "Refutation," which was written in response to Hegel's essay, seeks to ward off from this constitution, so excellent "for peace," the very invectives that Hegel rained down upon the old Empire in his opening sentences, and reminds Hegel of the apparently quite forgotten existence of a German Confederation and of the paragraph of the Federal Act on constitutions for landed estates.[70] Certainly, there were historical rights and wrongs on all sides: on the side of the Estates, which held on to the German idea, even if partly only for the sake of their own desires and merely as a means to pressure the King; on the side of the King, who, defiant against past history, externally created independence for his land, which later drove Württemberg towards Bismarck's new Germany, itself without a past, and internally created the unity of a people's state, by way of which the Swabians could again enter into that genuine federal state as a tribe in the old sense. For both of these things, the historical significance of the European sovereignty of the German states after 1815 meant that, on the one hand, they were withdrawn from the Habsburg imperial tradition, and on the other, that they were prepared to move over and down from the republic of princes of the old Empire into the new alliance of dynasties and tribes. And finally, the philosopher, who treated the German Federal Act of 1815 as empty air and saw the state of the future in the individual German state, also had historical right on his side, even if he now indiscriminately transferred this future-oriented concept of state to the semi-nature of the state that was directly before him. The situation was different when the philosopher, carried away by the admiration he had always and everywhere been accustomed to pay to the political strongman, and by the innocent equation of his own ideal of the state with the state intentions of the King, defended the King even when the horse's foot all too visibly protruded from under the King's cloak. If Hegel could brush aside with a cool smile the terrible mismanagement of the decade without Estates, which the Estates' complaints now uncovered, if Hegel, in view of the shameless precaution of the despot who wanted to make sure that taxes would be raised excessively for the duration of his government, largely to pay for court expenses, could only retrospectively advise the Estates of 1815 that they should have to endure all of this "out of thankfulness," then what is missing here, even if everything could be reduced to Hegel's desire to honor the deceased King and maintain that attitude towards the living, is that self-caution by means of which, at least according to today's more demanding notions, Hegel's essay could been differentiated from a commissioned panegyric.

Was it that? This is the second and, externally, the most absorbing question before us. It is to be answered essentially on the grounds of Hegel's position towards ministerial policy. A contemporary rebuttal letter, emanating from a distinguished member of the dismissed Assembly, was readily available,[71] remarking on Hegel's occasional comment on the costs that the Estates, through their prolonged existence, were unscrupulously imposing on the country, and that they should be repaid to the country with interest, and the anonymous member, as long as he remained anonymous, would be "remunerated" for the part he played. Also, Hegel's essay seems to have been distributed as an offprint in Württemberg, available more cheaply than it was sold by the publishing house,[72] with the consequence that the government would have certainly seized on the published essay as a welcome weapon in the battle for public opinion. The rumor that was affiliated with the rebuttal letter, according to which the whole thing was a commissioned work, seems to have been widespread elsewhere as well. Hegel's second biographer adopted a news report stating that Hegel was charged to write the text by Wangenheim himself, in order that thereby he might commend himself to succeed the minister for the Tübingen curatorship. He soon convinced himself of the implausibility of his source, but only retracted the accusation quite incidentally in a text published almost half a century later, thereby staining the image of Hegel's ethical personality to this day.[73] Since the rumors do dissolve upon closer inspection, but also since a position taken from the top down rarely remains free of such suspicions, and given the fact that the government would have used Hegel's essay for its own purposes, all of this does not allow anything certain to be claimed about the occasion and origin of the essay. What remains, then, is to investigate the essay according to the content itself and thereby conclude to what extent Hegel was even connected with the intentions of the Ministry, which, by the way, Wangenheim had left while Hegel's essay was being published.

It is to be noted from the outset that, with regard to the Ministry, Hegel shows practically none of the same courtesies he showed to the King, who died a year earlier. Thus, it is with an almost comical zeal that the rebuttal letter pounces on the passage in the essay where a merely remote echo of Wangenheim's programmatic text of 1815 can be found. It is actually the only place where Hegel allows the philosopher to emerge, in that he pits the doctrine of state contract against the *"original, substantial unity"* that underlies the connection between prince and subject, government and people. It is a "connection that is an objective, necessary relationship, independent of arbitrariness and discretion"[74] and a duty "upon which rights depend," whereas with a contract, rights are reciprocally granted in an arbitrary manner "and only then do duties come about."[75] This is where the rebuttal immediately latches on and finds, where the text provides no occasion at all, "the 'Idea' that was already being admired elsewhere by the reading public" – Wangenheim's text was titled *The Idea of a State Constitution* – or the "familiar fixed boundary line, standard idea, provisional middle point," all of this in the sentence quoted above! There is no difference between the alleged conformity in language and the conformity to the intellectual basis and entire procedure in general. The difference is, in short, that Wangenehim, as a characteristically opportunistic philosopher, is far more philosophical in his text than the politicizing teacher of philosophy. While Hegel, in his "very unspeculative by-product,"[76] as he writes to Niethammer, visibly sought to eliminate not only all artificial expressions, but even all actual philosophical reasoning in favor of what was purely political and historical,

Wangenheim is keen to adorn his text with an opportunely appropriated manner of speaking and thinking from Schelling's philosophy of nature, in place of the all-too-colorless political-historical reality. For instance, in order to justify the philosophical necessity of the court, it is declared that, as governmental fantasy, the ideas of the Ministry, that is, of state reason, "are to be integrated into ideals, and these are to be handed over to the regent (to the will of the state) for enthusiastic action."[77] It is needless to point out how utterly remote this method of thinking must have been, even in purely scholastic terms, from the philosopher Hegel. If the judgment of later decades condemned Hegel and Schelling to the same circle of hell, at that time there was nevertheless no solidarity between the two when they were alive. But above all, Hegel's purely political-historical starting point is far removed from Wangenheim's central idea of a state body, nicely structured into three-part paragraphs, so that when both texts are compared side by side there can be no talk of a response by Hegel to Wangenheim.

But it is not only text compared with text, but also political judgment versus political action that requires consideration. The trust that Wangenheim regained from the King through his foray into the land of natural philosophy caused a fundamental change in royal policy. In unnoticed contradiction to the audacious ascent of the "Idea," as already in the text itself, Wangenheim had successfully advocated to the King for the view of the internal validity of the old law, noting only its lack of external applicability. The constitution should no longer be taken as "given," but rather, as demanded by the Estates, it should be "compared." The message with which the King appeared before the newly convened Estates, on October 15, 1815, presented this new starting point for the negotiations and, from then on it remained unchanged in principle. This is Wangenheim's major contribution towards the realization of Württemberg's constitution. This is not the case with Hegel. He held unwaveringly, and with the full weight of his philosophical conviction, to the position which the government had abandoned more than two years ago. What interested him was the fundamental denial of the old right, the necessity of creating a new constitution, for a new state, "from a single cast." Hence, this explains the disproportionate detail with which he treated the negotiations of the spring of 1815, the period when Wangenheim was still in Tübingen, remote from the events. This alone fills almost nine-tenths of the entire space. And hence, the accusation relating to Hegel's "continual defense" of the first constitution, withdrawn by the King himself at Wangenheim's insistence, "throughout each paragraph" of the essay, points unequivocally towards only one thing, namely Hegel's independence from Wangenheim. When he finally does come to speak of the message of October 15, 1815, he deliberately underscores the legal protests that the King only incidentally included and, with a trivial comment, evades the edict's essential content, which Wangenheim had pushed through, namely the abandonment of the royal draft of the constitution and the fundamental acknowledgment of the Estates' position.[78] And in comparison, other issues come into even less consideration to this fundamental issue. The most important of these other issues is likely Hegel's attitude towards the bicameral system. Following the old constitution, the royal draft had wanted only one chamber. In a special text, using heavy-handed philosophical reasoning, and with Eschenmayer's blessing, Wangenheim had proposed, and constantly advocated for in opposition to the Estates, a House of Lords as the "hypomochlion," the calm center between the government and the people, in which the "intelligible nature of the state" would be expressed. It was one of the points against which the majority of the Estates had remained fixed in 1817. Hegel, in his brief survey of the period after the fall of 1815, makes no mention at all of the minister's pet idea, the same minister whom one suspected of being his patron. The only time he alludes to the bicameral system, and incidentally to the unicameral system present in the first royal constitution, is with a faintly commending remark that it "holds important authority, owing to its more general introduction and its age."[79] An agent for Wangenheim would have sounded a much different alarm here. The two points where Hegel criticizes the constitution of 1815, namely on the denial of eligibility for civil servants to be elected and on the form of the right to vote, which was uniformist and vague, both of these remain unchanged in that third draft of the constitution, which Wangenheim tried in vain to have accepted by the Estates during his term of office. Thus, a desire to protect the present Ministry does not surface there. And finally, Hegel excluded the last stages of the negotiations from his consideration, for which there is no formally known reason. Indeed, in a private letter from the end of January 1818, Hegel confesses that he had "not yet studied" this "second period" of the negotiations at all, and that he will hardly get to it. This "second period," which he had not, nor would study, is the exact term of office of the minister who had supposedly commissioned him to write the text![80]

Thus, the only thing that could commend the writing to the Ministry, and the reason it was also apparently distributed by it, is the hopeful concluding section, which will be discussed below, that points to a future agreement, and then also the unbelievably fierce attacks against the Estates, which are based on a serious historical-political conviction. Such an abrasive ally would, after all, have been welcome to the Ministry, even if he were to walk his own path when it came to the details and his basic mindset. In this, Hegel and the Ministry were bound against the same opposition. Let us now take a closer look at Hegel's stance towards this third power, the Assembly of the Estates.

As it were, the Estates did not form a completely united body. As early as 1815, there were faint beginnings of an opposition party. Representative Gleich even supported the royal position in principle, but admittedly soon disappeared from the Assembly because of it. Representative Cotta dissented at least on the question of the Estates treasury. From the Estates themselves, through the efforts of representative Griesinger, a sharp investigation into the notaries occurred, by way of which the Estates also did injury to themselves. However, these were the only attempts at opposition until the period of Wangenheim's Ministry. Only the latter succeeded in forming the beginnings of a party from within the Estates, namely in a decisive final vote where, for the first time, a strong minority, led by the already unreliable Cotta and by the previously steadfast Weishaar, stood on the side of the government with 42 votes. It could have been expected that Hegel, if he wanted to intervene decisively and in the government's favor in that moment, would have at least sparingly treated Wangenheim's supporters and the leaders of a future governmental party after their conversion. Instead, we find him attacking not only Weishaar, but even Cotta when the occasion arises, harshly criticizing their behavior during the early negotiations. A theoretical interest in the great contrast in views on the state, which emerged in 1815, outweighs all possible concerns. Only in this way, out of an almost improbable inner detachment from the present situation, can it be explained how Hegel occasionally praises, in full sincerity, the head of the opposition, Varnbüler, the same person who, during the previous summer and after the dissolution of the Estates Assembly, had returned the requested chamberlain's key to the King through the mail as an "object without value." Even the highly venomous "rebuttal letter," which sought everywhere to draw out personal connections, could only explain this lack of consideration for the current situation by assuming it was highly cunning, and in this manner creating a semblance of impartiality.[81] For indeed, those 66 members who voted in the majority, displaying that same steadfastness in 1817 that almost the entire Assembly had at the beginning, must have felt the most affected. Even if those bitter remarks on the Estates were not aimed at their latest behavior, they certainly felt them all; indeed, those Estates, who, like the French emigrants, "had learned and forgotten nothing"[82] from the tremendous upheaval of the last twenty years and, "in the entire course of their long and precious life together," have not managed a single decision "on any content of a constitutional subject."[83] It was not surprising then, that when they learned of Hegel's authorship, perhaps through Paulus, they replied in just as crude manner, or even cruder, from within their circle. Hegel had to endure the suspicion of being "remunerated"[84] and had to tolerate barbs, as he could only receive in his own homeland; for instance, that the "newest" writings of the ideologues wanted nothing more to do with contracts and the equality of humankind, or even a friendly reminder of the celebration that the young philosophers, who have since become old and obsolete, had once held in Germany at the news of the execution of Louis XVI.[85] And if Hegel had been upset about how in the Estates Assembly there was the inability to speak freely and long lectures were read out, he now heard the mocking request that his name be called up so that one could admire his freely given lectures, for it was well known that while teaching in Jena Hegel was completely dependent upon the letters and words in his notebooks.[86]

But beyond such unavoidable personal jostling and friction – to which was added the break with his old friend Paulus and at least one contestation by Niethammer, who found a bad cause ingeniously defended by Hegel – beyond all of this, Hegel's essay was suddenly there, was read, and public opinion in Württemberg began to tire of the dispute, as had long since occurred in the rest of Germany, and was now inclined to be

instructed. This is the last thing to be examined in our context: within
the early formation of political parties in the land, what was the position
of Hegel's critical review? If we observe from the position that Hegel
occupied at the end of 1817, how does the history of political parties in
Württemberg emerge during the next few years?

As was already mentioned, it was only in its final pages that Hegel's
essay cast a somewhat friendlier light on the Estates Assembly. In working out their own draft of a constitution, which was so important for
Hegel that he could break off his account at that point, the Estates could
have "unconsciously," simply through being forced to come together so
coherently, exercised on themselves the work of political education, for
the sake of which "clairvoyant ministries [...] would disregard the previous manifestations of passion, prejudices, perverse notions, spiteful-
ness, etc."[87] This indication of a convergence of government and Estates
is Hegel's only allusion to an emerging minority party supportive of the
government, which had become apparent in the summer during the last
referendum of the Estates. The organizational edicts, by way of which
the government implemented a series of reforms after the dissolution of
the Estates Assembly, reforms especially to the notary office and to local
self-governance, choked off the party of the "Altrechtler" to the degree
that they were only insignificantly represented in the Estates Assembly
of 1819. Their legacy, however, did not simply fall to the minority of
the old Estates Assembly, but instead two new parties were formed, one
from the members of the minority and the other from the newly con-
verted "Altrechtler." The stronger of the two stood with the government
during the eventual concluding work on the constitution and essentially represented the educated and civil servants. They probably would
have described themselves as liberal. The opponents were rooted more
in the general populace, in the "citizens," as they themselves claimed.
The Liberals called them the "Gentlemen's Party" and they called themselves the "Friends of the People."[88] The essential thing is that both parties had all but abandoned the standpoint of the "old right," considered
as such. Significant remnants of the once so strongly defended ideas
were still to be found among the Liberals, although greater value was
henceforth placed on the rights of the individual, for instance, and establishing these rights, which were "just as old as they were natural," as
part of the constitution was of high value, in contrast to the position

of "Altrechtler." And in general, it was the "transmutable principles of natural right" before which everything historical had to prove itself.[89] They rejected the idea of popular sovereignty, but upheld the idea of the constitutional contract, against which Hegel had waged his fundamental struggle. Regarding the practical demands of the "Altrechtler," we again find that they demand a committee, at least in many cases, and just like their opponents, however, they altogether dropped the demand for an Estates treasury. The former, like the "Altrechtler," recognized in principle the privileges of the nobility and were partly inclined to concede to the first chamber. The bureaucratic bias in them was revealed in their defense of the suffrage of the civil servant. It is in line with Hegel's argument when we now hear from Weishaar that the civil servant serves the states, that is, the government and the people, just like the representative.[90] In the fight against the civil servants, on the other hand, the "Friends of the People" take up the legacy of the "Altrechtler." But this fight against the civil servants became for them, in contrast to their predecessors, a fight against the "Gentlemen" in general, and with this name they not only included the ducal civil servants, but also the oligarchic magistrate corporations, and above all "the notaries and their followers," that same "civic oligarchy" against which Hegel also fought with fierce severity, using a disproportionate amount of space, and which they, as well as Hegel, equated without further ado with the "Altrechtler."[91] It is obvious that they rejected the cornerstones of power of the old Estates, namely the treasury and the committee. The reasoning, however, that underlay their struggle now brings them very close to the same battle which the reviewer had waged in the *Heidelberger Jahrbücher*. It is therefore not surprising that a journal representing the viewpoint of the new party printed the essay from the *Heidelberger Jahrbücher* unabridged.[92] And just as these ideas now penetrated the breadth of the people, they now also found their poets. The deep-toned laments of Uhland about the sunken jewels of the good old law were countered by Justinus Kerner in fresh and bright songs of argument. Like Hegel, the "Friends of the People" proceeded from the idea of the unconditional unity of the state. That is why there is no right to revolution, even if under certain circumstances there is moral duty. For this reason, a constitution cannot really be imposed upon the people since, when it comes into force, it becomes "in a way two-sided." But the hereditary prince, as representative of the unity of the state, is not at all in a position "to enter into a contract (in the ordinary sense of the word) with the Estates, in that thereby a two-sidedness would be created."[93] With this complete rejection of the idea of a contract, the "Friends of the People" put themselves in sharp opposition to the Liberals as well as to the Ministry, whereas they thereby adopted the underlying idea of Hegel's review. Advocating for the unity of the state now further leads them, quite like Hegel, to the idea of the natural alliance of monarchy and people against the aristocracy, which in Württemberg was essentially composed of the "civic" notaries and magistrates. However, the attitude against the actual nobility was more hostile and more sweeping than that of the Liberals, since they did not even acknowledge the old law as such and, to them, just as with Hegel, every right that is contrary to the advancing culture becomes an "injustice." Thus, their ideals were a civil society, which, in the words of its poet, closes itself "tightly around the royal house" like the knights in earlier times; a strong monarchy, which through its unity, even in absolute form, is better than a gentlemen's regiment; and a state that is strong by means of the citizens' freedom, who are honor-bound to serve it. In addition, their distinguished demands were the popular administration of justice, the self-governance of congregations, and basing citizen rights on municipal rights, by way of which the individual first becomes politically mature for the state, and gains as much cooperative life as possible in newly formed guilds, and the like. Here, too, the "Friends of the People" are in accord with Hegel's ideals and demands, down to the last detail, diverging from him only in more pointed democratic training, especially regarding their demands.

Thus, in 1819, the ideas advocated by Hegel were mostly victorious across the board, namely, the rejection of the validity of the old law, the praise of reason, and the fight against treasury and committee, even if they were partially separated along party lines. The bureaucratic-rationalist branch of his ideas, namely the glorification of civil service and the establishment of the basic constitutional and natural rights of the citizen, is taken up by the Liberals. In contrast, among the "Friends of the People" we find Hegel's central idea – state unity, the rejection of constitutional contract – and, based on this, the alliance between royalty and the people, freedom of the individual for the state, the struggle against the aristocracy, especially the "civic" aristocracy, free administration of justice, and congregational freedom as the basis of civil rights. Thus, the origin of Swabian democracy, with respect to people as well as to ideas, can probably be found with the "Friends of the People," which embodied the opposition of 1819.[94] Therefore, a part of Hegel's text, and even the best part, does not lead here to the moderate, constitutionally ruling government, but rather to the extreme left of Württemberg's future political parties. Here, in a small way, we already find a prelude to what later occurred on a larger scale in the history of political ideas in Germany, namely, the division of the Hegelian school of thought into a governmental "Right" and into a Hegelian "Left," within which the most pointed democracy forged its intellectual armor.

Only one major piece of the essay did not find a place in the intellectual furnishings of Württemberg's political parties. The proposition that the power of the state itself as external power – for which the citizen must be free – is itself the purpose of the state, this glorification of foreign politics remains alien even to the "Friends of the People," who nonetheless were able to conceive of the strength of the whole and the freedom of the parts together. For Hegel this constituted, still under the idea of state unity, the strongest justification of his view. In the life of Württemberg's political parties this idea would have been unnecessary, even if it had formed the historical basis for all the constitutional work stemming from the royal edict of 1815. It was only a natural consequence of what was at most a mid-level state, despite Friedrich's aspirations, that in the Kingdom of Württemberg there was no place for the idea among the leaders of the parties and that it was thus, more or less, excluded from the state itself. In unison with the historical occasion, yet in contradiction to the historical essence of things, the fact that the thinker Hegel nevertheless based the state and its necessities on this idea, accounts in the end for the overall internal impossibility that ultimately clung to his position. The exalter of Bonaparte believed to have seen the German government's introduction of internal liberal regulations, which he expected everywhere from Napoleon, and he therefore praised Napoleon and considered it impossible that German states could carry out these regulations without Napoleon's solicitation. He saw with indignation "what kind of incredible damage" to public opinion and among governments the Estates were doing to the constitutional state through their incorrigible obstinacy "to the good cause."[95] Thus, his text became liberal and bureaucratic at the same time. It could extol the wisdom of government over the folly of the "rabble," discover in the civil servant the true disposition of the state, and at the same time see the debate on human rights as a major part of the constitution, while expressing nothing less than fraternal views on the uprising of 1813, when the educated German youth had also "bled for the cause of giving German states free constitutions, and had brought with them from the battlefield the hope for future work and efficacy in the political life of the state."[96] And just as the review was liberally and bureaucratically tinged by its subject matter, as well as by the political experiences of its author, it also contained the vigor of another view of the state, stemming from Hegel's political ideal and his personal development, a view that simultaneously asserted the inherent right and unity of the state along with its free, independent growth. And if that first group of thoughts tinged by Bonaparte was well-suited for the state towards which they were directed, the second group, more singular to the thinker, contained a surplus of ideas, which was even too much for an opposition party that agreed on the majority of everything else. Hegel seemed to have no awareness for the fact that the state, of whose inherent right and European autonomy he spoke, could at most claim these characteristics on paper, which could bear anything. What went askew with Hegel's position in the Württemberg affair was that he allowed his glorification of the new, uniformly independent state to become of benefit to something politically incomplete and without future. The fact that he once again broadly implemented the view of an inherent external right, as well as an organic internal structure, was already a departure from the comparatively indifferent stance towards the state that had reigned over him under the star of Napoleon. What was unfortunate was that he now transferred his new, or rather his pre-Napoleonic, state ideal to a state that was not a state. He would have had to develop this view of a constitutional monarchy, which was seen through and through from the whole of the state and its external administration of power, in light of an actual, major state. And as the threefold coincidence of place of origin, present moment, and social interaction had led him to associate with a minor state, now life would lead him towards a major state as the worthy object of his doctrine's striving – prepared to help form it, also prepared to let himself be formed by it.

## NOTES

1   Hegel to Niethammer, January 6, 1814 (Br. II).
2   Hegel to Niethammer, February 21, 1815 (ibid.).
3   Hegel to Niethammer, December 29, 1814 (ibid).
4   Ibid.
5   Niethammer to Hegel, June 16, 1816 (ibid.).
6   Hegel to Niethammer, July 5, 1816 (ibid.) (cf. also Lenz [1910/1918] vol. II, 1, 200).
7   Ibid.
8   Ibid. – verbatim: "busy and eager assemblage."
9   GW 18, 4; HW 18, 11.
10  GW 18, 6; HW 18, 13 – verbatim: "more unconcernedly."
11  GW 18, 4; HW 18, 11.
12  GW 18, 4; HW 18, 11 f. – verbatim: "also *pure science*."
13  GW 18, 5; HW 18, 12.
14  GW 18, 4; HW 18, 12.
15  GW 15, 30–125; HW 4, 462–597.
16  Hegel to Niethammer, August 29, 1807 (Br. I).
17  Hegel to Niethammer, November 1807 (ibid.) – verbatim: "this other half, which is the noblest, the freedom of the people, participation of the same in elections."
18  Hegel to Niethammer, April 19, 1817 (Br. II) – verbatim: "of base common sense"; cf. also the following pieces of Paulus' estate kept at the Heidelberg University Library: Wilken to Paulus, January 21, 1817 (Sign.: Heid. HS. 862, 766); Thibaut to Paulus (without date; begins: "Durch Herrn G.K.R. Paulus besonders aufgefordert ...") (Heid. Hs. 861, 702); Hegel, Wilken, Thibaut together to Paulus, January 29, 1817 (in Hegel's hand and probably written up by him) (Br. II); Hegel to Paulus, January 19, 1817 (ibid.); – Paulus' literary estate still contains unprinted letters by Hegel: July 20, August 22, September 13, and October 13, 1816 [now all in Br. II]. [JS & JS: "personally malicious [...] and as to the matter highly philistine and commonsensical"]
19  Niethammer to Hegel, December 27, 1817, Schlusssatz (Br. II).
20  Zahn (1818), 5, 8.
21  Admittedly, he says at the beginning of the review that the constraint is only temporary ("initially") (GW 15, 30; HW 4, 462), but after it was printed, he writes to Niethammer that he has "not yet studied" the "second period," and that he will hardly come to it. – Hegel to Niethammer, January 31, 1818 (Br. II).
22  It is described as a "horse's foot" [a drawback], through which the author "immediately reveals on the first pages of whose spirit he is child," in the clever and distinguished "Remarks by an Expert on the Assessment of the Negotiations of the Württemberg Assembly of Estates in 1815, 1816, specially printed from the *Heidelberger Jahrbücher der Literatur* No. 66–77. Frankfurt/M 1818, Hermannsche Buchhandlung." (cited in the following as "Remarks."

The motto is: Should philosophy become the handmaiden of politics after it has ceased to be the handmaiden of theology?)

23  Lenz (op. cit.), 203.
24  The title given in W.w. XVI, 158 reads: "Assessment of the negotiations published in print ..."
25  GW 15, 31; HW 4, 463.
26  GW 15, 31; HW 4, 464.
27  GW 15, 32; HW 4, 466.
28  Ibid.
29  GW 15, 33; HW 4, 466.
30  Ibid.
31  GW 15, 52; HW 4, 493.
32  GW 15, 31; HW 4, 463.
33  GW 15, 31; HW 4, 463.
34  GW 15, 31; HW 4, 463.
35  GW 15, 32; HW 4, 466.
36  GW 15, 66; HW 4, 513.
37  GW 15, 33; HW 4, 466.
38  GW 15, 33; HW 4, 467.
39  GW 15, 37; HW 4, 472.
40  GW 15, 44; HW 4, 482.
41  GW 15, 45; HW 4, 483.
42  GW 15, 46; HW 4, 485 – verbatim: "the sense [of the state and of the life of the people], the sense of governing and obeying."
43  Ibid.
44  Ibid.
45  Ibid.
46  GW 15, 51; HW 4, 492.
47  GW 15, 110; HW 4, 576.
48  Ibid. – verbatim: "notaries."
49  GW 15, 106; HW 4, 571.
50  GW 15, 110; HW 4, 576.
51  GW 15, 50; HW 4, 491.
52  GW 15, 51; HW 4, 492.
53  Ibid.
54  GW 15, 59; HW 4, 489.
55  GW 15, 48; HW 4, 488.
56  Ibid.
57  GW 15, 49; HW 4, 489 – verbatim: "than before, as they thereby [obtain] a relation to and influence on war and peace."
58  GW 15, 37; HW 4, 471.
59  GW 15, 76; HW 4, 528.
60  GW 15, 77; HW 4, 529 f.
61  GW 15, 76; HW 4, 531.

62 GW 15, 77; HW 4, 529 – verbatim: "a position stepping out of the organism of the state, confronting the government as an independent power."

63 GW 15, 46; HW 4, 485.

64 GW 15, 114; HW 4, 582.

65 GW 15, 115; HW 4, 582.

66 GW 15, 46; HW 4, 485.

67 The sharpness of this contrast is shown by its exact reversal in L. Uhland: "all negotiations of the landed estates from March 1817 onward were based on the idea that the constitution of the Württemberg hereditary lands is not merely something usable that one could use, but something on which certain rights existed" (quoted from List [1913], 98).

68 GW 15, 121; HW 4, 592.

69 Cf. Schneider (1896), 473.

70 Zahn (op. cit.), 48–50, 62.

71 Ibid., 7.

72 Ibid., 72 – The fact that the "*Volksfreund*" printed it (cf. Roques [1912]) proves nothing here, since the paper was not ministerial.

73 The speech is by Haym; the withdrawal was made in his self-biography, printed posthumously.

74 GW 15, 60; HW 4, 505 – verbatim: "The connection in the state, which is an objective, necessary relation, independent of arbitrariness and discretion, is essentially different from such a contract [...]"

75 Ibid.

76 Hegel to Niethammer, January 31, 1818 (Br. II).

77 The "Remarks" (loc. cit.), 21 make every effort to hear from Hegel's "rational" state law an echo of the "principle that ministers are the representatives of state reason."

78 He emphasizes: "which is not the case" (GW 15, 115; HW 4, 583).

79 GW 15, 37; HW 4, 472 – One might suspect, however, that the Heidelberg professor was so cautious here in order to handle the aversion of the Baden civil service against a House of Lords with care. – An allusion to what, according to Wangenheim-Eschenmayer, was the determination of an aristocracy in the state, is to be found in Hegel in GW 15, 110; HW 4, 576.

80 The "Remarks" already conclude from this constraint to the year 1816 that Hegel, in contrast to the "other adversaries of the Estates," at least does not want to "bestow knighthood upon them only in order to achieve some purpose: (loc. cit., 43) and that he "at least did not write for the sake of his own advantage" (ibid., 44) (reference also to an opposition of Hegel to the present governmental policy: ibid., 32).

81 Zahn (op. cit.), 10.

82 GW 15, 61; HW 4, 507 – verbatim: "they have forgotten nothing and have learned nothing." – HW "have not learned." 1039 GW 15, 125; HW 4, 597.

83 GW 15, 125; HW 4, 597.

84 Zahn (op. cit.), 64 (more subtly the "Remarks" [op. cit.], 33).

85  Zahn (op. cit.), 73 (perhaps the earliest reference to the familiar story).

86  Zahn (op. cit.), 70 (cf. "Remarks" [op. cit.], 25, 48).

87  GW 15, 122; HW 4, 592.

88  List (op.cit.), 102 f.

89  Ibid., 118 f.

90  Ibid., 102.

91  Ibid., 124.

92  The "Württembergischer Volksfreund" should not be confused with the "Volksfreund aus Schwaben," addressed by List (loc. cit., 123), although serving the same tendency.

93  List (op. cit.), 128.

94  Ibid., 159.

95  Hegel to Niethammer, January 31, 1818 (Br. II).

96  GW 15, 41; HW 4, 478 – verbatim: "for the purpose [...] partly bled along with it."

# 11

# PRUSSIA

Hegel and the Prussian state grew towards each other. But it was now an entirely different Prussia, different from the one that Hegel had transfigured in 1802 from the division of estates familiar in Common Law and espoused by political theorists. At that time, moreover, Hegel had managed to refrain from becoming confounded in his overall assessment, which was widely held and common to the best of minds, that this "leathery and spiritless" state had only been temporarily forced into existence as an "ephemeral energy" by a single genius.[1] While in Jena, in the midst of Hegel's unrestrained displays of joy, this Prussia collapsed, owing to the victory of culture over barbarism, of intellect over sophistry. Men, mostly of non-Prussian origin, set about erecting a new Prussia from the fragments of the old state, a Prussia which was to widely open its fortress gates to the new German spirit, so as to allow this strong ally to lead Prussia to victory in the coming Wars of Liberation. And yet Hegel, the newspaper writer from Bamberg, the pedagogue from Nuremberg, had received no account of this new disposition, which forced the state out of its narrow, one-sided drive towards power, and

DOI: 10.4324/9780429354724-13

placed it under the dominion of the spirit. Around 1809, Hegel depicted to his students and their parents those states, with clear reference to the Prussian state of 1806, that "neglect and scorn what their inhabitants sought to preserve and build up out of the inner backdrop of their soul, direct their inhabitants towards mere utility and towards the spiritual only as a means" and who therefore "cluelessly stand in the face of danger, collapsing in on themselves in the very midst of their multitude of utility."[2] He did not anticipate that just then, in Prussia, men were already at work who subscribed word for word to this critique of the old state, and who, just like him, were seeking a cultural remedy in order to ensure that "intellectual content has value and interest in and for itself," forming the soul into "a core of independent worth [...] which constitutes the foundation of usefulness for everything else, and which is important to plant among all estates."[3] So little did he anticipate this, that when this internally renewed Prussia commenced battle for Germany in 1813, Hegel stood aside apathetically, and even with hostility. This Prussia, which in that moment moved closer to Germany than in many subsequent decades, appeared to Hegel as a foreign state, external to Germany itself, which, under the pretext of liberation from foreign dominion, would only attract "Cossacks and Bashkirs" to Germany.[4] It had completely lost its "merely formal" culture, as well as what was hoped for in a future Northern Germany. The internal world conquest of the German spirit, in which Hegel believed, could only proceed, so he thought in 1807, from the South. Prussia's preliminary battle would not result in German supremacy. The state withdrew into itself, but certainly not like it was before 1806. The ideas which had previously been granted admittance remained silently influential in hundreds of places and prevented the great body of the state to again fall into decay. But the general course of its politics initially led it more and more back towards a purely Prussian existence. And, at least at the beginning of this period, it could not be kept from the bright minds of Germany that the choice between Prussia and Austria was a question of Germany's internal fate, not merely its external form. This was, as had been occasionally stated in the *Heidelberger Jahrbücher* while under Hegel's co-editorship, "the impending predicament of our age"[5] – namely, whether one should stand by Austria, as all that remained "from an expiring, beautiful past," or hope for a "new future"[6] in connection with Prussia.

Faced with such a choice, Hegel had once chosen Austria. This was when Hegel had wanted to guide the dying German Empire to a perhaps still possible recovery, and he was brought to such a position partly through his mistrust of the inner rigidity of the Prussian state. At that time, he believed that municipal freedom and popular representation, which he called for in a future Germany, could be more easily expected from Austria, which had preserved its old Estates, than from Prussia, which in this regard, as in all cases, had proceeded in a leveling and mechanized manner.[7] Additionally, it is likely that the understandable need prevailed of mitigating the harsh nature of such subversive and drastic proposals for reform, as Hegel had presented them, such that he did not expect these reforms from the historically and presently revolutionary Prussia, but rather from Austria, which had long been legitimate and, through its own history, tended towards preserving what was already in existence.[8] This is what those passages from the text on *The German Constitution* in 1802 refer to, namely where Prussian politics, "emerging from a bourgeois mentality," which it had acquired coin by coin through painstaking work, was opposed to the politics of the old Austrian Empire, and therefore the smaller Estates could safely affiliate themselves with the latter. A few years later, and no trace of this hope for Austria was to be found. The reason for this was not exclusively the Austrian defeat which it suffered against France in 1805, but more the change in Hegel's view of the state that had meanwhile occurred. Hegel no longer regarded the state, as he had before in Jena, as one of the highest, indeed perhaps the highest, manifestation of spiritual life. Already in *The Phenomenology*, under the influence of Napoleon, Hegel had developed and retained the idea that, from now on, the state was only an ordering of external existence, subordinate to what was actually independent life, within which spirit dwells in philosophy and religion, and that during the period when the state became more than that, it was overcome by the union of Napoleon and German Idealism.[9] Thus, what then became the essential aspect of this Austrian state was its Catholic character. And if it then seemed to him that the philosophical and religious future could only proceed from Protestantism, and that he had no reason to fear that Napoleon would suppress German Protestant spiritual life, Hegel considered an Austrian victory to be the greatest danger.[10] In 1813, Prussia was still outside of his horizon. He had no idea that ideas on the relationship of state and spirit which were very similar to his own notions had long since taken hold here, including in the same manner he had developed these ideas precisely against Prussia in his school address in Nurnberg, for example. His view of Austria was still the same as in 1809. Thus, the deep hopelessness that accompanied the success of the Alliance was understandable.[11] He no longer had a relationship with Austria, and still none with Prussia. Moreover, the state had to first regain its equal status with spirit. Indeed, his view on the recently stateless character of spiritual life, or at least of spiritual life beyond the state, still reverberated distinctly from his address in Heidelberg, which he held at the recommencement of his academic career. But then, in the review of the events in Württemberg, Hegel's familiar political concern again awoke to independent strength. When, during the first few years of the Restoration, the Prussian state again withdrew itself faintheartedly, and yet perhaps also with a sense of higher necessity – who would dare to decide here! – from the demands of the idealistic spirit, and instead focused on its own narrow and closest tasks,[12] during this period Hegel found his way back to his pre-Napoleonic view of the state, which presided in its post not beneath spiritual life, nor to the side or together with it, but rather at times even over spiritual life itself. Thus, Hegel was pointed towards Prussia, and directly towards that Prussia of 1815, which had again begun to detach itself from its position in connection with the entire nation and beyond the state, without thereby carving itself into pieces. The address that Hegel held in 1818, upon his acceptance of the professorship in Berlin, testifies that he himself was aware of this common bond.

For the first time, Hegel acknowledged here more broadly and more deeply than he had two years earlier in Heidelberg, those "*higher interests of actuality,*" those battles that had saved and restored "*the political totality of the life of the people and of the state.*"[13] He again designated nationality as the "foundation of all living life."[14] At the same time, he again found that the actual effect of those battles for nationality, after this "rebirth of Germany,"[15] as he now also called the events of 1813, was that "*within the state, next to the governance of the actual world, the free realm of thought is now* blossoming up independently for the first time."[16] While this still sounds like an echo of that separate historical viewpoint from Hegel's Napoleonic period that saw spiritual life in opposition to the state, and gained its own momentum, in truth, when one compares the corresponding passage from the Heidelberg address two years earlier, this is precisely where the change can be found. At that time in Heidelberg, it was said that one may now hope that "next to the *state* [...] the *church* [...], *next to the realm of the world* [...] *the Kingdom of God* [...], next to *the political, and other* interests bound to *common actuality, science, the free rational world of the spirit, are again blossoming up*."[17] Now, in Berlin, the realms, the political realm of the "actual world" and the spiritual realm of the "world of thought," are no longer "next to" each other, but instead, both are "within" the state. In this manner, the view of the greater Prussian state, with its deliberate care for its spiritual, and especially scientific life, compelled Hegel towards one of his earlier, pre-Napoleonic thoughts. Namely, the more agreeable inflection of the "independent" powers of state and spirit. Of course, the philosopher gave precedence to spirit. What is now to be valid must "justify itself before *insight and thought*."[18] But the Prussian state submitted itself to this justification, for through its spiritual supremacy it "lifted itself up to the level of its importance in *actuality and in politics*, making itself equal, in terms of *power and independence*, to such *states* which were previously superior to it in their *external means*."[19] Therefore, it really is this state that is "founded on intelligence."[20] "Here, culture and the bloom of the sciences are one of the essential *moments in state life* itself."[21] And still more: as Hegel learned to again see the reciprocal common bond of state and spiritual existence in the Prussian state, his thought also finally gained a fruitful way of relating to the ethical spirit of Prussian prominence. In the beginning, he did not wish to see this spirit, but he later came to terms with its outcomes, most likely influenced by the fraternal youth who surrounded him in Heidelberg, and made it intelligible to himself as the will to fight for free constitutions. He now saw this spirit otherwise and, if we may say so, more truly. In its historical rise to prominence, he now recognized in Prussia, in addition to that alliance of state and culture, the new development, the second "basic element in the existence of *this state*,"[22] namely, an alliance of state and disposition." What Hegel considers "invaluable" is that the great battle "for independence, for the destruction of mindless foreign tyranny, and for freedom, has found its higher cause"[23] "in the *minds*" [of the people]; that it "was *the ethical power of the spirit*" that here, "in the full feeling of its energy, stretched out its banner, and thus made its *feeling* valid as force and *power* in actuality"[24]; and "that the present generation has lived in this feeling, *acted and worked*" and that herein spirit was lifted "to its dignity."[25] The "substantial content" that time has now gained for itself makes up the core, "the further development of which, towards all sides of the political, ethical, religious, and scientific," is entrusted to the age.[26] This is how Hegel now speaks. For years he had almost forgotten both of the "basic elements" of spirit for the existence of the state, namely, inner adherence to the higher life of culture, as well as to the ethical power of disposition. Under the impression of Napoleon's rule, Hegel found the life of culture beyond the state, and the state was only to protect it, not suffuse itself with it. Furthermore, the ethical goals which the thinker had set at that time do not point the individual towards the state, but rather towards philosophy and religion as the true fields of his conviction and activity. Now, the state had won back both relations, namely that of ethos and that of disposition. The actuality of the Prussian state had finally forced the philosopher back into his original ways. Perhaps unintentionally, along with his commitment to Prussia, it was a commitment of Hegel's return to the state that he expressed here.

The new Prussian minister of culture had known very well why he offered Hegel, the serious Swabian, Fichte's vacated professorship around the turn of the year 1817, instead of offering it to the genteel and privy Savigny, or to the lively Schleiermacher, who could move agilely over depths, or even the sophisticated Solger.[27] One may question how Fichte himself, if he had lived longer, would have contended with Hegel's appointment in Berlin to those above and below him. From the first negotiations, which were led by Niebuhr and Raumer late in the year of 1816, until they broke down with Hegel's call to Heidelberg, there is evidence that allows one to recognize how, among the leading circles in Prussia and still in the direct shadow of the rise to prominence, there was a strong concern for how one could capture and direct the spirit of this prominence into the future. Raumer's complaint in his promotional letter, that many of those youth who had fought and bled for the state did not have the faintest notion of the state, almost sounds comical to us.[28] One was clearly concerned. Among those three professors of the Friedrich Wilhelm University, from whom the students of Berlin, who were those seen with such concern, could perhaps receive the "faintest notion" of the world of ethics and rights, Schleiermacher seemed in no way harmless and Solger was far too soft and without persuasive strength, which Savigny, in his noble composure, also did not possess. Fries, who in 1816 a group of professors under the leadership of his personal friend, the theologian De Wett, had thought to call away from Jena, had already become somewhat estranged to the minister at that time due to the political fancies of his *Julius und Euagoras* and, meanwhile, through his proximity to the student fraternities, had also made a call impossible. Savigny, who may still have recalled his disappointment with Fries, the philosopher of right, from his own academic youth, and Scheiermacher – thus, both of the men who would later become Hegel's major adversaries – both of these men campaigned for Hegel, and against Fries, during the first call for a professorship.[29] In 1818, they were no longer consulted. The new minister acted on his own when, after an incidental visit to Heidelberg, he gained the impression that Hegel, as he wrote to the King, was "just as removed from paradoxical, flamboyant, untenable systems as he was from political and religious prejudices, and that he taught his science with calm and prudence."[30] With the conclusion of *The Science of Logic* in 1816, and with the publication of the *Basic Outline* in 1818, Hegel had entered into the forefront of German philosophers; among the living, only Schelling was surrounded with an older and brighter glow of fame; a certain Reinhold was the only one remaining from the earlier years of the Kantian movement, living half-forgotten and secluded in Kiel; and the only others who could be named here, with the sole exception of Fries, were mostly from Schelling's school or circle of influence. Thus, after his great renunciation of Schelling, Hegel stood completely alone in the public eye, no one's pupil, with a strong claim to philosophical dominance. It might have been that Altenstein still had other prospects for Hegel, other than that of a professor, perhaps a position with a more practical circle of influence. In any case, Hegel faced his Berlin listeners in his inaugural address with that claim to theoretical dominance. From the "middle point," from the capital city, he wished to proclaim "the science of the middle point."[31] And it was precisely through this claim that he gradually won over the Berlin public. For the age pressed forward towards such an arrangement. Not in vain had the age pursued the presuppositions and fundamental questions of philosophy. Now the world itself, indeed the entire world, the "universe" – we can express it using Hegel's own words – would "set before its eyes the courage of recognition [...] its wealth and its depths [...] and offer it up for enjoyment."[32] Goethe, who followed these movements partially as an observer and partially with indulgence, and who steadily participated in the events of Berlin through Zelter's ongoing reports, gave his blessings to the intentions of the proud thinker, as it were, when he accepted for his part the word "middle point," which Goethe himself had recently used in a similar manner,[33] and with which Hegel had perhaps appealed to the centralization plans of the minister, when Goethe called out to the philosopher – precisely in those days when the *Philosophy of Right* had been unveiled – renewing their old acquaintance: "It is certainly necessary, in this curious age, that somewhere a doctrine is spreading from a middle point, whereby a life can be supported practically and theoretically."[34]

It was a distinctly mixed audience that Hegel, in the thirteen years that he taught in Berlin, gathered around himself. In addition to students, among which those from non-Prussian Germany, including the South, made up a sizable number, there were also scattered old men, officials, even officers. The privy councilor of the Ministry of Culture, Johannes Schulze, who impressed his kind of Hegelianism on the Prussian upper school system for decades, had sat through the entire series of lectures. It was perhaps through the mediation of Captain Karl Griesheim, likewise a zealous Hegel student and friend of Clausewitz, that Hegelian elements migrated into the foundations of German military science.[35] And behind the actual audience there stood an even bigger circle, the society of Berlin. In the 1820s, Hegel had become one of the personalities without whom life in Berlin could not be imagined. It was especially his lectures on aesthetics, which he had planned earlier, but only first delivered in Heidelberg, and which he was able to bring into close connection with his metaphysics and history of philosophy, that afforded him a circle of influence well beyond the university itself. A cool-headed observer could even later relay the report of Hegel's death with her mockingly exaggerated remark: the learned world of Berlin, and perhaps even more so, the unlearned world, have lost their philosopher.[36] It was not as if Hegel had consciously cultivated this side of his work. He was far removed from wanting to shine in society. After he had died, a woman reportedly complained to the old Zelter that in conversation with Hegel she had never heard him say anything meaningful. She thus had to put up with the crude answer from the old man that it was simply in his line of work to talk to men. But it was precisely this mannerism, which was in no way suited for a salon, this self-evident separation between professional seriousness and good-natured harmlessness in the hours of relaxation, between that man who "talked to men" and that other man, who among pretty women showed such an awkwardly bearish gallantry, that those who did not know him could be deeply appalled by him. Indeed, it was precisely this mixture of Hegel's nature, uncharacteristic of Berlin, that succeeded in granting him a place in the Berlin of aesthetic tea parties and witty playful feelings. The reports on the impression that the teacher was making tend to set him in contrast to Schleiermacher. One can hardly imagine a greater contrasting figure than this thoroughly acclimatized Berliner (still the subject of some classic Berlin jokes), the contrast, namely, between the swift-talking, fiery orator and the slow talking man from Stuttgart, who indeed often spoke more to himself than to his listeners, and who still felt like a Swabian in Berlin, to the degree that in 1831, upon encountering David Friedrich Strauss, Hegel immediately relaxed when learning that his young visitor was from Ludwigsburg. What was Swabian to him, namely that which was wrapped around his own genius like an honorable protective layer of old-fashioned civility, remained the foundation of his way of life as well as his manner of thought. Those passages of his heavily worded presentation, passages moving backwards and forwards, illuminating the darkness of the dialectical development, those passages appeared meteor-like in their grotesque imagery, in their surprising depth of meaning and striking formulation, in the manner they branded themselves to memory. That with him the spirit always retained what suddenly appeared, that it remained unpredictable when the oasis of intuition was reached in the desert of abstraction – and that it was always reached with certainty – all of this is what secured Hegel the attention of a city in which, already at that time, its intellectual tyrants took nothing as badly as when they were outsmarted. And yet, the face of this Berlin was more exclusively cast with this drive towards being intellectually mastered than the Berlin of later decades. One should above all remember how much more "Prussian" Prussia become after 1848, and how, at the time in question, the still scarce outlines of the trenchant and prosaic Margraviate appeared to be dissolved in the serene air of humanist culture that wafted over from Weimar. The entire generation of officers and officials was still infected with that spirit. Only when they gave way did that Prussia arise from which the unification of Germany could proceed, and this occurred without these new Prussians ever really noticing what had issued from them, or what had happened to them. In order to correctly perceive Hegel's standing in Berlin, it pertains to include that the Berlin at that time was the capital city of another Prussia, and that Hegel's combination, peculiar to him, of a strong relation to the state with a fully encompassed historical culture could be comfortably housed within the walls of the Prussian state at that time.

But an unresolved question sounded upon the walls of this state. The alluring image of a national commonwealth had shown itself to be within reach for a few intense months, vanishing again soon. Nevertheless, the youth who believed to have fought for this commonwealth on the battlefields of 1813 did not give up on the idea so quickly. And the demands of the youth were directed towards Prussia, towards the leader of the national struggle, which in the first years, until around 1817, had still shown some hidden sympathies towards the German movement in the minor states. However, in view of the impossibility of European unity, Prussia now fell short in meeting the expectations of a generation which, for its part, began to lose the sense for such a validation of greater politics and, in contrast to such external impossibilities, set their sight firmly upon internal necessity. This was the disposition with which the student fraternities lived. Hegel was in their proximity in Heidelberg and two of their leaders followed him to Berlin, creating an atmosphere among students for the master, whose doctrine of the state, despite those words from his inaugural address on the political power of enthused "minds," may have come across as highly suspicious in the common understanding of the fraternities as operating in princely servitude. Well-meaning words from trustworthy sources could only help in this regard. Meanwhile, there came the retaliations against the first persecutions in the wake of the Wartburg Festival: the assassinations carried out by Sand and Loening. The Sand assassination, in particular, for an age that was interested in the moral side of politics, must have caused great excitement. Could, indeed, should this act, which arose so visibly from a pure and enthused mind, be judged like a "common" murder? The Berlin theology professor De Wette, a friend and student of Fries, made himself the spokesman of that attitude, widely circulating among the educated, when, in his letter of condolence to Sand's mother, he decisively negated the above question. The letter was discovered during the investigation, in which De Wette was already entangled due to his relationship to the student fraternities; and the King, enraged by the behavior of his professor, oversaw his removal from office. What followed, as an implementation of the Carlsbad Decrees, were measures to curtail freedom at the university. The importance that both sides attached to this can only be understood if we remember that, at that time, when parliamentary life was still in its infancy and a press in the contemporary sense was still in the making, universities believed that they could stand in place of both of these; and governments, in that they affirmed this belief through their apprehension, transformed this belief from something imaginary into something with weight in reality. Thus, all at once the struggle for freedom of teaching became a focal point of political opposition.[37] And Hegel, who after the assassination had even attended a student fraternity celebration, with Schleiermacher and De Wette at his side, was now forced, for the first time and following upon his intermediary stance during his inaugural address, to take a decisive position in Berlin on account of De Wette's moral justification of Sand's actions. In company, towards the beginning of 1820, Hegel asserted the right of the government to remove a teacher, in opposition to Schleiermacher, and only criticized that they did not allow De Wette to keep his salary. To this end, Hegel himself had contributed a relatively substantial sum to the gathering held by the circle of professors for their unemployed colleagues, for in general, due to his own presence at that celebration and his relationship with several of the already implicated leaders of the student fraternity, Hegel could have been suspected of being one of the most disreputable demagogue informants. Following that assertion, the two opponents engaged in an exchange of words – they did not, admittedly, go at each other's throats, as the gossipers of court and university had wished – and, in short, Schleiermacher described Hegel's view as pathetic, as it seemed to him in no way to justify the high, independent value of freedom of teaching. And yet, Schleiermacher subsequently wrote to Hegel to ask for his forgiveness, which he received. It was now the beginning of continuous tension between Hegel and the great theologian, in whom the Berlin opposition, even if Schleiermacher himself resisted such an imposition, gradually came to see as their intellectual leader. This was also, as noted, the beginning of Hegel's decisive political position, as until then he had not followed in any of the separate ways of his colleagues, except in one case, regarding conflicts of the university with the government. De Wette was being defended by Fries, and if Hegel, as well as Fries, had sought to bury the hatchet upon Hegel's appointment to Heidelberg as Fries' successor, owing to the many bitter comments and discussions between the two,[38] for his part, Fries had now become, through his statement on the absolute right and value of "conviction" – which was made tangible for Hegel in Sand's actions and De Wette's defense – nothing less than the origin of political evil for the Berlin philosopher of state. Hegel, in order to lend his doctrine of state an apparent anchoring in present life, which such a work indeed required, now thought to unveil his work in opposition to this point. Thus, Hegel came to make that political decision which would stick to him more than any other decision, beginning already during his lifetime, and whose consequences would drive him more closely and unconditionally than he himself had originally thought into the arms of the Prussian government. Indeed, instead of merely polemicizing against the simple disposition in the Preface to his book, Hegel also polemicized against its messenger. In the previous year, Fries was already forced through an order from above to abandon his lecture courses in Jena. Thus, for a "denunciation," as it was then called, Hegel's advance already came a bit too late. In any case, Hegel let himself get carried away here by an unrefined passion, which justifiably hurt his legacy. For Hegel himself, who hardly felt that his polemic was a personal one, his attack against Fries was nothing more than a front and had nothing at all to do with the actual content of the Preface, let alone the book. He still thoroughly believed to be defending a position he had won for himself and did not at all consider himself to be an unconditional defender of the government. He ascertained with certainty that Berlin, where on account of his foreword he had come to see many "sour faces," was at a loss regarding "into which categories the matter should be brought," for, as he thought, "they cannot shove what I said off into a so-called association with Schmalz."[39] Thus, he thought it would protect the independence and elevation of his viewpoint on the philosophy of state, through thick and thin, from being mixed up with an unimaginative loyalty to the government, as was now the type associated with that efficient, but cramped lawyer, Schmalz, since he was disastrously awarded the Order of the Red Eagle.[40] But the philosopher had overestimated the concern of political parties in their classification of opponents. Indeed, what he had considered impossible happened: they cast Hegel's position as an "association with Schmalz."

We do not want to let ourselves be further distracted, indeed tempted, to explicate the content on "doctrine and life" that the famous foreword delivers. Only in this way can we understand how such diverse, and even opposed effects, could have found their origin in the book.

After an initial declaration on the academic occasion and form of the work, Hegel looks to demonstrate the need for a scientific doctrine of the state, which he is planning to accomplish. It should not deal with new "truths," as they were being proclaimed and suppressed daily – Hegel scornfully calls them "warmed up cabbage"[41] – but rather, with Goethe's somewhat later verses: it should deal with the already long-found "old truth," which only needs to be "taken hold of": "*truth about right, ethicality, [and] state [which] is just as old as it is openly demonstrated and familiar in public laws, public morals, and religion.*"[42] And in order for it to be "justified" for free thinking, this old truth only needs to be "grasped" [begriffen], "the rational form [must be gained] for content already rational in-itself."[43] As its direct adversary the philosopher sees himself in opposition to that notion that philosophy must proceed as if "there had never been a state, or state constitution, in the world nor presently at hand, but rather as if *now* – and this *now* always endures – one had to start anew from scratch."[44] When in comparison to this notion he now refers to nature, of which one generally admits that philosophy is to recognize it as it is, that it is rational in itself, and that knowledge is to research this actual reason in it and not the contingencies which show themselves superficially. This comparison of "reason" contained in nature and spirit could appear strange to someone brought up on today's sense of methodology. One could believe to have clearly found here the basic mistake of Hegel's doctrine of the state – and this would neverthe-less be a mistake, for, as we will now see, Hegel grounded this equation of nature and spirit much deeper than it at first appears. But in the pas-sage of the foreword where we are currently positioned, he evidently thought to have sufficiently positioned the reader against that "atheism of the ethical world" that exposes this world to chance and arbitrari-ness. He leaves the line of thought in order to voice a moving complaint that, for those who consciously find satisfaction in the state – because unconsciously "*everyone*" has this satisfaction – philosophy has come "into disrepute" through the activities of such irresponsible state reformers.[45] At this passage Hegel recalls the address that "Herr Fries," "the General of this shallowness,"[46] gave at the Wartburg Festival three years earlier, and Hegel is outraged that here the rich architectonics of the state are mixed together in the "puree of heart, friendship, and enthusiasm," and that the work of reason, ongoing for thousands of years, is "left to mere feeling."[47] Consequently, given that such views also take on "the form of piety"[48] – it appears here that, in addition to Fries and his student followers, Hegel tosses barbs at De Wette and most likely at Schleiermacher as well – and that through the constant use of elevated words such as spirit, life, and peoples all that is on display is a "bad conscience."[49] But the "shibboleth" "by way of which the false brothers and friends of the so-called people separate themselves" is the concept of "law," which those politicians of emotion perceive as a shackle.[50] Hegel recalls that he had taken note of this somewhere in his textbook, and one is amazed, in following up on this "somewhere," when one finds that the "denunciation" of Fries and the liberals is based on the same thoughts which in the book serve to dispatch the conservative theoretician who during these years was made into a leader by certain circles of court society: K.L. v. Hallers.[51] Hegel found his own thoughts on the state to be so self-contained that he believed he could proceed against even the most opposed sides in his manner of attack. Of course, in the foreword there is only talk of Fries and his political views, and Hegel expressly condones the position that, recently, governments "have finally turned their attention to his manner of philosophizing."[52] For as long as "shallowness" remains bearable with outer calm and order, it could not be objected to "by the police." But the state is not merely police, it is comprised of "the need for deeper culture and insight,"[53] and, over time, false doctrines spoil the general principles from which actions spring. The state is therefore justified and duty-bound to be mindful of the fact that, for us, philosophy is not a private matter as perhaps it was for the Greeks, but rather that philosophy has "a public existence, moving the audience primarily or exclusively as civil service."[54] In any case, the conflicts that arose from the contact of a sham philosophy with the actuality of the state was fortunate for true philosophy, for thereby governments are finally directed towards their duty to protect true philosophy against the indifference with which the "positive sciences," as well as "religious edification,"[55] believe themselves permitted to look down upon it. And here, finally, where the philosopher again sees his science and the actuality of the state directed towards each other, he turns from the excursion into the politics of the day back to his main line of thought, which he had left with the questionable equation of the ethical and natural world.

Because philosophy, he had said, "is the *grounding of the rational*," it is – not in spite of this, but rather precisely thereby – "the *grasping of the present and the actual*."[56] Hegel then provides the very rationale for this – almost always overlooked, even if it is in the most apparent place – which supports the understanding of everything else that follows. He recalls a remark made in the book on the Platonic state, according to which this state is not an empty ideal, but essentially nothing other than "the nature of Greek ethicality,"[57] thus a purified likeness of the Polis. But Plato, "aware that it was being penetrated by a deeper principle which, within this context, could appear immediately only as an as yet unsatisfied longing, and hence only as something destructive, had to seek the help of that very longing itself in order to oppose it."[58] The "deeper principle" that "penetrated" the ethicality of the Polis for Hegel is doubtlessly the autocracy of the rational self, tied to Socrates and the Sophists. As important as it is now for the Polis that in it "some" are free, according to Hegel's later catchphrase, it is just as removed from organizing or even wishing for the freedom "of all," as already in the modern state, necessarily presupposing slavery for its very existence. Thus, in it the demand that the rational, and on that account the universal "I," namely the human being as such, should be the measure of all things, can only have a corrosive effect. This demand remains an "unsatisfied longing." But Plato seeks, "from out of that very longing itself," namely from the same basic tendency that reason is to be the measure and guide of actuality – or that the philosopher must be king – help for the Greek state endangered by the insurgency of critical reason. But Plato only manages to renew this threatened state with an even more rigid, even less viable form. Plato sought for help "in a particular *external* form of that ethicality,"[59] namely in a division of estates, where even the existing freedom of the few in the actual Greek state was destroyed by the irrevocable decision on class affiliation, as well as by the abolition of private property and family. Thus, by that particular external form of Greek ethicality through which he "thought to control" what was destructive, Plato had actually inflicted the "gravest danger" upon the deeper – pointing towards the future – drive of that ethicality, namely that acknowledgement of the "free infinite personality" of the human being as such, which was based on the freedom of "some."[60] He could not come upon the truth that "everyone" should be free; it had to "come from above."[61] It had to be revealed to the world through Christianity before a new world-historical people, the Germanic, could take it up and actualize it. Thus, what Plato did not find was the means to cure the sick world. What he saw, as clearly as the Sophists had, was the sickness. However, in contrast to the Sophists and their all-encompassing, corrosive critique, what Plato alone did was to call the correct doctor to the sickbed, in so far as he did not demand of reason a critique of the present state, but rather boldly called for reason to help build the future state. This "principle, on which the distinctive aspect of his idea turns," and through whose establishment Plato "proved himself to be a great spirit," was the "pivotal point" in the world of antiquity for the then impending revolution of Christianity.[62] Namely, the thought that reason is to configure actuality. "What is rational, that is actual"[63] – for immediately out of this dispute on the world-historical meaning of Plato's ideal state there springs forth the famous and notorious expression, like a shot: "not in general and since eternity has this been the case, instead it became, through Christianity, an ethical demand and the standard of all human institutions in the thought of the Kingdom of Heaven on earth."[64] But ever since, it is *actually* the case, and because the person of action is tasked to work out the ways of reason in the world, cognition stands – since then! – before the task of investigating actuality – which has become actual since then! – and to discover how reason has worked itself out in actuality. Only because the rational has become actual – principle of the act – only therefore is now the actual rational – principle of cognition. The second half of the proposition, which in contrast to Hegel's own usage is always taken to be the core of the thought – "Hegel's assertion of the rationality of the actual" – is thus only the consequence of the innermost revolutionary thought of the actuality of the rational, which was expressed in the first half. The cognition-grounding second proposition, which shows how the state of our age should be recognized, presupposes the historical-interpretive first proposition, which expresses the ethical life-principle of this state.

And now, the previously mentioned methodological equation of nature and spirit also becomes understandable. The identity of reason and actuality, of cognition and object has not always applied, as it has to the realm of nature, to the realm of the spirit. The realm of spirit, to now use Hegel's expression, really was once "god forsaken." Only since Christianity appeared in the world did reason become the foundation of the spiritual world and this rationality the principle for cognizing this world. This also corresponds to Hegel's *Lectures on the Philosophy of History*, which first conceive of the state as actualized ethicality with the beginning of the Christian-German epoch, whereas up until then the state is comprehended in aesthetic and judicial concepts and concepts of natural philosophy. And this, in turn, corresponds to the overview of ecclesiastical history, which Hegel gave in his lectures on the philosophy of religion, and whose theme is solely the reconciliation of church and world, the "realization of the spiritual with universal actuality." And finally, this corresponds above all to the world-historical development of thought itself, which only since then displays to us those great doctrinal concepts, in which in fact, and with the consent of thought, ethics no longer triumphs over politics, nor politics over ethics, as in paganism, but rather both, namely doctrines of salvation and of community, of personality and of institution, are intertwined in each other, and at least in the will of the thinker one is no longer highlighted more than the other. From the holy people of the Torah and from Paul's mysticism of the body of Christ, this line continues with Augustine's city of God, Dante's civilizing of humanity and onward to Hegel's profound double-dictum.

Let us return to this. After Hegel had pronounced it, he initially refers briefly to the cognition-grounding meaning of the second half. The comparison of the spiritual with the natural "universe" is now bolstered by the justification − based on a philosophy of history − that "subjective consciousness," if it "considers the present as vain," would then saw off the very branch upon which it rests.[65] Then Hegel immediately springs again to this justification based on a philosophy of history, thus to the content of the first half of the proposition, opposes that the idea should be "only such an idea," and avows himself, in contrast to this view, to the most resolute idealism, for which "nothing [is] actual" but the idea.[66] Then it is important, again in accord with the methodological second half of the proposition, "to recognize the eternal, which is present [...] in the semblance of what is temporal and temporary."[67] This is not so simple, because − and he explains here, as already in his *Logic*, how he understands "actual" − "the rational [...] in that in its actuality it likewise enters into external existence, emerges in an infinite wealth of forms, appearances, and configurations and surrounds its core with the colorful bark in which consciousness is initially housed and which the concept first penetrates in order to find the inner pulse and to also feel it still beating in the external configurations."[68] Those "infinite manifold relations," as Hegel declares in contrast to the "ultra-wisdom" of Plato and Fichte, are "not the object of philosophy."[69] Philosophy can appear "liberal" therein and perceive the hate, which the "know-it-all"" fondly directs towards certain individual institutions, as beneath its dignity.[70] Rather, philosophy's object is "*to grasp and represent the state as in-itself rational.*"[71] It is not philosophy's task to teach us how the state should be, but rather – and now, after all that has preceded, we can understand the Kantian-sounding phrase as the methodological application of the great double-dictum – "how [the state] should be recognized."[72] Hegel again expounds upon this factually – and now in a completely un-Kantian manner – through a reversal of the philosophy of history: that no philosophy, just as little as an individual, can leap beyond its age, but rather that it is the essence of philosophy to be "*its age conceived in thoughts.*"[73] That this is not to be a unification with the age in the sense of a dead, spiritless inertia, is again clarified here (as if it has not been said enough) through a rash Greek pun; Hegel changes the "Rhodus" of the present and its state, where philosophy is to show whether it understands how "to dance," into the "rose" of reason, which is to be recognized by philosophy "in the cross of the present"[74]: the beautiful flower of divine life is found within the hard wood of earthly suffering. The endeavors of this recognition will then lead philosophy to the reward of a joyful, "warmer" reconciliation with actuality, and in this manner philosophy will satisfy the honorable "obstinacy" of the modern era, which "in any case is the unique principle of Protestantism," which wishes to acknowledge nothing "that is not justified through thought"[75] and will thus help spirit to that freedom by way of which it finds itself in the present.

"Unification with the age," "not better than the age, but this at its very best" – twenty years earlier, this is how Hegel had expressed his ideal of life, in that moment when, after many years of feeling adverse about the age and its actuality, and finally living a reflectively detached life, he again found himself in the world and recognized his place in it, discovering the philosopher in himself.[76] In Berlin, he now places philosophy and his role as a philosopher in Germany at the peak of his work, thereby designating the summit of the track he had begun in Frankfurt. Now, he also does not want to be "better than the age" – this is the Rhodus where he "dances." Instead, he wants to be this "at its best." It is not the cross of the present, but rather the rose therein that he has set out to recognize.

To recognize! Nothing more. To recognize and thereby, for his part, to work on that inner peace that he desired for a shattered world, and that he held to be the true freedom of spirit. Even here the roots of his attitude lead back into the decisive years of his life. In those dark introductory pages of the text on *The German Constitution*, which dealt with the two typically opposed figures of freedom seekers, Hegel came upon the insight that humans obtain the freedom they desire through the course of history itself. It was there that Hegel first discovered that the task of a person of his timber was to pursue this course of cognition, and to thereby identify for the world the reconciliation he had gained through this cognition. Others were bestowed with other tasks – we have already heard the doctrine on world-historical heroes – for him, the philosopher, it was cognition.[77] And so our foreword closes with the thought that philosophy – and mind you, only philosophy – always comes too late to instruct us in how the world should be. "When philosophy paints its gray in gray, a form of life has grown old, and with gray in gray it cannot be rejuvenated, it can only recognized; the owl of Minerva begins its flight only with the falling of dusk."[78]

Our initial task, however, will be to uncover to what extent, in carrying out this task, Hegel really held fast to this attitude and aim, and how far, for instance, that power of the will, which he did not wish to acknowledge as presiding over his thought and over thought in general, nevertheless had overtaken him, given that it now only showed him one side of the present and concealed others from him, and that it drove him beyond the present towards intuitions of the future. And it is this very knowledge of the development of his views and thoughts that will instruct us here to separate between that which he received from the immediate present, out of which he wrote, and all the rest, beyond the Prussia of 1820, whose origins lay further back.

Hegel's book deals with the state within his philosophy of ethicality. However, ethicality itself is only a part of the philosophy of "objective" spirit, which in turn is a part of the philosophy of spirit. Spirit is the collective term for the third and final part of the system, as it is developed in outline in the *Encyclopedia* of 1817. This system from 1817, the main features of which remained unchanged for Hegel in 1827 and 1830, places "spirit" as the overarching unity of thought and object, of logic and nature. Hegel derives self-consciousness from logic and actuality from nature. That the state is placed in this system within "spirit," which is thus neither mere thought nor mere actuality, already emerges as Hegel's first unexpressed claim about its essence. A naturalistic view of the state would already find this objectionable. Hegel himself, when earlier he was developing Jesus' consciousness of the state, had relived the opposite, namely the expulsion of the state from the realm of spirit, and it was from this very reliving of history that he personally fought his way through towards an affirmation [Bejahung] of the spirituality of the state. With this affirmation [Ja], Hegel certainly entered the rank and file of the Idealist movement beginning with Kant. None of Hegel's immediate predecessors, with the single exception of Schelling in his "System Program" from the spring of 1796, had wanted to remove spirit entirely and fundamentally from the state. Within the systematic totality that Hegel denoted as "spirit," it had been established since the beginning of this system that the doctrine of the individual soul should proceed from "subjective" spirit – therefore from psychology. For a while, Hegel took care here to differentiate between cognition and willing, theoretical and practical spirit. It stood to reason to address ethicality and, furthermore, the state directly under "practical" spirit. This was already effectively the case in the practical philosophies of Kant, Fichte, and the young Schelling. Yet, in contrast to his immediate predecessors, Hegel had already gone his own way in the first Jena System. From his struggles in Frankfurt, he had formed the basic ethical view that compelled him to understand the ethical world not on the premise of the "I," as his predecessors had done, but rather to understand the "I" on the premise of the ethical world, on the premise of this world which had become "fate" for the soul. Thus, the first system already depicted the acting, individual human being as the mere nucleus of the life of the ethical world, and this was a fundamental departure from the course of the Idealist movement until now – even if still in intimate contact with it – and it likewise stood in uninfluenced agreement with the great theoreticians of the outgoing Hellenism. This was then Hegel's unchanged position moving forward. It is the basic feature of his thinking on these matters.

But from within this basic fact a second, important modification still occurred in Jena. Originally, the "subjective spirit" had only been the practical spirit; Hegel had already dealt with the cognizing spirit in the Metaphysics, connected to the Logic. This was likely one of the final results stemming from Kant's and his followers' division of disciplines. Already the system outlines from 1804 show Hegel striving to make the concept of "consciousness" – which corresponds to the likewise all-encompassing primordial concept of "fate," yet now includes the entire life of the soul – cognition as well as the will – the cornerstone of his doctrine of the ethical world. And in 1805 this striving comes to an end. The conceptual pair of universal and particular – which in 1802 Hegel had used as the basis of his systematic development, to the degree that the concept of the will had all but disappeared under the intellectualizing power of those basic logical concepts – Hegel now merged this conceptual pair with cognition and will. He did not allow these both to be qualified as contrasting but, rather, both of them lay in the one "I," and the ethical world was rooted not in their separation, but instead in their mutual interdependence. The "will, which is intelligence," the will, which, acknowledged as this individual will by other individual wills and which itself acknowledges others, already formed the spiritual condition of common life beneath the state. The state raised this individual will into conscious harmony with the "universal" will. This was the case in 1805.

With that, Hegel took a major step. First, in a certain sense, the mature thinker finally reconnected here to the concept of the state of his youthful Rousseau period, and the word "universal will" already expresses it. Nevertheless, we know that he did not place his philosophy of the state into Rousseau's equation of the "general" will with the will "of all," as Fichte had done in Germany. What was important in a spiritual-historical sense in Hegel assimilating Rousseau's movement, and the emerging movement of natural right within this, was precisely that such an assimilation could occur with him irrespective of the Platonic-Aristotelian thought of prioritizing the whole above the part, of the state above the individual. Hegel had found his own way to this "ancient" insight into the essence of the state. That it was his own personal way now began to have an effect. Because while the great Greek thinkers had conceived of the personality of the state as a thoroughly cognizable view of life, Hegel was driven to it through the steadfast opposition that the world took against the will, thus he could now fill up the content of a theory of the state, which externally looked exactly like that of antiquity, with an entirely modern life. The will became for him that special juice [besondere Saft] which circulated through the veins of this state organism. From this there originated an image of the state which departed, following Hegel's conception, at a decisive point from the view of the ancients.[79] The fixed division of estates, which, with its implied slavery, was the presupposition of all formations of state, even the democratic, as well their theoretical mirror images in antiquity, gave way to the most plausible point of comparison between state and organism in ancient thought. The modern doctrine of the organism which, occurring already with Leibniz[80] and even more so with Kant, had unsettled the overly crude notion of the functional division of fixed organs and instead strove to form a finer concept of organic purposefulness, permitted just as little of that caste-like view of the essence of the division of estates as did the modern notion of "profession." When Hegel wanted to comprehend the estates as essential for the state – estates whose existence, indeed, despite the revolutionary challenge put to their fundamental political meaning, remains undeniable – instead of developing their necessity out of the state, he had to develop it out of the same necessity through which he also conceived of the state.

Thus, newer philosophy did not develop the organ out of the organism, but instead, as the interdependence between every point and the whole, developed organ and organism out of the same basic concept of the organic. Following upon this, Fichte was the first to try to explain the interrelationship between citizen and state with the concept of an organism.[81] And in 1802, Hegel then began to construct the estates out of the same basic concepts of the universal and particular – "intuition" and "concept" – from which he had developed the state in general. If in 1802 it had remained undecided whether he thought about these estates like locked castes, or like modern professional classes with open confines,[82] now it is otherwise. The power of the individual over the estate systematically shows itself thereby that Hegel's concept of the estate is now developed by way of the specific self-consciousness of the individual in the estate. That psychology of the estates, which in 1802 was more of an addition and was also externally separated from the actual structure, hence becomes the central issue; "estate" and "disposition" are already consciously brought together in the heading of the section.[83] Hegel now comprehends that the one-sidedness which the human being suffered through his professional class could again be sublated [aufgehoben] in that this human being becomes "a totality in his thinking," indeed, that a somehow complete self-consciousness, "a knowledge of his existence and actions," is connected with his narrowly defined work."[84] Within "morality" this human being can thereby again "move beyond his class," in so far as he makes the effort "to do something for the universal" in order to "further" himself and his class.[85] Through his concept of the respectively complete individual self-consciousness, Hegel had thus silenced the complaint, stemming from Schiller and Hölderlin, on the incompleteness of the modern professional. What the full citizen of antiquity, but also only this one, possesses through the essentially political supra-professional content of his life, the modern human being possesses very generally in his profession, which he chooses with a free will, and which he thereby completely fulfills with his own consciousness.

The ethicality of profession thus no longer appeared to Hegel as an indignity, but rather precisely as an expression of inner human freedom and as a necessary consequence of the free choice of profession.[86] In this regard, Hegel perpetually and consciously opposed antiquity. In particular, he hardly ever mentions Plato's state without insisting on this decisive divergence. Overall, for Hegel, the free choice of profession actually remains the crown jewel of personal freedom in the state. Indeed, it is only the individually unfettered seizing of profession that makes that undividedness of self-consciousness possible, in which alone Hegel accepted the modern form of freedom, objectively equivalent to that of antiquity, but superior in that it is fundamentally without exception. We can thus understand how a subsequent social freedom, which the Prussian state granted to its citizens following Stein and Hardenberg, could seem so important to Hegel that, in comparison, the actual political concept of freedom almost receded in significance. Hegel believed that the fundamental difference between the modern state and the state of antiquity was not actually to be found in the political, but instead in the social concept of freedom, in the modern reinterpretation of the professional class.[87] In this sense, Hegel could explain that the creation of civil society in general belonged to the modern world.

Thus, if the *Philosophy of Right* of 1820 still betrays its emergence from the Hegelian concept of the will through Hegel's pointed critique of the concept of the state of antiquity, which he felt to be so decisive, then it is first necessary to understand how Hegel conceived of the concept of the state proceeding from the concept of the will in general. The systematist Hegel considered the will, "which is intelligence," to be the completion of the subjective spirit, thus the sufficient determination of the essence of the individual soul.[88] In accord with the essence of his philosophical method, he now placed this same concept of will, which denoted completion for the individual soul, at the beginning of the next position, which carries the now famous name "Objective Spirit."

After 1817, for Hegel "objective spirit" is definitely not the collective name for all of culture, as is the case in today's academic language, but is instead the name for only that part of human life which is admittedly already beyond mere individual life, thus found in the world of psychology condensed into "subjective spirit," but then again not yet reaching into the area of pure ideas. The world of "objective spirit" lies between simple soulful life and pure spiritual life. It encompasses the areas of human existence that have their foundation within human community and likewise their goal as human community. If perhaps art, religion, and science presuppose the common life of humans – and Hegel is far from contesting that – their goal, however, is no longer community. Although, according to Hegel's conception, they are still concerned with the enhancement of human spirit and the humanity actualized within them still has community as its necessary ground, it is merely the ground beneath its feet. Thus, it is through the demarcation towards both sides, the soulful side as well as the side of pure spiritual life – "subjective" as well as "absolute" spirit – that the area of the "objective" is determined. Hegel had not always seen the demarcation so clearly. Above all, the upper limit, that which meets "absolute" spirit, first became immovably fixed for him during the Napoleonic phase of his thinking, with its tendency towards a devaluation of the state. Until that time, that is, still in the System of 1805, Hegel had attempted, under the broad term "constitution," to comprehend not only the life of the state but also that of religion and science, and accordingly brushed up against the Romantic thought of an imminent state-sanctioned separation of religion and science:[89] "like a special administration of justice, [...] so [there is] a special science – religion – [but] our states have not yet arrived at this point."[90] This was because Hegel conceived of the state at that time partly in reciprocal relation to "art, religion, science," whereas the "actual" spirit of 1805 encompassed, in contrast to its successor, namely, the "objective" spirit of 1820, only that part of common human life that was below the state, as well as that part of the state which the thinker held as lower, in comparison with the division of society into estates and the workings of the highest government. That lower part consisted of state administrative justice and the politics of finance and economics and, additionally, the later much differently integrated phenomenon of right. In 1805, this medley of things filled the space between the individual soul and the liberated spirit. The significance of this arrangement for the relation of the state to ultimate matters has been repeatedly touched on, and will need to occupy us again expressly. Here, however, what is presented is not yet the metaphysical but, instead, the psychological chain, into which the systematist had then set the common essence of humanity. For in grasping how the "actual" spirit of 1805 emerges from the "will, which is intelligence," we will likewise reach the understanding we are seeking on the emergence of the "objective" spirit of 1820.

The "will, which is intelligence," namely complete individual personality, seeks a world over and beyond itself, and entering into this world becomes its fate, is an idea that is sufficiently familiar to us as the outcome of Hegel's time in Frankfurt. It was developed in the first draft of the Jena system, in close connection to the feeling and tone of those thoughts from Frankfurt, as a hostile confrontation of the individual with an overarching power: at that time "transgression" had formed the middle part of the philosophy of spirit. In all four later versions of the Jena system, the merging of personality into community was developed into a doctrine on the lower forms of human life together. The state was always elevated above and beyond, in that it was somehow thought of as the place of reconciliation where individuals again find themselves.[91] How strictly Hegel proceeded conceptually, how little this main arrangement depended on the material of life at hand, is shown most clearly by those three versions of the system. In those versions, the entire middle part is imbued schematically with a repetition from the first version, furnished with the key signature "in the people." Even the last Jena version, when it allowed the middle part to peter out in the description of the state that was not yet true, namely the "state as wealth," this version nevertheless dealt with an important part of the doctrine of the state, that is, with the "powers." The same striving towards the conceptual division between human beings losing themselves and finding themselves in community can be recognized in this terminological and systematic intricacy.

That this conceptual separation of both thoughts was originally what was decisive for the classification is shown more clearly yet in the connection that Hegel sets up between the parts of the System in 1805.[92] There, the spirit as will, which as intelligence was still bound to a content foreign to it, received a form of its own. In the world of "being-acknowledged" and of "legislative law," the spirit again has a manifold content, yet not directly its own. The "constitution" first becomes the place within the world of the will where spirit is able to generate its own content out of itself. This free generation then happens consciously in the "government." Accordingly, for Hegel, the "government" then meant the full actualization of the idea of the state, because here the realm of the will, constructed within the constitution, and initially within the division of estates, is consciously taken as the domain of the will. It is the meaning of government that it wills, and that fundamentally there are no longer, and can no longer be, any obstacles for its will – nothing foreign, nothing insurmountable.

One can then say that it was in 1805 that Hegel first came to terms philosophically with the idea from the winter of 1800 to 1801, namely, that the state is power. The state cannot be understood simply as power if, in the end, one does not wish to fall back into a raw natural view. Rather, in so far as one grasps the state as a powerful will, one can integrate it into the overall Idealist view, without thereby abandoning the thought of power. Therefore, this will, which returned to itself in the state in 1805, had previously wandered through a world of content foreign to it. It begins with the work of the subject who is no longer individual, but rather active in the division of labor, and then goes on to contract, and from there to transgression, encountering in punishment "legislative law." The individual, the "person," is initially the true object for law as well. It is demonstrated how the individual stepped out of the family and entered into the world of economic commerce. Only here does the universality of the law first win that strength of "existence" over against the individual, which the individual alone had possessed before.[93] Here then, precisely in the middle of this central part of the philosophy of spirit, the great turn of events happens, which subjects the individual to a whole. And here, for the first time, the name "state" appears. It is not yet the actual state. It is the state only in so far as the individual disappears in it, the state only as a "hard necessity," as an "unconscious guardianship" over the individual. As such, the state engages in economic operations. As far as we can see, Hegel designates the state, and only the state – and here for the first time – with the later so important expression "society."[94] Hegel then works in civil justice through judicial authority, finally culminating in criminal justice, from which, and through the concept of pardon, he finds the transition to the concluding third part of the middle section.[95]

Hegel entitled this third section "the living people," which in 1802, and still beyond this year, designated the height of politics and ethics. The guardianship of the state over the individual ceases being "unconscious" in the power of the "people" over all "existence, property and life." Here, law is "self-conscious life," however, as law over against the individual and not as the individual through law. We still find ourselves in the realm of the "actual spirit," thus in the realm where the individual will is sublated in the power of the whole. For Hegel, in 1802, this sphere of the "people" signified the height of the ethical. Now, after writing the notebook of 1804,[96] he forcibly pushed himself into a deeper level, without, however, displacing the state from the highest rung of the whole, in fact terming it "constitution," giving it the highest designation. Such a delimited "people" could not yet encompass the area of political existence in which the human being would once again become the bearer of life, thus could not yet encompass the doctrine of the estates nor that of the government. On the other hand, all internal state life – economic policy, private and public administration of justice – was already dealt with in the middle part of the "actual spirit" under "authoritatively legislating law," that is, within the "state," according to his terminology at the time. And so, it is characteristic of the incompleteness of this system that this "people," constrained between "state" and "constitution," have no content of their own. In fact, a manuscript page at hand briefly shows the same content as six pages earlier, only with a different systematic signature. Namely, that the "people" also participate in the three functions termed economy, civil justice, and criminal justice. This demonstrates a similar parallel necessity of the system as was found

in the position between the individual human being and the "intermediate realm" [Zwischenreich], first developed between 1803 and 1804.
But just as then, in the rough framework of the building constructed out
of necessity, an important and enduring position of the Hegelian system
had been established for the first time, namely "civil society." Hence, the
schematic of the development at that time is the sign that something
in Hegel's system was not yet in tune. It is obvious with the systematic
division from 1805, which placed the state partly on the absolute level
of the system and then also partly in the sphere below it, that the relation between the concept of state and the concept of spirit was not yet
definitively resolved.

The point discussed above, however, does not seem to be the origin
of that ambiguity between state and spirit that continued throughout the
further development of the system. Instead, it was initially the relationship between the state and "morality." We may recall how in Hegel's manuscript of 1805 it was precisely this relation that contained distinctive
variations. What was decisively new in that system, at least as opposed to
the System of 1802, was that the individual will, which was previously
suppressed, once again becomes free in the "constitution." In this way,
the individual will is liberated in harmony with the will of the whole,
yet in a natural rivalry with the freedom that "morality," in the sense of
Kant and Fichte, had already promised to its bearers. Such a competition
between thoughts could have been avoided as long as Hegel had not
designated the state as the will completing itself in freedom but, rather,
as the will as completed power. The common grounding of the will now
made the conflict ripe for another outbreak. As we know, Hegel sought
to overcome this difficulty in the section "Konstitution" by emphasiz-
ing the individual freedom of disposition for each individual estate. A
further step in this direction was to regard the order of these dispositions among themselves, so as to present a progressive self-liberation of
the spirit from the estate-oriented bond of the disposition, a liberation
which reached its goal in the spirit of the three highest classes – "scholar,
soldier, government." In particular, all the Machiavelli-like features with
which Hegel had previously adorned the government now gained a distinctive moral foundation. The absolute sublimeness of the government
in determining good and evil now likewise took on the meaning of the
systematic place for the absolute freedom of the human being in the

Kantian-Fichtean sense – an interweaving of these antagonistic thoughts too forceful to endure. It was, finally, a last important step in the direction indicated when, in the description of religion, Hegel put the greatest emphasis on the fact that within the sphere of religion all authority and human order were fading away, and that the individual was more or less "equal to a prince." The executed System of 1805 had already sought to satisfy the claims of "morality" on the state to this extent, a state which henceforth – grounded on the will of the individual – could no longer simply close itself off to such claims. But Hegel's marginal notes already crept forward. There, going directly against all of Hegel's familiar views on ethics, the systematic conclusion was sketched out wherein "morality" was located above the state and only still beneath religion. We know how, in 1806, above all in The Phenomenology and, at least until the end of 1812, in the Nuremberg Encyclopedia, Hegel actually carried out this idea, and how the conception of the world-historical significance of the present, that is, the Napoleonic-moment, was intertwined with it. But we also know how the fall of Napoleon brought the thinker to definitively displace the overall image of world history. Therefore, the focal point of further changes is to be sought within the arrangement of history.

In 1805, and likewise in the concluding part of The Phenomenology, taken systematically, history is the highest and final element in the entire system.[97] This corresponded to the standpoint from which Hegel's overall picture of world history was taken, which did not value ecclesiastical history as consummation but, so to speak, only as an interlude, albeit a necessary one. Ultimately, there could thus be no power that could exist beyond history. With the fall of Napoleon, the view prevailed that the absolute epoch of the history of religion, beginning with Christianity, was the absolute, and thus everlasting, epoch of world history in general. Thereby, the division of world history into Orient, Occidental Antiquity, and a Christian-Germanic world, which hitherto was only valid from particular viewpoints, came to reign unconditionally, and all other divisions, for their part, were only valid from special points of view. And now history had lost its right to be at the end of the system. After Christian revelation, which was outside of history, had transformed itself from its overcome past into the everlasting, ruling present, the historical was now no longer the highest. History now acknowledged something as higher than itself. However, the "absolute spirit," or in the words of the

Nuremberg *Encyclopedia* – which first shows this shift in the version no earlier than 1813, but likely later – "spirit in its pure presentation,"[98] had thereby reached its final position. In 1805, this entire area where spirit produces the spiritual and nothing else, and is thus completely free from all relations to anything unspiritual, is still placed above the state, albeit belonging to it. Thus, this entire area of spirit's highest self-rule [Selbstherrschaft] was now principally extended beyond history.

At the same time, however, the theme that had been justified within the framework of the system of that time, and on the basis of which the "morality" had been able to claim a place above the state in 1805, was discounted: the individual will, which in 1805 had demanded acknowledgment not only within, but also beyond, the state – as it was the cornerstone of the state – could now learn that it would be granted the "auto-nomos" it demanded within art, religion, and science. Within these alone could the individual will be "self," whereas in its relationship to the state the highest thing this will could and should attain was "law." Thus, "morality" – this is the second result that the late Nuremberg *Encyclopedia* yields – could move beneath the state and become its necessary precondition, while the state became for morality the fulfillment it could not attain on its own.

Now that the state was thus freed from the demands of the "morality" of the individual, and placed above these demands, the state could abolish the unnatural division which coupled it – in so far as the state had helped the individual attain the highest position – with art, religion, and science. However, in so far as the state presented community to the human being as a superior, even incomprehensible, power, the state was now denied a place in the sphere of moral freedom. After the supra-historical powers as such had taken their place in the system above history, the state, as the true content of history, moved below these in the system, which for their part, as we will see later in more detail, could now become the consummators of the state. If in 1805 it was said of "government," and of the state in general, insofar as the state was dealt with under the section "Constitution," that government and state were the "cunning"[99] that the unconscious individual will made use of for higher purposes, then now, after the state had vacated its place within the absolute, it is replaced by the "cunning of reason." Thus, the place of "government" from 1805 is taken over by history: a succinct expression for the shift that has occurred.

Hence, the state as fulfillment of moral freedom, insofar as such fulfillment is possible within the sphere of history – in the "world" – and the state as a ruling power over the individual will, have both become one. Using both meanings, Hegel now concluded that part of the system which, in 1805, he termed "actual," then later "practical" in Nuremberg, and finally "objective" spirit after Heidelberg. In both meanings, political community was the superordinate power, in which the individual will only found itself when it bowed down. The sphere of absolute freedom, where spirit truly found itself, was now placed above the earth of historical life, within the absolute third part of the philosophy of spirit. In both meanings, as coercive power over the amoral individual will and as sought-after law for the moral individual will, it was one. This was expressed when the spheres of both of those individual wills now appeared within objective spirit as its two preliminary stages: "right" and "morality." The way in which "morality" had reached this place at the end of the Nuremberg period was already shown; we must now consider how this occurred for "right."

In general, Hegel's relation to right had been a hostile one since the turning point in Frankfurt; he saw in the view of private law the sharpest contrast to the political view. His oldest systematic attempts always brought right into close connection with economic life; for Hegel, in both cases the apolitical human being is the bearer of right. Already in the outline of the system provided in 1803 by the essay on natural right, the "system of needs," and the identically structured "system of justice," make up the two basic prerequisites of the state. And this close connection between economy and right would persist. Thus, in 1805, the entire systemization of "actual spirit," after the preceding psychological part had developed the foundations for it in the sections "possession," "labor," and "distinction of individuals,"[100] still forms a fine network of legal and economic terms. The main divisions are: "right," "labor as the production and enjoyment of all," and "personal right and wrong," and each of these sections is again divided along legal and economic lines in their subsections into respective divisions. The late Nuremberg *Encyclopedia* then attempts to tear this web apart. Right is given its own place as the single lower level of "practical spirit," whereas the economy enters into the upper level, which as a whole was called "state."

With this, a process begun long ago comes to an end. In the beginnings of his concept of the state in Frankfurt, Hegel had sought to simply deny the individual without distinction, and consequently, the bearer of rights and the bearer of property fell into the same condemnation in contrast to the ideal political human being. However, the politician in Hegel gradually regained a relationship to the self-interest of the property owner, as already described in detail. In Hegel's doctrine of estates, property as such became for him the, more or less, negative precondition of the state, the apolitical "bourgeois" became the basis for the activity of the political human "living in the state." This reciprocity and dichotomy, which Hegel perceived to be the very essence of the state – the "tragedy in the ethical" – really only properly affected the bearer of the economy, whereas the bearer of right was affected only insofar as it coincided with the former. To a certain extent, the philosopher only paid attention to the human being who acquires property – when he meets the property-owning human on the way to court instead of on the way to business, he continues to mock him, just as before, as a trial-addict. This different treatment now finally comes to systematic fruition. Hegel banishes only right, alongside morality, to the vestibules of the state. The economy, however, is handled in closer connection with the state, as now the economy and only the economy, not right, is acknowledged as a necessary prerequisite of the state. This much is already evident in the late Nuremberg *Encyclopedia*. Indeed, after having separated the economy from right, Hegel seems to want to connect it so closely to the state that he does not look to assign it a proper place, but evidently thinks about it partly in connection with the governing powers, and partly in connection with the societal estates.[101] This remarkable opposition, sharpened to "tragedy" between economic and political dispositions, between the "bourgeois" and the "human living in the state," would have wholly lost the dominance over the system which had existed since 1803. It did not come to that. It could no longer determine the overall division of the system of the philosophy of spirit; but within a part of it, and indeed a major part of it, it remained in force.

The system of the *Encyclopedia* of 1817, the first system to be published in print, and, as already explained, the essentially definitive version, provided a new and definitive name for the final position of "practical spirit," as well as this position itself. Whereas in the Nuremberg system the "state" had stood within "practical" spirit, in the Heidelberg system, "ethicality" stands within "objective" spirit. And these two new names meant a new possibility for the inner configuration of their content. It was consistent with how "morality" was projected above the state in the decade of Hegel's life after 1805, when the Nuremberg *Encyclopedia* derived "practical spirit," on whose summit the state was enthroned, from the psychology of the individual will. Thus, the attempt from 1805 to assign this psychology of the will to the first part itself, and to first open the second part with its finished result, namely the "will, which is intelligence," was dropped. It was also consistent with the definitive version, which allowed the state to flow into history, that the old attempt was again taken up. In 1817, the psychology of the theoretical and practical spirit again formed the first part, and the contrast between the two parts is now quite clearly conceived as "subjective" and "objective spirit."

In that the "objective," that is, worldly nature of the middle stage, is now strongly emphasized again in the final part of this stage, which in Nuremberg had still been called "state" as a whole, the "objective" again gains a claim to a richer, even more worldly form, a claim not yet met in 1817. The state's pure world of the will is to be supported by several will-less worlds. For although that pure world of the will remains the goal, now, corresponding to its discharge into history, it is no longer set, as before, into the development of the will but rather into the development of the world of the will. In general, this pure world of the will is indeed displaced from its position in the truly absolute, which it had occupied at least with a part of its content in 1805, and it is now only the "completion of the objective spirit."[102] Thus, the designation "objective spirit" actually only concludes what was initiated by the shift in history at the end of the Nuremberg period. The state can now, since it becomes the leader of the chorus in a round-dance of worlds, again tolerate economic-social life next to itself, which was swallowed up, so to speak, in Nuremberg. And at the same time, it can now again draw close to another world to be considered: the family. Together with family and society, and above the realms of right and morality, the state now forms, assuming an older name, the realm of "ethicality."

Initially, Hegel does not closely connect the "Family" to the state, to now pursue this last major part of the systematic division on the path towards its definitive position. Instead, the family was situated partly in the psychological, and partly in the legal-economic regions of the system. In any case, the view according to which the family is the building block of the state was not followed up on after its beginnings within natural right. To this end, the disciple of Kant and Fichte took the concept of the

free individual too stridently. It was thus, so it seems, a historical consideration that facilitated the change here. The proximity into which the
state and "morality" moved in 1805, and which manifested itself in 1806
in the historical-philosophical depreciation of the state, allowed Hegel to
see a problem in the representation of the state in general, a problem he
had partly set aside and had partly thought to have solved through the
opposition of the bourgeois and the political human within the tragedy
of ethicality. The distinctively modern moment of this necessary contrast
of economic-social self-interest and a political sense of community was
emphasized more strongly than ever by its historical-philosophical association with the state of Louis XIV in 1806. However, at the same time
and for the first time since Frankfurt, the state was once again swayed
by the claims of the individual. Thus, it was a matter of determining the
place of this general foray of the individual against the state, now even
for antiquity. And this place is now found with The Phenomenology in the
conflict within Antigone between the state and family. For the family as
such is not the victim of the conflict here, but rather the state and the
family, the "upper and subterranean gods" are the unconquerable powers
between which the human being is crushed. If the Polis was the lone justified power for the human being of antiquity, as Hegel himself initially
thought and some others after him, then conflict between the human
being and community would not have even been possible. But that is not
the case, as The Phenomenology teaches. The family, that second power which
lays claim to the human being and especially to his original existence,
provides the opportunity to take a stand against the Olympian gods of the
state under the protection of other gods, namely the "subterranean" gods.
Thus, the tragedy of the human family in antiquity appears in 1806 next
to the modern tragedy of the economic human in the state – the "tragedy in the ethical" of 1806. The individual of private right had acquired
a place in the state, whereas the individual of moral law had acquired a
place, likewise in and beside the state, and even if only in tragic strife, at
least truly their own place, in the family.

But while, in its relation to the state, right had never again caused
Hegel serious difficulties after 1799, as we know, the relation of moral
law to the state still became problematic for him in 1805. The Nuremberg Propaedeutic already moves state and family into close proximity. But
the late Nuremberg Encyclopedia, which first treated right and morality as

preliminary stages to the state, does not seem to want to touch the fruitful classification of economy and society under the state that came along with this systematic distancing of right from the state; however, the relationship between family and state developed in *The Phenomenology* is not yet systematically conceived within it. While the economy and the estates are treated together within the state as that side of private right directed towards the state, the family remains distant from the state. It appears under "morality." It is as though Hegel had not yet been able to detach the early idea that morality turned towards the state of antiquity under the protection of the family from the idea of the systematic connection between state and morality, which he sought to establish after 1805. When he gave up that connection, and morality took its place below the state, the systematist did not, as he had done in the case of right with the economy, allow that side of morality turned towards the state, namely, the ethicality of the family, to stand in close association with the state but instead made the systematic fate of the family dependent on that of morality. Only the next phase of the system, the Heidelberg *Encyclopedia* of 1817, carried things further here. Without changing the major division of "right, morality, state," and just as society was detached from right, now the family was detached from morality and brought into immediate proximity to the state, which now forms the realm of "ethicality" together with these two worlds, which are helpful to it precisely because of their independence. How Hegel thought of the relationship in detail is hardly recognizable from the sketchy design of these parts of the system in 1817. He seemed, at that time, to still want to bring the family into a special connection with society, in that he appends the family to the doctrine of societal estates as the public – "universal" – estate of civil service and the – "particular" – professional classes as an estate of their own, namely that phenomenon of "individuality."[103] The concept of "individuality" would then clearly echo its original classification in the doctrine of the moral "individual." But three years later and the system has become firm. Family, society, state: family as the dark night in which the ethicality of the state is produced; society as the dull workday, in which the state works out the external means of its existence; and the state as the bright feast day of ethical life.

These would be the ways through which the individual realms of ethical life, leading all the way up to the state, sought their place in the

Systems of 1817 and 1820. And now that they have taken their place, what kind of image do they offer to the viewer?

The system begins with logic as the doctrine of pure thinking, then goes on to the doctrine which, according to its concept, should be inaccessible to this pure thinking, namely the doctrine of natural philosophy. It then rises from here as the philosophy of spirit to the third stage, where the unknowability of nature itself is known as something thought. The consciousness of the inseparability of thinking and being is at the root here, as much as in the preceding stages it was their separateness. This consciousness of the solidarity of thinking and being is itself present in the concept – it is, paradoxically speaking, still unconscious. It is this consciousness that is already "spirit," ultimately the will, but a will that has not yet been poured into a world, not yet condensed into manifold forms, and still lonely in the dull hollow of its self: "subjective spirit," the subject of psychology, beyond nature, yet without the consciousness of this freedom. It must escape this narrowness, and its freedom must become for it a world of configurations of freedom. Subjective spirit thus gives way to "objective" spirit. We are at the level of the basic actuality of spirit, of nature within spirit, so to speak.

Subjective spirit was merely the form of the spiritual; the divine indeed lived within it, but it was not this itself. It remained indifferent to its contents and, as feeling, sensation, imagination, and thought, gave shelter with the same good will to the highest, as well as the most humble. Conversely, only objective spirit is mere content. The divine indeed appears in it, but as its ultimate truth; the ungodly, merely earthly transitoriness will be revealed to it: history. Initially, objective spirit is what it has become, a world that is external to the ego, or more precisely, to the will. This world in all its entire outwardness is the world of right. Subjectivity, however, has here transformed into a vivid multiplicity of subjects, will has transformed into a multiplicity of mutually recognizing "persons," but these subjects are subjects of right alone. Their freedom is empty equality. In this first world, which the "I" built for itself, subjectivity is without any content, without a soul. Therefore, the ensouled "I," the "heart," demands its right in contrast to this empty legal subject. It also builds up a world for itself, the world of morality, in which resolutions, intentions, and goodwill, in short everything that lives only in the innermost of the human being, demands external validity. But these particularities of morality, when they are placed in contrast to the universality of right as something eternally other, degenerate into arbitrariness, into subjectivity in the bad sense. Only when particularity realizes that it is only the particular of the universal, only when the moral "I" subordinates its freedom, without giving it up, to the dictates of right, and thus, on the other hand, when the cold compelling dictate of right is filled with the wealth of the individual will, then its spirituality emerges, which is equally beyond the cool universality of law as well as the heated particularity of conviction: the world of ethicality as the harmony of freedom and law.[104] After passing through self-referential "morality," the undifferentiated "person" has become ethical "individuality."

But this ethical human is still unconscious of himself. He does not expressly want his own oneness with the universal at this stage, but rather, he encounters it, he feels it. Thus, he is a member of the family, which shows itself as the world in which ethicality, as it were, leads a naturally dark life, a life of love, of piety. He steps out of this primordial darkness into the daylight of consciousness, and his relationship to the universal should be something conscious and only conscious. The sphere of society into which he thus enters is the world that he knowingly and willingly builds – and indeed knowing, willing, and building very specific, special things. It is the world whose highest wisdom, from the perspective of the individual, is the association [Verein], and from the perspective of the whole, is the purposeful despotism of the policing state. In this world of self-interested syndicates, ethicality, which in the family was previously partial towards the slumber of mere feeling, now seems to broach the opposite extreme, the all-too-conscious, merely actual, feelingless, and thereby again unethical. The ethical in the highest sense will thus be what the dull-feeling nature of familial ethics and the purposeful clarity of social ethics uniformly contains in itself as it appears in the "corporation" based on an economic syndicate. And this unification occurs in the state. Here the individual wants the unity of himself and the whole, both as the conscious purposeful companion to the social mechanism, and also as the son of native earth. And as here the ethical foundations of society and family first harmonize together, the state thus now first becomes, as the highest blossom on the tree of ethicality, the true unity of right and morality. Only in the state do those two become reconciled, the legal coercion of the will through right, with the desired coercion of law through the heart. Only in the state do external ethos [Gesittung] and internal disposition [Gesinnung] become united.

Thus, within Hegel's definitive system, the state emerges from the will. We must now observe how Hegel depicts the image of things on each individual stage of this systematic emergence, and which threads connect his images to the actuality configured within them.

Right, to begin with what comes first systematically, and after having genetically comprehended the system, is for Hegel the private right of Rome. The entire systematic status which he assigns to right rests on this factor, which, of course, is conditioned by the age. Despite the many collected works since the seventeenth century, and especially since the eighteenth century, the scientific study of Germanic right only began with Eichhorn's major work in the first decade of the nineteenth century. When this occurred, Hegel's fundamental view of the nature of right was already clear. And even if this had not been the case, those beginnings of understanding German right would not have been apt to unsettle Hegel's fundamental view. For these early works, barring the singular Jakob Grimm, who was likely unaware of these other works, were themselves still under the spell of juridical thought, which was, after all, versed in the most advanced Roman law. The fundamental knowledge of the essentially cooperative, more or less public character of German private right, as well as the insight into the spirit of Roman right originally determined in a thoroughly public, right-based manner, which today strongly determines our idea of the nature of right, are from a more recent time. At the very least, both views owe their origin either directly or indirectly to the conflict that Hegel saw between what he took to be the purely individualistic essence of right and the ethical claims of the state, and which induced the systematist to submit right to the state. By thus recognizing how the spirit of the state was above right, that is, above individualistic right, Hegel first created the ground for a prospective new knowledge of the essence of right from the essence of the state.[105]

Now, one must not imagine this dependence of Hegel on the peculiarity of Roman right as if he were to have lapsed into the error of consciously absolutizing this right, or into the desire to purify the present forms of right by going back to the pure originality of Rome's "classical" civil right. The philosopher is far removed from the kind of endeavors that flourished among Savigny's followers. Only in the concept of right in general does he adhere to the mature outcome of Roman jurisprudence: he begins with a philosophical deduction of the concept of the person, not without characteristically transforming it, incidentally.[106] Already here, and in general in the whole integration of jurisprudence into philosophy, Hegel knows himself to be in contrast to the young Historical School of Law, a contrast that is also manifested in the fact that Hegel prefixes the already disreputable name of "natural right" to his entire book. He disavows his substantive agreement with Savigny's tendency of recognizing the essentially "positive" principle of right by invoking Montesquieu for the "true historical view," which is likewise the "genuinely philosophical" point of view, and not the more modern ones.[107] He clearly separates himself here from Savigny when he sees legislation "in connection with all the other provisions that make up the character of a nation and an age."[108] Unlike Savigny, Hegel considers the character of the people to be the outcome, not the root of legislation, beginning already in his earliest thoughts. But he then sees himself obligated, in acknowledging what is historical in right as its true justification, to seek a proper "origin" for right, in contrast to Savigny, who was spared this by the mystical concept of the origin of folk spirit. Hegel found this origin in the deductibility of basic concepts of law from philosophy. This natural right could not have been conceived in opposition to positive right since it relates to the latter, as Hegel characteristically says, like institutions to pandects.[109]

Nevertheless, in that historic right was thus guaranteed the necessity of a supra-historical deduction and, despite the acknowledgment of the historical, here the natural consequence was a different evaluation of legislation than in Savigny's circle. If right itself belonged to the cultivating forces – "moments" according to Hegel's usage – of the character of a people, then the appeal to the spirit of a people could not fundamentally restrict the legislative will. Thus, Hegel objected to Savigny's text of 1814 in quite bitter tones, in agreement with Thibaut, with whom he had maintained friendly relations since Heidelberg: "To deny the ability of a well-educated nation, or judicial estate of the same craft, a code of law [...] would be one of the greatest abuses that could be done to a nation or that estate."[110] These views, and also their closer justification in the essence of all historical explanation, which precisely indicates the uselessness of the institution in question for the present, were not first forced upon Hegel in response to Savigny. Hegel had already gone on about them in 1802. And yet he nevertheless now opposed the celebrated member of the Berlin law faculty through those views. And there was another point of conflict, also politically significant, not with the head of the "Historical School" but with the author of the *Treaty on Possession*, in that concept of the person which Hegel placed at the forefront of his book, and from which he sought to derive property and ownership, both as a concept of private right and according to their relation to public right.[111]

Hegel conceived of the person, from which he proceeded just like Roman jurisprudence, as the free will indifferent to content and directed only toward itself, that is, toward its own freedom. He thus consciously stepped into contrast with the Roman definition of a legal personality – "the human being considered according to his *status*, that is, the human being in so far as he is either a slave or free."[112] If he thus pitted the concept of the equality of everything that has human countenance, in the sense of more contemporary natural right, against the concept from antiquity of the self-evident natural distinctiveness of humankind, he likewise consciously separated himself in this definition from the modern concept of natural right, as it had been developed by Rousseau, Kant, and Fichte. According to them, right was the mutual limitation of individual free will, and thus they understood individual free will to be incidental individual caprice as such, so that the concept of a rational general will could only proceed from the mutual limitation of the individual will. By using the will as the cornerstone of objective spirit only after he had already purified it of all accidental content in the doctrine on subjective spirit, Hegel could, conversely, immediately begin with the "universal will" – a general will, then, which is not, as with those thinkers, the result of irrational individual wills, but instead denotes that universal reason is already hidden in the individual will.[113] This was, strictly speaking, a tremendous intensification of the idea of natural right. The individual, no longer as such, but insofar as he is rational, became the bearer of community. If Kant and Fichte, by taking the arbitrary drive of nature as the jurisprudential starting point and not the ethically free human being they had discovered, came to a standstill with Rousseau,[114] whom they nevertheless overcame as moral philosophers, then Hegel now introduced their new concept of moral freedom into the philosophy of right as a basic concept. Hegel, as the philosopher of right, formulated the "commandment of right" not negatively, with a concept of limitation as is the case with Kant's philosophy of right, but positively, corresponding to the Kantian formulation of the moral imperative: "*be a person and respect others as persons.*"[115] This new concept of legal personality, however, came to have the most significant consequences for the deduction of the concept of property.

Since Hegel let the incidental determinateness of the human being be sublated from the outset in the concept of the person, the relation at the level of right of the human being to things [Sache] could no longer be one of these incidental determinations, which Hegel had just now pushed aside as insignificant from the point of view of the philosophy of right. He could no longer treat the person apart from things. Thus, the relation to things became, to a certain extent, a necessary attribute of the person within the philosophy of right.[116] In doing so, Hegel was forced to discard the time-honored division between personal rights and property rights, which Kant had still been able to adopt without hesitation. In 1820, Hegel's own division thus became property, contract, and the breach of rights. To Hegel, "property" was the exact field in which the right of personhood had an effect – "personal right [is] essentially *property law* [Sachenrecht]."[117] This now determined his doctrine of possession and property. For since the legal relationship of the human being to the "things" was determined through personality for Hegel, therefore ownership, that is, the natural relation of human beings to things, had to be what was actually important for Hegel in terms of legal rights. Whereas, for the view that saw in the relationship to things only an additional feature to the already existing legal personality, this natural relationship of "ownership" first attained legal connection through that aspect of "property" which was created by right itself.

Savigny, for example, in his famous first book, set forth the rapidly prevailing proposition that possession as such does not enjoy legal protection under classical Roman right, and that the modern development of pandect law, which protected the owner directly, and not only by detour through the property owner, was a falsification based on misunderstanding. The practical-political significance of this idea, which, however, had hardly been taken into consideration by Savigny himself, lay in the field of the manifold mixed property relations that had developed on German soil out of the spirit of lending rights, especially for the farmer. Here, it was really of the highest importance whether one derived a legally independent right from the use of a piece of land, even if encumbered, in contrast to the right of the landlord which, according to the classical view of right was the only original right, even if it may have become practically devoid of content. Possession and property, ultimately German and Roman concepts of right, the *usus modernus pandectarum*, as it had here distinctively entered into the language of General Common Law, stood in contrast with a retrospective historical desire to renew "classical" legal concepts of right. It was Hegel who took up this struggle in the field of the philosophy of right. Just as Prussia's General Common Law recognized any self-serving proprietorship as "incomplete possession," while the classical Romanists only allowed the "master" and not the "proprietor" to be legal owners, Hegel also readily addressed the functional user as the owner and rejected the idea of "property without use" as an "empty abstraction." For the politically most interesting relations – "*dominium directum* and *dominium utile*, the *emphyteutic* contract, and the further relations of estates held in fee to their hereditary wages, interests paid, commutations, and manual wages"[118] – Hegel again claimed, again in direct connection to the language of the Prussian code of law, and here, incidentally, also the Austrian code of law, which conceives of these relations as "divided property" (a language extremely annoying for a strictly Romanist mind) that "for the sake of encumbrances" in this case there should be "two *owners*," not, however, communal ownership.[119] Hegel hereby alienated the Roman concept of property so distinctively from its classical sense that, in the wake of the development of common and Prussian law, Hegel had dragged the concept of property over into the concept of possession. The feudal state of the Middle Ages could be regarded as a precursor to the ideas of 1789, both here and elsewhere, for example in the equation of medieval estates and modern popular representation. The concept of property, as an incidental determination added to the person, gave way to the new concept, which claimed, as the very essence of the "person," that it creates for itself a sphere of external existence. It is not too far-fetched to recall for the pupil of Adam Smith, who Hegel indeed was in his view of economic life, the consequential connection for world history between "wealth" and "labor" upon which the great Scot founded his economy of individualism. For Hegel, it was

the active use of something, not the inactive claim to it, that made someone the owner.

And the fact that with these views on the affiliation of political freedom and economic freedom Hegel knew himself to be in such great
historical context is shown strikingly in the passage where he depicts
both their earliest roots at the beginning of the new epoch, as well as
their immediate emergence in the recent present: "It is likely due to the
span of one-and-a-half thousand years that the *freedom of the person* began to
blossom through Christianity, and that it has become, under only a small
part of the human race, a general principle. *The freedom of property*, however,
has been acknowledged here and there as a principle only since yesterday, so to speak. This is an example from world history on the length of
time required for spirit to progress in its self-consciousness, contrasted
with the impatience of the opinionated mind."[120] By thus introducing
in full consciousness the individual idea of freedom into the philosophy
of private right through his distinctive concept of will, and allowing it
to become the concept of the free property owner, Hegel is thus the first
person in the movement of natural right to establish a connection with
what happened after the night of August 4 in over half of Europe. He
does not find this connection through a pale universality, that is, he does
not merely see the freedom of the person but seeks to unwind the subtle
conceptual threads between the freedom of the person and the freedom
of property. However, he was not moved by what the Prussian Edict of
October 1807, liberating the peasants, had dressed up in proud words,
namely that henceforth there would be "only free people" in Prussia.
Instead, what comes into consideration in Hegel's search for conceptual
connections, one could say, was the occurrence of this proposition in
a legislative act essentially directed towards the liberation of property.
Indeed, this was the basic political fact that the Prussian Reform Party
had been counting on since 1807, and which found its classic expression at the same time as Hegel's book was published in the records of the
Prussian Chancellor when he declared, as the starting point for a Prussian
constitution, the following: "We have nothing but free proprietors."[121] It
was not the incidence of free proprietors as such, but the unconditional
political necessity of having "nothing but" free proprietors that was fundamentally new in the world of Prussian reform. And from the view of
a philosophy of right, Hegel's service was to have initially grasped the

political significance of the idea of pure private right. Savigny was far removed from wishing to touch upon this foundation of the new Prussia. It was not the politician with Savigny, but the romantic-historical scholar who had lost thoughtful connection here to the living age, as Savigny's name stands at the opening of the historical work in which a brilliant historian fundamentally broke for the first time with the view that had been established since Machiavelli and Montesquieu on the unlawful character of Lizin's agrarian reform. Niebuhr's steady and pithy sentences of 1811 clearly indicate the greatness of Prussia's agricultural policy. And again, Hegel, albeit not quite so decisive in the question of right but here still in the sense of that Machiavelli-Montesquieu conception – which might appear less "terrible" to Hegel's austere sense of state than to that of the orthodox Fries – nevertheless placed himself in the matter on the same ground as Niebuhr's work of history when he saw in those events of Roman history a victory of "private property" over the "commonality" of land ownership. Nevertheless, it remains significant how the two, Savigny's friend Niehbuhr and his opponent Hegel, came to terms with the new fact that the Linzin Reform appeared to be a transition from domains to a private economy. Niebuhr showed the legitimacy of events and Hegel was pleased with the victory of the "rational moment," although it happened "at the expense of other rights."[122]

The relevant political questions are far from exhausted with this treatment of the concept of ownership. Above all, the major question remains how Hegel avoided being driven beyond the necessity of property further to the thought of the necessary legality of property.[123] The fact that practical politics did not progress from the individualist to the socialist state economy is less surprising than the fact that this was somehow avoided by a political theory working so strongly with the general concept of the person. The answer to this question is that Hegel, although he talks about it often, does not yet speak his final word on it in the section on "Right." It was the fact that he treats right as one of the basic conditions but nevertheless outside of actual "ethicality," and that he entirely withdraws both family and society from right. He withdraws them so entirely that ever since 1820 he altogether disowns the inherited concept of familial right altogether and hereditary law is treated in the philosophy of the family, not that of right. It was precisely this systematic separation that makes it possible for Hegel to allow right to come into its right, and yet confine it within fixed limits with respect to a higher sphere. As was said before, it was ultimately against the individualistic spirit of Roman private right of the classical epoch that Hegel's old political hostility turned, and this spirit was thereby both acknowledged and rendered harmless. The right that was absent from this spirit and a will that wanted more than itself, these things were indeed more than right and legal will.[124] For Hegel, the realm of "ethicality" – family, society, state – had already begun. The simply free proprietor, as such, was the simple precondition of this realm of the ethical; he himself was not yet within it: he was a "person," not a member of the family, not a professional, not a citizen: not an ethical human being.

If Hegel detached the family so completely from their relations of right, it was – as we observed – related to his idea that the right of Rome was the typical right in general and that according to the original essence of right it was oriented towards being rigorously individualistic. This idea in which the authority of the Roman father over his family was not so much the expression of an original family division, or clan-like organization, but instead an unlimited abundance of right of the admittedly privileged individual, was not characteristic of Hegel alone. Rather, it was widespread in the science of that time. As we know today, this idea was based on an erroneous understanding which, even at that time, was attacked by individuals such as Gibbon[125] and Montesquieu[126] but which itself goes back to the traditions of antiquity on the development of Roman hereditary laws. In the beginning, there existed a period of thorough testamentary freedom, which would have found its classical version in a proposition of the twelve panels which today, by the way, is understood in the opposite way.[127] Thus, by conceiving the development of the lawful right of inheritance of relatives in Rome as the mere correction of an originally purely individualistic concept of property, Hegel, from this proprietary standpoint, had to reject the apparent underlying concept of family. And indeed, because Hegel's concept of the person and the necessity of property was nonetheless surpassed, he was forced to systematically extricate the family and its right, as he thought it should be constructed, from the philosophy of right and assign it to another place. We already know in what sense he chose "ethicality" as such. We now move to observe the details of the contemporary historical context of this concept of family, a concept for the sake of which Hegel denied such a deeply rooted concept as that of family law.

Coming from the Enlightenment, the family was constructed in a strictly legalistic manner according to the scheme of a contract, especially by Kant. This corresponded to the general situation of the times, in which the traditional patriarchal rigidity of family relations coincided with the need for sound reasoning, as was appropriate to the Enlightenment. The marriage of convenience was both the rule and the ideal. When in the following period the thought of love again came into an obvious connection with that of marriage, this is attributable to the reaction against the mood of the times at the end of the century and its palpitation for the inalienable rights of the heart. As we know, during his Frankfurt years, Hegel had temporarily attributed a rather fundamental philosophical significance to this romantic concept of love. Even then, there were distinctive unmediated attempts by him to arrive at his own construction of the relations of rights for the family, attempts which, as we shall see, continued in their effects into the *Philosophy of Right* of 1820. But the philosopher did not provide his final assessment of the family directly from those writings. He first had to completely overcome the Romantic epoch of his thinking, including on this point. This is something we have already observed, especially how the knowledge of the state-founding life of the family arose for Hegel from Sophocles' *Antigone*. Yet the way family appears in the System of 1820 – as a separate ethical power with respect to the state and yet the one pillar on which it rests – is something completely new. It was certainly expressed in antiquity, and in the eighteenth century it was by no means forgotten, that the family is the foundational element of the state.[128] But this was quite distinct from Hegel's understanding. Aristotle – and it is Aristotle whom all subsequent ones follow – does not speak of the family as a community in the ethical sense, but of the "house," that is, of a unification of economics and right. Thus, what follows from Aristotle, and those who subsequently accepted his concept, is to a certain extent an acknowledgment of the family, of the "house," as an element of the constitution of the state. However, Hegel rejects this point in a very modern fashion, indeed, as a person living after 1789. For Hegel, the family – and this is the essence of its systematic position – is an entity external to the state. It is, as an organization, not a member of the state's body. Instead, its relation to the state is rooted in the fact that it is the workshop in which the spirit of the individual is prepared for the state. If before Hegel the house itself was a piece of the whole of the state, now, with Hegel, it is only that the human being is raised in the house. That is why Hegel, although he constructed the family as an existing world, could not forgo feeling as such, that is, could not forgo "love." The systematic place of the family arose from the fact that, resting on feelings, it itself could become a nursery of feeling from which ethical dispositions could grow. With this, the knowledge of the house once obtained from *Antigone* culminates as an independent ethical power with respect to the state. What to the Attic poet was a conflict between the holy dignity of the law, upon which a true civil state should rest, and the brute force of a "tyrant," this was what the modern philosopher – to whom the "tyrant" did not seem so terrible or so contrary to the state as he may have for the Athenian of the Periclean age – had unintentionally reinterpreted. Whereas for the Athenian, whose people claimed to be the most pious of all the Hellenes, the right of the state was certainly on the side of the pious sister, for the pupil of Machiavelli, Robespierre, and Napoleon – the great teachers of state law – had moved unnoticed to the side of Creon. The tyrant represented the state to him, the sister a completely different, nevertheless also justified, and with respect to the state, truly justified ethical order, namely the house. It is from this basic view, according to which the family appears as a feeling-based ethical body of its own, with its own purpose outside of the state, albeit for the state, that Hegel's critique of the then currently accepted family law proceeds.

It is clear from the outset that this doctrine of the family, however distinctive it always was, ultimately had certain things in common with this then-accepted law. In particular, Hegel's acknowledgement of "feeling" for the sake of the resulting disposition, the disposition upon which the state is founded, could surely be combined with the moderate tendency of Prussian Common Law from the Enlightenment, at times even with Napoleonic right, both of which acknowledged the idea of contract in marriage, as far as it was compatible with the state order or also compatible with ecclesiastical claims. Even if this encounter was external, or basically coincidental and based on completely different conditions, it nevertheless led to a series of exact parallels between Hegel and Prussian legal conditions, parallels which may of course have their bases in the fact that during his Frankfurt years of apprenticeship Hegel had closely studied this right. Thus, even the thoroughly unromantic definition of

the purpose of marriage, wherein it "can be rooted only in mutual love
and aid,"[129] corresponds in terms of Common Law and, with the exception of the characteristic Hegelian emphasis on "love," almost literally
with the proposition from the Frederician code of law: "A valid marriage
can also be entered into for reciprocal support."[130] The fact that in the
treatment of the church's involvement in marriage Hegel more or less
exactly agrees with the practice in place under Altenstein, this only needs
to be mentioned for now. In contrast, this is the place to talk about the
grounds for divorce. Common Law did not go as far as the Napoleonic
Code, which in its original version, and in the version that remained
valid in Germany, considered mutual consent to be sufficient. The judge
allowed divorce, at least in a pre-arranged marriage, only when "according to the content of the records the antagonism is so intense and deeply
rooted that there is no hope left for rapprochement and for the attainment
of the ends of marriage."[131] Hegel's paragraph reads like a philosophical commentary on this, starting from the necessity of the "intimacy of
subjective disposition and sentiment": "Just as little as there can be coercion to enter into marriage, just as little may there otherwise be a merely
legal positive bond that is able to hold the subjects together in the face
of adverse and hostile sentiments and actions that have arisen. Instead, a
third moral authority is needed, which preserves the right of marriage
against the mere opinion of such a disposition and against the accidental
nature of a merely temporary mood, distinguishing it from total alienation, and establishes the latter, in order in this case to be able to *dissolve
the marriage*."[132] However, the different starting points become clear when
one considers that in the case of an unarranged marriage Common Law
considers mutual consent to be sufficient. Here the fundamental stance
towards contract from the Enlightenment breaks through, whereas
Hegel, in his basic view, cannot of course allow such a facilitating exception for pure reasons of convenience. – Exact agreement from likewise
completely different starting points is found again in the question of
marriage-hindering degrees of relationship. Common Law contained the
general tendency to largely remove Romanticist and canonical obstacles,
whereby it left behind both the Napoleonic Code and the Austrian code
of law, likewise of the Enlightenment.[133] When Hegel declares marriage
of relatives to be forbidden, because marriage can only be taken as a free
commitment of personalities with no preexisting natural bonds, that is,

only if husband and wife belong to "separate families,"[134] he now seems to attribute the relevant paragraphs of the Prussian code of law to a view taken from his own basic view. In practice, with one justified exception, Common Law ruled out marriage only within the actual family, between parents and children, and between siblings, including the case of total lack of consanguinity, that is also including between stepparents and stepchildren. Contrary to Prussian law, Hegel carries out an account of marital property law. In an inversion to Common Law, he presupposes community of property – "common property"[135] – which is only limited through the marriage contract. Especially when one considers how those early reflections on "love" from Frankfurt ended in a construction of the inner conceptual necessity of marital community of property,[136] it is not too bold to see here an emergence of the distinctively Hegelian conception of family which is fundamentally opposed to the idea of a contract. It is also a contrast between Hegel and Common Law that the latter acknowledges "free assets" for children,[137] whereas Hegel does not want to grant particular property to any member of the family.[138] With the raising of children Hegel again follows, almost in the same order – "nutrition," "education," "children's services," "discipline"[139] – the arrangement of Common Law: subsistence,[140] education and instruction,[141] parental discipline, then three points not mentioned by Hegel, and then the duty of the children towards domestic chores.[142] These latter, which Common Law limits in the sense of the pre-industrial age to assistance with the economy and trade of the parents, Hegel also confines to "what is common to family support in general."[143] And just as Common Law acknowledges the legal ground of "parental rearing" only in the "education" of the children, so too does Hegel reject "justice" as the ground for parental rearing, and likewise acknowledges education, with a conveyance common to him – "the elevation of the universal into [...] consciousness and will"[144] – as the sole legal ground of "parental rearing."

Finally, with hereditary law, as already stated, Hegel follows the modern development of right resolutely and in full consciousness.[145] He may even have had an awareness at this point to represent Germanic right in opposition to Roman right. For it was Pütter's view, which Pütter had specially developed to historically support the modern rights of princes, that the illegality of the last testament in the oldest form of German right had to be explained by the Proto-Germanic principle of common family property.[146] And even before that, Thomasius had praised the German exclusivity of the legal line of succession in opposition to the Roman last testament.[147] Thus, Hegel also refers to inheritance as entering into "distinctive possession" of "inherently common assets."[148] Also here, again of course not in the reasoning, but in the matter itself, Hegel's view coincides exactly with Common Law, which also, in contrast to common right, as well as the Napoleonic Code and even the Austrian code of law, is not founded on the Roman principle of succession, but rather on the unconditional validity of the inheritance principle.

But Hegel's final reason for taking this position lies even deeper than its justification makes it seem. This becomes clear when Hegel fundamentally rejects the further enhancement of the family-like character of hereditary law, as it existed in the peasant inheritance law, as well as in the *fideicommissum*. It is not a matter of the "abstraction" of the tribe, of "what family is called in general," it is not a matter of the extended family, but rather of the concrete "singularly actual" [eigentümlich wirkliche] family.[149] Only this family can provide what Hegel requires: an ethical spirit can only emerge from the "sensibility for actually present individuals"[150] and this is not the spirit of one individual or of one estate but the ethicality of all, which the state requires. Therefore, "not this house or tribe, but the family *as such*"[151] must be preserved through hereditary law. The necessity of the family, in which the individual as such has no property, is as universal to the philosopher as the necessity of property is for the person. And in this case, Hegel's position against the free last testament with regard to hereditary law is to be understood as the balancing of these two universal necessities. The individual must have property, for only in this way does he prove himself as a person. But through the freedom of choice, which this individual possesses in his right and for whose most blatant expression Hegel adopts the "old Roman" freedom to draw one's final testament, the universality of property is in danger. The freedom to draw one's final testament is therefore to be eliminated in order to secure property for the "person" by securing this property – before securing the "person." Thus, property is anchored in the family, in which the human being is acknowledged as an individual, without thereby being "free" in the individualistic sense of right. The hereditary law of the family, based on the communality of family assets, serves to maintain the necessary connection between person and property without having to directly make use of the state or society. It is the first and decisive line of demarcation by way of which Hegel's thesis on the property necessary for each individual separates in advance from Communism, which some years later was to recognize in the person of St. Simon's disciple, Amand Bazard, familial hereditary law as its proper adversary. The next step in this direction, which Hegel takes in the section on "Society," is only the consequence of this first step.

Civil society – the word does not originate with Hegel but received its pronounced sense from him. No part of his system of the philosophy of state has received such unvarying acknowledgment through the changing assessments of the whole as this one. Nor has any other part had such far-reaching external repercussions. The word, to begin with, was very popular at the end of the eighteenth century, chiefly through a book by Ferguson. Hegel's deed [Tat] was that, in full consciousness, he gave it a strictly limited sense: he called society the life of common human beings in larger associations, even in the state and beyond the state, insofar as it was not the life of the state itself but stood more or less only in an encompassing connection to the state. In doing so, Hegel created the possibility of incorporating into his system the concept of the relation between human being and community in terms of natural right without letting this relation dominate. Hegel expressly proclaimed, he who as a pupil himself had once quoted from Sulzer's book, which consistently worked with the following confusion, that it was the failure of natural right to confuse society and state by imagining the state "as a unity of separate persons, which is only commonality."[152] For civil society, the view holds which only wants to know of independent individuals who are connected only "through their *needs* and through the *judicial system* as a means for the security of persons and property and through an *external order* for their special and common interests."[153] It is the "external" state, the "state of *need*," the "*state of understanding*."[154]

How Hegel himself had developed this systematic is known to us. The sharp distinction by way of which the right of the "mechanical" was preserved within an "organic" state view was at first imposed on him by the apparent irrevocability of Adam Smith's basic ideas. The economy, as it forms the beginning of this part, is its most original content. The economy initially determines, biographically as well as historically, the

concept which Hegel forms of the whole: the "system of total interdependence," based on the self-interest of all. But soon, other external
functions of the state crystallize around this core, namely legal protection and "policing," in the broad sense that the term then had when it
referred to the whole field of internal administration, as well as its counterpart, the self-governance of the "corporation." In 1820, however, one
last thing was added: the economy now draws into itself a part of the
doctrine of the state that had hitherto been regarded by the philosopher
as a piece of the "state constitution," indeed, at first in opposition to state
government as the true content of the former: the doctrine of the estates.
And with this, the idea of the "external state" comes to its conclusion:
not only the economic human being belongs to "society," looking for
security and right, but the professional human being in general, the
human being as a member of his estate. For the state he is not – directly
and initially – a part of any of this. As the state is of society, so, as a
bearer of the state, the human being separates himself from the "particular person" as a member of society.[155] In thinking this concept of society through, which incidentally belongs only to "the modern world,"[156]
there is now room for the modern concept of the citizen. This is the most
important consequence, and biographically what comes last, as a result
of the Hegelian concept of society.

Hegel sees economic life – the "system of needs" – through the eyes
of the classical national economists of the West, and honorably mentions
the constellation of Smith, Say and Ricardo.[157] Hegel adopts the assumption from which this school secured an almost one-hundred-year after-
life for the fundamental method of thinking about natural right in the
sphere of economics: the turning "of *subjective self-interest* into the *contribution towards the satisfaction of the needs of all others*" and the emergence of "*general
assets*" from this "total entwinement of everyone's interdependence."[158]
But just as in 1802, Hegel immediately emphasizes that the possibility for the individual to have a stake in general assets is conditioned by
"capital" and "skill."[159] Far from being a critique of the basic concept of
economic harmony, Hegel sees in this the justification of the equality of
people's assets.[160] He now conceives of the necessity of the estates based
on the general varieties of work as something purely economic. They
are still the three older estates from 1802, but they now look different. A significant reversal is that their structure is derived economically

and is no longer based on ethical and psychological considerations. The ethicality of the estates is now only a result and not a presupposition of the estates. The free choice of profession, already acknowledged as the modern principle in 1802, is only first truly carried out as a guiding idea through the purely economic conception of estate structure. Both of these, the free choice of profession and the economic concept of the estates, belong together.[161]

The politician likewise now also acknowledges differences in estates. Apart from the structure of popular representation based on estate to be discussed later, it occurs especially with a justification of jury trials peculiar to Hegel. For the most part, Hegel appropriated the revolutionary justification of the institution in Prussia's Rhenish province, of which the German liberals had recently made a programmatic claim: "*every cultivated person*"[162] is entitled to a statement of the facts, and it is the "right of the litigant's self-consciousness"[163] to know it will be judged by its peers. But this last idea on the necessary confidence of the litigant in the judge is bound up with another idea, namely, that confidence is based primarily on the equality of the litigant with the deciding party, "according to their particularity, estate, and the like."[164] Here Hegel takes the older, more Germanic than revolutionary, justified claim for an estate-based jury, as he had already formulated it in 1802, at that time perhaps with an eye towards Prussian Common Law. As far as the individual estates are concerned, the first had already lost the appearance of a landowning noble official in 1805 and had taken on highly bureaucratic features. The brief remark that Hegel now dedicated to this estate shows clearly that he essentially had a professional civil service in mind. The special relationship that the first estate had with peasants in 1802 has disappeared.[165] The peasantry, without altogether going beyond its sphere – except in the one case that more recently agriculture is run, "upon reflection, likewise as a factory"[166] – is no longer depicted with the same ridicule of 1802, and even of 1805. Now, the peasantry works a soil which is capable of being "exclusive private property."[167] The landed nobility seems ascribed to it instead of being held merely by the first estate alone, as in 1802. Even a special communication by the nobility for peasants for state legal protection, which was asked for in 1802, is no longer at issue. What remained was above all only that right, not in its content, but in its form as the administration of justice, somehow apparently encounters the peasant in a simpler manner than is the case with other estates. But this circumstance is now combined with the different manner by way of which common educational content and faith approach the individual estates in general. According to the sketches from 1805, the citizen, or as it is tellingly termed, the trade class, is split into the classes of craftsman, manufacturer, and merchant.[168] Hegel also no longer displays that same irony towards that estate, between noble officer and peasant soldier, which in 1802 he had taken as the estate "deprived of bravery." This is the image of the estates in 1820.

With this, Hegel reflects the image of a new German society, and in particular the image of society as it was housed within the Prussian state during these decades. This becomes clear precisely in comparing the philosopher's ideal of the estates from 1802, which was likewise strongly oriented towards the conditions in Prussia as mediated through Common Law. Initially, the estates are now regarded as such, not merely according to their significance within the framework of the state, but as independent economic and social formations. There is – and this is a very decisive difference between 1802 and 1820, as well as between the Prussia of then and the Prussia of now – no longer any difference in their military significance; whereas, in 1802 this was the most prominent feature. The first estate is the estate of civil service, no longer that of the landed nobility. Common Law already included teachers, clerics, and officers under "civil servants." Understood in this manner, in these years after 1815, the nobility of the general Common Law were no longer truly the "first" estate in the Prussian state. Instead, this was reserved for modern civil servants. The peasantry, in part already through the rationalization of operations – Albrecht Daniel Thaer had been working in Möglin since 1806 – had become a trade class, settling everywhere possible as their own proprietors together with the landlord in a community of estates, no longer dependent on landed nobility as such to administer justice. The patrimonial courts were appointed by the landlord, but without distinction between his civilian or noble birth, and made use of only as a transferred piece of state legal administration. Finally, the civilian estate was no longer an estate of fearful petty bourgeois, but instead its typical representatives were manufacturers, merchants, or craftsmen. All three were still equally characteristic of the estate and a difference of interest within the estate was not noticeable. Compared to the farmer, whose dependence on the rule of nature makes him easily inclined to subservience to people, the civilian estate as a whole is attributed a sense of self, a sense for freedom, and a claim towards conditions protected by law. One can see that the political difference between city and countryside has by no means yet been bridged. Then again, internal contrasts are still slumbering in the urban population, contrasts which will later divide them among themselves. The modern classes [Stände] of factory owner and wholesale merchant are already emerging from this population – but not yet as its leading and determining element. If one disregards the, albeit important, provincial differences of Prussia at that time, and takes into account the inner convergence of the spatially separated, societally interrelated layers of the monarchy in the east and west, which were to become apparent in the constitutional struggles of the 1840s, then the Hegelian image corresponds to this as precisely as is possible in an account that is, after all, philosophically generalized. It corresponds to this above all in that one characteristic that separates Prussian society most distinctly from that of England or France, disregarding those differences that were based on past history: a fourth estate, an estate of industrial laborers, did not yet exist as an estate in Prussia and it does not exist as an estate in Hegel's system.

Not as an "estate." But the appearance itself had not remained hidden from Hegel. This was already ensured through his attentiveness to political conditions, especially in England.[169] As early as 1802, Hegel had developed the idea, still quite remote from Adam Smith and perhaps first expressed by Jacques Necker in 1775, that wealth has a tendency to "accumulate" among "immensely rich individuals," and is thus necessarily "associated with the deepest poverty."[170] From this accumulation theory of capital Hegel developed the danger of the moral dissolution of the trade class, which the government must "work against to the highest degree."[171] At the time, Hegel saw the means to this, without failing to recognize the necessity that in any case a part of the class would be "sacrificed to factory work and relinquished to crudeness"[172] in a "Konstitution"[173] of the class. The now unavoidable economic relationships of dependency were to be personalized through guild-like groupings of employers and employees in the same entity and thus made ethical, while at the same time keeping in mind a statutory additional burden for the rich in the case of public charges. It was therefore necessary to reorganize the trade class in the early age of large-scale capitalist enterprises to provide it with a new class-character [Standescharakter]. All of these ideas, after they had receded in 1805, now return in 1820. In the meantime, the massive social shift that Hegel had already seen in 1802 had progressed so far that, at least in Western Europe, the age of the first comprehensive socialist economic theories soon drew near. Hegel partly expressed his old thoughts when he now develops a detailed theory of the "corporation," and makes the case for a renewal of the old guild system, which, however, must unite laborers and capitalists in common entities. He attributes the dissolution of the guild constitution to a "conspicuous" part of the frightening social phenomena of the dawning capitalist age. But only to a part. He sees the main reason for this dissolution in the advent of the machine and the change in labor relations thereby brought about.[174] Even apart from this, now only conditional, endorsement of the corporation as a remedy for the social damage of capitalism, it will be difficult today to brush aside this thought of Hegel's as "reactionary," as one was inclined to do in the era of economic liberalism. Above all, the fundamental difference between Hegel's proposal and all guild systems must be taken into account: namely, the inclusion of employer and employee in the same "corporation." Even the generation before the war, whose social utopians strove for "factory parliamentarism," whose social political realists strove for the collective agreement, could have recognized their forbearer in Hegel. And this is to say nothing of the present generation.

Hegel sees the actual cause of social misery, as already stated, in the "mechanization" of labor. He expressly refers to the conditions in England, from which much can be learned. As in 1802, he seeks to derive the concentration of "wealth" from the concepts of need, pleasure, and labor. The *"isolation and narrowness"* of work in the age of the machine on the one hand, and boundless needs on the other, are the reasons for "the *dependence* and *distress* of the class [Klasse] bound to this work, which is connected to the inability to perceive and enjoy other abilities, especially the intellectual advantages of civil society."[175] On this basis, the process now continues on its own. Hegel touches upon the idea of the conceptual connection between the theory of impoverishment, the industrial reserve army, and the iron law of wages, first developed by French theoreticians of the eighteenth century,[176] when he says in a separate paragraph about the "rabble" – the word "proletariat" was not yet in use – : "When a large mass of people sinks below a certain standard of living – a level regulated automatically as the one necessary for a member of society – and when there is a consequent loss of the sense of right, of honesty, and of the dignity of supporting oneself through one's own activity and labor, the result is the creation of a *rabble*, which in turn makes it much easier for disproportionate wealth to be concentrated in a few hands."[177] The psychological definition of the "rabble" that Hegel gives here already points to the reason that he rejects government assistance from the outset, in this case genuinely in the spirit of civil economics of the nineteenth century: it would be "against the principle of civil society" – precisely economic individualism – "and of its individuals' feeling of their independence and honor."[178] But he also rejects the acknowledgement of the right to work: it likewise only makes the malady worse, which rests on the abundance of production and the lack of consumption.[179] He summarizes the situation with an ingenious catchphrase, entirely in the spirit of a subsequent academic socialism, which comprehends the immediate phenomena – namely, "excess of poverty and the creation of the rabble"[180] – out of the essence of society as a whole, not as a condition of illness to be alleviated by small means directed towards individual parts: society is "not rich enough in its *excess of wealth*."[181] Only incidentally, and as evidence of his exasperation in all "direct" means of a charitable or economic reformist social policy, with the exception of the creation of modern guild organizations, does Hegel mention here the following as the "the most direct" means that have been "put to the test" in England, and especially in Scotland: "to leave the poor to their fate and to direct them towards public begging."[182] For Hegel himself, in seeing the matter grounded in the essence of civil society, also already knows the remedy, likewise founded in the essence, that is, in the inner "dialectic" of this society, and thus directed not at the symptoms but at the root of the malady. It is precisely "this, its dialectic," that is, these unavoidable deficiencies that come with the nature of civil society, that drives civil society beyond itself.[183] Initially, foreign trade, and furthermore colonization – things Hegel had previously known nothing about in this socio-political context – affected the transformation of civil society, through which civil society "partially created for itself the return to the family principle upon new ground for a segment of its population, and thereby partially created a new need and field for its diligent work."[184] Thus, the socio-political significance of world trade and colonies was the transformation of the industrial surplus of people into peasant colonists and the creation of new markets. And colonies, mind you, not in the "sporadic"[185] manner of German emigration of that time, which remains without benefit for the motherland, but as a conscious colonial policy.

With this solution of the social question, Hegel leaves the contemporary theory of his age far behind. Just as Hegel likewise, seen from the standpoint of today's economic theory,[186] also annuls in advance Marx's surplus-value theory of capitalism, which rests so entirely on the presupposition of a hopelessly closed economic system. In Germany, this idea was expressed in this context in an effective political manner only in the last decades before the war, and it is curious to see how Hegel, on the occasion of speaking on the significance of world trade for the character of a people, uses words of that same inner power of vision and worldly enthusiasm which came in those decades to the herald of this idea, Friedrich Naumann, when he accentuates the following: the sea, with its power to enliven peoples, how here "the consolidation on this clod of earth and the limited circles of civilian life are displaced by the elements of fluidity, danger and ruin"[187] and how therefore "all great, internally aspiring nations push towards the sea."[188]

If Hegel had been able to conceive of the necessity of free property in the sense of the leading tendency of his age, without letting himself be carried away by the thought of necessarily equal property, then this was made possible for him through his doctrine on the confinement of property to family.[189] This doctrine, however, he did not fail to recognize, was in danger of again falling apart with regard to Hegel's own concept of civil society. After all, according to his own concept, society emerges from the perpetual dissolution of the family; the emergence from the family makes the family member a member of civil society. As such, one could only find the natural basis of a professional life tied to fixed family property in the peasantry estate.[190] In the trade class, on the other hand, corresponding natural ties are lacking. This is where Hegel's doctrine of the "corporation" came into play: equipped with a certain self-governance vis-à-vis the state, it formed a "*second family*"[191] for the individual of the trade class. Only here is family life secured.[192]

The "reactionary" element of Hegel's doctrine of corporations is much more strongly pronounced here than in the relation to the problem of the fourth estate. It is true that Hegel is far from wanting to renew the "medieval" guild; under no circumstances should his corporation, like that one, possess its own entitlement vis-à-vis the state.[193] But still, from the perspective of the prevailing doctrine of free enterprise, this reactionary element was a forcible means. Hegel needed it to maintain the basic premise – the necessity of free property – without it confusing the concept for him. Freedom of trade, which to Hegel, as to his German contemporaries, at least those of Northern Germany, had been a self-evident requirement in theory since Adam Smith – "*on the whole*" the "right relationship" between production and consumption establishes "itself"[194] – still requires state oversight on price formation, food quality, etc., just as in 1802 and 1805, and for the same reasons as then. And if Hegel was still fundamentally aligned here with the classical political economics of England, he distanced himself greatly from his teachers Smith, Say, and Ricardo through the further restriction of free enterprise through guild-like corporations. Even if the protection of family assets was a prerequisite to all of them for the self-evident existence of private property, none had recognized this with the same sharpness as Hegel, and therefore they saw no necessity to bring about this protection with as strong means as Hegel had considered appropriate.

Aside from the socio-political significance of the corporation in a broader sense, part of the disposition presupposed by the state also arises from the "corporation," as from the family. Here, the individual knows himself to be "acknowledged, knows that he belongs to a whole that is itself a member of general society, that he is of interest and worth the endeavor for the unselfish purpose of this whole: – Thus, the individual has *its honor in its class* [Stand]."[195] Together, the family and the corporation form the root of the state, not as organizations that compose or erect the state, as all older social science had understood them but instead as generative sites for that disposition which the state presupposes. The corporation fulfills this task, in particular, as the ethicization [Versittlichung] of "civil society,"[196] which originally depends purely upon the egoism of the individual. The customs of the home train the human being for the natural, unconscious self-integration into a whole; the corporation teaches him conscious and purposeful work for the needs of a community. Hegel himself finely relates the opposition of family and corporation to that of countryside and city, peasant and citizen. The state establishes itself upon both; it presupposes both dispositions and both at the same time. That Hegel's philosophy of the state begins with the concept of the will, that it refuses to conceive of this will one-sidedly as the formal will of the legal personality or even as the free choice of the moral human – that it rather lifts the will of the ethical individual above the will of legal coercion and moral temperament, this all now leads to a decisive result. For its foundation, Hegel's state construction seeks the concept of a disposition towards the state [Staatsgesinnung].

The more recent movement of natural right, at the end of which Hegel placed himself with this academic feat, began with the individual and, as we have already explained and must now consider more closely, from there sought to gain the concept of community. In the individual human being, it knew of the impulses of the soul that indirectly, or directly, drove this individual towards community. However, in the beginning, it suspected nothing of a conscious, and likewise necessarily known, will towards community. It could not have wanted to know anything about it. For its aim was precisely to construct the development of community from the detached individual human as such, whose impulses, even where they had community as their object, consciously aimed only at this individual's own satisfaction. It was precisely the historical merit of natural right to have pursued this and nothing else. The intrinsic value, or at least the intrinsic right, of community was considered to be the unquestionable content of revelation. As a secular science, natural right had achieved great things in terms of those centuries when it demonstrated the same insight, but on the basis of purely secular presuppositions, whether it was in order to confirm the revealed truth or to make it superfluous. But the concept of the egoistic individual presented itself, as such, as a pure worldly presupposition with Roman law as its basis and also with the church as that which belonged to the human being outside of revelation. It was on this basis that the state constructions of Grotius, as well as Hobbes, Locke, and Rousseau, were undertaken. And then the task came to Kant and Fichte, and they also completed it. But in the case of the German thinkers, what had made good sense to their predecessors – starting from the "natural" human being – stood in contradiction to their own system. As the first in the field of Christian culture with minds completely detached from that dualistic presupposition, they had established a moral concept of the human being that no longer wanted any relation with being a foil to, or in opposition with, a revealed concept of the human being. With Kant and Fichte, for the first time in the new world, moral reason claimed to determine the law of life entirely through its own power, without admitting from the outset the possibility of other sources of such a law. Thus, the rug was basically pulled out from an older kind of natural right. The dualism of flesh and spirit had become a purely inner-human one. Reason found within its own womb its own self and the non-rational; it found intelligible and empirical character. Thus, a deduction of community also had to be at the basis of Idealism's new concept of the human being, one not based on the contrast of "empirical" and "intelligible," but rather one based on the "whole" human being. But the influence of the pre-idealistic science of natural right, and especially, in Kant's and Fichte's case, the impression from Rousseau was so strong that this necessary thing did not happen: both Kant's doctrine of the state from 1797 and Fichte's work on natural right from 1796 still proceed from a concept of the human being which could only be scientific abstraction and no longer scientific truth. It again came to a construction of community based on the "empirical human."

This is where Hegel inserted his objection from the outset. His polemic of 1802 in the essay on the "Scientific Ways of Treating Natural Law" divided Kant and Fichte from their predecessors precisely on the grounds that the older thinkers of natural right had naively assumed certain individual determinants of the natural human being. Kant and Fichte, on the other hand, had admittedly intended to hold the great thought that "the essence of right and of duty, and the essence of the thinking and willing subject, are more or less the same,"[197] but then themselves abandoned this great thought and set up natural right as a "system of coercion" in contrast to ethics as the "system of freedom." From the beginning, Hegel was aware that his task was to avoid this relapse into pre-Kantian ethics and to fertilize the fields of the philosophy of right and the philosophy of the state with that thought that he had recognized at that time as the "great aspect" of Kantian-Fichtean philosophy.[198] Even now, he again praised Kant's "thought of infinite autonomy" as the "firm ground and starting point" of all knowledge of the will.[199] On the other hand, Hegel also saw in Rousseau, as Kant and Fichte had as well, the crowned completion of the older efforts of natural right. The German philosopher held Rousseau's achievement to be that the great Genevan had made the will, and indeed the conscious will, the "principle" of the state. Nevertheless, in that Rousseau had also remained fixed on a conception of this will as irrational, Hegel recognized the "mistake" from which the French Revolution had proceeded.[200] For it all depended on grasping the will as "rational in and for itself."[201] What this meant for Hegel has just been demonstrated.

This conception of the will as now "rational in and for itself" readily demands that the "will" does not simply apply to the will of the individual. Since it is "rational" according to its total essence, this will is just as much overarching order as it is the individual who is integrated into this order. Or, to put it differently: because the will – but such a will as Hegel conceives it in contrast to all older theories of natural right – because this will is recognized as the essential content of the state, the state is likewise recognized as the essential content of the will. Thus, the will has its actuality in the "custom" of all, and at the same time in the "self-consciousness" of the individual. One may not be thought without the other – this is the essence of the state. The will's brightness of consciousness is not to be dimmed by firmly alloying it with "custom." From the very beginning, the ethical "sensibility," the "piety" prevailing in the family, is expressly contrasted with the conscious willing of higher purpose by way of which "political virtue" is distinguished from that "piety."[202] The basic nature of the will, as Hegel uses it to construct the state, is precisely its ambiguity, by which it is at every point likewise conscious and "rational," in and above the individual, personal and suprapersonal. This is why Hegel, when he first considers the state purely as an isolated entity, not yet as a state among states, can describe this concept of the will in more detail as "patriotism." This is also why later, when Hegel passes over to the consideration of the state according to its external conditions, he again finds this ambiguous concept of the will inwardly in the context of constitutional sovereignty, and externally in the concept of a sovereign power-state. Therefore, in the end, when he represents the state itself as a serving member of the world-historical whole, he can demonstrate the same duality of the will, namely, that it is as "actual" as it is "rational," in what seems to him to be the essence of world history: namely, the actualization of world-historical necessity – and that means: of reason – through the peoples' historical destiny, with both converging in the world-historical hero, who makes the world-historical necessity the object of his personal passion. Patriotism, sovereignty, the world-historical moment – or in other words: the citizen of the state, the prince, the great man – these are the focal points from which Hegel systematically allows the will, after allowing this concept to develop systematically in the lower levels of state formations, to radiate as the essence of the state.

"Patriotism" – this is what Hegel calls the unity of political disposition with its object, and he indeed sees in this, as already stated, the foundation of the entire state.[203] It is, as has also been indicated, one of those concepts of reciprocity which combine a subjective disposition and an objective world. Here Hegel specifically refers to this objective world in which patriotism lives as "*institutions.*"[204] The "*highest right*" of individuals coincides in the state with the "*highest duty.*"[205] It becomes significant at this point in the system that Hegel had not only substantiated the legal will, but also the "moral" will of the state – that will which wants to be active for what it is interested in, to find its "*subjective satisfaction*" in the execution of a higher purpose.[206] Institution and patriotism thus challenge and condition each other. Hegel explicitly rejects the use of the term "patriotism" for only extraordinary actions. Rather, patriotism is "the political disposition of willing that has become *habitual*" and thus "the result of institutions existing in the state."[207] "The trust and disposition of individuals" for the state rests on this fixed basis of "institutions" as the "pillars of public freedom."[208] Only with "consciousness which proves itself in the ordinary course of life" can "extending oneself towards an extraordinary effort then be grounded."[209]

The thoughts that Stein and his colleagues had implanted in the renewing entity of the Prussian state are unmistakably echoed in these sentences, which precede Hegel's construction of the ideal state constitution. The common view of the reformers was that only on the basis of free institutions could a spirit capable of "extraordinary effort" arise, which was needed for the imminent liberation from foreign rule. Belatedly, but nevertheless, Hegel had testified to the truth of this thought in his inaugural speech in Berlin. By basing his description of "institutions" on this thought, he ties his philosophy of the state to the recently concluded great epoch of the Prussian state. Admittedly, he is writing in the year 1820. And so, the subdued, prematurely satiated mood of the political present resonates as an undertone in those sentences. That "extraordinary patriotism" is then placed behind the uniform "*pro patria vivere*" [to live for the country] which the "ordinary course of life" requires and in which Hegel sees the "essential" disposition for the state. However, he does not seem to consider that there could still be tasks that would again make this "extraordinary" disposition into the "essential" one. Yet, be that as it may, Hegel based the concept of the constitution on the interrelationship of institution and disposition. This relation, although prepared by the entire development of Hegel's idea of the state, reminiscent in its entire moralistic-individualistic tendency, especially in the Nuremberg Propaedeutics – and above all in the first – could only become the systematic basis of the doctrine of the inner life of the state with the transition to Berlin. For only now has this idea become universally valid and visibly freed from all limitations of the estates. It is true that there is still an estate of civil service, and that in general there are differences in how each individual estate relates to the state. However, estates have become economic entities and, as such, have been cast out from the state into "society." There are no longer any fundamentally different dispositions for the individual, from which he may know himself to belong to the state or to be a stranger to it. There is only the one "secret of patriotism" by which everyone is bound to the state: namely, that in the state everyone has "the means of preserving their own particular ends"[210] – the constitutional institution.

This equality of disposition is now the only equality that Hegel acknowledges for the state, he does not acknowledge it for rights, nor for morality. It is only with respect to "patriotism" that he speaks of "citizens" as such,[211] in the new sense of being elevated above one's estate, a sense the word had acquired following upon the modern movement of natural right.[212] Apart from equality before the law,[213] as well as the right of individual particularity stipulated by morality, as it is actualized in the modern world through the free choice of profession, Hegel understands civic equality as beyond the judicial, beyond the moral and social, only here, only in the form of the equality of disposition. Additionally, it is precisely the essence of the state, and already of the family, that there are differences within the content of duties, and that admittedly a member of the government, for example, does not require a different disposition but rather a different kind of service than that required of the ordinary citizen. With rights and in morality everyone is subject to the same thing but with ethical relations each is different, and it is precisely from the diversity of the duties to be fulfilled that the consciousness of being a "citizen" is established for the "subject" [Untertan][214] as the highest ethical relation. And, within this relation the three equalities converge, namely, the human before the law, the individual in their choice of profession, and the "citizen" in their patriotic disposition. This results in a claim to the protection of one's person and property;[215] a claim to the consideration of one's particular well-being and satisfaction of one's essence;[216] and finally, a claim to one's self-awareness as a member of a greater whole.[217] Thus, Hegel connects the concept of the universality of state citizenship with that of the structured constitution. "Disposition takes its particularly determined content from the different sides of the organism of the state."[218] The systematic that erects itself upon this connection becomes of itself the systematic precisely of these "different sides." When Hegel now tries to present the individual elements of the state constitution as an objective correlation of institutions, patriotism remains the universal form. This correlation of institutions can only be considered ethical in so far as it rests completely, and at each single point, upon the unity of state disposition and institution, which is presumed for it in general.

Initially, Hegel had understood "constitution" [Verfassung] according to its usage in the eighteenth century to mean the social structure as it is available to the government as material. Already as part of Hegel's first deliberations, the new revolutionary meaning of the word, according to which it denotes the "piece of paper" placed at the head of all governmental actions, had blended with its previous meaning. This double meaning of the word had therefore prompted Hegel to define it so generally that it encompassed the old as well as the new meaning. Thus, in 1802, state-constitution meant to him both the order according to which the government operated, as well as the social structure of the people. In the same sense, in 1805, Hegel titled the entire philosophy of state "Constitution" [Constitution], in that for his own concept he now made use of the French name, which in 1802 must have still designated the revolutionary concept of a constitution, a meaning he was to reject. However, that clarification of the concept of the state, which in 1820 would lead to the concept of the citizen and his disposition, namely, to "patriotism," and which had as its prerequisite the shifting of the estates into the social doctrine, this now gave the concept of the constitution a new meaning, one much closer to modern usage. The concept no longer denotes the unity of government and people, but instead the unity of the human being and the state, of disposition and institution.[219] The "political constitution" is the existing "organism" from which disposition is to take its "determinate content," and it is, on the other hand, the order and activity of the "*powers*"[220] that form the state. Thus, more or less that which in 1802 appeared to him as "crude," namely using the word constitution [Verfassung] to not designate, or at least not only designate, the overall structure of the state, but instead, as the new French concept of "constitution" [Constitution] had done, a direct relation between the state and the individual.[221] It is precisely this immediate relationship that Hegel has now acknowledged as the essence of the constitution, and it is upon this relationship that the structure of the state is initially built. That this concept of constitution meant an approximation to that concept of "constitution" that had been rejected in 1802, is clearly shown by the designation that Hegel gave it in 1817 when he likewise warmed up to the idea of the modern written constitution during the Württemberg affair: "The *constitution*," he had said at the time, "contains the provisions by which the rational will, in so far as it is only in *itself* the universal one of individuals, becomes understood and found and, through the efficacy of the government and its particular branches, becomes preserved in actuality – and is also protected from its accidental individuality, as well as against that of individuals."[222] As already then – and then for the first time – so now in 1820, for Hegel the constitution is also the relationship between totality and individual will which is actualized in the state's organization. Admittedly, the Nuremberg *Encyclopedia* had already tried to describe the modern concept of the constitution, but just as it had not yet cleanly lifted the concept of the citizen from out of the division of estates, so it had also initially described the constitution as the "separation and relation of governmental powers," and designated only as its most distinguished content – not like after 1817, as its essence – the "rights of the individuals in relation to the state, and the share of participation of the same."[223] This separation of administration and individual rights might have been in accordance with the spirit of the new French state organization, as it prevailed in Bavaria at the time when Hegel wrote the *Propaedeutic*. The new Prussian state organization, however, at least as it was held by the heirs of Stein's ideals, corresponded to the concept of constitution which Hegel described in 1817 and 1820: the construction of the state upon the universally underlying relationship of individual disposition to the whole, the pervasive "unity of right and duty," to again express it with Hegel's words.

What is built up upon this basic relationship, namely, the "organism of the state," is in 1820 also a doctrine of "powers." Hegel's relation to this important concept contained within the more modern doctrine of the state had taken on distinctive transformations throughout. In 1802, in contrast to Kant, who had also taken up the movement of natural right, Hegel had rejected the classical separation of judicial, legislative, and executive power. And in that, on the one hand – and in this regard a forerunner to Benjamin Constant's theories – Hegel raised the top of the state above the region of the separation of powers, and on the other hand, in that he attempted to combine internal and foreign politics in every power or, as he preferred to say, in every "system of government," he had divided the activity of the state into economic-political, legal and war administration, cultural and colonial politics. This attempt, with its overbold coupling of disparate fields, could not last, despite the importance of the underlying idea. The System of 1805, in accordance with its strong moral-philosophical tendency in general, did not attempt to build up a state organization at all, but instead was content to also depict, alongside the other estates and estate dispositions, the disposition of the estate of civil servants. The Nuremberg *Propaedeutic* then speaks of the "separation and relation of governmental powers" as they are laid down in the constitution. Even so, it shows that Hegel had meanwhile again approached Locke's and Montesquieu's concept of the separation of powers, even if – in the two words "and relation" – as the old pupil of Rousseau, the defender of Machiavelli and Robespierre, and the unconditional advocate of the idea of internal unity of the state, he could not do so without reservation. What Hegel says about the separation of powers in general in 1820 also displays signs of the great event in France, which likely had originally not cut as deep, but which had gradually gained that gravity over the course of his life, as well as gaining in gravity for the entire age, which made it the ever-ready standard of all political judgments: "With the *independence* of powers, as one has also seen in general, the destruction of the state is immediately set, or in so far as the state preserves itself in essence, the struggle with which one power subjects the other power to itself thereby first brings about the unity, as it has otherwise been constituted, and thus alone saves the essential aspect, the existence of the state."[224] Hegel thus rejects this "independence," this mutual limitation and surveillance of powers and its liberal justification, already originating with Montesquieu, for the sake of the unity of the state, and because any disposition towards the state must not harbor mistrust. The relation of powers to each other must not be an equilibrium, but instead, a "living unity."[225] Each must be a "*totality*," which means holding the others as "active in itself."[226] Thus, an example of what Hegel wanted to exclude with his doctrine of the separation of powers was a provision like that of the 1791 constitution, which barred members of the legislative assembly and the holders of the high judicial offices from entering the ministry.

How this doctrine of state powers will now look in detail, how it will deviate from Montesquieu's triad, can already be seen from the objection against Kant's adoption of Montesquieu's division, which Hegel mentions in advance of his own doctrine of the "systems" of government in 1802. At that time, Hegel reproached Kant for having set up judicial power as the keystone of the state and, for his part, admitting at once the correctness of this division of power, advocated for the entitlement of the executive in place of the role assigned by Kant to the judicial.[227] That view of the state as power, which had risen against Kant's doctrine of the constitutional state, remained with the thinker. And if he now undertook a division of the state according to "powers," it was clear that Montesquieu's "executive" power would be the highest. Compared to 1802, that the "judicial" could be completely omitted as a special power, was now ensured by the rich systematic division of the whole, a division in which law, as well as the state administration of justice, was assured its own treatment. Furthermore, that the highest peak of the state could exist not only as a single power next to others was guaranteed by the systematic structure of the section "Constitution," for the section dealing with "powers" was only a subsection. Here, the head of the state exists only as a power among powers, that is, in the narrowest sense of the word, only in its "executive" function, namely as the "final decision of the will."[228] In that Hegel retained Kant's ordering of powers according to the structure of a logical syllogism, legislation was sure to have the same place for him as with Kant, namely that of the major premise: "the power to determine and establish the universal."[229] Between the conclusion and the universally justified first premise, there was thus still room for a middle term, which was to "subsume" "the individual cases under the universal."[230] Kant, who regarded judicial power as the conclusion, had left this middle place for the executive. Hegel, who does not recognize the judicial as a power of its own, sees here the place of "governmental power" or, as we may paraphrase, the administration. The latter thus systematically acquires the validation that Montesquieu denied it. If the Frenchman's *pouvoir exécutiv* was rebuked for designating only the foreign policy of the government, and ignoring the entire circle of internal administration, in this case, for someone who sketched an ideal image of the English constitution of his age, this may be understood by the conditions in England at that time with its parliamentary centralization of the administration. Hegel, with Prussian conditions in mind, could easily see what had escaped the Frenchman: namely, that civil service as such possesses its own political power which cannot be eliminated by legislation. Thus, Hegel arranged the powers in the order in which an action of the state takes place in the ordinary course of political life: law provides the norm, officials apply it, and the head of state makes the formal decision. However, in carrying out this arrangement, Hegel reverses the order: he begins with the highest decision-making power. The reason for this becomes clear if we now substitute Hegel's own designation of this power with the one we have used so far: Hegel simply calls it "*princely power*."[231] For Hegel, it is not a matter of a head of state of any kind, which could also be represented, for instance, by a corporation or by popular decisions, where his constructive deduction of the decision-making will as the third concluding power might then remain. Instead, Hegel tries to develop the monarchical character of this power as philosophically necessary: the individual, however, cannot be "last" according to Hegel's entire presupposition of thought. Systematically, the individual "I will"[232] is always only at the beginning, even if, according to its task, it has the meaning of a conclusion. And thus, Hegel does not begin his doctrine of the constitution with the concept of the head of state, but rather with that of the prince.

One must be clear about what that meant. No rationalistic deduction of monarchy had yet dared to hold both the highest authority of the state and the personality of the prince necessary as such. Whether for reasons of convenience, or whether the deduction here ended with theology or history: the actual rational deduction always only reached the point of supreme power. As we well remember, when Hegel first tried to deduce the supreme head of state partly according to republican principles, and now and again also according to prevailing monarchisms, he ended up framing it in corporate terms. But even then, the motives which he inserted into this odd theoretical structure were of such a nature that they could easily lead to a theory of monarchy. It was, above all, the thought that the incidentally rational state must have a "natural" peak outside of reason.[233] Hegel had not yet seen this peak as an individual. He could not, because the individual as such had no place at all in the image of the state of 1802. This had already changed in 1805. At that time, Hegel had already based his philosophy of the state on the concept of the will, and the multiplicity of individuals was confronted with "the one individual" in the power of the prince[234] – both, this multiplicity as well as that unity, were not themselves bearers of the whole, which "rather carries itself free of these perfectly fixed extremes, [...] independent of the knowledge of individuals, as well as of the quality of a regent."[235] The free state of antiquity, where the people and the head of state coincide, is thereby a lower form of state. Only through the separation of the people and the head of state does freedom, that is, the "independence" of the individual, become possible. The will of the individual now demands the equally individual will of the head of state as its counterpart. The deduction of 1820 essentially differs from this in that here, the personality of the prince is not deduced as an element of the state in general, that it is not merely deduced from the concepts of government, people, and freedom, but as a member of the state organization. In 1805, this was not even addressed in this manner – tellingly enough, because the new idea of the age, namely, to explain the state on the basis of the subjective will, did not easily fall into line with the fixed order of authorities and institutions. In 1820, Hegel then also found the way to integrate this world into the fundamental concept of the subjective will, namely by developing it based on the concept of princely power.

For Hegel, the prince is above all a personality. The whole doctrine of the forms of government, as it was treated earlier, is already discounted for him from the outset. Monarchy, aristocracy, and democracy do not stand side by side as equal possibilities. It is not, as Fichte had thought in his "Natural Right," and even as Hegel had at first thought, basically indifferent whether "one," "several," or "all" preside over the state. Modern "constitutional monarchy"[236] cannot, as is admittedly the case with the monarchy of antiquity, stand next to aristocracy and democracy as a third form. These three forms, including monarchy in that "limited meaning,"[237] all belong to the past. They presuppose a structureless state and any reign at all where it is admittedly indifferent how many carry this reign out. On the other hand, the fully formed entity of the state that Hegel endeavors to portray, must, because it is supposed to be a will that has come into existence, grow forth out of this germination of the personal will and everywhere be filled with it. In the entire deduction of which we are aware, this emergence occurs conceptually in the likewise naïve and unconscious production of state disposition in the family and social corporation. Being filled with personal will is thus guaranteed through social freedom, through the free choice of profession, which Hegel values so incredibly high that he emphasizes it again and again as the fundamental difference between the modern state and the state of antiquity. To this extent it is only a question of the state in general. But in that this state born and nourished by the will is also supposed to be organization, thus actual power in the sense of Hegel's old definition, then, in order that here too personal will may be justified, personality as such must be given a place in the world of institutions. Thus, the prince, for the sake of his personality, becomes a state institution, an "authorial power" in the sense of natural right. And in order that he make the world of institutions entirely into a world of the will, he must be conceived of as the root of all institutions, as the "first" of the three powers.[238]

Through this difficult intersection of thoughts, a characteristic ambiguity emerges with Hegel's image of monarchy, finding its full illumination only beyond the field of the internal constitution in the concept of external sovereignty. The prince, taken systematically, is the origin of all activity of the state – the "first" power – and at the same time, taken practically, is merely the near contentless concluding "formal will," who executes decisions reached through official channels by the government and the popular will. In turn, as such a "third" power, this prince is systematically the highest power. When Friedrich Wilhelm supposedly replied, in response to the denunciation that Hegel had described the office of the King as merely "putting the dot on the J," saying "well what would happen if the King did not dot the J," then the professor would have felt himself to be quite rightly understood by the King. And yet the prince, precisely insofar as he is the "first" power and origin of all government, is only the lowest, only the "mere" empty individual. His content, the "J" from that anecdote only in need of a dot, must first be presented to him out of the wealth of the objective historical necessities of the state so that he can prove himself effective and powerful by it. On the one hand, the essence of the state is freedom, and a living and growing spirituality [Geistigkeit]; on the other hand, its essence is also form, right, and guiding rule. These two opposing, and yet cooperating, forces condition Hegel's image of monarchy. This is most visible in that very noticeable reversal in the Hegelian system of the sequence of a disposition just established in the immediately following explication. This deep intellectual conflict makes Hegel's image of monarchy so scintillating. And only insofar as it is likewise a great, but eternal, historical conflict inherent in the essence of the state – precisely between freedom and form, between life and right, between spirit and guiding rule – only insofar may this conflict also be applied to the background of Prussia at that time.

Princely power, the will according to its innermost essence as well as its outermost actualization, is divided in itself in such a way that this power, like subsequently the two other powers as well, carries in itself what is characteristic of all three powers: princely power has a relation to existing law, to the official processing of details, and it is also the place of final decisions. Of these three "moments," the last one, in contrast with the other two, is therefore its "distinguishing principle,"[239] namely, taking a position with regard to the constitution and to the body of officials. It is essentially "absolute self-determination."[240] As such, princely power is closely determined by the three concepts of sovereignty, personality, and naturalness. Within the system of the "inner constitution of the state," notwithstanding all that has been discussed before, the first of these three concepts is the opening concept, the "basic determination of the political state."[241] Following Hegel's method of thought, just as in the complete system the first subordinate term of the initial section of the first part, "Being," is the nucleus of the whole, so the entire constitution must be derived from sovereignty, as its most general and emptiest determination. Hegel now explains sovereignty – it is, mind you, at first only the internal sovereignty of the state – as the underlying negation of its own division within the subdivided whole. That is to say, although the state collapses into many "particular authorities and affairs," and although these affairs are placed in the hands of particular, individual people, that collapse must nevertheless never mean a collapse of the state, that transference must never mean a dispossession of the state. The state remains at every moment the ruling universality with respect to its own particularity, both objective and personal. The individual affairs of the state must be determined "within the idea of the whole,"[242] the individual person must be entrusted with office only for the sake of his "universal and objective qualities."[243] This is sovereignty and, indeed, as Hegel may now say with a new expression, the *"sovereignty of the state."*[244]

The concept of sovereignty has come to rest at this point in its history. Ever since the modern era first established this concept of sovereignty as the essence of the state, in accordance with the conditions of the sixteenth century, the next question had always been that of the bearer of sovereignty. But precisely because the concept of sovereignty designated ruling power [Herrschaft] as the essence of the state, and thereby blurred the Aristotelian separation of the essence of the state from its form of government, the question of the bearer of sovereignty invariably merged into that of the bearer of ultimate official authority. In place of a purely formal theory of the state, one therefore obtained such highly material theories of government until, in the end, by the contrast of the prohibitive popular sovereignty or sovereignty of the ruler, the entire concept fell onto the dead track of an inner-political struggle for power. Hegel was the first to again give the concept of sovereignty scientific vigor. By initially developing sovereignty purely out of principle, still without any explicit relation to its human bearer, Hegel created the name and concept of "state sovereignty." The word initially denotes nothing other than the essence of the state.

It is highly characteristic of Hegel how he now seeks to grasp this essence more closely, namely, in connection with that relation of sovereignty to the "particularity" of state life. According to Hegel, this relation – which under ordinary peaceful conditions consists in the unconscious construction of the whole through the independent existence of the parts and the conscious self-preservation of the whole through recourse to the parts – contains a comparison and a generic term.[245] The state is compared to the relation of an organism to its organs. The state is designated as the relation that exists between free will and its decisions, which never cease to be free will decisions. Likewise, it is "substance" and "subject," existence and will. And it corresponds to Hegel's conscious motif of raising "substance to the subject," that is, of proving that the world is dominated and permeated by spirit, that namely, just as only "freedom of will," and not "organism," means more than a comparison, the state is only thereby "substance," only has existence in that it is "subject," namely, in that the state is will. The "substantial" sovereignty of the state is actualized in the "subjective" personality of the monarch.

The monarch is not "sovereign" – only the state is sovereign – but rather a person. The personality which is ascribed to the state in the concept of sovereignty – sovereignty as the free will of the state – this "personhood" exists only "as a *person*."[246] The "individuality of the state" – yet another expression for its sovereignty – requires an "individual," the monarch.[247] The individual is "*that which simply begins from itself*,"[248] it cannot be further deduced, cannot be put together from parts; it is to be accepted as it is. The head of state must be an individual precisely for this reason, so that the ultimate deciding will in the state has this unquestionable and unanswerable originality. He must be an individual; but with this, nothing is yet said about the nature of the origin of his ruling power. Nevertheless, at this juncture Hegel mentions the doctrine of divine right, although not as one might expect. Instead, Hegel mentions this doctrine with respect to the concept of heredity discussed later as the "closest applicable" conception of the essence of modernity he develops, severe "misunderstandings" notwithstanding.[249] Hegel is perhaps hardly aware that in transplanting this concept he completely uproots the concept itself. When in 1802 Hegel himself said of the highest authority of his system of ethicality that it sat in the council of the most high,[250] and that it derived its divinity directly through its "naturalness," through its position based purely on the natural process of aging,[251] he was then closer to the concept of divine right. Although he was not then a monarchist, he was at least closer than now, when he no longer endeavored to derive this concept from "naturalness" but instead from the "personality" of the prince.[252] The common conception, in which the doctrine of divine right and regulated accession to the throne belong together, strikes at the essence of the matter, namely, principality "in its own right." Hegel, who sought to understand the doctrine of divine right from the necessity of a supreme, non-grounded position of decision in the state, ultimately grounds this doctrine not upon "its own" right, but upon the right of the state. And if a basic feature of the more recent development in political ideas is recognized in the fact that the state strives to transform all independent entitlements into constitutional law, then Hegel's shifting of divine right's position belongs here. In a highly logical manner, this shift leads the thinker to the otherwise simply contradictory undertaking of also seeking the beginnings of divine right in the republic of antiquity, on the one hand, namely, in the "first man," and on the other, in the political role of oracles and omens.[253] And as Hegel sees in the daemon of Socrates in general the foreshadowing of the omnipotence of the "subject," which for Hegel characterizes the Christian world age, so he also sees the premonition of the idea of monarchy particularly in this unconditional claim of the "I" to decide.[254] In 1820, as well as in 1805, freedom of the prince and freedom of the citizen, both foreign to the state of antiquity, belong together. They are both rooted in the same concept of free will, unknown in antiquity, which propels the entire modern state, to which they both belong.

The monarch is not sovereign, only the state is sovereign. But sovereignty is monarchical: the sovereign state requires the monarchical individual. Because this individual decides without responsibility, but nevertheless also has the state as a prerequisite for his decisions, now and only now does a concept become necessary for Hegel in which the rational necessity of the state and the ungraspable contingency of the deciding person coincide. And as such, the right of primogeniture offers him a concept that consummates the essence of princely decision-making power and accentuates the sovereign will of the state as the personal "ultimate self."[255] The "legitimacy" or, as Hegel prefers to say, the "majesty" of the prince[256] is thus the reclassification of the contingent princely person, "this individual,"[257] into the rational legality of the state as a whole. The contingency of the prince, his "personality," was a political requirement: through "legitimacy" this contingency is reintegrated into a fixed order of rights, which is above coincidence. Only thereby is the unity of the state secured against the danger of being "dragged down into the sphere of particularity, its arbitrariness, purposes, and views," and "removed from the struggle of factions against factions for the throne."[258] If Hegel could still use the first man of the republic as a comparison for the monarchical "personality," this now ceases. The princely family becomes a necessary piece of the state ideal, and Hegel rejects as false and double-edged any utilitarian justification of an heir to the throne for the "well-being"[259] of the state or the people. Rather, the transition from the concept of princely power in general to its actualization in hereditary principality took place with the same logical consistency, without being interrupted for the purpose of other thoughts, as did the ontological proof of God in the transition from the concept of God to his existence. In opposition to Kant, Hegel had famously tried to save this proof. Incidentally, however, it remains the case that Hegel does not combine the concept of divine right with legitimacy, but instead with the function of the prince in the state. Legitimacy is necessary, but not of itself. It is necessary based on the essence of the state. By deliberately basing legitimacy on the "idea" and not "on a positive right,"[260] Hegel remains faithful, to an almost dangerous degree, to his basic principle of deducing the state, together with all that it contains, from the will.

The "three" moments of princely power which have been treated thus far – sovereignty of the state, personal contingency, and natural coronation – describe this power only in relation to itself, only in its "*self-determination.*"[261] However, according to Hegel's concept of authority [Gewalt], princely power must in itself also have a relation to the two other powers, namely to executive power and legislative power. The relation to executive power is expressed in that the highest advisory bodies, which are to submit to the prince the objective documents of his decisions and which, in that these bodies alone are responsible for the "*objective of the decision,*"[262] can and must be made "responsible," thereby in contrast to the prince who decides purely "subjectively," these advisory bodies are filled by the prince with unlimited discretion. The other relationship of princely power, namely that relation to "constitution and laws" in which the state actually proves its "universality," lies in the "*conscience of the monarch*" and in the "*whole* of the *constitution* and in the *laws*," which, just as the prince's right rests upon them, are in turn themselves also based on his existence.[263] This continual reciprocity, this reciprocal self-determination, for instance, of public freedom and of the heir to the throne, forms the foundation of the state. "Love for the people, character, oaths, and authority" can only be regarded as "subjective foundations," but the "objective guarantees" reside solely in "institutions."[264] Thus, princely power is carried out within the entire circle of state life. The same now occurs with "governmental power."[265]

This is the name Hegel gives to the administration [Verwaltung]. It has already been said how here, with regard to Montesquieu and in terms of content, Hegel also introduced something new into the science of the state; and not merely with regard to Montesquieu's doctrine of powers. It is true that the concept of "government," in its application to administrative affairs, dates to the eighteenth century, and that in this sense Hegel had earlier already moved beyond the older concepts. But the eighteenth century did not, and could not, see a fundamental difference between the state function of princes and that of "government," as Hegel now addresses this with his doctrine of powers. For the eighteenth century, the conception of officials as princely servants had stood in the way. In truth, this view did not necessarily prevail, at least in practice. Thus, in Hegel's homeland, for example, there were already the beginnings of a service law, and thus of an independent position of civil servants with regard to the prince. The younger Moser had fought with utmost journalistic passion against what he held to be a naïvely opposed principle: if the prince wanted to corrupt his country, then the "princely servant" had neither the duty, nor the right, to prevent this.[266] And in Prussia, Stein had sought to create an independent state ministry, even before Jena, and he was admittedly attacked on this account. Nevertheless, it is striking how early Hegel strives to give civil service an important place in his political system. If in 1802, the function of civil service was still considered as the mere outcome of the life of the people, which in 1820 is retained in the basic definition of administration as a "subsuming," and not a deciding or organizing function, then in 1805 it is already given its own validation, even if without systematic consequence. And so, in line with the central theme at that time, which was to show the connection between estates and estate dispositions in the state, it was presented as a separate estate. Like the related estates of the officer and the scholar, and unlike the trade classes that did not belong to the government, it was ascribed modern "morality," and that meant freedom from the ethical life of bondage by the estates. In this connection, and at that time in 1805, Hegel came up with the distinctive idea that within civil service what one calls public opinion is truly safeguarded. It is "the true legislative body,"[267] in a similar sense as how, a few years later, Hegel placed administrative "councils" and "imperial estates" on equal footing as mediators between prince and people.[268] This image from 1805 may in some respects – for example, in the not at all self-evident combination of civil servant and officer – have been sketched in accordance with Prussian Common Law. In essence, however, especially in the equation of bureaucracy and "universal will,"[269] as well as in the characterization of the civil servant's disposition as "morality,"[270] it could be better illustrated by the Prussia of 1820 than by any conditions or theories within Hegel's proximity in 1805. In all actuality, Hegel's theory of the civil service later moved away from this pre-Prussian, Prussian stance. The Bavarian period may have contributed to this owing to practical life experiences, considering it was in Bavaria that Hegel first systematically presented civil service as its own "state authority." Theoretically, however, it is especially the idea of self-governance – hardly touched upon by the systematist in 1805, although already strongly expressed in the text on The German Constitution – which, in 1820, permeates the philosophy of administration and transforms the image of civil service. Given that in 1820 self-governance again presents that equation of administration and "universal will" within the administration as a particular kind of institution, space is created outside of administration for a separate form of popular representation. And insofar as self-governance, especially in the cities, was indeed this important complement to state civil service in Prussia at that time, and was regarded as such, the image as Hegel sketched it really only corresponds to Prussian conditions in 1820.

How important self-governance is for Hegel is shown by the fact that he begins with it. In accordance with his concept of civil society, he considers the subject matter of self-governance to be the "particular communal interests" that belong to it and wants to see them exercised by "communities, [...] trades and estates, and their authorities, heads, administrators, and the like." Whereas, they are to be elected in that their "authority [...] is based on the confidence of their peers and citizens," the right of "confirmation and determination" is, however, reserved for the state – just as the entirety of self-governance requires state oversight.[271]

The "secret of patriotism" and, in this regard, "the depth and strength the state possesses in its disposition," rests on self-governance and the "corporate spirit" which, although awakened by the former, turns within itself into the "spirit of the state."[272] From this inner justification of the idea of self-governance, Hegel now gains the freedom, in contrast to his own earliest views on this aspect of the matter and in contrast to the prevailing view of the age, to pass over the question of the external functionality of self-governance with sovereign disregard. He does not mention the popular claim, once put forward by himself, that self-governance is less expensive. The other claim, that it does superior work, he even rejects as untrue. It is not at all about functionality, but instead, as he now says with a certain humor – which nevertheless rests upon a deep seriousness – it is the case that "the laborious or foolish handling of such trivial matters is in direct relation to the self-satisfaction and opinion derived therefrom."[273]

After this aspect of civil service, which in 1805 was regarded as its relation to "public opinion," was thus developed within self-governance, the actual organization of authorities is worked out. This organization is based on an internal division of labor. The lowest and "most concrete" business, that is, the business affecting life as a whole, must be further processed or prepared by special authorities according to the "abstract" parts into which they fall, which "again converge into concrete oversight in the supreme governmental power."[274] Positions in civil service are to be filled only according to proven ability, not according to birth. Among the majority of those qualified, the appointment is then at the discretion of the prince.[275] Through this connection with the sovereignty of the prince, "governmental power" [Regierungsgewalt] participates in "princely" power.[276] If the appointment was still "contingent," then after the appointment the official has "a right taken by contingency."[277] He is neither "an itinerant knight," who serves the common good without a commission, nor a *state servant* – Hegel thus rejects the still very common designation in Prussia – for that one who would be "bound to his service according to mere necessity, without true duty, and likewise without right." Instead, for the civil servant, as everywhere, the essence of the constitution is that his special interest, his right, is one with the universal, one with his duty. His relationship to the state should not be conceived as a contract of private right. Instead, he places "the main interest of his spiritual and particular existence into this relationship," as he, for his part, is thereby "liberated in his external situation [...] from any other subjective dependence and influence."[278] Thus, the "will" in the Hegelian sense, namely the individual's entire "spiritual and particular existence," also operates within this part of the state.[279]

That the power of civil servants does not become independent to the state and those governed, this is ensured partly through the hierarchy of authorities, and the inherent self-control herein, and partly through the authorization of municipalities and corporations; and furthermore, this is even ensured, in the case that self-control fails on account of the *esprit de corps*, through the direct intervention of the sovereign. The most desirable thing, however, is that "dispassion, lawfulness, and mildness of conduct become *habitual custom*," and this is partially achieved through "the cultivation of ethics and thought," which "holds the spiritual balance"[280] of the necessary "mechanism" of business, and furthermore through the physical size of the state, through which "subjective views" are wiped out and "the habit of general interests, views and business" is produced.[281] Through this then – and here Hegel again takes up that idealization of the governing and civil servant estate from the Jena system – this circle becomes "the main part of the *middle class*, which includes the educated intelligence and the legal consciousness of the population of a people."[282] The danger that this circle isolates itself into an "aristocracy" – Hegel had illustrated this three years earlier in the Württemberg "notary class"[283] and as a result also now falls involuntarily into the Württemberg appeal to "dominance" – is managed "by the institutions of sovereignty from above, and by corporate rights from below."[284] The idealization of 1805 is enriched here by a new feature, in that Hegel now attaches to civil service the honorary title of "middle class." The expression is still new at that time and, in the mouth of someone who knew Aristotelian politics well, the connection to the concept of *mesoi* [μέσοι], the very concept upon which the Greek bases his good state, is certain. With Aristotle, however, and more in line with how the liberalism of the nineteenth century adopted the idea, an economic middle class is meant. However, Hegel – and this is highly significant, since for the founder of that particular concept of society Aristotle's estates were expelled from the state, and within the state only political relationships were accepted – ignores the economic side completely and transfers the name "middle class" to civil service, that "true legislative body" of the System of 1805. We will soon address the historical context of this distinction.

With the third power, Hegel remains in line with Locke and Montesquieu, and essentially agrees in substance as well: "legislative" power.[285] This power is the most recent in Hegel's system, despite the extensive treatment of the same in the text on The German Constitution. The prince was already established in 1805 – and, in shadowy form, even in 1802 – and civil service was established as an independent factor in 1805. Popular representation, although problematic in Nuremberg, was not established unconditionally until 1817. Of course, the late date must not be overestimated. If the text on The German Constitution, which strongly advocated for popular representation, but purely for reasons of yielding to the spirit of the age, made it seem quite understandable how the systematist likewise, and later still, did not inform himself about this institution, then the letter exchanges of the Bavarian years would leave no doubt that a completed system in those years would not have bypassed popular representation. And the early Nuremberg Propaedeutic already claims that at least councils "or" imperial estates are superfluous.[286] Württemberg's internal battles had first forced Hegel into a detailed treatment of the idea of popular representation. For someone familiar with Hegel's system, this treatment, although not systematic in form, already clearly shows the systematic context into which Hegel places the idea, indeed, shows this even more clearly than the cursory treatment of popular representation in the System of 1817. It is the idea, ethical and revolutionary in its origin, that the state as "power" only complements the state as "will" through popular representation. In the Philosophy of Right of 1820, Hegel weakened this thought insofar as he correlates the unity of power and will, order and disposition, principally to each individual part of the "constitution," and no longer only allows them, as was the case with the Württemberg text, to emerge solely from the interaction of the individual parts. But even in 1820, popular representation is prioritized and is kept in a certain harmony with the modern concept of a constitution, as Hegel likewise grants it a particular relationship to his, albeit more antiquated, concept of a constitution. The legislative power is namely "itself a part of the constitution,"[287] and indeed the constitution is its precondition, on the one hand, and, on the other, this power is further developed in the work of legislation itself. This is a closer relationship to the constitution than could have been said of the other two powers, for both of which it would have been true only that they presuppose the constitution, not that the constitution is also their product. Again, the fact that Hegel emphasizes the indiscernible shift of the constitution at the very beginning of his work is a sign of his distinctive aversion to the revolutionary concept of the "written" constitution, which is fixed above all powers, in favor of that "general clause" which world spirit, as Hegel recently expressed in the Württemberg text, attaches to all written constitutions.[288] In comparison with "governmental power," one can easily carry out the interaction of the three powers with each individual power, which Hegel accepts in principle. Princely power makes the highest decision, governing power provides accurate oversight and preparation of the details – in his lecture, Hegel expressly rejects the banishment of the ministry from parliament, and in this regard praises the English custom that ministers are members of parliament. The proper organ of legislative power nevertheless remains popular representation or, as Hegel consciously says: the "element of the estates."[289]

The way Hegel justifies the necessity of this "element" again reveals the particular systematic connection that exists between the Hegelian concept of the constitution and precisely this part of the constitution. Whereas the reciprocal interpenetration of institution and disposition remains more of an incidental provision in the case of princely power, as well as in the case of governmental power – in the case of the former effectively in the "personality" of the prince, in the case of the latter partly in self-governance and partly in the professional ethics of the civil servant – in the case at hand, this interpenetration forms the actual essence of the matter with popular representation. Even more decisively than with self-governance, Hegel denies any justification of popular representation based on considerations of functionality. The people by no means understand best what serves them the most. On the contrary, it is precisely that part of the state "which does not know what it wants."[290] In the case of lower officials, control of the estates has a certain practical value, in that clear knowledge of the circumstances may be gained. Higher officials, however, can govern very well without the estates, and the actual work consists in their interaction. Even the idea that estates have the superior will is "rabble-esque." One could just as well suspect them of selfish impulses. Nor is the "guarantee of public welfare and rational freedom" any different with them, indeed even less so than with institutions such as monarchical sovereignty, the hereditary throne, and the constitutional judiciary.[291] Instead, the only essential point of view remains that in the estates "the subjective moment of universal freedom [...] and the distinct will of this sphere, which in this account has been called civil society, comes *into existence* [Existenz] *in relation to the state.*"[292] Therefore, the publicity of their negotiations is an unconditional requirement.

Thus, "*formal freedom*"[293] is to come into its own right politically in the estates. In 1817, it had been said that the power of the state is joined by its will through the estates. And now, Hegel determines the bearer of this will more precisely. His own system provides him with the name: the owner of this "singular will" [eigenen Willens], which is to be brought into political existence [Existenz], is "civil society."[294] Thereby, this tremendously important concept of Hegel's state system becomes, systematically, an extension of its content. Civil society had to be conceptually separated from the state so that the political essence of the state could emerge purely. Even so, now civil society receives a political meaning again. In the beginnings of Hegel's system, the division of estates within civil society had once been the basis and content of the state in general. The displacement of the estates and estate-dispositions into the sphere below the state then allowed the increasing politicization of the Hegelian state to be realized. But now this movement, which of itself should have led solely to the monarchical-democratic idea of the state, comes to a standstill; society now asserted its claims on the state. If society can no longer be the basis of the state, as it was in the *ancien régime*, it at least wants to exercise its power in the only place where it can still find access. A constitutive people born of the modern idea of the state which is beyond society cannot be the bearer of that "subjective moment of universal freedom."[295] Instead, the bearer must again be that same society which Hegel rightly claimed to have expelled from the concept of the state. Thus, the same thinker, who in his general justification thought quite modernly here about the state, again fell back into the sphere below the state when implementing this thought, admittedly in accord with the leading minds of the epoch – the conservative ones, as well as the progressive ones – and not in accord with the intellectual holdings Hegel had gained for himself, namely, the idea of the political state based on political disposition.

All these remarks on the estates, however, are not to be understood in isolation. Something further arises from the basic idea described above. Precisely because the estates do not actually represent the "people" as a mass, they must stand, as a mediating power, between this mass on the one hand and the government on the other. Furthermore, it is their task, together with the organized government, to mediate between the prince and the people. The estates must, therefore, combine "the *sense* and *disposition of the state* and *government*" with the "*interests of particular circles and individuals.*"²⁹⁶ Just as little as the prince, are they allowed to become "extreme."²⁹⁷ Instead, they must hold themselves like a mediating power – one notices Württemberg being recalled. With this second thought, Hegel's theory of the Estates Assembly now finds its way back from the *ancien régime* to the present. Although the estates depict civil society, and not the people of the state, the estates must not feel themselves to be mere representatives of their own interests – as the conservative theory explicitly demanded, for example, in Friedrich Wilhelm IV's famous opening address to the First United Estates Assembly – but should stand "in common with the organized governmental power" on the basis of "the sense and disposition of the state" and against such an "isolation" of the special interests of religious communities, corporations, and individuals. And admittedly, this path back from the estate-based system to the representative system, to use the catchwords of the immediately following period, is linked with the main idea in the following way: not despite, but rather precisely because the estates represent society, and not the people of the state, are they able to form the counterweight against that "isolation" which, in its progression, would finally have led to a "*mass*," and to "sheer masses of force, against the organic state."²⁹⁸

The details of the exposition are now based on this distinctively intricate foundation. The Estates Assembly must, for the sake of its mediating position, produce from itself "an existing middle," just as the prince, for a similar purpose, requires a governmental power independent of himself.²⁹⁹ Thus arises the necessity for people who possess individual votes [Virilstimmen], who have that "naturalness" in common with the prince; in this case, the hereditary seat in the estates adhering to family.³⁰⁰ For this political reason, the institute of primogeniture – the independence of property from all, including the possessor himself – which was rejected by Hegel in the doctrines of society, right, and family, must remain, insofar as it is likewise necessary for this political purpose.[301] With this Hegel touches on the idea which he himself had expressed in 1802 and in 1805, and which was expressed in the decades following the Revolution, namely, that the nobility could ultimately only again be made viable through politicization.[302] In addition to possessing individual votes, the estates are composed of "*delegates*," which civil society delegates "*as that* which it *is*," that is, according to its "already constituted cooperatives, municipalities, and corporations," which hereby, and for their part, "obtain political cohesion."[303] Nevertheless, the delegates – and here the modern idea again breaks through – must be independent of their delegators, they must not receive any instructions or mandates. The Assembly must be "lively, mutually educational, and compelling, jointly deliberative."[304] One may again notice Hegel recalling the Württemberg Estates of 1815, with their recited speeches and lack of debate. The guarantee of aptitude lies – note the prohibitions – most closely "in the disposition, skill, and knowledge of the institutions and interests of the state and of civil society, acquired through *actual management* in *offices of authority* or *state*, and proven *in deed*, in the *sense of authority*, and *sense of state* thereby formed and tested."[305] This was already Hegel's judgment in Württemberg in the case of the "notaries" within the estates. Regarding the census, Hegel is just as opposed to it now as he was in 1817. Even if personal assets remain a condition for the election to honorary offices, they will still carry weight for the estates that result from it.[306] Hegel is skeptical about the idea of elections. If the delegate belongs to the electing corporation itself, which is necessary both for the sake of trust and for the sake of expertise, then the election "either becomes something entirely superfluous, or it is reduced to a minor game of opinion and caprice."[307] After all, the delegates are not "*representatives*" of "*individuals*," but of "*spheres*."[308] We also hear again the reasons familiar to us from 1817, namely that the atomistic electoral law creates voter indifference, and thus enables the authority of "a few, of one party."[309] That a political party could be the organization not of the few but of the many is, as we already know, an unfamiliar thought to Hegel. He recommends the bicameral system partly for the practical reason of creating a path of proper channels, and partly, and above all, in order to make the basic principle of the individual vote, the "mediation" between government and people, visible and more effective.[310] It is most striking that Hegel

takes Wangenheim's idea as his basis here, originating from Eschenmayer, an idea that Hegel had once touched upon, merely in passing, in
the Württemberg text (which was supposedly inspired by Wangenheim)
and there not for the justification of the bicameral system.

Hegel suitably adds a few paragraphs on public opinion, freedom of
the press, and related matters to the doctrine of popular representation.
He does not hold these more unconstrained forms of "subjectivity" in
high esteem, precisely because he essentially regards the Estates Assembly as organized public opinion and because, according to his concept
of constitution, only a disposition that can organize itself seems important to him. However, although public opinion is treated with a strange
mixture of seriousness and irony, in the end irony, and even crassness,
have the last word: public opinion is the "contradiction on hand,"[311]
for although it contains "the eternal [...] principles of justice, the true
content [...] of the entire constitution, legislation, and the general condition, as well as the true needs and [...] tendencies of actuality," it also
contains the opposite of all of these.[312] It is thus both "*vox dei*," as well as
"*Volgare ignorante*"[313] and must – one could even recall Goethe's distinction
between peoplehood [Volkheit] and people [Volk] – "be *respected* as much
as *despised*."[314] According to a lecture addendum, to combine both practically is the secret of the great statesman, which today, after Bismarck, we
can easily understand.[315] In the treatment of the freedom of the press a
certain optimism peculiar to the pre-journalistic age, as well as a concern
for academic freedom, are mixed up with the philosopher's aversion to
a freedom allowing one to write whatever one pleases. After all, one is
not allowed to do whatever one pleases.[316] On the whole, the paragraph
emanates a certain sovereign indifference: through the publicity of the
Estates Assembly, newspapers will be left with little to say – a prophecy
which resulted in the exact opposite.

In addition to legislation and general state affairs, Hegel adds the
approval of taxes to the content of the estates' deliberations. He thereby
declared monetary tax to be the only levy appropriate to the modern concept of the state and freedom.[317] In addition to this rejection of services
and allowances in kind, which had gradually become self-evident since
1789, Hegel avoided, in a year when Prussian tax law was hotly disputed,
becoming further involved in debating the source of tax revenue, which
he had previously dealt with in greater detail. The payments that the

state requires of its citizens for defense against its enemies are expressly excluded from the discussion here.[318] It can be said that Hegel's entire concept of the constitution, and his entire doctrine of the Estates Assembly, depend upon this matter of distribution. The army does not belong to the internal constitution of the state. Where Hegel demonstrates that patriotism – that is, disposition towards the state – is the subjective side of the constitution, he expressly rejects the idea that patriotism is mainly understood as extraordinary efforts in extraordinary circumstances. For Hegel, patriotism is the state-oriented civic disposition already present in times of peace. In that the internal structure of state organizations, which are imbued with this disposition, appear to him as an articulated construct, disposition assumes different forms everywhere, and indeed should. Therefore, at this point, Hegel cannot address the democratic lack of patriotic differentiation during times of war; it would overturn his entire elaborate construct of the internal structure of the state constitution. It was not in vain that Hegel had thrown aside that abrupt, and one-sided, definition of "the state as power" following upon the text on *The German Constitution* of 1801.[319] At that time, he too could not fully deny the democratic-equalizing consequences of such a state concept; both the justification of popular representation and of personal freedom follow this line of thought. Henceforth, Hegel would consistently develop the already conceived idea of the state as an integrated entity until he arrived at the concept of "constitution" developed in 1820, which was just as "substantially" rational as it was "subjectively" enlivened. It was a magnificent solution that Hegel then proposed to the problem, after many futile attempts,[320] when he treated the state, and specifically the state of "internal state law," in two separate ways, namely once as an "internal constitution, for itself," and then as "externally directed sovereignty."[321] It is the same state both times; however, not yet the state among states, as it is treated in the section on "external state law," but the state still considered purely as an individual. But if the state was seen from the inside as the richly articulated organism of the "constitution," it is now seen from the outside as simple, unarticulated sovereignty. Sovereignty had also been the basic concept of the internal constitution, but there it had meant the uniform cooperation of all the members of the whole. Now the concept assumes a more austere appearance. Sovereignty now denotes the unconditional subordination, indeed the "disappearance," of all the members in the whole. Thus, the two manifestations of "state-individuality" converge in the princely "individual." In the peacetime state, this individual secured the "development" and the "persistence" of the individual members,[322] whereas in the wartime state, the princely individual embodies the negative power against all that is individual, "life, property, and its right."[323] The two definitions of the state, as a warlike power and as an ethically linked structure, had existed unconnectedly side by side in 1802, in the political pamphlet on the one hand, and in the System of Ethicality on the other. Now they are systematically forced together, both in the concept of the state as "individuality," which is inwardly manifold and rich, as well as outwardly uniform and exclusive, and in the vivid appearance of the princely "individual."

Thus, as princely power is first addressed here in its effectively absolute activity — and no longer integrated into any legal or constitutional context — as that position to which "it alone and directly falls to command armed power, to maintain relations with the other states through envoys, etc., and to determine war and peace and other treaties,"[324] this is then also where the army first appears. It is not within the framework of patriotism, to say it again, but instead from within the stern power of the state over everything "individual and particular"[325] that Hegel derives the duty of the individual to sacrifice "property and life, in any case what is theirs and everything [...] that is conceived by itself in the scope of life," for the independence of the state.[326] Therefore, according to Hegel's entire arrangement, logically it is not a matter of disposition here — this belongs instead to the "internal constitution." Here, it is simply a matter of necessity and duty. And indeed, a matter of universal necessity — Hegel recalls the old passages from 1802 on the philosophical justification of war in general, which, however, do not apply to a justification of a single war in particular — and a matter of universal duty. However, in line with the nature of the matter, because the wartime state is only one side of the state, particular duty appears next to universal duty: namely, the soldier class, the standing army. The justification for a standing army must also not be based on considerations of functionality. But to be sure, the standing army will have to be employed for minor conflicts. For wars, on the other hand, when "the state as such, its independence, comes into danger," and which pass on their own accord, "when the whole has thus become a power," from defensive wars into conquest, in this case "duty calls all its citizens to its defense."[327] Thus, the concept of the state is complete in the army and its commander [Heerfürst]. That this is not some external conclusion, but that the same force which animates the peacetime state actually reveals itself in the wartime state, this is proven for Hegel by the historically demonstrable connection between internal state politics and foreign policy. Thus, the systematist anticipates the leitmotif found in the lifework of the greatest of historians.

We have initially developed Hegel's image of the state from 1820, as far as it was possible, only in its inner systematic and biographical context. We have now reached the point where the description of the state itself is complete. Furthermore, since we have also addressed the systematic relation of the state to the spheres below the state, namely to the ethics of the state, all that remains is to describe the metaphysics of the state. Before doing so, it seems practical to take up the question of the Prussian traits of the Hegelian state from 1820, as all the material for addressing this question has been provided above.[328]

That such traits are present has been touched upon occasionally, and readers themselves will have noticed some of them. Let us begin with the last one addressed. The constitution of the army depicted by Hegel is the Prussian one, namely the Prussian one of 1820, which is in line with the prevailing view of the age. In those decades between Boyen and Roon, the Prussian army was characterized by the juxtaposition of two organizations, the Landwehr and the line regiment, which were established on different bases and, in principle, even for different uses. While the Landwehr rested on the idea of compulsory military service as had it been established under the extraordinary challenges of the age during Prussia's rise to prominence, and while in it the inner kinship of the new idea of the state with the democracy of antiquity was expressed, the line regiment was essentially the old standing army of the pre-revolutionary period. The two organizations were kept separate with respect to their training and peacetime organization. However, the intention was that this difference, even during times of war, should remain in force, if feasible. Mobilization was carried out separately under certain circumstances, and if the line regiments were already in front of the enemy, the Landwehr regiments might have just left their garrisons. At the same time, even the organizer of the Prussian militia army also had the goal, according to the words of his biographer, to bring the essence of the *miles perpetuus*, its mobility and rapid intervention, to its highest potential.[329] Moreover, and again especially with Boyen himself, the idea prevailed that the Land-wehr could only be used for wars of survival, that is, only for defending a state's independence. This made it the case, as one could now declare with satisfaction or with ire, depending on one's political position, that the Prussian government was incapable of a martial politics in a grand style, one imperceptible to the people being defended, since any defense could only be carried out by means of a line regiment. We see that this corresponds line for line to the Hegelian image, with the one curtail-ment that for Hegel, the democratic consequences of the idea of com-pulsory military service are weakened, in that he places this compulsory service outside of the framework of "patriotism" and "constitution." But in all other respects, the image and the archetype coincide exactly. It is true that Hegel had already praised the idea of compulsory military ser-vice in a speech at the Gymnasium from 1810, stating that in the context of general education it was something found "in the nature of things," which had only gradually become foreign to individual estates.[330] How-ever, as is shown by Hegel's demeanor towards the son of his friend Niethammer in 1813, and then also by the statement to his students in 1815, that they could be glad to pursue their academic studies in peace, and even by a turn of phrase echoing this thought in the Heidelberg inaugural address of 1817, it is hard to imagine that the "highly com-manded" recommendation from 1811 that the upper grades should be taught "military exercises"[331] really came from his heart. If one now adds that the dual military system underlying the *Philosophy of Right* existed only in Prussia at that time, and was regarded everywhere – in fear, contempt, or hope – as characteristic of this state, then one may assume in good conscience that the professor from Berlin relied on Prussia for this idea.

The matter is not so simple on other points. With respect to the details of rights, especially family law, in many cases we could refer to Prussian Common Law. However, Hegel's study of the Frederician code of law comes at the end of the 1790s, and we were already brought to presume that Hegel's image of the state from the System of 1802, that is, from the time when he was most decisively averse to the Prussian state, was partially dependent upon this code. On the other hand, with the final system from Jena, the Frederician idea of the estates ceased to be as firm and the nobility retreated behind the civil service, even before the great collapse of old Prussia had followed in all actuality.

Economic individualism and "social freedom" in general, which Treitschke has taught us to see as a basic feature of the Prussia at that time, are also basic forces in Hegel's *Philosophy of Right*. However, we find them effective in Hegel long before the ideas come to dominate Prussia; we saw them spring forth simultaneously with the origin of Hegel's idea of the state. We saw how the very inner development of Hegel's state system in Jena was driven forward by the thorn of balancing the ideas of political and social freedom. Adam Smith's influences, to which Hegel was subject in 1802, also became dominant in the Prussian civil service, and later in the state, around that very time. And this explains Hegel's greatest, and most fundamental, encounter with the state in which he would spend his most effective years. On the other hand, the counter-weights against economic individualism, especially Hegel's hopes for the "corporation," can be traced back to the System of 1802. The fact that Hegel, from the very beginning – and this remained apparent in 1820 – was looking for a way out of the dangers of modern industrial labor already rules out associating Hegel's hopes with Prussia's reaction to Hardenberg's destruction of the guilds, a reaction that could hardly be noticed at the time. Instead, Hegel's impulse, which was also evident in 1820, came from across the channel, and these thoughts can probably be traced back to his preoccupation with the English Poor Law and the attempts at reform, which attest to the year 1799.

With regard to "civil society," how little consideration Hegel gave to the state to which he belonged, and how he continued to present his old thoughts unchanged, is shown by the fact that in 1820, as already in 1812, Hegel again called for jury courts, yet this time, he did so with a partially new, namely liberal, justification. However, in Prussia, jury courts only existed in the Rhenish parts of the country and, shortly before, Gentz had called them the "axiom of the Revolution," and as such they had been unanimously rejected at the Carlsbad conferences.

It is a different matter entirely when dealing with the institutions of the "constitution." On this point, although the beginnings of Hegel's ideas essentially date back to the Jena period, the final highlights seem to have been added to the image in Berlin. More so than with the social questions, Hegel may have felt obligated here to reveal the relation between his thoughts and Prussian actuality. Let us take a detailed look.

The monarchy, with its fundamental absoluteness – which neverthe-less, especially in peacetime, is in fact limited to a mere execution of ministerial bills – initially reflects at least as much of the French *Charte*[332] as Friedrich Wilhelm of Prussia, if not more. And yet, already in his earliest deduction of the concept of monarchy in 1805, Hegel had expressed the withdrawal of the king's personal idiosyncrasy – and since then presented it time and again as the hallmark of a well-ordered state – as the most striking feature of his image of monarchy. A feature, moreover, which one could easily align with Friedrich Wilhelm. The free appointment of ministers, personal unaccountability, and the right to pardon are as much French and English as Prussian. Even if the concept of ministerial responsibility was in fact not possible to implement in the Prussia of that time, and therefore not yet developed constitutionally, it was nevertheless morally present with Stein, and had also manifested itself visibly, and almost publicly, in the great ministerial crisis at the end of 1819. The polemic against the concept of divine right shows the philosopher to be completely immersed in Stein's theories. On this point, Hegel unhesitatingly rejects such designations as "misleading," which the Prussian king, as well as all the others, were using to introduce every act of state.

At first glance, Prussian features seem to impose themselves in the description of civil service. When one thinks of how Treitschke portrayed those twenty-five years from 1815 to 1840 as the "aristeia of Prussian civil service" – as that epoch when a highly educated, unimpeachably honorable generation in Prussia's ministries and governments completed the great task of internal unification and strengthening of the motley state, or at least initiated the greater task of leading this state into German supremacy – one feels inclined to readily associate these years with Hegel's description of civil service. However, the unyielding chronology again stands in the way. The esteem for administrative work was probably already in the blood of the son of the Württemberg tax official. The first system had already at least presupposed, if not expressed, the incidentally pre-Hegelian idea that a good administration is better than any "constitution."[333] The text on *The German Constitution*, which mocks the multi-government system, nevertheless established a similar ideal of civil servants as the ideal that would later broadly appear in the System of 1805. Here, civil servants are called the true "legislative body" and, in the same way, the equality of good independent "councils" with "imperial estates" is expressed in the first Nuremberg *Propaedeutic*. Similarly, in the text on the Württemberg constitution, there is a vehement polemic against that provision from Wangenheim's draft which denied civil servants the eligibility to be elected to the estates. In contrast, it is precisely the civil servants who have that sense of the state which is necessary for the estates. The reference to the importance of the size of the state for the cultivation of a broadminded spirit among the civil service is a new factor, and one that decidedly grew from observing Prussian conditions. In addition, it has already been pointed out how Hegel's high esteem for the civil service is somewhat repressed in the *Philosophy of Right*, especially compared with earlier statements such as that of 1805, owing in particular to the importance that Hegel places on self-governance, which was not present in 1805. For this, one might assume the influence of Stein's municipal statutes. However, already in the text on *The German Constitution*, Hegel had included that great hymn of praise on the usefulness and political necessity of self-governance, and therefore, in place of direct influence, one must instead assume the commonality of influence, from English conditions, for example. As a counterweight against the rigid uniformity of administration, Hegel recognizes the free activity of citizens, initially in their closer affairs, as necessary (even in his letters from Bavaria), and laments that of those two results from the Revolution only the first was imitated by the German states of that time. Hegel himself does not conceal that in 1820 he sees self-governance, which he calls for not only in cities but for municipalities as well – and incidentally in contrast to what was then actually happening in Prussia – as a distinctive advantage of German state life over the French.

Regarding the demand for an Estates Assembly, it was never denied that Hegel goes beyond the conditions of contemporary Prussia in an important way. At most, Hegel was criticized from a later point of view for not advocating strongly enough for such an assembly; however, this claim was never proven. Moreover, it remains the case that ever since Hegel's Napoleonic period an Estates Assembly certainly always belonged to his image of the best state, if not already since 1802.[334] For the particulars, one must hold oneself to Hegel's hopes and aspirations, and not look to gain answers from the actual relations in Prussia. Now, it has to be said that Hegel's idea of basing the Estates Assembly on a society organized politically through self-governance, in order to preferably have delegates who had previously gone through this schooling of practical public life, was found in some form in all Prussian constitutional plans considered in the years leading up to 1820. Only the thought, drawn from Stein, that there can be "no popular representation without the substructure of self-governance" can just as well be found with Rotteck, the people's tribune of Baden, but again, Hegel had already expressed this same thought earlier, namely in the plan for a constitution of Württemberg. This is also where one can already find approval for the idea of single votes for nobles and for the idea of the bicameral system. Only the justification of entailments was new, and not substantiated anywhere in Hegel's views on property law and family law. Hegel's skepticism against voting may be partially ascribed to the impression he gained from English parliamentary relations of that time, and to their sham elections. The specific assertion that the only healthy form of opposition between the Estates Assembly and the government is the "factiousness of mere subjective interest, such as that of the higher offices of state," also points to the English.[335] The restraint shown towards the problem of the sources of taxation, which in 1802 Hegel had constructed to reflect the Prussian state, may be explained by the general uncertainty of views on the Prussian tax law of 1820. Several important questions of constitutional state law remain unanswered, such as that of the budget – at least in 1820 – the question of periodicity, and that of initiative. Strangely enough, however, there is no allusion to the right to approve "new taxes," which was limited for the Estates by the royal constitutional pledge of 1815. Hegel is silent on all these individual questions, some of which are important in praxis, especially for Prussia. What is most striking is that Hegel does not say a word about the central question of Prussia's internal politics, concentrated in the problem of the estates, namely, the question of whether there should be a centralized state or Prussian "states," if there should be imperial estates[336] or provincial estates. It is as if this problem – which, of course, had long since ceased to be a problem for France and England at that time, but by way of which Prussian constitutional policy of those years first becomes comprehensible – was not present at all for the "Prussian philosopher of state." Based on Hegel's idea of the state in general, and given the fact that his image of popular representation stems from a dependence on Western paradigms, there can be no doubt as to what position Hegel took. But his complete disregard for the central problem of internal Prussian politics throws a peculiar light on the relationship of his image of the state to the Prussian conditions of those years. Are we to assume that he shied away from making a statement? But then he would have more than likely had to suppress statements like the one about divine right, suppress the outburst against Haller, which will be discussed later, as well his decisive position in favor of the Estates in general. One must come to terms with the negative findings on these points as well.

However, when Hegel addressed the concept of "externally directed sovereignty," he did comment on another question of Prussian political life, a question which, over the decades, would displace the question of the single, centralized state as a main concern. Within his system, Hegel only once mentioned nationality as a political factor. Where he explains how "family communities" are gathered into a people, "either by imperious force or by voluntary union through the connection established by their interlinked needs and the reciprocal effect of their gratification,"[337] he then names another possibility alongside these two possible origins of the state. Along with the possibility of war-like violence, which Hegel had previously allowed to stand on its own, and the economic-social possibility, which in a certain sense now underlies his systematic outline of family, society and state, he names as another possibility the calm expansion of the family "into a people – a *nation*, which thereby has a common and natural origin."[338] He thus acknowledged, at least as a possibility, the idea of a natural nationality as the basis of the state, albeit without any systematic consequences. This idea is now brusquely placed within the limits of mere possibility when it seems to require its own rights with respect to the sovereignty of the state, that very "independence, which is the first freedom and highest honor of a people": "Those who desire to forfeit an entirety, which constitutes a more or less independent state and which has its own center, those who desire to forfeit this middle point and its independence in order to join with another state and make a whole, know little of the nature of totality and the sense of self a people has in its independence."[339] The applicability to Prussia and to Germany is so apparent that it is hardly unintentional. Yet nevertheless, one must admit – and we will address this in what comes – that it would have been impossible for Hegel, in accord with his entire idea of the state, to speak differently. This political particularism was not imposed upon him by the Prussian politics of the time. Three years earlier, he had expressed his opinion on Württemberg's "sovereignty" in an equally unconditional manner. It was not to the merit of the greater Prussian state, nor was it at fault, that in contrast to the tribal state of Württemberg, Prussia was more deeply qualified for Hegel's idea of the state. Here, as with almost all other points, the superficially obvious assumption of a direct, and even intended, model relationship between Hegel and his state-employer proves to be false. The truth is much more that Hegel and the Prussian state are contemporaries, in time and to a certain extent also in age, namely, contemporaries in fate. The same worldly storms erupted over both: they erupted over the philosopher's receptive and forceful spirit of workmanship, and over the strong and regenerating body of the state "founded on intelligence." Thus, it can therefore be said that Hegel was the philosopher of the Prussian state, but only insofar as it can equally be said that the Prussian state of 1820 was a thought of Hegelian philosophy. The one is as true and untrue as the other.

The state as a thought of philosophy – with this we now arrive at the last section of our account of Hegel's book from 1820. First, we accompanied the emergence of the state from the will, and traced this emergence throughout the entirety of the community structures below the state. We then saw how Hegel sought to grasp the organization of the state as an outcome of this concept of will. And we have now reached the point where the state as a whole, built up from the will and arranged by it, is placed upon the Chair of philosophy and confronted with the other spiritual powers.

The first of these powers is the state itself. For it is characteristic of the state that it is indeed something ultimate for the human being, who in a certain sense cannot see beyond it, but that it is likewise "individuality," and thus really nothing ultimate at all. Let us first try to clarify this without relying too heavily upon Hegel's own words. After the individual had left the sphere of individual psychology, that is, the sphere of the "subjective spirit," we find him again in the spheres of "objective spirit" as a sociable being. Within "right," he finds himself in a plurality, not a community, of those who are equal to him – we know that for Hegel this is the classical private right of Rome. His will can only claim to be actual in that it grants the same claim to the will of all others. This relation is now reversed into exactly the opposite in "morality" – and we know that for Hegel this is the morality of Kant and Fichte. Here, the individual knows of nothing outside of his moral will, a will that claims to be such that it could be the law of a community. He does not acknowledge a real multitude of willing people beside himself, but rather the will of an ideal community, and this not alongside his own will, but as one with it. In the sphere of "right" the individual presupposed the many outside of himself, and thus does not consider himself to be something ultimate without need of "acknowledgment." In the sphere of "morality" he indeed considers himself to be something ultimate, but only with regard to the ideal community whose will he equates with his own. It is only within the spheres Hegel calls "Ethicality" that the individual acknowledges the community as something existing outside of himself, and precisely because of his own self-acknowledgment does he desire to be acknowledged by the community. In other words, the individual and the community are something mutually ultimate for each other. But this reciprocity is initially only something conditional. It only exists for a while in the "family." Then the individual steps out of the family into "civil society." In doing so, he does not disown the family in general – indeed, he establishes a new one – but he disowns the unconditionality of the relation between himself and the house where he was born and educated. This disavowal of the family is the step that leads him into "civil" society, the term with which Hegel summarizes all external communal life, that is, as long as it is not of the home or the state. The individual does not leave civil society. He remains its member, even if and insofar as he is a member of the "state." Thus, it already appears that in civil society the reciprocity of the relation between the human being and community has become something unconditional.

But this is not the case. Indeed, the reason that the individual does not leave civil society is that it is only a community insofar as it continuously forms economic, professional, and social communities within itself. The individual is always within one or another of these. However, for him, society as a whole is not community. It is, in a way, limitless, or at any rate without the ability to be self-limiting. Thus, society is also not some kind of epitome of humankind. After the individual had to leave the family, because it was only a "single" community, he is then incorporated into society, which is not real community, but only a gathering place for all kinds of communities. Therefore, just as before his relation to family in general was something unconditional, and only the relation to his original family was something to be given up, now conversely the unconditionality of his relation to society is in belonging to a single community, namely that of the chosen profession, which he will not give up on his own, whereas he cannot give up belonging to society in general solely because it does not exist as true community at all. Or rather, to bring the dialectic of these Hegelian concepts to a close: just as the relation to the individual family is necessary – first to the original family and then to the established one – family life in general designates the ultimate community only for one stage of life, namely for childhood. So, conversely, entry into society is admittedly necessary in general; however, the specific place within a specific one of society's communities is purely a matter of random predisposition and the random fate of life, if not entirely arbitrary. Thus, as one can see, the relation between the individual and the ethical community in these two spheres is only ever unconditional in one regard, and missing in another.

For Hegel, the concept of the state is determined by the fact that this unconditionality of the relation between individual and community is inherent in every respect. The individual is faced with only one community of this kind and, as an ethical human, he cannot give up his relation to it. No ethical relation beyond this is conceivable to him and none of them are as self-contained as this. His relation to the state in general, and to the special duties which he owes to his state in his position, are fulfilled by exactly the same disposition, namely "patriotism." He is not allowed to separate between the "contingency" of his special position and the "necessity" of belonging to a state in general. Thus, the unconditional relation is the relation between state and human being.

But this unconditionality is the unconditionality of a relation. And now everything becomes shaky again. A relationship, however narrow and necessary it may be, still has an external precondition, namely its own components. What is truly unconditional must be something singular. If the state has no other ground than precisely that human being who stands as free will at the conclusion of "subjective spirit," and if, on the other hand, the ultimate human relation is given to humans in the state, then both the state and the human being are such that not one is made by the other, rather their relation is that each presupposes the other – the state presupposes the actual human being and the human being presupposes the actual state. Therefore, philosophy must hold the human being, in the manner found at the conclusion of "subjective spirit," ready-made and available to the state, whereas the same thing cannot happen with the state, since the system can only be presented in one direction. Thus, instead of the state being deduced in advance as "actual," as is the case with the human being, it is rather presupposed as actual, and philosophy, as it were, requests that it is provisionally exempted from demonstrating the proof of this actuality – instead, it should subsequently deliver this proof. However, what has been said here of the state equally applies to all previous spheres of ethical life, all the way back to right.[340] Here, too, the assumption that there actually is a plurality of people is not philosophically proven. But it is only with the state that it becomes a burning question, because hitherto every sphere of "objective spirit" had been able to pass the assumption along with reference to the fact that within the given sphere, the relation between the human being and the sphere at hand had not yet found any conclusive resolution. In the case of the state, however, this assumption can no longer be avoided, as the state is supposed to be the place of unconditional human relations. Therefore, its actuality as such must be grasped philosophically. For the philosopher, however, actuality – apart from that highest actuality, which the state, as relation, cannot be – really means the same thing that it means in practical life: individuality. And therefore, for Hegel, the state – not despite, but precisely because it was constructed out of the free will of individuals – must itself be an "individual," unconcerned about these individual wills: a state among states.

This is the systematic basis of Hegel's realist metaphysics of the state. After all, it is nothing other than what we have pursued from the beginning of Hegel's thought: the origin of the idea of the power state, mediated by the concept of fate, and grasped from within the spirit of a most broadly stretched individualism. There are two other motifs, also pointing biographically back to Frankfurt, which show by means of a counter-check that Hegel could not have acted otherwise systematically. More on that below. Here, it is still to be shown how Hegel implements the concept of the power state.

This time, Hegel attempts to develop his long familiar idea of the state as power – where he presents it within the framework of a "philosophy of right" as the only justified moral principle of politics, owing to the merely conditional validity of state treaties and the egoism of the state – from the concept of "external state law." This is indeed valid, however, in that there is "no praetor"[341] for states, and in that right is based here on not one, but "on *various sovereign wills*," it is valid only in the form of an "*ought*."[342] With "external state law," or international law according to common usage, where the subjects of law are states, the acknowledgment, which within private right everyone claims and everyone receives from everyone else, must indeed be demanded by all from all; however, whether this demand is fulfilled for it "depends on its content, constitution, condition, and the acknowledgment [...] depends [...] on the view and will of the other."[343] From this Hegel derives the other aspects of his basic ideas on external politics. There is plenty in the details here that is determined by the age, and also limited by the age. For example, there is a distinctly ambiguous bearing towards the principle of intervention, not saying yes and not saying no, which stems from the idea that although every state demands acknowledgment, not every other state must grant it. Indeed, Hegel speaks of the "legitimacy of a state," which, "insofar as it is turned outward," is that of its prince, and while admittedly "on the one hand" it refers entirely inward, "on the other hand" it must be completed through the acknowledgment of the other.[344] Along with this there comes a guarantee that a state likewise acknowledges the others who acknowledge it. Thus, "on the one hand," one state should not interfere in the internal affairs of the other, while "on the other hand" it cannot be indifferent to what is happening within the other." We find ourselves in late 1820, at about the same time as the Congress of Troppau. The division of the European powers seems to be reflected in the paragraphs at hand. The ambiguity is all the more striking when a few paragraphs later, it is declared that wars are not to be waged "against the internal institutions."[345] Today, an observation such as the one that state treaties differ from private ones by means of their "infinitely inferior variety," also appears to be determined by the age.[346] Hegel does not foresee that a half-century, and even an entire century, later these "primarily self-satisfying wholes," which he understands as the states, would, as much as with any private person, stand in relation to each other "in mutual dependence according to the most manifold considerations,"[347] and that state trade agreements will then rival any private contract in unmanageability and intricacy. In general, he only speaks of the commonality of states in passing. He only mentions the Holy Alliance in his lecture rather dryly – admittedly only at the end of the 1820s, when it visibly went to pieces – and in the same breath with Kant's project of "perpetual peace."[348]

Since rights among states remain an "ought," and thus the "ethical whole," the individual state, is exposed to the contingencies of "passions, interests, purposes, talents and virtues, violence, injustice and vice,"[349] there must be a power present – since the state is indeed "the ethical whole" – to relieve these contingencies from its fate. After the state was first confronted with the power of the state, and had revealed its true nature in this relation, Hegel now allows another force to visit upon it: "world history" as the "world's court of judgment."[350]

For the third time in the system of the "state" we encounter here, at its conclusion, the equation of substantive reason with subjective actuality. In the internal life of the state, the rational constitution was animated by the subjective disposition of patriotism. The state in its external activity was based on the oneness of the external power of its will with the internal reason of its constitution, as represented in the prince. Now, in the end, the assertion is made of the state as a whole, without distinction between its internal and external life, that its actual existence as a willing "individual" is the immediate appearance of the rational world order. The basic idea of the Preface – which in those two other forms still appeared ethically or pragmatically veiled, namely as the oneness of disposition and institution, as the oneness of internal and external state life – can now be felt with the entire metaphysical weight that it contains. The saying that the youthful revolutionary Schiller had threateningly directed into the face of the mighty of the earth, this same saying the mature Hegel now holds up as a Gorgon's head in the struggle between revolution and restoration, so that the groups now actively quarreling before him – he who recognizes – are frozen into stone: world history is the world's court of judgment.

We have seen how that foundational proposition of the reciprocal unity of the actual and the rational creates rest only for cognition, by no means wanting to take away the movement from living things. The form it now takes makes this quite clear. If world history is the world's court of judgment, then the present receives its judgment by becoming past; by ceasing to be actual, it renders itself abandoned by reason. Thus, the equation of reason and actuality only really becomes distinct in its application. Time is the variable that must be inserted into that double-dictum to make it applicable and, since it only goes in one direction and does not run backwards, to make it unequivocal. Thus, the dialectical double-sidedness of the thought that only what is rational is actual, yet also that only what is actual is rational, becomes the unequivocal proposition of world history as the world's court of judgment. Let us remember that the proposition from the Preface, at the place where it stood in the book, only first opened in its development and meaning when we drew a subsidiary line from the movement of world history. And, understood in this way, it followed that only because and where what is rational is acknowledged as that which is to be actualized, may and must the actual be recognized as the actualization of the rational. This is the case now as well. Only because world history is the world's court of judgment, only because its irrevocable verdicts are drawn according to the law of reason, only therefore is the actual rational.

World history is now, in point of fact, and according to Hegel's fondly used expression, the "praetor" between states: it limits itself to instructing the process. Judgment is passed by the court world history sets up, and this court consists of citizens. Spoken without image: "world history" makes use of the states themselves for its judgments. A people is "judged" by world history in being destroyed or displaced by another people. Thus, it initially seems here in principle that Hegel can continue his realistic view of political life. "World spirit" remains in the background of the unconscious; "justice and virtue, injustice, violence and vice, talents and their deeds, small and great passions, guilt and innocence, glory of individual and national life, independence, happiness and unhappiness of states and individuals have their definite meaning and value in the sphere of conscious actuality."[351] Likewise, the "*geographical and anthropological* existence"[352] of a people, as well as its rise, blossoming, decline, and finally the fact that "at the peak of all actions, thus also of world-historical ones," there stand individuals,[353] all these are acknowledged as necessary complements to this view, as its visible exterior, so to speak. But behind this view there then appears the secret of world history, the "cunning of reason," to use the famous expression from the lectures on the philosophy of history. And the seemingly acknowledged pure historicity of history is again reduced to mere appearance.

Because world history is supposed to be the world's court of judgment, the apparent chaos, the entirety of "colorful actuality,"[354] must in truth be cosmos. There, what is seemingly the bare court of power, the "irrational necessity of a blind fate," reveals itself as "development," as the "exposition and *actualization of the universal spirit*."[355] The principle of this "development" is then the principle of "spirit" in general, namely, that spirit becomes more and more itself, and evermore purely itself, that it becomes more spiritual and more free – a process which Hegel calls becoming conscious. The peoples' histories must now incorporate themselves into this progress of self-consciousness. A people is a stage in this process; as long as it remains so – that means, and again seen from the outside, as long as this people is doing well – it has "absolute right," and it itself and its deeds "are brought to completion and it receives fortune and fame."[356] The blossoming of a people consists in the fact that it reaches this stage where it becomes world-historical, where what is historically essential emanates from it. A people's decline consists in the fact that it perseveres on its stage while world history wants to move on. Whether it perishes or somehow drags on in its existence, it is no longer of interest to world history, which has meanwhile chosen a new people to be its bearer. The destiny of the great man is similar. He, too, who seemingly only lives for himself, in truth serves the necessities of his people and, if this people is world historical, serves the necessities of world history as a "world historical hero." In the figure of the great man, which has been familiar to us in this way since 1802, the relation between the individual and the community gains a final embodiment in Hegel's system, even if it is consciously presented only as an exception. It would be possible to compile an entire treatise on the ethics of heroes from the *Philosophy of Right* of 1820 and from the *Lectures on the Philosophy of History*.[357] But it remains fixed within the framework of history and is thereby rendered harmless. It is an ethics of primordial times when states are founded and transitional times when states are renewed. Nevertheless, for the third time, the interpenetration of "subjectivity" and "substance," which dominates the entire doctrine of "objective spirit," consolidates itself into human personality: the hero joins the citizen and the prince.

We have already pursued how this concept of history developed within the Hegelian system. It was the major event in Hegel's system when it was cast from the highest height and expelled to the line of demarcation where what is human and what is divine, where earth and heaven, "objective" and "absolute" meet. In general, we recognized as probable that this revaluation of history was only one side of the revaluation of the present forced by the fall of Napoleon. For in finally giving up the belief that the present moment signified the beginning of the epoch of final completion, and that consequently the position that was formerly held by the present belonged without reservation to the entrance of Christianity into world history, Hegel led Christianity and the Church out of their previous historicization. If for Hegel the latter had hitherto been a mere element in the construction of the future, and thus themselves of the past, they now became for him simply the present. Thereby, however, this living present, which had existed for eighteen hundred years, was now elevated beyond the sphere of the historical. Unlike in 1805 and 1806, the historicity of the world could no longer be the highest concept of the system. Above its historicity now came its spirituality, visibly manifested in Christianity. Or, in other words, the world, whose highest aspect was its historicity, its progress, and its self-development, was arranged in the system below the spheres where those concepts of progress and development cease to signify the ultimate essence and the ultimate truth of things. The ethical world finds and needs no higher answer to its insolubility than that which is guaranteed by its historicity. Thus, with cause, the thinker may call the existence of the state "the path of God in the world" – mind you, simply "in the world."[358] But beyond the ethical world, beyond the visible organization of ethicality, there is an ultimate realm which is no longer organization, there is an ultimate being-alone of the soul [Beisichselbersein der Seele]. A realm where the soul is solitary, as it was before it spread to the world of "objective spirit," and where, however, after wandering through this world, it is solitary in a different way than it could have been before. And it is precisely history that enters between these two worlds, between the world of organization and the realms of solitude. And history's content is, looking "downwards," to actualize ethical organization, while also, looking "upwards," allowing that life of the soul, which is solitary in art, faith, and knowledge, to become actual. Thus, the result is that Hegel now finds new formulas for the path of world history.

In the beginnings, when Hegel first questioned a three-part philosophy of history – paganism, Christianity, and the future – he established this upon the concepts of a pure valuation of this world, a pure devaluation of this world, and a future incorporation of this contrast into a disposition that knows anguish and, in order to overcome it, acknowledges and accepts the same. The first appearance in the text on *The German Constitution* of what was later to become the definitive division of world history worked quite externally with despotism, the republic, and the unification of both in a monarchy surrounded by imperial estates. In *The Phenomenology*, where the new division of history was also disclosed for the history of religion, the passive oriental religion of nature was fused together with the creative Greek religion of beauty in Christianity. They were brought together in such a manner that Christianity contained the condition of being overcome in the thought of revelation and the human God in the content of faith. At the same time, *The Phenomenology* still built its universal construction of world history along the same contours and with the same thoughts as the original philosophy of history: an unbroken worldliness, a dichotomy between the world and what is beyond the world, and a higher unity. Only that it likewise clearly conceived of this development as a struggle of the idea of the state for its systematic place: in the Polis, the struggle against the individual operating from the basis of the family; in the medieval and contemporary state, the struggle against the individual liberating itself into society; and in the future state, the subordination of the state to the spirit. The *Encyclopedia* of 1817, in more detail the final paragraphs of the *Philosophy of Right*, and later the *Lectures on the Philosophy of History*, all these texts draw up the ground plan in such a way that world history is both the becoming of the consummate state constitution and the consummation of the individual human being. This happens in that Hegel – now for the first time – represents history as the development towards "freedom." On the one hand, this freedom is actualized in complete ethical organization, on the other hand it is the presupposition of life within "absolute spirit." In that Hegel allows spirit to become truly free in history, to "come to itself," to experience "progress in the consciousness of freedom,"[359] he likewise, and systematically, turns this freedom into something found beyond this progress: in world history, the life of freedom is to develop itself; freedom is also developed in art, religion, and philosophy, but here its life consists in the simple fact that it is. This duality of the concept of freedom, namely, that freedom becomes, but can only become because it is, makes it capable of being the systematic bearer of a world history whose metaphysical essence now includes the double meaning that it is at once "earth" and yet "footstool under His feet."[360] Up until 1806, world history had been the absolute itself. The conclusion of The Phenomenology could use the term world spirit[361] – the later term for world history – and God interchangeably. Later, beginning at least in 1817, this no longer happens.[362]

Owing to the intermediary position that history now assumes, the concept of a people – of nationality – could be treated in more depth and detail. Admittedly, almost nothing happened to make this concept fruitful for the state. In this regard, despite the promising turn of the inaugural speeches in Heidelberg and Berlin on nationality as the basis of all living life, everything remained the same in the Philosophy of Right. In the Lectures on the Philosophy of History, however, the intermediate positioning between state and spirit made it possible to somehow bring both forces together, and the concept of the spirit of the people now served this purpose.

Systematically, this can be understood on an even deeper basis. One might say that cultural goods are to be acquired by the individual; however, the lives of these goods are not absorbed therein: these cultural goods are actual even without this. The Sistine Madonna and the Critique of Pure Reason can be preserved in museums and libraries. The family, moral will, and professional ethicality cannot be thus preserved. They are actualized by human beings and not given another possibility of existing. Now, it is also possible to construct the being of the state according to the manner of cultural goods. To do so, some entity, a people for example, with its distinctive context of cultural goods, must be taken as its bearer, while the state itself is basically only the meaningless form of organization of this already existing entity. Strong impulses in this direction could already be found in the idea of the nation state of the nineteenth century, and at the beginning of the twentieth century, these impulses had nearly triumphed in the idea of a populist foundation of the state. Hegel was far removed from all of this. For him, the state was an ethical organization, that is, although admittedly an entity, it was founded not upon its own being but upon the human will. That it also had being itself, and not only absorbed and embodied the will of the individual, this was first systematically conceived where the state entered into "external state law" as a state among states. However, there it was the being of a forceful power of the will which consciously seeks to assert its own ends. Thus, it could not appear as pure being elevated above all will. It first became such pure being only immediately before the conclusion of the doctrine on the actualization of the will, namely in "world history." Here, however, the state is ultimately only an existing entity: the self-serving will, which suffused it in foreign policy, is recognized here as the reflection of an unconscious being – namely the participation of the "spirit of the people" in the "world spirit" – reflected in the consciousness of the state. And with this we reach a point, likewise based on Hegel's foundations, where state and culture can meet.

From the very beginning, even while he was still at the Stift, Hegel had conceived of the spirit of the people, based primarily on Montesquieu's conception, as the epitome of what appeared to the life of the people. In this context, the state – the "constitution" – had been a subdomain. This relation of the state to the other spheres of life was not further clarified. The close proximity that the state obtained to the "people" in the philosophy of the state made a new construction necessary, which was first made possible in the final Nuremberg systematic. Now the relation could be established which the Introduction to the *Lectures on the History of Philosophy* would later broadly carry out.[363] The state now became the precondition of culture. Art, religion, and science all descended from their heavenly seats and consented to taking their place in the historical constitutional-form of a people. They gave up the purely soulful "element" of their true existence and incorporated themselves into a "spiritual actuality in its entire extent of inwardness and outwardness."[364] Hegel now calls the connection ordered in this manner – the state as form, culture as content – spirit of the people. This is why Hegel structured and developed world history, understood as the growth of the world spirit through the changing forms of the spirit of the people, only according to the ethicality of the individual, which is complete in the inner form of the state, whereas he does not grant culture as such its own development in the context of world history. Instead, he aligns a corresponding form of culture with each form of the state, each which originates with dialectical necessity out of a previous form, without wanting to develop this culture here from its own preliminary stage, such as, for example, developing the art of Greece from that of Egypt. Rather, cultural goods – Hegel's "universal" or "absolute" spirit – only attain historical actuality in relationship to the state. That they nevertheless have their own history, and indeed each area its own, namely that there is a history of art, a history of religion, and a history of philosophy, is something entirely different. Having their own history does not make them essentially historical. They become so only in so far as they become the content of a people's spirit in a form of community life. This explains the otherwise inexplicable fact that along with his universal world history of the spirits of people Hegel could, without concern, develop particular philosophical histories of art, religion and philosophy – not of religion itself – in a structure that more or less diverged from world history.

Not of religion itself. With this, and not by chance, the last decisive aspect for an inner understanding of Hegel's view of the state is disclosed. The specific history of religion has the same structure as universal world history because world history has the same structure as the history of religion. Within Hegel's biography, we are already familiar with the context. Apart from a systematically inconsequential remark in the text on *The German Constitution*, Hegel first absolutized the Christian present instead of a post-Christian future within the history of religion. Christianity, with its drive to actualize reason, became for Hegel the primordial phenomenon of the agreement between actuality and rationality. When he transferred this view to the content of universal world history, which is first evidenced in the *Encyclopedia* of 1817, the idea of the form of world historical events had been long formed and incurred basically no change, even now. The view to historicize everything remained in force, whereby an individual people was to be understood only as a phase of the world historical process – its development understood as growing into this course; its blossoming as life, weaving and being within it; and its passing away as falling out of this course of history. But this view of the incessant change of historical phenomena now met a dangerous adversary in the disciples of the supra-historicity of historical Christianity. This European, or as Hegel says, Germanic world dominated by Christianity can no longer pass away; no other "world historical people" can appear and displace it, copying how it had displaced the Roman world. Hence, there is a peculiar dichotomy in Hegel's definitive philosophy of history.[365] Whereas pre-Christian peoples each signify only a phase, and development takes place in the changeover of these peoples, in the Christian-Germanic ethnic group development takes place as an inner progress, a progress in which peoples admittedly emerge and recede, and within which history in general by no means comes to an end, but the Christian people as a whole does not die. Instead, this people only unfolds ever more completely and develops ever more towards ethical freedom. Thus Hegel, out of the fundamental recognition of the eternal value of Christianity, and yet not on the basis of this recognition, arrived at a kind of community of peoples beyond the state and without the forms of state organization. He arrived at a church, if you will, whose invisible leader is the law of world history, namely "world spirit." In this way, Hegel's "fourth world empire" differs from the past three just like the Danielic one: it is the empire which will have no end. But Hegel arrived at this final thought by way of the strict separation of the states. The invisible law that unites this invisible community of peoples, the law of world history, is the same that eternally separates the visible peoples. History grows only from the contrasts between independent states, and history alone is the bond that unites these independent "individuals." And therefore, with good reason, we hesitated when calling this community of peoples a "church." It would be "invisible" in almost an ironic sense. And Hegel likewise denied it this name. He would have implied thereby that there was still an ethical law for the human being beyond the individual state, and thus would have robbed the unconditional relation between the individual and his state of its unconditionality. Therefore, Hegel forms his concept of church in a strictly Protestant sense as a purely inner-human and supramundane one, which knows community only as a community of saints or believers. The unavoidable relationships of this church to the world are mediated only through the individual soul.

This is the basis of the relation that Hegel allows his state to adopt to the church.[366] It is already telling at which point of the state doctrine the problem arises for him. After having developed the concept of "political disposition" – of patriotism – in its necessary connection to the institutions of the "constitution" at the beginning of the doctrine on internal state law, Hegel expresses the spiritual self-sufficiency of the state, so to speak, on the basis of this reciprocal relationship between subjective disposition and substantial order, between particular and universal interest: "the state knows [...] what it wants, and knows it [...] as *something thought*; it is therefore effective and acts in accordance with known purposes, known principles [...]."[367] And now here "is the place to touch upon *the relation of the state to religion*."[368] The possibility of a conflict is set. The state, after all, is not an external and soulless mechanism; it lays claim to disposition and "knows what it wants." Or, as Hegel says in all clarity, and with deliberate rejection of the "medieval" view of the state as that of the "*lay person in and for itself*"[369]: the state also has a doctrine. On the other hand, religion, for its part, rightly claims that it contains "the absolute truth," and accordingly, that "the highest of dispositions" falls to it, and that therefore "everything [...] attains its confirmation, justification, and assurance in it."[370] How is this internal dispute, not yet between state and church, but between consummate state and consummate religion, initially resolved? Hegel provides us the solution as he had essentially outlined it already in 1805 and, since then, especially in the Napoleonic period, as he had used it for the basis of his religious-political statements. In a consciously Protestant manner, he explains that religion and state are different manifestations, "complementary manifestations,"[371] of the same spiritual content. However, it is the nature of religion that first within it the individual, as individual, becomes "conscious [...] of the highest freedom and satisfaction,"[372] and that within religion the inherent right of the individual, which was removed in "morality," finds its impregnable fortress. The state, on the other hand, reaches beyond this foundation of inner disposition, which is also indispensable for it, into external actuality, in order to unfold "into the actual configuration and *organization of a world*."[373] State and religion must therefore not come into conflict, because the state begins where religion ends, namely with actuality, and because each presupposes the other. The state presupposes religion, which first completes the state (as the twenty-five-year-old had already explained following Mendelssohn's *Jerusalem*) in preparation for "the deepest aspect of disposition," and religion presupposes the state, which signifies for religion "the immense cross-over of the internal into the external," the incorporation of "reason into reality" upon which "the entire history of the world has worked."[374]

The result is what Hegel understands as the "simple" relation between the state and the church, or, as he characteristically puts it: between state and "church congregation."[375] The state is obligated "to aid and abet the congregation in its religious causes and to grant it protection." On the other hand, as a corporation, the congregation is under the state's "right to policing supervision,"[376] and the state is "to demand of all its members that they adhere to a church congregation."[377] Theoretically, one would expect that Hegel, in view of his conscious Protestantism with regard to the relation between church and state, would somehow come to favor Protestantism here, since only Protestantism unconditionally acknowledges the worldly state as willed by God, as Hegel demands. But even if this entire theory is already visibly connected to the political equality of the Christian confessions, which was first implemented in Prussia (but by 1820 was also already adopted by most other European states) Hegel now also expresses, and in the same sense as King Friedrich, his own version of statement that "the *religions* must all be tolerated"[378]: the state should "demand of all its members that they adhere to a church congregation – and incidentally to *any* congregation, for with regard to content [...] the state cannot become involved."[379] Thus, the more strongly organized a state is, the more that state may "conduct itself liberally," even against smaller communities, "which themselves do not religiously acknowledge their direct duties vis-à-vis the state," and thus the state may allow them to fulfill these duties "through commutation and substitution."[380] Here, Hegel is thinking of the exemption of the Mennonites from military service, which existed in Prussia until 1868. Regarding the Jews, the former reader of Mendelssohn's *Jerusalem* sides against the elevated "outcry" – a hostile movement against Jews had recently passed through Germany in 1819 – in agreement with the "granting of civil rights," which existed in Prussia beginning in 1811, on the basis of which the "desired balance of thinking and disposition will come about." Here, too, he avowedly champions the "governments in their action," but not Prussia's actions in particular.[381] In the matter of ecclesiastical marriage, Hegel takes the position that "ecclesiastical assurance" is only something additional, and that the essential thing is the assertion of state rights, since what is at stake is an "ethical relation."[382] This solution corresponds most closely to the *Code Napoléon*,[383] whereas the General Common Law allowed for a fully valid marriage by means of a priest-led ceremony,[384] and although the Prussian government had not gone so far as to repeal the *Code*'s obligatory civil marriage for the Rhineland in 1814, it had made the outbound ecclesiastical marriage obligatory.[385] Montgelas' Bavaria upheld a law analogous to the one of Rhineland-Prussia, a law under which Hegel's own marriage was contracted.[386] And at that time, the Prussian government tended towards the abolition of civil marriage altogether, even in its still existing form in the Rhineland, moving in precisely the opposite direction than Hegel had desired.[387]

The deepest aspect of Hegel's view of state and church comes to light when he takes up the split in the church during the sixteenth century. It is again his old idea, already realized in 1802. At that time, this idea was perhaps developed in viewing Frederician Prussia and from the theory on the relation of the state to the "church societies" existing in the state, a theory found in the General Common Law. Additionally, this idea was partly developed in light of the conditions of the Empire, where tolerance and freedom of thought, as well as the modern self-sufficiency of the state – which until then was a "lay person" – can be traced back to the split in the church. Hegel now takes up this question in a broad manner. That "desired unity of state and church"[388] espoused by the Romantics – if by this more was meant than the unity of principles and disposition – is actualized in oriental despotism. But there "the state is not present, not its self-conscious configuration in right, in free ethicality, and in organic development, which is alone worthy of spirit."[389] In order for the state to be thus configured, however, it is not merely necessary for it to have its own separate existence from the church; instead, "what is necessary is the distinction between the form of authority and the form of faith. This distinction, however, only emerges insofar as the church, for its part, becomes separated within itself. Only in this manner, only over *particular* churches, does the state gain *universality* of thought, the principle of its form, and bring this universality into existence [...] It is, therefore, off the mark to think that the separation within the church was, or would have been, a misfortune for the state, for *only through this* could the state have become that whereby it is determined, namely, self-conscious rationality and ethicality. Likewise, with regard to freedom and rationality, it is the most fortunate thing that could have happened to the church and for thought."[390] Although Hegel explicitly says that for all three – the state, the church and freedom of thought – many churches is "the most fortunate thing," he actually only proves it for the state and for thought, but not for the church. He even deprives the church of its ideal in Catholicity, which Protestantism had allowed the church to retain. The church should in no way be one church, not even within hope. There must be many states and many churches, not in such a way that each state has its own church, but in such a way that each state is faced with several churches. All of the driving forces of the Hegelian idea of the state come together here: the spiritual self-sufficiency of the state, which "also has a doctrine"[391]; the unconditional ethical relation of the individual to the state; and the view that the state may only have one organization above it – which is not a visible organization, and which therefore does not destroy its self-contained nature – namely, the spirit of world history. For this, the ideal of the one and universal church must be broken, because none of these thoughts could be maintained if this ideal remained unbroken. Only a church broken into "churches" allows the threefold *character indelebilis* of the Hegelian state – complete integration, ethical omnipotence, self-limitation – to remain unaffected. Only a church broken into "churches" completes what Hegel had recently begun in his formulation of the concept of religion based on the individual soul. Conversely, seen from this perspective it becomes clear how Hegel's state also had become as it is in order to correspond to that individualistic formulation of the concept of religion. The cornerstones of the entire Hegelian system, the absoluteness of the individual and the absoluteness of the whole, mutually support each other. The will for the religious salvation of the individual soul, oppressed by the world and fate, requires the concept of the self-ruling, inherently ethical state. This, however, what we now recognize in the completed system as the key to its systematicity, we observed in its development as the origin of the idea of the state. What once occurred in Frankfurt – that internal history, which led from the confessed desire to counteract the union with humankind, in that letter of the twenty-six-year-old,[392] to the acknowledgement of the state as fate – this, which was once blood and life, has now become a crafted work [gewirktes Werk]. The process of becoming closes into the circle of being. In the beginning stood the growing pains of a human soul; at the end stands Hegel's philosophy of state.

Being falls into the history whence it arose, and history dissolves it again in becoming. As a whole, Hegel's natural right was only effective in the academy, not in life. Life had to first break apart the unity of thought in order to construct these broken pieces anew. A safeguard against this, towards which a thinker must naturally aspire who is concerned above all with interweaving, and not with the threads, does not exist. The thinker will always only be able to secure himself against the forces he knows and believes to have bound into his thought, he cannot secure himself against the unknown forces that he himself first awakens. Past and present may bend to him, but his will remains powerless against the future.

The Scylla and Charybdis of the present, between which Hegel tries to navigate, are legitimacy and popular sovereignty, those very concepts which, according to the saying of Hegel's great French contemporary St. Simon, owe their existence solely to the fact that they are juxtaposed. This sentence could also have been written by the Hegel who wrote the *Philosophy of Right*. He also sought to deal with the two tendencies together, at the same place, while likewise always seeking to evade them. For Hegel, Haller and Rousseau share a single paragraph.[393]

The older adversary was the man of the Revolution, and thus far Rousseau had always been the more dangerous one, because Hegel himself had once dwelled within his circle and, even after greatly deviating from him, had still consciously derived his main idea from him. The first state system from 1802 – which likely made an impression on Schelling – distances itself consciously from "revolution," despite features drawn from antiquity and the idea of a republic, while actually not distancing itself from "reaction." Indeed, Haller, this other adversary, had vanished from Hegel's field of vision to such a degree at the time that Hegel did not hesitate in constructing the state's supreme authority – the predecessor of the monarch of 1805 – as a priesthood based on the concept of divine right that sits "in the council of the most high." The pole contrasting the Revolution – which Hegel tries to avoid here as well as in the general remarks of the text on *The German Constitution*, and in the subsequent state systems – is not the idea of legitimacy for Hegel, but instead bureaucratic praxis: the determining-of-everything-from-above; the disregard for free activity from below. Perhaps even the thought in 1805 that the civil service should be appointed through "public opinion" is to be understood as much as the attempt to de-bureaucratize the concept of the civil servant as it is to be understood as a revaluation of the revolutionary concept of public opinion. That the other extreme of popular sovereignty is not the omnipotence of civil servants but instead the concept of legitimacy, only dawned on Hegel in 1815. His letters from this time bear witness to this. Thus, the first winter in Berlin was well-suited to firmly establish this view. For it was then that Berlin society, especially within the circle of the Crown Prince, became infected with the views of the aristocrat from Bern [Haller], who looked to understand the state as a purely private order of law with the prince as its proprietor. In this view, this prince possessed his right, like any other private right which was at his free disposal as the right of the stronger. However, this "right" indicated "by the grace of God" meant undisturbed by any state duties and only inhibited by conflicting rights of "other" private people and the general morality. It is unbelievable, but discontent with the recommencing convulsions of revolution in Europe even brought men like Gneisenau to temporarily accept these assertions, which seemed to offer a remedy against revolution but which, nevertheless, like a veritable drastic treatment, were worse than the malady itself. Hegel, in a bloody polemic, whose sharpness exceeds anything he had ever directed towards Friesen, Schleiermacher, or even Savigny, then took on the Bernese aristocrat, whom Hegel might have once met personally and with whose recently published "democratic" antecedents[394] Hegel was certainly familiar. Above all, Hegel disputed with Haller over: the unabashed naturalism of his main principle; over his hatred of laws; over his degradation of the administration of justice from a state task to a mere boon; over his glorification of the right to emigrate and the right to resist; over his contempt for the written basic law in the manner of the English; and over his contempt for an objective concept of the state based on the General Common Law.[395] Hegel recognizes the inner kinship of Haller with his own adversary Rosseau in the fact that for the former the "particulars [Einzelheiten] of individuals"[396] are also the basis of the state. For Rousseau, however, the basis of the state is the "idea" of these particulars, namely the will, and the great Genevan was only lacking in that he allowed the communal will to emerge as something conscious directly from this will, instead of allowing, as Hegel himself had, the conscious will of the whole to emerge from the unconscious will of the individual. For the Bernese man, on the other hand, the state is based only on "the empirical particulars according to their accidental qualities, strength and weaknesses, wealth and poverty, etc."[397] Now that Hegel had recognized this opposition as the great struggle of the age – and he was historically correct – that other contrast he had emphasized earlier, namely the contrast between popular sovereignty and bureaucratism, was forced to recede far into the background. In its place, and already discernible in 1805, came the endeavor to save the "sovereignty" of the state from revolution and legitimacy by placing the bureaucratic "government," as the owner of the "sense of state," into the middle between the two poles of danger. Therefore, it follows that one can justifiably claim that this image of the state from 1820 is neither ultraroyalist, nor ultraliberal, but instead ultra-governmental.

The person who said this is the thinker who liberated Prussian conservatism from the already loosened fetters[398] of Haller's theory: Friedrich Julius Stahl.[399] He drew the strength for this deed, even more than he could, or was allowed to admit, from Hegel. Schelling, to whom he preferred to refer, was hardly independent of Hegel, particularly with regard to the state doctrine of the period in question. Stahl considered it to Hegel's merit to have "eliminated [Haller's] feudalistic doctrine based on private right."[400] Stahl himself criticizes his predecessor, as the acting official theoretician of Prussian conservatives, essentially from the "Schellingian-Hegelian" perspective of the subordination of private interests and entitlements to the state. Like Hegel himself, Stahl places himself between Rousseau and Haller: "there is [...] a third thing above the fallacy of the Revolution and above the fallacy of Haller, and that is [...] the public character of state authority."[401] But he does not merely criticize. He praises Haller for having brought "the natural side of right and state" to clear consciousness and for thereby making observations that "can be made fruitful in relation to the abstract mode of apprehension, from which we all suffer in this age."[402] And this praise of Haller is likewise a starting point for attacking Hegel, as the last sentence already shows. Hegel, in that he tore out the state – like all the rest – from the context of divine creation, and left the state entirely to itself in denying a deity beyond the world, thereby also suppressed the "natural side" of the state. And thus, Stahl's attack, where it transitions from a critique of the foundations of the system to a critique of the state doctrine, essentially follows Haller's lead, admittedly with incomparably more spirit and scientific rigor. Just as in Hegel's "*pantheistic*" system in general "*personality and freedom perish*,"[403] so Hegel also does not consider that "in every human being much volition, allowance, and expectation remains that is not fulfilled and determined by the state."[404] Personality was only seemingly of great importance to him. In all actuality, however, for example in deriving a representative constitution, it is not important at all. Indeed, Hegel even rejects that "A and B and C, all of those who actually live [in the state],"[405] would have their "real rights"[406] protected through popular representation or that in the administration of justice the particular "relation of A and B in the matter X"[407] is treated fairly. Thus, Hegel also does not consider "positive traditional right and the acquired rights founded upon it";[408] hence his repugnance for the English constitution and Roman history and his partiality towards German sovereigns versus the old Empire. Thus, despite all acknowledgement of "public right," one can see that this critique of Hegel is nevertheless Haller's old rebellion in favor of "life, freedom, personality, and history" – as Stahl puts it himself.[409] And if one desires to take a closer look at this solemn tetrad, it acquires the more distinct traits of those "inviolable rights whose holders must first be brought to join what is common and beneficial through inner conviction."[410] From behind the theory emerge the figures of the Markish Junkers, who could only be persuaded to accept Stein-Hardenberg's reform at the fortress of Spandau. Friedrich Wilhelm IV's distrust for the "liberalism" of his privy councilors also emerges who, for him, feeling himself to be much more liberal than the liberals themselves, embodied that "varmint the state."[411]

In understanding Hegel, Stahl's conservatism is equally important both for what it acknowledges and rejects. Through Schelling's mediation, the philosopher forced upon Stahl his idea of the state and of the people.[412] With this, Stahl's conquest of Haller in the conservative political party likewise means Hegel's victory over Haller. But Hegel did not force upon Stahl his position regarding the state in the system. Stahl's critique of Hegel, with respect to Hegel's system, means that the systematically subjugated fields of right, morality, and society were all defects from the state. Now, they all raise their independent claims again. The difference from before is only that the state, in its self-assertion, now has a better conscience towards such claims than it did in the eighteenth century. In that this internal defection now also encounters an external adversary – insofar as Hegel produces a religion that cancels the contract through the peaceful acknowledgment of the common interest in mutually guaranteeing those fields and in the relinquishment of their political claims, thereby arming itself for a new campaign of conquest – this then completes the crisis. Hegel's idea of the state has triumphed, but at the price of its systematic self-sufficiency and its dominion over the spheres below the state.

If Hegel allowed both Rousseau and Haller to fall into the same dam-
nation in 1820, and only professed his old love to the extent that he
acknowledged Rousseau's merit "to have established a principle, which
is a *thought*, not only according to its form [...] but also according to its
content, which is indeed *thought* itself, namely the will as the principle of
the state,"[413] then this combination, especially from Hegel's perspective,
was historically vindicated. Admittedly, just as Hegel himself had laid
only "Rousseau" and not "Haller" into the cornerstone of his state structure, so now it is only Rousseau's successors and not Haller's who oppose
Hegel within his own school. However, in essence, the objections of
these liberal Young Hegelians are remarkably close to those of Hegel's
conservative adversary. The only difference is that their critique comes
across, and may only come across, as a critique from Hegel's own pupils
and that, as a result, can play off the "true" and "secret" Hegel against the
public Hegel who misunderstands himself, that they can appeal from the
latter to the former and that, finally, they have a certain historical right
to do so, owing to Hegel's actual and conscious connection to Rousseau.

Like Stahl, Hegel's liberal pupils also find Hegel lacking the proper
consideration for the particular will of particular individuals. For them,
Hegel likewise does not speak enough of "A and B and C, all of those who
actually live [in the state]." They, too, wish to see considered that "there
remains in every human being much volition, permission, and obligation that is not fulfilled and determined by the state." They, too, strive for
a popular representation that is not merely a necessary part of the state
as a whole but, instead, and above all, the actual protection of the "real
rights" of actual people and actual individuals. But in acknowledging,
again like Stahl, the intrinsic idea of the state, namely the internal and
external autocracy of the state, and insofar as they also see in Hegel the
academic conqueror of Rousseau, a necessity arises for the pupils which
did not exist for Stahl: namely, the necessity to somehow *unite* their critique with their acknowledgment. Stahl had been able to simply claim
that the "many important ethical and political truths" – and he points
to "Hegel as one of their first, or at least most important, representatives" – had their origin "neither in Hegel's dialectic, nor in his other
philosophical principles," nor were they conditioned by his "pantheistic
worldview."[414] It was not as easy for Hegel's pupils. They had to com-
press the idea of the state to the extent that what they presumed to be

the "authentic Hegel" became visible behind it. And it was precisely the origins of Hegel's main concept in Rousseau that made this possible. The "universal" and likewise "subjective" will of the *Philosophy of Right* which, refined to a certain extent as the precious metal of the universal from the hybrid rock of the will of individuals, turned into the *volonté générale* of the "*Contrat social*," which came into being, again to a certain extent, through a physical change in condition of the identically exact chemical composition of the *volonté de tous* — like ice from water. The "all-all" [All-Alle] of the organic state conception transformed back into the "we-all" [Wir Alle] of the democratic state conception. Accordingly, the theories of popular representation and of monarchy were always developed in connection to Hegelian formulations, and the importance of popular representation as the bearer of the "universal will" was increased, while the power of monarchy was diluted to a "mere" final decision. For them, as well as for Hegel in recent years, the "Protestantism" of the state manifested itself as self-ruling. But precisely because they democratize, or at least parliamentize this self-rule [Selbstherrlichkeit], the term now becomes a battering ram against "medieval" institutions which Hegel would have still completely accepted, at least under certain conditions, such as the importance of social estates for popular representation or the *fideicommissum*. Thus, they consistently believe, or at least give themselves the appearance of believing, that they retained the essence of Hegel's idea of the state and only disclosed its temporally conditioned manifestation. That this was a fallacy is self-evident. But it was a historically justified fallacy, in that Hegel's liberal pupils, without knowing it or attaching importance to it, actually returned to the origins of Hegelian thought. It is a case which has granted the history of the Hegelian school in general the most remarkable side pieces. Accordingly, Strauss was able to tie his theory of Christianity's emergence from the myth of the early Christian community to certain isolated and inconsequential propositions from Hegel's philosophy of religion, as he himself was aware. What he could not have known was that these thoughts, appearing here more in passing, had once been at the center of a broad treatment on this same subject for the young Hegel. Furthermore, within the school, the attempt appears more than once to eliminate from Hegel the division of history which absolutizes Christianity in favor of a new division that would allow the absolute age to first begin in the present. Stahl assumes this as a common dogma of the Hegelian Left as early as 1847.[415] Heine's well-known schematization of history according to Hellenism and the Nazarene also lies along this course of thought. But no one knew, although it could actually have been gathered from Hegel's later writings, that the master himself had originally established this division, and that it had only quite gradually given way to the later, familiar one.

If Hegel's liberal successors at least tried to cling to an "authentic" Hegel, then this itself is proof that they too, albeit only reluctantly and with a twinge of conscience, accomplished the same thing that Stahl's conservatism did: they acknowledged the idea of the state while cutting the systematic bond that tied the state to the spheres below it. As with conservatism, with them the powers of "life, freedom, personality, and history" likewise rebel against the omnipotence of the Hegelian state – indeed, the power of history as well. For as surprising as it must seem to an only superficial knowledge of this old conservatism, which was still in opposition to the spirit of the age and therefore still full of spirit, Stahl had also accused Hegel of being "an adversary of the free movement which emerges into order and luminous form only from the disordered and unclear."[416] And if, on the one hand, the conservative anti-Hegelian took the simple and clear position of an opponent, who, both distinguished and smart, does not disdain of learning from his adversary, then the position of the "Left" Hegelians, on the other hand, was a desperate half-measure and, in the long run, untenable for those of honest and grounded nature. It is certainly no coincidence that most of them – when they later intervened politically, and especially after 1848 – abandoned either their liberalism or their Hegelianism: Bruno Bauer and David Friedrich Strauss sat in the ranks of the conservatives; Marx and Lassalle washed themselves clean of contemporary civil society and its liberalism; and while Feuerbach admittedly continued to idolize the state, he understood the state solely as a republic. For all of them, their liberal Hegelianism had only the meaning of a political phase of development. The Hegelian system of the state, as it had taken up its position between the two opposites of "Rousseau" and "Haller," proved in the long run, with regard to the two powers with which it was familiar, that it had the strength to repel what was foreign to it, whether this was in the form of a pupil or whether what was foreign sought to disarm the state system in the form of an adversary by acknowledging commonalities. In the end, contested from the left and the right, often appearing defeated and yet not "overcome" in its own sense, the Hegelian state held onto the place it had taken.

The system of the state was first overcome by the powers against which it was not armed, as at that time these powers were not yet collected and intellectually ordered. Both conservatism and liberalism believed they had to destroy the cohesion of the system before they could begin close combat. The two new opponents now take the system as it wanted to be taken: namely, as a whole and as one – be it with its structure in full relief, or be it with its methodological principle. Thus, they seized upon the system's connecting bond and, instead of sending the ship to the bottom of the sea, they sought to capture it.

The political party which emerged in 1848 and formed in the excitement of February and March 1849, initially as a momentary cartel – the Kaiser Party of March 21, the Gothaer of the 1850s, the German National Association of the 1860s, and finally the National Liberal Party of the first decade of the German Empire – this party spreads its roots deep into German intellectual life. Just as it was mixed with the most diverse elements, just as its members came together from all over, and lastly, just as they were united only by the one, national idea and only through being coalesced in the moment of national decision through this idea, so also the most diverse intellectual tendencies flowed into this party. The old liberals, molted democrats, sharp Prussian particularists who sensed here the way to a greater Prussia – those who believed purely in the national ideal – all of these factions came together here. Their ideational leaders, the circle that gathered around the Prussian Yearbook ever since 1858, unanimously believed, like their leading voice [Haym], who was the founder of the Prussian Yearbook itself, that Hegel embodied the variety of Prussian spirit that they were fighting against. And yet, based on the content of Hegel's thought, they also acknowledged him as the great teacher of the state. This could seem even more astonishing, since Hegel offered them next to nothing for their main concern, namely for the idea of the nation. Initially, Hegel's idea of the state was simply political. Indeed, in the *Philosophy of Right* he had directed the strongest possible words against the "unreasonable demand" that a state be absorbed into a larger whole. Thus, at most, this party could be granted an intellectual weapon through the assessment that the major state was the one true state, an assessment which reappeared in the *Philosophy of Right* along the same lines as in the text on *The German Constitution*. In 1830, this assessment went so far as to equate the ethicality of service in a minor state with mere "private morality."[417] But even then, as in the text on *The German Constitution*, Hegel was not thinking about a major national state, but about a major state in general.

On the other hand, however, the national idea, especially in its form within the circles of the political party that founded the German Empire, the National Liberal Party, was also not really nourished, at least not exclusively, by a Romantic view of the living German nation, breathing through its entire history, as was, for example, King Friedrich Wilhelm IV. Instead, this idea was mixed with a good deal of purely political will. With the national state, one strove above all for the state, and actually more so for the strong state – which needed the individual for the sake of its ethos – and one strove less for the state that brings the nation to its perfect fulfillment. And they found the state they were striving after with Hegel. They alone were not tempted to detach the "idea of the state" from its systematic conditions. On the contrary, what seemed valuable to them about this doctrine was precisely the integration of the spheres of life below the state into the whole of the state, the careful delimitation, and thereby the firm assemblage, for example, into which Hegel ordered the life of society below and within the life of the state, how he ordered domestic ethicality together with a disposition towards the state. They were, after all, oriented towards such connections, delimitations, and subordinations by way of the entire politics they pursued. They were not concerned, like Liberals and Conservatives, with protecting existing life in the existing state, but rather with integrating existing life into a future state. Where the former were content to draw shielding ramparts, these had to order and build. What counted was building up the state from below; for they, as internal politicians, could not reckon with the thought that the state might be created more with a warlike hand from above than with peaceful construction work from below. And therefore, because it was to be from below, they, and they alone, could actually understand that lively development of the state from its ensouled roots, namely the legal will of the person, the moral will of personality, and the ethical will of the human being and citizen, all of which Hegel had wanted to portray. Even if they rejected countless details, even if they considered the "method" to be dead or spoiled: they recognized what was their own in the ethos of this politics. Haym's book from 1857, Rümelin's Hegel speech from 1870,[418] Treitschke's treatment in the third volume of *German History*,[419] these exemplify this. And beyond that, they also found here that the metaphysics of the state, the state's systematic relation to the higher powers, was drawn out essentially as they had thought it themselves. Those later ones, although not yet Haym in 1857,[420] who stood under the impression of Bismarck's rise, recognized in Hegel's "external state law" the philosophical justification of the state's outwardly turned firm nature of power – a connection in the history of thought which, under fire from German artillery at that time, even the "*Révue des deux mondes*" could not turn a deaf ear towards.[421] In Prussia-Germany, those passages on "Theseus" from the text on *The German Constitution*, which were of course directed towards a German hegemony of Austria – Theseus who creates "a state out of scattered peoples" – were now heard with new meaning, and it was gladly believed, under the impression of the battles of Königgrätz[422] and Sedan,[423] that world history was the world's court of judgment. Also, it could have become evident to the political party of the *Kulturkampf* that no higher organized earthly power could stand above the state. And Treitschke, who saw in the "idea of immanence" the indestructible result of the idealistic movement from Kant to Hegel, highlighted the sentence in his own copy[424] of Hegel's *Philosophy of Right* at the beginning of the 1870s where Hegel, with his final piece of wisdom on the matter of the relation of the state to the "churches," advises the state to *divide et impera* [divide and rule]. We saw how in this sentence the innermost secret of Hegel's doctrine of the state was revealed. Treitschke's penciled marginal note allows us to recognize which political party inherited the crown jewels of this state doctrine.

It was an inheritance without strings attached. The party was indeed not "Hegelian." One was conscious of being allowed to acknowledge Hegelian ideas as one's own without having to commit oneself to the thinker on that account. One believed that one could exhaust the "content" of the system without having to cling to the "formal aspect" of its method. And one had the historical right to do so. For as an innermost driving force one possessed a thought that had actually remained foreign to Hegel and that gave the bearers of this thought the authority to appropriate the Hegelian system as a whole, and yet not in the sense of the thinker. And that meant overcoming the historical past.

But appropriating the system was not the only possible way to over-come Hegel. The close connection between system and method in Hegel opened up another path to appropriate the whole without becoming subject to it. The will towards a national state, which was foreign to Hegel, possessed the force to hold together the pieces of the system, which Hegel had coerced together through methodical thinking, in the same relative position without any loss. In contrast, whoever grasped the unifying methodical bond and carried within himself not the strength of a will foreign to Hegel, but an outlook foreign to Hegel, this person was capable of disregarding Hegel's systematic structuring of the content of the political world and of ordering the material anew. And he could also go beyond Hegel by going through Hegel himself, and thereby settle uncharted political territory. That was the charisma of the founder of social democracy.

Karl Marx, as a young journalist in the early 1840s, was to write about the negotiations of the provincial Estates of the Rhineland over a timber theft law for the liberal "Rheinische Zeitung." The young Hegelian, who, like the master, regarded the state as the only place where the freedom of the individual – understood of course in the sense of contemporary liberalism – could be adequately actualized, recognized with horror the truth in actualizing the ideal of freedom. Instead of the civic idealism he was looking for, these negotiations expressed a "rejected material-ism, a sin against the holy spirit of the people and humankind": each Estate sought to perceive only its own advantage, none thought of the whole.[425] The pure advocacy for one's own interests, however, which so deeply offended the liberal's political idealism, corresponded perfectly to the ideas of the conservative Romantic who held Prussia's fate in his hands at that time. Thus and not otherwise should "German Estates" feel themselves to be, namely as the defenders of their own, and only their own, well-acquired rights. It was not by chance that Stahl pointed with a certain acknowledgment towards the new French "social theories." These theories would be manifested, "at least with some initiative," so that as with liberalism "owners had come to acknowledge their dignity and their due share in the commonwealth," so now "non-owners would [also] attain the measure of life-satisfaction due to them."[426] The under-lying contradiction of the conservatives with regard to the liberal view of the state – with its loosening of the economic-social bonds and its simultaneous tightening of the purely political bond between the state and the human being – now also appears with Marx at the site of the initial dismay over the "rejected materialism" stemming from the self-advocacy of the estates in the state. What Marx still denounced in 1843, he would regard a few years later as the normal and desirable condition: the individual should assert the interests of his class in the common-wealth. The revulsion towards "bourgeois" society, which Marx absorbed as an employee of the bourgeois-liberal newspaper, had opened his eyes to the existence of a new estate, an estate which, especially in Germany, was still immature, weak-willed, blind, but nevertheless already there, an estate which only had to be made conscious of its situation and its path, in order that the goals of freedom, which Marx had once believed to be attainable in the political state, could be actualized along this path. But in pointing towards an estate instead of towards the state, the basic idea of Hegel's systematics of "objective spirit" shifted for the Hegelian, who had initially held the *Philosophy of Right* at the center of his interests and who even described his new point of view for the first time in a *Critique of Hegel's Philosophy of Right*.[427] That the fate of the free future of humankind depended precisely upon the "fourth estate," this stemmed at first only from the personal experience of Marx, and would only be established further that great experience of the "proletariat," which meant that the fate of humankind would henceforth unfold at the site of an estate and no longer at the site of the state, a coerced transformation of the system occurred.

Marx never carried out this transformation in his unwieldy and oppressive books. At first, it was probably because other urgent thoughts did not leave him time for it. Later, it was because such a positive cri-tique of the dead lion would have no longer appeared contemporary. Nevertheless, it is henceforth the most self-evident aspect informing all of Marx's works. For Marx, society occupies the place where the state had stood for Hegel. Initially, it is the concept of society as Hegel had grasped it in connection with classical national economics – the hustle and bustle of selfish purposes – from which a balanced condition ultimately arose of itself, a condition in which the individual unconsciously participated as a balancing weight from his place. Yet while Hegel could calmly leave the naturalistic psychology of Western national economists in effect, for within the state he had built up a sphere above the state, a sphere which did justice to his idealistic ethic, indeed, while Hegel could, and had to calmy let this realm of unethicality exist within ethicality, this was impossible for Marx. This was the case because Marx put society in place of the state within the realm of ethicality. And here he demanded of the human being the conscious commitment which Hegel had demanded only in the state. That is, Marx placed "class consciousness" where "disposition towards the state" had stood. Therefore, Marx could not acknowledge the materialistic-individualistic conception of society which Hegel had adopted from "Smith, Say, Ricardo."[428] Nevertheless, the prophetic experience from which Marx philosophized about human community – the face of the proletariat rising out of the darkness – forced him to look to satisfy the ethical poverty of the human being in "society" and not from within the state or the family. How was this to be solved?

The solution came through the philosophy of history. When society took the place of the Hegelian state, it also became heir to its relation to history. Society now emerged as the vehicle of the world-historical course towards consciousness of freedom. The Hegelian concept of society was the reflection of the presently vanishing condition of society, collected by the "bourgeois national economics" of Smith, Say, and Ricardo. Its content, for instance the profound phrase that society is not rich enough in its excess of wealth, could therefore remain valid as a description of this historical condition, a condition which Hegel, by the way, himself understood as civil society. But the image of the future already beckoned from the other side. And this future-liberated society would gloriously reward the commitment of the human being who surrenders to the present society, be it as exploiter or as exploited. The Hegelian image of history had again become apocalyptic to such a degree. It was still the Hegelian image, despite the exchanged vehicle. All the noble qualities of the state, the old vehicle, were heaped onto society, the new vehicle of history. The individual found his ethical world in the historically progressing society. The phenomena of culture outside of society found their historical actualization within society. They were accessories – reflections – of solely historical and actual, solely diverging social conditions. In that history now stood at that great moment, shortly before entering into the ultimate age, the "third Empire," and in that this Empire had already arisen in the thinker's consciousness and that no human volition could hinder or avert this fate, all that could rather be done was to prepare human consciousness for this age: this proto-Hegelian thought, later deprived of its apocalyptic sting by Hegel himself, had already been brought to light by the Left Hegelian school, unaware of the historical context. The school, however, turned this thought into something of the will, and thus alienated it from its origin. Marx alone allowed the strength of Hegel's "quietism" – Hegel's belief in fate – to live on. Thus, none of the others had fulminated with such lightning, none of the others even possessed the strength in their own view as Marx possessed in the vision of the "proletariat": none but Marx had seen with his own eyes where and how and in which form, the end of days was looming in the sky of history.

And none other, not even Hegel himself, had considered to such an end the thought of the unconditional worldliness [Diesseitigkeit] of the ethical relation than this fanatical herald of the human future. Hegel, in that he had recognized the state as the highest ethical relation, could indeed, for the sake of the unconditionality of this relation, place the concept of church above the state in the system. However, in actuality, Hegel had to oppose the state to the plurality of churches, and thereby had to abolish the concept of the church itself. In that Marx replaced the necessarily limited state with the entity of society – which with Hegel was only to be enclosed within the state, but which is itself was already stateless, and through the economy reaches over the entire earth and is connected over the entire earth – because of this Marx was untroubled by such difficulties. With Marx, the highest ethicality of the individual issued into an actual world-spanning community. Claims of an ethical kind could no longer appertain to any other earthly community; even the most comprehensive ones could not be more comprehensive claims than the society of the future. Thus, the church did not have to be eradicated; its superfluousness was obvious. Marx first brought Hegel's system of human community to the point where it actually took on the form that Stahl had attributed to the original system itself. Only Marx could actually carry out what Treitschke called the "great idea of immanence." But of course, according to the profound parable of the great Christian poetess of the North, at the point where Marx left the matter, namely with cosmopolitan society, the imitated image, whose realm is only of this world, could now be brought home in the church to its genuine image, whose realm is not of this world.[429]

Hegel had seen both the social question and the national question particularly early, indeed, already in 1802. But he had not anticipated in either the social or the national thought a power that could generate systems and communities. This is the reason that the state and the community systems that grew from these two thoughts could exercise a full right of inheritance over the Hegelian system, that they could possess it completely and remain masters over it, which was what went amiss for the successors of both "Haller" and "Rousseau," whom Hegel had expressly excluded from the inheritance and who sought to contest his last will. Thus, the figures of the Diadochi, who were once to fight over the inheritance, now gathered, partly visible and partly still hidden, in a circle around Hegel's state system. But it had not yet come to that point. The single spirit of the thinker still held the realm together, he was still master over the whole, reigning proudly in calm repose. Then came the July Revolution.

## NOTES

1 Arndt (1913) is mentioned here in place of many others. On the citations, see Section 7, note 87.
2 GW 10, 460; HW 4, 319.
3 Ibid.
4 Cf. Section 9, note 94.
5 *Heidelbergische Jahrbücher der Literatur* (1817), 888.
6 Ibid. 887.
7 Cf. Vol. I, 146.
8 Cf. Bd. I, 155 f.; 159 f.
9 Cf. p. 276 f.
10 Cf. p. 292 ff.
11 Cf. p. 297 ff.
12 Cf. p. 306.
13 GW 18, 11 f.; HW 10, 399.
14 GW 18, 12; HW 10, 400.
15 GW 18, 15; HW 10, 402 – verbatim: "But even in Germany the *flatness of the earlier age* has come so far *since its rebirth*, that ..."
16 GW 18, 12; HW 10, 400.
17 Cf. Section 10, note 12.
18 GW 18, 12; HW 10, 400.
19 Ibid.
20 GW 18, 4; HW 10, 18, 12 annotation – verbatim: "Prussia [is] built upon intelligence."

21  GW 18, 12 f.; HW 10, 400 – verbatim: "one of the most essential moments even in *state life*." Cf. also Gneisenau's familiar saying on the triple primacy ["of arms, of the constitution, and of the sciences," under which the Prussian state had to stand, according to Gneisenau"].

22  GW 18, 13; HW 10, 400 – verbatim: *"basic moment."*

23  Ibid – verbatim: "but more exactly, that great struggle of the people in union with their prince for independence, for the destruction of mindless foreign tyranny, and for freedom of *mind* has found its higher cause."

24  Ibid – verbatim: "asserted itself as the force and power of actuality."

25  Ibid.

26  GW 18, 14; HW 10, 401.

27  Cf. on the following up to page 351 Lenz (loc. cit.), vol. II/1.

28  V. Raumer to Hegel, August 7, 1816 (Br II).

29  Cf. to Savigny and Fries, Section 3, note 32.

30  Altenstein to the King, February 20, 1818 (op. cit.), vol. IV, 334.

31  GW 18, 13; HW 10, 400 – verbatim: "at this university, the university of the middle point, *philosophy*, the *middle point* of all intellectual cultivation and all science and truth, must also find its place and exquisite care."

32  GW 18, 18; HW 10, 404.

33  Goethe, "Über Kunst und Altertum" (Goethe [1985 ff.], Vol. XX).

34  Goethe to Hegel, October 7, 1820 (Br II).

35  Cf. Creuzinger (1911); but in addition, Rothfels (1920), Annotation 58.

36  Adelheit Zunz to Meier Isler, November 19, 1831 (Glatzer [1964], 156).

37  See, for example, Schelling to Cousin, 28 January 1819 (Plitt [1869], vol. II), as well as Schleiermacher to Arndt, 14 March 1818 (Lenz [op. cit.], vol. IV, 410).

38  Cf. Hegel to Paulus, May 2, 1816: "Extend [...] Herr Fries my return-compliment for the one which he had Siebeck make for me; he will be as happy to receive it as I was to receive his." (Br. II).

39  Hegel to Daub, May 9, 1821 (ibid.) – verbatim: "a so-called Schmalz association."

40  [The speech is by the Berlin jurist Th. A. H. Schmalz; cf. Br. II, 480, Annotation 8.]

41  HW 7, 13.

42  HW 7, 13 f.

43  Ibid., 14.

44  Ibid., 15.

45  Ibid., 16 f.

46  Ibid., 18.

47  Ibid., 17 – verbatim: "With the simple home remedy of leaving to *feeling* that which is the work of reason and its intellect [...], which has been ongoing for thousands of years."

48  Ibid.

49  Ibid.

50  Ibid., 20.

51  Ibid., § 258 footnote.

52   Ibid., 21.
53   Ibid.
54   Ibid.
55   Ibid., 22.
56   Ibid., 24.
57   Ibid.
58   Ibid. – verbatim: "and thus could only appear as something destructive, *Plato* had to seek help against it precisely from that longing."
59   Ibid.
60   Ibid.
61   Ibid.
62   Ibid.
63   Ibid.
64   Only G. Lasson, in his edition of the *Philosophy of Right*, has hitherto recognized the passage on Plato's state as the springboard for understanding the double-dictum of the rational and the actual. The fact that this passage has often been overlooked – Treitschke, e.g., who furnishes this part of the Preface in his personal copy held by the Leipzig city library with ongoing markings, fails to underline precisely the two lines "In the course of the following treatise …" and "But by doing this he has…" (ibid.) – explains the general misunderstanding of this double-dictum, namely that it is drastically expressed in the fact that one almost always cites it in reversed order, and when it is cited in abbreviation one finds it written as "what is actual, that is rational," namely as "Hegel's dictum on the rationality of the actual." Hegel himself belongs to the rare exceptions, who in his self-interpretation from 1827 (GW 19, 32), through the form of his letter spacing, and above all substantively, brings the "actuality of the rational" to the fore (cf. also § 360 of the *Philosophy of Right* itself [HW 7, 512].

   The interpretation given in the text itself, which of course could also be extended to GW 19, § 552 and 563, is admittedly not entirely in accord with G. Lasson, whose reading of the "rose in the cross of the present" in the Hegel Archive [what is meant is probably Lasson [1909], 43 ff.] I incidentally follow on p. 340.
65   HW 7, 25.
66   Ibid.
67   Ibid.
68   Ibid.
69   Ibid.
70   Ibid., 25 f.
71   Ibid., 26.
72   Ibid.
73   Ibid.
74   Ibid.
75   Ibid., 27.
76   Cf. Vol. I, 130 f.

77  Cf. Vol. I, 124–129 on the German constitution.

78  HW 7, 28.

79  Haym's doubt about the seriousness and truth of this departure (Haym, 377 f.) already seemed unjustified to the young Treitschke, who probably read the book in 1858. He adds a question mark in the margin of his copy (Leipzig State Library) next to Haym's sentence: "[Hegel] rises above the view of antiquity only to immediately sink back into it."

80  Cf. the familiar explanation of the organism as a machine, whose smallest parts are in turn machines" (e.g. Leibniz [2002], § 64).

81  FW 4, § 17 (on the civil-political contract) Corollaries.

82  Based on the entire mood of the 1802 image of the state, and based on its pervasive dependence upon the *ancien régime*, the former is probable.

83  GW 8, 266, SE III, 243.

84  Ibid.

85  GW 8, 281, SE III, 256.

86  Cf. e.g. B. HW 7, § 124.

87  HW 7, § 172 Addition; cf. already the construction of history in *The Phenomenology*.

88  Plato's state, Hegel formulates (in a marginal note to GW 8, 263; SE III, 240), "is not feasible because it lacked the principle of singularity [Einzelheit]" (verbatim: "Plato did not establish an ideal, but instead grasped the state of his age internally – but this state has passed away – it is not the Platonic Republic that is not feasible [sic] – because it lacked the principle of absolute singularity.").

89  Or perhaps what was being thought of was the particularity of the estates.

90  GW 8, 272; SE III, 248 – the omitted passage was deleted; it reads: "– and later from religion – [but] our states have not ... (cf. GW 8, 272 note).

91  For the System of 1804 and its alterations, the "how" of this is not clear due to the fragmentary transmission of manuscripts.

92  Main passage (GW 8, 277 f. SE III, 253): "As intelligence, being [das Seiende] has the form of another – as the will of its self – *being acknowledged* is the spiritual element; but still indeterminate in itself, and therefore filled with manifold content – the authoritative law is the movement of this content – or the universal intuiting itself as mediation – the constitution [Constitution] is its generation of the *content* out of itself, it constitutes *itself*, but in the form of the subject-matter – it *makes itself* the content, and as government it is spirit certain of itself, which knows that this is *its* content, it has the power over it, *spiritual content*. So it now has to produce this content as such knowingly itself. Thus it is *directly* art [...]."

93  GW 8, 242; SE III, 221 f.

94  GW 8, 243; SE III, 222.

95  GW 8, 272; SE III, 248.

96  Prepared through the concept "within the people" [im Volk] from 1803 ("Natural Right" essay) and 1804 (first draft of the notebook) (cf. SE I).

97  GW 8, 286 f.; SE III, 260 ff.

98    HW 4, 65.

99    GW 8, 276; SE III, 240; SE III, 240, 252 (in each case at the margin).

100    GW 8, 222 ff.; SE III, 204 ff.

101    HW 4, § 197 f.

102    GW 13, § 430.

103    Ibid., § 433.

104    Cf. HW 7, § 431: "The *ethical* is subjective disposition, but of right which exists in itself."

105    He does not seem to have bothered too much with literature on the history of law. The manner in which he makes the most of Hugo's short textbook paragraphs and even of the definitions from the outdated Hinnecius does not speak for a very far-reaching literary knowledge. I would like to conclude almost with certainty from the silence of § 217 (HW 7) that German right, for example Jakob Grimm's foundational findings on the formalistic-intuitive essence of right, did not come into view for Hegel.

106    HW 7, § 40.

107    Ibid., § 3 verbatim: "genuinely philosophical point of view."

108    Ibid.

109    Ibid.

110    Ibid., § 211 (cf. in addition ibid., § 215, the praise given to the General Common Law disparaged by Savigny). – The parenthesis omitted from the text – "in that it cannot be about making new *laws* for a system according to its *contents*, but rather about recognizing the given legal content in its particular universality, i.e. to grasp it *in thought*" – shows Hegel, for the superficial observer, to be in much closer contact with Savigny than he himself would like to admit. The personal antagonism between the two would not yet have been strong enough to elicit an intentional veiling of a kinship between viewpoints. For clarification, one must return to the different views on the meaning of "*Volksgeist.*" For Savigny, law is not allowed to be "made," because that would mean preempting the *Volksgeist*, which, when left in peace, would make its laws itself anyway. Hegel knows no *Volksgeist* that would exist without laws; for they make up a necessary component without which it would not be at all; and therefore Hegel knows an "cultivated nation" as such to be in possession of laws in advance, even if they are unwritten.

111    It is not said that Hegel consciously directed his theory of possession [Besitztheorie] against Savigny, which, however, his pupil Gans later did (1827, 220 ff.). Hegel's handwritten additions do not show any reference to Savigny's text, and with Hegel's probable narrow legal knowledge, this would likely be the case if he had been familiar with Savigny's text. Of course, it is possible.

112    HW 7, § 40 [an allusion to Heineccius' "Elementa Juris civilis"; see ibid.

113    HW 7, § 29.

114    Hence Kant's strange, historical-philosophical belief in nature, entirely incompatible with the *Critique*, which probably already does this. This belief befit Leibniz and Rousseau, and Hegel and Schelling – because they proceeded

methodically-dialectically or mystically-principally from the equation of thinking-being – likewise. But Fichte, and Kant as well, were not warranted to hold such a belief.

115   HW 7, § 13.

116   Ibid., § 35.

117   Ibid., § 40 – In 1817, the concept of person was not yet "negative against reality," and therefore at that time the traditional division into personal law and property law was still possible.

118   Ibid., § 62 – verbatim: "the relations of the *dominii directi* and the *dominii utilis*." [JS & JS: direct ownership and utilitarian ownership]

119   Ibid.

120   Ibid.

121   Treitschke (1912 f.), Vol. II, Supplement IV.

122   HW 7, § 46 – verbatim: "at the expense of others' rights."

123   Ibid., §, 46, 49 – the passage is characteristic (ibid., § 46) where he himself admits that the community of goods could here "easily present itself to the disposition."

124   Interesting in this connection is the addition to § 37, which reads like a protest against Ihering's "struggle for right"; nevertheless, one would not be allowed to quote the passage in this sense. For Ihering's concept of right is quite different from the concept that is consciously a private-law and against which Hegel's disdain is turned.

125   Gibbon translated by Hugo (1807 ff.) Vol. III, 116.

126   Montesquieu (1949 ff.), Vol. II, 27. Book.

127   Cf. Hugo (op. cit.), § 82, cf. on the Law of the Twelve Tables from the Roman inheritance law: *Institutiones Iustiniani*, Liber II, Tit. XXII f. (Behrends et al. [1993], 115 ff.); likewise Gaius (1904), §224 and Pamponius (D. de VS. [I, 16] and I.120 D. 50, 16 in: Mommsen et al [eds] [1985], vol. 4, 993a).

128   In Rousseau (1959 ff.), vol. III, I. book. ch. 2, 353 ff. Archetype [Urbild], itself unassociated with the state; he already applies the concept of the dissolution of the family in a similar way as Hegel did later; he also has the concept of love here, but finds no bridge from it to the state: he sees only the antithesis: here love, here obedience.

129   HW 7, § 164.

130   ALR II, I, § 2, against it § I Inst. (I, 9); (Behrends et al [1993], 13: "I. Matrimony or Marriage is the Connection of Man and Woman to Undivided Communal Life."); and therefore L. 39 § I D (23.3), ("*De iure totium*" – laws concerning the dowry, cf. Mommsen [loc. cit.], Vol. II, 668 ff.), against it A. L. R.; cf. furthermore ABGB § 44.

131   ALR II, I, § 718a.

132   HW 7, § 176.

133   ALR II, I, § 3 ff.; ABGB § 65 f.; CC, § 161 ff.; according to Roman law, affinity by marriage and quasi-affinity are impediments to marriage. The specially justified exception in Common Law is in ALR II, I, § 8; it already falls through

the condition of its occurrence as well as through the gender restriction under another point of view than that of the degree of kinship, which is also expressed in the allowance of dispensation.

134   HW 7, § 168.
135   Ibid., § 171; ALR II, I, §345.
136   HW I, 246 f.; N 381, f.
137   ALR II, 2, § 147 ff.
138   HW 7, § 171.
139   Ibid., § 174.
140   ALR, II, 2, §§ 65 ff.
141   Ibid. § 86.
142   Ibid., §§ 121 ff.
143   HW 7, § 174.
144   Ibid – verbatim: "The purpose of punishments is not justice as such; but subjective, moral nature, the determent of freedom still caught up in nature and elevating the universal in its consciousness and will."
145   Ibid., § 178 ff.
146   Pütter (1777 ff.), Vol. II, Sections IIVII (p. 259), XXXVI (p. 228), his view, however, was disputed by Professor Majer, who taught during Hegel's time at the *Stift* in Tübingen, in "*Germaniens Urverfassung*" (Majer [1798], §§ 59–64).
147   Thomasius (1705), §§ XLIV, LIX; the same (1803), 57 f. (59 f.); cf. Section 9, note 127.
148   HW 7, § 178.
149   Ibid., § 180.
150   Ibid.
151   Ibid.
152   Ibid., § 182 addendum.
153   Ibid., § 157.
154   Ibid., § 183.
155   Ibid., § 182.
156   Ibid., addendum.
157   Ibid., § 189.
158   Ibid., § 199 – verbatim: "the *general, permanent assets*."
159   Ibid., § 200.
160   Ibid.
161   Ibid., § 201 ff.
162   Ibid., § 227.
163   Ibid., § 227.
164   Ibid.
165   Ibid., § 205.
166   Ibid., § 203 addition.
167   Ibid., § 203.
168   Ibid., § 294.
169   Ibid., §§ 244 f.

170  GW 8, 353 f.; SdS, 77 f. – Stahl (1847), 321 speaks from his own experience of the year 1829 as the time "when we in Germany knew nothing of the social theories."

171  GW 8 354; SdS, 78.

172  Ibid., – verbatim: "and if it sacrifices a part of this class [Stand] to mechanical and factory work, and relinquishes it to crudeness."

173  Ibid.

174  HW 7, § 253.

175  Ibid., § 243.

176  Linguet (1767); Necker (1775).

177  HW 7, §244.

178  Ibid., § 245.

179  Ibid.

180  Ibid.

181  Ibid.

182  Ibid.– verbatim: "to instruct them."

183  bid, § 246; cf. also § 185.

184  Ibid., § 248

185  Ibid.

186  Plenge (1911), 159 ff.

187  HW 7, § 247 – verbatim: "the limited circles of civilian life, its pleasures and desires, by the element [...]."

188  Ibid. – verbatim: "internally aspiring nations push themselves towards the sea."

189  Ibid., § 170.

190  Ibid., § 203.

191  Ibid., § 202.

192  Ibid., § 253.

193  Ibid., § 278.

194  Ibid., § 236.

195  Ibid., § 253.

196  Ibid., § 255; cf. § 201 addendum.

197  GW 4, 441; HW 2, 469 f.

198  GW 4, 441; HW 2, 470.

199  HW 7, § 135.

200  Ibid., § 258.

201  Ibid.

202  Ibid., § 257.

203  Ibid., § 268.

204  Ibid., § 263.

205  Ibid., § 258.

206  Ibid., § 124.

207  Ibid., § 268; cf. also ibid., § 289.

208  Ibid., § 265.

209  Ibid., § 268 – verbatim: "this consciousness, which proves itself in all rela-
     tions during the ordinary course of life, is the basis for extending oneself
     towards an extraordinary effort."
210  Ibid., § 289.
211  Already in Kant: citoyen – bourgeois = citizen – citizen of the city (Kant [1902
     ff.], vol. VIII, 295). Accordingly, Hegel uses "bourgeois" in the 1802 *System of
     Ethicality* and now in the *Philosophy of Right* (HW 7, § 190), only that he erases
     the element of the estates from the term and expresses the contrast as the
     universal of humankind in "civil society" over against the human being in the
     state.
212  HW 7, § 289.
213  Ibid., § 209; cf. *Philosophy of History* on China: "our states guarantee equality
     before the law [...] universally" [presumably the following passage is meant
     (HW 12, 158): "With us, human beings are equal only before the law and in
     *the* connection that they have to property; besides, they still have many inter-
     ests and many particularities that must be guaranteed if freedom is to be
     present for us. In the Chinese Empire, however, these particular interests are
     not legitimate in themselves, and the government emanates only from the
     emperor, who operates it as a hierarchy of officials or mandarins."].
214  HW 7, § 261.
215  Ibid., § 109.
216  Ibid., § 124.
217  Ibid., § 261.
218  Ibid., § 269.
219  Ibid., § 265; cf. also § 267.
220  Ibid., § 269.
221  GW 5, 340; SdS, 63 f.
222  GW 13, § 439.
223  HW 4, § 199 – verbatim: "separation and relation of state powers."
224  HW 7, § 272 – verbatim: "With the *independence* of the powers, e.g. as they
     have been called, the *executive* and the *legislative* power, is, as one has also
     seen in general [...]"
225  Ibid.
226  GW 5, 341; SdS 72.
227  HW 7, § 273.
228  Ibid.
229  Ibid.
230  Ibid. – verbatim: "(b) subsumption of the particular spheres and individual
     cases under the universal – the *governmental authority*."
231  Ibid.
232  Ibid., § 279.
233  GW 8, 263 ff.; SE III, 240 ff.
234  GW 8, 262; SE III, 239 – verbatim: "the One individual."
235  GW 8, 263; SE III, 240.
236  HW 7, § 273.

237   Ibid.
238   Cf. to the following ibid., § 279.
239   Ibid., § 275.
240   Ibid.
241   Ibid., § 276.
242   Ibid.
243   Ibid., § 277.
244   Ibid., § 278.
245   For this is what it comes to when ibid., § 278 finds in the organism the same "determination," in the freedom of the will the same "principle."
246   Ibid., § 279.
247   Ibid. verbatim: "the individual [aspect] of the state."
248   Ibid.
249   Ibid.
250   GW 5, 345 f.; SdS, 70.
251   GW 5, 340 ff.; SdS, 64 ff.
252   Cf. also the addition to HW 7, § 281, where the grace of God as well as the positive justification are still explicitly rejected.
253   HW 7, § 279.
254   Ibid.
255   Ibid. § 280.
256   Ibid. § 281.
257   Ibid. § 280.
258   Ibid., § 281 – verbatim: "removed from the struggle of faction against faction for the throne and the weakening and shattering of state authority."
259   Ibid.
260   Ibid. – verbatim: "Birthright and inheritance law constitute the foundation of *legitimacy* as the foundation of not merely a positive right, but likewise within the idea."
261   Ibid., § 275.
262   Ibid., § 284.
263   Ibid., § 285.
264   Ebd., § 286 – verbatim: "*subjective* guarantees."
265   Ibid., § 287 ff.
266   Moser (1796), Vol. I, Vf.
267   GW 8, 263, SE III, 240 – verbatim: "The spiritual bond is *public* opinion; – this is the true legislative corps […]."
268   GW 10, 402; HW 4, 249.
269   GW 8, 263; SE III, 240.
270   GW 8, 266 f.; SE III, 242 f.
271   HW 7, § 288.
272   Ibid., § 289; cf. also the addendum to § 290.
273   HW 7, 289 – verbatim: "with the self-satisfaction and opinion of itself."
274   Ibid., § 290 – verbatim: "The *organization* of the administrative bodies has the formal, but difficult task, insofar as that from below, where civil life is

concrete, the same is governed in a concrete manner, but that this business is divided into its abstract branches which are treated by singular administrative bodies as distinguished middle points, whose effectiveness downwards as well as in the supreme governmental authority converges again in a concrete overview."

275    Ibid., § 291.
276    Ibid., § 292 – verbatim: "state authority [Staatsgewalt]."
277    Ibid., § 293.
278    Ibid., § 294.
279    Ibid.
280    Ibid., § 296.
281    Ibid., § – verbatim: "These subjective sides are wiped out for themselves."
282    Ibid., § 297 – verbatim: "The members of the government and the state civil servants constitute the main part of the middle class, in which the educated intelligence and the legal consciousness of the mass of a people fall."
283    GW 15, 39; HW 4, 474.
284    HW 7, § 297.
285    Ibid., § 300.
286    GW 10, 402; HW 4, 249.
287    HW 7, § 298.
288    GW 15, 121; HW 4 592.
289    HW 7, § 300.
290    Ibid., § 301.
291    Ibid.
292    Ibid.
293    Ibid.
294    Ibid.
295    Ibid.
296    Ibid., § 302.
297    Ibid.
298    Ibid. – verbatim: "Their [the estates] determination exacts of them as much of a *sense* for and *disposition* towards the *state* and the *government* as for the *interests* of *particular circles* and of *individuals*. At the same time, the significance of the estates' position is that, in common with the organized executive power, they are the mediator preventing both the *extreme* isolation of the prince's power – which otherwise might seem an arbitrary power of domination – and also the isolation of the particular interests of communities, corporations, and individuals. Or more important still, they prevent individuals from presenting themselves as a *mass* or *aggregate*, unorganized in their opinions and volition, and from moving as sheer masses of force against an organized state."
299    Ibid., § 304 – verbatim: "As from the side of princely power the governmental power (§ 300) already has this determination, so also from the side of the estates must a moment of it be turned according to the determination, in order to essentially exist as the moment of the middle."

300    Ibid., § 305.
301    Ibid., § 306 f.; cf. also ibid., § 181.
302    Ibid., § 312.
303    Ibid., § 308.
304    Ibid., § 309.
305    Ibid., § 310.
306    Ibid.
307    Ibid., § 311.
308    Ibid.
309    Ibid.
310    Ibid., § 312 f.
311    Ibid., § 316.
312    Ibid., § 317.
313    Ibid.
314    Ibid., § 318.
315    Ibid., addendum.
316    Ibid., § 319.
317    Ibid., § 299.
318    Ibid.
319    Cf. ibid., § 326: "when thus the whole has become the power [...]"
320    Like the one from 1802 in the doctrine of powers.
321    HW 7, § 321 ff.
322    Ibid., § 321.
323    Ibid., § 323 – verbatim: "life, property, and its rights"; cf. also ibid., § 326.
324    Ibid., § 329; cf. also ibid., § 228. On the addendum of § 329, cf. Moltke's famous
       opening sentence from "Geschichte des Krieges 1870–1871" (Moltke 1895).
325    Ibid., § 323.
326    Ibid., § 324.
327    Ibid., § 326.
328    It hardly needs to be stated that the text here (pp. 411–418) consistently relies
       on Treitschke's "Deutsche Geschichte" (Treitschke 1912 f.) with respect to
       Prussian relations.
329    Cf. Meinecke (1896/99), Vol. II, 169.
330    GW 10, 470; HW 4, 331 [Rosenzweig mistakenly provides the year of the
       Gymnasium speech as 1811; in fact, the quote comes from the speech from
       September 14, 1810].
331    GW 10, 469; HW 4, 330.
332    [Charte constitutionelle, the constitutional basis of the French monarchy since
       1814.]
333    Cf. Pope's well-known verse: "For Forms of government let fools contest;
       whatever is best administered is best" (Pope [1734], Epistle III).
334    Also the Encyclopedia of 1827 as well as the third edition completed in Sep-
       tember 1830 do not weaken anything. Cf. also the remarks, to be placed
       before the publication of the Philosophy of Right – within them on p. 272
       the date "17/3/19" is written – in the annotated author's copy of the 1817

*Encyclopedia* (Lasson 1912 ff.) on p. 274: right [...] municipal constitutions [...], landed estates, the one as necessary as the other."

335   HW 7, § 302.
336   At most, it might be noticeable that he avoids this expression, which is common to him.
337   HW 7, § 181.
338   Ibid.
339   Ibid., § 322.
340   But not further. In the subjective spirit, for example, the actuality of the next highest sphere is not the precondition of truth of the next lowest one; instead, here the parallelity of natural and conceptual development prevails, which is downright denied by Hegel for the philosophy of the objective spirit (cf. addendum to HW 7, § 182).
341   HW 7, § 333.
342   Ibid. § 330.
343   Ibid., § 331.
344   Ibid.
345   Ibid., § 338.
346   Ibid., § 332.
347   Ibid.
348   Ibid., § 333.
349   Ibid., § 340.
350   Ibid., § 341 ff.
351   Ibid., § 345.
352   Ibid., § 346.
353   Ibid., § 348.
354   Ibid., § 341.
355   Ibid., § 342.
356   Ibid., § 345.
357   Cf. ibid., § 348, 79, 93, 102, 118, 218, 350.
358   Ibid., § 258 addendum.
359   HW 12, 32.
360   [Cf. Matt. 5:33–35: "You have heard further that it was said to the ancients, 'You shall not take a false oath, and you shall keep your own to God.' But I say to you that you shall not take an oath at all, neither by heaven, for it is God's throne, nor by the earth, for it is His footstool, nor by Jerusalem, for it is the Great King's city."]
361   Of course, not to be confused – as has occurred – with "world-soul," the term for Napoleon in the well-known letter passage (Hegel to Niethammer, October 13, 1806 [Br I]); spirit and soul are two different things.
362   Cf. the sharp and clear separation in the 1827 *Encyclopedia* (GW 19, § 552).
363   Cf. GW 18, 121 ff.; HW 12, 543 ff.
364   HW 7, § 341.
365   Already seen often, recently thoroughly misinterpreted by Dittman (1909) in the sense of a propaganda for Lamprecht's methodology.

366    Cf. on the following also V 3, 339–347 and HW 17, 329 ff.
367    HW 7, § 170.
368    Ibid.
369    Ibid.
370    Ibid.
371    Ibid., § 360.
372    Ibid., § 270.
373    Ibid.
374    Ibid.
375    Ibid.
376    Ibid – verbatim: "policing supervision."
377    Ibid.
378    Frederick the Great in a marginal gloss in 1749: "All religions must be toler-
       ated, and the fiscal must be alert that none of the others do harm, because
       here each must live as they see fit."
379    HW 7, § 270.
380    Ibid. – verbatim: "A state, developed in its organization and therefore a strong
       state, can herein act more liberally, it can overlook individual matters that
       that might impact it, and even tolerate congregations within it (depending,
       of course, on the number of these) whose religion does not acknowledge
       even their direct duties towards the state. It is able to do so by entrusting the
       members of such congregations to civil society and its laws and is content if
       they fulfill their direct duties towards the state passively, either by means of
       having the services commuted, or having them substituted."
381    Ibid., footnote 2.
382    HW 7, § 270.
383    CC § 165.
384    ALR § II, 1, § 136.
385    Decree of August 25 (September 6) 1814.
386    Royal edict from September 8, 1808, § 18 (cf. Mages, E.: Gemeindeverfassung
       [19th/20th century] In: Historisches Lexikon Bayerns [2006]).
387    Cf. Treitschke (1912 f.), Vol. II, 411.
388    HW 7, § 270. – verbatim: "unity of the church and of the state."
389    Ibid.
390    Ibid.
391    Ibid. – verbatim: "However, the state also has a doctrine [...]."
392    Hegel to Nanette Endel, July 2, 1797 (Br I).
393    HW 7, § 258.
394    [Hartmann/Hasler (1863 ff.) according to which Haller is attributed the "nick-
       name 'Democrat'"].
395    HW 7, § 257 (esp. the footnote on v. Haller), § 219.
396    Ibid., § 258.
397    Ibid.
398    Cf. Meinecke (1908), 226 ff.
399    Stahl (1847), Vol. I, 470.

400   Ibid., 476 – verbatim: "But no less does he eliminate *Haller's* feudalistic doctrine of private law."

401   Ibid., § 559 – verbatim: "and this is precisely the public character of state authority in its true understanding."

402   Ibid., § 560 f.

403   Ibid., § 453.

404   Ibid., § 458.

405   Ibid., § 456.

406   Ibid., § 459.

407   Ibid., § 456.

408   Ibid., § 467.

409   Ibid., § 474.

410   Ibid., § 470.

411   Cf. Hoffmann (1868): 299: "A farmer from the administrative district of Merseberg, to whom the king, invoking 'the state and its order,' could not grant an undue promotion that he proffered verbally, had namely replied: 'Oh, I knew well that my beloved King does not oppose me, but that varmint the state.' The King often used this farmer's words in jest, also often ironically."

412   For Savigny, whom Stahl mentions, would probably have also been influenced by Schelling's "Vorlesungen über das akademisches Studium," as discussed above in the text.

413   HW 7, § 258.

414   Stahl (op. cit.), 472.

415   Ibid., § 481.

416   Ibid., § 470.

417   Cf. perhaps HW 10, § 539.

418   "Über Hegel," in Rümelin (1907).

419   Treitschke (1912 f.)

420   He had not recognized therein how the theory emanates from the state as power, but rather – in a truly doctrinaire manner – from personal resignation.

421   Cf. also Beaussère in the January 1871 edition; the reference to this is found in the Hegel book of the Frenchman P. Rocques (1912).

422   [Battle of Prussians against the Alliance of Austrian and Saxon troops at Königgratz (Bohemia) on July 3, 1866, from which Bismarck's army emerged victorious and Prussia rose to become the leading German power].

423   [Battle of the Franco-Prussian War in the Ardennes near Sedan on September 1, 1870; on the day the French troops surrendered, the German army captured French Emperor Napoleon III].

424   The copy can be found in the Leipzig City Library [according to information from the library, it can no longer be found in storage].

425   Plenge (1911), 60.

426   Stahl (op. cit.), 323 ff.

427   Marx (1844).

428   HW 7, § 189.

429   Lagerlöf (1985).

# 12

## JULY REVOLUTION

The three-day uprising, during which Parisian Liberals had the legitimate king chased away by the metropolitan proletariat and put the national king on the throne, came as a surprise to the participants themselves. In Europe it had the effect of a thunderstorm in winter. For the past fifteen years, one had seen the devil of the revolution painted on the wall so often that, even if revolution was actively rumbling on the southern periphery, people no longer really believed in its physical existence. In this "halcyon" epoch, bountiful in refined art and comprehensive knowledge, revolution had somewhat played the role of the mummy who was paraded around in Herodotean Egypt at feasts, causing the reaction that one's zest for life and sense of being was heightened. But now revolution had arrived. A special newspaper edition – the Prussian state already had an optical telegraph connection – reported the major event to residents of Berlin in brief, while meanwhile for three days the newspapers reported solely on the final governmental actions of Charles X, which were not prepared for revolution. After that, the newspapers could then finally provide the details, and thus those eager to know were thronging

DOI: 10.4324/9780429354724-14

to the reading rooms of the Josty[1] and Steheli[2] cafes. So, it actually was true. The ornate edifice of European peace – with its well-measured and calculated pillars, its legitimacy of the crown, its Christian sense of monarchs united in Holy Alliance, and its peoples who, each according to their historical character, had their legal share in public life – this edifice, cared for by some, hated by others, which had even seemed to have survived the dangerous shock of the Greek uprising against their legitimate sultan, finally collapsed. Art, wisdom, and ethos, which had found their protection within it, seemed to be in danger once again. Niebuhr predicted nothing less than a relapse into barbarism and a new Thirty Years War.[3] And perhaps, from the perspective of his generation, both were not all that inaccurate. Indeed, the emerging generation, hostile towards Goethe on both the right and the left, could well have been called "barbaric" by the fellow members sitting at that brilliant round table of the German spirit, which Goethe had presided over like the king in the Celtic legend. And the chain of revolutions and wars leading up to 1871, by way of which this new generation conceded in its own sense to Europe, actually stemmed from the definite delegitimization of France of 1830 and now found in this country, which had made revolution constitutional, a perpetually renewing impetus. Hegel was also deeply shocked. After the three and a half decades of warlike upheaval that he had experienced since youth, he too might have counted on calmness, at least external calm, which would have allowed the world spirit – that, as he put it in 1816, had been ever so engaged in actuality – to again turn inward and gather itself. And now all of this again became uncertain.

In the past decade, ever since he had published his work on the philosophy of state, Hegel's life in Berlin had continued along the same lines that he himself had set for himself through his initial demeanor.[4] The connection with the broader fraternity circles Hegel had maintained in the early years was considerably exposed on account of his approach towards Fries, even if he remained on good terms with the leaders, such as Carové[5] and especially Friedrich Förster.[6] The relationship with Schleiermacher did not improve after their poorly settled encounter. The two intellectual adversaries and rivals continued to fight against each other with all available means, both publicly and privately. And while Hegel lost ground with the liberal Romantics, he also gained no ground from the conservative Romantics. Savigny, who himself had won out over

De Wette for a professorship in Berlin, experienced little joy in Hegel. Indeed, Hegel's ruthless polemic against the basic ideas of the Historical School of Law, especially against Savigny's position on Prussian Common Law and on legislation in general, must have embittered the strongman of the Faculty of Jurisprudence. The fact that in his polemic Hegel used the strange means of blurring the boundaries between liberal and conservative Romanticism through the common shibboleth of "hatred towards the law"[7] only resulted in equal hostility towards him from both sides. It is also worth mentioning here the fact that Hegel seasoned the first paragraphs of the book with malice towards Hugo, the acknowledged elder from Göttingen of the Historical School of Law, despite his entirely pre-Romantic tendencies. The already somewhat senile scholar countered his reception in an infinitely dispirited and undignified "Critique," which was only a retort, in the *Göttinger Gelehrten Anzeigen*. This conflict reached its peak when Hegel gained, in the person of the young Eduard Gans from Berlin – who moreover was still a Jew at the time – a brilliantly spirited pioneering opponent against the "Historical School" and when Hegel tried to bring him onto the faculty. This attempt developed into an entire game of political intrigue, in which Hegel ultimately triumphed over Savigny, albeit only externally. But the Crown Prince, who had played a role in the state beginning in the 1820s, became interested in the affair on Savigny's behalf. Savigny's defeat was only possible due to the coincidence of the Prince's absence. In this way, as far as it was even still possible after the diatribe against Haller in the *Philosophy of Right*, Hegel had spoiled his chances before the sun had even risen.

Therefore, isolated in the conflict from both the left and the right, Hegel was constrained to become his own faction, that is to say, to set his own precedent. So that is what he did and, as was rightly observed, what he did consciously. This was the first means. The other was in seeking help from the only other power that could still offer it to him: the government, which was the only thing that Hegel had not yet made a mess of. Even if the *Philosophy of Right* stood on its own two feet, there was, for the reasons given in the previous section, an elective affinity between this work and the spirit reigning over the highest offices in Prussia at that time, which seemed to make an alliance more possible here than anywhere else. Owing to Hegel's diplomatic skill, he was able to hold himself distant from the antagonisms and feuds that prevailed

within the bosom of the Ministry of Culture itself. His trait, akin to
Goethe, of accepting the superiority of clever people and tyrants, those
who simply cannot be banished from the world, took care of the rest.
And both clever people and benevolently patronizing tyrants, though
not in the grandest sense, were abundant in Prussia. The Minister who
had appointed Hegel and who constantly protected him, all in all not
an unworthy successor of Wilhelm von Humboldt, had his fair share of
both. Already in Bavaria, and even earlier, Hegel had looked longingly to
the French model in hopes of managing a state-funded critical and literary newspaper. Later, the Heidelberg professor justified his resignation to
the Baden government with the opportunity offered to him in Prussia
to leave the "precarious situation of lecturing on philosophy at a university"[8] and, where required, to enter in Prussia into actual civil service.
It is likely that Hegel's dispirited sentiment towards the teaching profession, and even towards the profession of philosophy itself, had gradually
faded in Berlin as his success grew. During his final years, those closest
to him would never again hear the discontented expression: "they who
are damned by God to be philosophers!" But Hegel's desire to unite his
philosophical science with governmental authority had already been at
least partially fulfilled, even while he was still "lecturing on philosophy
at a university." This desire was not merely fulfilled because Hegel had
served for some years on Brandenburg's academic board of examiners,
nor merely because he was called upon by the Ministry as a consul-
tant; and again, it was not fulfilled merely because Altenstein, at Hegel's
request, had earnestly cautioned the *Halle Literary Journal*, which had dared
to accuse Hegel of intentionally slighting Fries in the passage from the
Preface to his *Philosophy of Right*. Instead, Hegel's desire had been fulfilled
above all on account of the *Jahrbücher für wissenschaftliche Kritik*, which were
first published in 1827. They were not exactly published by the government itself, as was the once hoped-for scientific *Moniteur*, which Hegel
had again tried to establish in Berlin at the beginning of the 1820s. Also,
in line with Hegel's original intention, they were also by no means
merely an organ of his school of thought, since an entire series of completely independent scholars – among them Wilhelm von Humboldt,
Böckh, Bopp, August Wilhelm Schlegel, Boisserée, Thibaut, Creuzer, and
Gesenius – were to work alongside Hegel. But nevertheless, the government showed a very benevolent interest in the enterprise, even to the

point of financial support, which Hegel himself half-jokingly perceived as a political piece in the moral conquest of Southern Germany, and as such limited the enterprise to what would later be the borders of the German Customs Union and the Bismarckian Empire. And the Hegelian character of the journal, even if Hegel had genuinely wanted to avoid this, soon came fully into its own.

And just as Altenstein's government had already supported Hegel in the affair with the Halle Literary Journal, and had promoted him to such a degree that Creuzer, for example, was able to call on Hegel to speak to the Minister as an advocate against an impending ban on Prussian students stemming from Heidelberg,[9] Hegel likewise came to defend this government, especially in the years following the publication of the *Philosophy of Right*, marked as they were by the tribulations surrounding the persecution of "demagogues." Even more so than the subtle-minded Minister himself, who restricted the freedom of the university more out of pressure from overall politics than out of personal conviction, and was visibly conflicted thereby, Hegel could at times represent the government's policies in a more credible manner. Only recently, in order to explain this apparently so unphilosophical attitude of the philosopher, one has rightly pointed towards Hegel's keen conviction that world history will continue its unstoppable progress within consciousness of freedom, no matter whether the individual, including Hegel himself, "smears a bit of shoe polish on the seven-league boots" of this "colossus,"[10] so that Hegel could afford to act on this attitude at times "in order to build up comradery."[11] Thus it came about, especially in 1822, the year during which the persecution led by Grano, Tzschoppe, and Kamptz[12] turned against Schleiermacher,[13] that some of Hegel's statements were almost reminiscent of that "association with Schmalz," which he had thought himself to be entirely free of when the book was first published. This association seemed evident when Hegel expressed that he had enjoyed giving the "demagogic people a great prod"[14] with his *Philosophy of Right*; or when he mocks the fact that "one" – Schleiermacher! – describes the present as "the times of oppression";[15] or even when he writes the following, verbatim, to a foreign student who is seeking entrance into a Prussian university and who entirely satisfied the condition of being without known "demagogic activities and dispositions": "our hallmark – that is, in a certain, and indeed very important sphere – is speculative attitude and depth, partly in and of itself, partly also because it does not give any impetus to the outside world and thereby does not cause those openings that can too easily lead to misunderstanding through popular representation."[16] It was not an "association with Schmalz" then, nor is it this now. But this separation of true internal content from "popular" representation, which Hegel praised as protection against "misunderstanding" in the letter just quoted, was nevertheless very worrying. And worrying especially from the exalted viewpoint of the philosopher himself. Precisely this philosophy of unconditional unity and universal actualization of the spirit must not of itself promote such separations between the initiated and the uninitiated; not freedom in general, but the freedom of all was the goal that was written with luminous letters at the end of history. And Hegel sensed the dangers that were rising against him here, albeit from the wrong side. A year before that letter, Hegel had told a high official that one could demonstrate the consequence of atheism from the malevolence associated with all speculative philosophy towards religion, and he had thereby foreseen the resurgence of this "almost forgotten catchphrase,"[17] which had once tripped up Fichte in Jena. And yet "atheism" was not the catchphrase that was soon actually to be used against Hegel, it was "pantheism." And it was not the "demagogues, among whom, as is well known, piety highly flourishes,"[18] not De Wette and Schleiermacher who accused him of this; it came instead from the circles of a rejuvenated pietism, from the nascent Conservative Party. They came and cut off access for Hegel to the future bearers of the crown. No matter how carefully Hegel's students and he himself worked out the conformity of his philosophy of religion with the prevailing dogma, Hegel was forced to recognize that in those "higher circles" the effect went only as far "as to silence."[19] They did not believe him on the harmlessness of his "speculative explanation of theology."[20]

As late as the first half of the 1820s, the European pressure began to fade under which the Prussian government had erringly strayed into a political policy which stood in contrast to the great traditions of the age of reform and upheaval, as the example of the persecution of demagogues had shown. Even Hegel's letters in the following period no longer contain any allusions to such a policy; after all, there was no longer any reason for it. Another point of opposition had since become apparent, an opposition which seemed to have so strongly drawn the practical interest of the politician Hegel that his conduct during the outbreak of the July Revolution was largely determined by it.

At the end of the previous section, in the overview of the relationship between the *Philosophy of Right* and the political parties of the nineteenth century, what was still missing was the clerical element. During Hegel's time in Bavaria – he had never before lived in a Catholic region – Hegel became familiar with, and learned to fear, the power of clericalism in political life, and during the Congress of Vienna some of his doubts and concerns were voiced in this direction. However, the stay in Heidelberg and the years in Berlin seem to have repressed these impressions. The *Philosophy of Right* called for a plurality of "churches" in a free state, which corresponded to common law, as well as to the governmental policy with respect to church politics. Where the book speaks of the relation of religion to the state, it is apparent that only Protestant Christianity is considered, in line with the earliest expressions of Hegelian thought. Indeed, the real concern of the politician turns here precisely against internalized Christianity, as for instance Schleiermacher had taught it, against the "highly flourishing" pious conviction "of the demagogues." But nowhere does the *Philosophy of Right* speak of Catholicism specifically. In fact, the historical-philosophical outline treats it as something over-come, as a preliminary stage for the present. And in doing so, to a certain extent, it denies Catholicism its actuality, in the more profound sense of the word. If anywhere, then the philosopher showed himself here to be bound to Prussian conditions. For at that time, the Curia – even if it had returned from its latest Babylonian exile with renewed strength and new possibilities – had ever so quietly changed its tune that even up into the 1830s, and just before the outbreak of the major conflict from which the Catholic Fraction was later formed, that an observer as far-seeing as Ranke (likely because, despite it all, he was still observing from Berlin) could still hold the power of the church in his day to be harmless for the Protestant state. As the Pope was first settling again in the Papal States, Niebuhr, as the Prussian envoy in Rome, was confident in reporting that the spiritual arsenal of the decrepit Papacy had become corroded. At the beginning of the 1820s, according to his own testimony, Hegel had come to a good understanding with the future leaders of the Catholic Fraction, with Windischmann and Ferdinand Walter. And in 1824, with an amiable turn of phrase that was neither Protestant nor Catholic, Hegel had still described the philosophers and, in a certain sense, the governments as belonging to the "priesthood." If suddenly, namely beginning in April of 1826, Hegel's correspondence teemed with outbursts against the "clerics," and if from then on, the problem of the state and Catholicism moved nearly to the center of his political interests, then this may have been prompted by the wayward practice of Rhenish and Westphalian priests in response to the royal decree of August 1825 on mixed marriages. However, the direct cause seems to be an incident that Hegel experienced personally.

In March of 1826, in his lecture on the history of philosophy and its development in the Middle Ages, Hegel elaborated on the Catholic doctrine of the Lord's Supper in its scholastic formation and characterized it in a very rough, even contemptuous manner. A listener, who was the chaplain at St. Hedwig Cathedral, had thereupon denounced Hegel to the Minister "for public disparagement of the Catholic religion." For confidential treatment, Altenstein placed the matter in the hands of Hegel's friend, Johannes Schulze, who also habitually frequented Hegel's lectures, and Hegel, informed of the incident, issued a defense of his position from the lectern. In the middle of this, the chaplain stood up and looked at Hegel "sternly and, as it were, menacingly." Whereupon Hegel responded: "I am not impressed in the least that you are looking at me in this manner," and whereupon the chaplain left the battleground amid general chatter. The matter was then settled in a communication to Altenstein, wherein Hegel had very proudly defended his position, a communication which essentially functioned as an oral defense at the college and reserved the right of the professor, "who is known to have been baptized and raised as a Lutheran, is and will remain so," "to be allowed, in philosophical lectures at a Protestant university," under a government "towards which all Protestants direct their eyes and see in it their main support and firm standing, to declare that the Catholic doctrine of the host is Papist idolatry and superstition."[21] Notwithstanding the good relationship with Altenstein, the courage that belonged to such an elevated tone against the government in this matter at that time was not that egregious. For, as may be recalled, in the past winter a petty war had already begun between the church and the government on the question of mixed marriages in the western part of the monarchy. And above all, shortly before the incident, there was a harsh letter of disapproval from the King to his half-sister, the Duchess of Anhalt, addressing her conversion to Catholicism, and news circulated of the expulsion of the King's half-brother from court on the same grounds. Two days after Hegel's letter of defense, entirely satisfied, Hegel reported to Cousin, his friend and Parisian professor of philosophy, on the royal course of action taken in those two cases; and from then on, and not earlier, an uninterrupted series of remarks on the advance of clericalism appears in letters to and from Hegel.[22] In France, in the Netherlands, and in England, Hegel sees strides being taken within the clerical movement, and his correspondents assume of Hegel that he is aware of how "detrimental it must be to the state." In one case, what caused concern was an unfavorable concordat; in one case it was the political emancipation of the Catholics in the hitherto purely Protestant state; and in another it was the Catholicization of neo-Romantic philosophy. Hegel's dealings in Berlin are likely echoed in a playful allusion to his wife a year and a half later[23] and hostile remarks were also made against Windischmann. Above all, however, the treatment of the relation between state and religion in the second edition of the *Encyclopedia*, published in 1827, bears witness to this new trait in his image of the state.

The changes that Hegel made to this second edition of the book, whose first edition was published in 1817, in so far as they relate to the subjects treated in the *Philosophy of Right*, are aimed at transforming the doctrine of objective spirit – which was still systematically undeveloped in 1817 – in accordance with how it is laid out in the *Philosophy of Right* of 1820. In part, however, some relatively extensive additions, compared to the general brevity of the overall approach, obviously pursue the purpose of providing supplemental material to the major work on the *Philosophy of Right*. While most of these additions actually do deal with questions that had been entirely omitted from the *Philosophy of Right* – such as the theory of the budget – the extensive note on the state and religion, which is, moreover, quite forcibly placed, was obviously intended less to supplement the amply detailed presentation of the problem in the *Philosophy of Right* than in some respects to replace it. Initially, the note seems to recall only the subjective necessity of religious disposition for the objective fulfillment of one's duty towards the state, already emphasized beginning in 1805, and again in 1820. But suddenly, for those who are familiar with the *Philosophy of Right*, and thereby recall that juxtaposition of the one state and the many churches, and also the emphasized indifference of the state towards the particular content of religious disposition, the following sentence comes as a surprise: "What is religious is [...] not only to be understood as *disposition*."[24] Religion is more than disposition, it is the state's firm "basis [...] the source and power [...] which has established and produced the state and its constitution."[25] And before the reader really knows what this distinct relationship should be between religion, which is not only disposition, and the state as objective institution − instead of the relation from 1820 between personal piety and personal disposition towards the state − the reader already finds themselves in the middle of a terribly fierce polemic against Catholicism, whose fundamental "unfreedom of spirit in religion" is consistent "only with a legislation of legal and ethical unfreedom."[26] Quite rightly − thus says the adversary of Haller, and also of Niebuhr − quite rightly has "the Catholic religion been so loudly praised, and is often still praised, as the sole religion in which the strength of governments is secured − but in fact, only for governments that [...] are founded on the unfreedom of the [...] spirit."[27] If then, for instance, "worldly wisdom [...] that is, wisdom about what is right and rational in actuality" awakens in the spirit of governments and peoples, and thus there arises a quarrel "of the needs of right and ethicality [...] against the religion of unfreedom," then it is useless, "if the principle of unfreedom in religion is not abandoned, that the laws and forms of government are transformed into rational organizations of right."[28] The justification of this entirely new idea, in light of 1820, opposing above all the legitimist glorification of political "authority" [Autorität] grounded in Catholicism, is essentially the same justification as the old one: the "principles of the reason of actuality" find "their ultimate and utmost verification in religious conscience."[29] What is new, however, is the complete skepticism that is now brought to bear upon the power of the institution, which was regarded with such confidence in 1820 and even in the Württemberg text in 1817: everything now comes down to "*individuals*," and thus what matters most is the "spirit of their religion" and not the "meaning of legislation."[30]

The affinity between the rational state and the Protestant religion remains connected to the older conception of faith, albeit in a looser connection, which is a matter of pure conscience and its political value a matter of pure disposition. What is new becomes fully visible when

Hegel, in the further course of his paragraphs, now undertakes to renew and reshape the relation between reason and actuality from the version of world history laid out in the Preface of 1820.

Hegel again proceeds from Plato's state. As in 1820, he sees the significance of this state in the fact that there philosophy attempted for the first time to ground the state upon the eternal Idea. Again, Hegel sees the deficiency of Plato's structural design in the fact that Plato did not, and could not, consider the free self-conscious individual will, as it was Christianity that brought this concept to bear on humanity. But while earlier Hegel had grasped the tragic nature of Plato's position in its uniqueness within world history, he now situates this position under the general idea that state and philosophy always follow religion in their historical development, so that therefore the philosopher Plato could not have anticipated Christianity's idea of the state. Thus, the state, since religion precedes it, cannot initially contain the consummate relation with religion. On the contrary, the state will of necessity first have to develop itself in "distinction" to religion. And only then, when this epoch has been passed through, can the state come to the "reconciliation of actuality [...] with spirit, of the state with religious conscience."[31] Thus, by asserting now, and now for the first time, the law of history that the state must necessarily come later than religion, Hegel goes beyond the simple view of world history from the Preface of 1820. The Preface had ordered the course of events as follows: the actuality of the Greek state; the Sophistic individual's attack upon this actuality; Plato's resistance, which however, although fed by the spirit of reason and thereby ingenious and future-oriented, misjudged the justified content of the Sophistic attack and is therefore without a future; and finally, the fulfillment of the Sophistic idea, as well as the Platonic, in Christianity, which acquires in the Teutons, with their natural idea of freedom, the people for the new state. Now, in 1827, the development has not yet come to an end, but the "decay"[32] internal to Christianity now first begins, because initially all that is present is religion. Thus, the Catholic Middle Ages becomes a culminating point of this construction. For the same reason that Plato could not recognize the true state, Catholicism too is unable to bear this true state. The historical construction, which is the foundation for the basic idea of the entire *Philosophy of Right* in 1820, is now erected for the sole purpose of proving the incompatibility of Catholicism with the state.

What Hegel had printed here for the first time, and was still contained within the husk of a difficult academic form, was expressed in magnificent simplicity, and with a clear application to the questions of life, in the Latin speech that he delivered as Rector of the University on June 25, 1830, on the occasion of commemorating the tercentenary of the Augsburg Confession – one month before the outbreak of the new French Revolution.[33]

Due to the connection of the celebration with a religious denomination, which contained the Lutheran doctrines of differentiation not only towards the Papists, but also towards the sacraments themselves, the celebration was not without its internal difficulties in settling the state of union between Lutherans and Reformed Protestants. Hegel, as a Lutheran himself, avoided these pitfalls in that he left aside everything that was actually dogmatic, and paid tribute to the Reformation as a whole, from the standpoint of a non-theologian, as a world historical turning point. After all, the significance of the day was not to be found in dogmatic stipulation, but in the fact that princes and free cities had declared that they stood by the *Augustana* – this "Magna Carta" of the Protestant Church – and thus for the first time claimed for the layperson the exquisite right to decide for themselves on matters of faith. With this association, which Hegel established at the beginning of his speech between the role of state powers in the age of Reformation and the idea of the general priesthood, Hegel had set his topic. To begin with, in the manner long common to him, Hegel addressed the second point first, namely the abolition of the difference between priest and layperson and its importance for the internalization of faith. This was above all how Hegel had previously understood the world historical meaning of the Reformation. This concept of Protestant freedom, which Hegel now equated with the modern concept of freedom of thought [Geistesfreiheit], was the foundation for Protestantism in its first decidedly Protestant epoch, namely during the Napoleonic period. It was only in this sense, even before the second edition of the *Encyclopedia*, that Hegel had regarded his own state as Protestant. For Hegel, this is now only one aspect of the matter, an aspect he even consciously abandons at the point where it becomes difficult. What interests him now is the other aspect: namely, what influence a restored Christianity exercised, and continues to exercise, on the progress of the state constitution and civil order. Therefore, beginning with praise for Protestant freedom and inwardness, Hegel soon moves to the role played by the princely and civic heads of state for the Protestant people. It is to their merit if lasting and ensured freedom develops from the liberation. The new piety required a new state. For just as since 1827, Hegel had already no longer wanted to restrict religion to a disposition, so he now declared that faith can no longer remain in the recesses of interiority and be closed off from the action and order of life. Hegel now allows the state to gain its inner unity and self-legislation from Protestantism itself, and not, as was the case in 1820, from the separation of churches and the existence of several churches in the one state: indeed, in our time, the ingenious men who want to separate state and religion are grossly mistaken – and we know in what sense Hegel himself was one of these men merely a decade ago; instead, the free unanimity of state and religion, and admittedly only of the state and Protestant religion, which alone demands such unanimity, this is the precious heritage of a great past of three hundred years. In that Hegel now sees the true state and Protestant faith as unconditionally bound, it is not surprising that he now applies this view to history and the present itself: state freedom can only prosper on the ground of religious freedom, and to misjudge this was the error of all those in Catholic empires who in past ages, punished by terrible outcomes, sought to renew the state and its ethos by means of reform and revolution. Conversely, as a Protestant state, and only as such, Prussia was able to improve laws, increase freedom, and to develop the constitution in a richer and more liberal way – Hegel was evidently thinking of free enterprise, the abolition of serfdom, and of municipal statues. And these reforms, which were likewise indicated by the progressive spirit and required by necessity, could come here from above, from the bearers of state power themselves and could be accomplished through their intelligence and human disposition. The state, as befit the state of Frederick the Great, which Hegel had praised twelve years ago in his inaugural address as being founded upon intelligence, and whose actuality Hegel had soon thereafter used as the model for describing the single free secular-organization of ethicality above the plurality of churches, this same state Hegel now founds upon the single Protestant faith. The "intelligence" was – as the sentence cited above from the address shows – only a servant to the work, no longer its foundation and origin. Hegel's state had lost its secular soul, indeed, had lost its autonomy. A new spirit had entered into it, a spirit which now had to create a new body for itself. The unconditional and conclusive ethical relation of 1820 between the individual human being and the community had found its appropriate completion in the relation of the one particular state to the many general churches. When this keystone was pulled away, the entire arch faltered. Hegel did not know how things stood when he concluded that brilliant speech, and when the chorus of students, in tune with Master Zelter's baton, answered with the resounding tones of Luther's latinized song. Five weeks later, on the King's birthday, the Rector was to announce the student prize winners from the various faculties. When he opened the envelope that contained the work crowned by the philosophical faculty, he read the name of one of his students, Gutzkow, the future leader of the Young Germany. That same late afternoon brought the first detailed news of the event that would force Hegel to bring his half-transformed idea of the state into battle with that very master he had once praised, and held accountable, for never refusing a challenge: with actuality.

Hegel had long followed with concern the internal tensions in France, which eventually erupted. The correspondence with Cousin, the apostle of German philosophy in Paris, shows exactly how familiar Hegel was with French parliamentary politics. The Frenchman Cousin, whom Hegel had advocated for years earlier in Berlin when Cousin was suspected of demagoguery by a high-ranking constable, and who in turn had become the ever-accommodating guide for Hegel during his stay in Paris, was well aware that his political principles were "a little less mature" than those of his venerated master and friend. Nevertheless, he could openly reveal his moderately liberal heart to Hegel: Cousin is "invariably attached to the matter of liberty," but no one will be able to entice him into becoming a "foil" for the same.[34] When Cousin's political party came into power along with the Ministry of Martignac in 1828, his friend in Berlin knew him to be "near the music of the liberal energy that was sounding the alarm reverberating throughout Paris, and throughout all of France and Europe," and believed to see in Cousin "a beaming satisfaction at the victories that arrived anew each mail day."[35] And yet, given Hegel's amicable participation in the events, which for Cousin also included the prospect of his reinstatement in the teaching post taken away from him by the clerical reactionaries, he subtly disassociated himself from the liberal victories by limiting his personal share in that "satisfaction" to the detail that a philosophy professor, namely Royer-Collard, was the head of the new chamber.[36] Cousin must have sensed this quiet reticence, and in his reply he goes into great detail in addressing Hegel's concerns, which were really only hinted at: it was not, as Hegel had maintained, an unexpected turnaround due to the random outcome of the elections; rather, the old government had mismanaged the economy; the election result could only have come as a surprise to the old government itself; the new government would take a middle-of-the-road policy, both internally and in European questions; his task – that is, Cousin's task – would be to insist on caution, moderation, and reconciliation, so that it could finally be shown that no one need be afraid of liberalism, neither private individuals nor governments, and that liberalism is capable of taking the reins of the state into its own hands; Hegel could rely on the fact that one would act rationally, and that France's future will not contain anything alarming: "remain calm regarding France, whatever you are told, and whatever it seems to you from afar."[37] This letter shows to what extent the internal politics of individual states and the liberal-conservative opposition were perceived to be a general concern for all of Europe, and especially to what extent people had become accustomed to seeing in Paris the hearth of European development. At the same time, it is precisely the manner in which the French liberal seeks to reassure the German thinker that makes Cousin's personal position clear. In principle, Cousin considers Hegel to be a likeminded person in the fight against an anti-intellectual reaction, but the Frenchman likewise presupposes that Hegel fears revolution as such, and that Hegel no longer wants to give in to progress at such a price. By consoling him with the prospect of calm development – which, according to his hope, would unfold in France after the victory of the liberals – Cousin believed he could win Hegel over.

It is a fear of revolution in general that frames the few statements passed down in letters and conversations from the period after July 1830. Admittedly, the generally good behavior of the student body during Hegel's rectorate, which came to an end during this period, provided him with little difficulty whatsoever. The only case he was required to deal with, which nevertheless deeply troubled him for a few days – a student had been walking around Berlin wearing a blue-white-red cockade! – vanished into thin air: the young traitor declared that the blue-white-red was only meant to refer to the colors of the Mark Brandenburg. Yet Hegel was all the more frightened by the opposition emerging among his own pupils. Gans, in particular, approved of the Revolution, and personally traveled to Paris in order to experience the reshaping of France firsthand and to again take up personal contact with the leaders he had once befriended in the past. The fear that the fire would not be confined to its hearth and that the world would once again be bathed in its flames, just as it was forty years ago, seemed to be justified when in August the Revolution made its incursion into Belgium which was also most joyfully met by Gans. Prussia already seemed to be directly involved here, not only by the proximity of its Rhine province to Belgium but above all by the close familial relation of its King to the ruler of the Dutch state, not to mention the fact that the adjacent event opened up unforeseen possibilities for a revolutionary France to resume the political policies of 1792. A cloud of new revolutionary wars seemed to loom on the horizon. While in September the closing words of the Preface to the new edition of the Encyclopedia had lamented that "superficiality and vanity were permeating the public,"[38] in mid-December Hegel wrote in a resigned mood to a supporter about the "tremendous political interest" that had currently "swallowed everything up." Philosophy cannot oppose "the ignorance, violence, and evil passions of this loud clamor."[39] In the meantime, the situation in Belgium had somewhat cleared up. The ambassadors' conference in London gave its retrospective blessing to the division carried out by the Revolutionaries. In January, with Prussia at the vanguard, the foundations of the future Belgian state were being laid by a united Europe. But in the meantime, a new threat of war had developed from the Polish uprising. Indeed, on January 29, Hegel still believed – owing to an increase in funding, which had continued right up until that moment – that there was no need to furnish an "interruption of the political peace and calm on the eastern border." However, he failed to recognize that there was "an oppressiveness about these relations."[40] On the evening of that very day, letters from Warsaw – newspapers could not make it through – informed Berlin of the removal of the Romanovs from office. In the morning before this news broke, what had mainly kept Hegel worried about war were the "exacerbated dispositions towards glory and conquest, still embittered against what was justified humiliation, making themselves so loudly heard" in France, and which had come to light on the occasion of the Belgian question.[41] In general, Hegel must have expressed himself on the emergence of an independent Belgium in such a manner that would have explained why an essay on this subject signed with the letter "H.," which was published in the editions of January 26 and 27 in the Prussian state newspaper, could be attributed to him within his immediate circle.

In this connection, I would like to make reference to a remark by Heinrich Laube from an 1834 feuilleton comprised of gossip from school and society.[42] It is unlikely that Laube's remark was accurate. Although the essay in question appears in very assured form, the language does not actually sound Hegelian. However, it seems highly probable to me that Laube's remark refers to Hegel. For even apart from the suggestive signature, and apart from the fact that very detailed knowledge of the circumstances in Belgium could be attributed to Hegel on account of his two visits to the country, the content also coincides precisely with thoughts which Hegel was thinking just at that time, thoughts which would have been heard by Hegel's acquaintances from his own lips. And just as Hegel had for some years declared true political freedom to be possible only on a Protestant foundation, and especially just as Hegel had sympathetically followed the struggle of his old pupil van Ghert, who was serving as an adviser to the Dutch Ministry of Culture and working towards establishing state influence over the education of the Belgian clergy: the writer of the essay also recognizes, in the most visible passage, the danger of founding the new state "upon the influence of hierarchy, which, under the pretext of zeal for the purity of doctrine, seizes the minds of the people in order to establish dominion over the spirit of the governments themselves by means of dominion over the spirits of its subjects." For the writer, to direct this influence is nothing less than "a European affair." "Any government, whichever confession its leader may have, is threatened by it. France has no less an interest than Great Britain and the German powers in avoiding the spread of a fanaticism which ultimately seeks, with open violence, to gain the freedom to develop on its own in opposition to the government of the Kingdom of the Netherlands." Indeed, the entire essay ends with words that are remarkably Hegelian: "It is impossible that a state should exist in the midst of Germany, France, and Great Britain, in which the guiding principle of the government would be the perpetuation of a coercion of conscience, of intolerance, and of ignorance for a large mass of its people. The nobler sense, which inevitably develops through free prosperity and through the growing insight of the higher classes in the country itself, if it is not to degenerate through fruitless struggle into a blind power that does not understand itself, needs the support of a government independent of hierarchy. And in the present condition of the country this independence can only be warranted by connection with other landed property wherein the government is already fortified upon the basis of universal education." If it is evident that the actually deeper justification for the author's opposition to an independent Belgium is found within the above idea, and if for its sake he takes the trouble to refute in detail the reasons given for the secession, then the immediate, and more timely reason for the essay can be found in the opening sentences on the importance for the security of German borders of a Belgium that has withdrawn from the French sphere of rule: "In fact, the Jura, the Vosges, and the Ardennes are so unmistakably the natural frontiers of the French Empire to the northeast that the occupation of Alsace and the present *Departement du Nord*, consisting of former Dutch lands, can only be regarded as the result of the political predominance which France acquired through the House of Austria in its German and Spanish line since the Peace of Westphalia, or rather since it was rid of its internal unrest. Even disregarding this, the less it has been attempted to wrest this one-hundred-and-fifty-year-old possession from the French Empire, even during the disastrous crisis lasting from 1814 to 1815, the less France, for its part, could look with jealousy at the institutions of defense whereby the German Empire seeks to prevent the further narrowing of its borders. *Institutions of defense*, because the German Confederation, by its very nature, is only concerned with preservation, and because no German power has any reason to wish to make acquisitions at the expense of France." Hegel had expressed himself in this same manner, only a little more strongly, in the above-mentioned letter on French dispositions, when incidentally – and in these very days – even French diplomats, and not merely public opinion, once again sounded undisguised demands to claim part of the "Rhine border." And it was exactly those sentences from the essay that aroused the ire of the Parisian "National," and drove it towards a vehement rejoinder, in response to which the Prussian state newspaper was forced to call Friedrich von Raumer, the Berlin historian and member of the regional censorship committee, to its defense.

Over the course of the winter, Hegel seems to have concluded, despite all his reservations, that the July Revolution had been a necessary and irreversible step. The *Lectures on the Philosophy of History*, as proof of the law of history that great judgements, in order to legitimize themselves to human consciousness as irrevocable, must occur twice, casually mentions the "two-time" expulsion of the Bourbons – namely in 1792 and in 1830 – along with the two-time founding of the Roman monarchy by Caesar and Augustus, and the two-time fall of Napoleon.[43] During his lectures in the waning hours of the Winter semester, Hegel even offered a critique of the Bourbon's restoration state, which he describes as a "fifteen-year farce," commenting on the relation between the government and the people. The reason for this was "the opposition of disposition and mistrust": "the French were lying to each other when they issued addresses full of devotion and love for the monarchy, full of blessings for the same." And Hegel initially finds the deeper reason here, again in line with his thoughts over the last five years, in the general impossibility of bringing about a rational constitution through the Catholic religion, which separates the sacred and the secular: "For the government and the people must have this final, mutual guarantee of disposition, and can only have it in a religion that is not opposed to the rational constitution of the state." Thus, even during that "fifteen-year farce," although the Charter was the general panacea conjured up by both sides, the prevailing "disposition was Catholic for one thing, which made it a matter of conscience to destroy existing institutions."[44] It is the same as in other Catholic states: without exception, liberalism remained "forged to political unfreedom through religious slavery."[45] Everywhere it is the same basic error: "that the fetters of right and freedom are cast off without the liberation of conscience, that there could be revolution without reformation."[46] And so, however much an "old heart" can rejoice "after forty years of wars and immense confusion," Hegel does not expect a permanent end to those revolutionary confusions and wars – rightly so, as subsequent history has shown – even from the new government of France, which agrees in principle with his own constitution.[47] For Hegel, it is precisely the "Catholic principle" that remains the unresolved question, the "rupture" in France's constitutional future.[48]

It is not the only unresolved question. The other question lies in the very essence of liberalism itself, in the demand that individuals as such should govern, or participate in government. The existence of a government itself seems to him to be called into question through this demand, which makes those who obey into those who command. And in parliamentarianism – at least in a parliamentarianism with a democratic basis and its eternal unrest, where the government is instituted by the will of the many and then, as government, stands in opposition to this very will – Hegel recognizes "the collision, the knot, the problem which history faces, and which it has to solve in the coming age."[49]

There is a reasonable explanation why Hegel's political concerns are not merely connected to the Catholic undertones of the new movement, which came about in 1830, but that he also senses trouble in the movement itself, in its pure political essence. For the movement was already longing after that form of state which could be the most tenacious and successful after 1789, and this state, if not Protestant in the German sense, was also certainly not Roman Catholic. On April 26, the state newspaper published the first installment of an article on the British Reform Bill, with subsequent installments published on April 27 and 29. However, nothing came in the latest publication after the notice "next installment to follow," and thus during Hegel's lifetime, his article – for he was the author – was complete only in manuscript form and was only made public after his death. It is Hegel's last political work.[50]

In the years before the July Revolution, England's strict Tory government, which its interior had been tied to by its position against revolutionary France, had already experienced a few knocks. Under the leadership of its old chief Wellington, the political party had recently lost ground, especially with regard to the Irish question and the related Catholic question. Under strong impressions from the July Revolution, the elections of the year 1830 resulted in victories for the opposition and, in the latter part of the year, the Wellington cabinet yielded to a Whig cabinet.[51] It was known that this meant an election reform bill would be brought to the table.

After England's parliament had adopted its oligarchic character at the end of the seventeenth century and the royal privilege of creating new parliamentary seats had been abolished, voices were raised, from around the middle of the eighteenth century onwards, calling for a change in electoral privileges that would correspond to the new conditions in the population, especially regarding better representation of the "middle classes."The younger Pitt – and subsequently, Fox – championed the idea. But the revolution in France, instead of fostering its actualization, had instead set this idea back decades. It was not until the 1820s, especially when the privileged status of the High Church was abolished in 1829, thereby toppling one of the foundations of the old oligarchic power, that the political agitation was able to emerge with a better chance for victory and, during the election campaign in the summer of 1830, this political agitation grew to full strength.

On March 1, 1831, the Ministry, after diligently soliciting public opinion, sought permission from Parliament to submit the bill. The reform would not fundamentally affect the corporational components of electoral law, which only recognized communities as voters and not individuals, instead was practically limited to balancing out the most blatant gaps between the corporate vote and the personal vote: electoral constituencies with less than two thousand inhabitants were to lose the right to vote; a number of hitherto unrepresented urban and rural districts with larger populations were to become electoral constituencies; eligibility to vote in the countryside was to be determined according to property type; and eligibility in the city on the basis of a census. This was the proposal. Under the pressure of public opinion and under fear of revolution, which was powerfully fomented by the reformists, the bill passed after a second reading on March 22, albeit following fierce debates and with only the trivial majority of a single vote. The prospects for the third reading were looking better, as it was possible that the majority would increase by then. Following the dissolution of the parliament, the Ministry, taking with them an electoral slogan certainly evident to the voters, now had a weapon they could use against the minority, and simply holding this weapon might preclude the need to use it – as long as the King could remain in place. And a strengthened majority in the House of Commons would also put pressure on the resisting majority in the House of Lords. This was the situation as the two houses entered the Easter holidays on March 30. But the minority did not remain inactive. When the Parliament reassembled on April 12, the minority mounted a strike that hit the government where it was most vulnerable: the majority in favor of the very moderate reform plan depended on the support of the leader of the Catholic Irish – O'Connel, the powerful man of the people – whose support for the Bill would entail the diplomatic postponement of his continuing interests. Even before the holidays, it was noted in passing by the opponents of reform that the governmental proposal would reduce the number of English Lower House seats in favor of seats for the Welsh-Scottish-Irish. But the argument had little effect. Now, at the start of the first session, a member of Parliament, Gascoine – not opposed to reform as such, but fanatically anti-Irish, – again raised the issue. O'Connel immediately countered. But Russell, the Minister who had brought the Bill to the table, had hoped that Gascoine and the Ministry would amend the governmental proposal to suit him, to the surprise of Gascoine himself. Prime Minister Grey confirmed this two days later and added the further explanation, going against the concerns of the reformists, who suspected that the Ministry would give in on the question of the abolished electoral rights, which were largely English: on no account would the government drop this principal point. But the mistrust aroused by the apparent vacillation of the Ministry was not so easy to allay. When, on April 18, the government presented its draft with the amendment that the current total number of delegates should remain unchanged – in appearance taking its opponent Gascoine into account but in truth accommodating its ally O'Connel and the Catholics – Gascoine proposed an "amendment" that this number should not be achieved by means of an increase in the number of Irish or Scottish delegates, however small. The Ministry claimed, apparently again deferring to O'Connel's group, that this would be a blow against the essence of the governmental proposal. And when the motion never-theless passed, by an eight-vote majority, the following day the ministers ordered the King to dissolve Parliament. On April 22, the monarch per-sonally administered this royal right, which had long remained unexer-cised, yet under the boisterous fury of the betrayed majority of April 19, who now openly accused the Ministry of betraying the country to the Irish and the Catholics.

The first installment of Hegel's essay was printed on April 25. He could not have begun writing it before April 7, that is, before the negotiations that occurred before the holidays were fully known in Berlin. The nego-tiations after the holidays, which on the day of April 26 were available in Berlin covering up until April 15, are not addressed by Hegel at all. A newspaper note from April 14, not referring to England, is used in pass-ing in the text and a note, which could have been known on the evening of April 23, was added as a footnote in the printed text, whereas it was still missing in the manuscript. Thus, the manuscript was already completed on April 23, although it was probably still in progress on April 14. However, the treatment of the subject does not go beyond March 30 and its subject matter is generally the parliamentary negotiations in March.[52]

England, as we know, had always been the target of Hegel's lively interest. The average person from Württemberg believed that in their own landed estates they possessed the exact counterpart to the British parliament. Hegel, however, just as he had long been critical of the Estates of his homeland, also followed England's parliamentary life without any true admiration. As early as 1798, in one of the notes to the Cart translation, he pointed out, quite in the spirit of the demands made by the opposition in the English Parliament itself, the wide gap that existed between the parliamentary majority and the popular will it claimed to represent. In his text on the Württemberg constitutional crisis of 1798, Hegel had also cited Charles Fox's major speech for parliamentary reform of 1796. Hegel seems to have been more preoccupied with the beginnings of the social question than with those political problems surfacing from the "imperfect representation of the nation," which, incidentally, had also strongly receded in England in the following period. Hegel's first biographer, Rosenkranz, could still look firsthand at Hegel's excerpts on the parliamentary negotiations on the poor tax, and we have run across numerous traces of this interest in the political systems of the subsequent period leading up until 1820. In addition, in the text on *The German Constitution*, we recognized a possible influence of the English ideas of self-governance and popular representation, the influence of both, however, remained mostly doubtful. In any case, Hegel never lost this sense of critique. Whenever England's treatment of social problems comes up for Hegel, he presents his critique more as a cautionary tale. Additionally, when Hegel does follow an English line of thought, he does not name the influence – unlike when addressing French matters – so that one is left here to conjecture. In the 1817 text on the Württemberg constitution, it was said of the English constitution that it had been preserved precisely because of its "abuses."[53] The *Philosophy of Right* from 1820 occasionally alludes to England, even outside of the social question, and Hegel, especially in the oral addenda to his lectures, was probably catering to the interests of his listeners during the following decade.[54] When the Reform Bill was introduced, Hegel was seized, according to good testimony, by the most agonizing restlessness. In the opinion of our correspondent,[55] it was in order to let off steam that Hegel wrote the essay for the state newspaper.

Only a part of everything that was stirred up in England on the occasion of the Bill makes its way into Hegel's essay. Initially, according to his own explanation, only the "elevated points of view which have been raised in the debates of Parliament up until now" were to be compiled, the prospective changes by the Bill to the "noble viscera, the vital principles of the constitution and the conditions of Great Britain."[56] In truth, certain points of view were then entirely omitted. For example, the linking of electoral reform to the question of the parliamentary representation of individual united kingdoms in the London Parliament, and in particular the problem of the Irish stepchild, and problem child of the British Crown, which was complicated by the question of denomination. We saw how this question, which, incidentally, was indeed addressed even before the holidays, was brought to the forefront of the negotiations through Gascoine's advance after the first days following the holidays. Hegel was probably still working on the essay when the opening days of these negotiations became known in Berlin, but he no longer took them into account. Only once does Hegel mention, and with bitter pathos, the treatment of Ireland as one of the sins of the English parliamentary government. What escaped him was the highly effective, indeed for that moment, decisive integration of Ireland's special politics with England's general policy. Completely detached from these relations, which are highly important for English history – and solely for English history – Hegel imparts his subject matter in such a way that only the general European significance stands out. This significance is bound to the major questions which the July Revolution has incessantly raised, questions that had hitherto also been the focus of Hegel's political thinking: the struggle between historical right and rational right, and the relation between constitutional powers. Using England as an example, Hegel addresses them anew. The essay, despite the continuous connection to the Reform Bill, does not so much revolve around England as around the political problem of liberalism in France, and especially in Prussia. But whereas otherwise, when dealing with France – and, if that January essay in the state newspaper did really originate from him, with

Belgium – Hegel takes the question of Catholicism in its relationship to liberalism as his starting point, here he treats liberalism purely as a political problem, indeed, one could say as a technical political problem. What characterizes the essay is more Hegel's doubt for the feasibility of liberal reform in England in general than for the justification of this liberal reform itself.

He indeed acknowledges the justification. Hegel finds the impetus for reform in the "sense of justice"[57] that opposes the "present" "irregularity and inequality"[58] of the electoral process – in the unprinted manuscript the words are "most bizarre, most irregular." Moreover, he does not fail to recognize the power of the concern stoked by the July Revolution, namely the desire to accommodate the admittedly "general voice"[59] of the English people. Hegel praises the fact that the matter is taken up so thoroughly, namely at the level of the "institution," and that it does not seek its salvation in individual measures, or even in mere moral influence.[60] He does not appropriate the Parliament's criticism of the present state of affairs in the sense which he once did in 1798: namely that the nation had seemed to him insufficiently "represented" and that he found a worrying sign in the overwhelming interference of "foul monetary advantage,"[61] and that he saw a good sign for the English people in the awakened aversion to such shamelessly admitted corruption. This time, no one in Parliament had dared to cite either the otherwise so popular "wisdom of the forebears," or the money interests connected with privilege, as reasons for adhering to the abuses of the currently existing state law.[62] In response to the widespread argument that it is precisely because of these abuses, which are now to be abolished, that numerous talented individuals have thus far found their way into the Parliament and from there into the government, we find Hegel rejecting this argument as belonging to the realm of "coincidence," incidentally following Macaulay's speech verbatim.[63] Nevertheless, even though Hegel adopts the reformists' critique of the ongoing conditions, he is far from approving of the law. That in England a wide field of social and political reform was possible, this Hegel undervalues least of all. But even if in England itself one hoped for or feared – as the case might be – that the realization of these reforms would come about through parliamentary reform, Hegel was not dissuaded in this regard. In a Parliament established on the basis of the reformed electoral law – Hegel thought this owing to

statements given in Parliament itself and carried it out point for point –
it would be no easier than in the previous Parliament for these reforms
to find a majority. Thus, the significance of the planned electoral reform
was limited to the fact that it would introduce a new "principle" into
English constitutional life. Whereas hitherto in English state law, as well
as private law, "the character of the positive"[64] had been predominant, and
even constitutional laws such as the Magna Carta or the Bill of Rights
bore the stamp of their historically accidental origin in private right, this
"formal foundation of what exists"[65] would be shaken by the Bill, and
all institutions would be threatened with the question of whether they
"are also in and of themselves right and rational."[66] This, then, is where
Hegel sees the crucial issue. But how does he react to it?

One might expect Hegel, with his familiar critique of what is merely
"positive" in law, to welcome the fact that henceforth in England the
"principles of real freedom"[67] will have a prospect of implementation.
In fact, his entire critique of English conditions always comes down to
this point. Hegel demonstrates England's backwardness in a consistent
comparison with the institutions of the continent, especially those of the
German states, and more particularly those of Prussia. Not even in the
former German Empire – which was "likewise a shapeless aggregate of
particular rights"[68] – have the symptoms of such political "depravity," of
such "selfishness pervading all classes of people," ever been seen.[69] Hegel
chides the Anglomania of the continental peoples, who "for so long have
allowed themselves to be impressed by the declamations of English liberty and the pride of the nation in its legislation."[70] Hegel shows point
by point how what was achieved on the continent partly through the
French Revolution, partly already – in Germany and Prussia – through
the Thirty Years War, and more recently through "rational education,"[71]
as well as through "the great sense of princes […] to allow the feeling of
a justice existing in and for itself to be the guiding star of their legislative activity,"[72] how in England sorry conditions still prevail to this day,
and how in England the Bill does not directly improve the prospects for
such reform. In this comparison, Germany is considered by him to be
the model country, a country where the ideas which in France only prevailed "when blended with many broad abstractions and in connection
with the known acts of violence," are "unmixed […] and have long since
become firm principles of inner conviction and public opinion, and have

brought about the actual, calm, gradual, and legislative transformation of those legal conditions."[73] As noted, Hegel does not expect such reforms from the Bill. For him – and this results in his critique – the Bill either goes too far, or not far enough.

The Bill does not go far enough. For although it fundamentally breaks with the view based purely on private right, which sees in a parliamentary seat nothing other than just some piece of private property, in breaking with this view it does not, however, continue in a logical manner, being only a "mixture of old privileges with the general principle of the equal eligibility of all citizens,"[74] and the Bill "places that which simply stems from the soil of the old feudal law in the much more glaring light of inconsistency, as if all entitlements as a whole were based on one and the same foundation of positive right."[75] Hegel does not consider it beneath his own dignity to reiterate a crude personal suspicion concerning the senior Minister on the scope and limit of this "mixture," which was mentioned as political gossip by a London correspondent to the state newspaper.[76] The Bill goes simply too far for Hegel in that it introduces an electoral law based on a census – we are familiar with Hegel's aversion to this – instead of a law based in some way on the lived class-distinctions of modern society. Hegel would like to see preserved the principle hitherto prevailing in England that it is not individuals who should be represented, as is the modern demand, but rather the "great differentiated interests of the nation,"[77] though not as to entrust its actualization to chance and the inethicality of bribery, as is the case in England, but in such a way that this principle be consciously acknowledged and constitutionally formed. In opposition to an electoral law that is not based on estates, Hegel still uses the argument stemming from the indifference of the individual towards a right that gives him such an infinitesimal share in the power of the state – as Hegel had already argued in 1817 in the Württemberg affair – and defends this argument "of healthy common sense,"[78] in an almost sophistic manner, against a political idealism that invokes the "elevated viewpoints of freedom, duty, the exercise of sovereign rights, and a share in the general affairs of the state."[79] In general, one would have to characterize Hegel's analysis of an extension of the electoral law as sophistic, starting as he does from the viewpoint of "original, inalienable"[80] right: he supports the concept of eligibility with a concept of inalienable rights, which the first concept opposes.

At first, a further democratization in addition to the one mentioned above does not seem to come up in the Bill. But Hegel, in connection with Wellington's speech in the House of Lords shortly before the holidays, already sees it rising in the background. The essentially closed circle of families, which was until now equally dominant in both "political parties," must give way to "new people,"[81] in that a part of its customary access to Parliament is now being taken away, and along with this – although that initially means only a replacement or expansion of one oligarchy with another – also come "heterogeneous" principles.[82] The fact that by departing from the previous principle, which was based solely on positive right, the door to Parliament was opened to new people, this in itself will have a far-reaching effects. The opposition, which hitherto stood on the same ground with the governing party and fought only for power and not over maxims – a condition described by Hegel in the *Philosophy of Right* as "exemplary" – this party will become an opposition party of continental character. England will come to know the "opposition between the *hommes d'état* and the *hommes à principes*."[83] In Hegel's view this in itself is not a misfortune, for England can stand a dash of "ideas." And England, despite fears coming from the opponents of reform, is protected against the cycle of contradiction inherent in the necessary obedience of democratic thought through the practical sense of its residents, as well as by the ample self-governance which consistently nurtures and maintains this practical-political sense. If, of course, these safeguards should prove ineffectual, then Hegel considers revolution to be a certainty in England. For the mediating position – and here Hegel touches on a point that cannot even be mentioned in England, because it concerns a national prejudice, Hegel, however, devotes almost the entire concluding part of his essay to it – is missing in England to which other states "owe the transition from a former legislation based only on positive right, to one based on the principles of real freedom – and indeed a transition kept pure of shock, violence, and robbery": namely, a strong monarchy.[84] For Hegel, the position of the king is the true Achilles heel of the English constitution. The Reform Bill will change nothing about it; the monarchical principle "has nothing more to lose in England";[85] owing to the position of the Ministry, and in Hegel's view that ultimately means the Parliament, royal prerogatives are "more illusory than real."[86] The king in actual English constitutional life, and soon it seems this will

apply to the king in France as well, holds office in a constitution modeled after Sieyès; and Napoleon likened the bearer of this office, with a
judgment Hegel says is "soldierly," to a fattened pig.[87] This exclusion of
the king – which goes as far as disallowing the public mention of his
approval or disapproval of governmental policy – now makes the people
into the only outside entity to which a suppressed political party within
the government could appeal. If the success of the Bill does indeed
impair the preexisting homogeneity of the ruling class, then the specter
of revolution stands waiting in the background of English liberty.[88]

These last considerations make up the concluding part of the essay,
which is no longer printed in the newspaper. The reason it was not
printed was due to a personal intervention of the King. Friedrich
Wilhelm considered it questionable, as the author was informed, that a
ministerial paper should set forth a rebuke against English conditions.[89]
Indeed, the state newspaper's London correspondents had taken a generally favorable position towards the reform plan;[90] and while Hegel's
critique showed general concern with regard to the reform, as is evident
from our account and also from the impression the article later made
on readers – for example on Stahl – it was not entirely disapproving.[91]
One might assume that the further course of the matter, not yet considered by Hegel, had made printing the final part inadvisable. In fact,
during the very days that the article appeared, the newspaper published
the report on the parliamentary sessions leading up to the dissolution.
In the Royal Right of Parliamentary Dissolution, which Hegel did not
mention at all in his enumeration, lay one, and perhaps the strongest,
constitutional possibility for the English monarchy to intervene in the
destiny of the state. Here, particularly in the present moment, the King
was free to decide whether he wanted to go with the Cabinet against the
Parliament or with the Parliament against the Cabinet. By standing up
for the Ministry at that time, the King dealt a serious blow to the power
of this Parliament. Hence the doubts, reported several times in the state
newspaper, whether the King would dare to take such a step; and hence
the tremendous excitement when he did so. It would have been highly
unfitting to simultaneously print the report on this impressive expression of the power of the English Crown alongside Hegel's account of its
complete powerlessness. And unfitting indeed to publish Hegel's use of
Napoleon's phrase cochon d'engrais [fattened pig].

But be that as it may, in any case the print of the essay was suspended; Hegel's most vigorous glorification of Prussian monarchy found no place in Prussia's government gazette. All in all, Hegel's political and news-paper pamphlets had their own unique destiny. The publication on the canton of Vaud with its "*discite justitiam*" appeared after it would have been too late for those responsible to learn justice. The text on the internal conditions of Württemberg from 1798 remained unprinted; the reason is no longer apparent. The major text on the reform of the Empire, which occupied Hegel for almost four years, also remained unprinted, prob-ably out of exasperation for its subject matter. Only the 1817 critique of the Württemberg Estates, the most decisive political piece Hegel wrote, was published, and even reprinted, and found both friendly and hostile resonance. And now this text – if one disregards the uncertain essay on Belgium – Hegel's next and final political publication, was interrupted in the middle. Its destiny is the most curious. The entire difficulty of Hegel's internal position was expressed in it. A reform was imminent, whose general aim he was forced to accept; a condition was to disappear which, in his opinion, no longer could claim the right to exist. Nevertheless, Hegel could not find a courageous "no" for the previous conditions, nor a resolute "yes" for the reform. The theoretically clear conditions became entangled for him through the fear of practical possibilities and dangers. A Hamletic tendency, otherwise foreign to him, looms over his behavior. Basically, Hegel must acknowledge the justification of the liberal striv-ing, regardless of all the restrictions and individual objections he must make. But he makes this acknowledgment impossible for himself by no longer having any real inner confidence in the future. Thus, his glance wavers between possibilities. What he demands of the reform is basi-cally that it should not be needed in the first place; it should have been done long ago. The fact that it is now making up for it causes Hegel to become its suspiciously observing adversary. It is that fear of revolution that had become increasingly visible in his remarks in recent years; and here it manifests in a classic manner. Hegel remains the glorifier of the ideas of 1789, but in 1830 these ideas are unwelcome, even if they go no further than those of 1789. Indeed, they would like to go further. The year 1789 was followed by 1793, by Napoleon's wars. At no cost can the year 1830 be followed by anything similar. In truth, Hegel has become what he called himself in the final class of the winter semester:

an old heart. The danger of revolution has been inserted between his thoughts and their goal. He is no longer able to follow the actualization of the rational without fear. For the first time, what had never happened to Hegel in forty years happened: he had to deny the silent question of actuality the clear and definite answer of the spirit. He who had followed the course of the Revolution, the rise and fall of Napoleon, and the Restoration of the old state's society step by step, with comprehension and affirmation – the "secretary of the world spirit" – covers his face before the new "surge" that history now undertakes. He hears it, but he can no longer see it, no longer interpret it. Instead of the event, he sees the "knot" at which history stands. He had otherwise cut such world-historical knots, a philosophical Alexander, with the sword of the spirit. This time he leaves it to history to deal with. He still sees the question but finds only an either–or as an answer. In the threatening confusion of the world, Hegel now directs his gaze to the rock that seems to stand firm: to Prussia and its monarchy. Here, liberal ideas are actualized into institutions of true freedom, and in the wake of the progressive education of the people, into insight and the good will of rulers. And so it happens, just as Hegel prepares to praise the Prussian monarchy, that this very monarchy demands his silence. And as a reason he is told that one should not desire to offend the foreign country by criticizing its institutions. Its anti-, or rather, a-monarchical institutions! Without willing it, Friedrich Wilhelm, or the one who allowed him to be heard by the philosopher, denied the international similarity of internal politics, the acknowledgment of which the past epoch had rested upon: for the sake of the general relation of the government to England, the Prussian king forbids a glorification of the Prussian monarchy.

Personal acknowledgment had made ample amends for the author. Hegel received the greatest "eulogies" during the private distribution of the essay, which was still allowed.[92] Also, the goodwill of the King, who shortly before had awarded Hegel the third class of the Red Eagle Order, which was then uncommon – incidentally at the same time as Schleiermacher – was hardly diminished by the incident. However, the note of discord, the reasons for which we have just seen, does not seem to have left the thinker. This discord was fed all too much by matters in the political world, and especially by the undeniable opposition in judgment found among some of the students. On his final birthday, one of his most devoted followers sent him a poem which, referring to the general agitation in Europe, called upon the master to name aloud the right word that would magically banish the unleashed spirits.[93] Hegel answered with a verse that thanked the stalwart follower for his "demand to resolve things upon an act of words, to summon the many, even friends themselves, who have gone mad with outrage."[94] But will a word that falls into this maelstrom not only increase the misery, which consists precisely in the fact that everyone desires to hear only themselves? If, however, it were to happen, if he would indeed "strike a blow," as he has long been urged to do, then for him such a calling would be …

> … a pledge to dare again
> with hope that spirits will still meet that word
> and that it does not fade into empty lamentation,
> that they carry it to the people, to be a work.[95]

> *ein Pfand es noch zu wagen*
> *mit Hoffnung, daß noch Geister ihm entgegenschlagen*
> *und daß es nicht verhall' in leere Klagen,*
> *daß sie's zum Volk, zum Werk es tragen!*

Hegel hopes that the spirits will "still" meet him. He no longer possesses that self-evident certainty of feeling from earlier that his word would find its place in time. He only dares to have "hope" that it will succeed in reaching "the people, to be a work." This is no longer the man who knows his self and the age to be so united that he tasked the former, namely the self, with the tremendous demand "to be" the latter, namely the age. The unification upon whose solid ground he had placed his life, the unification with the age, is torn asunder. He is now – although currently at an appreciable height, surrounded by adoring youth, whereas earlier an unknown individual – a solitary old man, an "old heart." However, for someone like Hegel, someone who from one's youth on was never really young and, once he had found himself, was never old in the sense of being behind the times or wanting, or allowed, to be obsolete, for someone such as this, when the inner ground of life, which had been carved out in rigorous storms of development and had thus far been asserted throughout all turns of fate, when this inner ground slips away from under one's feet, such a sentiment is the messenger from Hades, a warning of the coming departure. On November 7, Hegel concluded the Preface to the new edition of the first volume of *The Science of Logic* by openly admitting to the "inescapable distraction caused by the magnitude and many-sidedness of current affairs" and raising the doubt "whether the loud clamor of the day [...] still leaves room to participate in the dispassionate tranquility of cognition in thought alone."[96] Seven days later he died.

## NOTES

1   [An artist's cafe at the former Berlin City Palace].
2   [Cafe with a rather middle-class clientele at Berlin's Gendarmenmarkt].
3   In the preface to the second edition of the second part of his "Römische Geschichte" (Niebuhr 1830).
4   Cf. (up until 494) Lenz (1910/1918), Vol. II, 1.
5   Friedrich Wilhelm Corvé (1789–1852), jurist and philosopher.
6   Friedrich Wilhelm Förster (1791–1868), historian and long-time friend of Hegel.
7   HW 7, Preface.
8   Hegel to the Baden Ministry of the Interior, April 21, 1818 (Br II) – verbatim: "precarious function of lecturing on philosophy at a university."
9   Creuzer to Hegel, June 8, 1823 (Br III).
10  Following Hegel to Niethammer, July 5, 1816 (Br II).
11  Ibid.
12  [Prussian officials responsible for the "persecution of demagogues" and press censorship, who were extremely unpopular among the liberal student youth: Privy Councilor Grano, Gustav Aldo Tzschope (1794–1842), Karl Alber von Kampz (1769–1849).
13  [The theologian Schleiermacher (1768–1834) became the focus of Prussian "demagogue" persecution beginning in 1821 due to "liberal" tendencies in his lectures (cf. Reetz [2002], Schleiermacher/Jaeschke [1998])].
14  Hegel to Dubocs, July 30, 1822 (Br II).
15  Hegel to Hinrichs, April 4, 1822 (ibid.).
16  Hegel to Hinrichs, August 13, 1822 (ibid.).
17  Hegel to Creuzer, draft from the end of May 1821 (ibid.).
18  Ibid.
19  Hegel to Göschel, December 13, 1830 (Br III).
20  Hegel to Creuzer, draft from the end of May 1821 (ibid.).
21  According to HW 2, 68 ff. ("On a charge of public denigration of the Catholic religion").
22  Cf. the following letters: Hegel to Cousin, April 5, 1826; Seber to Hegel, June 3, 1826; Hegel to his wife, October 7, 1827 and October 18, 1827; Niethammer to

Hegel, January 1828; Carové to Hegel, 8. April 1828; Hegel to Förster, June 22, 1830; Günther to Hegel, July 30, 1830 (all included in Br III); cf. also the oral statement to Cousin in the fall of 1827 (Ww, XIX, 2. Theil, 388).

23  Hegel to his wife, October 12, 1827: "We have looked to these universities (Liège, Louvain, and Ghent) as future resting places if the parsons in Berlin take the *Kupfergraben* itself away from me [Hegel's Berlin residence near the university]. The Curia in Rome would in any case be a more respectable opponent than the wretchedness of a wretched parsonage in Berlin." (Br III).

24  GW 19, § 552. [JS & JS: Lachmann does not note that Rosenzweig may have provided the wrong citations for the reference to "the extensive note on the state and religion" that is central to the argument in this paragraph. The quote actually refers to the 1830 edition and can be found in GW 20, § 552.]

25  Ibid. – verbatim: "founded and produced."

26  Ibid. – verbatim: "Unfreedom of the spirit in religious matters [...] legislation and constitution of legal and ethical unfreedom."

27  Ibid.

28  Ibid. – verbatim: "the laws and state order [...] would be transformed."

29  Ibid.

30  Ibid.

31  Ibid.

32  Ibid.

33  Cf. to the following GW 16, 311–322.

34  Cousin to Hegel, August 1, 1825 (Br III) [*invariablement attaché à la chose de la liberté*].

35  Hegel Cousin to Hegel, March 3, 1828 (ibid.)

36  Ibid.

37  Cousin to Hegel, April 7, 1828 (ibid.) [*soyez tranquille sur la France quoinqu'on vous dise et quoi qu'il vous semble de loin*].

38  GW 20, 32; HW 8, 38.

39  Hegel to Göschel, December 13, 1830 (Br III) – verbatim: "But at present the tremendous political interest has swallowed up everything else, – a crisis in which everything that was once otherwise valid seems to be rendered problematic."

40  Hegel to Schultz, January 1831 (ibid.).

41  Ibid.

42  Laube (1837), Vol. I, 413: "[...] especially passionate against the emergence of Belgium [...] and fighting words against it and against the Reform Bill were probably the most important things he last wrote." – In the censorship files at the Secret State Archives of Berlin, nothing was found about the essay, nor, incidentally, about the one on the Reform Bill [cf. to the essay on Belgium: *Hegel Studien* 11–12 (1976), 88 ff].

43  HW 12, 380.

44  Ibid., 534.

45  Ibid., 535.

46  Ibid.

47  Ibid., 534.

48  Ibid.

49  Ibid., 535 – verbatim: "This collision, this knot, it is at this problem where history stands and which it must solve in future times."

50  GW 16, 323–404; HW 11, 83–128.

51  [The "Whigs" were the forerunners of the subsequent "Liberal Party" and consequently today's "Liberal Democrats" in the English Parliament. Beginning in 1830, after 30 years of uninterrupted Tory government, they provided the new Prime Minister in Earl Gray].

52  The state newspapers were distributed the evening before in Berlin. The exclusion of the delegates for Liverpool mentioned by Hegel, as well as the Wellington talk heavily utilized by Hegel, are first to be found in the edition from April 7. From this one can glean the *terminus a quo*. In the text, a report from the state newspaper from April 14 is used (in the second-to-last paragraph), relaying how the "*Courier français*" charges "that once zealous liberals, since entering into civil service, were now completely transformed and now found all of the minister's measures admirable; in particular, he complains about two privy councilmen, one of whom he not so subtly names as Herrn Thiers. The left side is becoming even weaker by means of these incomprehensible defections." (Cf. GW 16, 400; HW 11, 126) That Hegel's sentence is inspired by this report from the state newspaper, with his literal recollections ("charges," "left side") and the material "so many distinguished individuals" (state newspaper: "Herrn Thiers"), is without question. On the other hand, the comment added under the text, "in one of the last meetings of the parliament [...]" (Footnote to GW 16, 370; HW 11, 110), alludes to a report from the paper on April 24. The comment is still missing in the manuscript. Accordingly, the manuscript was completed between the 14th and the 24th [for dating cf. Jaeschke (2003), 313 f.].

53  GW 15, 40; HW, 476.

54  Addendums to HW 7, §§ 211, 248, 277, 300, 329.

55  Rosenkranz, who himself was in Berlin at that time.

56  GW 16, 325; HW 11, 83.

57  GW 16, 326; HW 11, 83.

58  GW 16, 325; HW 11, 83.

59  GW 16, 326; HW 11, 84.

60  GW 16, 330; HW 11, 86 – verbatim: "changes in the institutions."

61  GW 16, 329; HW 11, 85.

62  GW 16, 332 f.; HW 11, 87 f.

63  GW 16, 385: HW 11, 119 [Thomas Babington Macaulay (1800–1859), a politician close to the "Whigs," in the Assembly of the Lower House on March 2, 1830: "It has also been said that there have been many great and famous men among the holders of castled properties; I readily admit that, but we have to look not at contingencies but at general tendencies"].

64  GW 16, 333; HW 11, 88.

65  GW 16, 357; HW 11, 90.

66   GW 16, 334; HW 11, 88.
67   GW 16, 89; HW 11, 121 – verbatim: "foundations of a real [reellen] freedom."
68   GW 16, 329; HW 11, 86.
69   GW 16, 329 f.; HW 11, 86 [In the printed version of the "*Staats-Zeitung*," the word "*Verdorbenheit*" (depravity) used in the manuscript has been replaced by the supposedly less dramatic "*Eigensucht*" (selfishness) – on the interventions into the manuscript itself on the part of the editors and/or of Hegel himself, cf. the editorial report to GW 16, 482 f.].
70   GW 16, 334; HW 11, 88 f.
71   GW 16, 348; HW 11, 97.
72   GW 16, 335 f.; HW 11, 89.
73   GW 16, 390; HW 11, 121.
74   GW 16, 367; HW 11, 108.
75   GW 16, 367; HW 11, 109.
76   GW 16, 366 f.; HW 11, 108.
77   GW 16, 361; HW 11, 105.
78   GW 16, 375; HW 11, 113.
79   Ibid.
80   GW 16, 379; HW 11, 115.
81   GW 16, 399; HW 11, 126.
82   Ibid.
83   GW 16, 392; HW 11, 122 [statesmen and men of principle].
84   GW 16, 404; HW 11, 128.
85   GW 16, 393; HW 11, 123 – verbatim: "On the other hand, the monarchical principle no longer has much to lose in England."
86   GW 16, 383; HW 11, 117.
87   GW 16, 383 f.; HW 11, 117 f.
88   GW 16, 404; HW 11, 128.
89   Marie Hegel to Niethammer, December 2, 1831 (Nicolin [1970], 498).
90   Cf. the issue of March 11, 1831.
91   Cf. GW 16, 336 f.; HW 11, 107 f.
92   Marie Hegel to Niethammer, December 2, 1831 (Nicolin [op. cit.).
93   Stieglitz to Hegel, August 27, 1831 (Br III).
94   Hegel to Stieglitz, August 28, 1831 (ibid).
95   Ibid.
96   GW 21, 20; HW 5, 34.

# 13

## CONCLUDING REMARKS

*... from thoughts the act ...*

We are at the end. We feel how very much so now that the century of Bismarck has collapsed, a century on whose threshold Hegel's life stands like the thought before the act. If we recall that Hegel's life spans the exact timeframe within which Goethe's *Faust* came to be – 1770–1831 – then it becomes evident how this life itself and its work was constrained more exactly within the history of the nineteenth century than the life and work of the greatest German of that epoch. Admittedly, Hegel's students in Berlin gladly used the coincidence of the dates to celebrate both birthdays on a single holiday – in truth, the arc of Hegel's historical influence played out with much more shallowness, and therefore more briefly, than the influence of the poet two decades his elder. That Goethe could still spread his roots deeper into the spiritual world of the eighteenth century – into the pre-revolutionary and pre-Kantian world – provided for him an independence with respect to the new age, elevating him above and beyond that century, despite all that he had devoted

DOI: 10.4324/9780429354724-15

to it. The fruitful expanses of his life were spread equally broad on both sides of the great epochal divide, which we regard to be the classical moment of modern German intellectual history. And for the recollection of history, and thus as a possession of the nation, Goethe's life is bound neither one-sidedly to the ascent to that height nor to the descent from the same – neither to the ascent, as is the influence of Klopstock, Lessing, and perhaps even Kant; nor to the descent, as is the influence of Hegel. One can only do justice to Goethe's life if, as with Luther, one sees it in connection to a comprehensive spiritual history of the nation. Hegel himself can be framed more narrowly, at least regarding his national-historical significance – but not his world-historical significance. In every area of Hegel's influence, and not only the political, alongside an enduring personal position a guiding thought of the German nineteenth century is likewise expressed, and precisely at that moment of libera-tion from within the circle of the previous century. But the thinker's historical greatness also contains his historical constraint, and especially his constraint for the nineteenth century itself. We should not conceal to ourselves, nor do we want to – and have often indicated as much over the course of the book – that Hegel's thoughts did not so much guide the development of the entire century as merely disclose its course. May what little remains for us to say render visible where the thoughts of the politician Hegel linger behind the acts of Bismarck's century and render tangible how in this lingering-behind there was necessity, precisely the necessity that Hegel dwelt within the well-chamber of time.

As we have already said, the century's progress in political ideas had not actually been carried out from within Hegel's school. What hap-pened to Hegel's ideas here was much more of a conceptual spike, and perhaps even a toppling-over, than their further development. Regarding the actual school, in most cases the ideas of the master led down bypaths – especially in the most important case of all, that of Marx – which led only decades later back to the great military road [Heerstraße] of histori-cal life. Meanwhile, the most active travelers on this road were not part of the school and, indeed, thought themselves to be opposed to it and its master, to greater or lesser degrees. In what follows, it will be shown how the thoughts of a sampling of leading state-thinkers from 1830 to 1870 were divided from Hegel with respect to the state – not necessarily in conceptual opposition, but certainly in lively engagement.

The path we aim to follow is that shown to us by Friedrich Meinecke – the path from Hegel to Bismarck. It leads through the year 1848/49, with

Frankfurt and Berlin as the two transition points. Bismarck's era arose from both the National Liberalism of the hereditary-imperial party and the Prussian conservatism of the Gerlach Circle, and both were jointly compelling. These steps in national development are marked by three major treatises within the history of German academics which deal with the being and essence of the state. Dahlmann's *Politics* signified the hope-filled attempt to raise the liberalism of the pre-March era [Vormärz] into the maturity of a statesman's way of thinking – an attempt whose successes, despite everything, were attested to in the negotiations at St. Paul's Church, the first major testimonial of the following two decades. Stahl's *The History of the Philosophy of Right* led the conservatism of Prussia from its pre-March quietude to the resounding battleground of new constitutional life, thus transforming the Christian-German "circle" into the "small but powerful party" which became the wellspring of Bismarck's act. Finally, as herald of this act, Treitschke appeared on the scene – at first a fiery disciple of Dahlmann, but in his older age forced closer to Stahl's position – and laid out the academic outcomes in his lectures on politics. Given that the political development of the century is mirrored in these three men's ideas on the state, so they will help us to recognize the relation of this century's end to its beginning, the relation of its act to its thought; for not "as lightning from clouds" did the former spring from the latter. The path of history was longer and more gradual than the longing of the poet had dreamt it.

The state, as Dahlmann explained it, is an "original," "superior order, above humankind."[1] He rejects every attempt to reduce the state to a "creation of human caprice."[2] Stahl bases his doctrine of the state on the thoughts of the "moral realm,"[3] a moral realm whose existence and law do not merely subsist "through the will of its single members."[4] He concluded that the founders of Platonic "objectivity" within state theory – Hegel and Schelling – missed one aspect whereby the state first presents itself to Stahl as a "moral empire," namely the "handling of required ordinances."[5] And he grasps the state as ethical realm precisely in how it is a "real and free" governing power, "however, on the ground of ethically understandable order."[6] With regard to this "however," Stahl does not hesitate to find a "double element"[7] in the state's dominion: "*the government or state authority, – that is, the authority which is exercised by human beings – and the law.*"[8] In this "and" as in that "however," it becomes clear what separates Stahl from Hegel's strictly uniform derivation of the state-as-law from the state-as-authority, his derivation of the ethical order from the concept of the will. Instead of derivation, Stahl consciously provides a juxtaposition, and one which unmistakably contains its ultimate source in a religious perspective; however, considered purely on political terms, it is also a juxtaposition which allows the substantive existence of the state to emerge just as powerfully as in Dahlmann's formulation, referenced above. Finally, Treitschke, who knew well enough that "the state is power and that it belongs to the world of the will,"[9] was nevertheless dissatisfied with such concepts, which immediately pointed back to Hegel. Instead, he conceived of the state as "the rightfully unified people,"[10] or, as he more robustly expressed it at first: "that life of the people which is consolidated into a collected power."[11] It is plain to see how both of these – rightfully unifying power and existing people – are certainly not conceived of in Stahl's sense as a "double element." Nevertheless, the will, which is effective here in right and power, rather than being bound up simply in itself and its rational actualization, is bound to an existing entity, something outside of itself, namely the "people." Thus, in their emphasis on substantive existence and the elimination of the will, it should now become clear towards what Dahlmann and Stahl were unconsciously both being driven: namely, towards a state which is not merely founded upon its own will, but instead a state founded upon the nation, which prevails outside of the will and comes before it. What is illuminated here is where and how the century resolutely went beyond – and could go beyond – Hegel's thoughts on the state. Hegel's firmly held derivation of the state from the will was the implicit reason why his idea of the state did not become the idea of the national state and why, therefore, when it came to the idea of the nation, Hegel had earned for himself the role of philosopher of history rather than philosopher of state. The concept of the will had to be cut from the state's network of roots so that this idea could open its buds to the light of the idea of the nation.

Hegel himself certainly knew that the concept of the will, in the way that he placed it in his doctrine of the state, was a product of the eighteenth century and thus, in effect, a product of Rousseau and the Revolution. Here, when they claimed that the master's state doctrine was cast from the metal of freedom, the students could justifiably pick up a thread. Precisely because of this "liberal" element, we saw how Hegel failed to connect with those thoughts on the nation. This concept of the will, however, was far removed from Rousseau and Robespierre: as rational will, it had no other business than to raise itself up and away from its form as a contingent, individual will into the totality of the state – as rational, and not merely as general will. Its rationality is what first makes the will sovereign, not – as with Rousseau – that its sovereignty makes it rational. Thus, the individual was only called forth to merge with the state. And here we can once again grasp the connection which binds Treitschke to Hegel: for both, the state is still a goal. Hegel leads the individual will in this direction, Treitschke the nation. Both the individual human being and the nation can only first fully become what they are in the state: the individual first becomes truly moral, and the nation first becomes an actual people. Both individual and nation are thus, in a certain sense, to be sacrificed to the state – the inherent right of the human being, as well as the totality of the nation, to the divinized state. The dreadful schism of 1866[12] occurred in this spirit and – this comes above all into consideration here – was carried on in this spirit. Only an age that finally found humankind to be familiar and self-evident, after it had long been the object of "proper study,"[13] could so recklessly subjugate the human being to the distant goal of a yet-to-be created state. Only after the labor of the Romantics had formed the people into a common factor could one so easily, and almost without conscience, abandon the uniform subsistence of this people for the one thing that was necessary – the state.

Thus, it came about that the state which Bismarck created was not merely something more with respect to the state Hegel had conceived of, just as little as it had become mere fulfillment. In its national foundation, the new Empire had something that was foreign, or at least unnecessary, for the Hegelian state ideal, which in the end was content to arrive into the harbor of Prussian particularism. But given that this national foundation was the life-condition for the new Empire – and yet according to historical coincidence it had to purchase its life-strength at the very cost of destroying the totality of this very foundation – voices could be heard, even before the War, that did not want to recognize in Bismarck's act the simple fulfillment of German desire. Rather, the separation of state and nation seemed to them to be a sign of that other separation – which perceptive spirits had already sensed with anxiety immediately after 1870 – namely, the separation of state and culture. The bitter necessity of external history had hindered the German state from emerging with inner necessity out of the life of the nation, and therefore – once again – one did not find adequate space within this state. And therefore, from the beginning of the century onward, those voices could be heard, both familiar and foreign, which sought to realize their longing for the German state, a longing that seemed more in tune with the generation before 1914 than with the fulfillment which surrounded them. Those born around 1770, confounded in the "I," sought to conjure the state into existence around the year 1800 with passionate belief; but insofar as the state became the image of that faithful desire, it bore the characteristics not of a state, but of a nation. Perhaps it was because one called so exclusively for the state as a solitary human, for the sake of one's very solitariness, that the image of the nation as an independent power, set over against this personal longing and seeking, did not suffice. Perhaps, precisely because of that longing, the state could at times assume the face of a national-communal civilization which, even after Bismarck's act, remained only a hope. Perhaps it could therefore have also been the case that those who, at that time, held this hope resting deep in their hearts, could not anticipate the political form of fulfillment as it would occur through Bismarck. This could then be the reason why Hegel never succeeded in granting the nation its own proper right: he found too strongly in the state itself – and even the non-national state – the satisfaction of the will, the utter fulfillment of that for which the individual longed. Hegel felt this still too strongly to grant the nation its own place as the necessary content of the body politic. It was first those who came later – those who had already denied the will of the individual as departure point for their thoughts – who, in their derivation of the state, could create a place for the nation within the ideal of the state. Hegel had not yet done so.

In those years of the outgoing eighteenth century, as the new idea of the state arose for Hegel in proximity to Hölderlin, one can already find the causes that would limit the historical effects and consequences of this state idea when it emerged in the nineteenth century. And while the spiritual history of the new Empire most likely originated here, it nonetheless turned away from those beginnings. When the dream of 1871 became the first historical fulfillment – when "out of thoughts the act"[14] sprang – it did not, however, come to pass as the poet had hoped, it was not "lucid and mature." The hoped-for "creative genius" certainly did appear, and was powerfully revealed, but it was not yet the genius of "the people." What the Swabian youths, both together and tightly bound, had dreamt of with this appearance of genius, this had not yet been fulfilled: how …

    … our cities now
    are bright and open and awake, full of purer fire
    and how the mountains of German lands
    are the mountains of Muses,

    like those glorious ones of before, Pindus and Helicon, and Parnassus,
    and under the Fatherland's golden sky
    the free, clear joy of the spirit is shining.[15]

    *unsere Städte nun*
    *hell und offen und wach, reineren Feuers voll*
    *Und die Berge des deutschen*
    *Landes Berge der Musen sind,*

    *Wie die herrlichen einst, Pindos und Helikon*
    *und Parnassos, und rings unter des Vaterlands*
    *goldnem Himmel die freie,*
    *klare, geistige Freude glänzt.*

This dream remained unfulfilled even on the path from the collapse of the old Empire to the foundation of the new – from Hegel to Bismarck. When this book was begun, it still seemed a prophetic dream, one of those dreams which, precisely as dream, could remain alive to one day become what dreams may become: history-creating power. Today, as the book is published – 150 years after Hegel's birth, 100 years after the appearance of the *Philosophy of Right* – that dream seems to have dissolved itself without resistance into the foam of waves which flood over all of life. When the structure of a world crashes down, the thoughts that thought it, as well as the dreams which are woven through it, are buried under its collapse. What a more distant future brings, whether something new or unthought of, whether the renewal of something lost – who would allow themselves to predict that? Today, in the darkness that surrounds us, only a glimmer of hope falls from the at one time barely noticed conclusion of Hölderlin's verse, whose opening lines we chose in past, better days for the guiding word of this presentation. Only a glimmer – and yet the prisoner in the dungeon is still able to fix their glance upon it:

> Our lifetime is indeed narrowly limited,
> We see and count the number of our years,
> Yet the years of the peoples,
> Has these a mortal eye seen?[16]

> *Wohl ist enge begrenzt unsere Lebenszeit,*
> *Unserer Jahre Zahl sehen und zählen wir,*
> *Doch die Jahre der Völker,*
> *Sah ein sterbliches Auge sie?*

## NOTES

1   Dahlmann (1847), 4.
2   Ibid.
3   Stahl (1856), Vol. 11, 10.
4   Ibid., 141.
5   Ibid., 149.
6   Ibid., 186.
7   Ibid., 187.
8   Ibid., 187 f. – verbatim: "*State authority* (imperium [...] and the *law* (lex)."
9   Treitschke (1912 f.), Vol. II, 15.
10  Treitschke (1898), 449.
11  Treitschke (1859), 94.
12  German war between Austria and Prussia and the subsequent dissolution of the German Confederation.
13  Goethe in *Elective Affinities*: "The proper study of humankind is the human being."
14  Hölderlin "*An die Deutschen*" ["To the Germans"] (Second Version) (Hölderlin 1992 f.), Vol. I, 265 ff.
15  Ibid.
16  Ibid.

# AFTERWORD

Franz Rosenzweig, who was just 43 years old when he died of a serious illness, is known today as one of the most significant figures of Jewish thought in the twentieth century. His book *The Star of Redemption* has become a classic work in the philosophy of religion and its influence on both sides of the Atlantic only seems to be growing.[1] It is also well known that together with Martin Buber he prepared a groundbreaking new translation of parts of the Bible, which divided intellectuals from the very beginning.[2] Finally, and just as well-remembered, is the prominent role he played in 1920 in Frankfurt am Main during the founding of the Free House of Jewish Learning, which grew under his leadership during the early years of the Weimar Republic into a major center of activity for a notable group of Jewish intellectuals.[3] In the history of Jewish Thought in the twentieth century, Franz Rosenzweig thus occupies, next to Martin Buber, Gershom Scholem and Emmanuel Lévinas, one of the foremost, if not the primary place. There is the risk of forgetting, however, that this same Franz Rosenzweig, before his decisive turn towards Judaism, set about to rescue the legacy of German Idealism for the new century. We owe this early period of his work to the study at hand, which presents one of the most vivid, judicious, and exact investigations into the development of Hegel's political thought. Largely finished already before the First World War but first published in 1920 on account of the political turmoil, today the book has lost nothing of its original luster. One is still quickly captured by the masterful style, the power of historical enlivening, and the artfully developed interpretation as a whole.

Despite all of these grand traits, the fact that Rosenzweig's study is only known today to a small group of specialists is due, aside from an increasingly stunted awareness for intellectual-historical contexts, to a series of further reasons. The first of these to consider is certainly the simple fact that the original two-volume edition of the book was published in Gothic type, which was retained in the photomechanical reprints in German from 1962 and 1982.[4] The hindered readability of this script most likely discouraged many potentially interested readers from turning to the work. A second, equally important reason is surely that Rosenzweig completed his study before the historical moment when, with the collapse of the German Empire and the founding of the Weimar Republic, the philosophical entryway into Hegel's political thought had also radically changed. After 1918, all attempts at depicting the development of Hegel's social-theoretical work were written either from the perspective of a materialist reworking through Marx or, at the very least, arose under the effect of the incisive impact of historical materialism. For Rosenzweig, this point of reference is peripheral and almost foreign, to the extent that an atmospheric element of the newly overcome nineteenth inevitably clings to his interpretation. For the contemporary reader, engaging the study at hand first requires that one work through the crust of antiquated viewpoints and interpretive perspectives, before one can reach the actually productive, living kernel. And the related effort this entails may help explain why the most excellent depictions of Hegel's intellectual development today often fail to even mention Rosenzweig's book.[5]

And finally, a third reason in helping to understand why Rosenzweig's book has meanwhile been almost totally forgotten may lie in the subject-matter already stated in the book's title. Of all the issues that today are being raised anew in conjunction with Hegel's political philosophy, the idea of the "state" certainly plays the smallest role. Presently, almost everything in Hegel's *Philosophy of Right* is found worthy of reconstruction: his conception of "civil society";[6] the concept of "work" contained within this conception;[7] his construction of "ethicality";[8] the notion of "family" directed against Kant[9]; indeed, even the concept of "property";[10] just not his substantialist idea of the "state." It seems that this idea did not outlive the ensuing epoch, filled as it was with the gradual implementation and establishment of democratic constitutional states, due to its anti-individualistic tendencies and its organicistic construction.[11] In any case, there are but a few noticeable voices today that express the intention to renew Hegel's political philosophy in view of his concept of the state. Therefore, a study which already in its title claims to do precisely this evokes in the moment nothing more than an all-too-empty reverberation. The spirit of the age, to speak with Hegel, would have proceeded along above it, without us having to somehow lament the associated loss.

And yet, it would mean to underestimate the substance of Rosenzweig's book if we understood it merely as a contribution to the historical-theoretical reception of the Hegelian concept of the state. Admittedly, at first it was indeed Rosenzweig's sole intention, as we will still see, to reconstruct the development of Hegel's political thought under the guidance of the incremental emergence of his specific concept of the state. But in the course of the young author's work on this study, his engagement with the in-part newly accessible writings of the philosopher began to take on a life of its own, such that his field of attention also quickly began to broaden. In the end, it was no longer only the concept of the state that interested Rosenzweig in Hegel's intellectual biography but, rather, everything that contributed to Hegel's political conception of the modern world. To this there also belonged the novel role and intermediate position of the political economy, the changed function of the family, and, not least, the form of political organization that could integrate all of these parts. And thus, in the end, surely in contrast to the author's original intention, Rosenzweig's work became the first broadly expressed investigation into the intellectual emergence of the Hegelian concept of ethicality [Sittlichkeit]. Thanks to the admirable work that Josiah Simon and Jules Simon have invested in the translation of Rosenzweig's comprehensive book, there is now the chance to study his highly original and pathbreaking interpretation of Hegel's social and political philosophy in English for the first time. Let us hope that the book will hereby receive the attention that it undoubtedly deserves.

## I. CONTEXT OF ORIGIN

Rosenzweig's study on Hegel is dedicated "in grateful admiration" to Friedrich Meinecke, thus not to a philosopher or expert in law, but to a then already highly respected and later world-famous historian. The young Rosenzweig, born in 1886 in Kassel and raised there as an only child within a Jewish-liberal family home, decided during the winter semester of 1907/08, influenced by his cousin Hans Ehrenberg, to discontinue his initial course of study in medicine and to pursue the study of history and philosophy.[12] The decision was not really a surprise, as Rosenzweig was already engaged in the humanities during his studies of natural science in Munich and Freiburg and regularly visited seminars with similarly relevant topics. He was deeply impressed by the seriousness and rigor of Kant's philosophy, even if, entirely in the spirit of the contemporary rapture surrounding Nietzsche, the existential dimension seemed to be missing.[13] Finally, the student was led onto the trail of Hegel, again by his cousin Hans Ehrenberg, who at the time was pursuing his studies in philosophy under the mentorship of Wilhelm Windelband. In 1910, Windelband would hold his famous Heidelberg Academy address and, through the detection and declaration of a systematic "Renewal of Hegelianism,"[14] would lay the foundation for the short-lived movement of a German neo-Hegelianism.[15]

But in contrast to the aims of this movement, which could be found in the fields of cultural philosophy and ethics, Rosenzweig was initially interested in the political-historical impact of Hegel's philosophy. After a short interlude at the University of Berlin, he enrolled again in 1908 at the University of Freiburg in order to study history under the mentorship of Friedrich Meinecke and philosophy under Heinrich Rickert. Rosenzweig was immediately electrified by Meinecke's major study *Cosmopolitanism and the National State*, published in 1908.[16] He read it many times in those years, raved about it in letters to his mother,[17] and took it as the model for his own philosophical studies. In his book, Meinecke attempted to reconstruct the historical-intellectual process that led in Germany to the overcoming of the long dominant idea of a comprehensive cosmopolitanism and would thereby lay the general foundation for the emergence of a conception of the national state. It was Meinecke's conviction that the "unpolitical-universal"[18] ideas of cosmopolitanism prevented the establishment of a German national state in the eighteenth and early nineteenth century, so that a breakthrough towards a realist conception of the state was first necessary before Bismarck could erect a state structure on a national foundation. In this comprehensive, suggestively written history of ideas – which seems foreign from today's perspective, already because there is no discussion of the social and political causes of the belated formation of the national state in Germany[19] – Hegel now played the role of a bold trailblazer of political realism. With Hegel's "rationalization" of the "folk spirit" [Volksgeist], through which he removed the mustiness and political outdatedness of the concept, with his emphasis on the unconditional right of the sovereignty of the state – which made any thought of an "eternal peace" impossible – Hegel became, according to Meinecke, the first thinker in Germany who dared to take into view the rigorous requirements of a state striving for power.[20] Rosenzweig was taken by this political-philosophical interpretation of Hegel, which was developed in the 11th chapter of Meinecke's book. And yet, he did not agree point-for-point with the position worked out in that chapter, as some letters he had then written attest to.[21] Above all, Meinecke's intention to utilize Hegel's concept of the state for the purpose of legitimizing Bismarck's politics appeared to Rosenzweig as rather suspect. But he showed unreserved admiration for the superior way his teacher had planted Hegel within the political and cultural tensions of the nineteenth century in only a few brief pages. From this perspective, Rosenzweig was also able to recognize, through such a form of contextualization, that philosophical authors, in offering up interpretations beyond purely theoretical issues, invariably hold the intention to intervene into the conflicts of the self-understanding of their times. In other words, a historicism based on the history of ideas, as Meinecke had undertaken in his study, allowed Rosenzweig to perceive within all philosophy the existential side of a political position, that is, a tarrying with the direction of history's development. And this is exactly what interested the young student in those days at the intersection of philosophy and history.

Of course, during the years 1909 and 1910 it was not only Rosenzweig's enthusiasm for Meinecke's book that led him to develop a plan to pursue a doctorate under Meinecke on Hegel's political philosophy at the University of Freiburg. Within the same timeframe, Rosenzweig also joined his cousin Hans Ehrenberg in the plan to form a discussion circle of young philosophers and historians, which was to observe contemporary culture under the viewpoint of its sustaining and forward-looking ideas. Rosenzweig immediately saw the chance in this intellectual circle, and not entirely independent of Meinecke's Hegel interpretation, to make Hegel's philosophy fertile again for the present — if not in its content, then certainly in its history-oriented, intervening spirit.[22] Thus, the Freiburg student took up everything he could to help his cousin bring a circle of that sort into existence. Baden-Baden was deliberately chosen as the place for the regular gatherings, where members of the southwest German school of neo-Kantianism had often already met. Only young historians and philosophers from Germany were to be admitted as members, because fellow specialists from other countries (and women) would lack the intellectual qualifications to analyze German culture in the form of "self-recognition."[23] But, despite all the effort put towards productive working conditions, the first meeting of the "Baden-Baden Society," in which Ernst Robert Curtius and Werner Picht also participated, apparently ended in a fiasco. At any rate, Viktor von Weizäcker, another participant, reported in his memoirs that after Rosenzweig's presentation many of the historians indignantly announced an end to their collaboration, because he came across to them as too concept-heavy and anti-historical.[24] After this incident, therefore, the intellectual circle did not meet again. It shattered under the tensions between historicism and historical-philosophical ambitions before it really ever came into existence.[25]

For Rosenzweig, admittedly, who was certainly not lacking in terms of intellectual confidence, the fierce reactions to his lecture did not end in discouragement but, rather, impetus. In a letter to Hans Ehrenberg, he even says that Baden-Baden was the "*experimentum crucis*" of his own "theory."[26] As he wrote these lines from Berlin, the student had just received the approval from Friedrich Meinecke to work under his mentorship on his doctorate on Hegel's concept of the state. According to the records we possess, it was agreed upon that Rosenzweig would work from the perspective of intellectual history and reconstruct the development of Hegel's thought up until the point where a sufficiently differentiated doctrine of the modern state is delineated in the *Elements of the Philosophy of Right*. The work on this project made it necessary for the doctoral student to now spend some time in Berlin, where many of Hegel's still unpublished manuscripts could be found in the *Königliche Bibliothek*. In a letter to his cousin, which Rosenzweig must have written at the very beginning of his stay in Berlin, we learn how Rosenzweig had then divided his work days: beginning at ten in the morning he would sit in the manuscript wing of the library in order to study Hegel's original writings; after the wing closed he would proceed to the main reading room at three o'clock, where he would devote himself to works dealing with the historical and political background of his theme; late in the afternoon he would occasionally attend seminars at the university, with preference for those of the art historian Heinrich Wölfflin; and finally, in the evening, he would primarily attend theater productions.[27] But in essence, the doctoral student spent the year from the fall of 1910 to the fall of 1911 when he was in Berlin undertaking purely philological tasks: "I'm excerpting, collating, experiencing commas, pausing throughout, graphologizing, and, like Wagner, am a fool for the worthy parchment [...] It is really something magnificent to be so immediately close to him [Hegel, A.H.], to observe him in the attempts to formulate his thoughts."[28]

This elaborate engagement with Hegel's original manuscripts, which were preserved in numbered cartons in the *Königliche Bibliothek*, seemed necessary to Rosenzweig, because he had more than just intellectual history in mind with the goals for his dissertation. His ambition was much more to provide a chronology of Hegel's intellectual development in combination with working out Hegel's understanding of the state. Admittedly, Wilhelm Dilthey had already attempted to do something of the sort at the beginning of the century with his *History of the Young Hegel*, but in doing so limited himself more or less to Hegel's theological writings and, out of caution, refrained from making any suggestions on the periodization of individual manuscripts.[29] But now Rosenzweig, in order to present an ordered and detailed chronological account of Hegel's entire philosophical process of formation, wished to remove all these constraints. To this end, the only published works available to him, besides Dilthey's work, were the volume on *Hegel's Theological Writings*,[30] edited by Dilthey's student Herman Nohl, the well-known biographical documentations of Rudolf Haym and Karl Rosenkranz,[31] as well as the two collected works available at that time.[32] Thus, for Rosenzweig, in order to actually reconstruct Hegel's path of development at the chronologically detailed level of the different versions of his manuscripts, the daily trip to the manuscript wing of the Berlin library was unavoidable.

After concluding these philological studies, Rosenzweig returned to Freiburg in the winter semester of 1911/1912 in order to complete his dissertation under Meinecke's mentorship. At that time, he must have already had in mind not just the immediate task of turning in a completed dissertation but also the much more demanding goal of a comprehensive manuscript. As there are no comments from Rosenzweig's letters, we know next to nothing about the period of work on the dissertation during the year of 1912, only that the doctoral student was successfully promoted by presenting a later part of the work to Meinecke at the end of that same year. But Rosenzweig did not seem to allow himself any kind of rest in view of this external success. Rather, his engagement with the planned manuscript continued immediately afterwards. The new graduate again filled the winter semester of 1912/1913 with intense study, this time at the university of Leipzig, where, apparently, he wished to deepen his juridical knowledge for the sake of his continuing work on his book. During this uneasy period, he constantly scheduled stopovers in places like Tübingen and Stuttgart, where some of Hegel's original manuscripts or documents on his pressing political concerns could still be found.[33] It must have been within that same time period that Rosenzweig took up contact with the Berlin pastor Georg Lasson, who during those years was occupied with publishing Hegel's *Writings on Politics and Philosophy of Right* from the archives.[34] In any case, Lasson is thanked in the Preface to this present edition "for valuable suggestions," without it being further evident of what the collaboration consisted or when it may have taken place.

In order to work on the second volume of his Hegel book, Rosenzweig again spent the time period from the spring of 1913 until the outbreak of the First World War in the summer of 1914 in Berlin.[35] And yet, in Berlin he now regularly took part in Hermann Cohen's seminars and, in general, sought more intimate contact with Jewish philosophy of religion, as for him theological and religious problems now began to shift to the foreground.[36] One can already easily gain the impression from the letters of that time that the completion of the monograph was increasingly felt only as a burden and no longer an expression of what was actually internally being experienced. This distance to the Hegel project was then fully absorbed through the lived experience of the war, which Rosenzweig underwent towards the beginning as a voluntary nurse in Belgium and then subsequently as a soldier, first in France and then later in the Balkans. The time before the war – and with this the world of experience within which his engagement with Hegel's concept of the state was philosophically rooted – is now taken by Rosenzweig to be a definitively fallen epoch, so that the strains of thought and the arrangement of tasks from that time period had largely lost their force of validity. More or less overnight, the grand, engaged plan for a comprehensive study on the development of Hegel's political understanding became a mere burdensome duty, reluctantly followed against his will. What actually occupied Rosenzweig philosophically during these years of the war, what took hold of all his intellectual attention, was poured into the work *The Star of Redemption*, published in 1921.[37]

Returning from the War from a Belgrade military hospital to Germany, where he alternatively lived in Freiburg, Kassel, and Heidelberg, Rosenzweig rid himself of the remaining work on the book manuscript with an openly admitted feeling of resistance and alienation. In a letter there is talk that the "book as a whole" is behind him and any effort put towards it could only be a "lie."[38] In another letter, the "energy towards the Hegel book" is described as a mere expenditure for "old people."[39] Rosenzweig only improved upon the nearly finished manuscript in a few places and filled in gaps in content that he still found missing. He further accounted for Montesquieu, and above all Hölderlin, as their influence on Hegel's thinking did not come across adequately enough for him in the version of the book before him.[40] But in essence, Rosenzweig's engagement with the text during this time of finalizing the work is really only technical in nature. The greatest obstacle for the planned publication soon proves to be that publishers would demand a not insignificant subsidy for printing costs to be able to publish the extensive manuscript in the desired form of two separate volumes. After a series of failed applications for financial subsidy, which already led him to consider alternative forms of publication for his Hegel work,[41] Rosenzweig finally received the needed funds with the help of Heinrich Rickert through the Heidelberg Academy of the Sciences. In the second half of the year 1919, already occupied with plans for the founding of the Free House of Jewish Learning in Frankfurt, Rosenzweig takes up the final additions and revisions to his manuscript.

It is published in the year 1920 with the title *Hegel und der Staat* by the Munich- and Berlin-based publishing house R. Oldenbourg.

## II. SIGNIFICANCE

Although Franz Rosenzweig had received the impetus for his major study from reading the Hegel chapter in Meinecke's *Cosmopolitanism and National State*, his own intent and procedure were of a completely different kind than that of the teacher and mentor he so admired. Meinecke, who was only superficially familiar with Hegel's work, wanted with his portrait of the German idealist to depict the pioneer of that German concept of the power-state that he then saw attain historical actuality in the writings of Ranke and the deeds of Bismarck. The method of a history of ideas Meinecke used for this was of a certain simplicity, as he sought to prophetically disclose the abiding intention of Hegel's entire work from only a few of his formulations. In his own study, Rosenzweig's method is almost the opposite. He avoids inserting an underlying aim into the beginnings of Hegel's writings. Rather, in Rosenzweig's view, Hegel arrives neither deliberately nor single-mindedly at his actual theme, the political, but only on the winding road of repeated failure at alternative solutions and approaches. Therefore, Rosenzweig, in order to interpretively advance towards Hegel's concept of the state, cannot hold to the interpretive scheme of a continuous maturation of an original idea, but must rather take a central, lifelong problematic as the guiding principle of his reconstruction. For Rosenzweig, Hegel's key question emerges from the experience of cultural and societal division, to which the thought on the state then attempts a relatively late answer.[42]

But Rosenzweig's study differs quite fundamentally from his teacher's interpretive outline not only in terms of method but also with regard to its substantive perspective. As was mentioned, Meinecke wanted to honor Hegel's philosophical contribution in Germany towards the development of a positive idea of the national state. For this purpose, he collected all the passages from the philosopher's works, above all from the *Encyclopedia* and the *Philosophy of Right*, that inclined to highlight the world historical right of states grounded upon the "national principle."[43] In contrast, when he became Meinecke's student, Rosenzweig already showed considerable skepticism towards Bismarck's imperial politics.

He saw in this a sign of a German "Imperialism" and found the thought of a "national state" as too narrow to take into account the pluralism of different peoples in a territory.[44] Unlike his teacher, for Rosenzweig it could not come down to reconstructing the basic tenets of Hegel's concept of the state in order to thus encounter a basis for the legitimization of the German national state. On the contrary, Rosenzweig was concerned with evidencing that this state model remained extremely fragile, and he especially looked to avoid the obvious answer of anchoring it in a "national principle." Accordingly, in the Preface, written in 1920, Rosenzweig says of his own plans that the Hegelian thought on the state "was supposed to undermine itself" both "in its development throughout the life of its thinker and at the same time under the watchful eye of the reader."[45] And, in order to subsequently distance himself from his former teacher, Rosenzweig adds that he is undertaking such an internal deconstruction "so as to open the outlook upon an internally as well as externally more spacious German future,"[46] thus a Germany without national state foundations.

Of course, that which in the above sentence is called "life" is related for Rosenzweig to Hegel's intellectual development. He wants to follow the intellectual, not external process of experience through which the philosopher, after many failed attempts at sublimating the previously diagnosed division, finally arrives at a concept of the state. Surely "external" experiences and incidents also play an important role in this process – intellectual friendships, political events, socio-economic conditions – but central to the account remains how these were mirrored in Hegel's conceptual procedures. Rosenzweig was fully aware of the stylistic difficulties inherent in the intention of such an enlivening of factual content. As a future reader of his own book, he initially saw himself more as historian and less as professional philosopher, so that in writing the book he must have avoided allowing the purely conceptual aspects of Hegel's development to step too far into the foreground, and instead always skillfully mediated these aspects with empirical, external events. The extraordinary level at which Rosenzweig engaged these compositional challenges is articulated very nicely in some reflections he expounded upon in a letter from the early summer of 1914 to Hans Ehrenberg. There, the talk is not only of the constant difficulties of interlacing external-empirical events with conceptual-systematic developments but, rather surprisingly, the method for presenting Hegel's system is often compared to a "film," whereby apparently certain claims to form are connected – "I am," the letter states, "especially in this section [intended is presumably the sub-section "The development of the system" in Section 11, A.H.], rather smug with regard to content and form (precisely qua film)." Later, refer-encing the same chapter, there is even talk of "Kintopp" [the movies].[47]

At first glance, it is not entirely clear which stylistic elements of the admittedly newly founded medium of film it may be that Rosenzweig believes can help him determine his own method. In the section he refers to with his comments, it is a matter of the difficult task of describing in a few pages the step-by-step change in position that the "individual realms of ethical life" (morality, family, right, civil society, estates, profession, etc.) went through for Hegel beginning with the firsts drafts of the sys-tem in Jena and leading up to the completed structure of the system in the year 1820. When one reads these remarks, one is surprised at how they maintain a remarkably tension-laden liveness, despite the cum-bersome nature of the material. Within the course of the fifteen years described here, the various instances of ethicality constantly change their roles, are brought in turn into the fore- and background – at times more strongly illuminated, at times placed back into half-shadow – without the reader ever losing oversight with respect to the constantly new arrangements. The refined style of the implied chapter comes from the fact that it treats the respective reconstructions of the system like stage directions, whereby Hegel again and again looks to arrange the roles of the individual instances until he has brought them into a suitable relation. In this manner the reader, or better yet the viewer, is invited to witness the genesis of the definitive system like events on a film set, by way of which the director Hegel communicates with his actors, the ethi-cal powers, about their roles. If such an interpretation of Rosenzweig's reflections on method initially sounds far-fetched and out of place, there are certainly several formulations on the pages in question that seem to verify it. Again and again the author allows the ethical instances to enter like dramatic actors who seek to claim their right to Hegel, in order to then say at the end of his presentation that "these would be the ways through which the individual realms of ethical life, leading all the way up to the state, sought their place in the Systems of 1817 and 1820."[48] Of course, it is not readily apparent that a comparison with "film" should be called up in order to explain this dramaturgical foot hold. On the other hand, the very consciously chosen expression that Rosenzweig uses no less than four times in his letter to Hans Ehrenberg makes clear the degree to which Rosenzweig approached his task – namely, presenting to the reader of the newly dawning twentieth century the development of Hegelian thought – with a consciousness for modernity.

It was with related thoughtfulness that Rosenzweig's chose to title the first volume of his book, which follows Hegel's intellectual development up until 1806, "Stations of Life (1770–1806)," and to give the second volume, which deals with the time from the end of the Jena period up until Hegel's death, the title "Epochs of the World" (1806–1831). Ferdinand Tönnies, who wrote a review of Rosenzweig's monograph four years after its publication,[49] already chafed at this idiosyncratic choice of titles. According to his conviction there were "also epochs of the world in the time period between 1770–1806," just as inversely "stations of life" also came to pass for Hegel in the period between 1806 and 1831, wherefrom it follows that the peculiar dichotomy could not have happened "according to logical considerations."[50] Of course Rosenzweig was well aware of the suggested connections this implied. It was certainly not the case that he wanted to deny the significance of world-epochal events for the first phase of Hegel's development, nor deny the role of decisive biographical turning-points in Hegel's second phase – quite on the contrary, in dealing with the young Hegel the event of the French Revolution constitutes a formative event for a theory of history, and in dealing with the later part of Hegel's life Rosenzweig repeatedly emphasizes the decisive significance of being called to a professorship at the University of Berlin. The reasons by which Rosenzweig was moved to give the two volumes, respectively, such strongly contrasting titles, therefore must have been of an entirely different nature than those that could be brought about by such obvious objections. Rather, they relate to a very specific interpretation of the historical development of Hegel's work, which Tönnies evidently had not even considered. For Rosenzweig, namely, it is the case that Hegel came to the realization shortly after the completion of his middle years in 1806 that he could now function philosophically in step with the world-historical development of the spirit. For with the invasion of Napoleon into Germany, for Hegel, in a very physical sense, "the spirit of history has gone over into

Germany," in order to "begin there the work of the new, highest age," namely the definitive actualization of reason on earth.[51] And therefore, Rosenzweig further argues, Hegel now first, at the end of his time in Jena, held a key in hand in order to allocate a precise location for his own deeds and work within the process of world history: it is his own philosophy from which, like a mirror, the newly dawning epoch of Germany can form a picture of itself. From here, it is only a short step to Rosenzweig's claim that for Hegel, on the basis of this changed self-perception, what previously were only the stations of his life now show themselves to be "epochs of the world."[52] Hegel is now able, as surprising as it may sound, to rediscover in his own childhood, youth, and adulthood the three phrases that the world-spirit must have traversed in order to arrive at the historical moment at which its structure could first be completely grasped. Rosenzweig's decision to give the two volumes of his study the contrasting titles "Stations of Life" and "Epochs of the World" is thus anything but a mere whim or the result of logical negligence, as Tönnies had assumed. Rather, this decision expresses with utmost precision an insight into the development of Hegel's work that reveals something of Hegel's self-conception that hitherto had remained unseen.

As with the methodical reflections on film, so do the hidden considerations on the choice of title show the degree of theoretical discretion und stylistic prudence used to reconstruct Hegel's intellectual life path as a whole. There is hardly another book, and this is certain, that could have achieved something similar, at such a level of language, and with the same clarity. Rosenzweig's extraordinary craftsmanship consists in his exposition of the gradual maturation of Hegel's system in constant counteraction between historical-political experience and conceptual-philosophical processing. In the study, no historical event that caught Hegel's attention remains without repercussion for his thought, and no new turn in Hegel's thought is presented without simultaneously discussing its influence upon his perception of historical events. Rosenzweig was capable of achieving this very uncommon interlacing of contemporary history and intellectual development because he had trained himself equally as historian and philosopher. In contrast to many other authors who have tried to describe Hegel's intellectual development, Rosenzweig commanded over a broad range of historical knowledge, in addition to having a detailed expertise of philosophical context. In the

historical passages, where he presents the formative events for the development of Hegel's theories, Rosenzweig shows himself to be a faithful
pupil of his teacher Meinecke: the political events, be it the French Revolution, Napoleon's campaign of conquest, or the Carlsbad Decrees, are
portrayed as far as possible in historical manner and from the perspective
of their time, without overarching valuations, but in return always in
the most dense, extremely intimate liveliness. But never do such passages function independently, such that they would be presented in the
form of excursions or separate chapters, but instead they almost always
remain seamlessly bound within the stream of reenactment of Hegel's
political understanding. This is, namely, the actual theme of the study. It
determines its structure, characteristic style, and process of argumentation from the first line to the last. And yet, with all Rosenzweig's talent at
narrative presentation, the systematically oriented philosopher still holds
the upper hand over the historian of ideas. The historical-political events
are narratively interwoven in such a manner as to bring motives into play
and to discuss what may have prompted a change of perspective in Hegel
over and against the political sphere.

In the foreground of this thematic, which is decisive for the entire
study, lies the consideration – already raised shortly after Hegel's death –
if Hegel's ideal of the state aligns with the restorative or with the
progressive tendencies in Prussia at that time. It was sometimes the
regressive, indeed, totalitarian side of Hegel's political understanding,
sometimes the progressive-liberal side that was highlighted, depending
on the position one took towards Hegel's philosophy as a whole.[53] What
is then special about Rosenzweig's argumentation can be seen in how he
tries to wrest Hegel's conception of the state entirely free from the opposition surrounding it. For Rosenzweig, who was intimately familiar with
the debates of the time, it made little sense to adjoin the political theory
of his protagonist to either one side or the other, as it stood entirely on
its own two feet and, even in the Berlin period, did not allow itself to
be led astray by strategical considerations. According to Rosenzweig's
conviction, Hegel was far too interested, already from relatively early
on, in the construction of a spiritual-philosophical system than to allow
himself to be persuaded by the political developments in Germany in
drafting his model of the state. Rather, in conceiving individual instances
in the arrangement of his state, Hegel takes up what seems to fit in an

exemplary manner into his system from the governmental institutions of territories he is familiar with, without thereby paying particular attention to the political conditions in Prussia. And where at times it does in fact come to an overlap between conceptual elements of Hegel's rational state and real components of the Prussian state, for Rosenzweig this is in essence a result of "the commonality of influence, from English conditions, for example,"[54] and not an adaptation of Prussian state constructs by the philosopher. With his construction of the state, as Rosenzweig repeats in many passages of the study at hand, Hegel remains consistently true to his own convictions, justified on the basis of his system, and does not betray these convictions to political purposes of critique or to an affirmation of the Prussian state. Hegel does not wish to undertake a critique of the times with his political philosophy, but instead, using concrete models, to draft the best possible arrangement for a state construct that is to be conducive for the actualization of reason under modern conditions.

If hereby Hegel's concept of the state is removed from the dispute surrounding his political relation to Prussia, then the question still remains as to why one still encounters therein a certain tendency to assimilate to what exists, despite all theoretical autonomy. Although Rosenzweig does not directly address this problem in his study, he implicitly develops a solution over the course of his reconstruction that belongs to the most original and best among what Hegel scholarship has to offer – Michael Theunissen had already repeatedly pointed out that in the relevant passages of the book one finds a groundbreaking, and today still underappreciated, interpretation of Hegel's concept of politics and praxis.[55] For Rosenzweig, it is obvious that the key to Hegel's mature understanding of the state must be sought in that famous principle from the "Preface" to the *Philosophy of Right*, according to which "what is rational" is also "actual" and "what is actual" is also "rational." Within Hegel scholarship, in order to reach a clarification on Hegel's philosophical self-understanding, it is normally the second component of this formulation that is highlighted, that is, the talk of the rationality of what is actual. The consequence in general is then to imply that the author of the *Philosophy of Right* wants to ethically or morally endorse everything about the given social order. In contrast to such an implied reading, Rosenzweig begins with the first component of the principle and then takes it upon himself to give a plausible interpretation for speaking about the actuality of what is rational. In doing so, Rosenzweig takes advantage of a further series of formulations from the "Preface," above all religious and theological, in order to eventually arrive at the conclusion that with his notorious dictum Hegel referred to the event of Christian revelation: "not in general and since eternity has this been the case [the actuality of the rational, A.H.], instead it became, through Christianity, an ethical demand and the standard of all human institutions in the thought of the Kingdom of Heaven on earth."[56] Interpreted in this sense, namely as the identification of the "historical-factual anticipation of the Kingdom of God through Christ,"[57] the first clause contains, in the words of Rosenzweig, nothing less than the "revolutionary" meaning of summoning humankind to the ethical actualization of reason in its state order. Everything, so it might seem, that did not correspond in the existing conditions to the egalitarian principles of the Christian faith must be practically overcome, in order that the objective, already existing, rationality may carry through "subjectively" in actuality. In Rosenzweig's interpretation, however, this is already opposed by the meaning of the second clause, which he tries to understand to the effect that through this clause philosophy is merely obligated to recognize the previously outlined events. Philosophy cannot, and may not actively contribute to political-historical change, as is later the case with Marx, because due to its own capacities it is limited to only observing how the advances in the actualization of the Kingdom of God play out for the "state of our age."[58] Thus, if we follow Rosenzweig's extraordinary reconstruction, Hegel's doctrine of the state is the ambivalent result of a political-theological interpretation of human history: on the one hand, according to its deepest insight, it would need to welcome every practical upheaval in the existing societal order, and on the other hand it is summoned to merely sanction that which exists.

Even this explosive interpretation represents only one example from the abundance of groundbreaking insights Rosenzweig attends to in the study at hand. From beginning to end, Rosenzweig finds systematically highly productive, occasionally also highly surprising, explanations for all the new course-changes that Hegel undertakes in gradually working out his model of the state. In doing so, the details are just as important to Rosenzweig as the major lines of interpretation. He is interested in changes in Hegel's conception of the function of the individual estates or the role of the monarch, as well as in transformations in Hegel's construction of the systemic whole.[59] But the guiding principle that Rosenzweig follows in his artful interlacing of intimate and overarching views is the presentation of a gradual self-undermining of Hegel's original intentions: although Hegel, from early on, as we can read here, sought for the sake of the freedom of all individual wills to understand the state as a self-legitimizing, powerful organization, and therefore tried to abstain from rooting the state in anything national, in the end, with the construction of his system, he had to sacrifice "the inherent right of the human being [...] to the divinized state."[60] The adherents to Hegel's practical philosophy are still toiling away today on the dichotomy this brought about. It is to Rosenzweig's credit to have first worked it out in all its acuity, and to have accounted for it within all the riddles of the work.

## III. RECEPTION

In the short obituary Friedrich Meinecke wrote for his former student and published in 1930 in the *Historische Zeitschrift*, it states at the very end that "the philosopher and renewer of the Jewish spirit" left us "with that book on Hegel [...] a work of lasting value for German intellectual history."[61] That these words would not prove true, indeed, that since then Rosenzweig's study fell victim to being almost completely forgotten, can already be explained by the fact that for nearly a century it was only available in photomechanical reprints in its original German language, but never in an edition suitable for the current state of Hegel scholarship. The further the distance to the original edition of the book from the year 1920, the increasingly smaller the circle became of those who even took notice of it for their research. Today, the name Rosenzweig is often not even mentioned in the most relevant treatises on Hegel. But even given all of this, it might have seemed that the book would have a bright future in the years directly following its publication. Among experts, as Ferdinand Tönnies' review attests, it was received as an important study on political philosophy and was rightly praised as a milestone in Hegel scholarship. It was most likely two independently arising factors, which were set into motion soon after its publication, that contributed to the diminishing effect. On the one hand, the scholar's turn towards the Jewish spirit caused the early Hegel researcher to disappear almost entirely out of public perception behind the now steadily more visible philosopher of religion. On the other hand, with the onset of Western Marxism's engagement with Hegel in the 1920s, an entirely different interpretive perspective than the one Rosenzweig had followed in his study became dominant.

However, before the effect of either of these two tendencies could fully unfold, the Nazi takeover did its part in bringing the reception of Rosenzweig's work to an almost complete standstill. The author died at the height of his life in 1929 from an incurable sickness. As a Jewish philosopher of religion, he was already held in high regard at that time, but in the years after 1933 the quickly intensifying antisemitism ensured that his fame and his works could not spread any further. If a faithful legion of friends and relatives had not agreed at that time to keep the memory of Rosenzweig alive through the publication of his letters and smaller writings, then he may have fallen to the fate of permanently being forgotten. The two volumes that were published thanks to the efforts of this circle by the Schocken publishing house in 1935 and 1937[62] thus acted as supporting pillars for Rosenzweig's historical reception to help it bridge the national-socialist dictatorship. However, the same could not be said of the Hegel study. Based on the increasing polarization of thinking at that time, the book's differentiated tone and access-point seemed to fit less and less into the intellectual landscape. Neither the intellectual Left nor the ideological spokespeople on the Right saw themselves in a position to harness a book of such cut for their own purposes, and so it fell by the wayside equally between both fronts. Thus, as Herbert Marcuse prepared to write a monograph on Hegel shortly before the Second World War, in which he wanted to preserve Hegel's fundamental concepts from fascist appropriation, even for him Rosenzweig's highly relevant book was hardly still present. In Marcuse's account, it is only mentioned once and marginally, even though Marcuse labored with the exact same interpretive problems that are central to the work.[63]

After the Second World War, it thus seems that in fact only that part of Rosenzweig's work remained present that had the character of a philosophy of religion. In any case, the first monograph dedicated to the philosopher, Nahum N. Glatzer's study *Franz Rosenzweig. His Life and Thought*, published in 1953,[64] leaves the Hegel book practically unmentioned and almost exclusively focuses on *The Star of Redemption*. This privileging of the philosophy of religion was not changed by the fact that, as a result of the defeat of national socialism, Hegel's political philosophy now entered more strongly into public consciousness, as debate arose around it as to the intellectual causes of totalitarianism. Although concerning such an issue nothing would have made more sense than to fall back on Rosenzweig's study, it did not play a significant role for any of the factions involved in the discussion.

On the part of the Left, the tendency still prevailed, as it had already before the interregnum of the Nazis, to primarily interpret Hegel's philosophy retrospectively under the viewpoint of its preparatory role for Marxist theory. Therefore, the focus here was on topics that Rosenzweig certainly touches on but did not make into guiding threads of his reconstruction. Typical of this detachment is already the first major monograph that, shortly after the end of the Second World War, opens the series of Marxist inspired studies on the prerevolutionary character of Hegel's philosophy. Indeed, in his book The Young Hegel, still an indispensable source for the study of Hegel's early work today,[65] Georg Lukács can spare only polemical remarks for Rosenzweig's attempts at interpretation. Over the course of his presentation, Lukács repeatedly mentions Hegel and the State, which appeared only 28 years before his own work, and situates it quite disparagingly in line with the Right Hegelians, accusing it, entirely unwarranted, of concealing Hegel's national-economic interests as well as his republican tendencies.[66] The author of History and Class Consciousness appears to have absolutely no feel for Rosenzweig's efforts to gain as differentiated a picture as possible of his protagonist's development, that he allows Hegel to work through each political event independently with his own philosophical means. All in all, regarding how it references Rosenzweig, Lukács' book represents a document of gross indignation and crude prejudice.

If the fate of the study at hand had thereby been provisionally determined on the side of the Left Hegelians, it did not look much better during the same time period on the other side. As Karl Popper undertook his simplified attempt during the final years of the Second World War to ascribe to Hegel the decisive role in ideologically preparing the way for National Socialism, thereby officially declaring him an enemy of the "open society,"[67] for him, Rosenzweig's subtle argumentation would have of course remained entirely locked away. Popper deals with Hegel's concept of the state so ignorantly and superficially, as in fact should have been unthinkable a quarter of a century after the publication of *Hegel and the State*. Furthermore, the followers of the Critical Rationalists, who at least sensed the necessity to theoretically substantiate their theses, did not see the need twenty years later to take a closer look into the already extant scholarly literature. Therefore, in his book on *Hegel's Social Philosophy*, published in 1967, Ernst Topitsch could repeat all the prejudices of his teacher, despite a slightly improved understanding of the texts, without even once allowing himself to become agitated by Rosenzweig's study, which was dedicated to the same topic.[68] The early monograph of the Jewish philosopher of religion, so it could have appeared, had not survived the period of the National Socialist dictatorship unscathed. It was caught between the fronts in the fierce confrontation over the theoretical-political role of Hegel's philosophy, too deliberative and differentiated for the one side, and too subtle for the other to even have taken notice.

If it was to have remained in this state of reception, Rosenzweig's study would have soon thereafter fallen into desuetude, even among the more intimate professional public. Every bit of philosophical attention seemed to now be directed so exclusively towards the philosopher of religion, whose book *The Star of Redemption* so strongly shaped his image in compendiums and lexicons, that his early book on Hegel was treated at best as a precursor to the mature work. It was not much different even within the circles of those who increasingly came together beginning in the 1970s in order to ensure a lasting memory for Rosenzweig's eminent accomplishment. Even here, the Hegel study was not honored as an independent work but interpreted from the perspective of the later philosophy of religion as a work of philosophical preparation.[69] It is thus thanks only to the vigilant awareness for tradition of but a few Hegel scholars that Rosenzweig's book did not fall victim to being forever forgotten through this one-sidedness. Above all, Joachim Ritter and Michael Theunissen are to be named, who through important treatises on Hegel's philosophy both contributed to granting the early work of the Meinecke student and later philosopher of religion its due place in the philosophical literature of the twentieth century.[70] A direct path leads from these publications to the decision to make Rosenzweig's profound study available one hundred years later in a masterful English edition.

*Axel Honneth (translated by Josiah Simon)*

## NOTES

1   Franz Rosenzweig, *Der Stern der Erlösung*, 1921 (today idem, *Der Mensch und sein Werk. Gesammelte Schriften*, vol. II, Haag, 1976).

2   See, for example, Martin Jay, "Politics of translation – S. Kracauer and W. Benjamin on the Buber-Rosenzweig Bible," in *Leo Baeck Institute Yearbook* 21 (1976), pp. 3–24.

3   Cf. Raimund Sesterhenn (ed.), *Das freie Jüdische Lehrhaus-eine andere Frankfurter Schule*, Munich, 1987.

4   Franz Rosenzweig, *Hegel und der Staat*, first edition in two volumes, Munich and Berlin 1920 (photomechanical reprints: Aalen, 1962, 1982).

5   For example with Terry Pinkard, *Hegel: A Biography*, Cambridge, 2000.

6   Zbigniew A. Pelczynski (ed.), *The State and Civil Society. Studies in Hegel's Political Philosophy*, Cambridge 1984.

7   Hans Christoph Schmidt am Busch, *Hegels Begriff der Arbeit*, Berlin 2002.

8   Robert Pippin, *Hegel's Practical Philosophy. Rational agency as Ethical Life.* Cambridge 2008; Jean François Kervégan, *L'Effectif et la Rationnel. Hegel et l'Esprit Objectif*, Paris 2007.

9   Cf, among others, Axel Honneth, "Zwischen Gerechtigkeit und affektiver Bindung. Die Familie im Brennpunkt moralischer Kontroverse," in idem, *Das Andere der Gerechtigkeit*, Frankfurt/M. 2000, pp. 193–215.

10  Jeremy Waldron, *The Right to Private Property*, Oxford 1988, Chap. 10.

11  Cf. the presentation in: Charles Taylor, *Hegel*, Frankfurt/M. 1978, pp. 574–604. 12.

12  The biographical information is mainly taken from the compilation of letter quotations, which aided Nahum Glatzer in his description of Rosenzweig's intellectual development in his youth: Nahum H. Glatzer, *Franz Rosenzweig. His Life and Thought*, New York 1961. pp. 1–22. On his cousin Hans Ehrenberg, who will play a central role in Rosenzweig's development, see Günter Brakelmanm: "Leben und Werk von Hans Ehrenberg – eine biographische Skizze bis 1932," in Werner Licharz/Manfred Keller (eds.), *Franz Rosenzweig und Hans Ehrenberg. Bericht einer Beziehung*, Frankfurt/M 1986, pp. 81–119.

13  Cf. the letter to his mother of 18 November 1907, in: Franz Rosenzweig *Briefe*, selected and edited by Edith Rosenzweig, Berlin, 1935, 33 f.

14  Wilhelm Windelband, *Die Erneuerung des Hegelianismus. Festrede in der Heidelberger Akademie der Wissenschaft*, Heidelberg 1910.

15  Heinrich Levy, *Die Hegel-Renaissance in der deutschen Philosophie mit besonderer Berücksichtigung des Neukantianismus*, Berlin 1927.

16  Friedrich Meinecke, *Weltbürgertum und Nationalstaat. Studien zur Genesis des deutschen Nationalstaates*, München 1908 (quoted here from the Werkausgabe, Vol. V, Munich 1962).

17  Letter to his mother, Nov. 13, 1908, in Franz Rosenzweig, *Briefe*, op. cit. p. 41.

18  Friedrich Meinecke, *Weltbürgertum und Nationalstaat*, op. cit. p. 236.

19  Cf. Helmut Plessner, *Die verspätete Nation. Über die politische Verführbarkeit bürgerlichen Geistes*, Frankfurt/M. 1974 (original edition 1959).

20  Friedrich Meinecke, *Weltbürgertum und Nationalstaat*, op. cit., Chapter 11 (pp. 236–243).

21  Cf. for example the letter to Hans Ehrenberg of 4. 8. 1909 in: Franz Rosenzweig, *Briefe*, op. cit.

22  Cf. the letter to Franz Frank (undated) in: Franz Rosenzweig, *Briefe*, op. cit. p. 50 f.

23  Letter to Hans Ehrenberg 21. 12. 1909 in: Franz Rosenzweig, *Briefe*, op. cit. p. 47 f.

24  Viktor von Weizäcker, *Natur und Geist*, Munich 1977, p. 19. Von Weizsäcker, however, also mentions in the same passage that he had already at that time associated the hostile reactions to Rosenzweig's lecture with anti-Semitic resentments.

25  Viktor von Weizäcker, *Natur und Geist*, op. cit., pp. 18f.

26  Letter to Hans Ehrenberg, October 28, 1910, in: Franz Rosenzweig *Briefe*, op. cit., p. 59.

27  Letter to Hans Ehrenberg, 11 Nov. 1910, in: Franz Rosenzweig, *Briefe*, op. cit. p. 57 f.

28  Ibid.

29  Wilhelm Dilthey, *Die Jugendgeschichte Hegels* (1905), in: idem, *Gesammelte Schriften*, vol. IV, Leipzig and Berlin 1925, pp. 5-187

30  *Hegels theologische Jugendschriften*, edited by Hermann Nohl, Tübingen 1907.

31  Rudolf Haym, *Hegel und seine Zeit. Vorlesungen über Entstehung und Entwicklung, Wesen und Wert der Hegelschen Philosophie*, Berlin 1857 (reprint of the 2nd, expanded edition: Darmstadt 1962); Karl Rosenkranz, *G.W.F. Hegel's Leben*, Berlin 1844 (reprint Darmstadt 1963).

32  G.W.F. Hegel, *Werke*. Complete Edition by a Society of Friends of the Deceased, 18 vols., Berlin 1932–1945; idem, *Sämtliche Werke*, ed. by Georg Lasson, Leipzig 1907 ff.

33  Cf. Letter to Hans Ehrenberg from mid-July 1913, in: Franz Rosenzweig *Briefe*, op. cit.

34  G.W.F. Hegel *Schriften zur Politik und Rechtsphilosophie*, ed. by Georg Lasson, Leipzig 1913.

35  A more precise dating is provided by the letter to Hans Ehrenberg of May 29, 1917, in: Franz Rosenzweig *Briefe*, loc. cit.

36  Cf. for example: Ulrich Bieberich, *Wenn die Geschichte göttlich wäre. Rosenzweigs Auseinandersetzung mit Hegel*, Ottilien 1990, p. 42 ff.

37  On the war years, Nahum N. Glatzer, *Franz Rosenzweig. His Life and Thought*, op. cit. p. 32-85.

38  Letter to Gertrud Oppenheim, May 4, 1919, in: Franz Rosenzweig, *Briefe*, op. cit. p. 358.

39  Letter to Rudolf Ehrenberg, May 14, 1919, in: Franz Rosenzweig, *Briefe*, op. cit. p. 360.

40  Letter to Gertrud Oppenheim, June 8, 1919, in: Franz Rosenzweig, *Briefe*, op. cit.

41  Cf. Letter to Gertrud Oppenheim, May 4, 1919, in: Franz Rosenzweig, *Briefe*, op. cit. p. 358.

42  Page 129, this volume.

43  Friedrich Meinecke, *Weltbürgertum und Nationalstaat*, op. cit., p. 238.

44  Cf. letter from Hans Ehrenberg, August 6, 1909, in: Franz Rosenzweig, *Briefe*, op. cit. p. 43; Letter to Amschel Alsberg (grandfather), November 6, 1910, in: ibid. pp. 52 f.

45  Page 12, this volume.

46  Ibid.

47  Letter to Hans Ehrenberg, early summer 1914; in: Franz Rosenzweig, *Briefe*, op. cit., pp. 85 ff, here pp. 86–87.

48  Page 357, this volume.

49  Ferdinand Tönnies, "Besprechung von Franz Rosenzweig, Hegel und der Staat" in: *Zeitschrift für Politik*, 13 (1924), pp. 172–176.

50  Ibid., p. 172.

51  Page 249, this volume.

52  Page 250, this volume.

53  In the twentieth century, the first reading is represented, among others, by Ernst Topitsch (ders. *Die Sozialphilosophie Hegels als Heilslehre und Herrschaft-sideologie*, Neuwied und Berlin 1967), while the second reading is represented by Eric Weil (idem *Hegel et l'Etat*, Paris 1950). An excellent overview of the entire debate is given by Michael Theunissen, *Die Verwirklichung der Vernunft. Zur Theorie-Praxis-Diskussion im Anschluß an Hegel* (Beiheft 6 of the *Philosophischen Rundschau*), Tübingen 1970.

54  Page 415, this volume.

55  Michael Theunissen, *Die Verwirklichung der Vernunft. Zur Theorie-Praxis-Diskussion im Anschluß an Hegel*, op. cit., pp. 22–28; idem, *Hegels Lehre vom absoluten Geist als theologisch-politischer Traktat*, Berlin 1970, pp. 439–447.

56  Page 338, this volume.

57  Michael Theunissen, *Die Verwirklichung der Vernunft. Zur Theorie-Praxis-Diskussion im Anschluß an Hegel*, op. cit., p. 26.

58  Page 338, this volume.

59  It should be given that Rosenzweig was not able to always correctly solve the extremely difficult task of periodizing Hegel's still unpublished manuscripts and writings. On the more recent state of affairs, see, for example, Heinz Kimmerle: "Zur Chronologie Hegels Jenaer Schriften," in *Hegel-Studien* 4 (1967), pp. 125–167.

60  Page 505, this volume.

61  Friedrich Meinecke, "Nachruf," in: *Historische Zeitschrift* 142 (1930), p. 219 f.

62  Franz Rosenzweig, *Briefe*, op. cit.; idem, *Kleinere Schriften*, Berlin 1937.

63  Herbert Marcuse, *Reason and Revolution. Hegel and the Rise of Social Theory*, New York 1941 (German: *Vernunft und Revolution. Hegel und die Entstehung der Gesellschaftstheorie*, Neuwind und Berlin 1962).

64  Nahum N. Glatzer, *Franz Rosenzweig. His Life and Thought*, op. cit.

65  Georg Lukács. *Der junge Hegel. Über die Beziehungen von Dialektik und Ökonomie* (1943), in: idem, *Werke*, vol. 8, Neuwied und Berlin 1967.

66  See, for example, ibid, pp. 68, 82, 386.

67  Karl R. Popper, *Die offene Gesellschaft und ihre Feinde.* Vol. II: *Falsche Propheten* (Engl. 1945), Bern 1958.

68  Ernst Topitsch, *Die Sozialphilosophie Hegels als Heilslehre und Herrschaftsideologie,* op. cit.

69  See, for example, Wolfdietrich Schmied-Kowarzik (ed.) *Der Philosoph Franz Rosenzweig (1886-1929). International Congress – Kassel 1986.* 2 vols. Freiburg/Munich 1988.

70  Joachim Ritter, *Hegel und die französische Revolution,* originally Köln und Opladen 1957, revised Frankfurt/M 1965; Michael Theunissen, *Die Verwirklichung der Vernunft. Zur Theorie-Praxis-Diskussion im Anschluß an Hegel,* op. cit.

# Translators' Note on Abbreviations and Secondary Sources

*Hegel und der Staat* was published in 1920 with the support of the *Heidel-berger Akademie der Wissenschaften*. For this translation we consulted the most recent, reprinted edition (1982) of that original work, but in order to provide a more accessible, up-to-date, and easy-to-use text for an English-language audience, we primarily relied upon the Suhrkamp edition edited by Frank Lachmann and published in 2010. That edition provides many useful, comprehensive, and careful editorial modifications that situate the text in a research framework that recognizes the lasting value of Rosenzweig's interpretive and scholarly work. Our intent in relying directly upon Lachmann's updated scholarly version of this important text is to link this English-language translation with a straightforward connection to a broader range of readers and scholars who will look to Rosenzweig's interpretations of the origin and development of Hegel's political philosophy, philosophy of history, and phenomenology that culminated in his *Philosophy of Right*.

Given these choices, some comments are in order on the arrangement of endnotes, citations and listings of primary and secondary sources, and the extensive scholarly corrections and emendations of Lachmann's text. Lachmann notes that in order to improve the scholarly accessibility of the text, he altered Rosenzweig's style of connecting endnote references to supporting texts and annotations on significant words, phrases or references to events, people or places in the main body of Rosenzweig's text. As Lachmann further notes, in the original edition of the text, Rosenzweig often constructed his endnotes by providing an appropriate keyword and merely the page from his text where that word or concept occurred. It was then the reader's responsibility to search through the respective page to connect the information from the endnote to its referent in the text. Lachmann rectified this cumbersome arrangement by finding the specific place in the text that was referred to in this or that endnote and appending an endnote numeral either at the conclusion of the sentence or identifiable phrase where the idea occurred. He further addressed the confusions in Rosenzweig's non-prioritization of multiple references to primary or secondary sources within each endnote by ordering the sources in such a way that each citation has within itself a clearly unambiguous and efficient successive listing of sources. Lachmann also reordered the enumerations within the endnotes by providing more accurate citations (such as, for example: "Cf. Section 10, note 12").

We also directly followed the style of abbreviations used by Lachmann with respect to quotations from primary sources, from Hegel as well as from Fichte, Haym, Nohl, Rosenkranz, Schelling, and various codes of law. Specifically, references from Hegel's Works, Hegel's Letters, and certain selections from other authors are designated by an abbreviation followed by a volume number in Arabic numerals and page number(s). The Jenaer Systementwürfe and the Briefe, however, are quoted using Roman numerals. Lachmann notes that, where possible, he followed a hierarchical ordering beginning with the Gesammelte Werke (abbreviated GW) and then for the sake of convenience for the reader, a parallel specification to the Werke in 20 Bänden (abbreviated HW) follows.

Again, for the sake of consistency and faithfulness to Lachmann's extensive editorial work, we have provided the entirety of Lachmann's list of secondary sources in this edition in order to facilitate cross-referencing. Thus, citations to secondary sources take the form of: author surname, year of publication, and page number(s). For multi-volume works, the specification of the volume number follows the date of publication in Roman numerals while specifications such as book, selection, or chapter are respectively listed following the publication date.

Where appropriate, references to earlier editions or transmissions of Hegel's writings that were collected and published – such as those from Nohl, Rosenkranz, Haym, and Lasson – are additionally referred to. Lachmann notes that Hegel's orthographic idiosyncrasies were left in place in Rosenzweig's original text, almost all of which do not transfer to the English translation. In general, when a word in its German context was ambiguous or equivocal, we provided the German in brackets directly following the word in question. In many cases, Lachmann provides corrections of the words or phrases quoted by Rosenzweig with direct transmissions from Hegel's primary texts, which we have marked with "verbatim."

We should also note the important work that Lachmann did with respect to the peculiarities of Rosenzweig's style of writing and citation, most of which is not apparent in the English translation. Wherever possible and without distorting the meaning of a passage, Lachmann corrected Rosenzweig's texts for grammatical mistakes and printing errors, as well as unpacking compound adjectival forms, such as *kantischfichtesche* to *kantisch-fichtische*. We followed that protocol but used anglicized forms, such as Kantian-Fichtean. Throughout the text, many foreign language phrases in Latin, French, or Greek were italicized by Lachmann but not in Rosenzweig's original text, nor did Lachmann italicize such phrases comprehensively. In our translation, we italicized all non-English words and phrases. In order to facilitate the best possible reading experience for English readers, we provide either English translations of foreign words and phrases in brackets directly following the foreign language words in the main body of the text or in brackets in an endnote if the words are associated with a cited author or idiom.

Some final remarks about Lachmann's handling of the scarcity and incompleteness of Rosenzweig's bibliographic references need to be made. Lachmann comments that Rosenzweig does not provide an independent bibliographic list but, instead, often provides shortened versions of full titles of secondary literature or works by foreign authors that he consulted. Lachmann added to the body of Rosenzweig's text full bibliographic information where a citation was missing or fragmentary. In cases where references to certain editions were ambiguous, such as in cases where a publishing date was missing, Lachmann provides the missing information. In cases where multiple editions may have been available to Rosenzweig at the time of writing his book, Lachmann chose to provide the most probable version – as book, journal selection, or chapter — that Rosenzweig may have had available at the time of his research. For example, he indicates that Adam Smith's *An Inquiry into the Nature and Causes of the Wealth of Nations* (1776) was one such text and that he chose not only the most probable edition that may have been available but, if appropriate, the most recent edition that faithfully reproduces the original. This latter point explains, in part, the extensive bibliography that Lachmann provides since he sought to include the most relevant or important recent editions of the works in question. The final, essential point in this regard is that Rosenzweig's work itself provides a reading of the origins and chronology of Hegel's manuscripts that was limited in Rosenzweig's case since several of Hegel's primary works had not yet been edited in 1914, which was the technical *terminus ad quem* for his research efforts. Accordingly, when Rosenzweig's own commentary related to the dating of manuscripts was in question, Lachmann provides the most up-to-date bibliographic information that would not have been available at the time that Rosenzweig brought his research on the book to completion. Importantly, Lachmann omits and edits several endnotes relating to the chronology of Hegel's manuscripts from Rosenzweig's original edition that could be the source for potential future lines of research.

Finally, we provide a selection of primarily English-language sources and English translations of Hegel's texts that informed and helped to guide our own work in translation. In doing so, we hope to not only contribute to existing research but to stimulate future research efforts in Hegel and Rosenzweig studies.

# Abbreviations

## HEGEL'S WRITINGS

| | |
|---|---|
| Br | *Briefe von und an Hegel (Letters from and to Hegel)*. Edited by Johannes Hoffmeister. Vol. I–III: Hamburg 1969, Vols. IV1 and IV/2: ed. by Friedhelm Nicolin. Hamburg 1977 and 1981. |
| CH | Cart, Jean Jacques; Hegel, Georg Wilhelm Friedrich; Wieland, Wolfgang: *Vertrauliche Briefe über das vormalige staatsrechtliche Verhältnis des Waadtlandes (Pays de Vaud) zur Stadt Bern (Entrusted Letters on the Former Relationship under Constitutional Law of Vaud to the City of Bern)*. Facs. Göttingen 1970. |
| GW | *Gesammelte Werke (Collected Works)*. Published in conjunction with the German Research Foundation by the North Rhine-Westphalian (1968–1995 Rhine-Westphalian) Academy of Sciences. Hamburg 1968 ff. |
| HW | *Werke in 20 Bänden (Works in 20 Volumes)*. New edition based on the works from 1832–1845. Edited by E. Moldenhauer and K.M. Michel. Frankfurt/M 1969–1971. |
| Nohl | *Hegels theologische Jugendschriften nach den Handschriften in der Kgl. Bibliothek in Berlin (Hegel's Theological Writings based on the manuscripts from the Royal Library in Berlin)*, edited by Hermann Nohl. Tübingen 1907 (reprint Frankfurt/M. 1966). |

| SdS | *System der Sittlichkeit* [Critik des Fichteschen Naturrechts] (*System of Ethicality*) [Criticism of Fichtean Natural Law] Hamburg 2002. |
| --- | --- |
| SE | *Jenaer Systementwürfe (Jena System-Drafts)*. Volume I (*The System of Speculative Philosophy*): ed. by Klaus Düsing and Heinz Kimmerle. Hamburg 1986; Volume III (*Philosophy of Nature and Philosophy of Spirit*): Ed. by Rolf-Peter Hörstmann, Hamburg 1987. |
| V | *Vorlesungen. Ausgewählte Manuskripte und Nachschriften.* (Lectures. Selected manuscripts and postscripts) Hamburg 1938 ff. |
| Ww | *Sämtliche Werke (Complete Works)*. Ed. by G. Lasson, subsequently by J. Hoffmeister. Leipzig 1911 ff. |

## OTHER WRITINGS

| ABGB | General Civil Code (1812). 37th edition, Vienna 2009. |
| --- | --- |
| ALR | General Common Law for the Prussian States from February 5, 1794. 2nd, expanded edition. Neuwied 1994. |
| CC | Code-civil (online edition on the French government's website: wwwlegi.france.gouv.fr). |
| FW | Johann Gottlieb Fichte: Gesamtausgabe der Bayerischen Akademie der Wissenschaften (Complete Edition of the Bavarian Academy of Sciences). Edited by Reinhard Lauth, Erich Fuchs, and Hans Gliwitzky. Stuttgart 1962 ff. |
| Haym | Rudolf Haym. Hegel und seine Zeit. Vorlesungen über die Entstehung und Entwicklung, Wesen und Werth der Hegelschen Philosophie (Hegel and his Age. Lectures on the Origin and Development, Essence and Value of Hegel's Philosophy). Berlin 1857. |
| RB | "Bibliothek von Franz Rosenzweig vor 1933 angeschafft, auf der Name Rafael Nehemiah Rosenzweig nach Palästina geschickt, eingeordnet in die Stadtbibliothek Tunis." ("Library of Franz Rosenzweig, acquired before 1933, in the name of Rafael Nehemiah Rosenzweig sent to Palestine, placed in the Tunis Municipal Library.") Typescript, 56 pp., 1938. Manuscript Department of the University Library of Kassel (Sign.: 2° Ms.Philos.39 [A 46]). |

Rosenkranz    Karl Rosenkranz. *G.W.F. Hegels Leben* (*G.W.F. Hegel's Life*).
                       Berlin 1844 (Darmstadt 1969).

SHK           *F.W.J. Schelling: Historisch-kritische Ausgabe* (*F.W.J. Schelling*
                       *Historical-critical Edition*). Supported by the Schelling
                       Commission of the Bavarian Academy of Sciences and
                       Humanities, edited by Jörg Jantzen. Thomas Buchheim,
                       Wilhelm G. Jacobs and Siegbert Peetz. Stuttgart 1976 ff.

# SECONDARY SOURCES

Allgemeine deutsche Biographie & Neue deutsche Biographie. Gesamtregister auf CD-ROM. 2. Ausg. (2005). Berlin: Duncker & Humblot (Neue deutsche Biographie, hg. von der Historischen Kommission bei der Bayerischen Akademie der Wissenschaften; Gesamtregister).

Allgemeine preußische Staats-Zeitung (1819–1843). Berlin, Königliche Expedition.

Archiv für Rechts-, und Wirtschaftsphilosophie. Mit besonderer Berücksichtigung der Gesetzgebungsfragen 1907–1933). Berlin: Rothschild.

Aristotle; Grumach, Ernst; Flashar, Hellmut (1991 ff.): Werke in deutscher Übersetzung. Berlin: Akademie-Verlag.

Arndt, Ernst Moritz (1913): Geist der Zeit. 4 Bände. Berlin [u.a.]: Bong.

Bamberger Zeitung (1795–1865): Bamberg, Reindl.

Bayerisches Hauptstaatsarchiv München: Akten des Bayerischen Hauptstaatsarchivs aus den ehemaligen Königlichen Kreis-, und Staatsarchiven München.

Beaulieu-Marconnay, Carl von (1879): Karl von Dalberg und seine Zeit. Zur Biographie und Charakteristik des Fürsten Primas. o.O.

Behrends, Okko; Knütel, Rolf; Kupisch, Bertold; Seiler, Hans Hermann (1933): Corpus Juris Civilis. Die Institution. Text und Übersetzung. Heidelberg: C.F. Müller Juristischer Verlag.

Beilage zur Allgemeinen Zeitung (1798–1803; 1807–1908). München: Allgemeine Zeitung.

Bericht und Jahrbuch des Historischen Vereins über die Pflege der Geschichte des Ehemaligen Fürstbistums Bamberg (1911 ff.). Bamberg, Duckstein: Verein.

Beyer, Wilhelm Raimund (1974): Zwischen Phänomenologie und Logik. Hegel als Redakteur der Bamberger Zeitung. 2., erg. und erw. Aufl. Köln: Pahl-Rugenstein Verlag (Kleine Bibliothek. Politik, Wissenschaft, Zukunft, 51).

Bitterauf, Theodor; Müller, Karl Alexander von; Riezler, Sigmund von (1913); Riezler Festschrift. Beiträge zur Bayerischen Geschichte. Gotha: Perthes.

Brentano, Lujo (1871 f.) Die Arbeitergilden der Gegenwart. 2 Bände. Leipzig: Duncker & Humblot.

Brie, Siegfried (1874): Der Bundesstaat. Eine historisch-dogmatische Untersuchung (Neudruck 2001). Leipzig: Engelmann.

Burckhardt, Jacob; Oeri, Jakob (1905); Weltgeschichtliche Betrachtungen. (ND Wiesbaden 2009). Berlin: Spemann.

Constant de Rebecque, Benjamin (1814): Réflexions sur les constitutions, la distribution des pouvoirs, et les garanties dans une monarchie constitutionnelle. Paris: Nicolle [u.a.].

Creuzinger, Paul (1911): Hegels Einfluss auf Clausewitz. Berlin: Eisenschmidt.

Dahlmann, Friedrich Christoph (1847): Die Politik, auf den Grund und das Maß der gegebenen Zustände zurückgeführt (Neuausgabe Berlin 1924). 2. verb. Aufl. Leipzig: Weidmann.

Daire, Eugène (1846): Physiocrates. Quesnay. Dupont de Nemours. Mercier de la Rivière. L'abbé Baudeau. Le Trosne. (ND Genf 1971). 2 Bände. Paris: Guillaumin.

Dalberg, Carl Theodor Anton Maria von (1802): Über Bestimmung der Schädigungsmittel für die Erbfürsten. 2. Aufl. Meersburg.

Danz, Wilhelm August Friedrich (1797): Etwas über die bisherigen Landschaftlichen Ausschüsse in Wirtemberg. An die Deputirten zum bevorstehenden Landtage. o.O.

Danz, Wilhelm August Friedrich (1797): Freymüthige Betrachtungen über die Organisation der landschaftlichen Ausschüsse. o.O.

Dilthey, Wilhelm (1905): Die Jugendgeschichte Hegels. (ND Göttingen 1990). Berlin: Verl. d. Königl. Akad. d. Wiss.

Diogenes Laertius (1998): Leben und Meinung berühmter Philosophen. Hamburg: Meiner (Philosophische Bibliothek).

Dittmann, Friedrich (1909): Der Begriff des Volksgeistes bei Hegel. Zugleich ein Beitrag zur Geschichte des Begriffs der Entwicklung im 19. Jh. Zugl.: Leipzig, Univ., Diss., 1909. Leipzig: Voigtländer.

Dizinger, Carl Friedrich (1833): Denkwürdigkeitn aus meinen Leben und aus meiner Zeit. Ein Beitrag zur Geschichte Deutschlands vornämlich aber Württembergs und dessen Verfassung. Tübingen: Osiander in Komm.

Eber, Heinrich (1909): Hegels Ethik in ihrer Entwicklung bis zur Phänomenologie. Univ., Diss. Strassburg: Müh.

Eden, Frederick Morton (1797): The State of the Poor (ND Bristol 1994). London: Printed by J. Davis for B. & J. White u.a.

Euphorion. Zeitschrift für Literaturgeschichte (1894 ff.). Heidelberg: Winter.

Falkenheim, Hugo (1909): Eine unbekannte politische Druckschrift Hegels. Preußische Jahrbücher 138.

Fischer, Hans (1911 f.): Katalog der Bibliothek des Freiherrn Emil Marschalk von Ostheim. Bamberg, Büchner.

Fränkischer Kreiscorrespondent von und für Deutschland (1804 ff.). Nürnberg. Fränkischer Merkur. Ab 1834 Bamberger Zeitung (1809–1834). Bamberg.

Gaius; Poste, Edward; Whituck, E.A.; Greenridge, A.H.J. (1904): Gia Institutiones or Institutes of Roman Law. 4th ed. Oxford: The Clarendon Press.

Gallais, Jean Pierre; Anquetil, Louis Pierre (1819): Histoire de France depuis la mort de Louis XI. [Nouvelle éd. rev. et. Corr.]. Paris: Janet et Cotelle.

Gans, Eduard (1827): System den römischen Civilrechts im Grundrisse einer Abhandlung über Studium und System des römischen Rechts (ND Goldbach 1999). Berlin: Dümmler.

Gazette nationale, ou le moniteur universelle (1789 ff.). Paris: Leriche.

Gesellschaft der Wissenschaften (Hg.) (1753–1803) Göttingische Anzeigen von gelehrten Sachen. Göttingen: Dietrich [u.a.].

Gibbon, Edward (1776 ff.): The history of the demise and fall of the Roman Empire. (Neuausgabe New York 1994). London.

Gibbon, Edward (1788): The history of the demise and fall of the Roman Empire. 6 Bände. Basel: Tourneisen.

Gierke, Otto von (1902): Johannes Althusius und die Entwicklung der naturrechtlichen Staatstheorien. Zugleich ein Beitrag zur Geschichte der Rechtssystematik. (7., unveränderte Ausgabe Aalen 1981). 2. Durch Zusätze verm. Ausg. Breslau: Marcus.

Glatzer, Nahum N. (Hg.) (1964) Leopold Zunz. Jude, Deutscher Europäer; ein Judisches Gelehrtenschiksal des. 19. Jahrhundert in Briefen an Freunde.Herausgegeben und eingeleitet von Nahum N. Glatzer. Tübingen: Mohr (Schriftenreihe wissenschaftlicher Abhandlungen des Leo Baeck-Instituts, 11).

Goethe, Johann Wolfgang von (1985 ff.): Sämtliche Werke. Briefe, Tagebücher und Gespräche. 40 Bände. Frankfurt am Main: Deutscher Klassiker-Verlag (Bibliothek Deutscher Klassiker).

Gönner, Nikolaus Thaddäus (1804): Teutsches Staatsrecht (ND Stockstadt/ Main 2004). Landshut: Krüll.

Gross-Hoffinger, Anton Johann (1847): Erzherzog Karl von Oesterreich und die Kriege von 1792–1815. Leipzig: Lorck (Historische Hausbibliothek).

Häberlin, Karl Friedrich (1794 ff.): Handbuch des Teutschen Staatsrechts. Nach dem System des Herrn Geheimen Justizrath Pütter; zum gemeinnützigen Gebrauch der gebildeten Stände in Teutschland mit Rücksicht auf die neuesten merkwürdigsten Ereignisse. Berlin: Vieweg.

Hartmann, Alfred; Hasler, Friedrich (1863 ff.): Gallerie berühmter Schwizer der Neuzeit. 2 Bände. Baden: Hasler.

Hass, Damian Ferdinand (1786 ff.): Vorschläge wie das Justizwesen am Kammergericht bey künftiger Visitation oder am Reichstage nach den schon vorhandenen Gesetzen einzurichten und zu verbessern sey, wenn zu baldigen Entscheidung aller Rechtsanhängigen Sachen Hoffnung seyn sole. Wetzlar.

Haym, Rudolf (1902): Aus meinem Leben. Erinnerungen; aus dem Nachlass herausgegeben. Berlin: Gaertner.

Heeren, Arnold Hermann Ludwig (1803 ff.): Kleine historischen Schrifte. 3 Bände. Göttingen: J. F. Röwer.

Hegel-Studien (1964 ff.). Hamburg, Bonn: Meiner, Bouvier.

Heigel, Karl Theodor von (1881): Aus drei Jahrhunderten. Vorträge aus der neueren deutschen Geschichte. Wien: Braunmüller.

Heigel, Karl Theodor von (1886): Die Memoiren des bayerischen Ministers Grafen Montgelas. München.

Herder, Johann Gottfried von; Suphan, Bernhard (1884 ff.): Herders Ausgewählte Werke (ND Freiburg/Basel/Wien 1978). Berlin: Weidmann.

Hilsenbeck, Adolf (1913): Register zu den ersten 50 Jahrgängen der Sitzungsberichte der Kgl. Bayerischen Akademie der Wissenschaften (1860–1910). München: Verl. d. Königl. Bayer. Akad. D. Wiss., Reg.-Heft).

Historische Zeitschrift (HZ) (1859 ff.). München, Berlin: Oldenbourg.

Historisches Lexikon Bayerns (2006). München: Bayerische Staatsbibliothek.

Hoffmann, Wilhelm (1868): Deutschland einst und jetzt im Lichte des Reiches Gottes. Berlin: Stilke & van Muyden.

Hölderlin, Friedrich; Knaup, Michael (1992 f.): Sämtliche Werke und Briefe. 3 Bände. München: Hanser.

Holzhausen, Paul (1900): Der erste Konsul Bonaparte und seine deutschen Besucher. Ein Beitrag zur literarischen Würdigung des Konsulats. Bonn: Selbstverlag des Verfassers.

Hugo, Gustav (1807 ff.): Lehrbuch eines civilistischen Cursus. (ND Goldbach 1998). 7 Bände. Berlin: Mylius.

Humboldt, Wilhelm von (1903 ff.): Gesammelte Schriften. Hg. v. d. Kgl. Preuss. Akad. d. Wissenschaften. (Nachdruck Berlin 1968). Berlin: Behr.

Internationale Wochenschrift für Wissenschaft, Kunst und Technik (1907–1911). Berlin: anfangs München, Bayerische Druck- und Verlag-Anstalt: Scherl.

Jaeschke, Walter (2003). Hegel-Handbuch. Leben-Werk-Schule. Stuttgart: Metzler.

Joachimi-Dege, Marie (1908): Hölderlin Werke. In vier Teilen [in 1 Band.]. Berlin: Bong.

Kant, Immanuel (1902 ff.). Gesammelte Schriften. Herausgegeben von der Preußischen Akademie der Wissenschaften. Berlin: Reimer/Walter de Gruyter.

Klaiber, Julius (1877): Hölderlin, Hegel und Schelling in ihren schwäbischen Jugendjahren. Eine Festschrift zur Jubelfeier der Universität Tübingen. (unveränderter Nachdruck Frankfurt/M. 1981). Stuttgart: Cotta.

Köpke, Rudolf (1855): Ludwig Tieck. Erinnerungen aus dem Leben des Dichters nach dessen mündlichen und schriftlichen Mittheilungen (unveränderter Nachdruck Darmstadt 1970). Leipzig: Brockhaus.

Krämer, August (1821): Carl Theodor, Reichsfreiherr von Dalberg, letzter Churfürst von Mainz und Kurkanzler des deutschen Reichs. Grundzüge zu einer Geschichte seines politischen Lebens. Leipzig: Brockhaus.

Lagerlöf, Selma (1985): Die Wunder des anti-Christ Roman. München, Nymphenburger.

Landsberg, Ernst (1910): Geschichte der Deutschen Rechtswissenschaft. (Neudruck Aalen 1978). München: Oldenbourg.

Lassalle, Ferdinand (1863): Was nun? Zweiter Vortrag über Verfassungswesen (ND Berlin 1907). Zürich: Meyer & Zeller.

Lasson, Georg (1909): Beiträge zur Hegel-Forschung. 2 Bände. Berlin: Trowitzsch.

Lasson, Georg (1912 ff.): Hegel-Archiv. Leipzig: Meiner.

Laube, Heinrich (1837): Neue Reisenovellen (ND Frankfurt/M 1973). Mannheim: Hoff.

Lehmann, Max (1903): Freiherr vom Stein. Band 2. Die Reform. 1807–1808. Leipzig.

Leibniz, Gottfried W. (2002). Monadologie und andere metaphysische Schriften. Discours de métaphysique; Monadologie; Principes de la nature et de la grace fondes en raison. Hamburg: Meiner.

Leist, Justus Christof (1805): Lehrbuch des Teutschen Staatsrechts. (ND Goldbach 2004). 2. Aufl. Göttingen.

Lenz, Max (1910/1918): Geschichte der königlichen Friedrich-Wilhelms-Universität zu Berlin. Hall: Verlag der Buchhandlung des Waisenhauses.

Leser, Emmanuel (1874): Der Begriff des Reichthums bei Adam Smith. Eine national-ökonomische Untersuchung. Heidelberg: Winter's Universitätsbuchhandlung.

Linguet, Simon Nicolas Henri (1767): Théorie des lois civiles ou Principes fondamentaux de la société. (ND Paris 1984). London.

List, Albrecht (1913): Der Kampf um's gute alte Recht (1815–1819). Nach seiner ideen- und parteigeschichtlichen Seite. Tübingen: Mohr.

Majer, Johann Christian (1782): Autonomie vornehmlich des Fürsten- und übrigen unmittelbaren Adelsstandes im Römischen deutschen Reiche. Tübingen: Herrbrandt.

Majer, Johann Christian (1798): Germaniens Urverfassung. Mit einer Vorrede über den akademischen Vortrag der teutschen Reichsgeschichte. Hamburg: Bohn.

Majer, Johann Christian (1800): Teutsche Staatskonstitution. Hamburg: Bohn.

Marx, Karl (1844): Zur Kritik der Hegel'schen Rechtsphilosophie. (Vgl. MEW Bd. I, Berlin 2009.) In: Deutsch-Französiche Jahrbücher, S. 71–85.

Mayer-Moreau, Karl (1910): Hegels Socialphilosophie. Tübingen: Mohr.

Mehlis, Georg (1906): Schellings Geschichtsphilosophie in den Jahren 1799–1804. Gewürdigt vom Standpunkt der modernen geschichtsphilosophischen Problembildung. Heidelberg.

Meinecke, Friedrich (1896/1899): Das Leben des Generalfeldmarschalls Hermann von Boyen. 2 Bände. Stuttgart: Cotta.

Meinecke Friedrich (1908): Weltbürgertum und Nationalstaat. Studien zur Genesis des deutschen Nationalstaates. (ND München 1995). München (u.a.): Oldenbourg.

Mendelssohn, Moses (1783): Jerusalem oder über religiöse Macht und Judentum. (Neuauflage Hamburg 2005). Berlin: Maurer.

Michelet, Carl Ludwig (1884): Michelet's gesammelte Werke. Vollständige Ausgabe letzter Hand. Berlin: Nicolai.

Mitteilungen des Instituts für Österreichische Geschichtsforschung (1885 ff.). Wien, München: Oldenbourg.

Moltke, Helmuth von (1895): Geschichte des deutsch-französischen Krieges von 1870–71. (ND Wolfenbüttel 2005). Berlin: Mittler.

Mommsen, Theodor; Kreuger, Paul; Watson, Alan (Hg.) (1985). The Digest of Justinian. 4 Bände. Philadelphia: University of Pennsylvania Press.

Monatsblätter für innere Zeitgeschichte. Studien der deutschen Gegenwart für den socialen und religiösen Frieden der Zukunft (1867–1879). Gotha: Perthes.

Montesquieu, Charles Louis Secondat de; Caillois, Roger (1949 ff.): Œuvres complètes. 2 Bände. Paris: Gallimard (Bibliothèque de la Pléiade).

Montesquieu, Charles Louis Secondat de; Caillois, Roger (1992): Vom Geist der Gesetze. In neuer Übertragung eingeleitet und herausgegeben von Ernst Forsthoff. 2 Bände. Tübingen: Mohr.

Moser, Friedrich Carl von (1796): Politische Wahrheiten. Zurich: Orell Gessner Füssli u. Co.

Moser, Johann Jacob (1766): Neues Teutsches Staats-Recht. (ND Osnabrück 1967). Stuttgart: Metzler.

Moser, Johann J. (1770): Neueste Geschichte der teutschen Staats-Rechts-Lehre und deren Lehrer. Frankfurt, Main: Garbe.

Müller, Johannes (1787): Darstellung des Fürstenbundes. Leipzig: Weidmann.

Necker, Jacques (1775): Sur la législation et le commerce des grains. (ND Paris 1820). Paris: Chez Pissot.

Neuer Nekrolog der Deutschen (1824 ff.). Ilmenau: Voigt.

Nicolin, Günther (1970): Hegel in Berichten seiner Zeitgenossen. Hamburg: Meiner (Philosophische Bibliothek).

Niebuhr, Barthold Georg (1830): Römische Geschichte (Berlin 1853). 3 Bände. Berlin: Reimer.

o. V. (1817): Heidelbergische Jahrbücher der Literatur. Heidelberg: Mohr und Winter.

o. V. (1818): Bemerkungen eines Sachkundigen über die aus den Heidelberger Jahrbüchern 1817 Nr. 66–77 besonders abgedruckte Beurtheilung der Verhandlungen der württembergischen Ständeversammlung im Jahr 1815, 1816. Frankfurt: Hermannsche Buchhandlung.

Österreichische Rundschau (1904–1924). Wien: Konegen.

Pahl, Johann G.; Pahl, Wilhelm (1840): Denkwürdigkeiten aus meinem Leben und aus meiner Zeit. Nach dem Tode des Verfassers herausgegeben von dessen Sohne Wilhelm Pahl. Tübingen: Fues.

Paulsen, Friedrich (1897): Geschichte des gelehrten Unterrichts aus den deutschen Schulen und Universitäten vom Ausgang des Mittelalters bis zur Gegenwart; mit besonderer Rücksicht auf den klassischen Unterricht. (ND Berlin 1965). 2., umgearb. und sehr erw. Aufl. Leipzig: Veit.

Plato; Eigler, Gunther (2005); Werke in acht Bänden. Griechisch und deutsch. 8 Bände. Darmstadt: Wissenschaftliche Buchgesellschaft.

Plenge, Johann (1911): Marx und Hegel. (Neudruck Aalen 1974). Tübingen: Laupp.

Plitt, Gustav Leopold (1869): Aus Schellings Leben. In Briefen. (ND Hildesheim 2003). Leipzig: Hirzel.

Pope, Alexander (1734): An Essay on Man. Being the First Book of Ethic Epistles. (eng.-dt.: Vom Menschen. Hamburg 1977). London: printed by John Wright for Lawton Gilliver.

Posselt, Ernst Ludwig (1795–1820): Europäische Annalen. Monatsschrift. Tübingen, Stuttgart: Cotta.

Pütter, Johann Stephen (1777): Beyträge zum teutschen Staats- und Fürstenrechte (ND Hildesheim 2000). Göttingen: Vandenhoeck.

Reetz, Dankfried (2002): Schleiermacher im Horizont preussischer Politik. Studien und Dokumente zur Schleiermacher's Berufung nach Halle zu

seiner Vorlesung über Politik 1817 und zu den Hintergründen der Dema-
gogenverfolgung. Waltrop: Spenner.

Revue des deux mondes (1829 ff.). Paris u.a.

Roques, Paul (1912): Sa vie et ses œuvres. Paris: Alcan.

Roscher, Wilhelm (1874): Geschichte der National-Oekonomik in Deutschland. (ND Düsseldorf 1922). München: Oldenbourg (Geschichte der
Wissenschaften in Deutschland, 14).

Rosenstock-Huessy, Eugen (1914): Königshaus und Stämme zwischen 911
und 1250. (ND Aalen 1965). Leipzig: Meiner.

Rothfels, Hans (1920): Carl von Clausewitz. Politik und Krieg. Eine ideenge-
schichtliche Studie. (ND Bonn 1980). Berlin: Dümmler.

Rousseau, Jean-Jacques (1964): Œuvres complètes. Paris: Gallimard (Bibliothèque de la Pléiade, 153).

Rümelin, Gustav (1907): Kanzlerreden. Tübingen: Mohr.

Sartorius, Georg (1796): Handbuch der Staatswirtschaft. Zum Gebrauch
bei akademischen Vorlesungen, nach Adam Smiths Grundsätzen aus-
gearbeitet. (ND Bristol 1998). Berlin: Unger.

Schelling, Friedrich Wilhelm Joseph; Plitt, Gustav Leopold (1870): Aus Schellings
Leben. In Briefen. (ND Hildesheim 2003). 3 Bände. Leipzig: Hirzel.

Schelling, Friedrich Wilhelm Joseph (1803): Vorlesungen über die Methode
des academischen Studien. Tübingen: Cotta.

Schelling, Friedrich Wilhelm Joseph (1804): Philosophie und Religion.
(Neuauflage Freiburg/München 2008). Tübingen: Cotta.

Schelling, Friedrich Wilhelm Joseph (1985): Ausgewählte Schriften. I. Aufl.
Frankfurt am Main: Suhrkamp (Suhrkamp Taschenbuch Wissenschaft).

Schelling, Friedrich Wilhelm Joseph (1990): Vorlesungen über die Methode
(Lehrart) des akademischen Studiums. 2., erw. Aufl. Hamburg: Meiner
(Philosophische Bibliothek).

Schiller, Friedrich (1904 f.): Schillers Sämtliche Werke. Säkular Ausgabe in
16 Bänden. Stuttgart, Berlin: Cotta.

Schiller, Friedrich (2004): Sämtliche Werke in 5 Bänden. München: Carl
Hanser.

Schlapp, Otto (1901): Kants Lehre vom Genie und die Entstehung der
"Kritik der Urteilskraft." Göttingen: Vandenhoeck & Ruprecht.

Schleiermacher, Friedrich; Jaeschke, Walter (Hg). (1998): Vorlesungen über
die Lehre vom Staat. Berlin [u.a.]: de Gruyter (Kritische Gesamtausgabe).

Schleiermacher, Friedrich; Meisner, Heinrich (Hg). (1922): Schleiermacher
als Mensch. Sein Werden und Wirken. Familie- und Freundesbriefe.
Gotha: Perthes [u.a.].

Schmalz, Theodor Anton Heinrich (1805): Handbuch des teutschen
Staatsrechts. Zum Gebrauch academischer Vorlesungen. Halle: Renger.

Schmollers Jahrbuch für Gesetzgebung, Verwaltung und Volkswirtschaft im Deutschen Reiche (1871 ff.).

Schneider, Eugen (1896): Württembergische Geschichte. (ND Stuttgart 1986). Stuttgart: Metzler.

Schubert, Heinrich von Gotthilf (1854 ff.): Der Erwerb aus einem vergangenen und die Erwartungen von einem zukünftigen Leben. Eine Selbstbiographie (ND Erlangen-Nürnberg 2003). 3 Bände. Erlangen: Paln & Enke.

Smith, Adam; Garve, Christian; Dörrien, August (1810): Untersuchung über die Natur und Ursache des Nationalreichthums. (Neuauflage Berlin 1933). 3., verb. Ausg. 3 Bände. Breslau, Leipzig: Korn.

Speidel, Christian Friedrich (1797): Inbegriff von Wünschen, Winken und Vorschlägen in Beziehung auf den bevorstehenden Landtag Wirtembergs. [Stuttgart].

Spittler, Ludwig Timotheus; Wächter-Spittler, Karl Eberhard von (1827 ff.): Ludwig Timotheus Freiherrn v. Spittlers sämmtliche Werke. Stuttgart: Cotta.

Stahl, Friedrich Julius (1847): Geschichte der Rechtsphilosophie. (ND Hildesheim 2000). 2. Aufl. Heidelberg: Mohr.

Stahl, Friedrich Julius (1856): Die Philosophie des Rechts. (ND Hildesheim 2000). 2. Aufl. Heidelberg: Mohr.

Steuart, James (1913 f.): Untersuchung über die Grundsätze der Wirtschaftslehre. [Orig.: An inquiry into the principles of political economy. London 1767]. Jena: Fischer (Sammlung sozialwissenschaftlicher Meister, 16).

Stoll, Adolf (1890): Friedrich Karl von Savignys sächsische Studienreise 1799 und 1800. Kassel: Döll.

Strauss, Friedrich; Zeller, Eduard (1876 ff.): Gesammelte Schriften. Bonn: Strauss.

Thaulow, Gustav (1854): Hegels Ansichten über Erziehung und Unterricht. (ND Glashütten/Taunus 1974). Kiel: Akadem. Buchhdlg.

Thomasius, Christian (1705): Die origine successionis testimentariae. Halle/Saale, Univ. Diss. Halle/Magdeburg.

Thomasius, Christian (1738): De captatoriis institutionibus. Halle/Saale. Univ.-Diss. 1696. Halle/Magdeburg.

Treitschke, Heinrich von (1859): Die Gesellschaftswissenschaft. Ein kritischer Versuch (ND Darmstadt 1980). Univ., Habil., Leipzig, 1859. Leipzig: Hirzel.

Treitschke, Heinrich von (1912): Deutsche Geschichte im 19. Jahrhundert. (ND Essen 1997). 7. Aufl. (Staatengeschichte der neuesten Zeit, 24).

Treitschke, Heinrich von (1908): Bilder aus der deutschen Geschichte. (Neuauflage Leipzig 1922). 2. Bände. Leipzig: Hirzel.

Trescher, Hildegard (1918): Hegel und Montesquieu. Leipzig.

Uhland, Ludwig; Brandes, Friedrich (o.J.): Uhlands gesammelte Werke. In zwei Bänden (Neuauflage Leipzig 1914). Leipzig: Reclam.

Varnhagen von Ense, Karl August (1868 f.): Blätter aus der preußischen Geschichte. (ND Hildesheim 2009). Leipzig: Brockhaus.

Weiser, Christian Friedrich (1916): Shaftesbury und das deutsche Geistesleben. (ND Darmstadt 1969). Leipzig: Teubner.

Württembergische Vierteljahrshefte für Landesgeschichte (1878–1936). Stuttgart: [anfangs] Kohlhammer, Lindemann.

Zahn, Christian Jakob (1818): Freymüthige Widerlegung der in den Heidelbergischen Jahrbüchern im November und December 1817 erschienenen Beurtheilung der Württembergischen Stände-Verhandlungen. Frankfurt/M.: Boselli.

Zeitschrift für die gesamte Staatswissenschaft. ZgS (1844–1985). Tübingen: Mohr/Laupp.

Zeller, Eduard (1903): Die Philosophie der Griechen in ihrer geschichtlichen Entwicklung. (ND Darmstadt 2006). 4. Aufl. Leipzig: Reisland.

Zinkernagel, Franz (1907): Die Entwicklungsgeschichte von Hölderlins Hyperion. Straßburg: Trübner.

Zweig, Egon (1909): Die Lehre vom Pouvoir Constituant. Ein Beitrag zum Staatsrecht der französischen Revolution. Tübingen: Mohr.

# TRANSLATORS' BIBLIOGRAPHY

Avineri, Shlomo. "Rosenzweig's Hegel Interpretation. Its Relation to the Development of His Jewish Rewakening." In *Der Philosoph Franz Rosenzweig, Bd. II*. München: Verlag Karl Alber, 1988, pp. 831–838.

Avineri, Shlomo. *Hegel's Theory of the Modern State*. London: Cambridge University Press, 1972.

Beiser, Frederick. *Hegel*. New York: Routledge, 2005.

Bieberich, Ulrich. *Wenn die Geschichte göttlich wäre. Rosenzweigs Auseinandersetzung mit Hegel*. Erzabtei St. Ottilien. EOS Verlag: 1990.

Bienenstock, Myriam. "Rosenzweig's Hegel." *The Owl of Minerva* 23 (2) (1992): 177–182.

Bollnow, Otto Friedrich. *Die Lebensphilosophie F. H. Jacobis*. Stuttgart: W. Kolhammer, 1966.

Cristaudo, Wayne. *Religion, Redemption, and Revolution*. Toronto: University of Toronto Press, 2012.

Crites, Stephen. *Dialectic and Gospel in the Development of Hegel's Thinking*. University Park: Pennsylvania State University Press, 1998.

Dilthey, Wilhelm. *Das Erlebnis und die Dichtung*. Heidelberg: Springer Berlin, 2013.

Ehrenberg, Hans. *Die Parteiung der Philosophie*. Essen: Die Blaue Eule, 1998 (1911).

Ehrenberg, Hans. *Disputation. Fichte. Schelling. Hegel*. München: Drei Masken Verlag, 1923–1925.

Ehrenberg, Hans. "Einleitende Bemerkungen." *Hegels Erstes System*. Heidelberg: Carl Winter, 1915.

Fackenheim, Emil L. "On the Actuality of the Rational and the Rationality of the Actual." *The Review of Metaphysics* 23, no. 4 (1970): 690–698.

Glatzer, Nahum N. *Franz Rosenzweig*. New York: Schocken Books, 1970.

Gordon, Peter. *Rosenzweig and Heidegger*. London: University of California Press, 2003.

Haym, Rudolf. *Hegel und seine Zeit: Vorlesungen*. Darmstadt: Wissenschaftliche Buchgesellschaft, 1962.

Hegel, G.W.F. *Elements of the Philosophy of Right*. Trans. by H.B. Nisbet. Cambridge, UK: Cambridge University Press, 1991.

Hegel, G.W.F. *Heidelberg Writings*. Trans. by Brady Bowman and Allen Speight. Cambridge, UK: Cambridge University Press, 2009.

Hegel, G.W.F. *Lectures on Natural Right and Political Science. The First Philosophy of Right*. Trans. by J. Michael Stewart and Peter C. Hodgson. Oxford: Oxford University Press, 2012.

Hegel, G.W.F. *Natural Law*. Trans. by T.M. Knox. University of Pennsylvania Press, 1975.

Hegel, G.W.F. *Political Writings*. Trans. by T.M. Knox. London: Oxford University Press, 1964.

Hegel, G.W.F. *Theological Writings*. Trans. by T.M. Knox. Chicago: University of Chicago Press, 1948.

Hegel, G.W.F. *The Phenomenology of Spirit*. Trans. by A.V. Miller. Oxford: Oxford University Press, 1977.

Hegel, G.W.F. *The Phenomenology of Spirit*. Trans. and ed. by Terry Pinkard. Cambridge, United Kingdom: Cambridge University Press, 2018.

Hegel, G.W.F. *The Philosophy of Right*. Trans. by Alan White. Newburyport: Focus Publishing, 2002.

Hegel, G.W.F. *Political Writings*. Trans. by H.B. Nisbet. Cambridge, UK: Cambridge University Press, 1999.

*Hegel's Elements of the Philosophy of Right: A Critical Guide*, ed. by David James. Cambridge, United Kingdom: Cambridge University Press, 2017.

*Hegel on Ethics and Politics*. Ed. by Robert B. Pippin and Otfried Höffe; trans. by Nicholas Walker. Cambridge, United Kingdom: Cambridge University Press, 2004.

Heidegger, Martin. *On Hegel's Philosophy of Right: The 1934–35 Seminar and Interpretive Essays*. Trans. by Andrew J. Mitchell and ed. by Peter Trawny, Marci Sá Cavalcante Schuback, and Michael Morder. London: Bloomsbury, 2014.

Heinrich, Dieter. "Hegel and Hölderlin" in *The Course of Remembrance*. Stanford: Stanford University Press, 1997.

Herzfeld, Wolfgang (Ed.) *Franz Rosenzweigs Jugendschriften (1907–1914). Philosophie: Teil I – Kant; Philosophie: Teil II – Hegel; Teil III – Arbeiten zu Geschichte und Kultur*. Hamburg: Verlag Dr. Kovac, 2015/2017.

Kavka, Martin. "A Note on Religion and the State in Rosenzweig's *Hegel und der Staat.*" In *Rosenzweig Jahrbuch/Yearbook*, Freiburg/München: Verlag Karl Alber, Vol. 8/9, 2014.

Knowles, David. *Routledge Philosophy Guidebook to Hegel and the Philosophy of Right.* New York: Routledge, 2002.

Mendes-Flohr, Paul. "Franz Rosenzweig and the Crisis of Historicism." In *The Philosophy of Franz Rosenzweig.* Hannover: University Press of New England, 1988.

Mosès, Stéphane. "Hegel beim Wort genommen." In *Zeitgewinn. Messianisches Denken nach Franz Rosenzweig.* Frankfurt am Main: Verlag Josef Knecht, 1987.

Navarrete Alonso, Roberto, "'Der Jude, der in deutschem Geist macht.' Das Hegelbuch Franz Rosenzweigs und seine Wirkung." *Naharaim* 10 (2) (2016): 273–302.

Pöggeler, Otto. "Rosenzweig und Hegel." In *Der Philosoph Franz Rosenzweig, Bd. II.* München: Verlag Karl Alber, 1988, 839–853.

Pöggeler, Otto. "Between Enlightenment and Romanticism: Rosenzweig and Hegel." In *The Philosophy of Franz Rosenzweig.* Mendes-Flohr, Paul, ed. Hannover: University Press of New England, 1988.

Pöggeler, O. "Hegel Editing and Hegel Research." In: O'Malley, J.J., Algozin, K.W., Kainz, H.P., Rice, L.C. (eds) *The Legacy of Hegel.* Springer, Dordrecht, 1973.

Pollock, Benjamin. *Franz Rosenzweig's Conversions.* Bloomington: Indiana University Press, 2014.

Pelczynski, Z.A. (Ed.) *Hegel's Political Philosophy. Problems and Perspectives.* Cambridge, UK: Cambridge University Press, 1971.

Rahel-Freund, Else. *Franz Rosenzweig's Philosophy of Existence.* Hague: Martinus Nijhoff, 1979. (1933)

Ritter, Joachim. "Morality and Ethical Life." In *Hegel and the French Revolution: Essays on the Philosophy of Right.* Cambridge: MIT Press, 1984.

Rosenstock-Huessy, Eugen. "Hegel und unser Geschlecht." *Der Neue Merkur* 8 (1924–1925): 360–362.

Rosenzweig, Franz. *Franz Rosenzweig, Der Mensch und sein Werk. Gesammelte Schriften.* Bde I–IV. The Hague: Martinus Nijhoff, 1976–1984.

Rosenzweig, Franz. "Notizen zum Barock." *Rosenzweig Jahrbuch/Yearbook*, Vol. 4, 2009: 260–302.

Rosenzweig, Franz. *Philosophical and Theological Writings.* Trans. and ed. with notes and commentary by Paul W. Franks and Michael J. Morgan. Indianapolis, Cambridge: Hackett Publishing Company, Inc., 2000.

Rosenzweig, Franz. *The Star of Redemption.* Notre Dame: University of Notre Dame Press, 1985 (1921).

Rosenzweig, Franz. *Hegel und der Staat*. Berlin: Suhrkamp Verlag, 2010. First published: München and Berlin: Verlag von R. Oldenbourg, 1920. Facsimile reprint: Aalen: Scientia Verlag, 1962 (1984).

Rosenzweig, Franz. *Hegel e l'Etat*, trans. and ed. by Gérard Bensussan. Paris: Presses Universitaires de France, 1991.

Rosenzweig, Franz. *Hegel e o Estado*. Trans. by Ricardo Timm de Souza. Alameda Santos: Editora Perspectiva, 2008.

Rosenzweig, Franz. *Hegel e lo Stato*. Trans. by Anna Lucia Kunkler Giavotto and Rosa Curino Cerrato. Bologna: Il mulino, 1976.

Samuelson, Norbert. *An Introduction to Modern Jewish Philosophy*. Albany: State University of New York Press, 1989.

Schmied-Kowarzik, Wolfdietrich. "Brief Illuminations on the Dialogue between Franz Rosenzweig and Hans Ehrenberg." Trans. by Josiah Simon. In *Rosenzweig Jahrbuch/Yearbook*, Vol. 8. Verlag Karl Alber, 2014, pp. 87–111.

Shanks, Andrew. *Hegel's Political Theology*. Cambridge: Cambridge University Press, 1991.

Simon, Josiah. *Franz Rosenzweig's Hegel and the State: Biography, History and Tragedy*. University of Oregon Scholars' Bank, 2014.

Simon, Josiah. "On 'Philosophical Biography' as Form. The New Thinking in Franz Rosenzweig's *Hegel and the State*. In *Rosenzweig Jahrbuch/Yearbook*, Freiburg/München: Verlag Karl Alber, Vol. 10, 2024.

Simon, Josiah; Simon, Jules. "Foreword" for *Franz Rosenzweigs Jugendschriften (1907–1914) Philosophie: Teil II – Hegel: Schriften zur politischen Philosophie*, Ed. Wolfgang Herzfeld. Hamburg: Verlag Dr. Kovac, 2015, pp. 7–19.

Simon, Josiah; Simon, Jules. "Hegel und der Staat" in *Franz Rosenzweig. Religionsphilosoph aus Kassel*. Eds. Schmied-Kowarzik and Schulz-Jander. Kassel: euregio verlag, 2011, pp. 31–37.

Simon, Jules. *Art and Responsibility: a phenomenology of the diverging paths of Rosenzweig and Heidegger*. Continuum International Publishing, 2011; reissued in paperback and e-book: New York: Bloomsbury Academic, 2013.

Simon, Jules. "From Hegel to Rosenzweig: *From what is Rational ... and what is Actual*, to what is Ethical." In *Rosenzweig Jahrbuch/Yearbook*, Vol. 8/9. Freiburg/München: Verlag Karl Alber 2014, pp. 112–128.

Simon, Jules. "Hegels Familienbegriff vermittelt durch Rosenzweig: eine eigentümliche Geschichte" ("Hegel's concept of family, mediated through Rosenzweig: a peculiar story/history"); in *Rosenzweig Jahrbuch/Yearbook: 2006*, Freiburg: Verlag Karl Alber GmbH, 2006, pp. 218–231.

Simon, Jules. "Rosenzweig's *Midrashic* Speech-Acts: From Hegel and German Nationalism to a Modern-Day *ba'al teshuvah*" chapter for *Cambridge Companion to Jewish Theology* edited by Steven Kepnes. Cambridge, UK: Cambridge University Press, 2020, pp. 213–238.

Stewart, Jon. *The Hegel Myths and Legends*. Evanston, Ill: Northwestern University Press, 1996.

Vieweg, Klaus. *Das Denken der Freiheit. Hegels* Grundlienen der Philosophie des Rechts. Paderborn: Wilhelm Fink, 2012.

Waszek, Norbert (Ed.) *Rosenzweigs Bibliothek*. Freiburg: Verlag Karl Alber, 2017.

Weil, Eric. *Hegel and the State*. Baltimore: The John Hopkins University Press, 1998.

White, Hayden. *Metahistory: The Historical Imagination in Nineteenth-Century Europe*. Baltimore: Johns Hopkins University Press, 1973.

Windelband, Wilhelm. *Aufsätze und Reden zur Philosophie und ihrer Geschichte*, Tübingen: J.C.B. Mohr, 1924. [Ergänzung der Ausgabe von 1907].

Žižek, Slavoj; Ruda, Frank; Hamza, Agon. *Reading Hegel*. Cambridge: Polity Press, 2022.

# Index

formal existence 210–211
formal freedom 405
formal right 144
formal will 393–394
formlessness 164
Förster, Friedrich 7, 466
Forster, Georg 7, 96, 466
Fox, Charles 26, 75, 81, 307, 485
Frankfurt 89–123
Frankfurt publishing house 71
Frederician code of law 370
Frederick the Great 158, 477
freedom 66, 140, 185, 333, 337, 427,
    434; absolute 226, 245–247, 350,
    353; abstract 274; of choice 372;
    of conscience 129; to emigrate
    57; free choice of profession
    345, 375, 386, 393; measured
    22; moral 352, 362–363; of
    person 365; and power 162; of
    property 365; of religion 57–58;
    and satisfaction 432; of spirit
    341; of teaching 333; of thought
    278, 476; of trade 214, 381;
    unfreedom 474, 483; of will
    63, 396
free infinite personality 338
free monarchy 281
free property owner 365
free proprietors 365–366
free state of antiquity 65
French: abstractions 301; emperor
    282–283; immigrants 74;
    liberalism 139; nobility 162;
    parliamentary politics 478;
    republic 137
French Enlightenment 21
French Revolution (the Revolution)
    6, 27, 247, 259, 261, 384, 476,
    490, 496
Friedrich Wilhelm II 6

Friedrich Wilhelm III 24, 270,
    393–394
Friedrich Wilhelm IV 148, 187, 406,
    439, 444
Friedrich Wilhelm University
    328–329
friendship 91–93, 97, 99–100, 119,
    336
Friends of the People 314–317
Fries, Jakob Friedrich 329, 332, 334,
    336, 366, 437, 466, 468
Fury of disappearance 246

Gans, Eduard 467, 480
Gascoine, Isaac 486, 488
General Common Law 364,
    433–434, 437
general will 139, 221, 245–246, 261,
    343, 362, 505
genius 37–38, 40, 92, 134, 145, 147,
    149, 190, 192, 278–279, 283–284,
    323, 331, 506–507
geographical and anthropological
    existence 424
German Confederation 307
*German Constitution, The* 115–116,
    121, 130, 133, 141–143, 156, 158,
    161–162, 180–181, 184–185, 188,
    190, 192, 229, 260, 325, 341,
    400, 403, 409, 414–415, 427,
    430, 436, 444–445, 487
German Customs Union 469
German Empire 57, 112, 114–115,
    120, 132–133, 143–144, 229, 232,
    298, 307, 325, 443–444,
    482, 490
German Enlightenment 20, 22
"German Estates" 446
German Federal Act 307–308
"Germanic forests" 140
Germanic right 360, 371

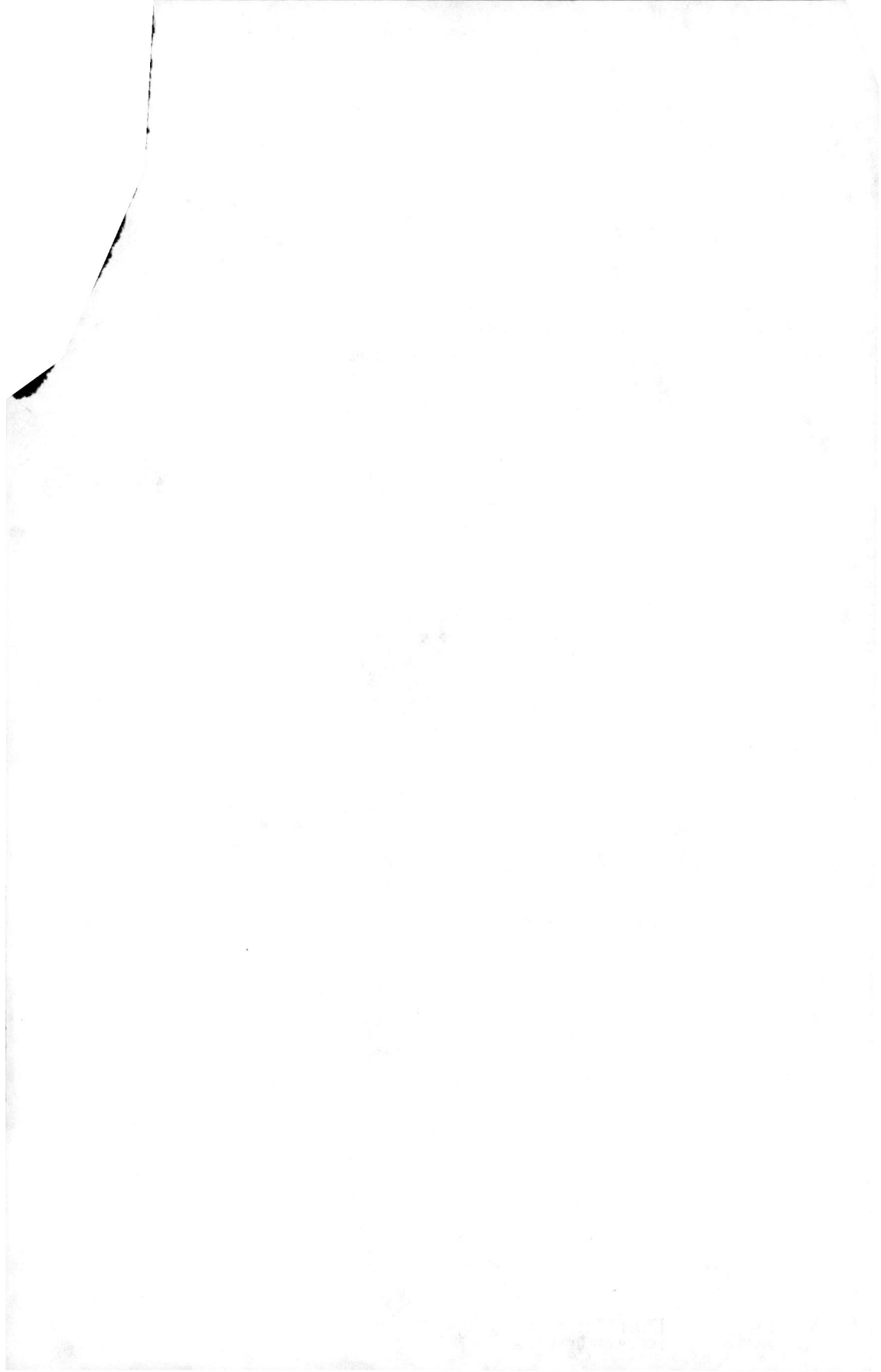

For Product Safety Concerns and Information please contact our EU
representative GPSR@taylorandfrancis.com
Taylor & Francis Verlag GmbH, Kaufingerstraße 24, 80331 München, Germany

www.ingramcontent.com/pod-product-compliance
Lightning Source LLC
Chambersburg PA
CBHW050622280326
41932CB00015B/2487